# Popular Religious Libraries in North America

## A Statistical Examination

John F. Harvey
with the assistance of
Jo Ann Mouridou

The Scarecrow Press, Inc.
Lanham, Maryland, & London
1999

WITHDRAWN
HIEBERT LIBRARY
FRESNO PACIFIC UNIV.-M. B. SEMINARY
FRESNO, CA 93702

# SCARECROW PRESS, INC.

Published in the United States of America
by Scarecrow Press, Inc.
4720 Boston Way
Lanham, Maryland 20706

4 Pleydell Gardens, Folkestone
Kent CT20 2DN, England

Copyright © 1999 by John F. Harvey

*All rights reserved.* No part of this publication may be reproduced,
stored in a retrieval system, or transmitted in any form or by any
means, electronic, mechanical, photocopying, recording, or otherwise,
without the prior permission of the publisher.

British Library Cataloguing in Publication Information Available

**Library of the Congress Cataloging-in-Publication Data**

Harvey, John F. (John Frederick), 1921–
    Popular religious libraries in North America : a statistical
examination / John F. Harvey with the assistance of Jo Ann Mouridou.
        p.    cm.
    Includes bibliographical references and index.
    ISBN 0-8108-3342-5 (cloth : alk. paper)
    1. Religious libraries—United States—Statistics.  2. Religious
libraries—Canada—Statistics.  I. Mouridou, Jo Ann.  II. Title.
Z675.R37H46   1998
027.6′7′0973—dc21                                          98-20144
                                                               CIP

♾ ™ The paper used in this publication meets the minimum requirements of
American National Standard for Information Sciences—Permanence of
Paper for Printed Library Materials, ANSI Z39.48–1984.
Manufactured in the United States of America.

(There are) more books upon books than upon all other subjects, we do nothing but comment upon one another.

—Michael Eyquem de Montaigne, *Essays*

Books must follow sciences and not sciences books.

—Francis Bacon, *Proposition*

And out of olde bokes, in good feyth, cometh al this newe science that men lere.

—Geoffrey Chaucer, *The Parliament of Fowls*

# CONTENTS

# PREFACE

This book is intended for all North American religious libraries and librarians in academic, special, school, and public libraries. Religious popular librarians should be interested in one of the few extant analyses of the libraries in their field. A significant part of it is devoted to congregational libraries, and all congregational librarians and many congregational leaders should be interested in this analysis. This book demonstrates that religious librarianship is indeed to some degree a discrete and separate occupational field.

All religious librarians should welcome a friendly opinion of their field. Popular religious library association leaders and their workshop and conference instructors will find useful material here. Library school faculty members may be interested in the description and analysis of a relatively new and developing field and a proposed publication program. Religious publishers and journalists should welcome a discussion of the libraries that serve as their primary market. It is to be hoped that the present work will stimulate further attention to the popular religious library field and will spark an interest in research on it.

## Data Collection and Analysis Policy and Procedure

Initially, the author was faced with the problem of obtaining detailed data on popular religious libraries that could be analyzed for greater understanding. No set of data on these libraries was readily available. A questionnaire could have been sent to several thousand libraries to obtain information, but the size of the return probably would not have exceeded 20 to 25 percent, at most.

In the popular religious library field, the percentage return on once-only mail questionnaire surveys has generally been poor. Dorothy Rodda received 23 percent in 1965, Martin Ruoss got 39 percent in 1966 from a scholarly library group, Joyce White obtained 18 percent in 1971–75, and the 1986 Church and Synagogue Library Association (CSLA) membership survey brought in 24 percent.[1-3] As a way of compensating for the low return in his directory, Ruoss printed the names and addresses both of libraries that returned questionnaires and libraries that did not.

Therefore, the author decided to take advantage of the fact that the *American Library Directory* (*ALD*) carried out a North American mail survey annually, which included three hundred to four hundred popular religious libraries. Analyzing the data taken from the *ALD* printed volumes was simpler, cheaper, and more satisfactory than using a personal mail questionnaire.

This book uses two *ALD* editions—the 31st (1978) and the 41st (1988)—thereby enabling the author to carry out a longitudinal study as well as an analysis of the information provided for each library. Copies of *ALD* were either purchased (1988) or donated by the Wayne State University Library, Detroit (1978), for which donation the author is grateful. In preparing this book, the author visited no library and no librarian was contacted directly, except for those libraries and librarians included in the CSLA survey covered in chapter 4.

Copies of the data collection forms used for the CSLA survey and the *ALD* study are shown in appendices D and E. Claudia Hannaford, American congregational librarian, designed the CSLA form. For the *ALD* form an attempt was made to include all information found in the fuller *ALD* listings that would be useful in understanding popular religious libraries. Even more detailed or varied types of information would have contributed to a larger and more generally comparable analysis, but this information was not available. Information on scholarly North American religious libraries was collected at the same time as the popular religious library information. The library information and subject areas covered by the *ALD* study data form are shown in appendix D.

The author completed questionnaires from the two *ALD* editions and then the data was keyboarded and recorded with assistance first from the Fachhochschule für Bibliothekswesen in Stuttgart, Germany, under the supervision of Saiedeh and Wolfgang von Keitz and later in Nicosia under the supervision of Jo Ann Mouridou. CSLA questionnaires were keyboarded and analyzed by Jo Ann Mouridou in Nicosia.

Each chapter in this book contains information that shows the popular religious libraries' distinctive character, that of certain types of these libraries, or that of special interest for other reasons. The distinctiveness, strengths, and weaknesses of each type of library are considered important here, also. They allow the author to develop the outlines of a profile in the field of North American religious libraries and its subdivisions. This profile should also establish acceptable working parameters for future studies.

## The *American Library Directory*: Its Strengths and Limitations

Since 1923 the *ALD* has enjoyed a long and honorable history among North American reference books. It provides the best-known and most comprehensive collection of information about scholarly and popular religious and nonreligious libraries. It covers public, academic, and special libraries. The most notable *ALD* limitation is its almost complete disregard of school libraries. As far as this author knows, there is no comprehensive school media center or library directory for the United States or Canada, although certain states and provinces may have their own state-specific directories.

The *ALD* also contains the occasional printing error affecting its factual integrity. For example, in the 41st edition, page 1300, the Maria Regina College Library total expenditure figure is one zero deficient. Work on the 43d edition for 1990 on another project suggested that it may contain more errors than the 41st edition. The directory editions also suffer from the tendency for a certain proportion of the libraries to be inconsistent in completing the annual questionnaire form and mailing it in to the publisher. As the years go by, some smaller libraries, including many popular religious libraries, apparently move in and out of the directory for that reason. Perhaps it is thought, erroneously, that a library that has reported to the *ALD* once need not report regularly in the future. The directory's present policy is to include all libraries returning questionnaires and all information reported on them.[4]

## Notes

1. John F. Harvey, *Church and Synagogue Libraries* (Metuchen, N.J.: Scarecrow Press, 1980).

2. The *World Almanac 1988* (New York: Pharos Books) listed the denominations of private U.S. religious and parochial schools. While the vast majority of them were Roman Catholic, the following denominations were well represented also: Baptist, Lutheran, Christian, Jewish, Seventh-day Adventist, and Episcopal/Anglican.

3. Joyce White, "Church Libraries," in *Encyclopedia of Library and Information Science* (New York: Marcel Dekker, 1970), 4: 662–73.

4. As a way of providing a concise background for both the author and the reader, a capsule (and therefore considerably oversimplified) summary was made of the history and beliefs of each one of the fourteen North American religious denominations that figure prominently in this study. All information comes from the *Yearbook of American and Canadian Churches*, ed. Constant H. Jacquet Jr. (Nashville: Abingdon Press, 1993). The author is aware that certain of these denominations are no longer completely independent but work in cooperation with certain other groups. The nature of the interrelationships among the denominations presents a complex and constantly evolving situation.

a. The *Baptists* (about 22 million members in North America) are numerous, the Southern Baptist group being the largest non-Catholic religious denomination in the United States. This evangelical group displays fragmentation among local communions. It is not a hierarchical group. In the United States alone there are at least twenty-five discrete Baptist bodies differing in various ways, including the expression of fundamental tenets, and representing historical subdivision. The first Baptist church in North America was opened by Roger Williams in Providence, Rhode Island, in 1638. Current leaders in this group include the Southern Baptist Convention (strong in house-of-worship media centers), which was organized in 1845 in Georgia. Southern Baptist churches are located in all fifty states and most Canadian provinces. The convention exists in order to help the churches to lead people to God through Jesus Christ.

The other leading Baptist groups include the Baptist Bible Fellowship International, which was organized in 1950 in Texas; the National Baptist Convention of America, organized in 1880 and composed primarily of African-American Baptists; the Canadian Baptist Federation, which was founded in Ontario in 1763 but was reworked into its present form in the Maritime provinces in 1888; the National Baptist Convention, U.S.A., an African-American group; the American Baptist Churches in the U.S.A., which started in 1814; and the National Association of Free Will Baptists founded in the late eighteenth-century in New Hampshire by one of the author's lineal ancestors, Rev. Benjamin Randall, along with Rev. Paul Palmer, who founded an earlier group with the same principles (no formal connection) in the early eighteenth century in North Carolina.

b. The *Christian* (Disciples of Christ) denomination (U.S. membership is about 1.1 million persons) was born on the American frontier in the early

nineteenth century. It developed from two branches originally located in
western Pennsylvania and Kentucky, which later united in Kentucky in 1932.
This group has existed in Canada since 1810. The church is known for its in-
formality, openness, individuality, and diversity. It has no official doctrine
of a type such as the Church of England's hard-line Thirty-nine Articles of
the Faith, although it calls for the reunion of the church on the basis of a return to New Testament faith and order.

    c. The *Churches of Christ* (1.6 million members) shared a common fel-
lowship with the Christian churches in the nineteenth century, but this fellowship was abandoned with the introduction of instrumental music into the
worship services. Its individual churches are autonomous, and the Bible
alone guides their faith and practice. Members believe in the divinity of Jesus
Christ and immersion into Christ for the remission of sins. The New Testament pattern is followed in worship and church organization. There are no
central denominational offices or church publications. The church organized
in Canada in the central provinces soon after the year 1800.

    d. The *Congregationalists* (0.4 million members) became prominent
in England during the civil war of the 1640s and later were among the
seventeenth-century migrants to New England in opposition to European
state control of their religious worship. The group became a recognized denomination by the 1850s. They were influenced by the Calvinist Puritans and
Separatists of the early seventeenth century. This group united with the
Christian Churches in 1931 and later joined with the German Reformed
Church and the Evangelical and Reformed Church in 1957 to become the
United Church of Christ in Ohio. However, Congregational churches are still
allowed to use the Congregational name and to lead a somewhat separate ex-
istence. The Church recognizes two sacraments: baptism and the Eucharist.

    e. *Episcopal/Anglican* churches (total North American membership about
3.6 million) take separate expressions north and south of the forty-ninth parallel. The Church of England was represented in the Jamestown colony in
Virginia in 1607 and soon developed representation in other colonies also.
After the American Revolution, the church became autonomous in 1789 as
the Protestant Episcopal Church. Church beliefs are both catholic and reformed (as distinct from Reformed, below). The historic creeds of Christianity (as they developed from the time of the early church fathers to the present day) represent the essential elements of faith along with the holy Scripture
and the two chief sacraments of baptism and the Eucharist. Anglicanism arrived in Canada about the year 1700 in Newfoundland and Nova Scotia and
has been self-governing in that country for more than a century.

    f. *Independent* is a designation used in this study to indicate Christian re-
ligious institutions that have no specific denominational affiliation.

    g. Much of what was said about Baptists regarding size and fragmenta-
tion applies as well to *Lutherans* (at least 12 million members). Eighteen or
more separate Lutheran denominational groups exist in the U.S. and Canada,

including the Evangelical Lutheran Church in America, Lutheran Church—Missouri Synod, and the Wisconsin Evangelical Lutheran Synod. Their predecessor organizations can be traced back to the mid-seventeenth century in New York and the early eighteenth-century German migrations to Pennsylvania, New York, and North Carolina.

Most Lutheran groups still adhere to the beliefs inherited from their European predecessors, particularly those from Germany and the Scandinavian countries. The Wisconsin Evangelical Lutheran Synod believes that the Bible is the infallible word of God, and it does not promote ecumenism. Latvian Evangelical Lutherans adhere to the Apostles', Nicene, and Athanasian Creeds, the Augsburg Confession, and Martin Luther's Small and Large Catechisms. Lutherans are strong in publishing and in media use (as well as house of worship libraries). Women are important in professional church activities, although they do not occupy clergy positions.

h. The *Mennonite* Church (0.3 million members in the United States and Canada) groups are relatively small in number but are large in number of separate subdenominations, Canada and the United States together accounting for at least twenty-eight of them. The Mennonite Church traces its beginning back to sixteenth-century Europe, the Protestant Reformation, and the Anabaptists. Some of them arrived in the United States as early as 1683. Mennonites believe that the word of God is central and that a new life in Christ is available to all who believe.

They generally refuse to serve in military forces but are strong in missionary work. They try to follow the way of Jesus in their daily lives. The church is evangelical, guided by the Bible and led by the Holy Spirit. The General Conference Mennonite Church was formed in 1860 and includes persons of many different ethnic backgrounds. Canadian Mennonites are represented in all provinces and trace their history back to the European Anabaptists of the early sixteenth century. The pioneer Mennonites arrived in Canada in the early eighteenth century.

i. The *Methodist* Church (at least 12 million members in the United States and Canada) too is fragmented and is represented in North America by at least seventeen distinct groups, of which several are good-sized. The individual subdenominations include the United Methodist Church (formed in 1968 in Texas); the African Methodist Episcopal Zion Church; the African Methodist Church; the Christian Methodist Episcopal Church; the Free Methodist Church of North America, and the Wesleyan Church. The Methodist Church originated in eighteenth-century England under John Wesley, but the American branch was founded at the Christmas Conference of 1784 in Baltimore. The Methodists arrived in Canada in the late eighteenth century. The church stands for human freedom and simplicity in worship. It emphasizes the teaching of the sanctification of man's entire life by means of grace through faith.

j. *Other Denominations* is another artificial group formed for this study to collect together all of the smaller denominations into one sizeable but manageable group. It includes a great variety of faiths and denominations and even certain artificial subgroupings of its own. Several of the larger of these groups will be described briefly here in order of size. The *Unknown* group was simply an arbitrarily formed group that contained all libraries for which no specific denominational affiliation, Christian or otherwise, could be identified by the author. The *Friends* (Quakers) group arrived in the United States in the mid-seventeenth century after starting in England. Only five subgroups are listed for this small but vocal and well-educated denomination. This group stresses Inner Light, rejects the sacraments and an ordained ministry, and opposes war.

*Reformed* church members owe their existence to various Calvinist churches formed in European countries. The group arrived in the United States in 1628 with a primarily Dutch heritage. The *Seventh-day Adventist* Church grew out of a worldwide religious revival in the mid-nineteenth century. The church is strong in missions, parochial schools, and publications (as well as healthful vegetarian living). The *Church of the Brethren* and related groups date from the 1708 Pietists-Anabaptists in Germany. Their creed is spelled out in the New Testament. The evangelistic *Church of Jesus Christ of Latter-day Saints* was organized in 1830 in New York State by Joseph Smith. Several of its prominent genealogical microform libraries (but none of its many smaller meetinghouse libraries) appear in many of the tables in later chapters. The *Assemblies of God* is a modern Pentecostal and evangelical group and dates from a worldwide religious revival in the World War I period. It was started in Canada in 1919 and is part of the charismatic renewal movement. There are at least 3 million persons in the movement and it is growing rapidly. The *Church of God*, a Holiness church, unlike the Assemblies of God, has many splinter groups. Nevertheless, it has at least 5 million members. The *Church of the Nazarene* is a Holiness and Pentecostal group that arose soon after the American Civil War. It stresses the importance of a devout and holy life and is Wesleyan Arminian in theology, representative in church government, and warmly evangelistic. Eastern Orthodox, Theosophist, Unitarian-Universal, United Church of Canada, Moravian, Christian Science, Salvation Army, Shaker, Baha'i, Church of Scientology, International Church of the Four Square Gospel, Jehovah's Witnesses, Islam, Pillar of Fire, Rosicrucian, and Schwenkfelder are among the remaining component denomination-type groups, many of them represented by no more than one or two libraries each in this study.

k. A large group, the *Presbyterians* (about 4 million members) claim a dozen separate subdenominations in Canada and the United States. Leading subgroups include the Presbyterian Church in America, the Cumberland Presbyterian Church, and the Second Cumberland Presbyterian Church. The Presbyterian Church in Canada is one of the largest Protestant groups in that country. The first Presbyterian group in North America was organized in

Philadelphia in 1706. Strongly ecumenical in outlook, the present church represents the result of many mergers, some reflecting the Great Revival of 1800.

Different divisions of the church have different beliefs. Some of them profess the Westminster Confession of Faith while others do not. Presbyterianism is part of the Reformed tradition, and one of its Canadian denominations is committed to world evangelization. Its officers must subscribe to the Westminster Confession of Faith and Catechism. Other subdenominations believe that the Bible is the only infallible rule of faith and practice. Its missionary interest is strong.

l. The *United Church of Christ* (1.7 million members) dates its existence from a 1957 conference in Ohio. However, its predecessor organizations are numerous and date back to the civil wars of the 1650s in England and even to the Heidelberg Catechism of 1563. It has a strong Lutheran and Reformed heritage. Its immediate precursors were the Congregational Church, the Christian Churches, the German Reformed Church, and the Evangelical and Reformed Church.

At the present time, apart from the semi-independence of the Congregational Church, there seem to be no splinter groups, though the various Reformed churches are closely related to the UCC. The United Church of Christ has no Canadian counterpart. The church acknowledges its debt to the Protestant Reformation and stresses an evangelistic approach. It recognizes two sacraments, baptism and Holy Communion, and combines the unity of the church and liberty of conscience.

m. A *Jewish* synagogue (about 6.1 million members in Canada and the United States) existed in New York City by 1654. Jewish synagogues can be divided into four major subgroups: Orthodox, Conservative, Reformed, and Reconstructionist, according to their degree of adherence to ancient religious customs and dietary laws. Jews trace their history back to the year 1800 B.C. in Palestine. They read from the Torah (the Pentateuch) and its commandments.

Jews believe in God and his oneness, in the changeless Torah, in the words of Moses and the prophets, in reward and punishment, the coming of the Messiah and the resurrection of the dead. This is the only separate non-Christian religious group of any size among the fourteen leading denominations in this study. Jews are well represented in Canada, especially in Montreal and Toronto. The history of the Canadian Jewish community began in 1760 in Quebec.

n. The *Roman Catholic Church* (about 71 million Canadian and U.S. members) constitutes the largest single religious body in the United States and Canada and works presently under the spiritual leadership of Pope John Paul II in the Vatican. Catholics trace their history back to St. Peter, St. Paul and the apostles of Rome. Catholic priests arrived in the New World with Columbus on his second voyage in 1493. The first continuing church was established at St. Mary's, Maryland, in 1634. In Canada the church began in 1534 when the first Mass was celebrated on the Gaspé Peninsula. The Canadian hierarchy is divided along linguistic lines between French and English and also along ethnic divisions.

Roman Catholic belief stresses the authority of the Pope and other officers of the hierarchy of the church, and the tenet that their church is the one holy, catholic, and apostolic church. Their faith is reflected in the Bible. The two Vatican Councils have further defined Roman Catholic beliefs. Sacraments include the celebration of the Mass, Baptism, Confirmation, Confession, Matrimony, Ordination, and Extreme Unction. The Virgin Mary and the saints are highly venerated. The Church is not divided into separate denominations, although there are many priestly, monastic, and sisterhood orders, for example, the Benedictines, Franciscans, Jesuits, Dominicans, and the Carthusians.

# Acknowledgments

The author would like to thank a large number of people for many contributions and specifically: Claudia Hannaford of Toledo (now deceased); Susan Zambakides (the entire book was in her word processor's memory unit at one point); Anne Gale, Carol Georgiou, Memna Hadjiharou, Donna Koulinos, Lorna Shearman, Karen Stephanou, Marie Claude Vidaillet, Janet Assadourian, Maria Damianou, Anthi Ellinidou, and Sahar Yanekian, all of Nicosia; the late Theodore Samore of Milwaukee and the late Frank Schick of Washington, D.C.; Richard Snyder of Philadelphia; Saiedeh and Wolfgang von Keitz, information scientists of Paris, France, and Stuttgart and Onkel, Germany, and Kobe, Japan; and Wendy Scott of the Library Development Centre at the National Library of Canada.

Special thanks go to Jo Ann Mouridou for her helpfulness in applying research methods as well as for all computer analyses. However, only the author, from outside the scholarly religious library and information field, is responsible for any misconstructions, misstatements, or poor judgments.

TABLE 1.1

A Religious Library Classification Scheme with Examples

---

SCHOLARLY LIBRARIES

*COLLEGES AND UNIVERSITIES (ACADEMIC)*

   Al Ashar University Central Library, Cairo, Egypt

   Catholic University of Louvain Library (French-speaking), Louvain, Belgium

   Haigazian College Library (Armenian), Beirut, Lebanon

   International Christian University Library, Tokyo, Japan

   University of Minnesota Newman Center Library, Minneapolis, MN, USA

*SEMINARIES, DIVINITY SCHOOLS AND RABBINICAL COLLEGES*

   Baltimore Hebrew College Library, Baltimore, MD, USA

   Catholic Higher School Faculty of Theology Library, Tilburg, The Netherlands

   Heythrop College Library (Jesuit), London, United Kingdom

   Islamic University Faculty of Theology Library, Cereban, Indonesia

   Ontario Theological Seminary Library, Willowdale, Ontario, Canada

*MONASTERIES, ABBEYS AND CONVENTS*

   Bibliothèque du couvent des Dominicaines, Toulouse, France

   Kykkos Monastery Library, Kykkos, Cyprus

   Monastery of St. Savior Library, Saida, Lebanon

   St. Anthony's Friary Library, Bangalore, India

   St. Benedict's Monastery Library, Rio de Janeiro, Brazil

*RELIGIOUS HISTORY LIBRARIES AND ARCHIVE CENTERS*

   Benedictine Order Central Principal Library, Pannonhalma, Hungary

   Canadian Baptist Archives, Hamilton, ON, Canada

   Gulbenkian Armenian Patriarchate Library, Aurelias, Lebanon

   United Methodist Historical Society Library, Baltimore, MD, USA

   United Society for the Propagation of the Gospel Library, London, United Kingdom

*DENOMINATIONAL HEADQUARTERS AND ADMINISTRATIVE OFFICES*

   American Congregational Association Library, Boston, MA, USA

   Anglican Church in Canada Library, Toronto, ON, Canada

   Baptist Missionary Society Library, London, United Kingdom

   Ecumenical Patriarchate Library (Greek Orthodox), Istanbul, Turkey

   Lutheran Evangelical Association Library, Helsinki, Finland

---

TABLE 1.1 (continued)
A Religious Library Classification Scheme with Examples

---

POPULAR LIBRARIES
>  *HOUSES OF WORSHIP (CONGREGATIONAL: CHURCHES AND SYNAGOGUES)*
>  Baptist Church Library, Tripoli, Libya
>  Church of Jesus Christ of Latter-day Saints Meetinghouse Library, Taipei, Taiwan
>  Congregation Kenesseth Israel Library, Allentown, PA, USA
>  Eman-e-zamin Mosque Library, Tehran, Iran
>  Lutheran Church Library, Swift River, SK, Canada
>  *PAROCHIAL SCHOOLS*
>  Allayyah Girls School Library (Episcopal), Amman, Jordan
>  Baptist Temple Academy Library, Fairfax, VA, USA
>  Catholic Education Office Library, East Melbourne, Victoria, Australia
>  École Saint-Florent Library, Saverne, France
>  Seventh-day Adventist Parochial School Library, Nicosia, Cyprus
>  *PUBLIC LIBRARIES*
>  Canberra Catholic Library, Watson, ACT, Australia
>  Christian Science Reading Room, Bulawayo, Zimbabwe
>  Evangelische Öffentliche Büchereien (Lutheran), Bremen, W. Germany
>  Senor de los Malagros Parochial Public Library, Comas, Peru
>  Union Nationale Culture et Bibliotheques Pour Tous (Roman Catholic Public
>  Library), Lille, France

---

Source: John F. Harvey, "Scholarly and Popular Religious Libraries," *International Library Review* 19 (October 1987), pp. 359–86.

TABLE 1.2

Core Activities Required for Full Scholarly and Popular Religious
Library and Bibliographic Development in Canada and the
United States

1.  Existence of a market ready to demand modern and professional religious library reference and circulation service.
2.  Religious library education available at graduate and undergraduate technician levels.
3.  Short continuing education courses for introductory education and practitioner updating.
4.  Local and national library conference programs.
5.  A comprehensive international library association.
6.  National library associations by level and denomination.
7.  National advisory library offices for major and minor denominations.
8.  At least one hundred superior academic libraries named to serve as models.
9.  At least two dozen superior seminary and two dozen superior Bible college libraries named to serve as models.
10. At least a dozen superior convent and a dozen superior monastery libraries named to serve as models.
11. At least a dozen superior religious organization administrative office libraries named to serve as models.
12. At least a dozen to one hundred superior congregational libraries of each denomination named to serve as models.
13. At least one hundred superior parochial and private school libraries named to serve as models.
14. Current and comprehensive adult and children's book and serial bibliographies.
15. Comprehensive bibliographies of significant books useful in each library type.
16. A current and comprehensive religious periodical index.
17. A current and comprehensive religious library periodical index.
18. One or more critical book reviewing periodicals.
19. A library journal, bulletin or newsletter published by each major denomination.
20. Several comprehensive surveys of library characteristics.
21. Comprehensive directories of the various types of libraries.
22. National biographical directories of religious librarians.
23. Several essays clearly defining and explaining the nature of religious librarianship.
24. Guidelines or performance standards for each type of library.
25. Model library policy and procedure manuals for each type of library.
26. Annual library budgets equaling at least 1–5% of the total institutional budget.
27. Comprehensive book classification schedules adapted for these libraries.
28. Comprehensive subject heading lists or thesauri.
29. Comprehensive library statistical collection, analysis and publication programs.
30. Library and information service research programs.

# 1

# AN INTRODUCTION TO THE RELIGIOUS LIBRARY WORLD

Before beginning to discuss aspects of the popular religious library picture, we must clarify this book's use of several key words and phrases and of several acronyms. Readers are urged to study carefully the glossary in appendix B to ensure that they understand these words and phrases thoroughly as they are used in the text.[1,2] Some terms can cause confusion, such as *congregational,* which may refer either to a specific denomination or to a type of library organization. *Denomination* may be used to describe all Baptists, for instance, or else only one of many North American Baptist groups, such as the Free Will Baptists.

The basic objective of this book is to describe and to analyze the fundamental characteristics of prominent groups of popular North American religious libraries. The characteristics to be examined are relatively basic, since this is a pioneering study and the groups of libraries are delimited and evaluated through the use of samples—in some cases large and in some cases small—of the population in each popular religious library subfield.

Emphasis is placed on identification and measurement of basic characteristics because these characteristics have not yet been firmly established as existing to any degree for these religious library groups. The study methodology is by sample because only samples of each population are available to the researcher without requiring unreasonable effort and expense. Nevertheless, in most cases the samples that were used clearly mirror the many dimensions of the targeted subfields.

The religious library field has not previously been identified by library and information leaders as comprising a distinct group sharing common characteristics. The field, therefore, needs to be defined as samples of the relevant subfields are described and analyzed here. The book takes the religious library field seriously. While the typical general library staff member may believe that the religious library field is small, specialized, and localized, the field is actually large and extensive. There are at least forty thousand North American religious libraries in at least 118 countries around the world.[3] In most of these countries, both scholarly and popular religious libraries can be found.

The author hopes that this book will make a distinct contribution to library literature in the following seven separate dimensions:

1. In addition to the traditional list of four basic types of libraries — public, school, academic, and special — this book proposes for consideration *a new type* of North American library based on library affiliation with or sponsorship by a religious institution or organization. Further, it divides the proposed category into two major subfields, scholarly and popular, plus five subdivisions for scholarly and three for popular religious libraries. Table 1.1 shows the author's classification. Careful study of this classification and its examples is essential to a clear understanding of the library categorization used in this book.

2. This book examines the characteristics of many North American popular religious public, congregational, and parochial school libraries, and its companion volume published earlier, *Scholarly Religious Libraries in North America,* examines the characteristics of the scholarly libraries.

3. All of this book's analyses and most of the conclusions drawn are *founded on objective library data obtained from three questionnaire surveys.*

4. To the limited extent possible with the data available, the analysis carries out an *international library comparison* between Canada and the United States.

5. It carries out a *ten-* or (in certain cases) *thirteen-year longitudinal comparison* of these sample libraries.

6. It compares and contrasts several *types* of popular religious libraries.

7. It proposes *a program of professional literature development* for the religious library field.

Much of the book's discussion is based on the author's analysis of 1) the information provided by the 1978 and 1988 editions of the *American*

*Library Directory* (*ALD*) and 2) the 1985–86 Church and Synagogue Libraries Association (CSLA) membership survey carried out by Claudia Hannaford.[4] Some of the material discusses and develops concepts already introduced by the author in previous books and papers.[2,3,5,6]

## The Larger Religious World

Generally speaking, religious libraries in the North American library world appear to be little discussed, written about or researched. Every issue of *Library Literature* (*LL*) contains a few citations to material about religious books and libraries, but the list is usually short and is made up primarily of scholarly library citations.[7] Further, religious libraries seem to maintain few ties with other kinds of libraries and to contribute only rarely to the significant journal, paper, and book literature of their own field. One seldom sees their libraries in positions of authority in general academic or special library associations, and one seldom reads their papers on religious library management, scholarly or popular.

Certain religious academic librarians, e.g., those heading large libraries, seem to be active in the large national academic and general library associations, but seldom in any religious library connection. As a group, some seminary librarians are distinctive in being active in seminary library associations, but only a small minority of these people merit scholarly notice. Certain Roman Catholic and Jewish librarians are active in local and national associations also, such as the Catholic Library Association (Cath LA) and the Association of Jewish Libraries (AJL), but again these are small groups of leaders active in largely parochial associations.

The larger religious world sees relatively few of these librarians either.[8] This world is the world of "the cloth"—ministers, priests, rabbis, and sisters—of the denominational hierarchy and of lay religious groups and their own sets of clergy and other leaders. The denominations become the libraries' sponsoring groups, and their leaders are the ones to whom the librarians must look for guidance and inspiration. The larger religious world takes its theological beliefs, practices, architecture, ceremonies, sacraments, and honors very seriously, and so must the librarian practicing therein.

This is a world of doctrine and dogma, of pomp and pageantry, of denominations and administrative divisions, of actors and diplomats. Each library is an emissary in the religious world, an organization standing between the institutionalized church and synagogue world and the lay or user arena and is expected, to some extent at least, to represent each one to the other with integrity and fidelity. Of course library representation is usually carried out as a unit of a larger institution, of a seminary or a synagogue, a college or a parochial school. The library's material collection has been selected at least in part to enable it to bridge the gaps between the secular and clerical worlds. This outlook and behavior describes all kinds of religious libraries to a greater or lesser extent.

Religious adherents may be subdivided among the various faiths, such as Christian, Jewish, or Muslim, the three largest North American religious systems.[8] Within each faith exist larger or smaller denominations or sects, such as Shiite Muslims and Reformed Jews. These groups differ somewhat among themselves in their forms of organization and in the articles of their faiths. In some cases, their insistence on the importance of these differences sets off the related groups from each other.

In other cases, groups, denominations and subdenominations have arisen out of regional, cultural, language, ethnic, or historical affinities and variations. Subdivision and further subdivision has been the North American Protestant rule, but in the present century a number of amalgamations have occurred also, for example, between the Universalists and the Unitarians, among several cooperating Lutheran groups, and among the groups that formed the United Church of Christ. Merely keeping track of whom is aligned with or separate from whom among certain Christian groups, such as the Baptists, Lutherans, and Mennonites, may be a frequent task.

The larger North American religious world contains a considerable variety of local, regional, and national administrative offices, organizations, and persons, both clerical and lay, male and female, in the headquarters of the many small and large denominations that are represented in Canada and the United States and where much of each denomination's power lies. The many central offices serve the clergy who are representatives of the denominations and the lay members who belong both to the worldwide denomination and to their own local houses of worship. It is not possible to be more specific than this, since so many different organizational forms occur.

Often the denomination's headquarters not only supervises the clergy out in the local churches and synagogues but also influences the many colleges and universities that may be directly sponsored by the denomination, affiliated closely with it, or affiliated with a specific house of worship. The central or regional office, such as a diocesan headquarters among Anglican churches, also supervises directly or influences various of its charitable organizations, such as hospitals, orphanages, retreat houses, benevolent societies, and other social service agencies, and its North American or foreign missions as well. This may give the headquarters officials much hierarchical authority over these organizations and the people who work in them, depending on the nature of the relationship between the superviser and the supervised.

To mention only a few other examples of the hierarchical system, we can list the Church of Jesus Christ of Latter-day Saints (LDS or Mormons), the Church of Christ, Scientist (Christian Science), Episcopal/Anglican, the Southern Baptist Convention, and the Roman Catholic Church, all of which seem to be large and well organized. Of course, denominational organization may take a centralized, a decentralized, or a congregational form.

After considering denominational headquarters, we must look at the many individual houses of worship that bring clergy and laypeople together. Certain aspects of this relationship are discussed later in this chapter. Most of the denomination's income is received in the individual house of worship unit, at the bottom, but in many cases its ecclesiastical authority is derived from the top, at the district or diocese or even at the regional or archdiocese level where a bishop or an archbishop may preside, for example, the Provincial Elders of the U.S. Moravian Church. In the end, however, the larger religious world consists primarily of individual house of worship members, most of whom consider themselves to be free agents taking what they want and returning the same to their local, regional, national, or worldwide church or synagogue groups.

An important part of the religious world is made up by the groups of sometimes more and sometimes less formally educated and ordained ministers, pastors, priests, rabbis, mullahs, imams, and other "holy" men. These religious leaders are further subdivided by rank into cardinals, archbishops, bishops, district superintendents, vicars, deans, and ministers among Roman Catholic or Protestant groups and deacons, elders, presiding elders, and other titles used sometimes for religious and sometimes for lay figures, making this a rank-and-title-conscious segment of North American society.

These ranks show the hierarchical, conservative, and traditional nature of the religious world and of most clergy. While denominations vary, and some have no formally appointed clergy (Baha'i adherents, the Salt Lake City Mormons, and the Christian Scientists, for instance), apparently few laypersons have more than a minimum amount of political influence in the affairs of most denominations, especially in the areas of doctrine and theology. The full-time professional clergy are the most powerful factors in local religious affairs, though a few lay leaders may exert influence in certain areas.

Outside the ministerial hierarchy, yet not very distant from it, are the religious orders of clergy, monks, and nuns, such as the members of the Society of Jesus and the Order of Friars Minor in the Roman Catholic Church. Religious order priestly functions may be similar to those of diocesan priests in serving churches, but, on the other hand, the individuals may work primarily on special missionary, publication, educational, or charitable projects and only secondarily as parish clergy.

In addition to the clergy, several denominations have full-time religious professionals such as monastery and convent members, priests' assistants, or charity administration assistants. They may have such titles and fill such roles as monks, brothers, sisters and nuns, or deaconesses. The denominations with these special professionals include Roman Catholic, Anglican, Lutheran, Salvation Army, Mennonite, and Greek Orthodox, among others. In addition, many denominations have full- or part-time lay administrative-religious employees with titles such as director of religious education, Sunday school superintendent, sacristan, verger, organist or director of music, for instance.

The clergy are persons, predominantly men, who have entered the service of their deity as a permanent vocation. They have a vested interest in institutionalized religion and represent both scholarly and popular library sponsors as well. They can be expected to push forward the religious aspect of library service and to regard a religious college library, for instance, as being primarily an organization with the basic mission of propagating a religious philosophy through reading and inspiring students and faculty members to lead more devout lives.

The basic mission of the religious library is to provide reading and viewing material on religion and the devout life. Whatever the level of the discussion, the primary focus is on spiritual development and on encouraging the spiritual and ethical development of the institutional members. Apparently the North American religious world's primary purpose is to assist the laity in saving its souls, or at least that is one way of perceiving it. The denominational clergy get together frequently in conferences for serious business discussions, to try to improve the status of their organizations as well as to discuss such practical things as job reassignment, building construction, fund-raising, and budgets.

Many laypersons are organized into one or more of the many permanent or temporary subgroups such as a Chicago Baptist Men's Breakfast Prayer Group, the Dominican Laity, or an Anglican Holy Land pilgrimage group. Another group of the laity falls under the heading of youth. Local youth clubs of many different kinds provide evidence of concentration on young age-groups and provide the house of worship with a continuing focus for its activities and a source of new memberships. Those of the Greek Orthodox Church in Cyprus provide interesting examples.

Opportunities for devoted leadership are numerous in all denominations, the houses of worship, and the lay groups. The conscientious library leader who is sufficiently resourceful can find many occasions to press library use and service on religious leaders, as well as exercising his or her leadership role within the library and within a specialized function of the church. A strong internal and external public relations program is needed to take the library ministry's service, as some congregations call it, to a large number of persons.

## The Importance of Libraries in the Religious World

Religion has a longer history than most other recognized fields of study, since several of the major faiths have existed for many centuries, such as the Hindu religion, which dates back to 1500 B.C. Other ancient religions trace their roots back several millennia before that. Many of the modern seminary library's titles were produced in the medieval, Reformation, or post-Reformation periods, certainly long before the twentieth century. Contrast the age of the average chemistry library's holdings!

In the scripture-oriented and conservative world of religion, where books and reading are thought to have widespread usefulness in presenting the sacred word and where daily reading is almost a requirement, the religious library and librarian should enjoy great importance and widespread respect. Both North American Christians and Jews are said by different writers to be "people of the book." At some time in most daily or weekly religious services the holy scripture used by the denomination or faith is read out in part, and in other sections of the service songs are sung that depend on or are inspired by the same holy writings.

Religion is more heavily dependent on the written word than are most other subject fields, so surely this should be an ideal field in which to be a librarian. The written word is all-important and the library has it! Libraries are significant in the religious world not only because they house the sacred books of the faith or the denomination but also because they provide service for the many theological commentaries and explanations, exhortations, and treatises that support and extend the sacred works.

Few persons teaching, preaching, or performing other tasks within the religious world can function properly without access to a good selection from the extensive literature of the field. Many of its main practitioners, the clergy, have small private book collections to assist them in carrying out their responsibilities. Most other fields are less book-bound, especially practical fields such as engineering and chemistry, so presumably they need fewer titles.

Certain categories of persons use religious libraries heavily. Seminary students study the large output of religious presses and their own holy book by day and by night in coursework preparation, while the clergy is expected to prepare ideas and quotations for weekly if not daily talks and sermons. Synagogue and church school teachers must regularly prepare the popular library material supporting their lessons, and seminary professors must read both religious and nonreligious material extensively in order to support their class and research work.

A large proportion of both house of worship laymen and laywomen (including a few librarians) are conscientious in reading their holy books regularly. Librarians in all kinds of religious libraries must read through the library's new additions in order to catalog them or to carry out reference work. Certain of these persons write reviews or annotations for publication about the new books arriving each month.

As a consequence of its pivotal role, the library occupies an honored place in the religious world and should receive strong support both by word and by funding from house of worship, academic, and other religious organization officials. However, this is not always the case, as we shall see in later chapters.

In what types of religious world institutions should popular or scholarly libraries be found? Denominational libraries may include one or more each in the national and lower-level headquarters offices, in each seminary, in each college or university, in each private synagogue or parochial school, in each monastery and convent (if the religious group has such institutions), and a few libraries to service historical and archive material. Perhaps the largest library category will consist of popular libraries serving denomination members directly in individual houses of worship. In addition, Mormon churches may support genealogical libraries, Catholic parishes may develop parish public libraries, and Christian Science churches may have reading rooms.[9,10] Larger denominations and those whose beliefs encourage wide reading will have many more libraries than those that are small or else more exclusively holy book oriented.

In general terms, what special functions should a library serve for its religious constituency? Functions differ according to type of denomination and type of library. Certain denominational libraries have the obligation to preserve significant religious material of all kinds originating within the denomination, and for the individual house of worship there is a need to preserve and service its own archives and publications. In addition, each library is obligated to select, acquire, organize for use, and service a collection of appropriate recent material representing its own faith and denomination, and perhaps material from the historical and wider religious world as well.

Religious academic and school libraries of all kinds, including church and synagogue schools, are expected to follow closely their parent organization's curricula, which may be either slightly or more extensively religious. In addition, on certain college and university campuses, some students take noncredit religion courses in denominational centers, such as a Hillel Jewish center or a Roman Catholic Newman center. At all levels these libraries can include recreational reading material that may or may not be religious. Of course, religious libraries may have further obligations, also, and may be required to provide service for research material in universities and seminaries, this year's Sunday school material in Protestant churches, and practical texts to assist daily operations in religious organization administrative office libraries.

In chemistry libraries a pressing need often exists for the most current information to be made available immediately, whereas in religious libraries there may be pressure to assemble an extensive collection, but usually not for either rush service or for new book service. And only in a seminary library, a religious college library, or a university library serving a theological department is there need for a truly extensive collection. Most religious libraries are small and have modest reputations locally, much less so in the larger religious world. The popular religious library almost never boasts a large collection, ten thousand volumes being large for a congregational or religious school library. As a consequence of restricted need, most parochial, convent/monastery, or religious public libraries also develop collections of this size or smaller.

Books and libraries vary greatly in their centrality to the religious institution that they serve and in religious officials' recognition of their value. Seminary libraries are probably given more attention and respect than any other religious library category, but typically they serve one of the smallest user groups. North American colleges and universities support their libraries relatively well, though centrality to the curriculum and research program is seldom of a high order. Individual houses of worship vary greatly in respect to funding, with the vast majority of them providing only a quiet supplementary service.

When a Presbyterian church library, for example, is able to influence the local minister or the women's Sunday school class through its librarian's personality or its judicious selection policies, then it may achieve some local recognition. Certain other religious libraries provide superior service, also, with live and useful material collections. As an example, the Cambridge, Ontario, Forward Baptist Church library circulated an average of 166 volumes each Sunday morning in 1983 and thereby must have earned a position of respect in that community.[11]

Typically, religious libraries of all kinds possess relatively small serial collections, such as the Wisconsin Lutheran Seminary Library which listed 37,000 book volumes but only 1,700 bound periodical volumes, a 21.8:1.00 ratio. Their book volume to serial volume ratio is the opposite of that in chemistry, for instance, where the ratio is relatively small. Therefore, scholarly religious libraries need a good card or computerized catalog or index much more than they need extensive serial indexes. It must also be true that a good theology library requires a larger collection to cover essential material than that needed for most other subject fields, simply because the theological literature is so vast.

Partly as the result of so much book writing, apparently the religious field contains more printed bibliographies than do most other fields. Bibliographies are needed to guide the reader through a field's extensive literature. As another result of past publishing and bibliography making, American Theological Library Association (ATLA) members' attention is directed toward reprinting and microfilming older but still useful monographic material as well as certain indexing projects for recent serial material.[12]

Many clergymen do not read extensively in their field, in some cases because their beliefs are holy book centered, that is, extensive reading of the holy book is enough to answer their questions. In other cases reading is not essential for them professionally or spiritually. And in still other cases throughout the world reading is not expected of them because they are illiterate. In addition, the range of literature relevant to their faith may be difficult to locate or pay for. Therefore, even though libraries may be thought by some to be religious institutions of special importance, they are not necessarily heavily used or awarded adequate budgets. They may be important for only a few leaders and students, while other persons may endorse their role without personally feeling the need to use them.

In fact, in many places religious libraries seem to be treated like repositories rather than like live, active, and helpful information centers. Few library users desire to read extensively on a religious topic, though some nonlibrary users extensively read religious material, which they have obtained from other sources. No leadership role is expected of the librarian in such a library, merely quiet, dedicated and often modestly paid or even volunteer service. In general, the library seems to occupy a place at the edge of the North American religious world, of central importance in a few cases but often no more than an optional or little-used service in others.

The greater religious world has much power over the library and its sponsoring institution. For the librarian to become acquainted with that world and eventually to develop some degree of familiarity with several parts of it would be beneficial for both sides. The outside religious world also provides opportunities to further the goals of the house of worship or academic institution by carrying out useful projects. The dedicated religious librarian should seek fulfillment in both the outside library and the outside religious worlds.

Greater library staff member activity might lead to cooperative projects and could involve the library more fully in the mainstream of religious world activities. Such activity would also provide recognition that both the religious and the library fields are strongly service oriented and that such an orientation is common not only to them but is also unusual in many other professional and business fields. Both library and religious practitioners are expected to approach their tasks in such a user- or clientele-oriented spirit.

Many religious academic librarians seem to have few close, direct working contacts with the *religious* leaders under whom they serve. Partly due to their passive nature, few library staff members have played a strong and forceful role in the religious world. As far as this author can tell, only a small number of religious library staff members are active in formal church or synagogue library or nonlibrary organizations or associations, and an even smaller number seeks leadership roles in them. Often the activists seem to be clergy or religious order members working from an academic or parochial school library base.

## The Larger Library and Information Service World

Space does not permit a full introduction to the larger library and information world or to the larger religious world. We are limited to sketching a general outline of the library and information service world in order to provide a basis for certain religious and other library world comparisons. The "larger library and information world" contrasts with the more modest religious library field and refers to all North American libraries and library and information activities. This is the world of some large and many thousands of small libraries, of library associations both general and specialized, and of library schools both with and without doctoral programs.

Though smaller than the religious world, the religious library and information world is also rich in variety and of considerable size. It includes a range of libraries from the quite specialized such as the Ames Orchid Library of Harvard University to the heterogeneous collections such as the New York Public Library. It is a world of occasional scholarship, at least in a few of the leading library schools, such as the University of Illinois Graduate School of Library and Information Science, and much routine clerical and semiprofessional work.

In contrast to the religious world of doctrine and faith in abstract or unprovable concepts, the information world is one of pragmatism and technique. In contrast to the religious institution's considerable independence, the library and information service institution is heavily dependent on a local parent institution, such as a university or a house of worship. It is a world in which the large public and university library directors and department heads customarily play a major role while the smaller elementary school and public librarians play a more modest one. It is a world of many politicians but only a few statesmen and women.

This world is one of large and small associations, several with over four thousand members, for example, the Canadian Library Association (CLA) with membership above four thousand, while others are specialized and small, for example, the Theatre Library Association of five hundred members. Generally, association memberships are growing, especially as these groups move further into continuing education. Certain large national associations take positions on national political, educational, and social issues, and their conferences attract hundreds of exhibitors and thousands of library staff members.

Several larger libraries have staffs of over a thousand persons, such as the Chicago Public Library with more than two thousand staff members, yet many other libraries have staffs of a single person, for example, the Center for Computer Law Library in Manhattan Beach, California. Probably most large libraries are not experiencing growth in staff size, while the number of one-person libraries is still growing. This world is a welter of varied personalities, ethnicity, and educational mores, with educational qualifications rising rapidly each year.

Gender emphases vary from the all-male administrative staff, for example, at the Coastal Plain Regional Library, Tifton, Georgia, to the all-female administrative staff at the Alsip-Merrionette Park Library, Alsip,

Illinois. Staff members' educational specializations can vary widely both in nature and in scope with practical subjects increasing slowly in popularity, for example, more MBA and MPA degrees and more social and computer science majors.

The larger library and information world includes the library press, which issues periodicals and reports of many kinds as well as books. Its influence on the field is growing. There are hundreds if not thousands of small North American university and congregational, association, and chapter newsletters and acquisitions lists, periodicals, and continuations, such as the *International Leads,* most of them ephemeral and aimed at local or denominational audiences. Many of the most substantial publications, such as the University of Illinois's *Library Trends,* are produced by universities. A surprising number of book publishers concentrate in this field—Bowker, Dekker, Greenwood (in part), JAI, Knowledge Industry, Libraries Unlimited, McFarland (in part), Neal-Schuman, Oryx, Scarecrow, Shoe String, and Wilson, as well as the American Library and the Special Libraries Associations.

In North America are concentrated more libraries, including religious libraries, than can be found on any other continent. The larger North American library and information world is one in which school libraries predominate in terms of separate units followed by numerous public libraries. There are more school libraries in Canada and the United States than all of the other kinds of libraries combined.[13,14] The total number of Canadian and U.S. libraries is about 158,000, of which about 28.8 percent have previous or present religious affiliation or sponsorship. Probably many institutions and libraries that are now largely secular had religious affiliations at some point in the recent past.

## Religious Library Importance in the Library and Information World

As a discrete group, scholarly and popular religious libraries are of some importance for several reasons. One of these reasons is the sheer number of these libraries in North America and elsewhere. (See chap. 2.) Religious topics occupy an entire section in most book classification schemes. In addition, religious librarians and their libraries form an interesting and distinctive group. Further, seminary library users are moving increasingly into interdisciplinary material use on university campuses and thereby bridging the gap with other subject fields. The policies and procedures followed in most large or small religious libraries differ little from those followed in libraries in other subject fields elsewhere. Their user group differs a little, however, and emphasizes persons who are working or studying in this field as house of worship members or students in church or synagogue parochial schools.

Despite their large numbers, religious libraries in most nations form a relatively small and less important segment of the national library and information world. Even in a nation with a state religion, such as Cyprus, religious libraries are of little importance. Especially if we judge by median sizes of budget, staff, and collection, their rank is surprisingly low. For instance, in most religious libraries staffing is usually no more than one to three persons per library, and in the popular religious libraries probably all of these staff members are volunteer clerks.

The largest religious libraries in this study are those located in universities, such as the University of Notre Dame Library in Indiana, with almost two hundred staff members. On the other hand, in Canada and the United States the occupational specialty of scholarly religious librarianship is a small one, small in numbers of people participating, smaller at least than legal, musical, medical, science and technology, art, rare book, archive, media, serial, government publication, armed forces, and government agency librarianships.

Religious academic libraries range from the grossly inadequate to the superior. In the college and university departmental library field, religious libraries occupy a respectable but hardly outstanding place, in part because their collections are relatively large but more nearly because their user groups are usually relatively small. Monastery and convent libraries, such as the St. Benedicts Monastery Library in Colorado, are certainly religious, if any libraries are, but they are usually small and may not always be fully professionalized or automated.

Even professional religious librarians seem to pay attention primarily to their own small "sideshows" within the larger library and information world. They do not mingle very much with other kinds of librarians. Religious library leaders seldom reach high office in national associations, except in national religious library associations. As far as this author can determine, no American Library Association (ALA) president in the past half-century has come from a religious library. Religious librarians are more likely to attend a conference sponsored by a religious library group, especially a group from the librarian's own denomination, than one sponsored by a general library group.

The only groups of religious librarians known to this author who attend conferences regularly or frequently are those from seminaries and parochial schools. A small group of U.S. and Canadian seminary librarians attends ATLA conferences faithfully, no matter how far away they are held. However, this group constitutes only 1–2 percent of the entire North American seminary library population, and a much smaller proportion of all religious librarians. Of course, ATLA seminary librarians may be considered to be the "cream" of the religious library world, in terms of educational background (many of the librarians have both graduate theology and graduate library and information school degrees), prestigious positions, and salary, and so we should expect much of them.

Full-time parochial school librarians turn out in large numbers for a *local* parochial school library conference, such as a Cath LA Brooklyn-Long Island Chapter meeting, less so for general school and other kinds of local conferences, and in small numbers for more distant conferences. Many popular religious librarians are part-time, nonprofessional volunteers who lack sufficient time or interest (and sometimes the funds) to attend general conferences where, in addition, religious library matters are seldom discussed.

Another characteristic of religious librarians is that they almost invariably have a humanities-oriented educational background. They may thus be qualified for work in a religious library, but they have a poorer background for management and may be less comfortable in front of a computer terminal than are business librarians. Nor, apparently, do the majority of them have educational qualifications in religion, and some lack library educational qualifications also.

Religious librarianship has an additional distinction. A thread runs through all of theology and through the work of all religious librarians. This is a common historical or developmental thread. Certain other fields also have similar historical threads or frameworks to follow. An entire curriculum can be hung on an outline of the history of religion. While the social sciences, "hard" sciences, and technical fields have their histories too, in designing course work and curricula, they do not necessarily show consciousness of such frameworks. Religion and theology librarians do.

To the author's mind, most religious librarians share one other common characteristic. Many of them are very cooperative, agreeable, and humble persons. In the process of editing nine collections of other people's papers on chapter topics of his own choosing in the past quarter century, the author has become aware of the difficulty of finding well-qualified persons who will agree to prepare these papers. Sometimes he must go through a dozen names before finding one who is both well qualified and amenable. So far, the one exception to this generalization was a book that used a group of popular religious librarians as authors. Almost without exception, the first choices agreed to prepare the chapters soon after being asked.[5]

To supplement the library press, there exists a popular religious library press publishing mostly thin, insubstantial, and bland newsletters, with usually favorable book review sections plus thin pamphlets and bibliographies; this group too is growing in size and market penetration. Several examples are listed in appendix A. Few full-length religious library and information science books and indexes are produced by the religious library press (except for Cath LA and ATLA), but the general library press publishes a few books in this religious library field each year.

## Religious Library Similarities and Differences from Nonreligious Libraries

Based on the data available for this book, which will be discussed in detail in later chapters, religious libraries seem to be similar in most areas to nonreligious libraries of the same type. In fact, they seem to bear many more similarities than differences to corresponding nonreligious libraries. They use the same cataloging rules and classification schemes (for most of the collection); they buy from several of the same book and serial publishers and dealers; the staff organization and work assignment principles are similar, financial policies are similar, and their charging systems are similar. However, certain differences and contrasts should be mentioned.

Most religious library material collections of all kinds (except those of colleges, universities and schools) are composed primarily of religious material. The Agudath Israel Congregation Malca Pass Library in Ontario, for example, probably contains little other than religious material, most of it Jewish. Typical nonreligious college, university, and school libraries devote only a small percentage of their collections to religious material. It would be surprising to find a large religious collection in the Texas A and M University Library, College Station, for instance. So religious material dominates certain library collections, but others concentrate on nonreligious material.

Many monastery, convent, congregational, and religious history libraries maintain no active selection or acquisition programs but depend on gifts to enlarge the library, since no book funds are regularly made available. Other libraries order a few books each year from a local religious bookshop with the small funds provided by their supervisors, for example, St. Paul's Anglican Cathedral Library, Nicosia, Cyprus.

Both seminary and congregational libraries patronize certain religious book and serial publishers, in many cases denominational. Classification activities in most religious libraries are similar to those in nonreligious libraries except for the problem of the many Bible editions contained in the seminary library and the special classification schemes that it may use for certain special religious collections.

Seminary libraries may have their own buildings (Ruoss found that 68 percent of them did have in 1968), and religious college and university libraries usually do have, but other kinds of religious libraries seldom have separate buildings.[15] In general, religious library circulation is small. Most Church and Synagogue Library Association (CSLA) congregational libraries averaged no more than twenty-five loans per week. On the other hand, certain parochial school libraries circulate one book per student per week.

Before completing the discussion of how religious libraries differ from nonreligious libraries, we must look at how religious institutions and their libraries vary among themselves in their emphasis on religion in the curriculum and in campus life. Many of them vary considerably. We might expect Laval University in Quebec, French speaking and Roman Catholic, to give strong emphasis to Catholic viewpoints. On the other hand, Bishop's University, also in Quebec, English speaking and Anglican, probably emphasizes Anglican viewpoints much less than we might expect.

On certain campuses the particular denominational affiliation is strong and its influence permeates campus life, such as at Seton Hall University (Roman Catholic) in New Jersey and at most independent Bible colleges, such as the Mennonite Brethren Bible College in Manitoba. On certain evangelical campuses a religious focus permeates daily life from breakfast prayers to evening religious services. However, on many other campuses, religious connections are weak and so is religious influence on faculty and students, e.g., at the University of the Pacific (Methodist) in California. On some campuses, many students spend four years studying without ever entering the campus chapel or the central library. Generally, on Roman Catholic, Jewish, Mormon, Baptist, Adventist, Christian, charismatic, evangelical, and Bible college campuses the religious presence is relatively strong, whereas at many other religiously affiliated educational institutions it is weak, often very weak.

After having discovered differences among religious colleges and universities, we can say that these differences represent their greatest contrast, since, for the most part, North American religious and nonreligious academic libraries are much alike. However, religious libraries generally possess a larger proportion of religious library material in the collection than do

nonreligious libraries. Further, the religious library may have special religious collections, at least pertaining to its own denomination or faith. Religious order nuns, priests, and brothers may work on the faculty and library staff, and probably the student body contains more than the usual
share of religiously committed or else "saved" Christian persons also.

Roman Catholic, Lutheran, Quaker, Episcopal/Anglican, and other
*parochial school* libraries are similar to public school libraries in their
book and serial collections, in using the Dewey decimal classification, in
using standard cataloging policies, and in providing the same variety of
public services in curriculum support to students and faculty members.[16]
However, parochial schools differ primarily in the following ways: (1)
the curriculum contains a stronger religious element, (2) the collection
may contain a larger emphasis on religious material and probably concentrates on material from the school's own denomination, (3) the librarian may belong to a religious order, and (4) certain of the faculty, library staff, and student body share a common religious heritage.

Many private parochial schools try to maintain a common frame of
reference that is not found in nonreligious private schools — a uniformity
of denominational emphasis affecting material collection, library staff,
student body, and faculty. A Roman Catholic library such as the one at
the St. John Neumann High School in Pennsylvania, for instance, has
many books written or edited by Catholics, has one or more sections of
books on Catholic thought and leaders, avoids church-proscribed books,
and buys most of its material from Catholic publishers and agents.

In certain important ways, religious *public* libraries are exceptions to
the above generalizations. In these ways and others, they also differ
sharply from municipal and state government-sponsored public libraries.
They have little or no tax support, and usually they offer no children's
service. The religious public library book collection is heavily slanted toward the publications of the sponsoring religious group, and most of
these are Christian Science or Roman Catholic libraries.

Christian Science reading room books and periodicals seem to be al-
most entirely restricted to those published by the Mother Church in
Boston, as found, for instance, in the First Church Reading Room in
Guadalajara, Mexico.[17] All of these libraries contain copies of the current and back issues of the fine *Christian Science Monitor* newspaper, the
*Christian Science Journal,* and the book writings of founder Mary Baker
Eddy. These reading rooms are always sponsored by a local church or
group of churches and may often be found either in a church or near it in
a storefront location on a busy business street. The material available may
be read there or purchased and taken away.

A large city may have a half dozen or more Christian Science libraries, as does Oklahoma City. Hours open weekly vary from two to sixty. One gets the impression that sponsoring the library is a major church activity. Each library appears to be much like the others, but they do not relate closely to each other in synergistic terms. Instead they cooperate more closely with their specific parent churches. They seem to be used by different groups of people but primarily by Christian Science church members. Many reading rooms are very small. Although their operation is simple compared with other congregational libraries, Christian Science reading rooms have an advisory office at the church headquarters in Boston that assists new churches in establishing their libraries and in educating library personnel.

Catholic reading rooms differ from Christian Science libraries in that they have a greater variety of books and publishers represented and are less single-mindedly evangelistic. Most Catholic public libraries, however, seem to emphasize introductions to Catholicism, Catholic thought on contemporary issues, and Catholic best-selling biographies and fiction such as are found in the Catholic Information Center on East Market Street in Philadelphia. Catholic libraries are not part of an international system as, to a certain extent, are Christian Science reading rooms. Most Roman Catholic reading rooms are supported by their fee-paying members, by a group of financial sponsors, and by healthy discounts from book suppliers.

There is no nonreligious group with which to compare congregational libraries, such as the large Blumenthal Library of Sinai Temple in California. However, libraries that serve primarily a Sunday school or a synagogue school may be compared to those in a private religious elementary or secondary preparatory school. Most congregational libraries serve a part-time one-morning-a-week school in which perhaps no one is paid a regular salary. They are typically smaller than private or public school libraries, concentrate primarily on religious material, especially denominational material, and may serve all house of worship congregation members, including children and young adults. Private religious school libraries serve full-time curriculum, faculty, and student groups. Of course, nonreligious school libraries have relatively few religious materials, staff members, or users.

Religious history and archive centers, such as the Oregon Province, Society of Jesus Archives Library, Spokane, differ little from nonreligious history and archive centers except for the nature of the parent organization and the material stored. Most of these are either national or regional denominational centers.

Religious organization administrative office libraries, such as the Anglican Church of Canada Harris Memorial Library in Toronto, differ little from other special libraries other than by containing a large percentage of religious material.[18] They stock much practical religious and nonreligious reference and historical material about a particular denomination. Many of them relate to the publishing, communication, or public relations arm of a particular denomination. In most cases, they are staffed by religiously affiliated persons who provide service to religiously affiliated users.

## Is Religious Librarianship a Cohesive and Narrowly Focused Field?

What about the cohesiveness of religious librarianship? Does religious librarianship have the single-minded focus and unity that a unique or discrete professional field should have? Can we define a cohesive or uniform library field? The following criteria can be used to examine the cohesiveness of a group of religious libraries: shared (1) religious institutional sponsorship, (2) library objectives, (3) material collection emphases, and (4) nature of the user groups. Also, the field should be served by (5) a limited number of specialized religious library associations. If all five of these factors were unfailingly required as criteria, religious librarianship would have difficulty in qualifying as an organized and cohesive field. However, if the standard to be applied were not quite that rigorous, then perhaps religious librarianship might qualify as being generally cohesive.

Perhaps common religious institutional sponsorship is the criterion most broadly applicable to the group of libraries discussed in this book. All (or almost all) of their parent institutions have formal religious denominational or house of worship sponsorship or affiliation, although their degree of closeness to the denomination or of religious observance in daily affairs varies. With religious sponsorship or affiliation, all parent institutions must be to a large degree religious. In all cases, therefore, these libraries have objectives that include religious material service to users for primarily religious purposes, meeting the second criterion, though in many academic libraries this objective is included only in a blanket service statement covering all kinds of library services and users.

House of worship, convent, and monastery libraries strongly emphasize religious books, the third criterion, but many of the former also contain a proportion of nonreligious children's books for their public library-type users, such as the Carmel Presbyterian Church, Glenside, Pennsylvania. Most religious college and university and parochial school libraries contain collections in which religious books constitute only a small proportion of the whole: (1) a modest number of books directly in the religious field, (2) some books in specific subject fields that were produced by a denominational author or press, and (3) many books that have no religious connection but relate to the institution's educational programs. The fourth criterion, uniformity in the nature of the clientele, includes many religious libraries but not all. Most academic libraries have only a few religiously connected users, but house of worship, monastery, and convent libraries serve almost no other kind. Parochial school libraries serve varied proportions of religiously oriented users.

Concerning organization of librarians into a number of library associations, the criterion is fairly met by these librarians. Most of the associations are small and limited by nation, sometimes even by region, usually by denomination, and even by scholarly versus popular focus. Of course, organization into one large association or even into three by faith (Christian, Jewish, and Islamic) would show greater cohesion, but a fractionated picture is better than a field without organizations.

Of course, cohesiveness is a stiff requirement for any group of libraries. By definition, each religious library subfield is more cohesive than is the whole. We can conclude that the religious libraries in this book are uniform in having religious institutional sponsorship and affiliation, largely uniform in fitting themselves into library associations, and partially uniform in each one of the three other criteria. The entire field has a strong focus on religion, and cohesiveness varies somewhat for each subfield and by each criterion.

A problem with this situation is that the group of academic religious librarians in this study (and perhaps other religious librarian subgroups as well) do not see themselves as being composed of general religious librarians. Rather, these people see themselves as being general academic librarians who work in strongly or weakly religiously affiliated institutions. In many cases, they display little religious group consciousness. In most instances, they are well aware of the institution's religiosity and are happy to be there but think only rarely about their parent institution's religious status.

Usually the lack of religious interest is due, at least in part, to the lack of campuswide religious emphasis or interest. In contrast, other kinds of religious librarians feel that they are happiest when working in a religious institutional administrative office, Bible college, monastery, house of worship, parochial school, or religious public library. In any case, most of these library employees appear to feel no religious library solidarity with the staff members of another library of the same denomination.

Certain related groups face a similar dilemma for somewhat different reasons. They recognize the religious nature of their positions without difficulty, but they think of themselves primarily as being Mormon librarians, for instance, or Jewish, or Congregational or Moravian librarians, rather than general or broadly religious librarians. In these cases the particular denomination takes precedence over the general religious status in their thinking. In fact, most religious libraries are very conscious of denominational differences, even of factional differences within the denominations, such as the Independence Mormons versus the Salt Lake City Mormons, or the Free Will Baptists versus the American Baptists, and this concern often outweighs feelings of affinity with other religious librarians. Even ATLA annual conferences are well aware of the diversity of denominational interests and cater to them specifically.

Further, probably the Methodist seminary librarian feels relatively little affinity with the Episcopal/Anglican popular church librarian, for instance. In this illustration, not only have we jumped to a different denomination, a different library level and probably a part-time versus a full-time librarian, but also most Methodist head seminary librarians are men, while most Episcopal/Anglican church head librarians are women. Such feelings of narrow differences negatively influence the religious library group's thinking and inhibit its recognition of its cohesiveness as a general body of religious professionals. Many religious librarians prefer to emphasize the differences, setting themselves off from other religious groups, rather than the similarities that bind all of them together. For these and other reasons it is difficult to identify certain religious librarians as belonging to a fully cohesive group.

## Criteria for Study Inclusion

The reader may wish to ask how the author chose the libraries covered in this religious library study. Where did he find more than two thousand North American scholarly and popular religious libraries, cohesive or not? This question is especially cogent, since in certain of the study's academic libraries, for instance, the percentage of religious material held was less than 0.5 percent, it was little used, and no staff member devoted more than a few hours a year to technical or public service for it. In reply, the author would say that every library is a religious library to the extent that its sponsorship, collection, and user group come from that subject field. The libraries in this study represent both ends of the scale, from being religious to only a small degree to being almost entirely religious, i.e., wholly classified in the Dewey decimal classification 200s, for instance.

When organizing the study, the author saw that it would be unrealistic to quiz two thousand libraries about the size of their religious material collections and the amount of staff time, funds, and use devoted to them before deciding to include the library in the study or reject it. Ascertaining the attention a library gave to religious material may have been the best way to learn its degree of religiosity, but that method was too intricate and expensive to use in this study. Probably neither religion nor any other single subject field would occupy more than a small percentage of the library's collection, time, and funds, except in congregational, monastery, or seminary libraries. Nor was there any logical and practical way of deciding what standard should be established for religious collection size, use, staffing, and funding.

The criterion of sponsorship was used because of the reasonableness of the assumption that a religiously related institution's library had an obligation to see that both collection and service contained some representation of religion, no matter how small, and particularly that of the sponsoring denomination. Such faiths and denominations as were mentioned in the previous section—Catholic, Jewish, Mormon, Baptist, charismatic, evangelical, and Bible oriented—constituted a sizeable percentage of the academic libraries and more than half of all congregational libraries studied. They customarily made their religious influence felt throughout the parent institution and therefore could be included in the religious library group without qualms. Certain other denominations were less demanding in religious terms (religiousness) and so the libraries were included primarily on the basis of their formal or informal or sometimes historic affiliations.

## Religious Library Contacts with Popular-Level Library Groups

### Popular Religious Library Associations

Certain high-ranking librarians view the popular religious library field— house of worship, parochial school, and public libraries—as being made up primarily of nonprofessionals or paraprofessionals and therefore as being outside the proper area of concern of any library school or any professional librarian. Others view popular religious librarianship as a secondary or derivative field that follows the intellectual lead of the better known library types—public, school, special, and academic libraries. Still others view popular religious librarianship as a field with such small funds, collections, and readerships per unit as to render that field incapable of making more than a minuscule contribution to the overall service level of librarianship.

While these views are useful to know and contain several elements of truth, they do not represent any sort of final evaluation of popular religious library and information service, nor do they present the entire picture of that field. Furthermore, these attitudes tend to downgrade the field unnecessarily, to cast an unfavorable light on the professional and nonprofessional librarians working therein, and to place the critics in a snobbish and professionally untenable position. Just why school librarianship is respectable and parochial school librarianship is less so or is not respectable at all, according to this view, and why public librarianship is respectable and privately sponsored religious public librarianship is less so is unclear, for instance.

Perhaps it is more sensible to view popular religious librarianship as an emerging professional and paraprofessional field, as is scholarly religious librarianship or general academic librarianship, for that matter, though no doubt the latter two groups are further along in their professional development paths than is the former. But is the popular religious library field moving toward full professional status? Of course, little data is available that would allow charting any upward or downward movement either toward or away from professionalism, as defined in the sociological literature, so we cannot answer this question with full objectivity.

Is the percentage of professional librarians working in the religous field rising or falling? While the answer to that question cannot be determined for the field as a whole, the percentage is high among popular private and parochial school libraries, especially if bachelor's degree library science graduates are accepted as professionals. Among other popular religious librarians, at least among congregational librarians, the evidence (see chaps. 2–4) suggests that the percentage of professionals has been growing in recent years. (See chap. 6 for the house of worship and religious public librarians who are now library school graduates. The proportion in certain categories may surprise you.)

When working with popular religious library associations that can be helpful to them in a number of ways, religious librarians have a variety of choices. The AJL Synagogue, Center, and School Section is active in carrying out programs that support temple, synagogue school, and Jewish center libraries. Leadership roles often go to the capable librarians of the large synagogues. AJL's nine chapters are composed primarily of synagogue library staff members. Book review pages constitute 50 percent or more of the AJL *Newsletter, Judaica Librarianship's* sister publication, and cover Jewish adult and children's fiction and nonfiction, scholarly and popular books, and serials.[19] A job clearinghouse is included, and chapter news and publication announcements complete each issue. Members are given newsletter assistance in several areas—book and periodical selection, acquisitions, cataloging, and reference work.

The Cath LA has three sections of strong interest to popular Catholic librarians, the Children's Libraries Section, the High School Libraries Section and the Parish and Community Libraries Section. The Children's Section includes members from public, parochial, and private elementary school libraries and tries to improve children's work everywhere. Closely related is the busy group of parochial and private secondary school librarians, which is active in the state, regional, diocese, and archdiocese-wide chapters and wherever there are Catholics working in school libraries. The Parish and Community Libraries Section is the one in which both Catholic parish (congregational) and public librarians are active. It is small because both of the latter groups are small in the Catholic world, but it has been active for almost thirty years.

The fact that the Parish and Community Libraries Section is located in the Cath LA puts Catholic congregational librarians in a somewhat better position than that of CSLA or LCLA members, since they can cooperate closely with the other Cath LA sections and individuals. The Catholic library may use special Cath LA subject headings and Catholic Library of Congress classification expansions for canon law, St. Thomas Aquinas, and the sacraments.

CSLA has been an active force in popular religious librarianship for the past thirty-one years.[20] It is an ecumenical group with many denominations represented in thirty chapters and affiliates in many states. It provides book reviews in a news bulletin and annual conference programs for several hundred attendees and participants.[21] These programs cover a variety of subjects—archive management, book lists, budgeting, cataloging problems, chapter activities, computer use, mending techniques, new books, public relations, publication programs, storytelling, volunteer training, and others. Obviously, CSLA is a useful contact for popular librarians to make. It publishes a series of small bibliographies and manuals for its membership and also for other librarians.

Membership in the thirty-five-year-old LCLA should be useful for Lutherans also.[22] This group has more than two dozen chapters, publishes a quarterly bulletin with book and media reviews and chapter news as well as conference plans. Annual conferences that provide helpful programs are held in various northern districts of the United States. The LCLA has an annual budget of $50,000 and several full- and part-time paid headquarters staff members. ACL meets the needs of evangelical Christian librarians in academic and popular libraries and has three hundred members. The association publishes the *Christian Librarian,* a quarterly, and the *Christian Periodical Index,* a small index to evangelical periodicals. An annual conference is held each June.

Canadian congregational library associations include (1) The Congregational Library Association of British Columbia, (2) The Christian Church Library Association, (3) The Church Library Association of Toronto, (4) The Mennonite Librarians Association, (5) The Pacific Northwest Association of Church Libraries (with both Canadian and U.S. members), and (6) The United Church of Canada Conference of Manitoba and NW Ontario. Most of these groups publish newsletters and perform the same activities as the popular U.S. religious library associations. The primary difference in Canada is that the groups are smaller than those in the United States and less specialized.

Not all Canadian regions, however, are covered by these six associations. We may note further that no national popular religious library association exists there, the associations all being regional, provincial, or regional-denominational. Furthermore, few of the existing associations are strong enough in membership to be of maximum usefulness to their members.

## Popular Religious Library Denominational Headquarters Offices

While most denominations provide no congregational library assistance to their members, several others are affiliated with a library association, and a few provide some kind and degree of headquarters popular library advisory service. Of the various Baptist subgroups, the Southern Baptists have been both the largest and the most active in congregational librarianship for at least five decades. The Sunday School Board Church Media Library Department of the Southern Baptist Convention is located in Nashville, and in the summer the department sponsors weeklong library conferences at its centers in Glorietta, New Mexico, and Ridgecrest, North Carolina. Through the winter and spring, the department sponsors regional two-day conferences in various locations.

The Church Media Library Department includes several full-time professional congregational library advisors and publishes the quarterly *Church Media Library Magazine* featuring short articles and useful bibliographies, some practical and some inspirational.[23] In addition, the congregational librarians of many Baptist churches organize themselves on a city-by-city basis each year. Small groups of five to thirty Baptist church librarians get together several times a year to learn from each other and from occasional visiting speakers.

The LDS (Mormon) Church maintains an extensive library system with headquarters in Salt Lake City.[24] A secretariat advises local librarians and has published a handbook showing how to organize and operate a Mormon meetinghouse library. This library system numbers altogether at least twenty-eight hundred meetinghouse libraries in every geographic area of the world. In addition, several hundred Mormon genealogical libraries are maintained in a variety of countries, and they are open to the general public as well as to meetinghouse members. Only the Mormons and the Christian Scientists have extensive, well-organized, and centrally advised international popular religious library networks. Both systems are impressive.

Of course, popular religious librarians have frequent contact with both religious and nonreligious book and serial publishers and dealers. This contact exists through advertising and also though religious and general library conferences, where publishers' representatives arrive with exhibits prepared for face-to-face discussions. Certain representatives also visit specific libraries regularly to discuss recent publications. Such contacts are more frequent in academic and seminary libraries than in popular religious libraries, of course.

Bookstores provide another point of contact with the greater library and book world. This is especially true of religious bookstores, such as Baptist Book Stores, the Augsburg Publishing House, and the Provident Book Shops. Certain libraries buy from bookstores by mail, such as from the Broadman Library Book Service, Nashville, while others make purchases in the bookstores. There they may learn more about both the publishing and the library spheres.

## Lack of Other National- and International-Level Contacts

We have described the major national-level religious library contacts for popular religious libraries. There are several of them. While many popular libraries have national contacts within their own religious library associations, as we have said before, few of them relate closely to the larger and more general national library associations, that is, the CLA, ACRL, or the Special Libraries Association (SLA), for instance, or even to the regional, state, or provincial library associations, for example, the Atlantic Provinces Library Association or the Delaware Library Association.

Contacts with leading American and Canadian professionals in library associations should enable popular religious librarians to learn a variety of useful ideas from them and to participate in major national library projects as well. The religious librarians' viewpoints should be broadened as their range of first- and second-hand experience is extended. Certain ideas and viewpoints acquired at national conferences can be useful in the religious library setting. More can be learned about effective library computer use at an SLA conference than at a small religious library conference, for instance.

Smaller parochial school library staff members can learn from large public and parochial school librarians who are well represented at American Association of School Librarians (AASL) meetings held in conjunction with ALA summer and winter conferences. In much the same way, school of religion librarians should be able to learn useful policies and techniques from the staff members of other university schools and departments who are attending ACRL-ALA conferences. Religious organization administrative office librarians should participate actively in SLA activities as well. And for that matter, many Catholic and Christian Science reading room librarians might attend Public Library Association (PLA) conferences for the same sort of professional education and updating.

As well as displaying restricted involvement in national general library association activities, North American popular religious librarians show a lack of international library involvement. Of course, in a few cases, Canadian and American librarians see each other each year at North American conferences, but they seldom visit religious libraries on other continents. A problem with library attendance at international conferences is that the sponsoring institution can seldom pay the librarian's travel expenses. Many libraries have trouble budgeting money for both national and international conferences. Even so, the situation should not rule out attendance at intervals of three or four years.

While the International Federation of Library Associations and Institutions (IFLA) and the International Federation for Documentation (FID) hold annual conferences attended by one hundred to four hundred North American librarians, few of these conferees represent religious libraries. Neither organization has any section or committee on religious libraries, but both have sections and committees for more general and for other specialized kinds of libraries that may be relevant and useful in imparting new ideas and techniques.

European religious libraries should be interesting to North American religious librarians in both the scholarly and popular fields. Many active popular-level libraries are found in Europe. There are professional associations of seminary libraries in at least five countries.[25–27] Each group represents several dozen or even several hundred active librarians.

For popular religious librarians there are active European associations in at least three countries. These include the Working Group for Archives and Libraries in the Lutheran Church (Germany), the Working Group of Catholic Theological Libraries (Germany), the Working Group of Libraries of the Catholic Church (Germany), the German Association of Protestant Libraries (Germany), and the Dutch Center for Public Libraries and Literature (partially religious) (Netherlands).

While there are many house of worship libraries, there are probably even more parochial school and religious public libraries in Europe. Church-sponsored public libraries are especially numerous in Belgium, Netherlands, France, and Germany. Usually their collections are small and they depend heavily on part-time volunteer staff members, but they are strong in children's and media material and in providing personal service. Although sponsored by private church groups and supported in part by user fees, surprisingly, certain of these libraries receive local government tax support.

There is also the National Association of Culture and Public Libraries (France), which has a network of eighteen hundred private Roman Catholic public libraries.[28] This system publishes its own collection of development journals, carries on an interlibrary loan service and has several full-time paid professional librarians in charge. In England, some popular religious libraries resemble those in North America, but other house of worship libraries resemble religious history or archive centers, containing medieval, eighteenth- and nineteenth-century manuscripts and books.

Many European religious libraries differ in various ways from North American libraries, sometimes in positive and sometimes in negative ways. One can expect to find less useful card catalogs, fewer on-line databases to search, fewer computer-based catalogs, fewer circulating collections, and a smaller number of well-paid professional staff members per library. Use of electronic typewriters and computers is less common than in North America, but the ability to read the languages represented in the library collection is much more common there. Holdings of European religious materials are stronger, of course. An enjoyable study tour of either kind of religious library can be taken in Europe. If the interested librarian searches for them, intriguing scholarly and popular religious libraries can be found in many other countries also.

## The Problems and the Advantages of Partial Isolation

We may conclude from the discussions in the preceding sections of this chapter that staff members in popular North American religious libraries appear to suffer from at least partial isolation from both the larger religious and the larger library worlds. The problems of partial isolation are those of intellectual and professional poverty. Religious librarians associate primarily with local persons in other small and specialized religious libraries who are often poorly informed about the field in general and about other information fields, especially those operating at a higher level.

Popular religious librarianship (except for the parochial school field) is only somewhat professional in most locations. In such isolation the more important issues before the general library world, such as national and state library and book legislation, government library policies, library and information field definitions, standards, and research are almost completely outside the purview of the religious librarian.

Their status suggests that these popular religious library personnel groups are either educationally or otherwise inferior to many nonreligious library personnel groups. Many religious librarians leave themselves open to the criticism that they are not particularly capable of enriching the field but are merely maintaining the status quo therein. Isolation leaves the uninvolved persons without the inspirational or educational opportunities as well as the understanding of the most current ideas that close and active involvement with a more aware and experienced library group could provide.

Persons in limited circumstances do not customarily dream large dreams or launch large projects. This restricted orientation makes it difficult for the religious library group to improve itself—to move its members forward in knowledge and sophistication toward professional or at least paraprofessional status. Isolated from both the larger religious and the general library fields, lacking strong and well-focused effort, popular religious librarians are likely to remain at a relatively low educational and awareness level in both worlds and to be largely out of touch with the most sophisticated and effective thinking in the larger worlds.

As far as this author knows, no bold national initiatives have been taken by religious library groups. Attempts should be made to lift sights, to make these fields more demanding and professional and more sensitive to developments elsewhere. This is one of the most important challenges facing them now.

Several suggestions for upgrading the field can be offered to scholarly and popular religious librarianship for consideration. Certain of these ideas are more practical than others are at this time. Apparently no attempt has yet been made to (1) convert ATLA into a theological library section of the much larger and richer ACRL, (2) establish within ACRL (or CALCUL) a religiously affiliated college and university library section with at least one thousand (CALCUL-200) potential religious library members, (3) establish within the Cath LA a section for convent and monastery librarians, (4) establish a congregational library section within either ALA, CLA, SLA, or IFLA, or all four, (5) establish a parochial school library section in the American Association of School Librarians, the Canadian School Library Association, or the IFLA School Libraries Section, or all three, and (6) establish a religious public library section or committee in the U.S. Public Library Association or the Canadian Association of Public Libraries, or both.

These suggestions would serve both to bring these groups of religious librarians more nearly into the mainstream of national library association activities and to surround them with positive influences from related groups. However, several of these ideas may not be entirely feasible at the present time. For instance, associations that are composed primarily of professionals, such as ALA and its divisions, may not care to "dilute" their ranks with a group primarily composed of nonprofessionals from congregational libraries to the extent of inviting them to form a new section. Few nonprofessional religious librarians are likely to have a strong interest either in participating in general library meetings at distant conferences or in any job activity that does not pay most of its participants.

Much of the same thing can be said for religious librarians joining national religious associations, probably denominational, such as the Dominican Laity or the Jewish National Federation of Temple Sisterhoods. Individuals are welcome in these groups and can make useful contributions, but probably only a modest number of religious librarians, except certain academic, seminary, and parochial school library clergy and sisters, have the strength of professional convictions and interest needed to fully sustain such an effort.

Without the contacts, courage, and cooperative spirit needed for joining the existing larger professional groups, and with the need to pitch most programming at the nonprofessional level for popular level librarians, North American religious librarians in the past were motivated and obligated to form their own small and specialized popular associations. The religious library field's initial isolation may have forced it to develop its own associations, denominational offices, and religious contacts at appropriate levels. We can hope that the success of the small religious library associations will lead these librarians to move toward closer cooperation with the larger and more professionalized groups in the future. Perhaps a partial step in that direction can be made by providing professional-level programming at national popular library conferences for the no-longer-so-small group of professionals working in popular religious libraries.

Partial isolation is less damaging than full isolation, consisting of a complete absence of national, local, religious, or other library associations, including denominational offices with which the religious librarian could relate. So there is some advantage in having access in these fields to the existing infrastructure on which improvements can be built. Much freedom to maneuver is held by these groups without strong ties elsewhere. Perhaps, after some decades of partial isolation, they will begin to reach out, to move toward cooperation or even toward eventual amalgamation with other scholarly and popular groups in the two areas of which religious librarianship comprises a small part: library and information service and organized religion.

## A Religious Library Service Development Plan

The development of a professional field and its institutions, services, and literature is an interesting social history study area. The author once explored such a subject as applied to a particular country, laying out a basic list of the many professional services and publications that a country should develop before it can be said to have achieved a comprehensive and fully developed professional library and information science field.[29] The author will describe something similar here, but this exposition is adapted not to a country but to the occupational field of scholarly and popular religious library and information service in Canada and the United States. Such a program relates closely to the recommended religious library upgrading program that was discussed in the previous section.

This section discusses the services and publications that North American (Canadian and United States) religious librarianship needs to become a mature professional field. The plan for literature development includes all facets of a reasonably extensive development and provides most of the materials and services needed by conscientious professionals in order to operate well in this field. A field needs a literature that can explain its theory and practice to its practitioners so that they grasp its complexities and breadth, its present and past activities. The significant literature develops as the field's intellectual development, its administrative structure, and its operational policies evolve. Each required type of service (the core activities) is listed in table 1.2, and examples from the library and information field are given in the explanation. The general plan can be adapted for any library subfield.

The list constitutes a set of standards or criteria or even ideals for the full scope and the level of library and bibliographic progress. The items listed not only must exist but must exist in well-organized, fully rationalized, and first-class form. The author does not assume that the thirty items are necessarily of equal importance, nor are they listed in any priority order. Nor does the author assume that these are the only items needed for the full development of religious library literature. Far from it! This list assumes the existence of a complete infrastructure of basic and general library, religious, and bibliographic services on which the religious library literature development plan can be built.

There is no assumption that a service would necessarily be practical or financially profitable to establish, now or later—merely that its establishment would be helpful to the user. Nor does the listing of a service necessarily imply that it does not now exist in some form; a few services do exist, but most of them are merely suggestions to date. The entire list represents personal thought and opinion rather than the result of any carefully planned research project. No attempt will be made to specify the nature of each item in detail. The section takes an ecumenical and global view of its subject and applies to all types of religious libraries. The items will be taken up in table 1.2 order.

*A sizeable market of users* is needed who are ready to demand religious library material reference and circulation service before the establishment of these services becomes practical. This situation exists now among many seminary faculty members and students and, to some extent, and with great variations, among some congregational library users. Many parochial school libraries have such users also. About religiously affiliated academic libraries, the situation is more questionable and varies greatly by institution, with many evangelical campuses being ready now for such use.

Few accredited North American graduate library and information science schools have ever offered *religious library science courses.* Even elective courses in scholarly or seminary librarianship have been offered rarely, presumably because the market for them in any one information school's service area is so small. In several existing library and information science schools—Catholic University, Drexel, University of North Carolina, University of Texas, Texas Woman's University, and probably others—master's theses have been completed on popular religious libraries. Probably theses have been written at certain library and information science schools on seminary libraries and their book collections, too.

In 1988 AJL organized a series of Jewish library courses for Queens College in New York. However, the courses were given in the Queens Continuing Education Division rather than in the Graduate School of Library and Information Studies. Drexel and a few other schools have offered workshops or conferences, also, but most library schools have provided the field with almost no direct service on any level.[30]

The lack of leadership from library education professionals has left the religious library education field largely in the hands of religious library professionals or nonprofessionals who possibly are not well prepared to move it ahead as rapidly as professional library educators would have done. Both scholarly and popular fields need close contact with formal library and information education through credit and continuing education courses. Educational programs should be developed to supplement and extend the present program of religious library conference continuing education upward in terms of degree years. Both graduate library education and undergraduate technician programs should be developed for the religious field, the former for supervisory and academic librarians, and the latter for assistants and congregational librarians.

An elective course in scholarly religious librarianship should introduce the student to that field, its library policies, and its more significant literature. Several recent trends affecting all specialized library fields should be explained and their application to religious librarianship discussed. Certain of the larger and better organized scholarly and popular libraries should host internship training programs. Parochial and other private school librarians need either bachelor's or master's degree programs plus education courses and an introduction to denominational library literature. Library technician or paraprofessional education departments could attract many congregational library staff members. In all of these cases, some freedom should be allowed for students to use their religious library background in preparing course work.

*Short continuing education courses* on preservation, microcomputers, and the *Religious Index* database have been offered at ATLA annual conferences in recent years, three being given in 1987 in one preconference day, and six in 1992. CEUs (Continuing Education Units) were not offered for them, but they can be recommended to ATLA for the future. AJL has offered such short courses with CEUs at its conferences regularly, and CSLA began to offer continuing education courses several years ago. The provision of continuing education needs to be upgraded and formalized for both scholarly and popular librarians and CEUs given for satisfactory work.

In addition to their annual national conferences, the Cath LA, CSLA, AJL, and LCLA have extensive chapter networks that provide *local library programming*. As we have seen, Baptist librarians carry out local programs also. Altogether, throughout various denominations, several hundred of these local chapter meetings are held each year in all North American regions. This is one of the few items on table 1.2 that is realized extensively now, at least by the popular librarians.

Scholarly religious librarians seem to support few of these local programs, probably due to the low density level of scholarly religious librarians in most cities. They are relatively few in any one state or province. Since each seminary curriculum emphasizes its own theology, cooperation is difficult. ATLA has no seminary chapter nor is there any other national, regional, state, or province-wide seminary library association in North America, as far as this author knows. While a few of these programs are held in large metropolitan areas and go to the extent of inviting visiting lecturers, they are rare.

Religious library education should be closely coordinated for the scholarly and popular library groups at all four levels described here—graduate credit course work, technician and paraprofessional course work, informal continuing education courses, and local and national conference programs in order to derive optimal educational and information gains from it.

Item 5 on table 1.2 recommends the establishment of a *comprehensive international religious library association*. The international council mentioned in the scholarly library book serves only four to six European countries, and the chances of expanding it in the short term seem to be poor. Perhaps an IFLA religious libraries section could be established instead. An international association should be divided into two main sections—scholarly and popular—or else two separate associations should be formed. Probably the chances of establishing an international scholarly are better than those of establishing an international popular library group.

An international association is needed to carry out on a global basis the member services that are similar to those now being performed by U.S. national library associations and by Canadian regional and provincial library associations. These services include providing awards for superior work, book reviews, chapter-level activities, national conference programs, continuing education, guidance for individual librarians, promotion of religious library interests, and serial and book publications. The group should be able to provide these services for many countries that have no religious library associations now. International cooperation should be facilitated by denomination as well as by type of library. In addition, the association should be able to assist the publishers of several countries in producing the kinds of material that these religious libraries find to be most useful.

*North American religious library associations,* discussed in a previous section, can be divided by level between scholarly and popular, by denomination among Catholic, Jewish, and several Protestant divisions, affiliation by national vs. provincial and regional, and by country between Canada and the United States. All have annual conferences. What is needed to improve the present situation? A primary problem is the associations' lack of members and funds. On the popular level this is due at least in part to the unpredictable shifting in and out of membership by the volunteer members. Building features into the association that will attract more members and hold them longer is much needed, and many of these features must become a permanent part of local chapter service.

Since Canada has no national scholarly or popular religious library associations, perhaps Canadian librarians should start them. Canadian attendance at U.S. library association conferences seems to be small. Only eight Canadians per year attended the 1986 and 1987 ATLA conferences, and seven in 1992. In addition, there is no scholarly level North American association that makes special provision for the staff members of either (1) religiously affiliated general colleges and universities or (2) non-ATS member scholarly religious seminary libraries.

Interest by non-ATS member seminary and Bible college library staff members needs to be articulated and focused. A national association of all scholarly religious libraries could become a meeting place for seminary and religiously affiliated college and university librarians, and it could carry out many of the same kinds of projects for the religious group that ACRL carries out for all academic librarians. If a denomination can provide better service to its congregational librarians than the ecumenical CSLA provides for many different denominations, primarily Protestant, perhaps it should establish a separate association.

Three denominations already provide *headquarters library advisory services*—LDS, Christian Science, and Southern Baptist, at least on the popular level. Such offices can carry out for other denominations also many of the services provided by the general library associations. The need for library service in support of the Sunday school and other church departments can best be understood and carried out on a denominational level. Advisory offices can facilitate coordination between denominational Sunday school publication programs and library service programs. A denominational group can provide a unified approach to congregational library service that no other group is able to provide. All major denominations and several minor ones should consider this idea at both the scholarly and popular library levels.

Items 8–13 table 1.2 reflect the desirability of identifying a number of *"good" or superior or even leading libraries in each subfield to serve as models of excellence.* Study of their operation should be instructive for other libraries. Who will name these leading libraries? The national and regional denominational library associations and library advisory offices could do this with ATLA assistance. Those library associations with award programs (such as CSLA and Cath LA) are already identifying the kinds of libraries that fit into these selected groups. After selection, model library identities and attributes should be well publicized. The idea of selecting a sizeable number in each category is to distribute them across various denominations, scholarly vs. popular levels, and areas of each country so that every librarian can identify one that is near enough to visit and inspect.

Table 1.2, item 14, indicates the need for current and comprehensive *adult and children's* book and serial *bibliographies.* There is no separate, current, and comprehensive bibliography of religious material, only the general Library of Congress MARC list, *Books in Print,* and the *National Union Catalog.* The Bowker, Faxon, and EBSCO international periodical and serial directories are well known and available. Such a list could grow out of one of these comprehensive bibliographies and could be used primarily as a convenient selection and acquisition tool in libraries with large religious collections.

Development of national union catalogs of religious books, serials, and manuscripts, a similar idea, would also be helpful in sharing library holdings to support interlibrary loan service. Of course, these catalogs should be located in databases with wide library access. To some extent the Online Computer Library Center (OCLC) database solves this problem, at least for scholarly libraries, but many scholarly and most popular religious libraries have no direct access to that database. Only a small percentage of the *ALD* study libraries were part of the 1988 OCLC database. The small and independent library is seldom a member of such a system, yet it may need union catalog help occasionally. Printouts of certain religious book, serial, and manuscript union catalogs could be duplicated and made available for small library access and use.

More work should be done to prepare *comprehensive bibliographies of "good" or significant books* for each library subfield, item 15 on table 1.2. An example would be a list of current books on Pope John Paul II recommended for Roman Catholic convent reading or a list of material on Unitarian-Universalist biography for academic library use. Presenting titles on a religious subject in a special bibliography should enable the library to focus user attention on certain of its most useful titles and thereby enable users to profit more from their reading. If such lists are well publicized, they can encourage relatively wide distribution and usage. What books should be included in such a basic list for each denominational field? Note that CSLA and AJL have already published such lists.[31,32]

A related and larger selection tool project would be cooperative compilation of a standard catalog of recommended titles for the two religious library levels. The present popular library bulletin book review sections, the ALA *Booklist* and *Choice* are available already. *Choice* and *Booklist*, however, cover few religious titles and the popular library bulletin reviews are brief, superficial, denominational, and of only temporarily usefulness. On the other hand, Catholic parochial school librarians could profit from efforts to produce Catholic supplements to certain national school library publications.

Bill Katz identified three thousand religious periodical titles, so a *comprehensive index is needed to religious periodical literature.*[33] Such an index should cover all faiths, denominations, and sects. Among the present group of indexes, the *Index to Jewish Periodicals, Index to Articles on Jewish Studies, Catholic Periodical and Literature Index,* and especially the *Religion Index One: Periodicals* can be recommended. *Religion Index One: Periodicals* and *Two: Books* are two of ATLA's triumphs. We may be better off now in providing this item than we are for most of the other items on this long list. Coverage of religious periodicals by existing indexes is still relatively superficial, however, and it is aimed too often at the general rather than the religious library reader. Religious libraries and large public library religion departments would find such a comprehensive index invaluable.

A subject, author, and title *index to religious library periodicals* is needed by religious librarians and students. It should cover both scholarly and popular fields and perhaps be published annually. We already have *Library Literature* and *Library and Information Science Abstracts*, but their religious field coverage is light, and a supplementary index is needed that covers extensively the domestic and foreign religious library and information science titles and abstracts the material covered. Students will be able to study the religious library field more satisfactorily when such an index is available.

As a related subject, comprehensive scholarly and popular religious librarianship bibliographies seem to be generally lacking. The 1986 ATLA Annual Conference *Proceedings* contains a useful conference proceedings index 1947–86, useful partly because the literature about other scholarly religious library areas is so sparse. The ATLA index must record some of the major papers of the subfield in that time period. The *Catholic Periodical and Literature Index* covers useful bibliographies on the various types of Catholic librarianship. Both the present and the previous religious librarianship volumes by this author contain useful chapter bibliographies. There is an annual index to *Church and Synagogue Libraries* (Bulletin) also. J. Larry Murdock compiled a bibliography of early church and synagogue librarianship in 1970.[34] A comprehensive and definitive bibliography of North American religious librarianship would complete many present gaps and assist students in these fields.

Another cooperative bibliographic project should be undertaken to publish a combined *critical religious book review journal* (item 18). It should be aimed at both the scholarly and popular library levels. We have the first-class ATLA *Index to Book Reviews in Religion,* but this index is not always as current as might be desired and focuses on only one subfield.[35] In certain ways it is unfortunate that several popular denominational library groups publish their own book annotation or review bulletins—CSLA, AJL, LCLA, Baptist, ACL, and to some extent Catholic—when all of the publications reviewed annually could be put into one comprehensive bulletin with denominational labels and critical evaluations!

A cumulated and enhanced journal could probably be published for a lower cost than the present combined costs of the separately existing bulletins. In a combined journal the annotations or short reviews would not necessarily be tailored for a particular denomination, however, but is such a narrow focus essential? Such an ecumenical plan might trample denominational lines and many persons might be unhappy if it were carried out, of course!

If the popular denominational bulletins stopped publishing their own book annotations or published fewer of them (which constitute 50 percent of their present bulletin page space), this would free space in these titles for substantive articles, a desirable feature. Of course, critical reviews are already available for many religious titles through the general scholarly book review journals, though these journals may be slower to appear than the denominational bulletins. Perhaps reviews of religious books in the general press might simply be reprinted in two journals, scholarly and popular.

All major and many minor denominations should publish *a religious library journal, bulletin, or newsletter* to communicate with their libraries and assist in improving library service. Popular-level bulletins are common (see appendix A for examples), but scholarly libraries should be served also. We need more substantial journals; the field's journals should try to make significant contributions to either its bibliography or its religious library thought, policy, and practice. This sort of contribution may not come immediately from the popular library group, however, which seems currently to be happy with its small newsletters.

*Several comprehensive surveys and analyses,* item 20 on table 1.2, should be undertaken to identify the characteristics of the North American religious library and information field and to supplement the four popular library surveys described in later chapters. In spite of these surveys, much is presently unknown about these fields. Several surveys and analyses are needed in order to measure the characteristics of the major facets of each subfield. Apparently no other comprehensive national surveys of scholarly and popular religious libraries have been undertaken to date.

Denominational and geographic analyses should be made, as well as analyses by such variables as library age, staff and collection size, budget, and use per student or per house of worship member, not to mention the policies followed in selection, acquisitions, cataloging, classification, and preparation for the shelves. Analyses should attempt to clarify the relationships between denomination and size and between the types of religious groups being studied, such as evangelical versus conservative and the various geographic regions. Analyses of inputs and outputs would be revealing. The best of the house of worship libraries should be cardinal examples of low dollar input (an all-volunteer staff!) and both high circulation and exemplary reference service.

We need *comprehensive scholarly and popular religious library directories* for both North American countries. Such directories are needed in the same way that censuses of people are required—in order to learn more about the composition of the population, to learn "what is out there" so that generalizations can be drawn that are based on facts rather than on speculation. No one directory lists religious academic, theological, organizational administrative office, parochial and private school, public, convent, or monastery libraries with an extensive coverage. There is the 1968 Ruoss volume listing 1,788 seminary and other scholarly libraries worldwide, but it is now out of date and was never fully comprehensive. The present author hopes to produce a new edition of that directory in the near future.

The directory that covers most North American scholarly libraries is the *ALD*, but it is substantially incomplete for convent, monastery, congregational, and parochial schools, and somewhat incomplete for all other scholarly library categories. No recent congregational library directory exists.[36] The author also hopes to produce a new edition of such a directory in the future. No directory covers parochial, private school, or religious public libraries thoroughly, except for the Christian Science reading room directory.[10]

The next item recommends compilation of *biographical directories of religious library personnel.* This author has never seen a biographical directory of religious librarians. Who are these people?[37] Probably a few religious library leaders appear in *Who's Who in America,* or at least in its regional editions. Of course, the ALA *Who's Who in Library and Information Service* presumably includes many scholarly and perhaps even certain popular American and Canadian religious librarians, but it is more than a decade old and incomplete for the religious library field, due in part to the "second job" nature of certain religious library positions and to their paraprofessional status.

We need biographical directories in order to identify the field's leaders, to study their characteristics, and to recognize and honor them. The information is needed to facilitate analyses to discover the distinctive characteristics of these professional and technical groups. Often this information is useful to group chairpersons also. Compiling such a directory may turn out to be a task for the individual denominational library associations or offices.

*A series of essays is needed* that define and explain what a scholarly or popular religious library is and discuss the most important concepts involved. This is item 23. The essays should clarify the relationships of these fields with other kinds of library fields and with the world of organized religion. Some existing essays take these fields a certain distance toward this goal.[38–42] Apparently several recent essays have helped advance ATLA thinking.

Several of the titles cited in this chapter should be useful to any author who wishes to provide an appropriate explanation of the scholarly or popular library fields. Chapter 4 also provides useful data. An essay is especially needed in popular religious librarianship, since that field seems to be poorly understood around the world.[43] In many countries, professional librarians seem either not to understand the field as being different in important ways from scholarly librarianship or, if they do grasp the principle, then they have a high opinion of the one and a low opinion of the other, which is illogical and unfair, since the two fields serve different user groups and deserve respect for their own separate contributions.

Full sets of *religious library standards* or guidelines should be written for all scholarly and popular library subfields.[44,45] Standards set guidelines or parameters for libraries to meet in order to be considered acceptable, "good," or even superior in service when compared with other libraries of the same kind. Of course, among scholarly libraries, colleges and universities can use one of ACRL's sets of standards unless the librarian believes that the standards need to be modified for a religious (versus a secular) institution. Organizational administrative office and convent and monastery libraries need their own sets of guidelines and standards.

Standards should address questions of high-quality service in every library area and should be a continually evolving statement reconsidered at regular intervals. Both the British, Australian, and New Zealand theological library associations have sets of scholarly library standards or guidelines.

Among popular religious library groups, CSLA has a statement of desirable practices in a staff self-assessment program that leads to a certificate of commendation. This statement was developed by Claudia Hannaford and the Continuing Education Committee. These practices were calculated to be fairly simple for most libraries to establish and follow, though not many members have done so thus far. AJL adopted synagogue, school, and center library standards in 1968 and published a revised edition in 1970. In turn, these standards have been superseded by a 1989 set.[46] The Cath LA published standards for parish and lending libraries in 1971. Again these standards seem to need updating. Of course, parochial school libraries can use the AASL media center guidelines if they wish to do so. The reader will find a brief listing of certain suggested congregational library standards in table 1.2.

Item 25 calls for *model scholarly and popular religious library policy and procedure manuals* that are essential to guide library practice.[47] They are especially useful in situations with changing procedures or large and changing staffs. The word "model" means that the library is adapting a similar library's ideas for its own use or that it is using a manual written as a "standard," one designed to be adaptable for others to use. College and university library policy and procedures manuals are available from many institutions, for example, the Arizona State University Library. Many university library manuals cover only one large department per volume. Watch *Library Literature* for other listings.

Congregational library manuals have been produced by organizations such as the Southern Baptist Convention, the Jewish Book Council of America, and the Abingdon, Augsburg, Bethany, Cokesbury, Drexel, Moody, Westminster, and Zonderva presses. CSLA has a 1980 model manual that was written by Martin Ruoss. While many house of worship and parochial school libraries possess such manuals, this is a management area that needs upgrading and completion in many religious libraries.

Setting a standard for *library income or expenditure* is especially difficult. To do so with justification requires the analyst to calculate what is required to stock, staff, and pay for the service level demanded by an individual library's sponsoring institution in a specific place and year. Developing a standard for an entire group of libraries can be done primarily by generalizing from many examples for which full statistical information is available, or else by estimation, since the large volume of supporting data needed for an objective analysis is seldom available. A third method is by being quite arbitrary.

Neither of the latter two methods can be recommended. In the present case, the 5 percent of the sponsoring institution's total budget (5 percent of the educational expenditures for academic institutions) recommended for the library is essentially a first guess about what may be adequate, since we know too little about these libraries to be more specific than that.

Five percent is a common academic library budget baseline standard, so it may fit some seminary and religious academic libraries reasonably well. This figure may be less useful in other areas. For congregational libraries, since their present "slice of the pie" is so small, chapter 4 suggests that one percent of congregational income be chosen as a reasonable standard. In any case, the percentage being sought is one designed to provide a "reasonably adequate" income for the typical religious library of a specific type. Certainly individual library situations vary a great deal.

A comprehensive *book classification schedule* and a comprehensive *subject heading list or thesaurus* are needed for North American religious libraries to replace the present piecemeal approach to solving the book indexing problem (items 27 and 28). Or perhaps three classification schedules and thesauri are needed: Christian, Jewish, and Muslim. Such schedules should spell out expansions of the religious sections (such as the Dewey 200s) in considerable detail. In addition to religion, they should cover religious biography, bibliography, sociology, art, music, literature, mythology, history, fiction, philosophy, and several other subject fields. Subject headings should cover the same subject fields.

That we have schedules and lists, certain of them having been published in several successive editions, means that this area of need is met to some extent now. Whether or not the schedules listed below fully solve these classification and subject heading publication problems is unclear to this author, however. Probably certain schedules do and others do not. In addition to the Library of Congress, Dewey, and universal decimal classifications, we have the following religious library classification schedules and subject heading lists:

1. ATLA publishes its own list of current and useful Library of Congress subject headings.[48]
2. AJL sells Mae Weine's *Classification,* which includes subject headings. Also, the Elazar, Bolub, and Celnik classification schedules serve Jewish libraries.[49–52]
3. The Cath LA has published *Catholic Subject Headings* and *The Dewey Decimal Classification 200 Schedules Expanded.*[53,54]
4. LDS churches use their own library classification schedule for Mormon material.[9]
5. Erwin John's classification schedule is used by certain Lutheran libraries.[55]
6. Many libraries use a special or borrowed classification schedule for certain special collections.
7. Other libraries use a locally made schedule for part or all of the collection, especially for local material.

The idea of special and local schedules is that they may accommodate sizeable collections that emphasize specialized subjects, such as the Holocaust, Canadian Methodist history, or local archives, much better than does a standard classification schedule. A comprehensive subject heading list or thesaurus is needed and special subject thesauri should be compiled for specialized situations. Some literature has appeared in the ATLA *Proceedings* and in *Judaica Librarianship* on religious library cataloging and subject headings. Standard book and periodical sources can be cited for scholarly library cataloging and classification information, though not very much of it is available for the religious library field.

An annual systematic scholarly and popular *religious library data collection, analysis, and publication program* is needed. Such a program has been carried out for its members by ATLA since 1962. Let us hope that the number of ATLA statistical categories can be expanded in the coming decade, that their definitions will be clarified and published, and that the privilege of participating in this (or a new) annual survey can be extended to a much larger and more varied group of seminary and department of religion libraries in the future. We may note the annual *ALD* publication of information also.

No such annual survey is presently available for popular religious libraries, again excepting for the *ALD*. Each denomination and headquarters may carry out its own survey if it wishes, but most now show little interest in the statistics of any kind of library. We are still in a rudimentary stage of statistical development for all kinds of religious libraries, so the question must be asked, In the absence of such information, how are we to understand these libraries?

At several seminaries and graduate library and information science schools, there should be ongoing *research programs in scholarly and popular religious library and information service,* the thirtieth and last item on table 1.2. This program should enhance the present scattered and sporadic efforts to study this field. Certain faculty members and students should focus their attention on specific current religious library and information problems and situations, especially in connection with student thesis preparation. Only through research programs can we achieve full understanding of religious librarianship. A religious library research agenda must be developed on which these research programs can work. Some of the projects can be carried out in cooperation with the university school of religion faculty and with university library staff members. After a few years of activity, progress should have been made in several areas.

## Notes

1. Several definitions were adapted from *Webster's New Collegiate Dictionary* (Springfield, Mass.: G & C Merriam, 1977) and *Harrod's Librarian's Glossary* (Aldershot, U.K.: Gower, 1987).
2. For a further definitional discussion, see John F. Harvey, "Scholarly and Popular Religious Libraries," *International Library Review* 19 (October 1987): 359–86. The close student of the author's religious library publications will realize that a few of his definitions have been modified or elaborated over time. Some of them are still evolving.

The author is using the designation "Protestant" loosely here. What is included is any discrete religious group that is neither Jewish nor Roman Catholic, nor Muslim nor Buddhist. Thus the word "Protestant" is being used as a catch-all category. The author does not wish to offend or misclassify any group, sect, faith, or denomination by arbitrarily calling it a Protestant or denominational group, though most of the groups in the Protestant category are normally called Protestant denominations. However, it is clearly much more practical to develop analyses and tables with thirteen or fourteen subgroups rather than with twenty-four or more, especially when many of the additional groups are quite small in this study's samples.

Practicality has ruled here, so the author apologizes if he has given offense to any group, including the following—Baha'i, Buddhist, Church of Scientology, Eastern Orthodox, Mormon, Muslim, Rosicrucian, Theosophist or United Church of Religious Science. All Christian and non-Christian sects, groups, and faiths except Jewish and Catholic are included in the "Protestant" group as used in this study. The category of "Other Denominations" is used in much the same way and includes about forty different religious groups or denominations.

3. John F. Harvey, "An Introductory World Survey of Popular Church and Synagogue Libraries," *International Library Review* 18 (October 1986): 347–72.

4. *American Library Directory* (New York: R. R. Bowker, annually).

5. John F. Harvey, ed. *Church and Synagogue Libraries* (Metuchen, N.J.: Scarecrow, 1980).

6. John F. Harvey and Shahr Azar Musavi, "Tehran Mosque Libraries and a Comparison with American Christian Church Libraries," *International Library Review* 13 (October 1981): 385–95.

7. *Library Literature* (New York: H. W. Wilson Company, quarterly).

8. *Yearbook of American and Canadian Churches 1988,* ed. Constant H. Jacquet Jr. (Nashville: Abington, 1988, 1993). *Statistical Abstract of the United States* (Washington, D.C.: Government Printing Office, 1984), pp. 134–36.

9. David M. Mayfield, "The Genealogical Library of the Church of Jesus Christ of Latter-day Saints," *Library Trends* 32 (Summer 1983): 111–27.

10. ". . . Christian Science Reading Rooms," *Christian Science Journal* 106 (May 1988): 9–30.

11. Report dated 20 December 1983 from Mrs. Anita Dalton, 41 Aberdeen Road North, Cambridge, ON, N1S 2X1, Canada.

12. American Theological Library Association, *Summary of Conference Proceedings* (Evanston, Ill, annually).

13. *Statistical Abstract,* pp. 156–57.

14. L. Jones Milbrey, "NCES Survey of Private School Library Media Centers 1979," *Bowker Annual* (New York: R. R. Bowker, 1983), pp. 352–55. The 1979 U.S. National Center for Education Statistics survey found about 14,200 private school libraries with approximately 28,400 employees and

2.0 employees per library. In this study, incidentally, the NCES found that Catholic schools were most likely to have a library (97 percent), schools with another religious affiliation were next most likely to have libraries (68 percent), and schools without religious affiliation were least likely to have libraries (62 percent).

15. *The World Directory of Theological Libraries,* ed. L. Martin Ruoss (Metuchen, N.J.: Scarecrow, 1968).

16. The *World Almanac 1988* (New York: Pharos Books) listed the denominations of private U.S. religious and parochial elementary and secondary schools. While the vast majority of them were Roman Catholic, the following denominations were well represented also, in order: Baptist, Lutheran, Christian, Jewish, Seventh-day Adventist, and Episcopal.

17. Personal letter from Nathan A. Talbot, manager, Committees on Publication, First Church of Christ, Scientist, 175 Huntington Avenue, Boston, MA 02115 USA, dated May 13, 1988.

18. Alice Hedderick, "Library Spreads Gospel Truth," *Canadian Library Journal* 44 (June 1987): 183–85.

19. Association of Jewish Libraries, *Newsletter* (New York: National Foundation for Jewish Culture, quarterly).

20. Ruth S. Smith, "The Church and Synagogue Library Association," in *Encyclopedia of Library and Information Science,* vol. 4 (New York: Marcel Dekker, 1970), pp. 674–81. See also Church and Synagogue Library Association, *Membership List* (Portland, Ore.: 1988).

21. *Church and Synagogue Libraries* (Portland, Ore.: Church and Synagogue Library Association, bimonthly).

22. *Lutheran Libraries* (Minneapolis: Lutheran Church Library Association, quarterly).

23. *Church Media Library Magazine* (Nashville: Southern Baptist Convention, quarterly).

24. See Harvey, "An Introductory World Survey," p. 350 n. 2.

25. J. R. Fang, *International Guide to Library, Archive and Information Science Associations* (New York: R. R. Bowker, 1976).

26. Association of British Theological and Philosophical Libraries *Bulletin* (Oxford: New College Library, 3 times a year).

27. *A Guide to the Theological Libraries of Great Britain and Ireland* (London: ABTAPL Publishing, 1986). See also *Collections of Religion and Theology in Australia and New Zealand* (Adelaide: Auslib Press, 1992).

28. Harvey, "An Introductory World Survey," pp. 354–58.

29. John F. Harvey, "Core Activities for National Library and Bibliographic Development," *UNESCO Bulletin for Libraries* 28 (March/April 1974): 79–86.

30. In this connection it is heartening to see a recent public relations announcement that tells us that Drexel University and Gratz College (of Jewish Studies), both in Philadelphia, have inaugurated a cooperative certificate program in synagogue librarianship. Bravo!

31. *A Basic Book List for Church Libraries: A Core Collection,* comp. Bernard Dietrick, 4th ed. (Portland, Ore.: Church and Synagogue Library Association, 1991).
32. *Creating a Collection: A Resource Booklist for a Beginning Judaic Library* (New York: Association of Jewish Libraries, 1983).
33. William Katz, comp., *Magazines for Libraries* (New York: R. R. Bowker, 1986), p. 857.
34. J. Larry Murdock, "The Literature of Church and Synagogue Libraries," *Drexel Library Quarterly* 6 (April 1970): 166–75.
35. American Theological Library Association, *Index to Book Reviews in Religion* (Evanston, Ill. bimonthly). See also *Books and Religion* (New York: Trinity Church, quarterly), another reviewing source.
36. *Directory of Church and Synagogue Libraries,* ed. Dorothy Rodda and John F. Harvey (Philadelphia: Drexel, 1967). Includes 3,240 libraries. Was still the most complete national U.S. directory of its field in 1975, according to *Guide to Reference Material,* by A. J. Walford (London: Library Association, 1975), p. 85.
37. However, see the recent Association of Jewish Libraries *Membership Directory* (New York: 1992).
38. Joyce White, "Church Libraries," in *Encyclopedia of Library and Information Science,* vol. 4 (New York: Marcel Dekker, 1970), pp. 662–73.
39. Joyce White, ed., "Church and Synagogue Libraries," *Drexel Library Quarterly* 6 (April 1970), entire issue.
40. Stephen L. Peterson, "Life Begins at 40? The Institutional Context of ATLA," American Theological Library Association *Proceedings* (St. Meinrad, Ind.: 1987), pp. 148–55.
41. Robert Wood Lynn, "The Future of Theological Research and Theological Libraries," American Theological Library Association *Proceedings* (St. Meinrad, Ind.: 1986), pp. 145–47.
42. Claude Welch, "The Theological Library—Servant or Partner?" American Theological Library Association *Proceedings* (St. Meinrad, Ind.: 1987), pp. 156–69.
43. Harvey, "An Introductory World Survey," pp. 368–71.
44. Joanne Klene, "Standards for Parish and Lending Libraries," *Catholic Library World* 42 (May/June 1971): 574.
45. See The Association of British Theological and Philosophical Libraries *Bulletin* 2 (June 1990): 1–31 and The Australian and New Zealand Theological Library Association *Newsletter* 6 (December 1988): 3–10.
46. Jewish Book Council of America, *Standards for Jewish Libraries in Synagogues, Schools and Centers* (New York: 1970). Superseded by *A Guide to Excellence: Standards for School, Synagogue and Jewish Community Center Libraries,* ed. Merrily Hart (New York: AJL, 1990).
47. See also John T. Corrigan, *Guide for the Organization and Operation of a Religious Resource Center* (Haverford, Pa.: Catholic Library Association, 1987).

48. *ATLA Current LC Subject Headings in the Field of Religion* (Denver: Iliff School of Theology, quarterly).

49. See Rebecca Dassa, "LC Subject Headings of Interest to Judaica Librarians," *Judaica Librarianship* 4 (Fall 1987): 40–45 and Paul Maher, *Hebraica Cataloging: A Guide to ALA/LC Romanization and Descriptive Cataloging* (Washington, D.C.: Library of Congress, 1987).

50. Mae Weine, *Weine Classification Scheme for Judaica Libraries* (New York: Association of Jewish Libraries, 1982).

51. David H. Elazar, *A Classification Scheme for Libraries of Judaica* (Ramat Gan, Israel: Turtledove, 1978).

52. Jewish Library Association of Greater Philadelphia, *Subject Headings for a Judaica Library* (New York: Association of Jewish Libraries, 1982).

53. Catherine M. Pilley and Matthew R. Wilt, eds. *Catholic Subject Headings* (Haverford, Pa.: Catholic Library Association, 1981).

54. Mary Celia Bauer, *Dewey Decimal Classification: 200 Schedules Expanded for Use* (Haverford, Pa.: Catholic Library Association, 1988).

55. Erwin E. John, *The Key to a Successful Church Library* (Minneapolis: Augsberg, 1967), pp. 7–11.

# 2

# THE GEOGRAPHY AND DEMOGRAPHY OF POPULAR RELIGIOUS LIBRARIES

This is a chapter of basic facts—facts that are basic to an understanding of popular religious libraries. In this work, the geography of religious libraries refers to the urban-rural areas, cities, states, regions, and countries in which North American libraries are found. The demography of these libraries refers to statistical data concerning their basic social characteristics, such as age and income level.[1] This chapter's discussion answers such questions as, In which states and provinces are these libraries found? How many exist? What are their denominational affiliations? Their founding dates? Their chief city centers? Often these attributes need to be broken down by type of library, region, denomination, and sometimes by total expenditure, volumes or chief librarian's gender before we can grasp them usefully.

This study examines the geography and demography of religious libraries thoroughly because these are among the most basic characteristics of libraries in a field about which little is known. While the study does not complete our knowledge of the field either in whole or in part, it should advance knowledge and understanding of it, at least for the population covered by the three databases being examined here: the *American Library Directory (ALD),* the thirty-first and the two-volume forty-first editions, and the Church and Synagogue Library Association (CSLA) 1986 survey. An analysis of library density, distribution, statistical deaths, and other characteristics will enable us to understand these libraries more fully, especially if we can thereby obtain some understanding of the variations and convergences among them.

51

The present chapter provides only basic geographic and demographic information and analyses. The information presented to the reader should help set the stage for the study of more specialized popular religious library characteristics in later chapters. More intensive analyses will be performed in later chapters and in the longitudinal comparisons included therein, and additional variables will be taken up there also. Because of their somewhat varied nature, as well as the generally smaller amount of information available on popular libraries, the reader will find that chapter sections which might be expected to be directly and easily comparable from scholarly to popular libraries are not necessarily comparable at all.

This chapter discusses the following aspects of the geographic and demographic dimensions:

## Geography: Where Were the Popular Religious Libraries Located?

After an initial discussion of library density and religious versus nonreligious library data, this section will take up the various subsections of geography in descending order from nation to city.

## Library Density

*ALD* religious libraries were found almost everywhere, in most but not quite all North American states and provinces and in a great many cities and towns. Rather than asking where the libraries were, perhaps it is more expedient to ask where the religious library density was greatest? In general, although it is begging the question, library geographic density followed density of congregations, since there could hardly be institutional libraries of any kind present without reaching a certain numerical density of houses of worship and of congregation membership.

Similarly, academic houses of worship of all kinds were concentrated primarily in high population density states. This means specifically that church libraries of a particular denomination were found in areas with large concentrations of the houses of worship of that particular denomination. So, to a considerable extent, the location of religious colleges and universities followed the population density of the houses of worship and the congregations of the college's own denomination. Presumably this not-very-profound correlation had a fundamental influence on library location.

The phenomenon of congregations preceding libraries in time ensured that denominational churches were usually located in places of high general population density and as well as in areas of strong denominational support. So we are saying that Pittsburgh, Pennsylvania, probably contains more religious libraries of all kinds than does Pittsburg, Kansas, because of the difference in overall population density. Several Reformed church libraries are found in Michigan, which has many of them, and few or none are found in Mississippi, where there are few or perhaps no churches belonging to that denomination.

The proximity of denominational population density centers with a large supply of potential students was presumably an important reason for establishing a denominational college nearby. Such an influence varies in strength according to denominational policy, the presence of competing colleges, and other locational characteristics, such as rates of regional and denominational growth. We are speaking of the conditions existing when colleges are founded, not necessarily those pertaining a century later, by which time the particular denominational constituency may have moved elsewhere. Although the degree of correlation was not perfect, a heavily populated state like Pennsylvania had more congregations and libraries per square mile than did the sparsely populated state of Wyoming, for instance. In sparsely populated areas, of course, there were no houses of worship, congregations, or libraries.

North American denominational density and location varied greatly
from one denomination and from one locality to another. Certain groups
were found in only a limited number of areas. For instance, the Mormons
were strong in the Rocky Mountains area of Idaho and Nevada but weak
in the White Mountains area of New Hampshire. Certain other denominations were represented in almost all regions of North America with a reasonably high degree of density. In fact, several of them, for example, the
Methodists and the Presbyterians, were so widely distributed that local concentrations could be found for them in almost every state and province.

We can extend the argument and speculate further that college and congregational library distribution varied as did the density of denominations
with or without a strong emphasis on books and libraries. For instance,
Lutheran and Jewish congregations may have emphasized religious books
and libraries more strongly than did such religiously conservative groups
as the Assemblies of God and the Church of the Nazarene congregations.
The latter groups were more likely to be holy book-centered with disci-
pleship training courses than to favor more general religious reading. The
latter denominations had few of either academic or popular libraries. Consequently, many religious libraries were presumably to be found in cities
with strong Lutheran or Jewish populations and fewer in cities with prominent Assemblies of God or Church of the Nazarene populations. Or at
least, that is how the theory goes.

Finally, density of religious libraries varied according to type of library.
Academic religious libraries were much less dense or common than popular religious libraries: many towns had one or more of the latter but none
of the former. Density of convent and monastery libraries was even lighter
yet, although this study's *ALD* list of convent and monastery libraries must
have been far from complete. Evidence will be presented in later sections
of this and other chapters that tends to support all of these generalizations.

A detailed answer to the locational question (where were the popular
religious libraries located?) is provided by tables 2.1 (for 1978) and 2.2
(for 1988), showing Canadian and U.S. library concentrations by state
and province together with a short list of the most popular denominations
therein.[2] The percentage of libraries in each state or province is calculated and supplied, as well as the regional code.

## Religious versus Nonreligious Library
## Geography and Demography

In practical terms, how do religious and nonreligious library geography
and demography differ? The answer to this question is largely outside the

scope of this study. All the author can do is to make a guess based on experience. Overall, there would seem to be little difference between them beyond a few obvious points. Naturally, there are many more nuns and priests working in the religious than in the nonreligious libraries, and the religious libraries may have more religious library material than do the nonreligious libraries; in fact, they carry a higher proportion of such material by definition. A comparison of the two varieties for school libraries may suggest that the religious libraries are smaller in some ways and that their growth rate may be slower than that of secular libraries. However, these ideas cannot be generally validated, and they constitute only the author's brainstorming.

The author knows of no body of nonreligious library data structured in a way that facilitates comparison with this book's religious library geographic and demographic data. It is difficult even to compare the *ALD* seminary libraries as a whole with ATLA seminary libraries in particular, in the companion volume on scholarly libraries, though both were listed in the *ALD*, because the latter was an elite group and the former was a more general and only somewhat selected group. Another handicap in comparing the libraries is that their frequency in many of the subcells of various tables was so small as to make detailed comparisons unreliable. Only gross comparisons with other libraries could be made validly. On certain tables the No Response column (no questionnaire response received from the library) was unacceptably large, thereby leaving few positive responses to be counted.[3] In addition, of course, large No Response proportions generally indicate skewed data.

Notice, incidentally, that the study contains little data in any subfield that would enable it to analyze these libraries' quality, in addition to size. Desirable as that sort of analysis might be, it could not be one of the objectives of this study because the appropriate quality information and standards were not available beyond the quantity and per-library information to be found in this and later chapters. Further, the author has no way of comparing these statistics usefully at this point in the development of the field. We are not currently at a stage where quantity data can be used to evaluate library quality.

## National Comparison: Canada versus the United States[4,5]

With the help of a number of tables and ten pages or so of text, this chapter section will discuss national geographic comparisons for the 1978 and 1988 popular libraries together and also individually. First we will discuss the basic and general information and then we will discuss the more specialized information. How many popular libraries existed in each country—Canada and the United States—and where were they located?

While the regional tables in this and other chapters included Canadian national data from which a comparison could be made with U.S. national data, such a comparison would be more easily understood by the reader if it were made separately and directly between the two nations on several variables rather than merely deriving it from other regional comparisons. Several analyses can usefully be made to show the nature of the national comparisons and the significant differences between the two countries. Of course, the basic difference between the U.S. and the Canadian religious library databases was that the former was so much larger than the latter.

Tables 2.1 (1978), 2.2 (1988), 2.3 (1978), 2.4 (1988), 2.5 (1988), and longitudinal study 2.6 covered each database as a whole and clarified its relative size and certain of its developments between 1978 and 1988. The longitudinal analyses will discuss change rates in tabular information between the 1978 and the 1988 databases, changes in variable scores over time. Certain of the 1988 results were similar to those in 1978 and so need not occupy our attention in a longitudinal analysis. These will already have been covered in the basic description of each variable on which the analysis will build. Certain other variables, however, changed significantly during the course of the decade, and this fact will be brought to the reader's attention.

We will examine the popular library group with the help of tables 2.7 (for 1978) and 2.6 (for 1978 and 1988). The total number of popular libraries in the *1978* database was 687 (100 percent). Of the 1978 popular libraries, 660, or 96.1 percent were American and 27, or 3.9 percent, were Canadian.

The total number of popular libraries in the *1988* database was 642 (100 percent). Of the 1988 popular libraries 621, or 96.7 percent, were American and 21, or 3.3 percent, were Canadian. The U.S.-Canadian ratios between the two nations were therefore 660:27 in 1978 and 621:21 in 1988, and these ratios boiled down to 24.4:1.0 and 29.6:1.0 for 1978 and 1988 respectively, quite a significantly increased contrast. In all cases, however, whether scholarly or popular, 88 percent or more of the *ALD* databases were libraries located south of the forty-ninth parallel, the U.S.-Canadian border. Therefore, this study was primarily one of U.S. libraries in both databases. Dominance by the United States was so great that it unbalanced the study, making it primarily a U.S. study, unfortunate as that may be. The scholarly domination over the popular library group was sufficient that certain database analyses that were possible for scholarly were reduced in usefulness for popular libraries due to low response rates and correspondingly small tabluar cell frequencies.

For another comparison, the grand total of *all kinds of libraries* listed in Canada and the United States in the 1988 *ALD*, religious plus nonreligious, was 34,366. Therefore, the religious libraries portion of this *ALD* total, the proportion that was analyzed in this book, 2,074 libraries, equals only 6 percent of the entire *ALD* list, a small fraction of the total.

For each edition year the United States had a much larger *scholarly* religious library world than did Canada. In fact, the United States had the largest national scholarly religious library group in the world, according to Ruoss.[6] Apparently Mexico, Central America, and the Caribbean added about one hundred scholarly religious libraries to those of Canada and the United States, but probably this addition did not bring the combined continental North American total up to the level of the European total.

The next longitudinal table shows the results of comparing the two nations on twenty-two growth variables (longitudinal table change percentages) for matched pairs of *popular* libraries. Results for 1978 showed a 7.22:1.00 ratio and for 1988 showed a 8.71:1.00 ratio favoring Canada by a large margin. Percentage change also favored Canada: see longitudinal table 2.8. Longitudinal table 2.9 shows library distribution for 1978 and 1988 for the United States and Canada. It indicates, for instance, that American congregational libraries declined in number between 1978 and 1988 in the United States, but in Canada they increased in frequency.

Now we can describe the *popular only* religious library geographic findings in the *ALD* databases. Again we must refer to tables 2.6 and 2.7 for 1988 for the information needed. Obviously, the United States had a much larger popular library group than did Canada. In fact, the total 1978 popular library ratio United States:Canada (24.4:1.0) was even larger than the scholarly United States:Canada library ratio (13.0:1.0). The popular religious library movement was younger in Canada than in the United States and was a regional rather than a national movement there. Certainly the United States supported a large popular religious library group, while the Canadian group was small even when compared through analyses with other popular religious library world leaders—France, Germany, and Iran, for instance.[7]

While the total number of popular libraries was about half of the number of scholarly libraries in the two 1988 databases (scholarly:popular ratio: 2.2:1.0), this fact should not be construed to mean that the ratio between the two groups was the same in actual population of libraries *in the field*. Instead, it meant only that this was the ratio pertaining within the two selected *ALD* databases, both of which were particularly small for the popular library group, especially within the 1988 database. Probably the ratio in the field—the reality—was closer to 1:20 scholarly:popular! This comparison demonstrated that the differences in strength among the scholarly and popular library groups were considerable in themselves, with the *ALD* popular library sample being weak in Canada and slightly stronger in the United States.

The Canadian popular library group lost in numbers during the decade, by 22 percent, while the American popular library group lost also, but only by 6 percent. Just why this double popular library loss occurred in the *ALD* databases is unclear, since the actual number of popular religious libraries in each country probably rose during that period, especially in the United States. Perhaps part of the reason lies with factors quite unrelated to either geography or demography. To some extent the loss may have represented a lack of enthusiasm on the part of the *ALD* editors for these small libraries, which usually had little interlibrary loan or research library interest.

If we examine the two national library groups further, we see several additional differences between them. While 31 to 34 percent of the 1978 and 1988 databases as a whole were popular, within the two Canadian databases the scores differed. In 1978, 28 percent of the Canadian sample was popular, while in 1988, only 13 percent of the Canadian database was popular. This finding simply reemphasized the weakness and small number of popular libraries in the Canadian databases, as compared with the United States. Both U.S. and Canadian popular libraries frequencies shrank somewhat during the decade. In total, Canadian scholarly and popular library numbers grew during this decade by 49 percent overall and United States libraries declined by 2 percent. Table 2.6 for 1978 and 1988 summarizes these longitudinal findings.

Table 2.6 is a curious kind of summary table. It attempts to show ratios and percentages between Canada and the United States for each *ALD* edition for popular libraries. The Canada:United States ratio was larger in 1988 than it was in 1978. The reason for this change was that the frequencies of Canadian popular libraries declined to a greater extent in 1988 than did the number of U.S. popular libraries for that year.

We have several more studies of national comparisons to consider. First, we will examine library age, city population, and staff sizes. Tables 2.10 for 1978 and 2.11 for 1988 show library age for the scholarly and popular databases combined with mean library ages of 72.9 and 71.0 years old. A Canadian/U.S. longitudinal table, table 2.12, shows popular libraries and the mean ages of Canadian vs. U.S. libraries. Canada averaged sixty-four and fifty-four years of age while U.S. popular libraries averaged only forty-three and forty-one years of age. Growth rate was poor for both groups but was poorest for the United States among popular libraries.

Table 2.13 presented two longitudinal tables dealing with *city population size* for Canadian and U.S. popular libraries. Population size was higher in Canadian cities in both 1978 and 1988, by 49 percent in 1978 and 83 percent in 1988. In fact, the United States vs. Canada city population difference was even greater here than for scholarly libraries. For popular libraries, city population growth was 20 percent in Canada while for the United States it was −2 percent.

We have arrived at the *library staff* section now. For professional staff members the results were almost even between the two countries. Continuing, table 2.14 shows a longitudinal study of popular library clerical staff members for Canada vs. the United States. In both years Canadian libraries averaged fewer clerks than did those of the United States, 2.0 to 4.3 clerks in 1978 and 1.7 to 2.9 in 1988. The U.S. clerical staff was larger than the Canadian clerical staff, though the latter sample was so small that its numbers were not statistically significant. Neither group showed a positive growth score. In summary for this subsection, we see that this series of national paragraphs was pretty much of a standoff, Canada vs. United States. Each nation came out ahead on several variables.

To summarize the national comparisons so far: after an introduction that outlined the chapter and discussed library density, we discovered that U.S. libraries outnumbered Canadian libraries 1,937:125 in 1978 and 1,888:186 in 1988. At least 91 percent of the entire database belonged to the United States. By count, the United States was ahead for certain of these tables, but Canada was ahead for more of them. The popular library subsample was much less well developed in Canada than in the United States. In the field, by contrast, the ratio of scholarly to popular libraries was probably more like 1:20. Presumably many of them possessed very minor libraries.

## Canada versus the United States: A Further Comparison of Forty-five Variables

In comparing the two nations in this study, a large number of international variables were analyzed to locate interesting or revealing relationships. This subsection will mention some of the findings briefly and then discuss the results. In order to save pages, most of the tables on which this discussion is based will not be reproduced here. The section will cover library age, city population size, consortium memberships, staff size, and material holdings for scholarly libraries and for popular libraries, often separately.

A longitudinal table for United States vs. Canada showed total staff size for 1978 versus 1988 for popular libraries. Where were the larger library staff sizes in North America? This table had also a popular library portion that showed the staff size for the United States and Canada. The scores were 4.0 and 2.7 staff members for Canada in 1978 and 1988 and 5.1 and 6.4 staff members for the United States for those years. The United States led in both cases. Again the positive decade growth belonged to the United States whereas Canada showed a −32 percent decade decline.

Examination of *library age* for matched pairs revealed a Canadian popular library triumph. The oldest libraries were Canadian for both years, with a mean of forty-two years for 1978 and the same for 1988. *City population* size was larger generally for library cities in Canada than in the United States. Similar ratios were seen for city population size run on matched pairs also. Popular library *total staff members* was clear-cut in its figures. The United States was ahead of Canada by 27.5 percent in 1978 and by 137 percent in 1988! The U.S. libraries grew on average and the Canadian libraries lost staff members during this period.

When we consider *library material,* we can start with library volumes in longitudinal table 2.15. It shows clearly that the Canadian popular religious book collections were much larger than the corresponding American collections. In 1978 the Canadian book collections were 638 percent larger than those of the United States, and in 1988 they were 368 percent larger. However, the U.S. libraries grew during this period and the Canadian libraries lost ground, by 23 percent.

For periodical title subscriptions we see that only the 1988 figures can be used. The Canadians forged ahead by 1988 to lead the Americans by 45 percent. And finally, a special study of *holdings* including books, periodical titles, vertical file drawers, and microforms combined was made that resulted in a total cumulative score for each nation. It showed the Canadians to be far ahead of the Americans. In 1978 the Canadians led by 514 percent and in 1988 they continued to lead by 303 percent. Again, however, we see that the Canadians lost impetus while the American popular libraries were gaining in holdings during the decade.

We continue the popular library subsection by studying the results of analyzing *library expenditures* per library for the two countries. However, only the 1988 part of the material expenditures table had a large enough library frequencies to warrant study. It showed the Canadians to be far ahead, $24,000 to $3,180 per library per year, or a ratio of 655 percent ahead of the United States, in spite of an American 175 percent growth rate for the decade.

Within this limited popular library survey, how did the two nations compare? Canada led in 1978 by 8:2 and in 1988 by 10:2 variables on a per-library basis, a clear-cut Canadian victory for a small group of libraries. These scores included all United States:Canada comparisons made in this section. Canada's strength was obviously in per-library scores, seldom in growth scores.

How did the two nations compare overall? For all variables covered in this subsection, Canada led in 1978 scores, 23:7, while in 1988 the two were almost tied, 15:17, Canada being slightly ahead. The pattern of Canada leading in 1978 and then being almost tied or else surpassed by the United States in 1988 occurred many times. Just what was happening can be seen in the Canada vs. United States discussion in the footnotes below. Either U.S. institutions made strong improvements in their scores or Canadian institutions ran into extensive financial problems and so improved only moderately during the decade. Or probably both of these trends developed to some extent. These scores include all United States:Canada comparisons made in this chapter.

We can see the battle of the sexes joined with the battle of the nations in longitudinal table 2.16, and perhaps also combined with the battle of the scholarly vs. the popular libraries and of 1978 vs. 1988. This is a combined table that shows in concise form many of the subjects that we have discussed in other sections of the book. Notice the contrast of the genders between the United States and Canada. And finally, two master national comparison tables were made, which listed all of the variables used in the analysis for popular libraries. They are not reproduced here, however, because each table is five pages long.

## Regional Comparison

The need to explore the nature of the two databases when viewed from a regional perspective justified a group of special analyses. Under the regional section the discussion will begin with scholarly and popular libraries combined and then proceed to cover popular libraries. The section will conclude with a further comparison by region and denomination. Tables 2.17 for 1978 and 2.4 for 1988 provide examples of these analyses. At the same time these tables will introduce the database analyses by state and province as well as by region.

The scholarly and popular analysis by region is in certain ways more complex than the analysis by nation. Each North American *ALD* database was divided into eight regions. In all, fifty-one states (including the District of Columbia) and twelve provinces were covered by these regions. The tables showed us that the largest regions by number were the Middle West and the Middle Atlantic, which together contained half of the libraries in each database. If we add the Southeast, third largest, then we have reached two thirds of the total. The smallest regions were the Rocky Mountains and the Northeast, totaling only 6 to 8 percent of the two databases.

In the Canadian, Rocky Mountains, and Southeast regions, about one fourth of the 1978 libraries were popular, while in the Middle Atlantic and Southwest regions two-fifths were popular. The same percentages applied to the 1988 database also, with the exception of Canadian libraries sinking in 1988 to become only 11 percent popular, as pointed out before, possibly indicating either changing *ALD* policy toward Canadian popular libraries or a lack of interest in the *ALD* on the part of the libraries themselves.

What religious denominations were most prominent in each region? In each Canadian province was a majority of popular libraries Roman Catholic, for instance? Tables 2.18 for 1978 and 2.19 for 1988 answer these questions for popular libraries. For 1978, Northeastern region popular libraries were only 11 percent Roman Catholic. Jewish and Congregational libraries added together contained 63 percent of the total number of Northeast libraries. Canadian libraries were also 63 percent Roman Catholic.

In which region(s) do the popular library denominations concentrate? We may look at this question by again studying tables 2.3 and 2.5 for 1978 and 1988. When the two tables are compared, we can see that there was little difference in the regional ratios between them. For popular libraries we can see that the Middle Atlantic and Middle West together contained more than half of the libraries, as pointed out above. If the Southeast and Southwest are added, we can account for four-fifths of all popular libraries in the sample.

The Middle Atlantic and Southwest regions contained large numbers of popular libraries. However, popular libraries were less numerous in the Southeast and Canada. Popular congregational libraries were located primarily in the Middle West, and parochial school and public libraries were located primarily in Canada. Where among the regions is each popular denomination strongest? Table 2.20 answered this denominational question for 1988. In column 1, the Middle West and Middle Atlantic led for the denominations as a whole. In column 2, the same two regions led and for column 3 the Southeast and Southwest led. These tendencies were true for both survey years.

Tables 2.18 for 1978 and 2.19 for 1988 presented the regional and denominational picture. In 1978, the Jewish and Presbyterian denominations led in all regions, especially in the Middle Atlantic, West and Middle West, but not in the Rocky Mountains region. Jewish libraries led in the Northeast and were also important in Canada. Congregational denomination libraries were important in the Northeast and Rocky Mountains regions, Baptist in the South, and Other Denominations in the West.

Table 2.19 shows what happens when we match popular library only denominations with region in 1988. The Jewish group led in popularity in the Northeast, Middle Atlantic, and Middle West. The Baptists led in the Southeast and Southwest. Other Denominations achieved prominence in the West and Rocky Mountains regions, and Roman Catholics predominated in Canada. Strong second-ranking denominations were the Other Denominations in the Northeast, Presbyterians in the Southeast and West, Methodists in the Southwest, and Jewish in the West and Canada. So Jewish and Other Denominations were somewhat stronger than other denominations overall in a regional analysis.

Table 2.21 for 1988 enables us to break down the popular library only portion of 1988 table 2.22 into its three component parts. There we discover that *congregational* libraries were made up primarily of Jewish (29 percent), Presbyterian, Baptist, Other Denominations, and Methodist libraries, with almost no representation from the Independent, Churches of Christ, Mennonite, or Roman Catholic libraries. For *parochial school* libraries only two denominations emerged: Jewish and Roman Catholic. For *public* libraries only three denominations contributed significantly: Roman Catholic, Jewish, and Other Denominations. The congregational library type was the most popular for the Episcopal/Anglican, Lutheran, Presbyterian, and Jewish denominations. What regions were most common with various popular library denominations? The Middle West and Middle Atlantic regions were most popular, with nine different denominations.

For popular libraries, which library regions had the largest city populations? Table 2.23 for 1988 shows the answers to this question. The overall mean in 1978 was 461,400 persons, and in 1988 it declined to 356,600 persons. Largest mean city population was for the Middle Atlantic region with 555,800, and smallest was the Northeast with 120,000 in 1978. For 1988 the largest mean was found in Canada with 663,900 persons average and the smallest was the Northeast again, with 131,500 city population.

Table 2.24 (1978–88) showed a summary longitudinal table for regional distribution of popular libraries. Note that Canada and the Southwest grew in proportional representation during the decade, while every other region shrank or remained static, the Rocky Mountains, Middle West, and Middle Atlantic losing the most libraries for the table as a whole. Canada lost six libraries in total. The West also lost popular libraries. State composition of each region was described as well.

Popular congregational libraries were located most densely in the Middle West and Middle Atlantic regions, and parochial school and public libraries primarily in Canada. Jewish popular libraries were strong in most regions and Baptist and Other Denominations were strong in several regions. Largest mean city population was located in the Middle Atlantic region and smallest in the Northeast for 1978. For 1988 Canada and the Northeast again had the honor of ranking highest.

In summary, by region for popular libraries, the Middle West and Middle Atlantic were largest, and the Rocky Mountains and Northeast were smallest in numbers of libraries. The Middle Atlantic and Southwest were 40 percent popular. Jewish and Presbyterian libraries were leaders in almost all popular regions. The Southeast and Middle West regions were oldest, and the West and Southwest regions were youngest. Table 2.6 showed the relevant ratios between the United States and Canada.

## State and Provincial Comparison

The next analysis follows the regional analysis above and concentrates on the states and provinces in the study. It opens with a discussion of scholarly and popular libraries together. Tables 2.1, 2.2, 2.4, and 2.17 (for 1978 and 1988), reviewed before, will be helpful in this section also. Tables 2.1 and 2.2 show for the two databases the number and the leading denominations of Canadian and U.S. libraries in each state and province. This is a comprehensive set of tables that shows fundamental information about the databases. Tables 2.4 and 2.17 for 1988 and 1978 show the number of libraries per state, province, and region, as well as the percentage that each one represents for all of the U.S. and Canadian libraries.

In general, the states and provinces with the largest numbers of religious libraries had the largest overall population bases, and the states and provinces with the smallest numbers of libraries had the smallest population bases. Hence, library frequency can be seen to follow population density. We can see the state and province breakdowns of the two databases if we examine the tables listed just above. As we see in table 2.25 (for 1988), many denominations were so small that their representation was limited to a few local institutions.

Which states and provinces were largest in producing popular libraries? Generally, those with the largest total number of libraries also generated the largest number of popular libraries. Table 2.26 for 1988 answers this question. Table 2.27 shows this information for 1978 and 1988. It shows that certain states, such as New Mexico, gained libraries in strong fashion, while others, such as Oregon, fell strongly between 1978 and 1988. Table 2.28 for 1978 and 1988 shows popular libraries per state/province. It encourages study by state or region.

In summary, for states and provinces, the largest in libraries were Pennsylvania, New York, California, Ohio, and Texas for 1978 and Pennsylvania, New York, Texas, California, and Ohio for 1988. These states made up about a third of the total in each database. Three-fifths of the libraries were found in only one-sixth of the states and provinces. State emphasises were brought out by denomination. Jewish (in popular), Methodists (in 20 states), Baptist (in the South), and Presbyterians (in 16 states) were found in most of the states and provinces. On the other hand, several states and provinces either showed no libraries or produced very few of them.

## City Comparison[8]

If we analyze the 1978 and 1988 *ALD* databases by city, what do we find? We would like to know several things about cities and religious libraries. For instance, does a difference exist in the average city population level by type of library? Which cities were the leading religious library centers in North America? The city population analysis will examine the entire situation first, then city vs. rural locations, then city population size by denomination, region, library type, total library expenditure, chief librarian's gender, and then specific cities. Finally, a section summary will be presented.

The overall 1978 mean city population size for popular libraries was 361,372 people, 1.3 percent larger than the 1988 mean size, 356,612, as seen in longitudinal table 2.29. We can see also that the mean popular library existed in a somewhat larger city than the mean scholarly library.

Interesting information can be gleaned from frequency charts by city population size (not shown). First, there were size differences between the mean and median figures, the latter being much smaller than the former. In this case, the median was the more useful measure where large numbers were used because the mean was more influenced by the few libraries in disproportionately large metropolitan centers of over one or two million persons. The popular library median city population was 93,700 for 1978 and 91,800 population for 1988. The trends differed from those displayed by the means. Table 2.30 for 1988 shows that popular religious libraries were somewhat more oriented toward larger cities than were scholarly libraries. Only 38 percent of all popular libraries were found in cities of under 50,000 persons. This leaves 62 percent of the sample spread over a rising and then declining curve over the balance of the distribution.

Only 7 percent of the popular libraries, however, were found in cities of over one million persons. Therefore, popular libraries preferred smaller centers than that, but it seems likely that popular libraries, depending on their congregations for support and funding, were unlikely to have libraries if they were located in small centers and hence these do not appear on the *ALD* lists!

We can express a rural-urban ratio by showing the number of libraries in (1) the village population category and then (2) all higher population categories. For popular libraries the ratio was 1:7, meaning that there was one popular library in a village for every seven popular libraries in cities.

Tables 2.31 and 2.32 by state/province show small and large cities for popular libraries for both 1978 and 1988. They reveal such information, for example, as that New Jersey contained many small library cities and that the mean popular library was located in a city of about 39,500 population — small. On the other hand, typical Texas libraries were located in cities of 350,000 or over for 1978. Another analysis by *region* and city population size can be seen for 1988 in table 2.33 covering popular libraries. The region with the largest mean 1988 population was Canada, at 634,700 persons, with the Middle Atlantic next. The Northeast region showed the smallest cities.

Let us examine the libraries by *type* for both database years in longitudinal table 2.29 and in table 2.33 (for 1978 and 1988). Among popular libraries, public libraries were located in the largest cities, averaging 846,000 in 1978 and 1.07 million people in 1988. Popular congregational libraries were located in the smallest cities, about 327,500 population — a figure that did not change for the two years. Popular library city size change was largest for parochial schools at 22 percent, and smallest for public libraries at −21 percent.

The mean congregational population figure was about 10 percent less than the popular population figure in general, but both parochial school and public library populations were much larger in size, parochial school by 60 percent and public by 137 percent. Public was the largest for city size of the ten scholarly and popular types of libraries, and parochial schools was the third largest. From tables 2.29, 2.34, and 2.35 (for 1978 and 1988), we can see the popular denominational library analysis picture. The primary effect of the time trend is to enlarge the effect of certain scores, not to reduce them.

What was the mean *popular* library city population size by denomination? Overall 1978 means was 361,400 people for popular libraries, as mentioned above. Table 2.34 for 1978 shows Roman Catholic at 561,200 to be the largest and Congregational at 141,600 to be the smallest population means. For 1988 in table 2.35 the overall mean was 356,600 people. Table 2.35, a denominational table, shows Independent at the top size, averaging 700,800, and Mennonite at the bottom level, averaging only 12,500. Therefore, the ratio of largest to smallest popular 1988 denominational population means was 56:1. These 1988 findings are similar to those for scholarly libraries and for the 1978 popular library database table 2.34.

Clearly the Independent, Roman Catholic, and Jewish groups were oriented around large cities while the Baptist, Christian, Congregational, Mennonite, Methodist, and United Church of Christ denominations preferred small cities or large towns. The popular Jewish/Roman Catholic library group city population level was significantly larger than the mean Protestant library group city population size.

If we look at tables 2.36 and 2.37 to study city population size by total annual library expenditure for popular libraries in 1978 and 1988, we see an uneven progression upward. The tables show that there was a strong positive correlation between the rise in library expenditure and the rise in mean city population level. Generally speaking, popular libraries spending under $1,500 were located in cities of about 256,000 people, and libraries spending $20,000 to $95,000 were located in cities of about 784,900 people.

For chief librarian's gender, longitudinal table 2.38 shows population size groups by librarians' sex. For popular libraries in 1978, males were strongest in the smallest and the medium-large library cities: 15 percent. They were smallest in the medium-sized group: 9 percent. For 1988 males ranked highest in the large cities, 24 percent, and lowest in medium-small and medium-large cities, showing a definite move toward preferring large cities.

## Chief Population Centers

Now we will turn to the final aspect of city population and the number of religious libraries. Where were the population centers of *popular* religious librarianship in North America? Table 2.39 answers this question for 1978 and 1988. In 1978, Philadelphia led by a comfortable margin with Washington, Dallas, Minneapolis, and New York City following in being the locations for the largest number of libraries. For 1988, the table reflects several interesting changes from 1978. New York City became the leader in terms of geographic concentration with Washington, Dallas, and Albuquerque following. Philadelphia ranked lower on this table. Albuquerque, which ranked lower in the 1978 table, now placed fourth, while New York City, Washington, and Dallas retained their previous high rankings for popular libraries.

Table 2.39's cities contained 39 percent of all popular libraries for 1978 and 35 percent for 1988. The anomaly in this table was the drop in libraries for the city of Philadelphia, which sank from nineteen to five libraries between 1978 and 1988. This was primarily a loss of representation among Jewish, Roman Catholic, and United Church of Christ popular libraries for reasons that are not completely clear. Basic trends in scholarly and popular libraries were similar in regard to city population level. A final comprehensive look at the most popular cities can be gained in longitudinal table 2.40 for popular libraries. Several cities showed dramatic changes during the decade, while others appeared to be stable.

The two subsamples, scholarly versus popular, were dissimilar in that only 35 to 40 percent of the popular libraries were located in cities of two or more popular libraries. This indicated that popular libraries had the tendency to congregate in larger cities. Otherwise, only 20 to 25 percent of all popular libraries would be found in cities with two or more popular libraries.

Table 2.41 shows four popular Baptist libraries in one specific city: Albuquerque. Methodist had two, Other Denominations five, Jewish five, and Roman Catholic two libraries in popular cities. Reformed church libraries in Grand Rapids and Jewish in New York City, with five apiece, led the table. Notice that two thirds of the popular libraries in Atlanta were Methodist, all of Grand Rapids belonged to the Other Denominations, mostly Reformed, all of the Miami libraries were Jewish, as were all of the popular libraries in Chicago as well as all of the libraries in Cleveland and in Ottawa. All Quebec City libraries were Roman Catholic.

We now turn to a final analysis of specific city populations, this time by denomination. By denomination we look at lists of cities that reported two or more libraries per denomination. For instance, in Chicago, Cleveland, Miami, and Nashville, all popular libraries listed were Jewish. There was a direct and positive correlation between library expenditure level and mean city population size. The chief cities by number of religious libraries were New York City, Washington, Philadelphia, Dallas, and Montreal.

## Geographic Section Summary and Conclusions

This section was expected to answer the question, Where were the popular religious libraries located? After a preliminary discussion of library density and nonreligious library geography, the explanation continued by pointing out that all data collected originated in Canada or the United States. Of the two nations, the United States accounted for 88 percent or more of all data collected and so dominated the study. The total number of scholarly and popular libraries covered in 1978 was 2,062 and in 1988 was 2,074.

On the other hand the ratio *in the field* was probably 1:20 scholarly:popular libraries. American libraries declined slightly in number between 1978 and 1988, but the Canadian library group grew by 59 percent. In addition, the popular library sample shrank by 6 percent. The popular library sample was weak and small in Canada but much larger in the United States. The study compared the United States and Canada on several variables, and Canada was the stronger of the two on most of them.

In general, the states and provinces with the largest overall population provided the largest numbers of libraries. By region the Middle West and Middle Atlantic were the largest and Rocky Mountains and Northeast were the smallest in size. By state and province, a third of the libraries were located in Pennsylvania, New York, Texas, California, and Ohio in both databases. State or province longitudinal increase in sample size between 1978 and 1988 was largest in Quebec.

Mean city population level was high for popular libraries. Libraries in the Middle Atlantic and Canadian regions were located in the larger cities on average and in the Northeast and Southeast regions in the smallest cities. Median population level was about 92,000 for popular libraries. Popular libraries were primarily an urban/suburban phenomenon with few of them being located in small towns distant from cities.

## Demography: What Are the Demographic
## Characteristics of Popular Religious Libraries?

This section on the demography of Canadian and U.S. religious libraries will discuss several basic and specialized variables by sample composition. They include the following: library deaths and births, library age, and the characteristics of chief librarians. Other demographic information has already been reviewed in the previous section on geography. We will begin appropriately with the apparent *ALD* "deaths" and "births" of religious libraries.

### Library Deaths and Births

Library *deaths* is a subject appropriate for a demographic discussion, but one that was not covered directly in this study. Nor was the attempt to analyze the groups of popular libraries that died with the 1978 *ALD* edition entirely productive. Religious libraries die, of course, just as other libraries and other social institutions do. But evidence of these deaths is hard to find in this or any other scholarly study known to the author. Of course, the death rate must be universally low; once started, almost all libraries keep on operating, year after year, as far as this author knows.

When a library dies, it means that its collection of material is either dispersed to a variety of locations, discarded, sold, donated to another library, or burned. An intermediate step would be to put the collection into inactive storage in its own quarters or elsewhere and release all library staff members. Whenever a seminary or monastery dies, for instance, its library usually dies also, although in certain cases the material collection (not the library) may be transferred or sold to another institution and merged with that institution's library. Or else, where no previous library existed, it becomes the new institution's new library.

This study produced evidence suggesting that some library deaths may have occurred between the 1978 and 1988 *ALD* data collection periods. See longitudinal table 2.42. Certain libraries (422, or 20 percent) reported their questionnaire information for the 1978 edition but did not do so for the 1988 edition. Of course, in most of these nonrepeat cases, the library probably continued to exist but simply did not report its information for the 1988 edition, although it may have reported to earlier or later *ALD* editions. In certain other cases, however, the library may have died in fact. Approximately half of these 422 "death" cases were popular libraries, a suggestively high percentage.

In most cases, the libraries died because their parent institutions closed, and that must have been what happened in certain of these *ALD* cases. Of course, we have no idea how many of the 1978 libraries that failed to appear in the 1988 edition actually died, as opposed to simply failing to report or undergoing some other change. We know that these 1978 libraries failed to report in 1988, and that is all. At least their data was not published in the 1988 edition.

In a few cases, we suspect that the nonrepeating library did not die but simply moved with its parent institution to another location. Or the institution may have changed its official name. In certain of those cases, perhaps the change was not recognized by the author. It is highly unlikely that the library died while the parent institution lived on. In conclusion, we know little about North American religious library deaths. But a few of them must have occurred every year in the decade studied. We can report only on the nonrepeat group, which is identified here as the "no longer listed" group. These libraries' characteristics will be described in chapters 2 and 5.

A similar demographic subject is library *births,* and again this author knows little about them, for religious libraries or for any other kind of library. Births occurred every year, probably more of them than deaths, but no measure of births was available to this author. A number of libraries (434, or 21 percent) appeared in the entire 1988 database that were not listed in the 1978 database. There were slightly more young libraries newly reported in the forty-first edition than old libraries deceased in the thirty-first edition. The matched pairs totaled 1,640 libraries in each database (1978 and 1988) and were part of neither the formerly listed nor the newly listed groups.

It is impossible to tell whether these newly listed libraries were new libraries or merely older libraries that failed to complete the 1978 edition questionnaire. Probably most of them were the latter, but certain of them must have been the former. Only very young libraries, those less than ten years old, were truly new, of course. It is interesting to note that 12 percent of the newly listed libraries were between eleven and twenty years old, and 39 percent were even older, many of them over fifty! See tables 2.43 and 2.44 for 1988 and longitudinal tables 2.45 for the entire sample and 2.46 for popular libraries. While the *ALD* marked each library appearing for the first time with an asterisk, that does not mean that all of them were necessarily new libraries, merely that they were new to the *ALD.*

## Library Age[9–12]

Popular library ages can be considered by type of library, by region, and by denomination. However, we need to know the average age of all popular libraries first. In tables 2.47, 2.48, 2.49, 2.50 and 2.51 (for 1978 and 1988) among popular libraries the overall mean ages shown were forty-four and forty-one years. Mean age for each *ALD* edition's databases can also be seen in other tables for 1978 and 1988. Table 2.49 shows 1978 mean ages (no longer listed) to differ from 1988 ages (newly listed) by ten years for the United States with the 1978 libraries being older. For Canadian libraries, 1988 shows much younger ages, twenty-six to sixty-nine years, the recently dead being much older than the newly born libraries(!).

For popular libraries, longitudinal table 2.48 showed public libraries to be oldest (at 56–63 years) and congregational to be youngest (at 40–42 years). Change was consistently toward an all minus (younger) sample, with public libraries revealing the largest decade age drop at −11.5 percent from 1978 to 1988. Age for popular libraries can also be seen for 1978 in table 2.52 and for 1988 in table 2.53. Roman Catholic led with a 1978 mean age of fifty-three and Baptist, Methodist, and Presbyterian followed with a mean age of forty. For 1988, Roman Catholic libraries led with fifty-two years and Lutheran and Methodist followed with age thirty-seven each. For congregational libraries we can look at longitudinal table 2.54. Mean age was forty-two for 1978 and forty years for 1988. During the decade, apparently, the group got younger!

We have two popular library tables for 1978 and 1988 on library age by region. For 1978, oldest by far was the Canadian region, with the Northeast second, sixty-four and fifty-six years respectively. Youngest were the Southeast and Rocky Mountains at thirty to thirty-seven years, young ages. For 1988, oldest were the Northeast at fifty-five and Canada at fifty-four. Youngest were the Southeast and the West at about thirty-seven. See tables 2.50 and 2.51.

One more table can be examined here showing age and library expenditure: table 2.55 for 1988. As we might expect, it showed age to increase as library expenditure rose, from means of thirty-eight to forty-six plus years. Another table (not shown) analyzed age and type of library and included both scholarly and popular groups in the 1988 database. Popular library age averaged 41.5 years in 1988, as contrasted with 80 years old for scholarly libraries in that same year, a 1.93:1.00 relationship.

A notable difference between scholarly and popular libraries concerned the need for scholarly institutions to establish a library immediately after institutional founding. Few houses of worship felt such a need until some years after their institutional life had begun. Founding a library was a high priority step for scholarly institutions but seems to have been a low priority need for popular, non-academic organizations. Also the popular library movement is much more recent than the scholarly library movement.

We have next a series of popular library tables addressing the two variables of library age and denomination in general. We will start with table 2.53 for 1988. The youngest popular library denomination was the Independents at twenty-five years of age. Roman Catholic and Other Denominations libraries were the oldest among the popular denominations in both databases. At fifty-two, Roman Catholic libraries were as old as many scholarly libraries for our samples despite earlier findings. Table 2.53 showed Protestant denominations to be only slightly younger than the mean. The range of ages was large for popular libraries. The highest denominational mean score was more than double the lowest one in both edition databases.

Now we can study the tables showing the oldest popular libraries for each denomination separately. The oldest *Baptist* libraries for 1988 are shown in table 2.56. One library, the First Baptist Church in Dallas, was a century old, as old as most scholarly libraries. The computer printout showed twenty-nine more libraries immediately below the three libraries listed on this table, all aged forty years. *Christian* libraries in 1988 ranged from twenty-five to sixty years old (table 2.57). These were young ages to find on an "oldest" table, but they were the oldest libraries in the Christian denominational portion of the database. Notice that most of these libraries were located in large cities.

Table 2.58, a short table dealing with *Churches of Christ* libraries, shows the ages of the only two Church of Christ popular libraries in the 1988 database. Both were relatively young: forty years old and fifteen years old. In other similarly short tables, however, the failure of many popular libraries to declare their ages (368 out of 687 in 1978, and 270 out of 643 in 1988 did not do so) has led to tabular material that says less about the *average age* of denominational popular libraries than about the *reporting habits* of congregational librarians. Of course, they might not have known the dates of founding of their respective libraries.

The *Congregational* church library table for 1978 lists five libraries, all of which were forty years of age. Young! *Episcopal/Anglican* popular libraries in 1988 table 2.59 present a long list, and the two oldest of them were about a century old: the Church of the Redeemer, Andalusia, Pennsylvania, and the Episcopal Church Center, Burlington, Vermont.

*Independent* libraries (1978) list two interesting libraries—the Montreal YMCA at 120 years old and the Auburn Theological Seminary Lending Library, a forty-year-old public library operated by the seminary. The oldest *Lutheran* library list, table 2.60 for 1978, included a 120-year-old congregational library, Hope Lutheran Church in Milwaukee.

The *Methodist* table for 1988 was another short list but contained one 140-year-old congregational library, Mt. Vernon Place Methodist Church in Washington, D.C. (table 2.61). The next library list, *Other Denominations* for 1988 (table 2.62), was long and listed a group of relatively old libraries including five of more than a century in years. Seven denominations were included on the list. The oldest library was the Friends Free Library of Germantown, Philadelphia, 140 years old. All of the oldest five *Presbyterian* libraries were sixty or more years old (table 2.63 for 1988). Another short list of young-old libraries is shown in table 2.64 for 1988 *United Church of Christ* libraries. Its sixth oldest library was just fifteen years old.

We come now to *Jewish* libraries for 1988. This was a long list of older popular libraries (table 2.65). Half of them (7) were a century or more old and one was 180 years old—Congregation Rodeph Shalom in Philadelphia. Finally, we conclude this series of tables with another long list of 1988 libraries (table 2.66) for *Roman Catholic*. It included the oldest popular library in the database, Petit Seminaire de Québec in Quebec City, 225 years old. It also included four libraries located in Connecticut and Rhode Island, 30 percent of the list, and together with an equal number of Quebec and Ontario libraries they totaled three-fifths of the libraries on the list.

In summary, we have two popular library databases averaging from forty-one to forty-four years of age. One library was 225, and eighteen were 100 to 199 years old. The oldest one was a Roman Catholic library. Two-thirds of the others were either Other Denominations or Jewish libraries. On the whole, Roman Catholic and Other Denominations libraries were oldest, and United Church of Christ libraries were youngest.

## Chief Librarians[13-15]

Often the only staff member listed for a library in the *ALD* was the chief librarian. So analyses of staff members' characteristics should include certain analyses of the chief librarians. Chief librarians' gender was identifiable (usually!) and could be studied. To which gender did these religious librarians belong? We can examine these matters by type of library, region, and city population size and then look at named chief librarians. Chief librarians' gender by type of library tells us several interesting things as revealed by tables 2.67 for 1978 and 2.68 for 1988. We notice a difference between these two tables in that many of the 1978 No Response libraries moved to either the male or the female column by 1988, mostly toward the female side. Overall, the 1988 popular libraries were led by women (1.6:1.0).

Within the popular library group, women held leadership positions by a 4:1 margin, a considerable contrast to the scholarly library scene. In summary, women dominated the entire popular library group. This fact is displayed in table 2.7 (for 1978). Much the same picture can be seen in table 2.67 for the 1978 and table 2.68 for the 1988 databases. Table 2.69 (for 1978–1988) is a master or summary chief librarian's gender table, which is also longitudinal. It shows the areas of overall strength for the female group. Further, it illustrates the apparently slow growth rate for the male group contrasted with the, again apparently, much faster growth rate for the female group.

What was the ratio between the chief librarians' gender by region? For popular libraries, Canada and Northeast led the male column, and the Southwest and Middle West led the female column. Some switching around of regional supremacy was obvious here. Popular libraries in both 1978 and 1988 present an interesting picture for chief librarian's gender. The reader will remember our discovery that popular libraries were heavily weighted on the side of female leadership by at least a 3:1 to 4:1 ratio. A table (not shown) tells us that even so the popular libraries in the larger cities were headed primarily by males. The ratio in these cities was close in 1978—1.03:1.00—but it was not as close in 1988—1.4:1.0. Surprising! Does that show a popular library trend toward male chief librarians?

A named chief librarian—another analysis category—means one whose personal name was shown in the *ALD* library entry. Although called for on the *ALD* information blank, many entries did not include that item, however, especially among popular libraries. Whether this omission was the fault of the local person who completed the information form or was due to deliberate omission by the publisher is not known, but it is thought to have been that of the library respondent. The percentage of chief librarians who were named in the *ALD* was 65 percent in 1978 but rose to almost 100 percent in 1988.

In summary, for chief librarians, women led in number for popular libraries. Table 2.42 is another master table, a summary of changes in library type for popular libraries for 1978 and 1988 that lists each entire database, matched pairs, no longer listed, and newly listed libraries. Notice also that the numbers of newly listed and history/archive libraries were larger for 1988, so that their 1978–88 growth rate was large. Popular library frequency in the decade was 216 to 174 libraries for no longer listed and newly listed instituions. For popular libraries, congregational library matched pairs remained the same, of course, but forty-one fewer newly listed than no longer listed libraries were listed in 1988 than in 1978. More than half of the 1978 no longer listed were popular libraries, and 40 percent of the newly listed libraries for 1988 were popular, a disproportionately heavy percentage suggesting *ALD* editorial policy as one souce of the apparent imbalance.

## Demographic Section Summary and Conclusions

The demographic section undertook to describe the databases in terms of basic population characteristics — library deaths and births, age, and chief librarian's gender. While deaths were numerous in the *ALD* (20 percent of the total) in terms of dropout from one edition to the next, it is almost certain that a much smaller proportion of the libraries ceased to exist in the real world. No firm information was available on the larger population, however, so little could be said about it. Much the same was true for library "births," although it seems likely that they were numerous in the real world. But speculation was all the author could offer in regard to the 434 *ALD* libraries in 1988 that had not appeared in the 1978 edition. However, the proportion of new libraries to the greater population was around 2 to 3 percent per year.

Age was analyzed for popular libraries and averaged between forty-one and forty-three years. The popular library movement did not get rolling until after World War II. Oldest popular libraries were most often Northeastern, Roman Catholic, and public libraries, and nineteen specific libraries were identified as being the oldest of them. The congregational, Southeast, Baptist, and Methodist libraries were among the youngest of the popular libraries.

Chief librarian's gender was decidedly female among popular libraries. Middle West and congregational libraries dominated the female, and Northeast and public libraries dominated the male popular library groups. The longitudinal study by chief librarian's gender focused on the changes in database composition by nation and library type from the earlier to the later period.[16]

## Decade Projections

In conclusion, this chapter provides not only the readings from the 1978 and 1998 *ALD* databases but also the projections of the same variables for 1998 as well as a short list of subject areas needing further study. The projected figures address the question of what level will have been attained for each variable by the year 1998 and are based on extrapolations from the 1978 and 1988 data. Tables 2.70, 2.71, 2.72, and 2.73 should be consulted. They are derived from the statistical discussion that constitutes appendix C.

Table 2.73 showed the statistical projections for *popular* libraries 1978 to 1998. Mean age should drop slightly from forty-three years in 1978 to thirty-nine in 1998. City population size should also drop somewhat. Total staff size should rise strongly, from a mean of 5.1 in 1978 to 7.7 in 1998, if current trends continue. Number of library professionals will remain stationary. Total library expenditures will rise significantly, from a mean of $2,664 in 1978 to $16,754 — by 529 percent! Volume holdings will rise strongly also from a mean of 4,965 volumes in 1978 to 7,105 volumes in 1998 — by 43 percent. These are U.S. figures only.

Most Canadian projections were based on figures that were too small to be taken seriously, but a few derived from more meaningful cell sizes. Age can be predicted to sink rapidly from a mean of sixty-four years to around forty-four by 1998. City population size will rise from a mean of 528,000 in 1978 to 741,400 in 1998, by 40.4 percent. Total database figures will show a mean rise of 162 percent for the decade from 1988 to 1998 for the United States but a loss of 24.5 percent for the decade for Canada.

In conclusion, this section for the United States and Canada extrapolated the data available for fourteen variables from 1978 to 1988 and on as far as 1998. Some of the variables were predicted to rise while others were predicted to fall. In all cases, however, variable change was based on the trend obtained between 1978 and 1988 and was only as valid and reliable as the data samples from which it was drawn.

## Subject Areas Needing Further Study

This chapter concludes with a section of suggestions for further study. Additional studies are needed to replicate this study and to examine certain aspects of it more closely. This chapter leaves many useful and reasonable questions unanswered or even unmentioned. They should be attacked, one by one. On the other hand, the following list is far from complete for the research needed. We have here a brief list of suggested research or exploration and analysis projects on North Amercian scholarly and popular religious libraries:

1. Within the states and provinces a further study of religious library geography would be helpful. Where within a specific state or province or group of them are its popular religious institutions concentrated? Where are its chief religious centers located?

2. Correlation studies should be made between congregational density, house of worship density, and library density, all within the same denomination. To what extent and under what conditions is it true that denominational density in a particular location determines the density of its libraries there?

3. From a geographic perspective, an analysis should be made to describe the location of religious libraries by denomination within several metropolitan areas in order to reach generalized conclusions.

4. Study library deaths and births. Learn why several hundred religious libraries dropped out of the *ALD* each decade and several hundred more were added that had not been represented the decade before. How many of them actually died and how many were actually newly born each year? And just how complete for certain cities are the *ALD* academic, public, and special library listings?

5. Work out correlations between institutional founding dates and library founding dates for each one of the ten types of libraries and see how these findings relate to library size, development, and services offered.

6. The researcher should attempt to identify the reasons why beyond the number of congregational members, certain states or certain denominations are strongly represented in the religious library world while others are not.

7. Ethnicity should be considered in the religious library world. To what extent do the scholarly or popular religious libraries in this study represent the North American Anglo-Saxon tradition vs. Hispanic-American, African-American, and French-Canadian traditions?

8. In 1998 a graduate student should carry out a further longitudinal study of the libraries in this study to reevaluate variable trends and determine at that time the status of the leading libraries of 1978 and 1988.

## Notes

1. The difference between geography and demography is real and should be apparent to the reader. However, the two fields overlap in that demographers study not only population statistics but also the distribution of populations throughout geographic areas. The various subtopics under these two main subject fields have been distributed between them here in such a manner as to facilitate chapter organization. As a result, the distribution of the religious library population has been assigned to geography, for instance, and other subtopics also may have been assigned to one or the other main field in rather arbitrary fashion.

    In fact, much of the entire book might fit into an extended chapter on demography. Much demographic information is covered in the geographic portion of the chapter. Further, certain subtopics that are discussed do not fit well into either main field and even less well anywhere else in the book. The author hopes the reader will forgive such "convenient" subject assignments.

2. The reader will note in this and later chapters that 1988 tables are used extensively, whereas 1978 tables are used much less often: the reader might have expected the study to employ the data from both years with the same frequency and more consistently. There are two reasons for our policy: (1) often the 1978 or 31st edition picture was much like that of the 1988 (41st) edition, so the older table was omitted to avoid unnecessary repetition, which would only confuse and bore the reader and add little to the argument: and (2) a simplified presentation was preferred.

3. Nonresponse may be the result of any one of several factors. Each one of them has a different effect on the statistics of the libraries that do respond. Therefore, a high nonresponse rate may or may not be catastrophic, depending on whether it is due to:

    1. Deliberate suppression of facts
    Number of volumes held
        *Mean*      *No Response*
        27,483    61 percent
    Result: *Mean too high,* as underachievers tend to be embarrassed or very sensitive and hence skip the question that embarrasses them
    2. Nonapplicability (e.g., they have no holdings of this type)

Number of films

*Mean*          *No Response*

129               71 percent

Result: *No effect on mean* but cell size becomes quite small

c) Ignorance or lack of data

Congregational Budget

*Mean*          *No Response*

1,625,450     39 percent

Result: *Slight effect on mean,* usually in an upward direction, as ignorance and overwork are generally associated with low budgets

4. The task of profiling for Canadian and U.S. scholarly libraries is easier than that for popular library samples simply because the scholarly sample sizes are larger than those for the popular libraries and data reliability is accordingly greater.

5. There is a distinct difference between the types of libraries that make up the Canadian and the U.S. popular library samples. For the United States for the years 1978 and 1988, there were 660 and 621 popular libraries respectively. The matching figures for Canada were 27 and 22—a regrettably small Canadian sample by any standard. However, and for several reasons, the libraries composing the Canadian group appear to be better libraries of their types. "Better libraries" here is not meant to imply better in a qualitative or normative sense, but simply to indicate that the Canadian libraries found in the two *ALD* samples were probably among the larger, more strongly supported libraries within the population from which they were drawn. About 92 percent of the U.S. popular libraries (for both editions) were congregational in nature—church and synagogue libraries designed to serve the needs of their congregations. There were only thirty and then thirty-four parochial school and public libraries cumulated within the two U.S. editions. For Canadian libraries, on the other hand, the distribution was quite different. In 1988 the number of Canadian congregational libraries composed only 27 percent of the total; parochial school and public libraries made up the balance of the total: 41 percent and 32 percent respectively. These latter two figures were even larger in 1978—48 percent and 37 percent. (This phenomenon is largely associated with Roman Catholic elementary and high schools in Canada.)

Roughly speaking, parochial school and public libraries (both of which can be expected to have been more strongly supported than were congregational libraries) composed between 73 percent and 85 percent of the Canadian samples. Hence, it is to be expected that the characteristics of the Canadian popular libraries differ proportionately with the difference in library type. That is, as the number of parochial school and public libraries increased proportionately within the sample, so did the characteristics or attributes of the sample assume a "bigger, better" configuration simply because congregational libraries tended to be smaller and less well supported. Among the U.S. libraries, Baptists accounted for 11 percent of the total in 1988, Other Denominations

12 percent, Presbyterian 16 percent, and Jewish 29 percent. Protestants made up 67 percent of all the U.S. popular libraries. The figures for 1978 were similar, with Protestant accounting for 72 percent of the total. In 1988 the Jewish libraries took an additional 5 percent of the U.S. sample. The Canadian denominational distribution was somewhat different. In 1988, Other Denominations accounted for 14 percent of all libraries: Protestant libraries accounted for only 27 percent of the total. The Jewish libraries took 27 percent—almost precisely the same as in the United States. The large difference in distribution between the two countries was found among the Roman Catholic libraries.

In the United States, the Roman Catholic libraries were only 4 percent of the total; in Canada these libraries constituted 45 percent—almost one-half of all Canadian popular libraries. Therefore, from the start we are confronted with the phenomenon of differences in makeup vis-à-vis the United States-Canada subsamples. The American group was largely Protestant and overwhelmingly congregational in nature. The Canadian group, on the other hand, was almost one-half Roman Catholic and largely parochial school or public libraries. We ought to expect, then, that the Canadian libraries will appear to be stronger than their U.S. counterparts. It might be wise, however, to remember, on balance, that the Canadian and U.S. libraries were only counterparts to a certain extent. This will help somewhat in understanding the differences to be found in the specific variable analyses.

6. G. Martin Ruoss, *A World Directory of Theological Libraries* (Metuchen, N.J.: Scarecrow, 1968), pp. 13–18.

7. John F. Harvey, "An Introductory World Survey of Popular Church and Synagogue Libraries," *International Library Review* 18 (October 1986): 347–72.

8. The questionnaire question "questionnaire returned" produced interesting results. Almost all libraries could be assigned a response to the question, either "yes" or "no." The percentage of libraries that returned their questionnaires in 1978 was considerably lower than that in 1988—about three-quarters of all libraries for both countries. By the time of the 1988 edition almost all libraries *did* return the required information—99 percent for the United States and 100 percent for Canada. Although it would be curious to try to analyze this outcome as the result of Canada versus United States activity, it seems more reasonable to conclude that the difference between the two editions may have been the result of a change in the *ALD* editorial policy.

"Library directory named" produced identical results for both countries for both editions. All libraries could be assigned either a "yes" or a "no" answer to this question on the basis of whether or not the name of the director appeared in the directory. In 1978 both countries produced directors' names for approximately 90 percent of their respective libraries. By 1988 this percentage had risen to 100 percent. In contrast to the preceding inquiry, the outcome of this question appears to have been the result of a spontaneous tendency among librarians to submit the desired names. Why this change occurred is unknown.

9. The author must point out that this discussion of ages is an analysis of the founding dates of the libraries, not those of their parent institutions. Sometimes the parent institution and the library were founded in the same year or even at the same time, but sometimes several years elapsed before the parent institution managed to establish its library. Therefore, parent institutional founding dates should not be confused with library founding dates wherever possible.

10. In each table, for the same variable value, the libraries were listed in exact alphabetical order by the name of the state or province and then by city with all Canadian libraries following all U.S. libraries.

11. Individual library scores on each variable were expressed in terms of the midpoint of each group within the entire group of scores. This fiction facilitated statistical analysis and data collection. The figure of 225 years of age is used because it represents the midpoint of the range of ages of those libraries founded in the year 1800 or before.

12. The following were among titles that were helpful to the author in preparing the chapters in this book:

Accredited Institutions of Postsecondary Education, 1980–1981 (Washington, D.C.: American Council on Education)

Accredited Institutions of Postsecondary Education, 1987–1988 (Washington, D.C.: American Council on Education)

American Association of Bible Colleges, Directory 1987–1988 (Fayetteville, Ark.: 1987) Ash, Lee, comp., Subject Collections (New York: R. R. Bowker, 1985)

Association of Advanced Rabbinical and Talmudic Schools, List of All Accredited Schools (New York: 1988)

Christian Resources Handbook (Mississauga, Ont.: Marc Canada, 1987)

Directory of Canadian Universities (Ottawa: Association of Universities and Colleges of Canada, 1986)

Education Directory, Colleges and Universities, 1980–1981 (Washington, D.C.: U.S. National Center for Education Statistics)

Fact Book on Theological Education (Vandalia, Ohio: Association of Theological Schools, 1986)

Graduate Programs in the Humanities and Social Sciences 1988 (Princeton, N.J.: Peterson, 1987)

Index of Majors, 1986–1987 (New York: College Entrance Examination Board, 1986)

Information Please Almanac (Boston: Houghton Mifflin, 1986), p. 315.

Mead, Frank S., Handbook of Denominations in the United States (Nashville: Abingdon, 1980)

Philosophy, Religion, and Theology: A Catalog of Selected Doctoral Dissertation Research (Ann Arbor: University Microfilms International, 1985)

Readers Digest Almanac (Pleasantville, NY: 1980)

13. Chief librarian's gender is an interesting variable where scholarly libraries are concerned. For the United States in both 1978 and 1988 the samples were

almost equally split between males and females, with males leading slightly (by exactly 6 percentage points in each case)—with 50 percent and 52 percent of the samples by proportion. In Canada, on the other hand, the proportion of males was somewhat higher than in the United States, 62 percent and 63 percent for the two editions. The proportion of females was curious, however, in that it rose from 28 percent in 1978 to 35 percent in 1988.

Given the fact that for *popular* libraries almost the entire shift between males-females was accounted for by greater numbers of female heads declaring themselves in 1988 (and producing No Response replies in 1978; this phenomenon was true for *both* Canada and the United States, as a point of interest), it is reasonable to assume that most of the 10 percent No Response group in 1978 was actually composed of female heads who later declared themselves in the 1988 edition. I believe that this interpretation of the statistics is correct as there is virtually *no change whatsoever in the proportions of male heads between 1978 and 1988 for either the United States or Canada or for either popular or scholarly libraries.*

If the configuration of proportions has been interpreted correctly above, then we are forced to conclude that there has been little swing in directorships toward either males or females where head librarianship is concerned. There has, however, been a distinct tendency for female chiefs to "come out of the woodwork," so to speak. The No Response rate for the United States in 1978 was 6 percent, followed by only one percent in 1988. The matching figures for Canada were 10 percent and 2 percent. Here again, Canada gave evidence of following the U.S. lead after a delay in time.

For popular libraries these rates were even more dramatically revealing. The No Responses for 1978 were 40 percent and 26 percent for the United States and Canada respectively. For 1988 the matching percentages were 9 percent and zero percent! Obviously, by 1988 the question of gender was no longer as subjectively sensitive a matter as in previous years. Also, it appeared to be less salient in Canada than in the United States. However, this appearance may be deceptive as it is clear that there were few weak libraries within the Canadian sample—and chief librarians of strong, healthy libraries had much to boast of and were unlikely to suppress either their gender or any other library information.

The interesting point about the question of gender is twofold: (1) there was no significant change toward more females—in fact over the decade there was a 2 percent increment toward males in the United States accompanied by a one percent growth in Canada; and (2) Canada had an 11 percent or 12 percent lead in terms of male over female heads. These figures were stable over the ten-year period. How to explain this pair of facts is difficult. It is clear that there was no *trend* in the United States that might be followed in Canada after an appropriate lag of a few years. And it is equally clear that Canada had more males than females and that the situation was not changing—except toward a larger proportion of males!

A study of the data at the end of the 1990s is necessary to resolve this interesting riddle. At the moment it looks as if the trend in both the United States and Canada was toward slightly more males and that Canada was leading in the race. An alternative explanation might simply be that the larger, better libraries attracted male librarians and that as the Canadian *ALD* libraries tended to be quite a lot "better" (larger) than the average library within the population, the percentage of males in the sample was even higher than in the United States.

14. In terms of chief librarian's gender for popular libraries, we find that the U.S. sample in 1978 was 12 percent male matched by a corresponding 12 percent in 1988. The U.S. change over this period regarding female library heads was 48 percent in 1978 swelling to 79 percent in 1988. Although the percentage of No Response fell dramatically in 1988, the entire fall was absorbed by the additional proportion of female library chiefs. This suggests that the percentage of males for the United States remained constant over the decade. This supposition is confirmed by the popular library data for Canada. In 1978 male library heads accounted for 33 percent of the Canadian sample followed by 36 percent in 1988. The figures for female chiefs were 41 percent and 64 percent—almost precisely the same pattern of change configurations as for the United States. It is interesting to see that there is a larger proportion of males in Canada (close to three times larger); however, this fact is probably accounted for by the correspondingly larger proportion of parochial school and public libraries in Canada, as pointed out earlier. It seems that congregational libraries tend more to be associated with female librarians. Among the samples of matched pairs we find the sample distributions to be almost precisely the same as for the larger United States-Canada configurations. Congregational libraries in the United States accounted for 96 percent of the samples in both editions; within Canada the matching figures were 19 percent and 14 percent, indicating an initially low proportion falling over time. For the subsamples, "no longer listed" (1978) and "newly listed" (1988), the total number of libraries was too small to do much with: 216 and 174. However, within these subsamples the distributions were similar for the United States and different for Canada.

In Canada, congregational libraries composed only 9 percent of those lost in 1978 (i.e., only one congregational library), followed by 50 percent of the newly listed libraries in 1988 (four libraries). These numbers cannot be used as anything but *indicators,* but the suggestion is that the proportion of congregational libraries for Canada may be rising over time. A look at the raw figures shows us that in 1978 there were four of these libraries followed by six in 1988—only an intensive study of the remaining editions in the series (the figure for the 1998 edition would be instructive!) would tell definitely if the trend toward a long-term increase in congregational libraries is more than illusory.

Proceeding to the variables describing popular library attributes, we find a number of interesting divergences interspersed with a larger number of Canada-United States congruences. "Library accreditation" for both countries was zero percent for popular libraries in 1988. "Formal denominational affiliation" approached unity—again as one might expect as these libraries were "religious" by definition. The question concerning "departmental library status" drew zero percentages for both states. "Questionnaire returned" and "library director named," on the other hand, produced 100 percent responses. To be included in the *ALD*, it is now necessary for all libraries to submit their questionnaires!

The question concerning the "religious order status" of the chief librarians (whether a priest or brother, sister or nun, etc.) elicited answers of zero percent and one percent for the United States (1978 and 1988), accompanied by 4 percent and 5 percent for Canada. A closer examination of the figures shows that there are several priests and nuns in the American sample in 1988 and only one priest in the Canadian sample for both editions. So much for the value and power of small samples as indicative tools where percentage analysis is used! At any rate, religious figures seemed to appear with surprising infrequency among library chiefs, especially when we consider that popular libraries were often attached to *churches and synagogues.* Once again, however, it is interesting that the religious who did appear were within the U.S. congregational library sector and did not seem to occur within the Canadian parochial school group. Perhaps this suggests a developing professionalism among popular library heads, but it is too early to say. Within Canada the indication is possibly more tenable simply because of the "better" nature of the Canadian *ALD* libraries.

Looking at total popular library staff, we find means of 5.1 and 6.4 persons for the United States, and 4.0 and 2.7 for Canada. This represents an increase in total staff size of 25 percent for the United States and a fall of one third for Canada! An examination of the staff breakdown by edition tells us that the United States showed 1.7 and 1.7 professionals matched by 2.0 and 1.8 professionals in Canada. Clerks and student assistants (or volunteers?) for the United States registered 2.9 and 7.4 persons in 1988; for Canada these figures were 1.7 and 2.2 staff members. These statistics appear solid enough, except when we notice that the No Response rate for the United States is particularly high—over 70 percent. No Responses composed 59 percent of the Canadian group, too.

The combination of the mean staff members and the No Responses suggests several things: (1) among the American popular libraries No Response was likely to be the result of smaller staff sizes: therefore, as the response rate for Canada was significantly higher, the Canadian libraries started to look *better* generally; (2) in terms of number of professionals, the countries ranked about equal, i.e., at approximately two professionals per library, although this figure was almost certainly much too high for those libraries not responding and for the general population of libraries; (3) Canadian libraries almost certainly had lower total staff sizes than their American counterparts, although not nearly as much lower as shown by the statistics.

A total of one hundred U.S. libraries (16 percent) reported student assistants, as opposed to three Canadian libraries (a corresponding 14 percent). We can conclude from this picture that the two countries varied greatly on this final staff variable (means of 7.4 versus 2.2) but that the number of such libraries with student assistants tended to be low generally. As the No Response rates within the 1978 edition were large (over 80 percent for both countries), it is impossible to conclude anything at all about *change over time* in terms of library staffing for popular libraries. However, there are three possible conclusions with a good amount of support within the 1988 edition considered alone: (1) a larger proportion (52 percent) of the Canadian libraries were "better" in terms of staff size—41 percent of these responded versus only 27 percent for the United States; (2) in terms of total staff size the U.S. libraries were 137 percent better off for those libraries reporting (6.4 persons vs. 2.7 staff members for Canada); and (3) there was virtually no difference between the two countries in terms of number of professionals per library.

Looking at city population size for the libraries in our samples, we find that mean city size for Canada went up from 530,000 to 635,000 between 1978 and 1988. This is an increase of 20 percent over the ten years. For the United States, on the other hand, mean city size was approximately 350,000 for both editions (and tending to fall slightly by the 1988 survey, by 2 percent). In fact, the mean Canadian city size was 1.8 times as large as that for the United States. As all libraries could be identified in terms of city size for their locations, the conclusion for this variable was inescapable. Canadian libraries reporting to the *ALD* were generally those located in the larger cities. Few small or medium-sized city libraries reported to the *ALD* for Canada.

For the United States, however, city population size was more spread out and more stable over time. The average size of U.S. cities fell slightly over time, and the distribution of libraries tended toward slightly smaller centers of population density.

Similarly, although still significant, city size seems to have had less influence on whether or not U.S. libraries were listed in the *ALD*. This last assertion, however, would be difficult to prove except in light of the mean city population size for the Hannaford (CSLA) group. In fact, the mean city population size for the CSLA (1985) libraries was 149,000 and bears out this observation.

Mean library age presents a different configuration. For 1978 and 1988 the United States reported popular library means of forty-three and forty-one years. For Canada, the matching means were sixty-four and fifty-four years. A total of 58 percent of U.S. libraries reported, as opposed to 68 percent of Canadian libraries. Obviously, not only were the Canadian libraries considerably older but they were also the "better" libraries among Canadian popular libraries, since there is no reason to think that Canadian libraries in general were older than were their U.S. counterparts, in fact, just the contrary obtains. This idea is already familiar to us and was expected.

What was not expected, however, was that the average age of popular Canadian libraries was falling somewhat (by about one year in age per year of the survey decade). This suggests that listing by Canadian libraries with the *ALD* was slowly becoming more common, and that *in time* (perhaps in another 15 to 20 years) a more representative sample of the population will be found on the *ALD* list of Canadian libraries.

The average U.S. *ALD* popular library appeared to be about forty years old. It is likely that this figure was somewhat higher than was true for the population mean. The average U.S. popular library in the field, however, was possibly *less* than thirty years old. Therefore, the U.S. sample was also "better" (at least older) than the overall library population. See chapter 6 and consider the matching age figures for the White (19.3 years) and CSLA data (17.5 years) to justify this assumption.

It is interesting that the mean library age in the United States was falling too (from 43 to 41 years over the decade). If this trend continues, we can expect to find that the *ALD* list for the USA may be slowly becoming more "democratic." On the other hand, the slight fall in mean age may simply indicate that libraries achieve "maturity" or prominence faster than they did formerly. Only further longitudinal analysis of the *American Library Directory* libraries into the 1990s would prove the issue.

For expenditures, on the other hand, we find that we have a similar configuration of No Response rates as for library staffing. The response rates for the United States were 23 percent and 40 percent for 1978 and 1988. The matching figures for Canada were 15 percent and 27 percent. In other words, most popular libraries in both countries did not respond! All we can do is look at the pattern that emerged from those libraries that *did* respond and assume that the average throughout the national populations was somewhat lower.

For the United States in 1978 the mean total popular library expenditure was between $2,650 and $2,800, depending on the method of cumulation. This figure rose by 270 percent to about $10,000 in 1988. Assuming an average book cost of approximately US $10.00, this sum represented an annual increment of a thousand books by the final year of the decade. However, if the entire library income were to be spent on books, there would be no funds left for salaries, other material, building costs, binding, etc. Divided several ways, $10,000 did not go far— it was equivalent to one part-time salary.

For Canada, the mean total annual expenditure rose from approximately $92,000 to $112,000 by 1988. This was an increase of about 22 percent. However, these figures were based on five libraries that responded in 1978 and ten in 1988. From this we can conclude very little except that five and then ten of the largest and most prosperous libraries reported their expenditures for the two editions under study! It appears that Canadian expenditures probably rose over the decade (there were certainly more "rich" libraries by 1988), but nothing significant could be concluded.

Considering that the Canadian dollar had a value of somewhat over US $0.80 and that inflation over the decade was in the realm of 60 percent, it appears that the average North American library was somewhat better off by 1988 than it was in 1978. However, we cannot say by how much or whether the average Canadian library was in a better or poorer position relative to its U.S. neighbors.

We find that mean volume holdings for the United States rose from five thousand to six thousand over the decade based on high response rates (96 percent in 1988). Hence, a mean of six thousand is a reliable estimate for the population, although probably somewhat high. The matching values for Canada were 36,600 and 28,200 based on similar response rates. Interestingly enough, as was predicted, a rise of 17 percent in response rate produced a 23 percent *fall* in volume holdings for Canada! This again may have indicated that libraries with less than outstanding holdings may have previously tended to withhold information about the sizes of their collections. It also suggests that over the decade more libraries of an ordinary profile were submitting the *ALD* questionnaire.

It is possible to conclude only that holdings in Canada were much greater for its elite group of libraries (many of which were either parochial school or public and correspondingly larger than for the average congregational library) and that there may or may not have been an increase in mean holdings over the decade. For the United States it appears that volume holdings increased significantly, probably by more than the 22 percent indicated as the response rate rose from 73 percent to 95 percent. Hence, probably the true rise in holdings approximated something in the nature of 30 percent for the congregational libraries making up the U.S. subsample (the same rise may have occurred in Canada). It is likely that this increase was also reflected in the general library population, but the extent of real growth there would be difficult to estimate.

The pictures for popular library periodical subscriptions and vertical files were almost identical as for the preceding variable. Canada reported a mean of ninety subscriptions versus sixty-two for the United States, almost 50 percent more. Vertical file drawers in Canada came up as 9.7, against 7.4 in the United States. Both variables showed similar response rates for the two countries. Again, the Canadian libraries reflected their larger types and their elitist natures.

For microform holdings the picture differed enormously. In 1988 only 2 percent of U.S. popular libraries reported microform holdings (mean of 47,700) and one Canadian library reported fifty microforms. Mean microforms for 1978 in the United States equaled 49,400. However, even in the United States there were only seven and then twelve libraries reporting microforms for the two editions with a slightly declining mean over the time period. Obviously, American popular libraries with microforms needed about fifty thousand of them on average, based on the present study, and Canadian popular libraries never joined the microform trend at all. More than that, who can say? It appears likely, however, that microforms will never catch on in either country among popular libraries. This is particularly probable given the rise of new storage media such as CD-ROMs, optical disks, etc.

Concerning media holdings (the cumulative of maps, media, and art reproductions), we find that in 1978 a total of 170 libraries reported holdings in any or all of the three component media categories. In 1978, however, the average library with media holdings had holdings in 2.0 of the three types — 169 libraries reported that they held "media" of some sort. In 1988, though, the mean number of types held was 1.7 out of a possible 3 types with 219 libraries reporting "media" holdings of one or another combination of types. About one-hundred popular libraries reported map holdings for both years; similarly, about fifty libraries reported art reproductions, again for both years.

For Canada only, three and then five libraries showed media holdings in any of the three types for the two editions. The means for Canada were 2.3 and then 2.0 — a slight decline in number of types held concurrently as the number of holding libraries increased. This pattern is similar to that shown in the United States, where the proportions of libraries holding media were 26 percent and then 35 percent; the figures for Canada were only 11 percent and 23 percent. Although both countries showed an increase, Canada was well behind the United States, and neither country did well in terms of the number of different media types held.

The questions concerning "restrictions on circulation" and "restrictions on reference service" produced little by way of response. In the United States only 8 percent and 6 percent of all popular libraries claimed to have restrictions of these two types in 1978. By 1988 these percentages had risen to 10 percent and 9 percent. For Canada, the matching statistics were 4 percent and 4 percent followed by 14 percent and 9 percent. Generally speaking, 90 percent of the popular libraries reporting applied no systematic restrictions on either reference service or circulation, and the two countries tended to be comparable in terms of results. Restrictions on circulation were slightly more common than on reference service. The consortium membership variable similarly came out rather poorly. In the United States, 2 percent and then 3 percent of popular libraries reported consortium memberships, with the means for the two editions being 1.0 and 1.2 memberships. The corresponding data for Canada for the two editions were 7 percent of libraries with 1.0 membership and 5 percent with 1.0 membership. Canada appears to have had a slight advantage here, but given the nature of Canadian libraries, this advantage was probably more apparent than real.

The question about OCLC membership brought in nothing for either state. Similarly, the query concerning automation projects showed only that in 1988 twenty U.S. libraries (3 percent of the total) claimed to be involved in automation projects. That Canada brought in nothing at all is surprising, since the average Canadian library *appeared* to hold so many more volumes (and to have more money) than many in the United States. Obviously computers entered the popular library field in Canada even later than for the United States.

Extended collections, on the other hand, showed some interesting traits. For example, 48 percent of all U.S. popular libraries had a mean of 1.9 subject interests in 1988. This was a rise over the 30 percent of libraries with subject interests in 1978. The Canadian mean for 1988 was identical with that for the United States, but the proportion of libraries was only 27 percent—considerably lower.

Special collections, to the contrary, showed the United States with 15 percent of the libraries reporting a mean of 1.4 special collections. The figures for Canada were 27 percent for a mean of 1.3 collections. One is inclined to wonder here if the meanings of the terms "subject interests" and "special collections" were quite clear to the respondents of the questionnaire. It appears unlikely, however, that there was any real confusion, since 27 percent of Canadian libraries reported that they had both "special collections" and "subject interests." In the United States more than three times as many libraries claimed to have "subject interests" as had "special collections."

As the actual number of libraries concerned in the Canadian sample was so small, it is tempting to think that the six or eight "well-heeled" Canadian libraries were those best able to afford these types of extended service to their members and so reported it. That rather facile conclusion, however, does not explain why U.S. libraries tended to favor subject interests over special collections so heavily, except if we consider that "special collections" were often bequests, whereas "subject interests" tended to be deliberate, planned concentrations of acquired materials designed to meet readership needs. In that case, a lower proportion of the U.S. libraries in this study benefited from the former, and a larger proportion of them were professional enough to encourage the latter.

Library publications produced less equivocal results. Neither country had any popular library publications at all in 1978. However, for 1988, 6 percent of the U.S. libraries registered 1.8 publications each. This trend was topped in Canada, where 32 percent of Canadian libraries claimed a mean of 1.1 publications. Hence, it can be said, with the usual qualifications, that the United States had *more* publications, but more of the Canadian popular libraries (by proportion) published material.

The "twenty-seven variable composite score" shows Canada far ahead for both editions, largely because of the great Canadian differential over the United States in terms of volume holdings and annual expenditure. The important facts here relate to the growth figures within the two countries over the decade. We know that the Canadian popular libraries were largely parochial school and public: their composite growth rate was 61 percent, or about 6 percent per year. A total of thirteen of the fifteen libraries seemed to be the *same libraries* for the two editions, and so we can truly speak of a real growth of about 60 percent for these thirteen libraries.

The figures for the United States were for 420 libraries in 1978 and 421 in 1988, almost all of them the same libraries reporting in both years. The change rate here was a real growth of 34 percent—a little more than one half of the Canadian rate. Given that the Canadian dollar was worth less than its U.S. counterpart, we can probably drop the Canadian *real* growth rate to about 50 percent, which is still significantly higher (at the 99 percent level of confidence) than the comparable U.S. figure of 34 percent.

Therefore, based on these composite growth rates, it is clear that the Canadian parochial school and public libraries were growing significantly faster than were the congregational-type libraries of the United States. Probably this is not surprising, since dedicated parochial institutions get more support, and it tends to increase at a faster rate. However, in order to demonstrate the point conclusively, another study needs to be done about the turn of the millennium, say, in 1998.

15. John F. Harvey and Elizabeth M. Dickinson, *Librarians' Affirmative Action Handbook* (Metuchen, N.J.: Scarecrow, 1983), p. 24 table 9.

16. It should be clear to all readers that the author produced more tables for this study than could be used in the published version of it. Additional tables are available for inspection by any reader on request to John F. Harvey, Suite 1105, 82 Wall Street, New York, NY 10005-3682, U.S.A., telephone 212-509-2612 or telefax 212-968-7962. Please specify either the exact tabular contents desired or your focus of interest.

TABLE 2.1

Total 1978 *American Library Directory* Questionnaires by State/Province and Region: Entire Sample

| State/ Province | State/ Province Abbreviation | Regional Abbreviation | Useable Questionnaires Obtained | % | Most Popular Denomination(s) |
|---|---|---|---|---|---|
| Alberta | AB | CA | 8 | 0 | Lutheran, Roman Catholic |
| British Columbia | BC | CA | 2 | 0 | Anglican |
| Manitoba | MB | CA | 6 | 0 | Roman Catholic |
| New Brunswick | NB | CA | 3 | 0 | 3 tied |
| Newfoundland | NF | CA | 1 | 0 | Anglican |
| Northwest Territories | NT | CA | 0 | 0 | — |
| Novia Scotia | NS | CA | 9 | 0 | Roman Catholic |
| Ontario | ON | CA | 36 | 2 | Roman Catholic, Anglican |
| Quebec | PQ | CA | 51 | 2 | Roman Catholic, Jewish |
| Saskatchewan | SK | CA | 11 | 1 | Roman Catholic |
| Prince Edward Island | PE | CA | 0 | 0 | — |
| Yukon | YT | CA | 0 | 0 | — |
| Alabama | AL | SE | 27 | 1 | Baptist, Methodist |
| Alaska | AK | W | 4 | 0 | 4 tied |
| Arizona | AZ | SW | 13 | 1 | Baptist, Jewish, Roman Catholic |
| Arkansas | AR | SW | 15 | 1 | Baptist, Methodist |
| California | CA | W | 116 | 6 | Roman Catholic, Jewish, Baptist, Presbyterian |
| Colorado | CO | RM | 27 | 1 | Lutheran, Roman Catholic, Congregational, Methodist |
| Connecticut | CT | NE | 36 | 2 | Roman Catholic, Congregational, Jewish |
| Delaware | DE | MA | 4 | 0 | Jewish |
| District of Columbia | DC | MA | 36 | 2 | Roman Catholic, Methodist |
| Florida | FL | SE | 42 | 2 | Baptist, Jewish, Presbyterian, Independent, Roman Catholic |

TABLE 2.1 (continued)
Total 1978 *American Library Directory* Questionnaires by State/Province and Region

| State/Province | State/Province Abbreviation | Regional Abbreviation | Useable Questionnaires Obtained | % | Most Popular Denomination(s) |
|---|---|---|---|---|---|
| Georgia | GA | SE | 38 | 2 | Baptist, Methodist, Presbyterian |
| Hawaii | HI | W | 11 | 1 | 9 tied |
| Idaho | ID | W | 5 | 0 | 5 tied |
| Illinois | IL | MW | 92 | 5 | Roman Catholic, Methodist, Presbyterian, Jewish |
| Indiana | IN | MW | 54 | 3 | Roman Catholic, Methodist |
| Iowa | IA | MW | 33 | 2 | Roman Catholic, Lutheran, Methodist |
| Kansas | KS | MW | 31 | 2 | Roman Catholic, Mennonite, Methodist |
| Kentucky | KY | SE | 39 | 2 | Baptist, Roman Catholic, Christian |
| Louisiana | LA | SW | 21 | 1 | Roman Catholic, Baptist, Methodist |
| Maine | ME | NE | 4 | 0 | Roman Catholic |
| Maryland | MD | MA | 31 | 2 | Roman Catholic, Jewish, Presbyterian |
| Massachusetts | MA | NE | 55 | 3 | Roman Catholic, Jewish |
| Michigan | MI | MW | 86 | 4 | Roman Catholic, Jewish, Reformed, Presbyterian |
| Minnesota | MN | MW | 51 | 2 | Lutheran, Roman Catholic, Baptist |
| Mississippi | MS | SE | 23 | 1 | Baptist, Methodist |
| Missouri | MO | MW | 69 | 3 | Baptist, Roman Catholic, Christian |

TABLE 2.1 (continued)
Total 1978 *American Library Directory* Questionnaires by State/Province and Region

| State/ Province | State/ Province Abbreviation | Regional Abbreviation | Useable Questionnaires Obtained | % | Most Popular Denomination(s) |
|---|---|---|---|---|---|
| Montana | MT | RM | 5 | 0 | Roman Catholic |
| Nebraska | NE | MW | 20 | 1 | Methodist, Lutheran |
| Nevada | NV | W | 2 | 0 | 2 tied |
| New Hampshire | NH | NE | 6 | 0 | Roman Catholic |
| New Jersey | NJ | MA | 51 | 2 | Roman Catholic Jewish, Presbyterian |
| New Mexico | NM | SW | 13 | 1 | Presbyterian, Roman Catholic |
| New York | NY | MA | 137 | 7 | Roman Catholic, Jewish, Independent |
| North Carolina | NC | SE | 60 | 3 | Baptist, Presbyterian, Methodist |
| North Dakota | ND | MW | 9 | 0 | Roman Catholic, Presbyterian |
| Ohio | OH | MW | 108 | 5 | Roman Catholic, Methodist, Jewish, Presbyterian |
| Oklahoma | OK | SW | 21 | 1 | Baptist, Christian |
| Oregon | OR | W | 22 | 1 | Baptist, Presbyterian, Roman Catholic |
| Pennsylvania | PA | MA | 173 | 8 | Roman Catholic, Jewish, Presbyterian, Methodist |
| Rhode Island | RI | NE | 7 | 0 | Roman Catholic, Jewish |
| South Carolina | SC | SE | 24 | 1 | Baptist, Methodist |
| South Dakota | SD | MW | 14 | 1 | Baptist, Lutheran, Roman Catholic |
| Tennessee | TN | SE | 59 | 3 | Baptist, Methodist, Presbyterian |
| Texas | TX | SW | 106 | 5 | Baptist, Roman Catholic, |

TABLE 2.1 (continued)
Total 1978 *American Library Directory* Questionnaires by State/Province and Region

| State/ Province | State/ Province Abbreviation | Regional Abbreviation | Useable Questionnaires Obtained | % | Most Popular Denomination(s) |
|---|---|---|---|---|---|
| | | | | | Methodist, Presbyterian |
| Utah | UT | RM | 5 | 0 | Mormon |
| Vermont | VT | NE | 4 | 0 | Roman Catholic |
| Virginia | VA | SE | 37 | 2 | Baptist, Methodist, Episcopal, Presbyterian |
| Washington | WA | W | 22 | 1 | Roman Catholic, Methodist |
| West Virginia | WV | SE | 9 | 0 | Presbyterian |
| Wisconsin | WI | MW | 58 | 3 | Roman Catholic, Lutheran |
| Wyoming | WY | RM | 0 | 0 | — |
| Total | | | 2,062 | 100 | |

TABLE 2.2
Total 1988 *American Library Directory* Questionnaires by State/Province and Region: Entire Sample

| State/ Province | State/ Province Abbreviation | Regional Abbreviation | Useable Questionnaires Obtained | % | Most Popular Denomination(s) |
|---|---|---|---|---|---|
| Alberta | AB | CA | 21 | 1 | Roman Catholic, Lutheran, United Church Canada |
| British Columbia | BC | CA | 6 | 0 | 6 tied |
| Manitoba | MB | CA | 15 | 1 | Mennonite, Roman Catholic |
| New Brunswick | NB | CA | 3 | 0 | 3 tied |
| Newfoundland | NF | CA | 1 | 0 | Episcopal |
| Northwest Territories | NT | CA | 0 | 0 | — |
| Novia Scotia | NS | CA | 8 | 0 | Roman Catholic |
| Ontario | ON | CA | 47 | 2 | Roman Catholic, Jewish, United Church Canada |
| Quebec | PQ | CA | 72 | 3 | Roman Catholic, |

TABLE 2.2 (continued)
Total 1988 *American Library Directory* Questionnaires by State/Province
and Region

| State/<br>Province | State/<br>Province<br>Abbreviation | Regional<br>Abbreviation | Useable<br>Questionnaires<br>Obtained | % | Most Popular<br>Denomination(s) |
|---|---|---|---|---|---|
| Saskatchewan | SK | CA | 13 | 1 | Independent,<br>Jewish<br>Roman Catholic<br>Lutheran |
| Prince Edward Island | PE | CA | 0 | 0 | — |
| Yukon | YT | CA | 0 | 0 | — |
| Alabama | AL | SE | 23 | 1 | Baptist,<br>Presbyterian,<br>Methodist |
| Alaska | AK | W | 4 | 0 | 4 tied |
| Arizona | AZ | SW | 15 | 1 | Baptist, Jewish,<br>Lutheran,<br>Roman Catholic |
| Arkansas | AR | SW | 13 | 1 | Baptist,<br>Methodist |
| California | CA | W | 116 | 6 | Roman Catholic,<br>Jewish,<br>Presbyterian |
| Colorado | CO | RM | 21 | 1 | Roman Catholic,<br>Congregational,<br>Methodist |
| Connecticut | CT | NE | 30 | 1 | Roman Catholic,<br>Jewish |
| Delaware | DE | MA | 6 | 0 | Jewish,<br>Methodist |
| District of Columbia | DC | MA | 30 | 1 | Roman Catholic,<br>Methodist |
| Florida | FL | SE | 48 | 2 | Jewish, Baptist,<br>Methodist,<br>Presbyterian |
| Georgia | GA | SE | 31 | 2 | Methodist,<br>Baptist,<br>Presbyterian |
| Hawaii | HI | W | 7 | 0 | Independent,<br>plus 5 tied |
| Idaho | ID | W | 6 | 0 | Roman Catholic |
| Illinois | IL | MW | 87 | 4 | Roman Catholic,<br>Methodist,<br>Jewish |
| Indiana | IN | MW | 58 | 3 | Roman Catholic,<br>Methodist |

TABLE 2.2 (continued)
Total 1988 *American Library Directory* Questionnaires by State/Province
and Region

| State/Province | State/Province Abbreviation | Regional Abbreviation | Useable Questionnaires Obtained | % | Most Popular Denomination(s) |
|---|---|---|---|---|---|
| Iowa | IA | MW | 35 | 2 | Roman Catholic, Methodist, Lutheran |
| Kansas | KS | MW | 28 | 1 | Roman Catholic, Mennonite, Methodist |
| Kentucky | KY | SE | 41 | 2 | Baptist, Roman Catholic, Christian, Methodist |
| Louisiana | LA | SW | 16 | 1 | Baptist, Roman Catholic |
| Maine | ME | NE | 3 | 0 | 3 tied |
| Maryland | MD | MA | 33 | 2 | Roman Catholic, Jewish, Presbyterian |
| Massachusetts | MA | NE | 53 | 3 | Roman Catholic, Jewish, Independent, Methodist |
| Michigan | MI | MW | 71 | 3 | Roman Catholic, Jewish, Reformed |
| Minnesota | MN | MW | 55 | 3 | Lutheran, Roman Catholic, Baptist |
| Mississippi | MS | SE | 22 | 1 | Baptist, Methodist, Presbyterian |
| Missouri | MO | MW | 70 | 3 | Baptist, Roman Catholic, Christian |
| Montana | MT | RM | 3 | 0 | Roman Catholic |
| Nebraska | NE | MW | 22 | 1 | Christian, Lutheran, Methodist |
| Nevada | NV | W | 2 | 0 | Mormon, Salvation Army |
| New Hampshire | NH | NE | 7 | 0 | Roman Catholic |
| New Jersey | NJ | MA | 46 | 2 | Jewish, |

TABLE 2.2 (continued)
Total 1988 *American Library Directory* Questionnaires by State/Province
and Region

| State/<br>Province | State/<br>Province<br>Abbreviation | Regional<br>Abbreviation | Useable<br>Questionnaires<br>Obtained | % | Most Popular<br>Denomination(s) |
|---|---|---|---|---|---|
| New Mexico | NM | SW | 17 | 1 | Roman Catholic,<br>Presbyterian<br>Baptist,<br>Methodist |
| New York | NY | MA | 140 | 7 | Roman Catholic,<br>Jewish,<br>Independent,<br>Episcopal |
| North Carolina | NC | SE | 63 | 3 | Baptist,<br>Methodist,<br>Presbyterian |
| North Dakota | ND | MW | 8 | 0 | Roman Catholic,<br>Presbyterian |
| Ohio | OH | MW | 96 | 5 | Jewish,<br>Roman Catholic,<br>Methodist |
| Oklahoma | OK | SW | 21 | 1 | Baptist,<br>Methodist |
| Oregon | OR | W | 19 | 1 | Baptist,<br>Roman Catholic |
| Pennsylvania | PA | MA | 162 | 8 | Roman Catholic,<br>Jewish,<br>Presbyterian |
| Rhode Island | RI | NE | 12 | 1 | Roman Catholic,<br>Jewish |
| South Carolina | SC | SE | 21 | 1 | Baptist,<br>Methodist |
| South Dakota | SD | MW | 13 | 1 | Baptist,<br>Lutheran,<br>Roman Catholic |
| Tennessee | TN | SE | 57 | 3 | Methodist,<br>Baptist,<br>Presbyterian |
| Texas | TX | SW | 117 | 6 | Baptist,<br>Methodist,<br>Roman Catholic,<br>Presbyterian |
| Utah | UT | RM | 5 | 0 | Mormon |
| Vermont | VT | NE | 6 | 0 | Roman Catholic |

TABLE 2.2 (continued)

Total 1988 *American Library Directory* Questionnaires by State/Province and Region

| State/ Province | State/ Province Abbreviation | Regional Abbreviation | Useable Questionnaires Obtained | % | Most Popular Denomination(s) |
|---|---|---|---|---|---|
| Virginia | VA | SE | 43 | 2 | Baptist, Methodist, Presbyterian |
| Washington | WA | W | 24 | 1 | Roman Catholic, Lutheran, Methodist |
| West Virginia | WV | SE | 10 | 0 | Presbyterian |
| Wisconsin | WI | MW | 52 | 3 | Roman Catholic, Lutheran |
| Wyoming | WY | RM | 0 | 0 | — |
| Total | | | 2,074 | 100 | |

TABLE 2.3

1978 *American Library Directory* Popular Libraries by Region

| Region | Popular Libraries | |
|---|---|---|
| | Number | Percentage |
| Northeast | 38 | 6 |
| Middle Atlantic | 168 | 25 |
| Southeast | 91 | 13 |
| Southwest | 77 | 11 |
| West | 63 | 9 |
| Rocky Mountains | 10 | 1 |
| Middle West | 213 | 31 |
| Canada | 27 | 4 |
| Total | 687 | 100 |

TABLE 2.4
1988 *American Library Directory* Regional Composition by
State/Province: Entire Sample

| Region and State/Province | Libraries | Percentage | Percentage of Total |
|---|---|---|---|
| Northeast | 111 | 100 | 5 |
| Massachusetts | 53 | 48 | |
| Connecticut | 30 | 27 | |
| Rhode Island | 12 | 11 | |
| New Hampshire | 7 | 6 | |
| Vermont | 6 | 5 | |
| Maine | 3 | 3 | |
| Middle Atlantic | 417 | 100 | 20 |
| Pennsylvania | 162 | 39 | |
| New York | 140 | 34 | |
| New Jersey | 46 | 11 | |
| Maryland | 33 | 8 | |
| District of Columbia | 30 | 7 | |
| Delaware | 6 | 1 | |
| Southeast | 359 | 100 | 17 |
| North Carolina | 63 | 18 | |
| Tennessee | 57 | 16 | |
| Florida | 48 | 13 | |
| Virginia | 43 | 12 | |
| Kentucky | 41 | 11 | |
| Georgia | 31 | 9 | |
| Alabama | 23 | 6 | |
| Mississippi | 22 | 6 | |
| South Carolina | 21 | 6 | |
| West Virginia | 10 | 3 | |
| Southwest | 199 | 100 | 10 |
| Texas | 117 | 59 | |
| Oklahoma | 21 | 11 | |
| New Mexico | 17 | 9 | |
| Louisiana | 16 | 8 | |
| Arizona | 15 | 8 | |
| Arkansas | 13 | 6 | |
| West | 178 | 100 | 9 |
| California | 116 | 65 | |
| Washington | 24 | 13 | |
| Oregon | 19 | 11 | |
| Hawaii | 7 | 4 | |
| Idaho | 6 | 3 | |
| Alaska | 4 | 2 | |
| Nevada | 2 | 1 | |
| Rocky Mountains | 29 | 100 | 1 |
| Colorado | 21 | 72 | |

TABLE 2.4 (continued)
1988 *American Library Directory* Regional Composition by
State/Province: Entire Sample

| Region and State/Province | Libraries | Percentage | Percentage of Total |
|---|---|---|---|
| Utah | 5 | 17 | |
| Montana | 3 | 10 | |
| Middle West | 595 | 100 | 29 |
| Ohio | 96 | 16 | |
| Illinois | 87 | 15 | |
| Michigan | 71 | 12 | |
| Missouri | 70 | 12 | |
| Indiana | 58 | 10 | |
| Minnesota | 55 | 9 | |
| Wisconsin | 52 | 9 | |
| Iowa | 35 | 6 | |
| Kansas | 28 | 5 | |
| Nebraska | 22 | 4 | |
| South Dakota | 13 | 2 | |
| North Dakota | 8 | 1 | |
| Canada | 186 | 100 | 9 |
| Quebec | 72 | 39 | |
| Ontario | 47 | 25 | |
| Alberta | 21 | 11 | |
| Manitoba | 15 | 8 | |
| Saskatchewan | 13 | 7 | |
| Nova Scotia | 8 | 4 | |
| British Columbia | 6 | 3 | |
| New Brunswick | 3 | 2 | |
| Newfoundland | 1 | 1 | |
| Total | 2,074 | 100 | 100 |

TABLE 2.5
1988 *American Library Directory* Popular Libraries by Region

| Region | -------------Popular Libraries------------- | |
| | Number | Percentage |
|---|---|---|
| Northeast | 35 | 5 |
| Middle Atlantic | 156 | 24 |
| Southeast | 93 | 15 |
| Southwest | 82 | 13 |
| West | 50 | 8 |
| Rocky Mountains | 8 | 1 |
| Middle West | 197 | 31 |
| Canada | 21 | 3 |
| Total | 642 | 100 |

TABLE 2.6
1978 and 1988 *American Library Directory* Longitudinal Popular
Library Geographical Data Summary

| Basic Data | ---------------1 9 7 8--------------- | | | ---------------1 9 8 8--------------- | | |
| | U.S.A. | Canada | Entire Sample | U.S.A. | Canada | Entire Sample |
|---|---|---|---|---|---|---|
| Number of Libraries | 660 | 27 | 687 | 621 | 21 | 642 |
| Ratios | 660:27 | | | 621:21 | | |
| | 24.4:1.0 | | | 29.6:1.0 | | |
| Percentage | 96.1 | 3.9 | 100 | 96.7 | 3.3 | 100 |

TABLE 2.7
1978 *American Library Directory* Chief Librarian's Gender by Region
for Popular Libraries

| Region | Male | % | Female | % | No Response | % | Number of Libraries |
|---|---|---|---|---|---|---|---|
| Northeast | 10 | 26 | 16 | 42 | 12 | 32 | 38 |
| Middle Atlantic | 21 | 13 | 84 | 50 | 63 | 37 | 168 |
| Southeast | 7 | 8 | 43 | 47 | 41 | 45 | 91 |
| Southwest | 8 | 10 | 43 | 56 | 26 | 34 | 77 |
| West | 12 | 19 | 26 | 41 | 25 | 40 | 63 |
| Rocky Mountains | 3 | 30 | 3 | 30 | 4 | 40 | 10 |
| Middle West | 15 | 7 | 104 | 49 | 94 | 44 | 213 |
| Canada | 9 | 33 | 11 | 41 | 7 | 26 | 27 |
| Total | 85 | 12 | 330 | 48 | 272 | 40 | 687 |

TABLE 2.8

1978 and 1988 *American Library Directory* Longitudinal Study Gross Popular Library Rating Points over Twenty-two Growth Variables for Canada and the United States for Matched Pairs[a]

| | -------------------1 9 7 8------------------- | | | | -------------------1 9 8 8------------------- | | | | |
| Region | Number of Libraries | No Response | Total Libraries | Mean Points | Number of Libraries | No Response | Total Libraries | Mean Points | Percentage Change 1978–88 |
|---|---|---|---|---|---|---|---|---|---|
| Canada | 15 | 1 | 16 | 49,250 | 13 | 1 | 14 | 79,490 | 61 |
| U.S.A. | 420 | 35 | 455 | 6,820 | 421 | 34 | 455 | 9,128 | 34 |
| Total | 435 | 36 | 471 | 8,283 | 434 | 35 | 469 | 11,240 | 36 |

[a]See Chap. 4 n.7 for the list of growth variables.

TABLE 2.9

1978 and 1988 *American Library Directory* Longitudinal Study Library Distribution for Canada and the United States[a]

| | ---------Canada--------- | | | ---------U.S.A.--------- | | | -Canada to U.S.A.- Ratio Value | | ---Totals--- | | |
| Library Type | 1978 | 1988 | % Change | 1978 | 1988 | % Change | 1978 | 1988 | 1978 | 1988 | % Change |
|---|---|---|---|---|---|---|---|---|---|---|---|
| Popular | 27 | 22 | −19 | 660 | 621 | −6 | .04 | .04 | 687 | 643 | −6 |
| Congrega-tional | 4 | 6 | 50 | 630 | 587 | −7 | .006 | .01 | 634 | 593 | −6 |
| Parochial | 13 | 9 | −31 | 14 | 16 | 14 | .93 | .56 | 27 | 25 | −7 |
| Public | 10 | 7 | −30 | 16 | 18 | 13 | .63 | .39 | 26 | 25 | −4 |

[a] The number of popular libraries may be either 642 or 643 depending on variable being considered. One library in 1988 can be considered as either scholarly or popular or both.

TABLE 2.10

1978 *American Library Directory* Popular Libraries by Age: Entire Sample

| Founding Date | Number of Libraries | Percentage |
|---|---|---|
| 1981+ | 0 | 0 |
| 1971–1980 | 38 | 2 |
| 1961–1970 | 183 | 9 |
| 1941–1960 | 435 | 21 |
| 1921–1940 | 236 | 11 |
| 1901–1920 | 171 | 8 |
| 1881–1900 | 180 | 9 |
| 1861–1880 | 124 | 6 |
| 1841–1860 | 126 | 6 |

TABLE 2.10 (continued)
1978 *American Library Directory* Popluar Libraries by Age:
Entire Sample

| Founding Date | Number of Libraries | Percentage |
|---|---|---|
| 1821–1840 | 49 | 2 |
| 1801–1820 | 16 | 1 |
| 0–1800 | 13 | 1 |
| No response | 491 | 24 |
| Total | 2,062 | 100 |
| Mean | | Year: A.D. 1905.1 or 72.9 years old |

TABLE 2.11
1988 *American Library Directory* Popular Libraries by Age:
Entire Sample

| Founding Date | Number of Libraries | Percentage |
|---|---|---|
| 1981+ | 9 | 0 |
| 1971–1980 | 87 | 4 |
| 1961–1970 | 210 | 10 |
| 1941–1960 | 422 | 20 |
| 1921–1940 | 233 | 11 |
| 1901–1920 | 163 | 8 |
| 1881–1900 | 183 | 9 |
| 1861–1880 | 125 | 6 |
| 1841–1860 | 120 | 6 |
| 1821–1840 | 60 | 3 |
| 1801–1820 | 17 | 1 |
| 0–1800 | 16 | 1 |
| No response | 429 | 21 |
| Total | 2,074 | 100 |
| Mean | | *Year*: A.D. 1917, or 71 years old |

TABLE 2.12
1978 and 1988 *American Library Directory* Longitudinal Study
Popular Library Age in Years for Canada and the United States

| | 1978 | | | | 1988 | | | | Percentage Change |
| Region | Number of Libraries | No Response | Total Libraries | Mean Years | Number of Libraries | No Response | Total Libraries | Mean Years | 1978–88 |
|---|---|---|---|---|---|---|---|---|---|
| Canada | 19 | 8 | 27 | 64 | 15 | 7 | 22 | 54 | −16.0 |
| U.S.A. | 300 | 360 | 660 | 43 | 358 | 263 | 621 | 41 | −4.7 |
| Total | 319 | 368 | 687 | 44 | 373 | 270 | 643 | 41 | −6.8 |

TABLE 2.13
1978 and 1988 *American Library Directory* Longitudinal Study
Popular Library City Population Size for Canada and the United States

|  | -----1 9 7 8----- | | | | -----1 9 8 8----- | | | | Percentage |
| Region | Number of Libraries | No Response | Total Libraries | Mean Persons | Number of Libraries | No Response | Total Libraries | Mean Persons | Change 1978–88 |
|---|---|---|---|---|---|---|---|---|---|
| Canada | 27 | 0 | 27 | 528,000 | 22 | 0 | 22 | 634,700 | 20.0 |
| U.S.A. | 658 | 2 | 660 | 354,500 | 621 | 0 | 621 | 346,200 | −2.3 |
| Total | 685 | 2 | 687 | 361,400 | 643 | 0 | 643 | 356,100 | −1.5 |

TABLE 2.14
1978 and 1988 *American Library Directory* Longitudinal Study
Popular Library Clerical Staff Members for Canada and the United
States

|  | -----1 9 7 8----- | | | | -----1 9 8 8----- | | | | Percentage |
| Region | Number of Libraries | No Response | Total Libraries | Mean Members | Number of Libraries | No Response | Total Libraries | Mean Members | Change 1978–88 |
|---|---|---|---|---|---|---|---|---|---|
| Canada | 2 | 25 | 27 | 2.0 | 6 | 16 | 22 | 1.7 | −15 |
| U.S.A. | 104 | 556 | 660 | 4.3 | 62 | 559 | 621 | 2.9 | −33 |
| Total | 106 | 581 | 687 | 4.3 | 68 | 575 | 643 | 2.8 | −35 |

TABLE 2.15
1978 and 1988 *American Library Directory* Longitudinal Study
Popular Library Volume Holdings for Canada and the United States

|  | -----1 9 7 8----- | | | | -----1 9 8 8----- | | | | Percentage |
| Region | Number of Libraries | No Response | Total Libraries | Mean Volumes | Number of Libraries | No Response | Total Libraries | Mean Volumes | Change 1978–88 |
|---|---|---|---|---|---|---|---|---|---|
| Canada | 21 | 6 | 27 | 36,640 | 21 | 1 | 22 | 28,230 | −23 |
| U.S.A. | 484 | 176 | 660 | 4,965 | 597 | 24 | 621 | 6,035 | 22 |
| Total | 505 | 182 | 687 | 6,282 | 618 | 25 | 643 | 6,789 | 8 |

TABLE 2.16
1978 and 1988 *American Library Directory* Longitudinal Study
Popular Library Chief Librarian's Gender by Nation

| Region/ Nation | ------1978------ | | | ------1988------ | | | -----Totals----- | | ----1978–1988 % Change---- | | |
|---|---|---|---|---|---|---|---|---|---|---|---|
| | Male | Fe-male | No Re-sponse | Male | Fe-male | No Re-sponse | 1978 | 1988 | Male | Female | No Response |
| U.S.A. actual | 76 | 319 | 265 | 75 | 492 | 54 | 660 | 621 | −1 | 54 | −80 |
| Percent-age | 12 | 48 | 40 | 12 | 79 | 9 | 100 | 100 | | | |
| Canada actual | 9 | 11 | 7 | 8 | 14 | 0 | 27 | 22 | −11 | 27 | −100 |
| Percent-age | 33 | 41 | 26 | 36 | 64 | 0 | 100 | 100 | | | |
| All actual | 85 | 330 | 272 | 83 | 506 | 54 | 687 | 643 | −2 | 53 | −80 |
| Percent-age | 12 | 48 | 40 | 13 | 79 | 8 | 100 | 100 | | | |

TABLE 2.17
1978 *American Library Directory* Regional Library Composition by
State/Province: Entire Sample

| Region and State/Province | Libraries | Percentage | Percentage of Total |
|---|---|---|---|
| Northeast | 114 | 100 | 6 |
| Massachusetts | 55 | 48 | |
| Connecticut | 36 | 32 | |
| Rhode Island | 7 | 6 | |
| New Hampshire | 6 | 5 | |
| Maine | 5 | 4 | |
| Vermont | 5 | 4 | |
| Middle Atlantic | 432 | 100 | 21 |
| Pennsylvania | 173 | 40 | |
| New York | 137 | 32 | |
| New Jersey | 51 | 12 | |
| District of Columbia | 36 | 8 | |
| Maryland | 31 | 7 | |
| Delaware | 4 | 1 | |
| Southeast | 358 | 100 | 17 |
| North Carolina | 60 | 17 | |
| Tennessee | 59 | 16 | |
| Florida | 42 | 12 | |
| Kentucky | 39 | 11 | |
| Georgia | 38 | 11 | |
| Virginia | 37 | 10 | |
| Alabama | 27 | 8 | |

TABLE 2.17 (continued)
1978 *American Library Directory* Regional Library Composition by
State/Province: Entire Sample

| | | | |
|---|---|---|---|
| South Carolina | 24 | 7 | |
| Mississippi | 23 | 6 | |
| West Virginia | 9 | 3 | |
| Southwest | 189 | 100 | 9 |
| Texas | 106 | 56 | |
| Louisiana | 21 | 11 | |
| Oklahoma | 21 | 11 | |
| Arkansas | 15 | 8 | |
| Arizona | 13 | 7 | |
| New Mexico | 13 | 7 | |
| West | 182 | 100 | 9 |
| California | 116 | 64 | |
| Oregon | 22 | 12 | |
| Washington | 22 | 12 | |
| Hawaii | 11 | 6 | |
| Idaho | 5 | 3 | |
| Alaska | 4 | 2 | |
| Nevada | 2 | 1 | |
| Rocky Mountains | 37 | 100 | 2 |
| Colorado | 27 | 73 | |
| Montana | 5 | 14 | |
| Utah | 5 | 14 | |
| Middle West | 625 | 100 | 30 |
| Ohio | 108 | 17 | |
| Illinois | 92 | 15 | |
| Michigan | 86 | 14 | |
| Missouri | 69 | 11 | |
| Wisconsin | 58 | 9 | |
| Indiana | 54 | 9 | |
| Minnesota | 51 | 8 | |
| Iowa | 33 | 5 | |
| Kansas | 31 | 5 | |
| Nebraska | 20 | 3 | |
| South Dakota | 14 | 2 | |
| North Dakota | 9 | 1 | |
| Canada | 125 | 100 | 6 |
| Quebec | 49 | 39 | |
| Ontario | 36 | 29 | |
| Saskatchewan | 11 | 9 | |
| Nova Scotia | 9 | 7 | |
| Alberta | 8 | 6 | |
| Manitoba | 6 | 5 | |
| New Brunswick | 3 | 2 | |
| British Columbia | 2 | 2 | |
| Newfoundland | 1 | 1 | |
| Total | 2,062 | 100 | 100 |

TABLE 2.18
1978 *American Library Directory* Popular Libraries by Region and
Major Denominations

| Popular Libraries | Number of Libraries | Percentage |
|---|---|---|
| Northeast Region | | |
| Jewish | 14 | 37 |
| Congregational | 10 | 26 |
| Episcopal/Anglican | 4 | 11 |
| Roman Catholic | 4 | 11 |
| Middle Atlantic Region | | |
| Jewish | 64 | 38 |
| Presbyterian | 38 | 23 |
| Methodist | 14 | 8 |
| Other Denominations | 14 | 8 |
| Southeast Region | | |
| Baptist | 31 | 34 |
| Presbyterian | 20 | 22 |
| Jewish | 12 | 13 |
| Methodist | 12 | 13 |
| Southwest Region | | |
| Baptist | 23 | 30 |
| Presbyterian | 14 | 18 |
| Episcopal/Anglican | 10 | 13 |
| Jewish | 9 | 12 |
| West Region | | |
| Other Denominations | 16 | 25 |
| Jewish | 12 | 19 |
| Presbyterian | 12 | 19 |
| Roman Catholic | 5 | 8 |
| Rocky Mountains Region | | |
| Congregational | 3 | 30 |
| Lutheran | 2 | 20 |
| Middle West Region | | |
| Jewish | 46 | 22 |
| Lutheran | 39 | 18 |
| Presbyterian | 30 | 14 |
| Other Denominations | 21 | 10 |
| Canadian Region | | |
| Roman Catholic | 17 | 63 |
| Jewish | 5 | 19 |
| Other Denominations | 3 | 11 |

TABLE 2.19

1988 *American Library Directory* Popular Libraries by Region and
Major Denominations

| Popular Libraries | Number of Libraries | Percentage |
|---|---|---|
| Northeast Region | | |
| Jewish | 18 | 51 |
| Other Denominations | 8 | 23 |
| Roman Catholic | 4 | 11 |
| Episcopal/Anglican | 2 | 6 |
| Middle Atlantic Region | | |
| Jewish | 69 | 44 |
| Presbyterian | 28 | 18 |
| Other Denominations | 17 | 11 |
| Methodist | 15 | 10 |
| Southeast Region | | |
| Baptist | 26 | 28 |
| Presbyterian | 22 | 24 |
| Jewish | 18 | 19 |
| Methodist | 12 | 13 |
| Southwest Region | | |
| Baptist | 21 | 26 |
| Methodist | 16 | 20 |
| Presbyterian | 12 | 15 |
| Jewish | 11 | 13 |
| West Region | | |
| Other Denominations | 14 | 28 |
| Jewish | 12 | 24 |
| Presbyterian | 10 | 20 |
| Baptist | 4 | 8 |
| Rocky Mountains Region | | |
| Other Denominations | 4 | 50 |
| Middle West Region | | |
| Jewish | 52 | 26 |
| Lutheran | 32 | 16 |
| Presbyterian | 24 | 12 |
| Other Denominations | 22 | 11 |
| Canadian Region | | |
| Roman Catholic | 9 | 43 |
| Jewish | 6 | 29 |
| Other Denominations | 3 | 14 |
| Independent | 2 | 10 |

TABLE 2.20
1988 *American Library Directory* Most Popular Library Regions by
Denomination

| Denomination | ----------------Popularity---------------- | | |
| | 1 | 2 | 3 |
| --- | --- | --- | --- |
| Baptist | Southeast | Southwest | Middle West |
| Christian | Middle West | Southeast | Southwest |
| Churches of Christ | Southeast | | |
| Episcopal/Anglican | Middle Atlantic | Southwest | Southeast |
| Independent | Canada | Middle West | |
| Lutheran | Middle West | Middle Atlantic | Southwest |
| Mennonite | Middle West | Middle Atlantic | |
| Methodist | Southwest | Middle Atlantic | Southeast |
| Other Denominations | Middle West | Middle Atlantic | West |
| Presbyterian | Middle Atlantic | Middle West | Southeast |
| United Church of Christ | Middle West | Middle Atlantic | Northeast |
| Jewish | Middle Atlantic | Middle West | Southeast |
| Roman Catholic | Middle West | Southwest | Northeast |

TABLE 2.21
1988 *American Library Directory* Popular Library Types by
Denomination

| Denomination | Number of Libraries | Percentage |
| --- | --- | --- |
| | Congregational | |
| Jewish | 170 | 29 |
| Presbyterian | 97 | 16 |
| Baptist | 71 | 12 |
| Other Denominations | 71 | 12 |
| Methodist | 64 | 11 |
| Lutheran | 42 | 7 |
| Episcopal/Anglican | 33 | 6 |
| Christian | 17 | 3 |
| United Church of Christ | 13 | 2 |
| Roman Catholic | 8 | 1 |
| Mennonite | 4 | 1 |
| Churches of Christ | 2 | 0 |
| Independent | 1 | 0 |
| Total | 593 | 100 |
| | Parochial School | |
| Jewish | 12 | 50 |
| Roman Catholic | 10 | 42 |
| Independent | 1 | 4 |
| Other Denominations | 1 | 4 |
| Total | 24 | 100 |

TABLE 2.21 (continued)
1988 *American Library Directory* Popular Library Types by
Denomination

| Denomination | Number of Libraries | Percentage |
|---|---|---|
| | Public Library | |
| Roman Catholic | 13 | 52 |
| Jewish | 5 | 20 |
| Other Denominations | 5 | 20 |
| Episcopal/Anglican | 1 | 4 |
| Independent | 1 | 4 |
| Total | 25 | 100 |

TABLE 2.22
1988 *American Library Directory* Denominational Breakdown for
Popular Libraries

| Denomination | Number of Libraries | Percentage |
|---|---|---|
| Jewish | 187 | 29 |
| Presbyterian | 97 | 15 |
| Other Denominations | 77 | 12 |
| Baptist | 71 | 11 |
| Methodist | 64 | 10 |
| Lutheran | 42 | 7 |
| Episcopal/Anglican | 34 | 5 |
| Roman Catholic | 32 | 5 |
| Christian/Disciples of Christ | 17 | 3 |
| United Church of Christ | 13 | 2 |
| Mennonite | 4 | 1 |
| Independent | 3 | 0 |
| Churches of Christ | 2 | 0 |
| Total | 643 | 100 |

TABLE 2.23

1988 *American Library Directory* City Population Size by Region for Popular Libraries

| Region | Number of Libraries | No Response | Total Libraries | Mean Number of Persons |
|---|---|---|---|---|
| Northeast | 35 | 0 | 35 | 131,500 |
| Middle Atlantic | 156 | 0 | 156 | 512,200 |
| Southeast | 93 | 0 | 93 | 165,000 |
| Southwest | 82 | 0 | 82 | 461,600 |
| West | 50 | 0 | 50 | 387,800 |
| Rocky Mountains | 8 | 0 | 8 | 196,300 |
| Middle West | 197 | 0 | 197 | 286,000 |
| Canada | 21 | 0 | 21 | 663,900 |
| Total | 642 | 0 | 642 | 356,600 |

TABLE 2.24

1978 and 1988 *American Library Directory* Demographics: Regional Distribution by Edition Showing Percentage Change for Popular Libraries

| | 1978 | % of Regional Sample | 1988 | % of Regional Sample | % Change |
|---|---|---|---|---|---|
| Northeast | 38 | 33 | 35 | 32 | −8 |
| Middle Atlantic | 168 | 39 | 156 | 37 | −7 |
| Southeast | 91 | 25 | 93 | 26 | 2 |
| Southwest | 77 | 41 | 82 | 41 | 6 |
| West | 63 | 35 | 50 | 28 | −21 |
| Rocky Mountains | 10 | 27 | 8 | 28 | −20 |
| Middle West | 213 | 34 | 197 | 33 | −8 |
| Canada | 27 | 22 | 21 | 11 | −22 |
| Total | 687 | 33 | 642 | 31 | −7 |

TABLE 2.25

Total 1988 *American Library Directory* Denominational Breakdown for Entire Sample Libraries

| Rank | Denomination | Number of Libraries | Percentage |
|------|-------------|---------------------|------------|
| 1  | Roman Catholic | 490 | 24 |
| 2  | Jewish | 232 | 11 |
| 3  | Baptist | 223 | 11 |
| 4  | Methodist | 213 | 10 |
| 5  | Presbyterian | 187 | 9 |
| 6  | Lutheran | 118 | 6 |
| 7  | Independent | 100 | 5 |
| 8  | Episcopal/Anglican | 66 | 3 |
| 9  | Christian/Disciples of Christ | 58 | 3 |
| 10 | Unknown | 43 | 2 |
| 11 | United Church of Christ | 38 | 2 |
| 12 | Churches of Christ | 29 | 1 |
| 13 | Mennonite | 26 | 1 |
| 14 | Congregational | 23 | 1 |
| 15 | Friends | 23 | 1 |
| 16 | Reformed | 19 | 1 |
| 17 | Seventh-day Adventist | 17 | 1 |
| 18 | Church of Jesus Christ of Latter-day Saints | 17 | 1 |
| 19 | Church of God | 15 | 1 |
| 20 | Brethren | 14 | 1 |
| 21 | Church of the Nazarene | 14 | 1 |
| 22 | Assemblies of God | 13 | 1 |
| 23 | Eastern Orthodox | 11 | 1 |
| 24 | United Church of Canada | 11 | 1 |
| 25 | Swedenborgian | 6 | 0 |
| 26 | Theosophist | 6 | 0 |
| 27 | Christian and Missionary Alliance | 5 | 0 |
| 28 | Moravian | 5 | 0 |
| 29 | Salvation Army | 5 | 0 |
| 30 | Unitarian-Universalist | 4 | 0 |
| 31 | Buddhist | 3 | 0 |
| 32 | Christian Science | 3 | 0 |
| 33 | Missionary Church | 3 | 0 |
| 34 | Moslem | 3 | 0 |
| 35 | Shaker | 3 | 0 |
| 36 | Evangelical Church of Canada | 2 | 0 |
| 37 | Evangelical Covenant | 2 | 0 |
| 38 | Evangelical Free Church | 2 | 0 |
| 39 | Pentecostal | 2 | 0 |
| 40 | Pentecostal Holiness | 2 | 0 |
| 41 | Rosicrucian | 2 | 0 |

TABLE 2.25 (continued)
Total 1988 *American Library Directory* Denominational Breakdown
for Entire Sample Libraries

| Rank | Denomination | Number of Libraries | Percentage |
|------|--------------|---------------------|------------|
| 42 | Unity | 2 | 0 |
| 43 | Atheist | 1 | 0 |
| 44 | Baha'i | 1 | 0 |
| 45 | Bible Fellowship | 1 | 0 |
| 46 | Christian Evangelical Church of America | 1 | 0 |
| 47 | Church of Scientology | 1 | 0 |
| 48 | Grace Gospel Fellowship | 1 | 0 |
| 49 | International Church of the Four Square Gospel | 1 | 0 |
| 50 | Jehovah's Witnesses | 1 | 0 |
| 51 | Open Bible Standard | 1 | 0 |
| 52 | Pillar of Fire | 1 | 0 |
| 53 | Schwenkfelder | 1 | 0 |
| 54 | Spiritualist | 1 | 0 |
| 55 | United Church of Religious Science | 1 | 0 |
| 56 | United Missionary | 1 | 0 |
| Total | | 2,074 | 100 |

TABLE 2.26
1988 Number of *American Library Directory* Popular Libraries by
State/Province[a]

| State/Province | Region | Popular Libraries 1988 | % of Entire State Sample |
|----------------|--------|------------------------|--------------------------|
| PA | MA | 55 | 34 |
| NY | MA | 46 | 33 |
| TX | SW | 50 | 43 |
| CA | W | 39 | 34 |
| OH | MW | 38 | 40 |
| IL | MW | 26 | 30 |
| PQ | CAN | 8 | 11 |
| MI | MW | 35 | 49 |
| MO | MW | 18 | 26 |
| NC | SE | 12 | 19 |
| IN | MW | 18 | 31 |
| TN | SE | 9 | 16 |
| MN | MW | 21 | 38 |
| MA | NE | 14 | 26 |
| WI | MW | 22 | 42 |

TABLE 2.26 (continued)
1988 Number of *American Library Directory* Popular Libraries by
State/Province[a]

|  | | Popular Libraries | |
| State/Province | Region | 1988 | % of Entire State Sample |
| --- | --- | --- | --- |
| FL | SE | 25 | 52 |
| ON | CAN | 9 | 19 |
| NJ | MA | 25 | 54 |
| VA | SE | 9 | 21 |
| KY | SE | 9 | 22 |
| IA | MW | 4 | 11 |
| MD | MA | 16 | 48 |
| GA | SE | 10 | 32 |
| DC | MA | 12 | 40 |
| CT | NE | 13 | 43 |
| KS | MW | 2 | 7 |
| WA | W | 6 | 25 |
| AL | SE | 10 | 43 |
| MS | SE | 5 | 23 |
| NE | MW | 6 | 27 |
| SC | SE | 1 | 5 |
| CO | RM | 7 | 33 |
| OK | SW | 5 | 24 |
| AB | CAN | 3 | 14 |
| OR | W | 1 | 5 |
| NM | SW | 15 | 88 |
| LA | SW | 5 | 31 |
| AZ | SW | 6 | 40 |
| MB | CAN | 0 | 0 |
| AR | SW | 1 | 8 |
| SD | MW | 4 | 31 |
| SK | CAN | 1 | 8 |
| RI | NE | 5 | 42 |
| WV | SE | 3 | 30 |
| NS | CAN | 0 | 0 |
| ND | MW | 3 | 38 |
| NH | NE | 2 | 29 |
| HI | W | 2 | 29 |
| ID | W | 0 | 0 |
| VT | NE | 1 | 17 |
| BC | CAN | 0 | 0 |
| DE | MA | 2 | 33 |
| UT | RM | 1 | 20 |
| AK | W | 0 | 0 |
| ME | NE | 0 | 0 |
| MT | RM | 0 | 0 |

TABLE 2.26 (continued)
1988 Number of *American Library Directory* Popular Libraries by State/Province[a]

| State/Province | Region | Popular Libraries | |
| | | 1988 | % of Entire State Sample |
|---|---|---|---|
| NB | CAN | 0 | 0 |
| NV | W | 2 | 100 |
| NF | CAN | 0 | 0 |

[a]"Percentage of sample" refers to the proportion of all libraries in each state that are popular relative to the entire number of sample libraries in each state, for example 34 percent of the libraries in Pennsylvania are popular and the remaining 66 percent are scholarly.

TABLE 2.27
1978 and 1988 *American Library Directory* Popular Libraries by Region, State, and Province[a]

| Region | State | 1978 Libraries | % | 1988 Libraries | % | Percentage Change 1978–88 |
|---|---|---|---|---|---|---|
| NE | CT | 18 | 47 | 13 | 37 | −28 |
| | MA | 12 | 32 | 14 | 40 | 17 |
| | ME | 1 | 3 | 0 | 0 | −100 |
| | NH | 2 | 5 | 2 | 6 | 0 |
| | RI | 4 | 11 | 5 | 14 | 25 |
| | VT | 1 | 3 | 1 | 3 | 0 |
| | | 38 | 100 | 35 | 100 | −8 |
| MA | DC | 14 | 8 | 12 | 8 | −14 |
| | DE | 3 | 2 | 2 | 1 | −33 |
| | MD | 17 | 10 | 16 | 10 | −6 |
| | NJ | 27 | 16 | 25 | 16 | −7 |
| | NY | 39 | 23 | 46 | 29 | 18 |
| | PA | 68 | 40 | 55 | 35 | −19 |
| | | 168 | 100 | 156 | 100 | −7 |
| SE | AL | 13 | 14 | 10 | 11 | −23 |
| | FL | 19 | 21 | 25 | 27 | 32 |
| | GA | 11 | 12 | 10 | 11 | −9 |
| | KY | 8 | 9 | 9 | 10 | 13 |
| | MS | 5 | 5 | 5 | 5 | 0 |
| | NC | 12 | 13 | 12 | 13 | 0 |
| | SC | 2 | 2 | 1 | 1 | −50 |
| | TN | 8 | 9 | 9 | 10 | 13 |
| | VA | 11 | 12 | 9 | 10 | −18 |
| | WV | 2 | 2 | 3 | 3 | 50 |
| | | 91 | 100 | 93 | 100 | 2 |

TABLE 2.27 (continued)
1978 and 1988 *American Library Directory* Popular Libraries by
Region, State, and Province[a]

| Region | State | 1978 Libraries | % | 1988 Libraries | % | Percentage Change 1978–88 |
|--------|-------|----------------|------|----------------|------|---------------------------|
| SW | AR | 3 | 4 | 1 | 1 | −67 |
|    | AZ | 7 | 9 | 6 | 7 | −14 |
|    | LA | 10 | 13 | 5 | 6 | −50 |
|    | NM | 10 | 13 | 15 | 18 | 50 |
|    | OK | 4 | 5 | 5 | 6 | 25 |
|    | TX | 43 | 56 | 50 | 61 | 16 |
|    |    | 77 | 100 | 82 | 100 | 6 |
| W | AK | 1 | 2 | 0 | 0 | −100 |
|   | CA | 41 | 65 | 39 | 78 | −5 |
|   | HI | 7 | 11 | 2 | 4 | −71 |
|   | ID | 0 | 0 | 0 | 0 | 0 |
|   | NV | 2 | 3 | 2 | 4 | 0 |
|   | OR | 4 | 6 | 1 | 2 | −75 |
|   | WA | 8 | 13 | 6 | 12 | −25 |
|   |    | 63 | 100 | 50 | 100 | −21 |
| RM | CO | 8 | 80 | 7 | 88 | −13 |
|    | MT | 1 | 10 | 0 | 0 | −100 |
|    | UT | 1 | 10 | 1 | 13 | 0 |
|    |    | 10 | 100 | 8 | 100 | −20 |
| MW | IA | 1 | 0 | 4 | 2 | 300 |
|    | IL | 24 | 11 | 26 | 13 | 8 |
|    | IN | 18 | 8 | 18 | 9 | 0 |
|    | KS | 3 | 1 | 2 | 1 | −33 |
|    | MI | 47 | 22 | 35 | 18 | −26 |
|    | MN | 20 | 9 | 21 | 11 | 5 |
|    | MO | 17 | 8 | 18 | 9 | 6 |
|    | ND | 3 | 1 | 3 | 2 | 0 |
|    | NE | 4 | 2 | 6 | 3 | 50 |
|    | OH | 50 | 23 | 38 | 19 | −24 |
|    | SD | 4 | 2 | 4 | 2 | 0 |
|    | WI | 22 | 10 | 22 | 11 | 0 |
|    |    | 213 | 100 | 197 | 100 | −8 |
| CA | BC | 0 | 0 | 0 | 0 | 0 |
|    | AB | 0 | 0 | 3 | 14 | 0 |
|    | MB | 0 | 0 | 0 | 0 | 0 |
|    | NB | 1 | 4 | 0 | 0 | −100 |
|    | NF | 0 | 0 | 0 | 0 | 0 |
|    | NS | 0 | 0 | 0 | 0 | 0 |
|    | ON | 6 | 22 | 9 | 43 | 50 |
|    | PQ | 19 | 70 | 8 | 38 | −58 |
|    | SK | 1 | 4 | 1 | 5 | 0 |

TABLE 2.27 (continued)
1978 and 1988 *American Library Directory* Popular Libraries by Region, State, and Province[a]

| Region | State | 1978 Libraries | % | 1988 Libraries | % | Percentage Change 1978–88 |
|---|---|---|---|---|---|---|
| | | 27 | 100 | 21 | 100 | −22 |
| Total | | 687 | 100% | 642 | 100% | −6.6% |

[a] The percentage columns in this table represent the percentage of all popular libraries in each region which are represented by a particular state, e.g., 47% of all libraries in the Northeast are found in Connecticut in 1978.

TABLE 2.28
1978 and 1988 *American Library Directory* Number of Popular Libraries by State/Province[a]

| | | Popular Libraries | | | | |
|---|---|---|---|---|---|---|
| Region | State | 1978 | % of State sample | 1988 | % of State sample | % change |
| NE | CT | 18 | 50 | 13 | 43 | −28 |
| | MA | 12 | 22 | 14 | 26 | 17 |
| | ME | 1 | 20 | 0 | 0 | −100 |
| | NH | 2 | 33 | 2 | 29 | 0 |
| | RI | 4 | 57 | 5 | 42 | 25 |
| | VT | 1 | 20 | 1 | 17 | 0 |
| MA | DC | 14 | 39 | 12 | 40 | −14 |
| | DE | 3 | 75 | 2 | 33 | −33 |
| | MD | 17 | 55 | 16 | 48 | −6 |
| | NJ | 27 | 53 | 25 | 54 | −7 |
| | NY | 39 | 28 | 46 | 33 | 18 |
| | PA | 68 | 39 | 55 | 34 | −19 |
| SE | AL | 13 | 48 | 10 | 43 | −23 |
| | FL | 19 | 45 | 25 | 52 | 32 |
| | GA | 11 | 29 | 10 | 32 | −9 |
| | KY | 8 | 21 | 9 | 22 | 13 |
| | MS | 5 | 22 | 5 | 23 | 0 |
| | NC | 12 | 20 | 12 | 19 | 0 |
| | SC | 2 | 8 | 1 | 5 | −50 |
| | TN | 8 | 14 | 9 | 16 | 13 |
| | VA | 11 | 30 | 9 | 21 | −18 |
| | WV | 2 | 22 | 3 | 30 | 50 |
| SW | AR | 3 | 20 | 1 | 8 | −67 |
| | AZ | 7 | 54 | 6 | 40 | −14 |
| | LA | 10 | 48 | 5 | 31 | −50 |

TABLE 2.28 (continued)
1978 and 1988 *American Library Directory* Number of Popular
Libraries by State/Province[a]

| Region | State | 1978 | % of sample | 1988 | % of sample | % change |
|--------|-------|------|-------------|------|-------------|----------|
|        | NM | 10 | 77 | 15 | 88 | 50 |
|        | OK | 4 | 19 | 5 | 24 | 25 |
|        | TX | 43 | 41 | 50 | 43 | 16 |
| W      | AK | 1 | 25 | 0 | 0 | −100 |
|        | CA | 41 | 35 | 39 | 34 | −5 |
|        | HI | 7 | 64 | 2 | 29 | −71 |
|        | ID | 0 | 0 | 0 | 0 | |
|        | NV | 2 | 100 | 2 | 100 | 0 |
|        | OR | 4 | 18 | 1 | 5 | −75 |
|        | WA | 8 | 36 | 6 | 25 | −25 |
| RM     | CO | 8 | 30 | 7 | 33 | −13 |
|        | MT | 1 | 20 | 0 | 0 | −100 |
|        | UT | 1 | 20 | 1 | 20 | 0 |
| MW     | IA | 1 | 3 | 4 | 11 | 300 |
|        | IL | 24 | 26 | 26 | 30 | 8 |
|        | IN | 18 | 33 | 18 | 31 | 0 |
|        | KS | 3 | 10 | 2 | 7 | −33 |
|        | MI | 47 | 55 | 35 | 49 | −26 |
|        | MN | 20 | 39 | 21 | 38 | 5 |
|        | MO | 17 | 25 | 18 | 26 | 6 |
|        | ND | 3 | 33 | 3 | 38 | 0 |
|        | NE | 4 | 20 | 6 | 27 | 50 |
|        | OH | 50 | 46 | 38 | 40 | −24 |
|        | SD | 4 | 29 | 4 | 31 | 0 |
|        | WI | 22 | 38 | 22 | 42 | 0 |
| CA     | BC | 0 | 0 | 0 | 0 | |
|        | AB | 0 | 0 | 3 | 14 | |
|        | MB | 0 | 0 | 0 | 0 | |
|        | NB | 1 | 33 | 0 | 0 | −100 |
|        | NF | 0 | 0 | 0 | 0 | 0 |
|        | NS | 0 | 0 | 0 | 0 | 0 |
|        | ON | 6 | 22 | 9 | 43 | 50 |
|        | PQ | 19 | 70 | 8 | 38 | −58 |
|        | SK | 1 | 4 | 1 | 5 | 0 |
| Totals |    | 687 | 33% | 642 | 31% | −7% |

[a]"Percentage of sample" refers to the proportion of all libraries in each state that are popular relative to the entire number of sample libraries in each state, for example, 34 percent of the libraries in Pennsylvania in 1998 are popular and the remaining 66 percent are scholarly.

TABLE 2.29
1978 and 1988 *American Library Directory* Longitudinal Study City Population Size by Popular Library Type

| Library Type | 1978 | | | | 1998 | | | | |
|---|---|---|---|---|---|---|---|---|---|
| | No. of Libraries | No Response | Total Libraries | Mean 1978 | No. of Libraries | No Response | Total Libraries | Mean 1988 | Percentage Change |
| Popular | 685 | 2 | 687 | 361,372 | 642 | 0 | 642 | 356,612 | −1 |
| Congregational | 632 | 2 | 634 | 327,670 | 593 | 0 | 593 | 327,251 | 0 |
| Parochial | 27 | 0 | 27 | 468,333 | 24 | 0 | 24 | 572,292 | 22 |
| Public | 26 | 0 | 26 | 1,069,519 | 25 | 0 | 25 | 846,000 | −21 |

TABLE 2.30

Total Number of 1988 *American Library Directory* Popular Libraries in Each City Population Size Group

| City Population Size Group | Number | Percentage |
|---|---|---|
| 1,000,001+ | 42 | 7 |
| 500,001–1,000,000 | 74 | 12 |
| 300,001–500,000 | 84 | 13 |
| 100,001–300,000 | 105 | 16 |
| 50,001–100,000 | 92 | 14 |
| 10,001–50,000 | 163 | 25 |
| 0–10,000 | 82 | 13 |
| Not classified | 0 | 0 |
| Total | 642 | 100 |
| Median | 91,300 | |
| Mean | 356,600 | |

TABLE 2.31

1978 *American Library Directory* State City Population Size: Number of Popular Libraries in Small Cities and Mean City Size

| State | Small Cities | Per- centage | Other Cities | All Libs. | Mean City Size |
|---|---|---|---|---|---|
| NY | 9 | 23 | 30 | 39 | 1,103,654 |
| DC | 0 | 0 | 14 | 14 | 850,000 |
| PQ | 4 | 21 | 15 | 19 | 587,368 |
| TX | 3 | 7 | 40 | 43 | 522,500 |
| ON | 0 | 0 | 6 | 6 | 500,000 |
| PA | 21 | 31 | 47 | 68 | 487,022 |
| IL | 0 | 0 | 24 | 24 | 446,667 |
| AZ | 0 | 0 | 7 | 7 | 410,714 |
| WI | 2 | 9 | 20 | 22 | 371,591 |
| WA | 0 | 0 | 8 | 8 | 357,500 |
| CA | 5 | 12 | 36 | 41 | 351,474 |
| HI | 0 | 0 | 7 | 7 | 348,571 |
| MI | 7 | 15 | 40 | 47 | 348,245 |
| OH | 1 | 2 | 49 | 50 | 321,450 |
| OK | 0 | 0 | 4 | 4 | 305,000 |
| MO | 4 | 24 | 13 | 17 | 297,059 |
| CO | 0 | 0 | 8 | 8 | 294,375 |
| IN | 2 | 11 | 16 | 18 | 289,444 |
| KY | 0 | 0 | 8 | 8 | 261,875 |
| TN | 0 | 0 | 8 | 8 | 257,500 |
| MD | 1 | 6 | 16 | 17 | 236,029 |
| MN | 4 | 20 | 16 | 20 | 228,750 |

TABLE 2.31 (continued)
1978 *American Library Directory* State City Population Size: Number
of Popular Libraries in Small Cities and Mean City Size

| State | Small Cities | Per- centage | Other Cities | All Libs. | Mean City Size |
|---|---|---|---|---|---|
| OR | 0 | 0 | 4 | 4 | 223,750 |
| IA | 0 | 0 | 1 | 1 | 200,000 |
| NV | 0 | 0 | 2 | 2 | 200,000 |
| RI | 0 | 0 | 4 | 4 | 200,000 |
| UT | 0 | 0 | 1 | 1 | 200,000 |
| AL | 2 | 15 | 11 | 13 | 185,769 |
| LA | 1 | 10 | 9 | 10 | 173,750 |
| FL | 1 | 5 | 18 | 19 | 170,658 |
| GA | 2 | 18 | 9 | 11 | 157,273 |
| MA | 1 | 8 | 11 | 12 | 147,292 |
| KS | 0 | 0 | 3 | 3 | 140,000 |
| NC | 3 | 25 | 9 | 12 | 137,292 |
| VA | 1 | 9 | 10 | 11 | 133,409 |
| NE | 1 | 25 | 3 | 4 | 105,625 |
| SC | 1 | 50 | 1 | 2 | 101,250 |
| NM | 0 | 0 | 10 | 10 | 100,000 |
| CT | 3 | 17 | 15 | 18 | 99,028 |
| AR | 1 | 33 | 2 | 3 | 92,500 |
| DE | 0 | 0 | 3 | 3 | 75,000 |
| ME | 0 | 0 | 1 | 1 | 75,000 |
| MT | 0 | 0 | 1 | 1 | 75,000 |
| NB | 0 | 0 | 1 | 1 | 75,000 |
| MS | 2 | 40 | 3 | 5 | 58,000 |
| WV | 0 | 0 | 2 | 2 | 57,500 |
| ND | 0 | 0 | 3 | 3 | 51,667 |
| NH | 0 | 0 | 2 | 2 | 47,500 |
| SD | 1 | 25 | 3 | 4 | 43,125 |
| AK | 0 | 0 | 1 | 1 | 40,000 |
| VT | 0 | 0 | 1 | 1 | 40,000 |
| NJ | 5 | 19 | 22 | 27 | 39,722 |
| SK | 0 | 0 | 1 | 1 | 20,000 |
| Total | 88 | 13 | 599 | 687 | 361,372 |

TABLE 2.32
1988 *American Library Directory* State City Population Size: Number
of Popular Libraries in Small Cities and Mean City Size

| State | Small Cities | Per-centage | Other Cities | All Libs. | Mean City Size |
|---|---|---|---|---|---|
| NY | 7 | 15 | 39 | 46 | 1,280,598 |
| PQ | 0 | 0 | 9 | 9 | 882,222 |
| IL | 3 | 12 | 23 | 26 | 645,096 |
| DC | 0 | 0 | 12 | 12 | 600,000 |
| AB | 0 | 0 | 3 | 3 | 600,000 |
| TX | 3 | 6 | 47 | 50 | 568,350 |
| ON | 1 | 11 | 8 | 9 | 466,944 |
| AZ | 1 | 17 | 5 | 6 | 450,417 |
| CA | 5 | 13 | 34 | 39 | 431,603 |
| IN | 1 | 6 | 17 | 18 | 373,472 |
| OK | 0 | 0 | 5 | 5 | 324,000 |
| TN | 0 | 0 | 9 | 9 | 295,556 |
| NM | 0 | 0 | 15 | 15 | 277,333 |
| WA | 0 | 0 | 6 | 6 | 273,333 |
| OH | 3 | 8 | 35 | 38 | 271,118 |
| WI | 3 | 14 | 19 | 22 | 260,795 |
| MO | 2 | 11 | 16 | 18 | 229,444 |
| HI | 0 | 0 | 2 | 2 | 220,000 |
| NC | 3 | 25 | 9 | 12 | 203,958 |
| NV | 0 | 0 | 2 | 2 | 200,000 |
| UT | 0 | 0 | 1 | 1 | 200,000 |
| MI | 5 | 14 | 30 | 35 | 197,929 |
| CO | 0 | 0 | 7 | 7 | 195,714 |
| PA | 23 | 42 | 32 | 55 | 189,500 |
| MN | 4 | 19 | 17 | 21 | 185,238 |
| VA | 0 | 0 | 9 | 9 | 180,000 |
| MA | 2 | 14 | 12 | 14 | 176,786 |
| LA | 0 | 0 | 5 | 5 | 175,000 |
| GA | 1 | 10 | 9 | 10 | 172,750 |
| NE | 1 | 17 | 5 | 6 | 170,417 |
| FL | 1 | 4 | 24 | 25 | 166,700 |
| MD | 2 | 13 | 14 | 16 | 144,688 |
| KY | 0 | 0 | 9 | 9 | 142,222 |
| RI | 0 | 0 | 5 | 5 | 132,000 |
| IA | 0 | 0 | 4 | 4 | 115,000 |
| CT | 1 | 8 | 12 | 13 | 102,500 |
| AL | 2 | 20 | 8 | 10 | 99,500 |
| AR | 0 | 0 | 1 | 1 | 75,000 |
| OR | 0 | 0 | 1 | 1 | 75,000 |
| ND | 0 | 0 | 3 | 3 | 63,333 |
| MS | 2 | 40 | 3 | 5 | 58,000 |

TABLE 2.32 (continued)
1988 *American Library Directory* State City Population Size: Number
of Popular Libraries in Small Cities and Mean City Size

| State | Small Cities | Per-centage | Other Cities | All Libs. | Mean City Size |
|---|---|---|---|---|---|
| WV | 0 | 0 | 3 | 3 | 51,667 |
| DE | 0 | 0 | 2 | 2 | 47,500 |
| NH | 0 | 0 | 2 | 2 | 47,500 |
| SD | 1 | 25 | 3 | 4 | 43,125 |
| VT | 0 | 0 | 1 | 1 | 40,000 |
| NJ | 3 | 12 | 22 | 25 | 38,300 |
| SK | 0 | 0 | 1 | 1 | 20,000 |
| KS | 1 | 50 | 1 | 2 | 11,250 |
| SC | 1 | 100 | 0 | 1 | 2,500 |
| Total | 82 | 13 | 561 | 643 | 356,612 |

TABLE 2.33
1978 and 1988 *American Library Directory* Longitudinal Study
Popular Libraries in Small Cities[a]

| Library Type | 1978 Number of Libraries in Small Cities | 1978 Percentage in Small Cities | 1988 Number of Libraries in Small Cities | 1988 Percentage in Small Cities | Percentage Change 1978–88 |
|---|---|---|---|---|---|
| Popular | 88 | 13 | 82 | 13 | −7 |
| Congregational | 81 | 13 | 76 | 18 | −6 |
| Parochial | 6 | 22 | 2 | 8 | −67 |
| Public | 1 | 4 | 4 | 16 | 300 |

[a]Small cities have a population of 10,000 or fewer persons.

TABLE 2.34
1978 *American Library Directory* City Population Size by
Denomination for Popular Libraries

| Denomination | Number of Libraries | No Response | Total Libraries | Mean City Population Size |
|---|---|---|---|---|
| Baptist | 83 | 0 | 83 | 221,100 |
| Christian | 19 | 0 | 19 | 427,600 |
| Churches of Christ | 0 | 0 | 0 | 0 |
| Congregational | 28 | 0 | 28 | 141,600 |
| Episcopal/Anglican | 42 | 0 | 42 | 419,900 |
| Independent | 5 | 0 | 5 | 1,409,000 |
| Lutheran | 53 | 0 | 53 | 267,100 |
| Methodist | 55 | 0 | 55 | 199,200 |
| Other Denominations | 67 | 0 | 67 | 403,700 |
| Presbyterian | 114 | 1 | 115 | 248,900 |
| U.C.C. | 13 | 0 | 13 | 289,200 |
| Summary | | | | |
| Jewish | 162 | 1 | 163 | 515,000 |
| Roman Catholic | 44 | 0 | 44 | 561,200 |
| All Protestant | 479 | 1 | 480 | 291,100 |
| Total | 685 | 2 | 687 | 361,400 |

TABLE 2.35
1988 *American Library Directory* City Population Size by
Denomination for Popular Libraries

| Denomination | Number of Libraries | No Response | Total Libraries | Mean City Population Size |
|---|---|---|---|---|
| Baptist | 71 | 0 | 71 | 218,900 |
| Christian | 17 | 0 | 17 | 383,200 |
| Churches of Christ | 2 | 0 | 2 | 110,000 |
| Episcopal/Anglican | 34 | 0 | 34 | 492,200 |
| Independent | 3 | 0 | 3 | 700,800 |
| Lutheran | 42 | 0 | 42 | 194,600 |
| Mennonite | 4 | 0 | 4 | 12,500 |
| Methodist | 64 | 0 | 64 | 181,100 |
| Other Denominations | 77 | 0 | 77 | 464,000 |
| Presbyterian | 97 | 0 | 97 | 240,900 |
| U.C.C. | 13 | 0 | 13 | 98,650 |
| Summary | | | | |
| Jewish | 187 | 0 | 187 | 479,800 |
| Roman Catholic | 31 | 0 | 31 | 577,900 |
| All Protestant | 424 | 0 | 424 | 286,100 |
| Total | 642 | 0 | 642 | 356,600 |

TABLE 2.36
1978 *American Library Directory* City Population Size by Total
Annual Popular Library Expenditure

| Library Expenditures | Number of Libraries | No Response | Total Libraries | Mean City Population Size |
|---|---|---|---|---|
| Under $1,500 | 110 | 0 | 110 | 341,500 |
| $1,501–$20,000 | 40 | 0 | 40 | 405,000 |
| $20,001–$95,000 | 4 | 0 | 4 | 1,385,000 |
| $95,001 and over | 1 | 0 | 1 | 1,500,000 |
| No Response | 530 | 2 | 532 | 352,300 |
| Total | 685 | 2 | 687 | 361,400 |

TABLE 2.37
1988 *American Library Directory* City Population Size by Total
Annual Popular Library Expenditure

| Library Expenditures | Number of Libraries | No Response | Total Libraries | Mean City Population Size |
|---|---|---|---|---|
| Under $1,500 | 139 | 0 | 139 | 256,000 |
| $1,501–$20,000 | 83 | 0 | 83 | 300,500 |
| $20,001–$95,000 | 23 | 0 | 23 | 784,900 |
| $95,001–$510,000 | 6 | 0 | 6 | 1,721,000 |
| $510,001 and over | 1 | 0 | 1 | 1,500,000 |
| No Response | 390 | 0 | 390 | 355,200 |
| Total | 642 | 0 | 642 | 356,600 |

TABLE 2.38
1978 and 1988 *American Library Directory* Longitudinal Study Chief Librarian's Gender by City Population Size for Popular Libraries[a]

| City Population Size | 1978 | | | | 1988 | | | | Percentage Change | | | |
|---|---|---|---|---|---|---|---|---|---|---|---|---|
| | Male | Female | No Response | Total | Male | Female | No Response | Total | Male | Female | No Response | Total |
| **Smallest** | | | | | | | | | | | | |
| 1–10,000 persons | 13 | 40 | 35 | 88 | 13 | 65 | 4 | 82 | 0 | 63 | −89 | −7 |
| Percent | 15 | 45 | 40 | 100 | 16 | 79 | 5 | 100 | | | | |
| **Medium-Small** | | | | | | | | | | | | |
| 10,001–100,000 | 25 | 135 | 108 | 268 | 25 | 203 | 28 | 256 | 0 | 50 | −74 | −4 |
| Percent | 9 | 50 | 40 | 100 | 10 | 79 | 11 | 100 | | | | |
| **Medium-Large** | | | | | | | | | | | | |
| 100,001–1,000,000 | 41 | 124 | 108 | 273 | 35 | 210 | 18 | 263 | −15 | 69 | −83 | −4 |
| Percent | 15 | 45 | 40 | 100 | 13 | 80 | 7 | 100 | | | | |
| **Large Cities** | | | | | | | | | | | | |
| 1,000,001 & over | 6 | 31 | 19 | 56 | 10 | 28 | 4 | 42 | 67 | −10 | −79 | −25 |
| Percent | 11 | 55 | 34 | 100 | 24 | 67 | 10 | 100 | | | | |
| No Response | 0 | 0 | 2 | 2 | 0 | 0 | 0 | 0 | N/A | N/A | −100 | −100 |
| Percent | 0 | 0 | 100 | 100 | 0 | N/A | 0 | N/A | | | | |
| Total | 85 | 330 | 272 | 687 | 83 | 506 | 54 | 643 | −2 | 53 | −80 | −6 |
| Percentage | 12 | 48 | 40 | 100 | 13 | 79 | 8 | 100 | | | | |

[a]Smallest: 1–10,000 persons, medium-small: 10,001–100,000 persons, medium-large: 100,001–1,000,000 persons and large: 1,000,001 persons and over

TABLE 2.39
1978 and 1988 *American Library Directory* Longitudinal Study Popular Libraries Located in Specific Cities

| City Name | State/Province | Region | 1978 | | | 1988 | | | Percentage Change 1978–88 |
|---|---|---|---|---|---|---|---|---|---|
| | | | Number in City | Number of Popular Libs. | Percentage Popular Libs. | Number in City | Number of Popular Libs. | Percentage Popular Libs. | |
| Philadelphia | PA | MA | 42 | 19 | 45 | 26 | 5 | 19 | -58 |
| Washington | DC | MA | 36 | 14 | 39 | 30 | 12 | 40 | 3 |
| Dallas | TX | SW | 20 | 13 | 65 | 19 | 11 | 58 | -11 |
| New York | NY | MA | 36 | 10 | 28 | 36 | 13 | 36 | 30 |
| Minneapolis | MN | MW | 16 | 10 | 63 | 15 | 8 | 53 | -15 |
| Detroit | MI | MW | 16 | 9 | 56 | 8 | 3 | 38 | -33 |
| Terre Haute | IN | MW | 9 | 9 | 100 | 5 | 5 | 100 | 0 |
| Milwaukee | WI | MW | 19 | 8 | 42 | 16 | 8 | 50 | 19 |
| Toledo | OH | MW | 8 | 8 | 100 | 4 | 4 | 100 | 0 |
| Cleveland | OH | MW | 11 | 7 | 64 | 8 | 4 | 50 | -21 |
| Grand Rapids | MI | MW | 12 | 7 | 58 | 10 | 5 | 50 | -14 |
| Montreal | PQ | CAN | 23 | 7 | 30 | 31 | 5 | 16 | -47 |
| Honolulu | HI | W | 9 | 6 | 67 | 4 | 1 | 25 | -62 |
| St. Louis | MO | MW | 22 | 6 | 27 | 21 | 6 | 29 | 5 |
| Erie | PA | MA | 9 | 5 | 56 | 6 | 3 | 50 | -10 |
| Rochester | NY | MA | 10 | 5 | 50 | 12 | 7 | 58 | 17 |
| San Antonio | TX | SW | 12 | 5 | 42 | 14 | 5 | 36 | -14 |
| Cincinnati | OH | MW | 13 | 5 | 38 | 14 | 7 | 50 | 30 |
| Columbus | OH | MW | 8 | 5 | 63 | 8 | 4 | 50 | -20 |
| Indianapolis | IN | MW | 10 | 5 | 50 | 15 | 7 | 47 | -7 |

| City | State | Region | | | | | | |
|---|---|---|---|---|---|---|---|---|
| Providence | RI | NE | 6 | 4 | 67 | 8 | 3 | 38 | -44 |
| Baltimore | MD | MA | 11 | 4 | 36 | 10 | 2 | 20 | -45 |
| Pittsburgh | PA | MA | 11 | 4 | 36 | 10 | 3 | 30 | -17 |
| Atlanta | GA | SE | 12 | 4 | 33 | 9 | 3 | 33 | 0 |
| Louisville | KY | SE | 9 | 4 | 44 | 11 | 5 | 45 | 2 |
| Birmingham | AL | SE | 9 | 4 | 44 | 6 | 3 | 50 | 13 |
| Albuquerque | NM | SW | 5 | 4 | 80 | 10 | 10 | 100 | 25 |
| Houston | TX | SW | 9 | 4 | 44 | 10 | 7 | 70 | 58 |
| Phoenix | AZ | SW | 7 | 4 | 57 | 7 | 2 | 29 | -50 |
| Seattle | WA | W | 7 | 4 | 57 | 7 | 3 | 43 | -25 |
| Chicago | IL | MW | 23 | 4 | 17 | 19 | 4 | 21 | 21 |
| Toronto | ON | CAN | 14 | 4 | 29 | 18 | 5 | 28 | -3 |
| Buffalo | NY | MA | 8 | 3 | 38 | 8 | 3 | 38 | 0 |
| Miami | FL | SE | 6 | 3 | 50 | 7 | 3 | 43 | -14 |
| Los Angeles | CA | W | 10 | 3 | 30 | 12 | 4 | 33 | 11 |
| Denver | CO | RM | 14 | 3 | 21 | 9 | 2 | 22 | 4 |
| Dayton | OH | MW | 7 | 3 | 43 | 4 | 1 | 25 | -42 |
| Boston | MA | NE | 10 | 2 | 20 | 14 | 3 | 21 | 7 |
| Memphis | TN | SE | 8 | 2 | 25 | 8 | 1 | 13 | -50 |
| Richmond | VA | SE | 6 | 2 | 33 | 8 | 2 | 25 | -25 |
| Lexington | KY | SE | 5 | 2 | 40 | 6 | 1 | 17 | -59 |
| Fort Worth | TX | SW | 6 | 2 | 33 | 8 | 2 | 25 | -25 |
| Oklahoma City | OK | SW | 8 | 2 | 25 | 6 | 3 | 50 | 100 |
| Portland | OR | W | 11 | 2 | 18 | 8 | 0 | 0 | -100 |
| San Francisco | CA | W | 6 | 2 | 33 | 6 | 2 | 33 | 0 |
| Springfield | MO | MW | 7 | 2 | 29 | 7 | 2 | 29 | 0 |
| Lincoln | NE | MW | 6 | 2 | 33 | 7 | 3 | 43 | 29 |
| Quebec | PQ | CAN | 2 | 2 | 100 | 7 | 2 | 29 | -72 |

TABLE 2.39 (continued)
1978 and 1988 *American Library Directory* Longitudinal Study Popular Libraries Located in Specific Cities

| City Name | State/ Province | Region | 1978 | | | 1988 | | | Percentage Change 1978–88 |
|---|---|---|---|---|---|---|---|---|---|
| | | | Number in City | Number of Popular Libs. | Percentage Popular Libs. | Number in City | Number of Popular Libs. | Percentage Popular Libs. | |
| Yonkers | NY | MA | 3 | 1 | 33 | 6 | 2 | 33 | 0 |
| Nashville | TN | SE | 18 | 1 | 6 | 19 | 4 | 21 | 282 |
| Winston-Salem | NC | SE | 5 | 1 | 20 | 6 | 1 | 17 | –17 |
| Austin | TX | SW | 8 | 1 | 13 | 12 | 3 | 25 | 100 |
| New Orleans | LA | SW | 9 | 1 | 11 | 7 | 0 | 0 | –100 |
| Kansas City | MO | MW | 8 | 1 | 13 | 10 | 2 | 20 | 60 |
| St. Paul | MN | MW | 10 | 1 | 10 | 11 | 2 | 18 | 81 |
| Lancaster | PA | MA | 5 | 0 | 0 | 6 | 1 | 17 | 0 |
| Edmonton | AB | CAN | 5 | 0 | 0 | 9 | 2 | 22 | 0 |
| Total libraries in specific cities | | | 660 | 255 | 39 | 648 | 224 | 35 | –12 |

TABLE 2.40
1978 and 1988 *American Library Directory* Longitudinal Study:
Change in Most Popular Cities in Alphabetical Order by City Name
for Popular Libraries

| City Name | State | Edition 31 No. of Libraries | Edition 41 No. of Libraries | Percentage Change |
|---|---|---|---|---|
| Albuquerque | NM | 4 | 10 | 150 |
| Atlanta | GA | 4 | 3 | −25 |
| Austin | TX | 1 | 3 | 200 |
| Baltimore | MD | 4 | 2 | −50 |
| Birmingham | AL | 4 | 3 | −25 |
| Boston | MA | 2 | 3 | 50 |
| Buffalo | NY | 3 | 3 | 0 |
| Chicago | IL | 4 | 4 | 0 |
| Cincinnati | OH | 5 | 7 | 40 |
| Cleveland | OH | 7 | 4 | −43 |
| Columbus | OH | 5 | 4 | −20 |
| Dallas | TX | 13 | 11 | −15 |
| Dayton | OH | 3 | 1 | −67 |
| Denver | CO | 3 | 2 | −33 |
| Detroit | MI | 9 | 3 | −67 |
| Edmonton | AB | 0 | 2 | |
| Erie | PA | 5 | 3 | −40 |
| Fort Worth | TX | 2 | 2 | 0 |
| Grand Rapids | MI | 7 | 5 | −29 |
| Honolulu | HI | 6 | 1 | −83 |
| Houston | TX | 4 | 7 | 75 |
| Indianapolis | IN | 5 | 7 | 40 |
| Kansas City | MO | 1 | 2 | 100 |
| Lancaster | PA | 0 | 1 | |
| Lexington | KY | 2 | 1 | −50 |
| Lincoln | NE | 2 | 3 | 50 |
| Los Angeles | CA | 3 | 4 | 33 |
| Louisville | KY | 4 | 5 | 25 |
| Memphis | TN | 2 | 1 | −50 |
| Miami | FL | 3 | 3 | 0 |
| Milwaukee | WI | 8 | 8 | 0 |
| Minneapolis | MN | 10 | 8 | −20 |
| Montreal | PQ | 7 | 5 | −29 |
| Nashville | TN | 1 | 4 | 300 |
| New Orleans | LA | 1 | 0 | −100 |
| New York | NY | 10 | 13 | 30 |
| Oklahoma City | OK | 2 | 3 | 50 |
| Ottawa | ON | 1 | 2 | 100 |
| Philadelphia | PA | 19 | 5 | −74 |
| Phoenix | AZ | 4 | 2 | −50 |

TABLE 2.40 (continued)
1978 and 1988 *American Library Directory* Longitudinal Study:
Change in Most Popular Cities in Alphabetical Order by City Name
for Popular Libraries

| City Name | State | Edition 31 No. of Libraries | Edition 41 No. of Libraries | Percentage Change |
|---|---|---|---|---|
| Pittsburgh | PA | 4 | 3 | −25 |
| Portland | OR | 2 | 0 | −100 |
| Providence | RI | 4 | 3 | −25 |
| Quebec City | PQ | 2 | 2 | 0 |
| Richmond | VA | 2 | 2 | 0 |
| Rochester | NY | 5 | 7 | 40 |
| San Antonio | TX | 5 | 5 | 0 |
| San Francisco | CA | 2 | 2 | 0 |
| Seattle | WA | 4 | 3 | −25 |
| Springfield | MO | 2 | 2 | 0 |
| St. Louis | MO | 6 | 6 | 0 |
| St. Paul | MN | 1 | 2 | 100 |
| Terre Haute | IN | 9 | 5 | −44 |
| Toledo | OH | 8 | 4 | −50 |
| Toronto | ON | 4 | 5 | 25 |
| Trois-Rivières | PQ | 1 | 0 | −100 |
| Washington | DC | 14 | 12 | −14 |
| Winston-Salem | NC | 1 | 1 | 0 |
| Yonkers | NY | 1 | 2 | 100 |
| Total | | 257 | 226 | −12 |

TABLE 2.41
1988 *American Library Directory* Most Popular Cities for Popular
Libraries by Denomination

| City Name | State/ Province | Region | Denominational Libraries in City | All Popular Libraries in City |
|---|---|---|---|---|
| Baptist Libraries | | | | |
| Washington | DC | MA | 2 | 12 |
| Louisville | KY | SE | 2 | 5 |
| Minneapolis | MN | MW | 2 | 8 |
| Albuquerque | NM | SW | 4 | 10 |
| Methodist Libraries | | | | |
| Washington | DC | MA | 2 | 12 |
| Atlanta | GA | SE | 2 | 3 |
| Albuquerque | NM | SW | 2 | 10 |
| Rochester | NY | MA | 2 | 7 |

TABLE 2.41 (continued)
1988 *American Library Directory* Most Popular Cities for Popular
Libraries by Denomination

| City Name | State/ Province | Region | Denominational Libraries in City | All Popular Libraries in City |
|---|---|---|---|---|
| Other Denominations Libraries | | | | |
| Washington | DC | MA | 3 | 12 |
| Grand Rapids | MI | MW | 5 | 5 |
| New York | NY | MA | 4 | 13 |
| Philadelphia | PA | MA | 2 | 5 |
| Jewish Libraries | | | | |
| Los Angeles | CA | W | 3 | 4 |
| Miami | FL | SE | 3 | 3 |
| Chicago | IL | MW | 4 | 4 |
| St. Louis | MO | MW | 3 | 6 |
| New York | NY | MA | 5 | 13 |
| Rochester | NY | MA | 4 | 7 |
| Cincinnati | OH | MW | 3 | 7 |
| Cleveland | OH | MW | 4 | 4 |
| Columbus | OH | MW | 3 | 4 |
| Nashville | TN | SE | 4 | 4 |
| Dallas | TX | SW | 3 | 11 |
| Roman Catholic Libraries | | | | |
| Dallas | TX | SW | 2 | 11 |
| Houston | TX | SW | 2 | 7 |
| Montreal | PQ | CAN | 2 | 5 |
| Quebec City | PQ | CAN | 2 | 2 |

TABLE 2.42
1978 and 1988 Demographics: *American Library Directory* Popular
Libraries by Edition Showing Percentage Change for All Sample Divisions

| | Matched Pairs | | | No Longer Listed | Newly Listed | | All Sample | All Sample | |
|---|---|---|---|---|---|---|---|---|---|
| | 1978 | 1988 | % Change | 1978 | 1988 | % Change | 1978 | 1988 | % Change |
| Popular | 471 | 468 | −1 | 216 | 174 | −19 | 687 | 642 | −7 |
| Percentage | 29 | 29 | | 51 | 40 | | 33 | 31 | |
| Congregational | 440 | 440 | 0 | 194 | 153 | −21 | 634 | 593 | −6 |
| Percentage | 93 | 94 | | 90 | 88 | | 92 | 92 | |
| Parochial | 16 | 13 | −19 | 11 | 11 | 0 | 27 | 24 | −11 |
| Percentage | 3 | 3 | | 5 | 6 | | 4 | 4 | |
| Public | 15 | 15 | 0 | 11 | 10 | −9 | 26 | 25 | −4 |
| Percentage | 3 | 3 | | 5 | 6 | | 4 | 4 | |

TABLE 2.43
1988 *American Library Directory* Popular Library Type by Age
Distribution Showing Percentage Breakdown

| | ------------------Type of Library------------------ | | | |
| Year Opened | Congregational Libraries | Parochial Libraries | Public Libraries | Total (%) |
|---|---|---|---|---|
| Before 1800 | 0 | 100 | 0 | 100 |
| 1801–1820 | 100 | 0 | 0 | 100 |
| 1821–1840 | 100 | 0 | 0 | 100 |
| 1841–1860 | 50 | 0 | 50 | 100 |
| 1861–1880 | 75 | 0 | 25 | 100 |
| 1881–1900 | 100 | 0 | 0 | 100 |
| 1901–1920 | 71 | 0 | 29 | 100 |
| 1921–1940 | 75 | 13 | 13 | 100 |
| 1941–1960 | 95 | 2 | 2 | 100 |
| 1961–1970 | 91 | 7 | 2 | 100 |
| 1971–1980 | 94 | 0 | 6 | 100 |
| 1981 and after | 100 | 0 | 0 | 100 |
| No Response | 94 | 5 | 2 | 100 |
| Total | 94 | 3 | 3 | 100 |

TABLE 2.44
1988 *American Library Directory* Popular Library Age for Newly Listed Libraries

| Library Type | 1–10 YRS | % | 11–20 YRS | % | 21–50 YRS | % | 51 YRS & over | % | No Response | % | Number of Libraries | Mean Years |
|---|---|---|---|---|---|---|---|---|---|---|---|---|
| Popular | 3 | 2 | 14 | 8 | 42 | 24 | 16 | 9 | 99 | 57 | 174 | 36 |
| Congregational | 3 | 2 | 12 | 8 | 36 | 24 | 11 | 7.2 | 91 | 59 | 153 | 34 |
| Parochial | 0 | 0 | 0 | 0 | 5 | 45 | 2 | 18 | 4 | 36 | 11 | 37 |
| Public | 0 | 0 | 2 | 20 | 1 | 10 | 3 | 30 | 4 | 40 | 10 | 55 |

TABLE 2.45

1978–88 *American Library Directory* Longitudinal Study Popular
Library Age for No Longer Listed and Newly Listed Libraries

| Library Type | No. of Libraries | 1978 No Response | Total Libraries | Mean Years | No. of Libraries | 1988 No Response | Total Libraries | Mean Years | % Change 1978–88 |
|---|---|---|---|---|---|---|---|---|---|
| Popular Congregational | 49 | 167 | 216 | 51 | 75 | 99 | 174 | 36 | −29.0 |
|  | 37 | 157 | 194 | 46 | 62 | 91 | 153 | 34 | −26.0 |
| Parochial | 6 | 5 | 11 | 46 | 7 | 4 | 11 | 37 | −20.0 |
| Public | 6 | 5 | 11 | 83 | 6 | 4 | 10 | 55 | −34.0 |

TABLE 2.46

1978 and 1988 *American Library Directory* Longitudinal Study
Popular Library Age by Denomination for No Longer Listed and
Newly Listed Libraries

| Denomination | No. of Libraries | 1978 No Response | Total Libraries | Mean Years | No. of Libraries | 1988 No Response | Total Libraries | Mean Years | % Change 1978–88 |
|---|---|---|---|---|---|---|---|---|---|
| Baptist | 2 | 20 | 22 | 25 | 6 | 4 | 10 | 33 | 32 |
| Christian | 1 | 5 | 6 | 60 | 2 | 2 | 4 | 50 | −17 |
| Churches of Christ | 0 | 0 | 0 | — | 2 | 0 | 2 | 28 | 0 |
| Episcopal/ Anglican | 6 | 9 | 15 | 63 | 3 | 4 | 7 | 15 | −76 |
| Independent | 2 | 2 | 4 | 80 | 1 | 0 | 1 | 25 | −69 |
| Lutheran | 3 | 15 | 18 | 67 | 0 | 7 | 7 | — | −100 |
| Mennonite | 0 | 0 | 0 | — | 1 | 0 | 1 | 40 | 0 |
| Methodist | 2 | 14 | 16 | 43 | 7 | 18 | 25 | 28 | −35 |
| Other Denominations | 7 | 32 | 39 | 48 | 10 | 14 | 24 | 43 | −10 |
| Presbyterian | 4 | 25 | 29 | 40 | 1 | 10 | 11 | 5 | −87 |
| U.C.C. | 1 | 2 | 3 | 40 | 1 | 2 | 3 | 5 | −87 |
| Summary | | | | | | | | | |
| Jewish | 13 | 30 | 43 | 43 | 38 | 30 | 68 | 40 | −7 |
| Roman Catholic | 8 | 13 | 21 | 56 | 3 | 8 | 11 | 40 | −29 |
| All Protestant | 28 | 124 | 152 | 53 | 34 | 61 | 95 | 32 | −40 |
| Total | 49 | 167 | 216 | 51 | 75 | 99 | 174 | 36 | −29 |

TABLE 2.47

1988 *American Library Directory* Popular Library Type by Library Age (Actual)

| Year Opened | -------------Type of Library----------- | | | Total (Actual) |
| | Congreg. Libs. | Paroch. Libs. | Public Libs. | |
| --- | --- | --- | --- | --- |
| Before 1800 | 0 | 1 | 0 | 1 |
| 1801–1820 | 1 | 0 | 0 | 1 |
| 1821–1840 | 1 | 0 | 0 | 1 |
| 1841–1860 | 1 | 0 | 1 | 2 |
| 1861–1880 | 4 | 0 | 1 | 5 |
| 1881–1900 | 7 | 0 | 0 | 7 |
| 1901–1920 | 8 | 0 | 3 | 11 |
| 1921–1940 | 29 | 4 | 5 | 38 |
| 1941–1960 | 179 | 3 | 6 | 188 |
| 1961–1970 | 81 | 6 | 2 | 89 |
| 1971–1980 | 25 | 0 | 2 | 27 |
| 1981 and after | 3 | 0 | 0 | 3 |
| No response | 254 | 11 | 5 | 270 |
| Totals | 593 | 25 | 25 | 643 |
| Mean Birth Year: | 1948 | 1935 | 1932 | 1946 |

TABLE 2.48

1978 and 1988 *American Library Directory* Longitudinal Study Popular Library Age by Library Type

| Library Type | --------------------1 9 7 8-------------------- | | | | --------------------1 9 8 8-------------------- | | | | Percentage Change 1978–88 |
| | Number of Libraries | No Response | Total Libraries | Mean Years | Number of Libraries | No Response | Total Libraries | Mean Years | |
| --- | --- | --- | --- | --- | --- | --- | --- | --- | --- |
| Popular | 319 | 368 | 687 | 44 | 373 | 270 | 643 | 41 | −6.8 |
| Congre- gational | 284 | 350 | 634 | 42 | 339 | 254 | 593 | 40 | −4.8 |
| Parochial | 14 | 13 | 27 | 55 | 14 | 11 | 25 | 53 | −3.6 |
| Public | 21 | 5 | 26 | 63 | 20 | 5 | 25 | 56 | −11 |

TABLE 2.49
1978–1988 *American Library Directory* Longitudinal Study Popular Library Age for Canada and the United States for No Longer Listed and Newly Listed Libraries

|  | 1978 | | | | 1988 | | | | |
|  | --------No Longer Listed------- | | | | ----------Newly Listed---------- | | | | |
| Region | No. of Libraries | No Re-sponse | Total Libraries | Mean 1978 | No. of Libraries | No Re-sponse | Total Libraries | Mean 1988 | Percentage Change |
| Canada | 8 | 3 | 11 | 69 | 5 | 3 | 8 | 26 | −62 |
| United States | 41 | 164 | 205 | 47 | 70 | 96 | 166 | 37 | −21 |
| Total | 49 | 167 | 216 | 51 | 75 | 99 | 174 | 36 | −29 |

TABLE 2.50
1978 *American Library Directory* Popular Library Age by Region

| Region | 1–10 YRS | % | 11–30 YRS | % | 31–50 YRS | % | 51 YRS & over | % | No Response | % | Number of Libraries | Mean Years |
|---|---|---|---|---|---|---|---|---|---|---|---|---|
| Northeast | 0 | 0 | 1 | 3 | 11 | 29 | 4 | 11 | 22 | 58 | 38 | 56 |
| Middle Atlantic | 0 | 0 | 22 | 13 | 49 | 29 | 12 | 7 | 85 | 51 | 168 | 44 |
| Southeast | 0 | 0 | 10 | 11 | 26 | 29 | 2 | 2 | 53 | 58 | 91 | 37 |
| Southwest | 0 | 0 | 7 | 9 | 25 | 32 | 6 | 8 | 39 | 51 | 77 | 41 |
| West | 0 | 0 | 9 | 14 | 8 | 13 | 7 | 11 | 39 | 62 | 63 | 41 |
| Rocky Mountains | 1 | 10 | 1 | 10 | 3 | 30 | 0 | 0 | 5 | 50 | 10 | 30 |
| Middle West | 0 | 0 | 23 | 11 | 50 | 23 | 23 | 11 | 117 | 55 | 213 | 45 |
| Canada | 0 | 0 | 5 | 19 | 4 | 15 | 10 | 37 | 8 | 30 | 27 | 64 |
| Total | 1 | 0 | 78 | 11 | 176 | 26 | 64 | 9 | 368 | 54 | 687 | 44 |

TABLE 2.51
1988 *American Library Directory* Popular Library Age by Region

| Region | 1–10 | % | 11–30 | % | 31–50 | % | 51 & over | % | No Re-sponse | % | Number of Libraries | Mean Years |
|---|---|---|---|---|---|---|---|---|---|---|---|---|
| Northeast | 0 | 0 | 3 | 9 | 12 | 34 | 6 | 17 | 14 | 40 | 35 | 55 |
| Middle Atlantic | 0 | 0 | 31 | 20 | 51 | 33 | 13 | 8 | 61 | 39 | 156 | 42 |
| Southeast | 1 | 1 | 16 | 17 | 32 | 34 | 4 | 4 | 40 | 43 | 93 | 37 |
| Southwest | 0 | 0 | 14 | 17 | 26 | 32 | 8 | 10 | 34 | 41 | 82 | 40 |
| West | 0 | 0 | 13 | 26 | 7 | 14 | 7 | 14 | 23 | 46 | 50 | 37 |
| Rocky Mountains | 0 | 0 | 1 | 13 | 2 | 25 | 2 | 25 | 3 | 38 | 8 | 53 |
| Middle West | 2 | 1 | 32 | 16 | 54 | 27 | 21 | 11 | 88 | 45 | 197 | 41 |
| Canada | 0 | 0 | 6 | 29 | 4 | 19 | 5 | 24 | 6 | 29 | 21 | 54 |
| Total | 3 | 0 | 116 | 18 | 188 | 29 | 66 | 10 | 269 | 42 | 642 | 41 |

TABLE 2.52
1978 *American Library Directory* Popular Library Age by
Denomination

| Denomination | Number of Libraries | No Response | Total Libraries | Mean Number of Years |
|---|---|---|---|---|
| Baptist | 33 | 50 | 83 | 40 |
| Christian | 8 | 11 | 19 | 39 |
| Churches of Christ | 0 | 0 | 0 | |
| Congregational | 5 | 23 | 28 | 40 |
| Episcopal/Anglican | 19 | 23 | 42 | 48 |
| Independent | 2 | 3 | 5 | 80 |
| Lutheran | 26 | 27 | 53 | 44 |
| Methodist | 23 | 32 | 55 | 40 |
| Other Denominations | 24 | 43 | 67 | 50 |
| Presbyterian | 52 | 63 | 115 | 40 |
| U.C.C. | 4 | 9 | 13 | 36 |
| Summary | | | | |
| Jewish | 98 | 65 | 163 | 45 |
| Roman Catholic | 25 | 19 | 44 | 53 |
| All Protestant | 196 | 284 | 480 | 43 |
| Total | 319 | 368 | 687 | 44 |

TABLE 2.53
1988 *American Library Directory* Popular Library Age by
Denomination

| Denomination | Number of Libraries | No Response | Total Libraries | Mean Number of Years |
|---|---|---|---|---|
| Baptist | 41 | 30 | 71 | 39 |
| Christian | 9 | 8 | 17 | 39 |
| Churches of Christ | 2 | 0 | 2 | 28 |
| Episcopal/Anglican | 20 | 14 | 34 | 39 |
| Independent | 1 | 2 | 3 | 25 |
| Lutheran | 26 | 16 | 42 | 37 |
| Mennonite | 1 | 3 | 4 | 40 |
| Methodist | 32 | 32 | 64 | 37 |
| Other Denominations | 37 | 40 | 77 | 49 |
| Presbyterian | 53 | 44 | 97 | 38 |
| U.C.C. | 7 | 6 | 13 | 29 |
| Summary | | | | |
| Jewish | 124 | 63 | 187 | 43 |
| Roman Catholic | 20 | 11 | 31 | 52 |
| All Protestant | 229 | 195 | 424 | 40 |
| Total | 373 | 269 | 642 | 41 |

TABLE 2.54

1978 and 1988 *American Library Directory* Longitudinal Study
Congregational (Type) Library Age by Denomination

| | ------------------1 9 7 8------------------ | | | | ------------------1 9 8 8------------------ | | | | Percentage |
| Denomination | Number of Libraries | No Response | Total Libraries | Mean Years | Number of Libraries | No Response | Total Libraries | Mean Years | Change 1978–88 |
|---|---|---|---|---|---|---|---|---|---|
| Baptist | 33 | 50 | 83 | 40 | 41 | 30 | 71 | 39 | −2.5 |
| Christian | 7 | 11 | 18 | 36 | 9 | 8 | 17 | 39 | 8.3 |
| Churches of Christ | 0 | 0 | 0 | — | 2 | 0 | 2 | 28 | 0 |
| Episcopal/ Anglican | 18 | 23 | 41 | 44 | 19 | 14 | 33 | 40 | −9 |
| Independent | 0 | 3 | 3 | — | 0 | 1 | 1 | — | 0 |
| Lutheran | 26 | 27 | 53 | 44 | 26 | 16 | 42 | 37 | −16 |
| Mennonite | 0 | 3 | 3 | — | 1 | 3 | 4 | 40 | 0 |
| Methodist | 23 | 32 | 55 | 40 | 32 | 32 | 64 | 37 | −7.5 |
| Other Denoms. | 24 | 62 | 86 | 41 | 33 | 38 | 71 | 46 | 12 |
| Presbyterian | 52 | 63 | 115 | 40 | 53 | 44 | 97 | 38 | −5 |
| U.C.C. | 4 | 9 | 13 | 36 | 7 | 6 | 13 | 29 | −19 |
| Summary | | | | | | | | | |
| Jewish | 90 | 60 | 150 | 45 | 112 | 58 | 170 | 43 | −4.4 |
| Roman Catholic | 7 | 7 | 14 | 51 | 4 | 4 | 8 | 33 | −35 |
| All Protestant | 187 | 283 | 470 | 41 | 223 | 192 | 415 | 39 | −4.9 |
| Total | 284 | 350 | 634 | 42 | 339 | 254 | 593 | 40 | −4.8 |

Median age = 40 years

TABLE 2.55

1988 *American Library Directory* Popular Library Age by Library
Expenditures

| Library Expenditures | Number of Libraries | No Response | Total Libraries | Mean Number of Years |
|---|---|---|---|---|
| Under $1,500 | 93 | 46 | 139 | 38 |
| $1,501–$20,000 | 63 | 20 | 83 | 46 |
| $20,001–$95,000 | 17 | 6 | 23 | 46 |
| $95,001–$220,000 | 5 | 1 | 6 | 50 |
| $220,001 and over | 1 | 0 | 1 | 80 |
| No Response | 194 | 196 | 390 | 41 |
| Total | 373 | 269 | 642 | 41 |

TABLE 2.56
1988 *American Library Directory* Oldest Popular Baptist Libraries

| Library | Age (in years) |
|---|---|
| First Baptist Church, Dallas, TX | 100 |
| First Baptist Church, Albuquerque, NM | 60 |
| First Baptist Church, San Antonio, TX | 60 |

TABLE 2.57
1988 *American Library Directory* Oldest Popular Christian Libraries

| Library | Age (in years) |
|---|---|
| Douglas Boulevard Christian Church, Louisville, KY | 60 |
| First Christian Church, St. Joseph, MO | 40 |
| First Christian Church, New Castle, PA | 40 |
| First Christian Church, Knoxville, TN | 40 |
| First Christian Church, Lubbock, TX | 40 |
| First Christian Church, Alexandria, VA | 40 |
| University Christian Church, Seattle, WA | 40 |
| Eaglewood Christian Church, Indianapolis, IN | 25 |
| High Street Christian Church, Akron, OH | 25 |

TABLE 2.58
1988 *American Library Directory* Oldest Popular Church of Christ
Libraries

| Library | Age (in years) |
|---|---|
| University Church of Christ, Murray, KY | 40 |
| Roanoke Church of Christ, Roanoke, VA | 15 |

TABLE 2.59
1988 *American Library Directory* Oldest Popular Episcopal/Anglican
Libraries

| Library | Age (in years) |
|---|---|
| Church of the Redeemer, Andalusis, PA | 100 |
| Episcopal Church Centre, Burlington, VT | 100 |
| Christ Church Cathedral, Indianapolis, IN | 60 |
| St. Thomas Episcopal Church, Battle Creek, MI | 60 |
| St. Paul's Episcopal Church, Washington, DC | 40 |
| St. Giles Episcopal Church, Northbrook, IL | 40 |

TABLE 2.59 (continued)
1988 *American Library Directory* Oldest Popular Episcopal/Anglican Libraries

| Library | Age (in years) |
| --- | --- |
| Church of the Holy Faith, Santa Fe, NM | 40 |
| St. John the Divine Cathedral, New York, NY | 40 |
| St. George's Episcopal Church, Schenectady, NY | 40 |
| St. Paul's Episcopal Church, Maumee, OH | 40 |
| St. Martin's Episcopal Church, Houston, TX | 40 |

TABLE 2.60
1988 *American Library Directory* Oldest Popular Lutheran Libraries

| Library | Age (in years) |
| --- | --- |
| Hope Lutheran Church, Milwaukee, WI | 120 |
| Oak Grove Lutheran Church, Richfield, MN | 80 |
| First Lutheran Church, Sioux Falls, SD | 80 |
| St. Martin's Evangelical Lutheran Church, Austin, TX | 60 |

TABLE 2.61
1988 *American Library Directory* Oldest Popular Methodist Libraries

| Library | Age (in years) |
| --- | --- |
| Mount Vernon Place United Methodist Church, Washington, DC | 140 |
| First United Methodist Church, Alhambra, CA | 60 |
| First United Methodist Church, Tulsa, OK | 60 |

TABLE 2.62
1988 *American Library Directory* Oldest Popular Other Denominations Libraries

| Library | Age (in years) |
| --- | --- |
| Friends Free Library of Germantown, Philadelphia, PA | 140 |
| New Church Union Swedenborgian, Boston, MA | 120 |
| Heritage Christian Reformed Church, Kalamazoo, MI | 120 |
| Unitarian Universalist Church, Binghampton, NY | 100 |
| Church of Jesus Christ of Latter-day Saints, Salt Lake City, UT | 100 |
| Pilgrim Congregational Church, Duluth, MN | 80 |
| Church of Jesus Christ of Latter-day Saints, Mesa, AZ | 60 |
| Theosophical Book Association for the Blind, Ojai, CA | 60 |

TABLE 2.62 (continued)
1988 *American Library Directory* Oldest Popular Other Denominations Libraries

| Library | Age (in years) |
| --- | --- |
| First Congregational Church, Colorado Springs, CO | 60 |
| Friends Meeting, Washington, DC | 60 |
| Crombaugh Memorial Public Church, Le Roy, IL | 60 |
| First Christian Reformed Church, Zeeland, MI | 60 |
| United Lodge of Theosophists, New York, NY | 60 |

TABLE 2.63
1988 *American Library Directory* Oldest Popular Presbyterian Libraries

| Library | Age (in years) |
| --- | --- |
| Westminster Church, Detroit, MI | 80 |
| First Presbyterian Church, San Diego, CA | 60 |
| First Presbyterian Church, Greensboro, NC | 60 |
| Westminster Presbyterian Church, Oklahoma City, OK | 60 |
| First Presbyterian Church, Yakima, WA | 60 |

TABLE 2.64
1988 *American Library Directory* Oldest Popular United Church of Christ Libraries

| Library | Age (in years) |
| --- | --- |
| St. John Evangelical United Church of Christ, Collinsville, IL | 40 |
| St. Paul's United Church of Christ, Evansville, IN | 40 |
| Trinity United Church of Christ, St. Louis, MO | 40 |
| United Church of Christ, Vermillion, OH | 40 |
| Plymouth Congregational United Church of Christ, Burlington, WI | 25 |
| Pilgrim Church, Toledo, OH | 15 |

TABLE 2.65
1988 *American Library Directory* Oldest Popular Jewish Libraries

| Library | Age (in years) |
| --- | --- |
| Congregation Rodeph Shalom, Philadelphia, PA | 180 |
| Congregation Mishkan Israel, Hamden, CT | 160 |
| Temple Beth El, Birmingham, MI | 120 |

TABLE 2.65 (continued)
1988 *American Library Directory* Oldest Popular Jewish Libraries

| Library | Age (in years) |
| --- | --- |
| Young Men's and Women's Hebrew Association, New York, NY | 120 |
| Temple-Congregation Shouner Emunim, Sylvania, OH | 120 |
| The Temple, Cleveland, OH | 100 |
| Temple Beth-el Congregation, Providence, RI | 100 |
| Temple Emanu-el, Birmingham, AL | 80 |
| Temple Emanu-el, Tucson, AZ | 80 |
| Temple Beth Zion, Buffalo, NY | 80 |
| Jewish Community Center, Nashville, TN | 80 |
| Temple De Hirsch Sinai, Seattle, WA | 80 |
| Jewish Public Library, Montreal, PQ | 80 |

TABLE 2.66
1988 *American Library Directory* Oldest Popular Roman Catholic
Libraries

| Library | Age (in years) |
| --- | --- |
| Petit Seminaire de Québec, Quebec City, PQ | 225 |
| Union St. Jean Baptiste, Woonsocket, RI | 80 |
| Oratoire St. Joseph, Montreal, PQ | 80 |
| Old St. Mary's Church, San Francisco, CA | 60 |
| Catholic Lending Library, Hartford, CT | 60 |
| Cardinal Ritter, St. Louis, MO | 60 |
| Commission des Écoles Catholiques, Montréal, PQ | 60 |
| Stamford Catholic Library, Stamford, CT | 40 |
| Our Lady Queen of Martyrs Church, Birmingham, MI | 40 |
| Catholic Information Center, Philadelphia, PA | 40 |
| St. Francis Chapel, Providence, RI | 40 |
| Church of the Incarnation, Dallas, TX | 40 |
| Catholic Information Center, Toronto, ON | 40 |

TABLE 2.67
1978 *American Library Directory* Chief Librarian's Gender for Popular
Libraries by Library Type

| Type of Library | ----------Chief Librarian's Gender---------- | | | | | | Number of Libraries |
|---|---|---|---|---|---|---|---|
| | Male | % | Female | % | No Response | % | |
| Popular | 85 | 12 | 330 | 48 | 272 | 40 | 687 |
| Congregational | 68 | 11 | 308 | 49 | 258 | 41 | 634 |
| Parochial | 7 | 26 | 10 | 37 | 10 | 37 | 27 |
| Public | 10 | 38 | 12 | 46 | 4 | 15 | 26 |

TABLE 2.68
1988 *American Library Directory* Chief Librarian's Gender for Popular
Libraries by Library Type

| Type of Library | -----------Chief Librarian's Gender----------- | | | | | | Number of Libraries |
|---|---|---|---|---|---|---|---|
| | Male | % | Female | % | No Response | % | |
| Popular | 82 | 13 | 506 | 79 | 54 | 8 | 642 |
| Congregational | 65 | 11 | 474 | 80 | 54 | 9 | 593 |
| Parochial | 6 | 25 | 18 | 75 | 0 | 0 | 24 |
| Public | 11 | 44 | 14 | 56 | 0 | 0 | 25 |

TABLE 2.69
1978 and 1988 *American Library Directory* Demographics: Chief
Librarian's Gender by Edition Showing Percentage Change

| | --------------------------Popular-------------------------- | | | | |
|---|---|---|---|---|---|
| | 1978 | % of Sample | 1988 | % of Sample | % Change |
| Male | 85 | 12 | 82 | 13 | −4 |
| Female | 330 | 48 | 506 | 79 | 53 |
| No Response | 272 | 40 | 54 | 8 | −80 |
| Total | 687 | 100 | 642 | 100 | −7 |

TABLE 2.70
1978 and 1988 *American Library Directory* Popular Libraries
Statistical Summary

| | Variable Range from 0— | Value of 1 Standard Dev'n | Percentage of Range | Value of 1 Standard Error of the Means |
|---|---|---|---|---|
| | ------------------All Popular Libraries------------------ | | | |
| Totals | 7,092,256 | 763,607 | 188.9 | 144,819 |
| Averages | 337,726 | 36,362 | 9.0 | 6,896 |
| | ----------All Popular Libraries: Matched Pairs---------- | | | |
| Totals | 7,092,256 | 734,458 | 190.60 | 178,506 |
| Averages | 337,726 | 34,974 | 9.10 | 8,500 |
| | ----Percentage Difference: All versus Matched Pairs---- | | | |
| Averages | | −3.8 | .9 | 23.3 |

TABLE 2.71
1978 and 1988 *American Library Directory* Popular Libraries Statistical Summary Extrapolated

| | ± 1.65 Standard Deviations (90% Accur.) | Percentage Growth (Ten Yrs.) | Projected Growth (1st Year) | P.A. Projected Unit Change | Projected Variable Minimum | Projected Variable Maximum | Actual 1978 Mean | Actual 1988 Mean | Extrapolated 1998 Mean |
|---|---|---|---|---|---|---|---|---|---|
| **All Popular Libraries** | | | | | | | | | |
| Totals | 1,259,952 | 207 | 21 | 2,246 | 357,262 | 623,002 | 433,258 | 455,720 | 478,183 |
| Averages | 59,998 | 10 | 1 | 107 | 17,012 | 29,667 | 20,631 | 21,701 | 22,771 |
| **All Popular Libraries: Matched Pairs** | | | | | | | | | |
| Totals | 1,211,856 | 310 | 31 | 4,939 | 324,736 | 677,996 | 399,204 | 426,100 | 499,490 |
| Averages | 57,707 | 15 | 1 | 235 | 15,464 | 32,286 | 19,010 | 20,290 | 23,785 |
| **Percentage Difference: All versus Matched Pairs** | | | | | | | | | |
| Averages | -3.8 | 49.8 | 47.6 | 119.9 | -9.1 | 8.8 | -7.9 | -6.5 | 4.5 |

TABLE 2.72

1978 and 1988 *American Library Directory* Longitudinal Study All Popular Library Accreditations by Library Type

| Library Type | No. of Libraries | 1978 No Response | 1978 Total Libraries | 1978 Mean Accreditations | No. of Libraries | 1988 No Response | 1988 Total Libraries | 1988 Mean Accreditations | % Change 1978–88 |
|---|---|---|---|---|---|---|---|---|---|
| Popular | 4 | 683 | 687 | 1.3 | 0 | 643 | 643 | — | −100.0 |
| Congregational | 2 | 632 | 634 | 1.5 | 0 | 593 | 593 | — | −100.0 |
| Parochial | 2 | 25 | 27 | 1.0 | 0 | 25 | 25 | — | −100.0 |
| Public | 0 | 26 | 26 | 0.0 | 0 | 25 | 25 | — | 0.0 |

TABLE 2.73
1978–1988–1998 *American Library Directory* Variable Projections for Canadian and U.S. Popular Libraries

| Variable | No. of Libraries 1978 | No. of Libraries 1998 | Mean 1978 | Mean 1988 | Projection 1998 | 10-Year % Change | 1st Year % Change | P.A. Unit Change |
|---|---|---|---|---|---|---|---|---|
| | | | Canada | | | | | |
| Library age | 19 | 15 | 64 | 54 | 44 | −18.5 | −1.9 | −10 |
| City population size | 27 | 22 | 528,000 | 634,700 | 741,400 | 16.8 | 1.7 | 106,700 |
| Total library staff | 2 | 9 | 4 | 2.70 | 1.40 | −48.1 | −4.8 | −1.3 |
| Library professionals | 2 | 4 | 2 | 1.80 | 1.60 | −11.1 | −1.1 | −0.2 |
| Institutional faculty size | 0 | 0 | 0 | 0 | 0 | | | 0 |
| Institutional enrollment | 1 | 0 | 450 | 0 | 450 | | | 0 |
| Total annual library expenditure | 4 | 6 | 92,130 | 111,800 | 131,470 | 17.6 | 1.8 | 19,670 |
| Annual library expenditure on material | 4 | 10 | 19,130 | 24,000 | 28,870 | 20.3 | 2.0 | 4,870 |
| Annual library expenditure on personnel | 1 | 5 | 15,000 | 74,500 | 134,000 | 79.9 | 8.0 | 59,500 |
| Library volume holdings | 21 | 21 | 36,640 | 28,230 | 19,820 | −29.8 | −3.0 | −8,410 |
| Library periodical subscriptions | 6 | 10 | 50 | 90 | 130 | 44.4 | 4.4 | 40 |
| Library microform holdings | 0 | 1 | 0 | 50 | 100 | 100 | 10 | 50 |
| Library consortium memberships | 2 | 1 | 1 | 1 | 1 | 0 | 0 | 0 |
| Subject ints + special coll'ns + lib. publications | 10 | 12 | 2.30 | 2.30 | 2.30 | 0 | 0 | 0 |
| Totals | 99 | 116 | 691,473 | 873,432 | 105,629 | 171 | 17 | 182,409 |
| Averages | 7.1 | 8.3 | 49,391.0 | 62,388.0 | 75,449.3 | 12.2 | 1.2 | 13,029.2 |
| Percentage of Difference from U.S. Averages | −95.7 | −96.2 | 65.1 | 102.2 | 137.4 | −24.5 | −24.5 | 1,291.6 |

TABLE 2.73 (continued)
1978–1988–1998 *American Library Directory* Variable Projections for Canadian and U.S. Popular Libraries

| Variable | No. of Libraries 1978 | No. of Libraries 1988 | Mean 1978 | Mean 1988 | Projection 1998 | 10-Year % Change | 1st Year % Change | P.A. Unit Change |
|---|---|---|---|---|---|---|---|---|
| | | | U.S.A. | | | | | |
| Library age | 300 | 358 | 43 | 41 | 39 | -4.9 | -0.5 | -2 |
| City population size | 658 | 621 | 354,500 | 346,200 | 337,900 | -2.4 | -0.2 | -8,300 |
| Total library staff | 115 | 165 | 5.10 | 6.40 | 7.70 | 20.3 | 2.0 | 1.3 |
| Library professionals | 78 | 91 | 1.70 | 1.70 | 1.70 | 0 | 0 | 0 |
| Institutional faculty size | 2 | 2 | 70 | 40 | 10 | -75 | -7.5 | -30 |
| Institutional enrollment | 2 | 2 | 150 | 300 | 450 | 50 | 5 | 150 |
| Total annual library expenditure | 151 | 246 | 2,664 | 9,709 | 16,754 | 72.6 | 7.3 | 7,045 |
| Annual library expenditure on material | 106 | 220 | 1,158 | 3,180 | 5,202 | 63.6 | 6.4 | 2,022 |
| Annual library expenditure on personnel | 33 | 78 | 5,758 | 18,620 | 31,482 | 69.1 | 6.9 | 12,862 |
| Library volume holdings | 484 | 597 | 4,965 | 6,035 | 7,105 | 17.7 | 1.8 | 1,070 |
| Library periodical subscriptions | 155 | 265 | 63 | 62 | 61 | -1.6 | -.2 | -1 |
| Library microform holdings | 7 | 12 | 49,390 | 47,680 | 45,970 | -3.6 | -0.4 | -1,710 |
| Library consortium memberships | 10 | 19 | 1 | 1.20 | 1.40 | 16.7 | 1.7 | 0.2 |
| Subject ints + special coll'ns + lib. publications | 216 | 344 | 2.10 | 2.20 | 2.30 | 4.5 | 0.5 | 0.1 |
| Totals | 2,317 | 3,020 | 418,771 | 431,879 | 444,986 | 227 | 23 | 13,108 |
| Averages | 165.5 | 215.7 | 29,912.2 | 30,848.5 | 31,784.7 | 16.2 | 1.6 | 936.3 |

# 3

# AN INTRODUCTION TO POPULAR RELIGIOUS LIBRARIES

This chapter opens the discussion of the study's findings for *American Library Directory* (*ALD*) popular religious libraries. Chapters 3–4 provide a statistical and table-driven analysis and interpretation of the information discovered in the *ALD* database. Chapter 5 provides such an analysis for the Church and Synagogue Library Association (CSLA) database, and chapter 6 provides a comparative analysis of the four major studies of popular religious librarianship carried out to this date in North America.

The objectives of chapters 3–4 are to analyze and discuss the essential characteristics of the popular libraries and to determine how they differed among themselves and with scholarly libraries from the thirty-first to the forty-first *ALD* editions. These chapters will search for positive relationships for the popular library field that are significant and lie within the scope of this discussion. These chapters will also make comparisons of many sorts among relevant variables in describing the new and discrete popular religious librarianship field. What is distinctive or unique about popular religious libraries? Are these libraries like nonreligious libraries? Well, yes and no, but we should have a better idea about the answer to that question by the end of chapter 4.

Since no accurate measure of the universe of popular religious libraries was available, the completeness of the list of libraries included in this study cannot be ascertained with certainty. The author assumes that it was quite *incomplete* in both 1978 and 1988, since it totaled only 642 and 687 libraries out of the twenty-five thousand (2–3 percent) estimated in chapter 1 to be the size of the U.S. congregational library universe. And Canada must be added to this group. See chapter 1 and chapter 6 for the frequencies discussed, chapter 2 for a discussion of the popular library data projections to 1998, and appendix B for the term working definitions used in the chapters.

In carrying out their objectives, the two chapters (3–4) attempt to discover the essential nature of popular religious librarianship. Both are introductory chapters. Popular religious libraries are like scholarly ones in certain of their information patterns but are clearly different from them in others. Of course, chapter 3 and 4 libraries must resemble nonreligious public and school libraries in certain ways, but there were no nonreligious library databases available with which to compare the entire popular library group. In any case, the present parochial school and public library databases were so small (often no more than 15–20 active cases per table) that comparisons were hard to make with any other group. And there was no group with which to compare the congregational libraries that could be regarded as representing a unique library type or as representing a hybrid form of special and school library.

The chapter's value will not be primarily in its displays of statistical findings but in the relationships discovered between the variables and in the implications of these relationships, to the extent that we can interpret them. However, many of the findings will be hard to interpret beyond the fairly obvious. While popular religious libraries have been studied in a serious manner before, the number of these studies is quite small. Chapters 1, 5, and 6 discuss earlier studies. Several aspects of the statistical picture described in chapter 2 apply similarly for this chapter and will not be repeated. Such important variables as type of library, region, chief librarian's gender, volume holdings, and denomination will dominate the analysis.

The three popular library types introduced in chapter 1 remain our viewing perspective here: (1) congregational, church, or synagogue or house of worship libraries, (2) private religious parochial elementary/secondary school libraries, and (3) private religious public libraries. We will also be dealing with the same breakdowns by library regions, personnel, expenditures, types of material, and denominations as were introduced in the earlier chapters. Certain basic information is provided about the variables here, including the limitations on their analysis. We will be dealing only occasionally with the contrasting scholarly religious library group.

For many variables chapter 2 provided extensive analyses and explanations. However, there is less to be said about related subjects in chapters 3–4. Many analyses were impossible to carry out here due to the lack of parent institutional information available to the scholarly library companion volume and due to the generally less active libraries existing in the popular group. Further, there were only three types of popular libraries, instead of the seven types found among scholarly libraries.

All of the study's *ALD* questionnaire questions will be used here except those dealing with the sponsoring institution's higher educational degrees, accreditation, faculty, and students (which were inappropriate to popular libraries). In all, 37 variables and 222 possible response categories and answers plus open-ended questions were studied for these libraries. The following questions or variables used in these chapters were directly relevant; they are listed in *ALD* study questionnaire order:

*American Library Directory:* Edition 31 (1978) or 41 (1988)
Nation: United States or Canada
Region: Northeast, Middle Atlantic, Southeast, Southwest, West, Rocky
    Mountains, Middle West, and Canada
State or province: Sixty-three covered
City population size: 0–3+ million
Library type: Popular—congregational, parochial school, and public denominational: thirty-two listed plus others as they occurred
Library age or founding date: 0–1981+
Staff size: Professional 0–10+; clerical 0–10+; and student assistant
    0–29+
Expenditure: Material $0–162,001+; personnel $0–300,001+; other
    $0–20,001+; and total $0–510,001+
Holdings: Book volumes 0–540,001+; periodical titles 0 –1,601+; microforms 0–100,001+; and vertical files 0–131+
Consortium memberships: 0–8
Religious subject interests
Religious special collections
Publications
Notes

Chapter 3 covers the following major and minor sections:
I.   Introduction
II.  Basic popular library characteristics
     A. Popular library information

    B. Type of library
    C. Matched library pairs
    D. Region
    E. Chief librarian's gender
    F. Denomination
    G. City population size by denomination
    H. Database analysis
III. Provision of questionnaire information
    A. Questionnaire returned
    B. Number of questions answered
    C. Library named
    D. Departmental libraries
    E. Chief librarian named
    F. Summary
IV. Library service
    A. Cooperation and automation
    B. Consortium memberships
    C. OCLC membership
    D. Local automation projects
    E. Subject interests
    F. Special collections
    G. Publications
    H. Restricted access to library service
    I. Summary
V. Special analyses
    A. Most active libraries
    B. Extended services and collections
    C. Twenty-seven growth variables combined
VI. Chapter summary
VII. Notes

## Basic Popular Library Characteristics

This section will describe popular library characteristics of two kinds—first, basic variables that include sponsorship, market, material collection, and staffing and second, several previously used variables like library type, region, chief librarian's gender, denomination, and city population size. The entire section is summarized at the end.

## Popular Library Information

How do popular religious libraries differ from scholarly ones? Sponsorship differs completely between the two groups of libraries; there is almost no overlap. Scholarly libraries are sponsored by scholarly institutions — universities, colleges, history/archive collections, denominational offices, and convents and monasteries. These are institutions operated by adults for use by other adults.

Popular libraries are sponsored and operated by adults for use primarily by children and young people, as well as some adults. They are sponsored by elementary and secondary schools and by public library-type institutions but mostly by houses of worship. These institutions collect, process, and make available material written for children and young people and to a lesser extent for adults. The philosophy of popular library service is oriented around popularization and service at a simple and introductory level. The scholarly library material collection is generally erudite, focused, and adult, while the popular library collection is simple and is aimed at less mature, less specialized readers.

Since higher educational information is not particularly relevant for popular libraries, less might be known about their institutional setting than is known about the setting of the scholarly library group. For popular libraries, the *ALD* gave no house of worship membership size, faculty, or Sunday school enrollment information, parochial school enrollment or faculty size, public library persons served, or other such information useful in profiling these institutions and their users. In lieu of *ALD* information, the author recommends that the reader study chapter 5 carefully for background information on the CSLA congregations and their associated institutions, which were similar in most ways to those of the *ALD* congregational libraries, similar even to the point of duplication of certain libraries in both databases creating *ALD*-CSLA matching pairs.[1]

Also in lieu of *ALD* information, the author will briefly summarize his present understanding of popular library sponsoring or parent groups, superficial though it is. Congregational libraries were usually sponsored by a house of worship in a specific denomination — a single church or synagogue. Since most such institutions were small themselves, much smaller than those groups sponsoring most scholarly religious institutions, it is not surprising that their libraries also were usually much smaller than scholarly libraries. On the other hand, a few congregations were surprisingly large and prosperous, employed a number of full-time paid staff members, and supported large and active libraries or media centers.

Specific parochial schools or religious or denominational boards of education that served an entire area or city sponsored most parochial school libraries. These may represent any denomination and may have a religious order or a house of worship or Catholic bishop as their sponsor. Institutional sponsors of public libraries were harder to characterize because they showed much less uniformity. Religious public libraries may have been established and supported by a private religious organization or society, by a YMCA, YWCA, or YMWHA, or a Catholic Newman Center, a church parish or other kind of house of worship, or another kind of group.

The market for popular library service differed significantly from that for scholarly library service also. Scholarly library users for the most part were higher education students and faculty members, plus researchers, for the most part, while popular library users were elementary and secondary school plus Christian Sunday school and Hebrew school students and faculty members, again for the most part. There is some overlap and an obvious mean age difference between the two groups of users.

The two types of material collections contrast in reading level, the scholarly being aimed at adults and the popular being aimed at children and young adults or at general recreational devotional reading. Two tables show popular library volume holdings, one by library type and one by total annual library expenditure. Table 3.1 for 1988 shows mean volumes for congregational libraries to be 5,737, mean parochial school volumes to be 20,490 and mean public library volumes to be 17,800. Overall popular library mean was 6,776 volumes. This library mean contrasts profoundly with the scholarly library mean of 112,600 volumes.

Table 3.2 for 1988 shows the relation between popular library volume holdings and total expenditure. Did these two variables correlate positively? Yes, they did. Libraries with expenditures under $1,500 averaged only 4,060 volumes held, whereas libraries with expenditures of $20,001–95,000 averaged 14,770 volumes holdings.

If we reverse the order of these two variables, longitudinal table 3.3 shows us the mean popular library expenditures per volume. We see there for those 1988 libraries with volume numbers under 3,500, that the mean total expenditure was $1,805. However, for libraries with 3,500–20,000 volumes, the mean expenditure was $12,070. Thus, the correlation between the two variables worked in both directions. Note that the top 9 percent of the congregational libraries had 10,000 or more volumes, a large number for such libraries, and further that the top three congregational libraries spent a total of $95,000 or more per year—large expenditures. In terms of expenditures per volume, it is clear that under 3,500 volumes expenditures were about $0.52 per volume, whereas at 20,000 volumes expenditures averaged somewhat more than $0.60 per volume. In other words, smaller libraries are more cheaply run per volume on the average.

Library staffing differed in subtle ways as well. It was composed primarily of adults in both fields, but most scholarly libraries contained one or more specialists in technical library work, while most popular libraries did not. The latter tended to attract staff members oriented to providing part-time, unpaid, public service for children or young adults, whereas scholarly libraries usually attracted full-time, paid and scholarly level staff members oriented to adult service.

## Type of Library

The type of library is a matter that can be dealt with easily. Master longitudinal table 3.4 shows 1978 and 1988 popular libraries' basic data. By percentage, popular libraries were composed of the congregational—92 percent, parochial school—4 percent, and public libraries—4 percent in 1978. In the combined scholarly and popular studies only the senior college group was larger than the congregational group and then only by one percent. Clearly, the popular library group was dominated by its congregational libraries except in renegade Canada.

The reader should remember, however, that the proportion of popular libraries was only 33 percent in 1978 and 31 percent in 1988 of the size of the entire scholarly-popular library database. The popular group was about half as large as the scholarly library group in each year. Note also that the number of popular libraries fell somewhat from 1978 to 1988, from 687 to 642, a loss of 45 libraries, or 7 percent of the total. The author does not know the reason for this drop. Congregational libraries absorbed most of this loss by dropping forty-one libraries, from 634 to 593, or a loss of 6 percent. Parochial school libraries lost three of their number during the decade, or 11 percent. Public libraries fell from twenty-six to twenty-four libraries, for a loss of 8 percent. One library was reclassified between databases (1978 to 1988) producing a gross decline of forty-five libraries.

Table 3.5 for 1988 shows that more than half of the public libraries were located in Canada and the Northeast. Canada also had almost half of the parochial school libraries but only one half of 1 percent of the congregational libraries! More than half of the congregational libraries were located in the Middle West and Middle Atlantic regions.

## Matched Library Pairs

For matched pairs of libraries (the same library in both the 1978 and 1988 editions), the number of libraries was not quite identical between the 1978 and 1988 databases, 471 to 468 libraries. Three parochial school libraries were reclassified as scholarly or as another popular type during the decade. Since the numbers in the entire databases were 687 and 642, the matched pairs constituted 69 percent and 73 percent of each total. The no longer listed and the newly listed groups were proportionately more numerous and qualitatively weaker for popular than for scholarly libraries.

The percentage of the parochial school and public libraries that were no longer listed from 1978 to 1988 was 42 percent, whereas the same percentage for congregational libraries 1978–88 was 27 percent. Therefore, the percentage of matched pairs for congregational libraries was 55 percent, higher than for parochial school and public libraries. This leads us to assume that the congregational libraries in the samples were of somewhat higher stability and quality than the corresponding parochial school and public libraries. For popular libraries, 31 percent of them were no longer listed or dropped out, almost a third of the total for 1978. Also, for popular libraries 27 percent were newly listed, new in the *ALD* for 1988. For congregational libraries only, 31 percent of them were newly listed and 26 percent were no longer listed. These were large percentages relative to the total sample sizes.

Longitudinal table 3.5 for 1978–88 showed a cross tabulation of popular library types and regions for the matched pairs group. Only congregational libraries had enough popular library cases to be statistically significant. Except for the Middle West and Middle Atlantic regions, all of the other regions were statistically small, and Canada and the Rocky Mountains regions together constituted only 2 percent of the total.

Table 3.6 1978–1988 showed matched pairs by region. Largest region was the Middle West with Middle Atlantic next. Smallest were Rocky Mountains and Canada with only small numbers of libraries, based on 1988 figures. Looking at table 3.7 1978–1988 by denomination and for matched pairs, the reader can make interesting comparisons between scholarly and popular libraries by year. Jewish and Presbyterians led the table in popularity. Churches of Christ, Independent, and Mennonite were the smallest popular library denominations.

## Region

Longitudinal table 3.8 shows the popular religious library database by year, 1978 and 1988, and its percentage breakdown by region. It enables the reader to compare the no longer listed (1978) and the newly listed (1988) libraries. The percentages are similar between the two percentage columns, but compare the West (53.5 percent for 1978 and 25.6 percent for 1988), and Canada (which shows 42.3 percent for 1978 and 9.2 percent for 1988) by their percentages. Each showed a significant change over the decade. Matched pairs and no longer listed and newly listed libraries can be compared using tables 3.6 and 3.8 also.

Additional tables show other aspects of what happens when popular library denominations are divided by region. Also, the popular library distribution differed from that of the scholarly libraries by region. See tables 2.30 for 1978 and 2.31 for 1988. In 1978 frequency, the Jewish group led the popular libraries in the Middle Atlantic, Middle West, and the Northeast. The Baptists led in Southeast and Southwest. Other Denominations led in the West and Rocky Mountains regions, and Roman Catholics led in Canada. See tables 3.9 for 1978 and 3.10 for 1988.

Strong second-ranking denominations were the Other Denominations in the Northeast, Congregationals in the Northeast and Rocky Mountains, Presbyterians in the Southeast and West, Methodists in the Southwest, Lutherans in the Middle West, and Jewish in the West and Canada. So Jewish, Baptist, and Other Denominations were more widespread in their regional popularity than were the other popular library denominations.

By 1988 the Jewish denomination was even stronger. It was strong in every popular library region except for the Southwest and Rocky Mountains. Congregationalists were again prominent in the Northeast and the Rocky Mountains. Baptists were strong in the Southeast and Southwest. Other Denominations emerged in the West, Lutherans in the Rocky Mountains and Middle West, and Roman Catholics in Canada.

Tables 3.9 for 1978 and 3.10 for 1988 show the regions most frequented by popular libraries by denominations and library type. The Middle West and Middle Atlantic regions led the first table and the Middle West and Canada regions led the second one. Table 3.11 for 1988 showed the most popular library regions by denomination for the popular religious libraries. The Southeast with six and the Middle West with five library listings dominated the 1978 table's first category. For 1988 the Southeast with five and the Middle West with six listings dominated the first category. In the second and third categories of popularity the Middle Atlantic ranked high.

Table 3.12 for 1978 and 1988 shows a distribution that is similar to the one discussed above. This table shows how each popular library denomination was divided among the regions in each year. For instance, for 1988, the Middle West laid large claims to the Lutheran group, as it did for the UCC. The table also suggests that the Jewish group dominated the Northeast region in 1988, as it did the Middle Atlantic region. Many data cells were occupied by small frequencies.

Table 3.13 for 1978 shows the volume holdings of popular libraries by region. The volume holdings were heavily weighted on the small side, overall mean size being 6,282 volumes. Almost half of the libraries had 3,500 or fewer volumes. Largest regional mean was that of Canada with 36,648 volumes, but that figure represented only twenty-one cases. The weakest or poorest regions, the Middle Atlantic and Southeast regions, averaged less than 4,000 volumes.

In summary, for this subsection by region and denomination, the results were complicated, but the Jewish group, especially, and also the Baptist and Other Denominations groups, were the regional leaders. We may note that the Canadian region was strong for parochial schools and public libraries as well.

## Chief Librarian's Gender

Type of library by chief librarian's gender showed popular libraries as a whole to reflect a male:female ratio of 1.0:4.0. Both parochial school libraries (1.0:1.4) and public libraries (1.0:1.2) proved to be much less female dominated than were congregational libraries (1.0:4.5). So much for 1978. For 1988, we see an even stronger overall popular library female domination, 1.0:6.2, and an even stronger corresponding congregational library female prevalence, 1.0:7.3. Even parochial school libraries had a ratio favoring females, 1.0:1.3, for that year. Table 3.14 shows a 1988 ratio of 1.0:6.2; for matched pairs we see a ratio of 1.0:6.4 in table 3.15; and for no longer listed and newly listed libraries, table 3.16 shows 1.0:5.7, all strongly favoring females and differing little, although in some cases significantly, from each other.

By region, popular libraries were uneven everywhere in terms of men vs. women chief librarians. They were most heavily male in Canada (1.0:1.2) (45 percent), and most heavily female in the Middle West (1.0:7.0) and the Middle Atlantic (1.0:3.8) regions. So much for 1978. In 1988 the results were similar; no region registered 1.0:1.0 male:female. The Middle West had the heaviest end of the male:female ratio, 1.0:8.3. Overall in 1988, the male:female ratio here was 1.0:6.2.

Finally, we can look at city population size by chief librarian's gender for popular libraries, table 3.17 for 1988. What we see there may surprise us. While the number of persons covered by the table is 86 percent female, the mean city population size for males is 39 percent larger than that for females! Males headed libraries in cities of 476,100 on the average, while females headed libraries in cities of 342,000 mean population. So, based on this table, we must conclude that males were found more often in larger and females most often in smaller cities. Notice the small number of No Response libraries here. In summary, females dominated popular religious library chief librarians' gender by at least a 4:1 ratio, although males held the best and most cosmopolitan positions.

## Denomination

Because denominational affiliation was a defining attribute of religious libraries as a study field, we must discuss the denominations in relation to several variables before we can claim to understand popular religious institutions and libraries well. Popular religious libraries are defined by reference to their parent institutions' denominations. Sometimes denominational tables reflected a special concentration by state or region for a particular denomination, as we have just seen above, as with the prominence of Congregational institutions in the Northeast region. At other times, little which was distinctive could be found in terms of denominational distribution.

The popular library databases differed in denominational emphases from those for scholarly libraries. Note that certain helpful introductory denominational tables that cover both scholarly and popular libraries are found in chapter 2. Longitudinal table 3.18 for 1978 and 1988 shows the denominations by frequency in alphabetical order.

Table 3.18 for 1988 shows some curious ratios between scholarly and popular libraries. For instance, those denominations in which the scholarly: popular ratio is much higher than would normally be expected: Baptist, Assemblies of God, Brethren, Churches of Christ, Churches of God, Independent, and Roman Catholic. On the other hand, the following are the denominations for which the scholarly:popular ratio is lower than one would expect: Congregational, Episcopal/Anglican, Jewish, and Presbyterian. This author can give no further reason for these differences in ratios except random occurrence, but a reader who is quite familiar with the psychology and sociology of each of these denominations can probably suggest certain influential factors for each one. Obviously, certain denominations tend deliberately toward either academic institutional or congregational library development, but not both.

Table 3.19 for 1978 breaks down the popular library database by denomination. The leading popular library denominations in size order in 1978 were, Jewish, Presbyterian, Baptist, Other Denominations, Methodist, Lutheran, Roman Catholic, and Episcopal/Anglican. Popular library leaders in size in 1988 were, in order, Jewish, Presbyterian, Other Denominations, Baptist, Methodist, Lutheran, Episcopal/Anglican, and Roman Catholic. The denomination at the bottom level by 1978 size was Independent, and in 1988 it was several smaller groups—Churches of Christ, Independent, and Mennonite. The major denominational difference between popular and scholarly groups was the preeminence of Jews in the popular groups and the prominence of Roman Catholics in the scholarly group.

Other tables showed the percentage of each denomination that belonged to each one of the three subtypes of popular libraries. For congregational libraries there was much variation among denominations, but Jewish and Presbyterian led, while Churches of Christ, Independent, and Roman Catholic were small in percentage. For parochial schools, Jewish and Roman Catholics led, and for public libraries Jewish, Roman Catholic, and Other Denominations led among their small proportions. Several tables (not shown) for 1978 and 1988 show the breakdown by denomination for the databases. Jewish libraries constituted almost a fourth of the total number of public libraries in 1978, whereas Roman Catholics constituted only one seventeenth of them. In 1988 the gap widened for Jews. They constituted 29 percent of popular libraries and Roman Catholic, only 1 percent of them.

Note that the Unknown group was larger than certain of the known denominations but was rejected for inclusion among the "top thirteen" because of its "unknown" nature. With the rise in number of Jewish libraries, a modest rise in the ratio of Jewish-Roman Catholic vs. Protestant libraries could be predicted. For popular libraries that ratio was 30 percent Jewish-Roman Catholic in 1978 and rose to 34 percent in 1988.

Note that the first three denominations in size in each year—Jewish, Presbyterian, and Baptist in 1978 and Jewish, Presbyterian, and Other Denominations in 1988—already accounted for more than half of the popular libraries. Note also that the Baptist scholarly library surge forward in the 1980s was not echoed in the Baptist popular library sample which dropped in frequency instead—eighty-three to seventy-one, or 14 percent—in that decade. Longitudinal table 3.20 enables us to compare scholarly with popular and 1978 with 1988 libraries by denomination. We can identify several interesting popular library changes. See how the number of Episcopal/Anglican, Lutheran, Roman Catholic, Baptist, and

Other Denominations libraries fell off in 1988, while Jewish and Methodist libraries grew in number, for instance.

Table 3.21 for 1988 shows a final analysis for denomination. The number of tables is listed on which each denomination's libraries appeared. Check the numbers in the 7–9 and 10+ columns. We can note that the mean number of tables per denomination was similar but Jewish led in number, with Presbyterian and Baptist following. This means that Jewish libraries appeared on the highest number of the book's "highest of the high" tables among all of the popular library denominations. Of course, in addition to having a number of excellent libraries, there were quite a lot of Jewish popular libraries, all competing for top ranks.

## City Population Size by Denomination

A series of tables was made that showed the libraries located in the largest cities for each denomination. It provided interesting information on these libraries and gave us a further idea of whether the denomination had libraries located primarily in cities or in rural areas and small towns. All tables were for 1988 only. For table 3.22 we see five *Baptist* libraries, and all were located in large cities. The *Christian* library table showed much the same thing, all libraries located in large cities. Only two libraries represented the *Churches of Christ* denomination, one in a small city and one in a town. Various interesting popular libraries were highlighted in these tables.

*Episcopal/Anglican* libraries can be seen in Table 3.23, and all were located in large cities. The three libraries at the top of the table were all located in cities of over one million in population. *Independent* library cities ranged down from 1.5 million to 2,500 in population, over a range of four libraries only. This is a different picture from the one found for scholarly libraries. *Lutheran* libraries were numerous in Milwaukee, as table 3.24 shows, but none were located in cities of over one million population. Small towns were the mode for *Mennonite* libraries. Large cities were most numerous among the *Methodist* libraries in table 3.25. The population level was highest for *Other Denominations* libraries, the eighth largest city on its list being the Middle Atlantic metropolis Philadelphia.

Popular *Presbyterian* libraries in table 3.26 were located in large cities ranging from 1.5 million down to 0.8 million population; from Detroit and Houston down to large cities in all parts of the United States. However, *United Church of Christ* libraries were not usually located in large cities, only the top three libraries being in cities of above 700,000 population. This was similar to the UCC picture for scholarly libraries. All *Jewish* libraries in table 3.27 were located in large cities, all of the table being made up of cities of four million plus. So we see again that most denominations contained several institutions which were located in large North American cities. The only exceptions were the Mennonites and the United Church of Christ.

Longitudinal table 3.28 shows city population size by denomination for the United States only. Removing Canada leaves much the same picture as before. However, in 1988 Roman Catholic had the largest mean population, 585,200, with Episcopal/Anglican next at 488,900 population. Smallest cities were found in the UCC and Methodist denominations, with 98,650 and 181,100 population. This leaves a ratio of 5.9:1.0 between the largest and smallest denomination population by city. Jewish and Roman Catholic mean city populations were much larger than Protestant populations.

In summary thus far, we have examined the three types of popular libraries and have confirmed the fact that the congregational library type dominated the entire database. In general, the matched pairs, no longer listed, and newly listed groups performed as follows. The matched pairs group constituted the majority of the popular libraries and were somewhat stronger in tables than was the entire database. Hence, the matched pairs constituted a somewhat superior group. The no longer listed (which were listed in the 1978 *ALD* but not the 1988) and the newly listed (which were listed in the 1988 *ALD* but not the 1978) groups were smaller and somewhat weaker than the entire database. The ratio of Jewish-Roman Catholic vs. Protestant libraries moved somewhat toward the Jewish-Roman Catholic side. By denomination we have found that Jewish and Presbyterian libraries were most numerous and that Roman Catholic, Churches of Christ, and Independent were least numerous in the popular library database.

## Database Analysis

Longitudinal table 2.42 enables us to compare 1978 and 1988, scholarly vs. popular, no longer listed vs. newly listed, matched pairs, the two editions, and the percentage changes by library type.[2] Note that certain decade reclassifications forced the matched pairs to match only within the entire samples and to be slightly deficient for popular libraries only. Also, note that the matched pairs averaged almost 70 percent of the size of the entire popular library database. The no longer listed and the newly listed libraries differed little between themselves in this table, but they were only a third of the size of the entire databases. Note also that the overall popular library 1978–88 change was small and that the number of popular libraries dropped slightly for 1988, by 6.6 percent.

We may consider popular libraries for no longer listed and newly listed libraries and consult longitudinal table 2.42 again. The first problem encountered with matched pairs, no longer listed, and newly listed libraries is the small size of the latter two subsamples. Often this makes it impossible to study any type of library other than congregational because the numbers of the other library types are too small to enable us to identify significant differences.

Table 2.42 shows matched pairs to have lost 19 percent of its number by 1988 for parochial school libraries. This suggests that three 1978 popular libraries changed their character to scholarly libraries by 1988. Very unusual but true. Ninety-three percent of the popular matched pair libraries were congregational. As for congregational libraries in table 2.42, the 21 percent drop in numbers from 1978 to 1988 was high. Note, however, that for both parochial school and public libraries in both years, 41–42 percent of the libraries were in the no longer listed or the newly listed group. That is a large chunk to find in either of those small, inferior, and changeable groups.

Forty-four percent of the 1978 congregational libraries were in the no longer listed group. For 1988 this percent was 35 percent newly listed, again a large percentage to find in this unstable group. This percentage contrasts with the comparable scholarly library figures of 18 percent and 22 percent. So the weakness and instability of popular libraries was greater than that of the scholarly libraries and showed up in their frequent location in the no longer listed and the newly listed groups. Otherwise, the cause of this instability was unclear.

## Provision of Questionnaire Information

In view of the greater instability of the popular libraries, we might predict that they would perform less well than the scholarly libraries on questionnaire return as well as on other variables. Certainly provision of popular library questionnaire information was not uniformly strong. Many libraries failed to complete the *ALD* questionnaires and return them to the publisher. This section will discuss the ability of popular libraries to provide the *ALD* information needed—questionnaire return, library names, chief librarians named, number of questions answered, and departmental libraries.

## Questionnaire Return

Among the phenomena that were investigated for this section were library questionnaire return to the publisher and the provision of the specific information requested. Scholarly libraries were poor at return in the 1978 edition but were almost perfect in the 1988 edition. Likewise, popular libraries were poor at return in the earlier but improved at return in the later edition. Almost all popular library denominations did poorly in 1978, only a third of the questionnaires having been returned, on the average. In the case of 1988, however, only one percent of popular libraries failed to return their questionnaires.

Just why the questionnaire return for 1988 improved so much over the return of 1978 is unclear. Presumably the 1988 *ALD* editors made a stronger effort to obtain a complete return than their predecessors did, or they made a determined effort this time to obtain the needed information elsewhere. Incidentally, the regions that were poorest to return differed between the scholarly and the popular libraries.

In more specific terms, we were concerned to identify the libraries that failed to return their questionnaires, primarily for 1978. What were their unique characteristics? We can examine these characteristics by library type, by region, by denomination, and by expenditure. Most 1978 popular *library types* did poorly here, as longitudinal table 3.29 shows. Two-thirds of all 1978 popular libraries failed to return their questionnaires, as compared with a third of the scholarly libraries. Two-thirds of the 1978 congregational libraries and 70 percent of the parochial schools failed to return their questionnaires. Public libraries did somewhat better since 46 percent of them returned the questionnaires.

If we examine the 1978 questionnaire return by *region* in table 3.30, we see that the Northeast was the poorest in return with the Middle Atlantic coming next. Canada (it led the scholarly library return list also), the West, the Southwest were best in questionnaire return. However, there was only a small difference between the various regions.

For 1978, which *denomination* was the worst offender in failing to return *ALD* questionnaires? The highest percentage of *nonreturn* was found in the Churches of Christ (100 percent nonreturn), Episcopal/Anglican, Independent (80 percent nonreturn), and UCC (85 percent nonreturn) denominations. Best return was made by Lutherans (60 percent nonreturn) and Presbyterians (63 percent nonreturn). See table 3.31 for 1978 and longitudinal table 3.32 for 1978 and 1988. Another table showed that most of the libraries that did not return their questionnaires were located at the bottom end of the library expenditure table and spent a total of only $6,300 or less per year on the library. The 1978 popular library nonreturns were primarily small congregational libraries.

If we look at congregational libraries alone, we can ascertain which denominations failed to return their questionnaires in the largest numbers. Independent, UCC, Congregational, and Episcopal/Anglican are the denominations that were poorest in returning questionnaires in 1978. In summary, *ALD* questionnaire return was poor in 1978 but high in 1988. No information was available to explain why it improved so much over the decade. Northeast, UCC, Independent, and those libraries spending little were among the poorest ones in questionnaire return.

## Number of Questions Answered

Popular libraries were not only poor in returning questionnaires but they were also poor in providing full sets of library data for the *ALD* (and, incidentally, for this study). The typical popular library provided only a fraction of the questionnaire data called for, most and probably all of which was available locally if the chief librarian chose to find and report it.

Longitudinal table 3.33 shows a special analysis of popular libraries which, incidentally, contains few No Responses. It also shows the mean number of questionnaire questions answered by the librarians and used in the study for each library type, not responses to *ALD*'s questionnaire but to the present author's questionnaire. In both years these numbers were much smaller than the total number of questions to which the questionnaire asked them to respond—forty-one. Longitudinal table 3.34 shows for 1988 that the mean number of questions answered rose from sixteen to twenty as *volume holdings* rose from under 3,500 volumes to 20,001–100,000 volumes per popular library. Obviously the two variables correlated positively. We see also that the libraries answering few questions were those of low incomes.

By type of library, public libraries in both years and parochial school libraries for 1988 exceeded the number of questions answered by con-gregational libraries. In 1978 these popular library figures were fifteen and seventeen questions, but by 1988 they were seventeen and nineteen questions. Parochial school libraries had the largest increase per library. Note that the scholarly library mean number of questions answered con-siderably surpassed the popular library means, twenty-six and twenty-seven questions vs. fifteen and seventeen questions answered, a margin of 58–73 percent. In summary, out of forty-one questions asked, the pop-ular libraries responded typically to no more than fifteen to seventeen of them, 37–41 percent. Public and parochial school libraries did somewhat better than congregational libraries here, but none of the three library types did well. In conclusion, the questionnaires were answered only par-tially in most cases, often because the library held none of certain mate-rial or else failed to list all of the information which it had available.

## Library Names

An additional and specialized analysis of the 1978 and 1988 database in-formation was made. It dealt with the title of the library, the house of wor-ship, or other sponsoring religious institution. Several different kinds of names were discovered in this survey. Many houses of worship were numbered, for example, First Baptist Church, Second Congregational Church, and so on. How many houses of worship were numbered this way? Almost 7 percent of the libraries were numbered First, but no sig-nificant percentage was numbered beyond that. In fact, there was a slight drop in the number of numbered names by 1988.

Table 3.35 for 1978 and 1988 shows the results of these name analy-ses and provides a list of the saints, such as St. John and St. Paul, for whom certain house of worship libraries were named. Libraries named for saints constituted about one-seventh of the total number of popular li-braries.

A variety of types of names were found. Certain libraries were simply known as the Los Angeles Methodist church library, while others were called the Los Angeles Methodist Church Procopiou Library, for in-stance. In many cases the library was named for a generous donor, and in a few cases for a former chief librarian. Certain libraries were called learning centers or media resource centers instead of libraries because, presumably, they contained media material. The percentage of libraries using this new title were small, 15 percent per year, but it seemed to be growing. Others were called memorial libraries, as in the Mourides Memorial Library. About 15 percent of the libraries were so called. Still others were named after the Trinity or the Godhead, about 6 percent of the total.

In all, 44 percent of the popular libraries had a special name of some kind, although probably some overlap existed here, also. Such special names were more common among Roman Catholic and Episcopal/Anglican denominations than among other denominations. In summary, houses of worship and other institutions and their libraries were called by a variety of names from First Presbyterian to Memorial to a saint's name. Some were simply called media center. Altogether about two-fifths of them had a special name, and this was a large minority.

## Departmental Libraries

Departmental libraries were found for about one in twelve scholarly libraries in each database. However, they were much less common among popular libraries. In a few cases, perhaps one in one hundred popular libraries, a house of worship had separate adult and children's sections, but that was all. Otherwise, popular libraries were too small to need departmentalized libraries.

## Chief Librarian Named

A named chief librarian means one whose personal name was shown in the *ALD* library entry. Although called for on the *ALD* information blank sent to each library, many entries did not include that information. Whether this omission was the fault of the local person who completed the information form or was due to deliberate omission by the publisher is not known, but it is thought to have been that of the local person. In any case, omission of this item, as well as any other item in the information form, left the library and the reader with an incomplete entry. The present investigation tried to characterize the libraries omitting this name, the delinquents, first by library type, by region, by expenditures, by volumes, and then by denomination.

As we saw for scholarly libraries and chief librarians named, there was a major difference between 1978 and 1988; in 1988 the percentage named was much higher than it was in 1978. For 1978 by *type of library* only 59 percent of the congregational libraries listed the chief librarian's name; for 1988, however, 91 percent of them listed that name, though that still did not get us to a 100 percent return. For parochial school libraries, the picture was almost as bad, 63 percent of them were listed in 1978, but 100 percent were listed in 1988! For public libraries, the picture was better, with 85 percent being listed in 1978 and 100 percent in 1988. The popular library totals showed that 60 percent named the chief librarian in 1978 whereas 92 percent named that person in 1988, still one-twelfth short of 100 percent.

By *region*, Canadians were most cooperative in returning the chief librarian's name (again!), with a 74 percent figure. The Southwest (1978), West (1978), and Middle West (1988) were least cooperative in providing this name, with a net 55 percent figure. Response improved in 1988 when Rocky Mountains and Canada responded with 100 percent figures. And further, when examined by *library expenditures*, the libraries at the two lowest general expenditure levels seemed to be the libraries with the highest percentage of "no names."

Table 3.36 for 1978 shows popular library chief librarians named by *volume holdings*. The table is difficult to interpret since the Yes and No columns look much alike. In fact, while most of the smallest libraries were in the Yes column, 38 percent of them were located in the No column. We sought to identify the characteristics of the libraries that failed to name their chief librarians. In fact, the No column seems to be heaviest at the small number of volumes end while the Yes column seems to be heaviest in the larger sizes. So small volume holdings was one of the characteristics of the libraries that failed to name their chief librarians. In fact, it is possible that a few church ministers with small libraries ran the library themselves and listed no one as the librarian.

For 1978 *denominations* the best return scores were made by the Jewish libraries, 72 percent, and the poorest by the Congregationalists, Churches of Christ, and Episcopal/Anglican with 39 percent and 45 percent. In 1988, Episcopal/Anglican and Roman Catholic had 100 percent scores, but Presbyterian had only an 85 percent and Lutheran an 86 percent score. Again, there was no pattern to 1988 failure, the two denominations being similar. As a group, Jewish-Roman Catholic libraries were 5 percent higher in mean scores than the Protestant denominations in 1978 and 14 percent higher in 1988.

By denomination, there were more significant differences in another category. In the popular library percentage improvement column of longitudinal table 3.37, for chief librarians named, the Baptists, Episcopal/Anglicans, and Methodists scored high. For congregational libraries, Independent and Mennonite had few libraries in any column.

## Summary

As a conclusion to this section on the provision of questionnaire information, the section covered questionnaire return, number of questions answered, libraries named, departmental libraries, and provision of chief librarian's names. Emphasis was on the kinds of libraries that failed to provide the needed information and their characteristics. Popular library return performance was often poor in 1978 but improved greatly in 1988. The libraries doing poorly had small total expenditures in 1978, and otherwise they differed among themselves by region, denominational, and library type. More than 44 percent of all popular libraries had special names representing memorials, saints, donors, media centers, or other numbers.

## Library Service

The library service section collects a number of small and miscellaneous variables for which data could be obtained on the *ALD* questionnaire and which relate to library service. It shows their performance for popular libraries and starts with cooperation and automation. In turn this category is followed by consortium membership, OCLC membership, and local automation projects. Then we move to the subject interests and special collections listed in the *ALD*, to popular library publications and then to the curious phenomenon of the libraries that restricted use. A summary concludes the section.

### Cooperation and Automation

The existence of several analyses related to cooperation and automation implies some degree of library interest in cooperation, service improvement, and modern computer use. Although the use of cooperation and automation as service-enhancing devices in popular libraries lagged well behind their use in scholarly institutions, by 1988 certain popular libraries had begun to use all of them for that purpose. Most scholarly libraries developed an interest in these fields due in part to their location in colleges and universities where cooperation and computer use were widespread. A few popular libraries had the advantage of guidance and support in these areas from other parent institutions, schools, and administrative offices. But others did not.

As a result of the growth of interest in both cooperation among libraries and local automation projects, the *ALD* gave these fields increased attention and space in the 1988 edition. So it was from that edition that we gained most of the information that was used on these topics in other chapters. Regrettably, little additional information was provided in either *ALD* edition on any additional library service aspects, for instance, circulation, reference, or interlibrary loan.

## Consortium Membership

This section will summarize the results of the measures of popular library service that were available in the *ALD* entries on consortium membership. While the author did not expect popular libraries to have cooperative consortium memberships in any number, a few of them did report such memberships. In 1978 the number of popular libraries with these memberships were twelve (2 percent), and in 1988 the number rose to twenty (3 percent). See table 3.38 for 1988. Fifty-eight percent of the 1988 scholarly vs. 3 percent of the 1988 popular libraries were consortium members. Therefore the ratio of 1988 scholarly to popular library consortium memberships was 826 to 20, or 41.3:1.0. In parochial school and public libraries the numbers of consortium members were 13 percent and 4 percent of the total of these types of libraries respectively. This meagre result was not surprising.

Twenty 1988 libraries were members of a consortium, but only two of the twenty were members of more than one consortium. Most of these few members were congregational libraries. Perhaps the congregational libraries should form their own library consortium! Of course, so few popular libraries were consortium or OCLC members because few of them (1) carried out a significant amount of reference work, (2) had collections large enough to enable them to offer interlibrary loan service to other consortium members, (3) cataloged large numbers of scholarly books, and (4) were open for service on any but the holy day each week. However, a few popular libraries were interested in such service and joined consortia to help them perform their chosen tasks better.

Among the twenty 1988 popular library consortium members, we discovered that seven denominations were included, with only one or two libraries apiece for most of them. In that group, we note that the Douglass Boulevard Christian Church in Louisville was a member of four consortia, and the English Lutheran Church in LaCrosse belonged to two consortia. Excellent! See table 3.39 for 1988. The exceptional group in this sparse picture was the Jewish group, which included a large number of consortium members. Even in the 1978 database, eight out of the twelve popular consortium members were Jewish.

In other tables we studied the relationship between the number of consortium memberships and the total library expenditures. The tables were designed to permit annual library expenditures to rise along with the number of consortium memberships. And conversely, as consortium memberships rose, so a rise in annual library expenditures appeared. And the tables showed these things validly.

## OCLC Membership

Nor did the author expect any popular libraries to be members of the specialized and well-known Online Computer Library Center group, the best-known North American library consortium. However, one 1988 congregational library was an OCLC member. It was the Episcopal Diocese of West Texas Cathedral Library in San Antonio. Probably this library preferred to obtain cataloging from OCLC rather than from other sources. Table 3.39 shows that this library was a member of a total of three consortia.

## Local Automation Projects

Local automation projects were uncommon among popular libraries, none existing in 1978. Parochial school and public libraries were involved in none even in 1988. Congregational libraries had twenty such projects, as table 3.40 for 1988 showed. This figure represented 3 percent of all congregational libraries. Surely that percentage has grown since 1988, however. These projects seemed to be located primarily in the Middle Atlantic and Middle West regions. In spite of this small number, congregational libraries reported more automation projects than did 1988 scholarly convents/monasteries, denominational headquarters, and history/archive libraries and as many as junior college libraries aggregated.

Finally, the projects were primarily those of libraries with medium-sized (but large for popular libraries) total annual expenditures—$20,000 to $220,000 per year. Automation had come to the popular library field! It was possible to learn little else about popular library local automation projects because the small numbers usually left us with statistically non-significant and therefore unreliable figures.

In summary of this subsection, there were few measures of library service in the *ALD* and most of those existing were indirect measures. Automation and consortium memberships were given greater attention in the forty-first than in the thirty-first edition. A fundamental factor was the weak service program of many congregational libraries. However, twenty of these libraries belonged to consortia. Generally, it seemed to be the medium-sized and larger libraries that were consortium members. Local automation projects showed a few *ALD* congregational libraries to have entered the computer world of the 1980s and 1990s.

## Subject Interests

We have several analyses of the subject interests (headings) listed for *ALD* library material collections. These headings were listed in order to show the *ALD* reader what were the libraries' specialized collection development and holdings interests. The interests and their analyses appear in tables 3.41, 3.42, 3.43, 3.44, and 3.45 and cover both 1978 and 1988. The study listed only the religious headings among subject interests.

In 1978 177 scholarly and popular libraries listed 241 subject interests, and in 1988 288 of them listed 545 interests. That was 9 percent and 12 percent of the total number of libraries in these databases. The mean number of interests in each entry for 1988 was 1.9 per library for those libraries having them. The entire sample library longitudinal average showed a 63 percent decade increase in the number of libraries reporting subject interests, a strong gain. For popular libraries, number of libraries reporting subject interests was sixty-two in 1978 and forty-nine in 1988.

By type of library, in table 3.41 public libraries averaged the largest number of interests per library in 1978 and 1988 (among those libraries having any at all). About half of the public libraries had subject interests. Congregational libraries averaged 1.9 interests and 30–48 percent of them listed headings. Almost all of the libraries in which the interests appeared were congregational, 90–93 percent of the total for 1978 and

1988. The number of congregational libraries reporting subject interests was sixty in 1978 and forty-six in 1988. Decade-long percentage change was −23 percent for that group, however. Longitudinal table 3.41 shows that the number of interests dropped 1978–88 by 21 percent for popular libraries, but not for parochial or public libraries.

Longitudinal table 3.42 shows a list of subject interests and shows their popular library status. An interesting study could be made by comparing the more popular scholarly with the more popular popular headings as well as the decade-long change in interests. Table 3.43 shows the mean interests per library. Public libraries lead with 2.2 and 2.3 subject interests per library.

Longitudinal table 3.44 shows the subject interests by volume holdings. Our hypothesis was that the mean number of subject interests and mean number of volumes would show a positive correlation. In 1988 they did so, but in 1978 apparently they did not, though the small number made it difficult to interpret the number of interests per library data. The 1988 mean went up as the volume holdings rose, thereby showing that the library that had more volumes also had more subject interests indicated in the *ALD* listings. Libraries with under 3,500 volumes averaged 1.7 interests apiece, while those with 20,001–100,000 volumes averaged 2.9 interests.

Certain longitudinal tables for 1978 and 1988 show for subject interests that the popular and scholarly libraries' overall number of 1988 means was exactly even. Many of the same interests were found in both popular and scholarly library table also. What interests can be seen in these popular library tables? The following interests were most common among popular libraries: theology, Bible, Judaica, Jewish history and literature, Christian life, general religion, and church history.

## Special Collections

Special collections contained unusual books and serials or collections of rare religious books and manuscripts focused on a specific subject. Again the number of special collection listings rose over the decade along with the number of subject interests. Probably this was a function of better 1988 cataloging and classification practices.

Special collection listings were also studied, and Tables 3.45 and 3.46

show these 1978–1988 results. Only a limited number of libraries listed special collections: fifty popular libraries listed them in 1978 and one hundred did so in 1988. Only the religious collection headings were listed here—7 percent and 16 percent of the total number of popular libraries. Again, the low participation of 1978 improved somewhat in 1988. Congregational collection listings declined by 18 percent in that period, although in public libraries, there was no decline and in parochial schools the number increased somewhat.

While special collections were listed by popular libraries of all kinds, most of these libraries were congregational. Parochial school libraries contained no collections in 1978, but five of them had such collections in 1988. About a third of the public libraries scored in each database. A companion longitudinal table to table 3.44 was made for special collections, but it showed no correlation between size in number of volumes and size in number of collection listings. Curious!

For special collections in 1988, the overall mean for scholarly was close to the same as that for popular libraries, 1.4 to 1.7 collections for those libraries having any of them, perhaps signifying nothing important. The number of special collections almost doubled 1978–88, also, 72 (5 percent) libraries having them for 1978 and 135 (9 percent) for 1988. Table 3.46 listed popular library special collections. The most popular special collections were Judaica, Bibles, Christian history, theology, and philosophy. Popular libraries seemed to have a majority of the listings for only one special collection: Judaism.

Longitudinal table 3.45 shows many small numbers but a few interesting and not so small numbers also. Congregational libraries made up 92 percent of all of these popular libraries in 1978 and 1988. About 15 percent of the congregational libraries had special collections in 1988, whereas 21 percent of the parochial school libraries had them and 36 percent of the public libraries had them.

In summary, the *ALD* entries of many libraries contained lists of that library's subject emphases and interests. They were found to be most numerous proportionately in public libraries, to correlate positively with volume growth, and to average about two interests per library for those libraries listing them. The number of all libraries reporting them averaged 9 percent and 12 percent of the total number of libraries. Special collections were studied also and were found to average 1.4 to 1.7 collections per library for 1978 and 1988. They were held by 7 percent and 16 percent of all popular libraries. Most of the libraries listing these collections were congregational.

## Publications

Books, pamphlets, and serials edited and published by the libraries themselves were unusual enough in the scholarly group, but surely they were rare in the popular library group. Popular library publications were nonexistent in the 1978 *ALD*, but forty-four libraries listed them in 1988, 7 percent of the total. These forty-four libraries issued seventy publications altogether. Most libraries listed only one publication, however. This picture contrasts with the number of scholarly libraries that had publications. Most of the popular libraries listing publications were congregational, but about 20 percent of the parochial school and public libraries listed publications in 1988 as well. The mean number per participating library was 1.6 publications.

Another table, 3.47, shows the types of publications issued by popular libraries in 1988. Two-thirds of the publications were bulletins/newsletters or periodicals. A surprising number of libraries issued monographs, and a few others issued bibliographies and catalogs. See table 3.48.

A longitudinal table examined popular library publications. Periodicals and magazines dominated in popular libraries, 24 percent of the public libraries having publications. See table 3.49. Three-fourths of the popular libraries listing publications were congregational. In summary, certain popular libraries issued book, pamphlet, or serial publications, about 7 percent of the total, a strong accomplishment for them.

The lack of more popular library service-enhancing programs leads the author to say that most of these libraries were in a much more elementary developmental stage than were most scholarly religious libraries. Their lack of reader services suggests something that may be called an immature or unsophisticated development level. On the other hand, since this author increasingly regards the congregational library as a kind of part-time private school library, perhaps we should simply say that the best of them had the developmental level of an average part-time school library and that the service level provided was appropriate for such a small and local clientele and such a volunteer staff.

## Restricted Access to Library Service

Not only was popular library service limited but some popular libraries restricted use in these small libraries to members of their parent organization or persons with a particular interest. Certain libraries restricted circulation of library material, while others restricted reference service. In all, the number of libraries restricting circulation to members equaled sixty-seven, or 10 percent of all 1988 popular libraries.

See longitudinal table 3.50 for 1988. This table shows large enough (statistically significant) numbers of libraries for only Presbyterian in 1978, Baptist in 1988, and Jewish in both years to be taken seriously. And practically all of these libraries were congregational, though 7 percent of them were located in parochial schools. An interesting thing about the libraries restricting circulation or reference service was that their numbers increased by 24 percent from 1978 to 1988. This was a strong increase in restrictions and was thought to be unfortunate by this author.

To obtain other views of these variables, we can examine restricted access by library type, region, and denomination. By type of library, we see that congregational and parochial school libraries showed strong percentages of libraries that restricted use, 10 percent of all congregational libraries, for instance. In what regions were these restricting libraries located? The Middle Atlantic and the Middle West contained 63–66 percent of them. Leading denominations among the libraries practicing such restrictions were Jewish, Presbyterian, Baptist, and Roman Catholic. The Jewish group seemed to lead in many aspects of popular librarianship, including exclusiveness.

Regarding the "reference service to members only" question, 43 of 687 libraries for 1978 answered yes, and 58 of 642 libraries answered yes for 1988. These figures make up 6 percent and 9 percent of each database. Of the libraries limiting reference service to certain users, the congregational libraries made up almost half—more than all of the scholarly libraries restricting reference service combined. In summary of the discussion concerning restrictions, certain of the libraries restricted access to library use for circulation or reference service, or both. Most of these libraries were congregational, Jewish, or Presbyterian, and were located in the Middle Atlantic and Middle West regions.

Now let us study the libraries that are listed on both circulation and reference service restriction lists. See table 3.51 for 1988 for the parochial school library list. All of these five libraries maintained both restrictions on use—two Jewish and three Roman Catholic (two of which were Canadian libraries). Regrettably, the congregational library list of libraries restricting both circulation and reference service includes sixty-two libraries, so no table was made. By denomination this list was led by Jewish, Baptist, and Presbyterian denominations and by state by Missouri, Texas, Ohio, and Pennsylvania.

## Summary

In summary of the library service section, we have studied cooperation and automation and have found that few measures of library service were available. Consortium membership was held by several libraries, mostly Jewish, and one Christian denominational library was an OCLC member. Local automation projects attracted a few libraries, also, and again 1988 had all of the action. Subject interests were listed for only some libraries, and they were helpful in understanding these libraries' subject matter emphases. Headings were similar or the same as those for scholarly libraries.

Special collections were similar to the subject interest headings, and again only modest percentages of these libraries reported them. Publication was an ambitious project for a popular library to carry out and led primarily to bulletins listing new books and to booklists on specific religious subjects. Restricted access to popular libraries was a strange subject, but about 10 percent of these libraries insisted on it. Other libraries, in contrast, welcomed not only any house of worship member from any institution but also the general public, for whom they willingly served a public library function. It is regrettable that *ALD* published so little information directly on reference service and use in these libraries.

## Special Analyses

### Most Active, Extended Service, and Growth Variable Libraries

This short concluding section takes up two special popular library studies. They deal with (1) the most active libraries (in automation), (2) those libraries presenting extended services and collections, and (3) the twenty-seven growth variables combined. Finally, we will conclude with the chapter summary. To determine the most active libraries, a new and brief analysis examined library consortium membership, OCLC membership, and local automation projects combined into a master automation or active measure.

On these three measures, which denominations and regions made the highest scores? These combined measures of the most active (in automation) libraries revealed that the Jewish and Other Denominations groups scored highest, with the Baptist and Roman Catholic denominations following. By region the most active libraries were found in the Middle West and the Southwest with the Middle Atlantic, Southeast, and West following. Only one table was made for the most active libraries, table 3.39 for 1988. This table showed three libraries leading the way: the Douglass Boulevard Christian Church in Louisville, the Episcopal Diocese of West Texas Cathedral in San Antonio, and the English Lutheran Church in LaCrosse. We salute them for their automation and cooperative activity!

Longitudinal table 3.52 showed small but uniform library scores, with congregational apparently somewhat stronger than the other library types. However, only congregational libraries had enough cases to warrant examination and study. The mean additional activities score was highest by region for the West and the Southeast and lowest for the Northeast and the Rocky Mountains regions.

## Extended Services and Collections

Table 3.53 for 1988 and longitudinal table 3.54 introduce another new type of table, one based on a combination of variables concerning subject interests, special collection listings and publications and which was analyzed by type of library and by region. These tables combined each popular library's scores on these three variables to obtain a comparative and cumulative score for each one. A further specialized table examined type of library. All popular library types showed lower No Response rates and prospered on extended services and collections. With more than 60 percent of the public libraries participating, that was a strong library type. Parochial school libraries doubled their participation between 1978 and 1988. Even congregational libraries grew in participation, from 32 percent to 55 percent.

Longitudinal table 3.55 examined 1988 mean extended services and collections by denomination for popular libraries. Which denomination had the highest mean score? Christian, Episcopal/Anglican, Lutheran, and Roman Catholic were highest in 1978; and Christian and Episcopal/Anglican (again!) were highest in 1988. A mixed result. Percentage change was highest for Lutheran and Episcopal/Anglican, if we avoid the very small Ns scattered throughout the table. Longitudinal table 3.56 shows the congregational library scores only on extended services and collections by denomination. The means were 2.1 services in both 1978 and 1988, and the gain 1978 to 1988 was zero. Table 3.56 closely resembles table 3.55.

Tables 3.57, 3.58, and 3.59 for 1988 show the popular libraries that had the highest scores for the special analysis on extended services and collections. The three tables analyze congregational, parochial school, and public libraries. The highest score of all three tables was earned by the Congregation Beth Akhim Library in Southfield, Michigan. Of the twenty-five libraries in the three tables, five were Canadian (or one-fifth), nine were Jewish, and seven were Roman Catholic. Of the six libraries with the highest scores, four were Jewish.

## Twenty-seven Growth Variables Combined

We may now introduce the third popular library analysis in this series. This is an analysis of the growth of *twenty-seven variables by chief librarian's gender* and was taken from longitudinal tables.[3] Based on their scores, points were assigned to each variable and then summed to obtain a gross total for it. Then these totals were compared. The libraries scoring highest on this measure were those with the highest longitudinal change percentage scores. The result shows males to have made many more points than females: 7,635 to 2,040 growth points (3.7:1.0) in 1978 and 16,470 to 11,120 (1.48:1.00) in 1988. By region, the twenty-seven growth variables showed Canada to have the highest number of growth points and that its variables were growing the fastest of all regions.

Longitudinal table 3.60 shows the mean scores made by the three types of libraries. Leader among the three was public libraries, which had a higher score (based on percentage change) than the other two library types. These libraries were moving ahead rapidly. Next were congregational libraries, which also made a good showing. Weakest by far in the entire table were parochial school libraries.

In summary for this short section, we have examined three special analyses of the variables studied in this chapter. These analyses were designed to identify the libraries which were more active or grew faster than the rest. Jewish, congregational, Canadian, and male chief librarian libraries usually rose to the top here.

## Chapter Summary

In this chapter summary we can explain what the chapter learned about popular libraries. The chapter opened with a brief look at the sponsors or parent institutions of congregational, parochial school, and religious public libraries. The libraries' ability to provide the information called for on the *ALD* questionnaire, and specifically the chief librarian's name, was analyzed. The number of questions answered was disappointing, as was the percentage of libraries providing the chief librarian's name for 1978, but these scores improved for 1988. The various types of library names existing in this subfield were explicated and then the next section dealt with basic library characteristics. The types of libraries were congregational in largest part, and the Middle Atlantic and Middle West regions were most prominent in this database.

The Jewish and Presbyterians led the denominations in numbers, while the Roman Catholics, so prominent in the scholarly database, were few here. No circulation, reference, or interlibrary loan figures were given for them in the *ALD*. Consortium membership was examined with popular libraries showing a modest number of memberships in this group. A few local automation projects existed. Subject interest and special collection listings were numerous here. Certain small libraries restricted access to house of worship members, and we tried to characterize them. Several special analyses were made to identify the most active and the fastest growing library groups, and they were listed and explained.

# Notes

1. Certainly some of the CSLA congregational libraries can be found in the *ALD* popular library database, but just which ones or just how many were repeated there has not been worked out. There may be several dozen of these duplicates altogether. See chapter 4.
2. As an extreme example of the differences between frequencies and means to be found in the entire database and those to be found in the matched pairs database for popular libraries, the reader should see table 3.61 for 1988. The matched pairs frequencies were smaller than those for the entire database. The dead or no longer listed group contained many congregational libraries, especially Roman Catholic, Presbyterian, Lutheran, Episcopal/Anglican, and Baptist, and was usually both the smallest of these categories and had the poorest quality libraries. The newly listed category of libraries was similar to the no longer listed category but was often somewhat larger and had somewhat better quality libraries.
3. See table 4.95 for a list of the twenty-seven growth variables.

TABLE 3.1
1988 *American Library Directory* Volume Holdings for Popular Libraries

| Library Type | Volume Holdings | | | | | | | | | | Number of Libraries | Mean Volumes |
|---|---|---|---|---|---|---|---|---|---|---|---|---|
| | 1–1,000 | % | 1,001–3,500 | % | 3,501–10,000 | % | 10,001 & over | % | No Response | % | | |
| Popular | 56 | 9 | 251 | 39 | 236 | 37 | 74 | 12 | 25 | 4 | 642 | 6,776 |
| Congregational | 52 | 9 | 243 | 41 | 221 | 37 | 53 | 9 | 24 | 4 | 593 | 5,737 |
| Parochial | 1 | 4 | 3 | 13 | 8 | 33 | 11 | 46 | 1 | 4 | 24 | 20,490 |
| Public | 3 | 12 | 5 | 20 | 7 | 28 | 10 | 40 | 0 | 0 | 25 | 17,800 |

TABLE 3.2
1988 *American Library Directory* Popular Library Volume Holdings by Total Annual Library Expenditure

| Library Expenditures | Library Volume Holdings | | | | | | | | | | Number of Libraries | Mean Volumes |
|---|---|---|---|---|---|---|---|---|---|---|---|---|
| | 1–3,500 | % | 3,501–20,000 | % | 20,001–100,000 | % | 100,001 & over | % | No Response | % | | |
| Under $1,500 | 78 | 56 | 54 | 39 | 0 | 0 | 0 | 0 | 7 | 5 | 139 | 4,061 |
| $1,501–$20,000 | 16 | 19 | 65 | 77 | 2 | 2 | 0 | 0 | 1 | 1 | 84 | 8,310 |
| $20,001–$95,000 | 1 | 4 | 17 | 74 | 5 | 22 | 0 | 0 | 0 | 0 | 23 | 14,770 |
| $95,001–$220,000 | 0 | 0 | 3 | 60 | 2 | 40 | 0 | 0 | 0 | 0 | 5 | 23,000 |
| $220,001–$410,000 | 0 | 0 | 0 | 0 | 0 | 0 | 0 | 0 | 0 | 0 | 0 | 0 |
| $410,001–$510,000 | 0 | 0 | 0 | 0 | 0 | 0 | 0 | 0 | 0 | 0 | 0 | 0 |
| $510,001 and over | 0 | 0 | 0 | 0 | 0 | 0 | 1 | 100 | 0 | 0 | 1 | 130,000 |
| No Response | 212 | 54 | 151 | 39 | 9 | 2 | 2 | 1 | 17 | 4 | 391 | 6,378 |
| Total | 307 | 48 | 290 | 45 | 18 | 3 | 3 | 0 | 25 | 4 | 643 | 6,789 |

TABLE 3.3
1978 and 1988 *American Library Directory* Longitudinal Study Total Annual Popular Library Expenditures by Volume Holdings

| Number of Volumes | 1978 | | | | 1988 | | | | Percentage Change 1978–88 |
|---|---|---|---|---|---|---|---|---|---|
| | Number of Libraries | No Response | Total Libraries | Mean Dollars | Number of Libraries | No Response | Total Libraries | Mean Dollars | |
| No Response | 2 | 180 | 182 | 35,130 | 8 | 17 | 25 | 906 | –97 |
| Under 3,500 volumes | 83 | 223 | 306 | 1,108 | 95 | 212 | 307 | 1,805 | 63 |
| 3,501–20,000 | 66 | 114 | 180 | 3,591 | 139 | 151 | 290 | 12,070 | 236 |
| 20,001–100,000 | 3 | 14 | 17 | 113,000 | 9 | 9 | 18 | 71,420 | –37 |
| 100,001–240,000 | 1 | 1 | 2 | 32,500 | 1 | 2 | 3 | 560,000 | 1,623 |
| Total | 155 | 532 | 687 | 4,973 | 252 | 391 | 643 | 12,140 | 144 |

TABLE 3.4
1978 and 1988 *American Library Directory* Demographics: Popular Libraries by Edition and Showing Percentage Change for All Sample Divisions

| | | | | ---Matched Pairs--- | | | | | |
| | 31st ed. 1978 | 41st ed. 1988 | % Change | 1978 | 1988 | % Change | No Longer Listed 1978 | Newly Listed 1988 | % Change |
|---|---|---|---|---|---|---|---|---|---|
| Popular | 687 | 642 | −7 | 471 | 468 | −1 | 216 | 174 | −19 |
| Percentage | 100 | 100 | | 69 | 73 | | 31 | 27 | |
| Congregational | 634 | 593 | −6 | 440 | 440 | 0 | 194 | 153 | −21 |
| Percentage | 92 | 92 | | 93 | 94 | | 90 | 88 | |
| Parochial | 27 | 24 | −11 | 16 | 13 | −19 | 11 | 11 | 0 |
| Percentage | 4 | 4 | | 3 | 3 | | 5 | 6 | |
| Public | 26 | 25 | −4 | 15 | 15 | 0 | 11 | 10 | −9 |
| Percentage | 4 | 4 | | 3 | 3 | | 5 | 6 | |

TABLE 3.5
1988 *American Library Directory* Popular Matched Pairs by Region: Congregational Type Libraries Only

| Region | --------------------Type of Library-------------------- Congregational Libraries | Parochial Libraries | Public Libraries |
|---|---|---|---|
| Northeast | 23 | 0 | 3 |
| Middle Atlantic | 103 | 4 | 2 |
| Southeast | 67 | 1 | 0 |
| Southwest | 58 | 0 | 0 |
| West | 37 | 1 | 2 |
| Rocky Mountains | 7 | 1 | 0 |
| Middle West | 143 | 1 | 2 |
| Canada | 2 | 6 | 6 |
| Total | 440 | 14 | 15 |

TABLE 3.6
1978 and 1988 *American Library Directory* Demographics: Regional
Distribution by Edition and Showing Percentage Change for Popular
Matched Pairs

| Region | 1978 | % of Sample | 1988 | % of Sample | % Change |
|---|---|---|---|---|---|
| Northeast | 26 | 6 | 26 | 6 | 0 |
| Middle Atlantic | 109 | 23 | 109 | 23 | 0 |
| Southeast | 68 | 14 | 68 | 15 | 0 |
| Southwest | 58 | 12 | 58 | 12 | 0 |
| West | 40 | 9 | 40 | 9 | 0 |
| Rocky Mountains | 8 | 2 | 8 | 2 | 0 |
| Middle West | 146 | 31 | 146 | 31 | 0 |
| Canada | 16 | 3 | 13 | 3 | −19 |
| Total | 471 | 100 | 468 | 100 | −1 |

TABLE 3.7
1978 and 1988 *American Library Directory* Longitudinal Study
Popular Libraries by Denomination

| Denomination | 1978 | % of Sample | 1988 | % of Sample | % Change |
|---|---|---|---|---|---|
| Baptist | 83 | 12 | 71 | 11 | −14 |
| Christian | 19 | 3 | 17 | 3 | −11 |
| Churches of Christ | 0 | 0 | 2 | 0 | 0 |
| Episcopal/ Anglican | 42 | 6 | 34 | 5 | −19 |
| Independent | 5 | 1 | 3 | 0 | −40 |
| Lutheran | 53 | 8 | 42 | 7 | −21 |
| Mennonite | 3 | 0 | 4 | 1 | 33 |
| Methodist | 55 | 8 | 64 | 10 | 16 |
| Other Denomina- tions | 92 | 13 | 77 | 12 | −16 |
| Presbyterian | 115 | 17 | 97 | 15 | −16 |
| United Church of Christ | 13 | 2 | 13 | 2 | 0 |
| Summary |  |  |  |  |  |
| Jewish | 163 | 24 | 187 | 29 | 15 |
| Roman Catholic | 44 | 6 | 31 | 5 | −30 |
| All Protestant | 480 | 70 | 424 | 66 | −12 |
| Total | 687 | 100 | 642 | 100 | −7 |

TABLE 3.8
1978 and 1988 *American Library Directory* Longitudinal Study
Popular Libraries by Region

| Region | 1978 | % of Sample | 1988 | % of Sample | % Change |
|---|---|---|---|---|---|
| Northeast | 12 | 6 | 9 | 5 | −25 |
| Middle Atlantic | 59 | 27 | 47 | 27 | −20 |
| Southeast | 23 | 11 | 25 | 14 | 9 |
| Southwest | 19 | 9 | 24 | 14 | 26 |
| West | 23 | 11 | 10 | 6 | −57 |
| Rocky Mountains | 2 | 1 | 0 | 0 | −100 |
| Middle West | 67 | 31 | 51 | 29 | −24 |
| Canada | 11 | 5 | 8 | 5 | −27 |
| Total | 216 | 100 | 174 | 100 | −19 |

TABLE 3.9
1978 *American Library Directory* Most Popular Popular Library
Regions by Denomination

| Denomination | First | Second | Third |
|---|---|---|---|
| Baptist | Southeast | Southwest | Middle West |
| Christian | Middle West | Southeast | Southwest |
| Churches of Christ | None | | |
| Congregational | Northeast | Middle Atlantic | West |
| Episcopal/Anglican | Middle Atlantic | Middle West | Southeast |
| Independent | Middle Atlantic | West | |
| Lutheran | Middle West | Middle Atlantic | Southwest |
| Methodist | Middle West | Middle Atlantic | Southeast |
| Other Denominations | Middle West | West | Middle Atlantic |
| Presbyterian | Middle Atlantic | Middle West | Southeast |
| United Church of Christ | Middle West | Northeast | |
| Jewish | Middle Atlantic | Middle West | Northeast |
| Roman Catholic | Canada | Middle Atlantic | Middle West |

TABLE 3.10
1988 *American Library Directory* Most Popular Popular Library
Regions by Type of Library

| Type of Library | First | Second | Third |
|---|---|---|---|
| Congregational | Middle West | Middle Atlantic | Southeast |
| Parochial School | Canada | Middle Atlantic | Middle West |
| Public | Canada | Middle West | Middle Atlantic |

TABLE 3.11

1988 *American Library Directory* Most Popular Popular Library
Regions by Denomination

| Denomination | First | Second | Third |
|---|---|---|---|
| Baptist | Southeast | Southwest | Middle West |
| Christian | Middle West | Southeast | Southwest |
| Churches of Christ | Southeast | Southwest | West |
| Episcopal/Anglican | Middle Atlantic | Southeast | Southwest |
| Independent | Southeast | Middle West | Middle Atlantic |
| Lutheran | Middle West | Middle Atlantic | West |
| Mennonite | Middle West | Canada | Middle Atlantic |
| Methodist | Southeast | Middle West | Southwest |
| Other Denominations | Middle West | Middle Atlantic | West |
| Presbyterian | Southeast | Middle West | Middle Atlantic |
| United Church of Christ | Middle West | Middle Atlantic | Northeast |
| Jewish | Middle Atlantic | Middle West | Northeast |
| Roman Catholic | Middle West | Middle Atlantic | Canada |

TABLE 3.12
1978 and 1988 *American Library Directory* Popular Libraries by Region and Denomination

| Region | Churches | | | | | | | Other | | | | | Roman | |
|---|---|---|---|---|---|---|---|---|---|---|---|---|---|---|
| | Baptist | Christian of Christ | Episcopal | Independent | Lutheran | Mennonite | Methodist | Denominations | Presbyterian | UCC | Jewish | Catholic | Total |
| Northeast | 2 | 0 | 4 | 0 | 0 | 0 | 0 | 13 | 0 | 1 | 14 | 4 | 38 |
| Middle Atlantic | 8 | 1 | 10 | 2 | 5 | 0 | 14 | 17 | 38 | 1 | 64 | 8 | 168 |
| Southeast | 31 | 6 | 5 | 0 | 1 | 0 | 12 | 4 | 20 | 0 | 12 | 0 | 91 |
| Southwest | 23 | 4 | 10 | 0 | 3 | 0 | 5 | 5 | 14 | 0 | 9 | 4 | 77 |
| West | 4 | 1 | 3 | 1 | 3 | 1 | 4 | 17 | 12 | 0 | 12 | 5 | 63 |
| Rocky Mountains | 0 | 0 | 1 | 0 | 2 | 0 | 1 | 4 | 1 | 0 | 1 | 0 | 10 |
| Middle West | 15 | 7 | 8 | 1 | 39 | 2 | 19 | 29 | 30 | 11 | 46 | 6 | 213 |
| Canada | 0 | 0 | 1 | 1 | 0 | 0 | 0 | 3 | 0 | 0 | 5 | 17 | 27 |
| Total | 83 | 19 | 42 | 5 | 53 | 3 | 55 | 92 | 115 | 13 | 163 | 44 | 687 |

TABLE 3.12 (continued)
1978 and 1988 *American Library Directory* Popular Libraries by Region and Denomination

| Region | Churches | | | | | | | Other Denominations | Presbyterian | UCC | Jewish | Roman Catholic | Total |
|---|---|---|---|---|---|---|---|---|---|---|---|---|---|
| | Baptist | Christian of Christ | Episcopal | Independent | Lutheran | Mennonite | Methodist | | | | | | |
| | | | | | | | | —————————1988 Denomination————————— | | | | | |
| Northeast | 1 | 0 | 2 | 0 | 0 | 0 | 1 | 8 | 0 | 1 | 18 | 4 | 35 |
| Middle Atlantic | 7 | 1 | 9 | 0 | 4 | 1 | 15 | 17 | 28 | 2 | 69 | 3 | 156 |
| Southeast | 26 | 4 | 3 | 0 | 1 | 0 | 12 | 5 | 22 | 0 | 18 | 0 | 93 |
| Southwest | 21 | 3 | 7 | 0 | 3 | 0 | 16 | 4 | 12 | 0 | 11 | 5 | 82 |
| West | 4 | 1 | 3 | 0 | 1 | 1 | 3 | 14 | 10 | 0 | 12 | 1 | 50 |
| Rocky Mountains | 0 | 0 | 0 | 0 | 1 | 0 | 1 | 4 | 1 | 0 | 1 | 0 | 8 |
| Middle West | 12 | 8 | 9 | 1 | 32 | 2 | 16 | 22 | 24 | 10 | 52 | 9 | 197 |
| Canada | 0 | 0 | 1 | 2 | 0 | 0 | 0 | 3 | 0 | 0 | 6 | 10 | 22 |
| Total | 71 | 17 | 34 | 3 | 42 | 4 | 64 | 77 | 97 | 13 | 187 | 32 | 643 |

| Region | Churches | | | | | | | Other Denominations | Presbyterian | UCC | Jewish | Roman Catholic | Total |
|---|---|---|---|---|---|---|---|---|---|---|---|---|---|
| | Baptist | Christian of Christ | Episcopal | Independent | Lutheran | Mennonite | Methodist | | | | | | |
| | | | | | | | | ———————Percentage Change Denomination——————— | | | | | |
| Northeast | -50 | N/A | -50 | N/A | N/A | N/A | N/A | -38 | N/A | 0 | 29 | 0 | -8 |
| Middle Atlantic | -13 | 0 | -10 | -100 | -20 | N/A | 7 | 0 | -26 | 100 | 8 | -63 | -7 |
| Southeast | -16 | -33 | -40 | N/A | 0 | N/A | 0 | 25 | 10 | N/A | 50 | N/A | 2 |
| Southwest | -9 | -25 | -30 | N/A | 0 | N/A | 220 | -20 | -14 | N/A | 22 | 25 | 6 |
| West | 0 | 0 | 0 | -100 | -67 | 0 | -25 | -18 | -17 | N/A | 0 | -80 | -21 |
| Rocky Mountains | N/A | N/A | -100 | N/A | -50 | N/A | 0 | 0 | 0 | N/A | 0 | N/A | -20 |
| Middle West | -20 | 14 | 13 | 0 | -18 | 0 | -16 | -24 | -20 | -9 | 13 | 50 | -8 |
| Canada | N/A | N/A | 0 | 100 | N/A | N/A | N/A | 0 | N/A | N/A | 20 | -41 | -19 |
| Total | -14 | -11 | -19 | -40 | -21 | 33 | 16 | -16 | -16 | 0 | 15 | -27 | -6 |

TABLE 3.13
1978 *American Library Directory* Popular Library Volume Holdings by Region

| Region | 1–3,500 | % | 3,501–20,000 | % | 20,001–100,000 | % | 100,001 & over | % | No Response | % | Number of Libraries | Mean Volumes |
|---|---|---|---|---|---|---|---|---|---|---|---|---|
| Northeast | 15 | 39 | 14 | 37 | 0 | 0 | 0 | 0 | 9 | 24 | 38 | 4,871 |
| Middle Atlantic | 79 | 47 | 37 | 22 | 1 | 1 | 0 | 0 | 51 | 30 | 168 | 3,959 |
| Southeast | 44 | 48 | 25 | 27 | 0 | 0 | 0 | 0 | 22 | 24 | 91 | 3,967 |
| Southwest | 29 | 38 | 29 | 38 | 2 | 3 | 0 | 0 | 17 | 22 | 77 | 6,421 |
| West | 27 | 43 | 15 | 24 | 1 | 2 | 0 | 0 | 20 | 32 | 63 | 5,762 |
| Rocky Mountains | 5 | 50 | 1 | 10 | 0 | 0 | 1 | 10 | 3 | 30 | 10 | 20,890 |
| Middle West | 106 | 50 | 49 | 23 | 4 | 2 | 0 | 0 | 54 | 25 | 213 | 4,689 |
| Canada | 1 | 4 | 10 | 37 | 9 | 33 | 1 | 4 | 6 | 22 | 27 | 36,640 |
| Total | 306 | 45 | 180 | 26 | 17 | 2 | 2 | 0 | 182 | 26 | 687 | 6,282 |

TABLE 3.14
1978 and 1988 *American Library Directory* Longitudinal Study Chief
Librarian's Gender for Popular Libraries

|  | 1978 | % of Sample | 1988 | % of Sample | % Change |
|---|---|---|---|---|---|
| Male | 85 | 12 | 82 | 13 | −4 |
| Female | 330 | 48 | 506 | 79 | 53 |
| No response | 272 | 40 | 54 | 8 | −80 |
| Total | 687 | 100 | 642 | 100 | −7 |

TABLE 3.15
1978 and 1988 *American Library Directory* Longitudinal Study Chief
Librarian's Gender for Matched Pairs of Popular Libraries

|  | 1978 | % of Sample | 1988 | % of Sample | % Change |
|---|---|---|---|---|---|
| Male | 63 | 13 | 58 | 12 | −8 |
| Female | 262 | 56 | 370 | 79 | 41 |
| No response | 146 | 31 | 40 | 9 | −73 |
| Total | 471 | 100 | 468 | 100 | −1 |

TABLE 3.16
1978 and 1988 *American Library Directory* Longitudinal Study Chief
Librarian's Gender for No Longer Listed and Newly Listed Popular
Libraries

|  | 1978 | % of Sample | 1988 | % of Sample | % Change |
|---|---|---|---|---|---|
| Male | 22 | 10 | 24 | 14 | 9 |
| Female | 68 | 32 | 136 | 78 | 100 |
| No response | 126 | 58 | 14 | 8 | −89 |
| Total | 216 | 100 | 174 | 100 | −19 |

TABLE 3.17
1988 *American Library Directory* Popular Library City Population Size
by Chief Librarian's Gender

|  | 1–10,000 | % | 10,001–100,000 | % | 100,001–1,000,000 | % | 1,000,001+ | % | Number of Libraries | Mean Persons |
|---|---|---|---|---|---|---|---|---|---|---|
| Male | 13 | 16 | 25 | 30 | 35 | 42 | 10 | 12 | 83 | 476,100 |
| Female | 65 | 13 | 203 | 40 | 210 | 42 | 28 | 6 | 506 | 342,000 |
| No response | 4 | 7 | 28 | 52 | 18 | 33 | 4 | 7 | 54 | 303,500 |
| Total | 82 | 13 | 256 | 40 | 263 | 41 | 42 | 7 | 643 | 356,100 |

TABLE 3.18

Complete List of *American Library Directory* Denominations in
Alphabetical Order for 1978 and 1988

| Denomination | 1978 | | | 1988 | | | Percent Change 1978–88 | |
|---|---|---|---|---|---|---|---|---|
| | Scholarly | Popular | % Diff. | Scholarly | Popular | % Diff. | Scholarly | Popular |
| Assemblies of God | 12 | 1 | 92 | 12 | 1 | 92 | 0 | 0 |
| Atheist | 0 | 0 | 0 | 1 | 0 | 100 | | |
| Baha'i | 1 | 0 | 100 | 1 | 0 | 100 | 0 | |
| Baptist | 140 | 83 | 41 | 152 | 71 | 53 | 9 | −14 |
| Bible Fellowship | 1 | 0 | 100 | 1 | 0 | 100 | 0 | |
| Brethren | 14 | 2 | 86 | 13 | 1 | 92 | −7 | −50 |
| Buddhist | 0 | 0 | 0 | 3 | 0 | 100 | | |
| Christian and Mis- sionary Alliance | 7 | 0 | 100 | 5 | 0 | 100 | −29 | |
| Christian Evangelical Ch. of America | 1 | 0 | 100 | 1 | 0 | 100 | 0 | |
| Christian Scientist | 1 | 2 | 100 | 3 | 0 | 100 | 200 | −100 |
| Church of Canada | 0 | 0 | 0 | 0 | 0 | 0 | | |
| Church of Christ | 27 | 0 | 100 | 27 | 2 | 93 | 0 | |
| Church of God | 12 | 1 | 92 | 14 | 1 | 93 | 17 | 0 |
| Church of J. C. of Latter-day Saints | 8 | 8 | 0 | 8 | 9 | 13 | 0 | 13 |
| Church of Scientology | 0 | 1 | 0 | 0 | 1 | | | 0 |
| Church of the Nazarene | 11 | 1 | 91 | 13 | 1 | 92 | 18 | 0 |
| Congregational | 5 | 28 | 460 | 5 | 18 | 260 | 0 | −36 |
| Disciples of Christ | 40 | 19 | 53 | 41 | 17 | 59 | 3 | −11 |
| Eastern Orthodox | 7 | 0 | 100 | 10 | 1 | 90 | 43 | |
| Episcopal/Anglican | 32 | 42 | 31 | 32 | 34 | 6 | 0 | −19 |
| Evangelical Church of Canada | 0 | 0 | 0 | 2 | 0 | 100 | | |
| Evangelical Covenant Church | 2 | 1 | 50 | 2 | 0 | 100 | 0 | −100 |
| Evangelical Free Church | 1 | 0 | 100 | 2 | 0 | 100 | 100 | |
| Friends | 19 | 6 | 68 | 17 | 6 | 65 | −11 | 0 |
| Grace Fellowship | 1 | 0 | 100 | 1 | 0 | 100 | 0 | |
| Independent | 82 | 5 | 94 | 97 | 3 | 97 | 18 | −40 |
| International Ch. of the Four Square Gospel | 1 | 0 | 100 | 1 | 0 | 100 | 0 | |
| Jehovah's Witnesses | 1 | 0 | 100 | 1 | 0 | 100 | 0 | |
| Jewish | 35 | 163 | 366 | 45 | 187 | 316 | 29 | 15 |
| Lutheran | 70 | 53 | 24 | 76 | 42 | 45 | 9 | −21 |
| Mennonite | 14 | 3 | 79 | 22 | 4 | 82 | 57 | 33 |
| Methodist | 147 | 55 | 63 | 149 | 64 | 57 | 1 | 16 |

TABLE 3.18 (continued)
Complete List of *American Library Directory* Denominations in
Alphabetical Order for 1978 and 1988

| Denomination | ------------1978------------ | | | ------------1988------------ | | | Percent Change -----1978–88----- | |
|---|---|---|---|---|---|---|---|---|
| | Scholarly | Popular | % Diff. | Scholarly | Popular | % Diff. | Scholarly | Popular |
| Missionary Church | 2 | 0 | 100 | 3 | 0 | 100 | 50 | |
| Moravian Church | 4 | 0 | 100 | 5 | 0 | 100 | 25 | |
| Moslem/Islamic | 1 | 0 | 100 | 2 | 1 | 50 | 100 | |
| Open Bible Standard Church | 2 | 0 | 100 | 1 | 0 | 100 | −50 | |
| Pentecostal | 3 | 1 | 67 | 2 | 0 | 100 | −33 | −100 |
| Pentecostal Holiness Church | 1 | 0 | 100 | 2 | 0 | 100 | 100 | |
| Pillar of Fire | 1 | 0 | 100 | 1 | 0 | 100 | 0 | |
| Presbyterian | 90 | 115 | 28 | 90 | 97 | 8 | 0 | −16 |
| Reformed | 9 | 10 | 11 | 9 | 10 | 11 | 0 | 0 |
| Roman Catholic | 469 | 44 | 91 | 458 | 32 | 93 | −2 | −27 |
| Rosicrucian | 1 | 0 | 100 | 1 | 1 | 0 | 0 | |
| Salvation Army | 2 | 1 | 50 | 4 | 1 | 75 | 100 | 0 |
| Schwenkfelder Church | 1 | 0 | 100 | 1 | 0 | 100 | 0 | |
| Seventh-Day Adventist | 16 | 0 | 100 | 17 | 0 | 100 | 6 | |
| Shakers | 3 | 0 | 100 | 3 | 0 | 100 | 0 | |
| Spiritual Frontiers Fellowship | 1 | 0 | 100 | 0 | 0 | 0 | −100 | |
| Spiritualist | 0 | 0 | 0 | 0 | 1 | | | |
| Swedenborgian Church | 3 | 2 | 33 | 3 | 3 | 0 | 0 | 50 |
| Theosophist | 6 | 1 | 83 | 4 | 2 | 50 | −33 | 100 |
| United Church of Canada | 7 | 0 | 100 | 9 | 2 | 78 | 29 | |
| United Church of Christ | 24 | 13 | 46 | 25 | 13 | 48 | 4 | 0 |
| United Church of Religious Science | 0 | 1 | | 0 | 1 | | | 0 |
| United Missionary | 0 | 0 | 0 | 1 | 0 | 100 | | |
| United Universalist | 2 | 5 | 150 | 2 | 2 | 0 | 0 | −60 |
| Unity | 2 | 0 | 100 | 2 | 0 | 100 | 0 | |
| Unknown | 31 | 20 | 35 | 29 | 14 | 52 | −6 | −30 |
| Wesleyan | 2 | 0 | 100 | 0 | 0 | 0 | −100 | |
| Total | 1,375 | 687 | | 1,431 | 643 | | | |
| Average Change (Libs. per Denom.) | | | | | | | .97 | .76 |

TABLE 3.19

1978 *American Library Directory* Denominational Breakdown for
Popular Libraries by Order of Descending Frequency

| Denomination | Number of Libraries | Percentage |
| --- | --- | --- |
| Jewish | 163 | 24 |
| Presbyterian | 115 | 17 |
| Baptist | 83 | 12 |
| Other Denominations | 67 | 10 |
| Methodist | 55 | 8 |
| Lutheran | 53 | 8 |
| Roman Catholic | 44 | 6 |
| Episcopal/Anglican | 42 | 6 |
| Congregational | 28 | 4 |
| Christian/Disciples of Christ | 19 | 3 |
| United Church of Christ | 13 | 2 |
| Independent | 5 | 1 |
| Total | 687 | 100 |

TABLE 3.20
1978 and 1988 *American Library Directory* Longitudinal Study Denominational Breakdown for No Longer Listed and Newly Listed Libraries Only

| | Scholarly | | | | | Popular | | | | | Entire Sample | | |
|---|---|---|---|---|---|---|---|---|---|---|---|---|---|
| | 1978 | % of Sample | 1988 | % of Sample | % Change | 1978 | % of Sample | 1988 | % of Sample | % Change | 1978 | 1988 | % Change |
| Baptist | 14 | 38.9 | 27 | 73.0 | 93 | 22 | 61.1 | 10 | 27.0 | −55 | 36 | 37 | 3 |
| Christian | 3 | 33.3 | 3 | 42.9 | 0 | 6 | 66.7 | 4 | 57.1 | −33 | 9 | 7 | −22 |
| Churches of Christ | 2 | 100 | 3 | 60 | 50 | 0 | 0 | 2 | 40 | 0 | 2 | 5 | 150 |
| Episcopal/Anglican | 5 | 25 | 8 | 53.3 | 60 | 15 | 75 | 7 | 46.7 | −53 | 20 | 15 | −25 |
| Independent | 14 | 77.8 | 28 | 96.6 | 100 | 4 | 22.2 | 1 | 3.4 | −75 | 18 | 29 | 61 |
| Lutheran | 10 | 35.7 | 16 | 69.6 | 60 | 18 | 64.3 | 7 | 30.4 | −61 | 28 | 23 | −18 |
| Mennonite | 0 | 0 | 8 | 0 | 0 | 0 | | 1 | 11.1 | | 0 | 9 | 0 |
| Methodist | 9 | 36 | 9 | 26.5 | 0 | 16 | 64 | 25 | 73.5 | 56 | 25 | 34 | 36 |
| Other Denominations | 38 | 49.4 | 52 | 68.4 | 37 | 39 | 50.6 | 24 | 31.6 | −38 | 77 | 76 | −1 |
| Presbyterian | 4 | 12.1 | 3 | 21.4 | −25 | 29 | 87.9 | 11 | 78.6 | −62 | 33 | 14 | −58 |
| U.C.C. | 1 | 25 | 2 | 40 | 100 | 3 | 75 | 3 | 60 | 0 | 4 | 5 | 25 |
| **Summary** | | | | | | | | | | | | | |
| Jewish | 6 | 12.2 | 15 | 18.1 | 150 | 43 | 87.8 | 68 | 81.9 | 58 | 49 | 83 | 69 |
| Roman Catholic | 100 | 82.6 | 86 | 88.7 | −14 | 21 | 17.4 | 11 | 11.3 | −48 | 121 | 97 | −20 |
| All Protestant | 100 | 39.7 | 159 | 62.6 | 59 | 152 | 60.3 | 95 | 37.4 | −38 | 252 | 254 | 1 |
| Total | 206 | 48.8 | 260 | 59.9 | 26 | 216 | 51.2 | 174 | 40.1 | −19 | 422 | 434 | 3 |

TABLE 3.21

1988 *American Library Directory* Popular Libraries Listed on the
Highest Number of Tables by Denomination

| Denomination | 1–3 | % | 4–6 | % | 7–9 | % | 10+ | % | No Response | % | Number of Libraries | Mean Tables |
|---|---|---|---|---|---|---|---|---|---|---|---|---|
| Baptist | 24 | 34 | 18 | 25 | 12 | 17 | 7 | 10 | 10 | 14 | 71 | 5.0 |
| Christian | 5 | 29 | 6 | 35 | 4 | 24 | 2 | 12 | 0 | 0 | 17 | 5.4 |
| Churches of Christ | 0 | 0 | 0 | 0 | 2 | 100 | 0 | 0 | 0 | 0 | 2 | 8.0 |
| Episcopal/ Anglican | 15 | 44 | 10 | 29 | 2 | 6 | 5 | 15 | 2 | 6 | 34 | 4.7 |
| Independent | 1 | 33 | 1 | 33 | 0 | 0 | 1 | 33 | 0 | 0 | 3 | 5.3 |
| Lutheran | 11 | 26 | 9 | 21 | 11 | 26 | 3 | 7 | 8 | 19 | 42 | 5.6 |
| Mennonite | 2 | 50 | 2 | 50 | 0 | 0 | 0 | 0 | 0 | 0 | 4 | 3.8 |
| Methodist | 26 | 41 | 12 | 19 | 7 | 11 | 5 | 8 | 14 | 22 | 64 | 4.2 |
| Other Denominations | 29 | 38 | 17 | 22 | 4 | 5 | 6 | 8 | 21 | 27 | 77 | 4.3 |
| Presbyterian | 36 | 37 | 16 | 16 | 13 | 13 | 7 | 7 | 25 | 26 | 97 | 4.6 |
| United Church of Christ | 6 | 46 | 4 | 31 | 2 | 15 | 1 | 8 | 0 | 0 | 13 | 4.9 |
| **Summary** | | | | | | | | | | | | |
| Jewish | 86 | 46 | 43 | 23 | 19 | 10 | 10 | 5 | 29 | 16 | 187 | 4.0 |
| Roman Catholic | 8 | 26 | 8 | 26 | 6 | 19 | 6 | 19 | 3 | 10 | 31 | 5.9 |
| All Protestant | 155 | 37 | 95 | 22 | 57 | 13 | 37 | 9 | 80 | 19 | 424 | 4.8 |
| Total | 249 | 39 | 146 | 23 | 82 | 13 | 53 | 8 | 112 | 17 | 642 | 4.6 |

*Column group header: ---------Number of Table References---------*

TABLE 3.22

1988 *American Library Directory* Popular Libraries Located in the
Largest Cities by Denomination for Baptist Only

| City | Library | Population |
|---|---|---|
| New York, NY | Riverside Church | 4,000,000 |
| Dallas, TX | First Baptist Church | 850,000 |
| San Antonio, TX | First Baptist Church | 850,000 |
| Washington, DC | Chevy Chase Baptist Church | 600,000 |
| Washington, DC | Shiloh Baptist Church | 600,000 |

TABLE 3.23

1988 *American Library Directory* Popular Libraries Located in the
Largest Cities by Denomination for Episcopal/Anglican Only

| City | Library | Population |
|------|---------|-----------|
| New York, NY | St. John the Divine Cathedral | 4,000,000 |
| New York, NY | Trinity Church | 4,000,000 |
| Houston, TX | St. Martin's Episcopal Church | 1,500,000 |
| Indianapolis, IN | Christ Church Cathedral | 850,000 |
| Dallas, TX | St. Michael and All Angels Episcopal Church | 850,000 |
| San Antonio, TX | Episcopal Diocese of West Texas | 850,000 |
| San Antonio, TX | St. Mark's Episcopal Church | 850,000 |
| Washington, DC | St. Paul's Episcopal Church | 600,000 |
| Toronto, ON | Church Army in Canada, Cowan Memorial Library | 600,000 |

TABLE 3.24

1988 *American Library Directory* Popular Libraries Located in the
Largest Cities by Denomination for Lutheran Only

| City | Library | Population |
|------|---------|-----------|
| Phoenix, AZ | Shepherd of the Valley Lutheran Church | 850,000 |
| Memphis, TN | Ascension Lutheran Church | 600,000 |
| Milwaukee, WI | Ascension Lutheran Church | 600,000 |
| Milwaukee, WI | Hope Lutheran Church | 600,000 |
| Milwaukee, WI | Mount Carmel Lutheran Church | 600,000 |
| Milwaukee, WI | Our Savior's Lutheran Church | 600,000 |
| Milwaukee, WI | Prince of Peace Lutheran Church | 600,000 |

TABLE 3.25

1988 *American Library Directory* Popular Libraries Located in the
Largest Cities by Denomination for Methodist Only

| City | Library | Population |
|------|---------|-----------|
| Houston, TX | Chapelwood United Methodist Church | 1,500,000 |
| Dallas, TX | Highland Park United Methodist Church | 850,000 |
| San Antonio, TX | Harlandale United Methodist Church | 850,000 |
| Washington, DC | Metropolitan Memorial United Methodist Church | 600,000 |
| Washington, DC | Mount Vernon Place United Methodist Church | 600,000 |

TABLE 3.26

1988 *American Library Directory* Popular Libraries Located in the
Largest Cities by Denomination for Presbyterian Only

| City | Library | Population |
|------|---------|-----------|
| Detroit, MI | Hope United Presbyterian Church | 1,500,000 |
| Detroit, MI | Westminster Church | 1,500,000 |
| Houston, TX | Central Presbyterian Church | 1,500,000 |
| Houston, TX | First Presbyterian Church | 1,500,000 |
| San Diego, CA | First Presbyterian Church | 850,000 |
| Indianapolis, IN | United Presbyterian Church | 850,000 |
| Baltimore, MD | Faith Presbyterian Church | 850,000 |
| Dallas, TX | Highland Park Presbyterian Church | 850,000 |

TABLE 3.27

1988 *American Library Directory* Popular Libraries Located in the
Largest Cities by Denomination for Jewish Only

| City | Library | Population |
|------|---------|-----------|
| New York, NY | Board of Jewish Education | 4,000,000 |
| New York, NY | Young Men's and Women's Hebrew Association | 4,000,000 |
| New York, NY | Congregation Emanu-el | 4,000,000 |
| New York, NY | Congregation Shearith Israel | 4,000,000 |
| New York, NY | Park Avenue Synagogue | 4,000,000 |
| Chicago, IL | Chicago Sinai Congregation | 4,000,000 |
| Chicago, IL | Congregation Kins | 4,000,000 |
| Chicago, IL | Congregation Rodfel Zedek | 4,000,000 |
| Chicago, IL | Ner Tamid Congregation | 4,000,000 |

TABLE 3.28
1978 and 1988 *American Library Directory* Longitudinal Study Popular Library City Population Size by Denomination for the United States Only

| Denomination | 1978 | | | | 1988 | | | | Percentage Change 1978–88 |
|---|---|---|---|---|---|---|---|---|---|
| | Number of Libraries | No Response | Total Libraries | Mean Persons | Number of Libraries | No Response | Total Libraries | Mean Persons | |
| Baptist | 83 | 0 | 83 | 221,100 | 71 | 0 | 71 | 218,900 | −1 |
| Christian | 19 | 0 | 19 | 427,600 | 17 | 0 | 17 | 383,200 | −10 |
| Churches of Christ | 0 | 0 | 0 | 0 | 2 | 0 | 2 | 110,000 | 0 |
| Episcopal/Anglican | 41 | 0 | 41 | 428,400 | 33 | 0 | 33 | 488,900 | 14 |
| Independent | 4 | 0 | 4 | 1,386,000 | 1 | 0 | 1 | 2,500 | −100 |
| Lutheran | 53 | 0 | 53 | 267,100 | 42 | 0 | 42 | 194,600 | −27 |
| Mennonite | 3 | 0 | 3 | 10,000 | 4 | 0 | 4 | 12,500 | 25 |
| Methodist | 55 | 0 | 55 | 199,200 | 64 | 0 | 64 | 181,100 | −9 |
| Other Denominations | 89 | 0 | 89 | 322,300 | 74 | 0 | 74 | 458,500 | 42 |
| Presbyterian | 114 | 1 | 115 | 248,900 | 97 | 0 | 97 | 240,900 | −3.2 |
| U.C.C. | 13 | 0 | 13 | 289,200 | 13 | 0 | 13 | 98,650 | −66 |
| Summary | | | | | | | | | |
| Jewish | 157 | 1 | 158 | 502,100 | 181 | 0 | 181 | 471,400 | −6.1 |
| Roman Catholic | 27 | 0 | 27 | 700,500 | 22 | 0 | 22 | 585,200 | −16 |
| All Protestant | 474 | 1 | 475 | 285,900 | 418 | 0 | 418 | 279,400 | −2.2 |
| Total | 658 | 2 | 660 | 354,500 | 621 | 0 | 621 | 346,200 | −2.3 |

TABLE 3.29

1978 and 1988 *American Library Directory* Longitudinal Study
Popular Library Questionnaires Returned

| Type of Library | -------------1978-------------- | | | | ------------1988------------- | | | | |
| | Number of Libraries Yes | % | No Response or No | Total Libraries | Number of Libraries Yes | % | No Response or No | Total Libraries | Percentage Change 1978–88 |
|---|---|---|---|---|---|---|---|---|---|
| Popular | 230 | 33 | 457 | 687 | 639 | 99 | 4 | 643 | 178 |
| Congregational | 210 | 33 | 424 | 634 | 590 | 99 | 3 | 593 | 181 |
| Parochial | 8 | 30 | 19 | 27 | 24 | 96 | 1 | 25 | 200 |
| Public | 12 | 46 | 14 | 26 | 25 | 100 | 0 | 25 | 108 |

TABLE 3.30

1978 *American Library Directory* Popular Library Questionnaires
Returned by Region

| Region | ------------Were Questionnaires Returned? Yes or No------------ | | | | | | Number of Libraries |
| | "Yes" | % | "No" | % | No Response | % | |
|---|---|---|---|---|---|---|---|
| Northeast | 8 | 21 | 30 | 79 | 0 | 0 | 38 |
| Middle Atlantic | 51 | 30 | 117 | 70 | 0 | 0 | 168 |
| Southeast | 36 | 40 | 54 | 59 | 1 | 1 | 91 |
| Southwest | 25 | 32 | 52 | 68 | 0 | 0 | 77 |
| West | 26 | 41 | 37 | 59 | 0 | 0 | 63 |
| Rocky Mountains | 4 | 40 | 6 | 60 | 0 | 0 | 10 |
| Middle West | 71 | 33 | 141 | 66 | 1 | 0 | 213 |
| Canada | 9 | 33 | 18 | 67 | 0 | 0 | 27 |
| Total | 230 | 33 | 455 | 66 | 2 | 0 | 687 |

TABLE 3.31

1978 *American Library Directory* Congregational (Type) Library
Questionnaires Returned by Denomination

| Denomination | Yes | % | No | % | No Response | % | Number of Libraries |
|---|---|---|---|---|---|---|---|
| Baptist | 24 | 29 | 59 | 71 | 0 | 0 | 83 |
| Christian | 7 | 39 | 11 | 61 | 0 | 0 | 18 |
| Churches of Christ | 0 | 0 | 0 | 0 | 0 | 0 | 0 |
| Congregational | 6 | 21 | 22 | 79 | 0 | 0 | 28 |
| Episcopal | 10 | 24 | 31 | 76 | 0 | 0 | 41 |
| Independent | 0 | 0 | 3 | 100 | 0 | 0 | 3 |
| Lutheran | 21 | 40 | 32 | 60 | 0 | 0 | 53 |
| Methodist | 20 | 36 | 35 | 64 | 0 | 0 | 55 |
| Other Denominations | 19 | 31 | 41 | 67 | 1 | 2 | 61 |
| Presbyterian | 42 | 37 | 73 | 63 | 0 | 0 | 115 |
| U.C.C. | 2 | 15 | 11 | 85 | 0 | 0 | 13 |
| **Summary** | | | | | | | |
| All Protestant | 151 | 32 | 318 | 68 | 1 | 0 | 470 |
| Jewish | 55 | 37 | 94 | 63 | 1 | 1 | 150 |
| Roman Catholic | 4 | 29 | 10 | 71 | 0 | 0 | 14 |
| Total | 210 | 33 | 422 | 67 | 2 | 0 | 634 |

TABLE 3.32

1978 and 1988 *American Library Directory* Longitudinal Study
Popular Library Questionnaires Returned by Denomination

| | ------------1978------------- | | | | ------------1988------------ | | | | |
| | Number of Libraries | | No Response | Total | Number of Libraries | | No Response | Total | Percentage Change |
| Denomination | Yes | % | or No | Libraries | Yes | % | or No | Libraries | 1978–88 |
|---|---|---|---|---|---|---|---|---|---|
| Baptist | 24 | 29 | 59 | 83 | 71 | 100 | 0 | 71 | 196 |
| Christian | 7 | 37 | 12 | 19 | 16 | 94 | 1 | 17 | 129 |
| Churches of Christ | 0 | 0 | 0 | 0 | 2 | 100 | 0 | 2 | 0 |
| Episcopal/Anglican | 11 | 26 | 31 | 42 | 34 | 100 | 0 | 34 | 209 |
| Independent | 1 | 20 | 4 | 5 | 3 | 100 | 0 | 3 | 200 |
| Lutheran | 21 | 40 | 32 | 53 | 41 | 98 | 1 | 42 | 95 |
| Mennonite | 1 | 33 | 2 | 3 | 4 | 100 | 0 | 4 | 300 |
| Methodist | 20 | 36 | 35 | 55 | 64 | 100 | 0 | 64 | 220 |
| Other Denominations | 27 | 29 | 65 | 92 | 77 | 100 | 0 | 77 | 185 |
| Presbyterian | 42 | 37 | 73 | 115 | 96 | 99 | 1 | 97 | 129 |
| United Church of Christ | 2 | 15 | 11 | 13 | 13 | 100 | 0 | 13 | 550 |

TABLE 3.32 (continued)
1978 and 1988 *American Library Directory* Longitudinal Study
Popular Library Questionnaires Returned by Denomination

| | --------------1978------------ | | | | ----------1988------------- | | | | |
| | Number of Libraries | | No Response | Total | Number of Libraries | | No Response | Total | Percentage Change |
| Denomination | Yes | % | or No | Libraries | Yes | % | or No | Libraries | 1978–88 |
|---|---|---|---|---|---|---|---|---|---|
| **Summary** | | | | | | | | | |
| Jewish | 61 | 37 | 102 | 163 | 187 | 100 | 0 | 187 | 207 |
| Roman Catholic | 13 | 30 | 31 | 44 | 31 | 97 | 1 | 32 | 138 |
| All Protestant | 156 | 33 | 324 | 480 | 421 | 99 | 3 | 424 | 170 |
| Total | 230 | 33 | 457 | 687 | 639 | 99 | 4 | 643 | 178 |

TABLE 3.33
1978 and 1988 *American Library Directory* Longitudinal Study
Popular Libraries Answering Questionnaire Questions

| | -----------1978------------ | | -----------1988------------ | | |
| Type of Library | Number of Libraries | Mean Questions | Number of Libraries | Mean Questions | Percentage Change 1978-88 |
|---|---|---|---|---|---|
| Popular | 687 | 15 | 643 | 17 | 13 |
| Congregational | 634 | 15 | 593 | 17 | 13 |
| Parochial | 27 | 15 | 25 | 19 | 27 |
| Public | 26 | 17 | 25 | 19 | 12 |

TABLE 3.34
1978 and 1988 *American Library Directory* Longitudinal Study
Popular Library Questionnaire Questions Answered by Volume
Holdings

| Number of Volumes | -----------1978---------- | | -----------1988--------- | | |
| | Number of Libraries | Mean Questions | Number of Libraries | Mean Questions | Percentage Change 1978-88 |
|---|---|---|---|---|---|
| No Response | 182 | 12 | 25 | 14 | 17 |
| Under 3,500 | 306 | 16 | 307 | 16 | 0 |
| 3,501–20,000 | 180 | 18 | 290 | 19 | 5.6 |
| 20,001–100,000 | 17 | 17 | 18 | 20 | 18 |
| 100,001–240,000 | 2 | 20 | 3 | 20 | 0 |
| 240,001–440,000 | 0 | 0 | 0 | 0 | 0 |
| 440,001+ | 0 | 0 | 0 | 0 | 0 |
| Total | 687 | 15 | 643 | 17 | 13 |

TABLE 3.35

1978 and 1988 *American Library Directory* Named House of Worship
Library Characteristics, All Samples

| Characteristics | 1978 | Percentage | 1988 | Percentage |
|---|---|---|---|---|
| Numbered Houses of Worship | | | | |
| 1st | 139 | 7 | 133 | 6 |
| 2nd | 3 | 0 | 2 | 0 |
| 3rd | 1 | 0 | 1 | 0 |
| Learning or media resource centers | 55 | 3 | 70 | 3 |
| Memorial libraries | 286 | 14 | 290 | 14 |
| Libraries named after saints | 303 | 15 | 281 | 14 |
| Libraries named after the Trinity or the Godhead | 127 | 6 | 128 | 6 |
| No special name given | 1,148 | 56 | 1,169 | 56 |
| Grand total | 2,062 | 100 | 2,074 | 100 |

| Popular Libraries that were named after Saints | | 1978 | 1988 |
|---|---|---|---|
| | All Saints | 3 | 2 |
| | Magdalen | 1 | 0 |
| | Notre Dame de Grace | 1 | 0 |
| | Our Lady of Light | 1 | 0 |
| | Our Lady Queen of Martyrs | 1 | 1 |
| | San Jacinto | 0 | 1 |
| | St. Albert le Grand | 0 | 1 |
| | St. Andrew | 3 | 0 |
| | St. Anthony | 2 | 0 |
| | St. Augustine | 1 | 1 |
| | St. Christopher | 1 | 1 |
| | St. Clement | 1 | 1 |
| | St. Cloud | 0 | 1 |
| | St. David | 0 | 1 |
| | St. Elias | 0 | 1 |
| | St. Francis | 2 | 2 |
| | St. George | 2 | 1 |
| | St. Giles | 1 | 1 |
| | St. Ignatius | 1 | 0 |
| | St. Ignatius Loyola | 1 | 0 |
| | St. James | 2 | 1 |
| | St. John | 7 | 6 |
| | St. John the Baptist | 0 | 1 |
| | St. John the Divine | 1 | 1 |
| | St. Joseph | 1 | 0 |
| | St. Luke | 4 | 4 |
| | St. Maria Goretti | 1 | 1 |
| | St. Mark | 4 | 3 |

TABLE 3.35 (continued)
1978 and 1988 *American Library Directory* Names House of Worship
Library Characteristics, All Samples

| Characteristics | 1978 | Percentage | 1988 | Percentage |
|---|---|---|---|---|
| | St. Martin | 2 | 2 | |
| | St. Mary | 4 | 3 | |
| | St. Matthew | 1 | 1 | |
| | St. Michael | 1 | 2 | |
| | St. Olaf | 1 | 1 | |
| | St. Patrick | 2 | 0 | |
| | St. Paul | 6 | 7 | |
| | St. Peter | 3 | 1 | |
| | St. Stephen | 0 | 2 | |
| | St. Thomas | 2 | 3 | |
| | St. Timothy | 0 | 1 | |
| Total | | 64 | 55 | |

TABLE 3.36
1978 *American Library Directory* Popular Library Chief Librarian
Named by Volume Holdings

| Library Volumes | Yes | % | No | % | No Response | % | No. of Libraries |
|---|---|---|---|---|---|---|---|
| Under 3,500 Volumes | 190 | 62 | 116 | 38 | 0 | 0 | 306 |
| 3,501–20,000 | 145 | 81 | 35 | 19 | 0 | 0 | 180 |
| 20,001–100,000 | 13 | 76 | 4 | 24 | 0 | 0 | 17 |
| 100,001–240,000 | 2 | 100 | 0 | 0 | 0 | 0 | 2 |
| 240,001–440,000 | 0 | 0 | 0 | 0 | 0 | 0 | 0 |
| 440,001 and over | 0 | 0 | 0 | 0 | 0 | 0 | 0 |
| No response | 64 | 35 | 116 | 64 | 2 | 1 | 182 |
| Total | 414 | 60 | 271 | 39 | 2 | 0 | 687 |

TABLE 3.37

1978 and 1988 *American Library Directory* Longitudinal Study
Popular Library Chief Librarian Named by Denomination

| Denomination | 1978 | | | | 1988 | | | | |
| --- | --- | --- | --- | --- | --- | --- | --- | --- | --- |
| | Number of Libraries | | No Response | Total | Number of Libraries | | No Response | Total | Percentage Change |
| | Yes | % | or No | Libraries | Yes | % | or No | Libraries | 1978–88 |
| Baptist | 44 | 53 | 39 | 83 | 68 | 96 | 3 | 71 | 55 |
| Christian | 13 | 68 | 6 | 19 | 15 | 88 | 2 | 17 | 15 |
| Churches of Christ | 0 | 0 | 0 | 0 | 2 | 100 | 0 | 2 | 0 |
| Episcopal/Anglican | 19 | 45 | 23 | 42 | 33 | 97 | 1 | 34 | 74 |
| Independent | 3 | 60 | 2 | 5 | 3 | 100 | 0 | 3 | 0 |
| Lutheran | 31 | 58 | 22 | 53 | 36 | 86 | 6 | 42 | 16 |
| Mennonite | 1 | 33 | 2 | 3 | 4 | 100 | 0 | 4 | 300 |
| Methodist | 31 | 56 | 24 | 55 | 56 | 88 | 8 | 64 | 81 |
| Other Denominations | 50 | 54 | 42 | 92 | 71 | 92 | 6 | 77 | 42 |
| Presbyterian | 71 | 62 | 44 | 115 | 82 | 85 | 15 | 97 | 15 |
| United Church of Christ | 7 | 54 | 6 | 13 | 12 | 92 | 1 | 13 | 71 |
| **Summary** | | | | | | | | | |
| Jewish | 118 | 72 | 45 | 163 | 176 | 94 | 11 | 187 | 49 |
| Roman Catholic | 26 | 59 | 18 | 44 | 31 | 97 | 1 | 32 | 19 |
| All Protestant | 270 | 56 | 210 | 480 | 382 | 90 | 42 | 424 | 41 |
| Total | 414 | 60 | 273 | 687 | 589 | 92 | 54 | 643 | 42 |

TABLE 3.38
1988 *American Library Directory* Popular Library Consortium Memberships by Library Type

| Type of Library | 1-2 Consortuim Memberships | % | 3-4 Consortuim Memberships | % | 5-6 Consortuim Memberships | % | 7+ Consortuim Memberships | % | No Response | % | Number of Libraries | Mean Membership |
|---|---|---|---|---|---|---|---|---|---|---|---|---|
| Popular | 19 | 3 | 1 | 0 | 0 | 0 | 0 | 0 | 622 | 97 | 642 | 1.2 |
| Congregational | 15 | 3 | 1 | 0 | 0 | 0 | 0 | 0 | 577 | 97 | 593 | 1.3 |
| Parochial | 3 | 13 | 0 | 0 | 0 | 0 | 0 | 0 | 21 | 88 | 24 | 1.0 |
| Public | 1 | 4 | 0 | 0 | 0 | 0 | 0 | 0 | 24 | 96 | 25 | 1.0 |

TABLE 3.39

1988 *American Library Directory* Congregational Libraries with the
Highest Cumulative Scores on Cooperation and Automation Activities[a]

| Library | Score |
| --- | --- |
| Douglass Boulevard Christian Church, Louisville, KY | 4 |
| Episcopal Diocese of West Texas Cathedral, San Antonio, TX | 3 |
| English Lutheran Church, LaCrosse, WI | 2 |

[a] Library cooperation and automation include consortium memberships, OCLC
membership, and local automation projects.

TABLE 3.40

1988 *American Library Directory* Local Automation Projects for
Popular Libraries

| Type of Library | Libraries with Automation Projects | % | Libraries with No Project/Reply | % | Number of Libraries |
| --- | --- | --- | --- | --- | --- |
| Popular | 20 | 3 | 622 | 97 | 642 |
| Congregational | 20 | 3 | 573 | 97 | 593 |
| Parochial | 0 | 0 | 24 | 100 | 24 |
| Public | 0 | 0 | 25 | 100 | 25 |

TABLE 3.41
1978 and 1988 *American Library Directory* Longitudinal Study Library Religious Subject Interests (Variable 2) for Popular Libraries

| Library Type | 1978 | | | | 1988 | | | | Percentage Change 1978-88 |
|---|---|---|---|---|---|---|---|---|---|
| | Number of Libraries | Percentage | No Response | Total Libraries | Number of Libraries | Percentage | No Response | Total Libraries | |
| Popular | 62 | 9 | 625 | 687 | 49 | 8 | 594 | 643 | -21 |
| Congregational | 60 | 9 | 574 | 634 | 46 | 8 | 547 | 593 | -23 |
| Parochial | 1 | 4 | 26 | 27 | 1 | 4 | 24 | 25 | 0 |
| Public | 1 | 4 | 25 | 26 | 2 | 8 | 23 | 25 | 100 |

TABLE 3.42

1978 and 1988 *American Library Directory* Subject Interests Broken Down into Categories for Popular Libraries[a]

| Subject Interest | 1978 | 1988 | % of All Subject Interests accounted for, 1988 |
|---|---|---|---|
| Religion: general | 7 | 63 | 12 |
| Theology | 39 | 51 | 9 |
| Bible | 49 | 57 | 11 |
| Judaica | 73 | 138 | 25 |
| Church History | 16 | 38 | 7 |
| Jewish history and literature | 37 | 54 | 10 |
| Missions and missionaries | 11 | 18 | 3 |
| Miscellaneous faiths and denominations | 7 | 18 | 3 |
| Religious education | 17 | 18 | 3 |
| Roman Catholicism | 3 | 4 | 1 |
| Christian life | 24 | 26 | 5 |
| Pastoral care | 4 | 4 | 1 |
| Church work | 5 | 1 | 0 |
| Biography and fiction | 12 | 17 | 3 |
| Baptist Church | 2 | 3 | 1 |
| Jewish life | 5 | 8 | 2 |
| Philosophy and psychology | 7 | 2 | 0 |
| Music | 4 | 1 | 0 |
| Devotionals | 14 | 15 | 3 |
| Mysticism | 2 | 2 | 0 |
| Sociology and religion | 2 | 6 | 1 |
| Other unclassified | 1 | 1 | 0 |
| Total | 341 | 545 | 100 |

| | 1978 | 1988 |
|---|---|---|
| Number of libraries with subject interests | 208 | 304 |
| Number of subject interests per library | 1.6 | 1.8 |

[a] These figures refer only to libraries that named their subject interests.

TABLE 3.43

1978 and 1988 *American Library Directory* Longitudinal Study
Popular Library Subject Interests

| Library Type | --------------------1 9 7 8-------------------- | | | | --------------------1 9 8 8-------------------- | | | | % Change 1978–88 |
| | No. of Libraries | No Response | Total Libraries | Mean Interest | No. of Libraries | No Response | Total Libraries | Mean Interests | |
| --- | --- | --- | --- | --- | --- | --- | --- | --- | --- |
| Popular | 208 | 479 | 687 | 2.0 | 304 | 338 | 642 | 1.9 | −5 |
| Congregational | 188 | 446 | 634 | 2.0 | 284 | 309 | 593 | 1.9 | −5 |
| Parochial | 6 | 21 | 27 | 2.2 | 8 | 16 | 24 | 1.8 | −18 |
| Public | 14 | 12 | 26 | 2.2 | 12 | 13 | 25 | 2.3 | 5 |

a This table refers to all libraries showing subject interests including those reporting them
but not providing the subject interest title.

TABLE 3.44
1978 and 1988 *American Library Directory* Longitudinal Study Popular Library Subject Interests by Volume Holdings

| Number of Volumes | 1978 | | | | 1988 | | | | Percentage Change 1978–88 |
|---|---|---|---|---|---|---|---|---|---|
| | Number of Libraries | No Response | Total Libraries | Mean Interest | Number of Libraries | No Response | Total Libraries | Mean Interest | |
| No Response | 9 | 173 | 182 | 1.6 | 4 | 21 | 25 | 1.3 | −19 |
| Under 3,500 | 98 | 208 | 306 | 1.9 | 124 | 183 | 307 | 1.7 | −11 |
| 3,501–20,000 | 93 | 87 | 180 | 2.2 | 163 | 127 | 290 | 2.0 | −9 |
| 20,001–100,000 | 6 | 11 | 17 | 1.5 | 12 | 6 | 18 | 2.9 | 93 |
| 100,001–240,000 | 2 | 0 | 2 | 1.0 | 1 | 2 | 3 | 1.0 | 0 |
| Total | 208 | 479 | 687 | 2.0 | 304 | 339 | 643 | 1.9 | −5 |

TABLE 3.45
1978 and 1988 *American Library Directory* Longitudinal Study Popular Library Special Collections by Library Type

| Type of Libraries | 1978 | | | | 1988 | | | | Percentage Change 1978–88 |
|---|---|---|---|---|---|---|---|---|---|
| | Number of Libraries | No Response | Total Libraries | Mean Collections | Number of Libraries | No Response | Total Libraries | Mean Collections | |
| Popular | 50 | 637 | 687 | 1.6 | 100 | 542 | 642 | 1.4 | −12 |
| Congregational | 42 | 592 | 634 | 1.7 | 86 | 507 | 593 | 1.4 | −18 |
| Parochial | 0 | 27 | 27 | 0 | 5 | 19 | 24 | 2.8 | 0 |
| Public | 8 | 18 | 26 | 1.1 | 9 | 16 | 25 | 1.1 | 0 |

TABLE 3.46

1978 and 1988 *American Library Directory* Special Collections Broken
Down into Categories for Popular Libraries

| Special Collection | 1978 | 1988 | % of All Special Collections Accounted For |
|---|---|---|---|
| Church history | 6 | 13 | 10 |
| Judaism | 28 | 61 | 46 |
| Miscellaneous faiths and denominations | 2 | 4 | 3 |
| Religion: comparative and other | 6 | 5 | 4 |
| Bibles | 11 | 15 | 12 |
| Methodist Church | 0 | 2 | 1 |
| Baptist Church | 0 | 0 | 0 |
| Theology and philosophy | 2 | 12 | 9 |
| Roman Catholicism | 3 | 3 | 2 |
| Missions and missionaries | 1 | 3 | 2 |
| Roman Catholic religious orders and groups | 1 | 1 | 1 |
| Music | 3 | 2 | 1 |
| Literature and art | 4 | 6 | 4 |
| Lutheran Church | 1 | 2 | 1 |
| Biography (Roman Catholic) | 1 | 0 | 0 |
| Quakers | 1 | 1 | 1 |
| United Brethren in Christ Church | 0 | 0 | 0 |
| Evangelism | 1 | 0 | 0 |
| Presbyterian Church | 1 | 3 | 2 |
| Adventism | 0 | 0 | 0 |
| Patristics | 0 | 0 | 0 |
| Biography and fiction | 0 | 2 | 1 |
| Other unclassified | 0 | 0 | 0 |
| Total | 72 | 135 | 100 |

| | 1978 | 1988 |
|---|---|---|
| Number of libraries with special collections | 50 | 100 |
| Number of special collections per library | 1.4 | 1.35 |

TABLE 3.47
1988 *American Library Directory* Popular Library Publications in
Descending Order of Frequency[a]

| Type of Publication | Number of Publications Listed | Percentage |
|---|---|---|
| Journal/periodical | 29 | 41 |
| Library bulletin/newsletter | 17 | 24 |
| Monographs | 6 | 9 |
| Bibliographies | 5 | 7 |
| Catalog | 4 | 6 |
| Acquisitions list | 3 | 4 |
| Annual report | 3 | 4 |
| Miscellaneous | 2 | 3 |
| Serials list | 1 | 1 |
| Library handbook | 0 | 0 |
| Library guide | 0 | 0 |
| Friends of the library newsletter | 0 | 0 |
| Total | 70 | 100 |

[a] The total number of publications represents all the publications listed including those
for libraries with several publications each.

TABLE 3.48

1988 *American Library Directory* Popular Library Publications Broken Down into Categories[a,b]

| Type of Publication | 1988 Popular | % of Total | Percentage of Total Publications Accounted for Popular |
|---|---|---|---|
| Library bulletin/newsletter | 17 | 24 | 15 |
| Monographs | 6 | 9 | 7 |
| Bibliographies | 5 | 7 | 6 |
| Library handbook | 0 | 0 | 0 |
| Miscellaneous | 2 | 3 | 3 |
| Library guide | 0 | 0 | 0 |
| Acquisitions list | 3 | 4 | 6 |
| Serials list | 1 | 1 | 2 |
| Journal/periodical | 29 | 41 | 94 |
| Annual report | 3 | 4 | 13 |
| Catalog | 4 | 6 | 21 |
| Friends of the library newsletter | 0 | 0 | 0 |
| Total | 70 | 100 | 10 |
| Number of popular libraries with publications | | | 44 |
| Number of publications per library | | | 1.6 |

[a] The number 70 represents all of the publications listed, including those for libraries with several publications each. It does not include untitled publications mentioned but not specified.

[b] The last column represents popular library publications as a percentage of all sample library publications for both scholarly and popular libraries together, i. e., popular libraries produce approximately 10 percent of all sample library publications.

TABLE 3.49
1978 and 1988 *American Library Directory* Longitudinal Study Popular Library Publications[a]

| | ---------1 9 7 8--------- | | | | ---------1 9 8 8--------- | | | | Percentage |
| Library Type | Number of Libraries | No Response | Total Libraries | Mean Publications | Number of Libraries | No Response | Total Libraries | Mean Publications | Change 1978–88 |
|---|---|---|---|---|---|---|---|---|---|
| Popular | 0 | 687 | 687 | 0 | 44 | 598 | 642 | 1.7 | 0 |
| Congregational | 0 | 634 | 634 | 0 | 33 | 560 | 593 | 1.7 | 0 |
| Parochial | 0 | 27 | 27 | 0 | 5 | 19 | 24 | 1.8 | 0 |
| Public | 0 | 26 | 26 | 0 | 6 | 19 | 25 | 1.7 | 0 |

[a] The means shown above include all popular library publications, whether named or untitled.

TABLE 3.50

1978 and 1988 *American Library Directory* Longitudinal Study
Popular Libraries Restricting Circulation to Members by Denomination

| | -------------1978------------- | | | --------------1988-------------- | | | Percentage |
| Denomination | Number of Libraries | % | No Response | Total Libraries | Number of Libraries | % | No Response | Total Libraries | Change 1978-88 |
|---|---|---|---|---|---|---|---|---|---|
| Baptist | 6 | 7.2 | 77 | 83 | 10 | 14.0 | 61 | 71 | 67 |
| Christian | 2 | 11.0 | 17 | 19 | 2 | 12.0 | 15 | 17 | 0 |
| Churches of Christ | 0 | 0 | 0 | 0 | 1 | 50.0 | 1 | 2 | 0 |
| Episcopal/Anglican | 2 | 4.8 | 40 | 42 | 0 | 0 | 34 | 34 | -100 |
| Independent | 0 | 0 | 5 | 5 | 1 | 33.0 | 2 | 3 | 0 |
| Lutheran | 2 | 3.8 | 51 | 53 | 3 | 7.1 | 39 | 42 | 50 |
| Mennonite | 0 | 0 | 3 | 3 | 0 | 0 | 4 | 4 | 0 |
| Methodist | 3 | 5.5 | 52 | 55 | 6 | 9.2 | 58 | 64 | 100 |
| Other Denominations | 5 | 5.4 | 87 | 92 | 6 | 7.8 | 71 | 77 | 20 |
| Presbyterian | 14 | 12.0 | 101 | 115 | 9 | 9.3 | 88 | 97 | -36 |
| United Church of Christ | 3 | 23.0 | 10 | 13 | 4 | 31.0 | 9 | 13 | 33 |
| **Summary** | | | | | | | | | |
| Jewish | 14 | 8.5 | 149 | 163 | 20 | 11.0 | 167 | 187 | 43 |
| Roman Catholic | 3 | 6.9 | 41 | 44 | 5 | 16.0 | 27 | 32 | 67 |
| All Protestant | 37 | 7.7 | 443 | 480 | 42 | 9.7 | 382 | 424 | 14 |
| Total | 54 | 7.9 | 633 | 687 | 67 | 10.0 | 576 | 643 | 24 |

TABLE 3.51

1988 *American Library Directory* Cumulated Restriction Scores for
Parochial School Libraries[a]

| Library | Restrictions |
|---|---|
| Bureau of Jewish Education, San Francisco, CA | 2 |
| Niles Township Jewish Congregation, Skokie, IL | 2 |
| Cardinal Ritter, St. Louis, MO | 2 |
| Edmonton Catholic Schools, Edmonton, AB | 2 |
| St. Gerard's Parish, Yorkton, SK | 2 |

[a] Library restrictions include both circulation and reference service restrictions.

TABLE 3.52

1978 and 1988 *American Library Directory* Longitudinal Study
Additional Activities for Popular Libraries[a]

| Type of Library | No. of Libraries | No Response | Total Libraries | Mean Activities | No. of Libraries | No Response | Total Libraries | Mean Activities | % Change 1978-88 |
|---|---|---|---|---|---|---|---|---|---|
| Popular Congregational | 12 | 675 | 687 | 1.0 | 39 | 604 | 643 | 1.2 | 20 |
| | 10 | 624 | 634 | 1.0 | 35 | 558 | 593 | 1.2 | 20 |
| Parochial | 1 | 26 | 27 | 1.0 | 3 | 22 | 25 | 1.0 | 0 |
| Public | 1 | 25 | 26 | 1.0 | 1 | 24 | 25 | 1.0 | 0 |

[a] Additional activities include library consortium memberships, OCLC membership, and local automation projects.

TABLE 3.53
1988 *American Library Directory* Popular Library Extended Services (Cumulative) by Region[a]

| Region | 1 | % | 2–3 | % | 4–5 | % | 6+ | % | No Response | % | Number of Libraries | Mean Services |
|---|---|---|---|---|---|---|---|---|---|---|---|---|
| | | | Religious and Other Special Collections, Subject Interests and Publications | | | | | | | | | |
| Northeast | 13 | 37 | 5 | 14 | 3 | 9 | 0 | 0 | 14 | 40 | 35 | 1.8 |
| Middle Atlantic | 51 | 33 | 30 | 19 | 14 | 9 | 4 | 3 | 57 | 37 | 156 | 2.1 |
| Southeast | 19 | 20 | 14 | 15 | 7 | 8 | 3 | 3 | 50 | 54 | 93 | 2.4 |
| Southwest | 22 | 27 | 22 | 27 | 1 | 1 | 2 | 2 | 35 | 43 | 82 | 2.0 |
| West | 9 | 18 | 8 | 16 | 5 | 10 | 2 | 4 | 26 | 52 | 50 | 2.6 |
| Rocky Mountains | 5 | 63 | 0 | 0 | 1 | 13 | 0 | 0 | 2 | 25 | 8 | 1.5 |
| Middle West | 49 | 25 | 33 | 17 | 14 | 7 | 8 | 4 | 93 | 47 | 197 | 2.3 |
| Canada | 5 | 23 | 5 | 23 | 2 | 9 | 0 | 0 | 10 | 45 | 22 | 2.3 |
| Total | 173 | 27 | 117 | 18 | 47 | 7 | 19 | 3 | 287 | 45 | 643 | 2.2 |

[a] The extended services (cumulative) variable represents the sum of positive or missing scores for 4 variables: general religious subject interests, subject interests, special collections and publications. Therefore, a library with a positive response on all four component variables would achieve a maximum score of 15 if it had, for example

| | |
|---|---|
| General religious subject interests | 1 |
| Subject interests (listed) | 5 |
| Special collections (listed) | 6 |
| Publications | 3 |
| Total (Cumulative) | 15 |

TABLE 3.54
1978 and 1988 *American Library Directory* Longitudinal Study Library Extended Services (Cumulative) for Popular Libraries

| Type of Library | --------1978-------- | | | | --------1988-------- | | | | Percentage Change 1978-88 |
|---|---|---|---|---|---|---|---|---|---|
| | Number of Libraries | No Response | Total Libraries | Mean Services | Number of Libraries | No Response | Total Libraries | Mean Services | |
| Popular | 226 | 461 | 687 | 2.1 | 356 | 287 | 643 | 2.2 | 4.8 |
| Congregational | 204 | 430 | 634 | 2.1 | 327 | 266 | 593 | 2.1 | 0 |
| Parochial | 6 | 21 | 27 | 2.2 | 12 | 13 | 25 | 3.1 | 41 |
| Public | 16 | 10 | 26 | 2.5 | 17 | 8 | 25 | 2.8 | 12 |

TABLE 3.55

1978 and 1988 *American Library Directory* Longitudinal Study Popular Library Extended Services (Cumulative) by Denomination

| Denomination | 1978 | | | | 1988 | | | | Percentage Change 1978-88 |
|---|---|---|---|---|---|---|---|---|---|
| | Number of Libraries | No Response | Total Libraries | Mean Services | Number of Libraries | No Response | Total Libraries | Mean Services | |
| Baptist | 24 | 59 | 83 | 2.3 | 36 | 35 | 71 | 2.2 | -4.3 |
| Christian | 6 | 13 | 19 | 1.9 | 11 | 6 | 17 | 2.9 | 53 |
| Churches of Christ | 0 | 0 | 0 | 0 | 2 | 0 | 2 | 1.5 | |
| Episcopal/Anglican | 10 | 32 | 42 | 2.6 | 14 | 20 | 34 | 2.9 | 12 |
| Independent | 1 | 4 | 5 | 1.0 | 1 | 2 | 3 | 1.0 | 0 |
| Lutheran | 13 | 40 | 53 | 2.2 | 18 | 24 | 42 | 2.7 | 23 |
| Mennonite | 0 | 3 | 3 | 0 | 2 | 2 | 4 | 4.0 | |
| Methodist | 12 | 43 | 55 | 2.3 | 21 | 43 | 64 | 1.8 | -22 |
| Other Denominations | 31 | 61 | 92 | 2.2 | 38 | 39 | 77 | 2.4 | 9 |
| Presbyterian | 29 | 86 | 115 | 2.0 | 43 | 54 | 97 | 1.9 | -5 |
| United Church of Christ | 2 | 11 | 13 | 2.0 | 4 | 9 | 13 | 2.8 | 40 |
| Summary | | | | | | | | | |
| Jewish | 87 | 76 | 163 | 2.1 | 153 | 34 | 187 | 2.1 | 0 |
| Roman Catholic | 11 | 33 | 44 | 2.4 | 13 | 19 | 32 | 2.6 | 8.3 |
| All Protestant | 128 | 352 | 480 | 2.2 | 190 | 234 | 424 | 2.3 | 4.6 |
| Total | 226 | 461 | 687 | 2.1 | 356 | 287 | 643 | 2.2 | 4.8 |

TABLE 3.56
1978 and 1988 *American Library Directory* Longitudinal Study Congregational (Type) Libraries Only with Extended Services by Denomination

| Denomination | 1978 | | | | 1988 | | | | Percentage Change 1978-88 |
|---|---|---|---|---|---|---|---|---|---|
| | Number of Libraries | No Response | Total Libraries | Mean Services | Number of Libraries | No Response | Total Libraries | Mean Services | |
| Baptist | 24 | 59 | 83 | 2.3 | 36 | 35 | 71 | 2.2 | -4.3 |
| Christian | 5 | 13 | 18 | 1.6 | 11 | 6 | 17 | 2.9 | 81 |
| Churches of Christ | 0 | 0 | 0 | 0.0 | 2 | 0 | 2 | 1.5 | 0 |
| Episcopal/Anglican | 10 | 31 | 41 | 2.6 | 13 | 20 | 33 | 3.0 | 15 |
| Independent | 0 | 3 | 3 | 0.0 | 0 | 1 | 1 | 0.0 | 0 |
| Lutheran | 13 | 40 | 53 | 2.2 | 18 | 24 | 42 | 2.7 | 23 |
| Mennonite | 0 | 3 | 3 | 0.0 | 2 | 2 | 4 | 4.0 | 0 |
| Methodist | 12 | 43 | 55 | 2.3 | 21 | 43 | 64 | 1.8 | -22 |
| Other Denominations | 26 | 60 | 86 | 2.1 | 34 | 37 | 71 | 2.4 | 14 |
| Presbyterian | 29 | 86 | 115 | 2.0 | 43 | 54 | 97 | 1.9 | -5 |
| U.C.C. | 2 | 11 | 13 | 2.0 | 4 | 9 | 13 | 2.8 | 40 |
| Summary | | | | | | | | | |
| Jewish | 80 | 70 | 150 | 2.0 | 140 | 30 | 170 | 2.0 | 0 |
| Roman Catholic | 3 | 11 | 14 | 2.7 | 3 | 5 | 8 | 2.0 | -26 |
| All Protestant | 121 | 349 | 470 | 2.2 | 184 | 231 | 415 | 2.3 | 4.6 |
| Total | 204 | 430 | 634 | 2.1 | 327 | 266 | 593 | 2.1 | 0 |

TABLE 3.57
1988 *American Library Directory* Congregational (Type) Libraries
with the Highest Cumulative Scores for Popular Library Extended
Services[a]

| Library | Score |
| --- | --- |
| Congregation Beth Achim, Southfield, MI | 11 |
| Grace Lutheran Church, Show Low, AZ | 8 |
| Church of the Holy Faith, Santa Fe, NM | 8 |
| Adath Israel Synagogue, Cincinnati, OH | 8 |
| First Baptist Church of Lakewood, Long Beach, CA | 7 |
| Eaglewood Christian Church, Indianapolis, IN | 7 |
| Central Presbyterian Church, Terre Haute, IN | 7 |

[a] Library service includes the listings of general religious and subject interests, special collections and publications published.

TABLE 3.58
1988 *American Library Directory* Parochial School Libraries with the
Highest Cumulative Scores for Popular Library Extended Services[a]

| Library | Score |
| --- | --- |
| Central Agency for Jewish Education, Miami, FL | 8 |
| Jewish Education Association, Louisville, KY | 8 |
| Bureau of Jewish Education, San Francisco, CA | 5 |
| Bureau of Jewish Education, Getzville, NY | 4 |
| Edmonton Catholic Schools, Edmonton, AB | 3 |
| Board of Jewish Education, New York, NY | 2 |
| Commission des Écoles Catholiques, Montréal, PQ | 2 |

[a] Library service includes the listings of general religious and subject interests, special collections and publications published.

TABLE 3.59

1988 *American Library Directory* Public Libraries with the Highest
Cumulative Scores for Popular Library Extended Services[a]

| Library | Score |
|---|---|
| Stamford Catholic Library, Stamford, CT | 5 |
| Minnie Cobey Library, Columbus, OH | 5 |
| Cecil Harding Jones, Jenkintown, PA | 5 |
| Oratoire St. Joseph, Montréal, PQ | 5 |
| Theosophical Book Association for the Blind, Ojai, CA | 4 |
| Catholic Lending Library, Hartford, CT | 4 |
| Crombaugh Memorial Public Church, Le Roy, IL | 3 |
| Flint Newman Center, Flint, MI | 3 |
| Toronto Jewish Congress, Willowdale, ON | 3 |
| Catholic Information Center, Philadelphia, PA | 2 |
| Jewish Public Library, Montreal, PQ | 2 |

[a] Library service includes the listings of general religious and subject interests, special collections, and publications published.

TABLE 3.60

1978 and 1988 *American Library Directory* Longitudinal Study Gross
Popular Library Rating Points Over Twenty-seven Growth Variables

| Library Type | No. of Libraries | No Response | Total Libraries | Mean Points | No. of Libraries | No Response | Total Libraries | Mean Points | % Change 1978–88 |
|---|---|---|---|---|---|---|---|---|---|
| | ----1978---- | | | | ----1988---- | | | | |
| Popular | 435 | 36 | 471 | 8,283 | 434 | 35 | 469 | 11,240 | 36 |
| Congregational | 408 | 32 | 440 | 6,021 | 408 | 32 | 440 | 7,976 | 32 |
| Parochial | 12 | 4 | 16 | 34,820 | 11 | 3 | 14 | 39,060 | 12 |
| Public | 15 | 0 | 15 | 48,570 | 15 | 0 | 15 | 79,510 | 64 |

TABLE 3.61

1988 *American Library Directory* Denomination by Library Type for Popular Library Matched Pairs

| Denomination | Congregational Libraries | Parochial Libraries | Public Libraries | All Popular |
|---|---|---|---|---|
| Baptist | 61 | 0 | 0 | 61 |
| Christian | 13 | 0 | 0 | 13 |
| Churches of Christ | 0 | 0 | 0 | 0 |
| Episcopal/Anglican | 27 | 0 | 0 | 27 |
| Independent | 1 | 0 | 1 | 2 |
| Lutheran | 35 | 0 | 0 | 35 |
| Mennonite | 3 | 0 | 0 | 3 |
| Methodist | 39 | 0 | 0 | 39 |
| Other Denominations | 51 | 0 | 2 | 53 |
| Presbyterian | 86 | 0 | 0 | 86 |
| United Church of Christ | 10 | 0 | 0 | 10 |
| Summary | | | | |
| Jewish | 109 | 6 | 4 | 119 |
| Roman Catholic | 5 | 8 | 8 | 21 |
| All Protestant | 326 | 0 | 3 | 329 |
| Total | 440 | 14 | 15 | 469 |

# 4

# POPULAR RELIGIOUS LIBRARY CHARACTERISTICS

This chapter is a continuation and extension of chapter 3 and takes up three additional major subjects as they relate to popular religious libraries— library personnel, library material, and library expenditures. Each section and subsection has appropriate introductions and conclusions to introduce and summarize what was learned about the subject in the chapter. In addition, a projection will be shown of future development, and additional research projects will be suggested for future consideration. Tables of many kinds were made for each section, and many of them are reproduced here.

## Library Personnel

"Library personnel" may be a rather formal or even pretentious designation for the handful of part-time volunteer ladies who gather in the typical North American congregational library once a week or so to carry out their assigned clerical tasks. On the other hand, since this field has been growing rapidly, it is true also in a surprising number of cases that there are not only paid full-time staff members in some of these libraries but even a few professional librarians. While most scholarly libraries are operated by full-time paid staff members, usually professionals with paid clerks and part-time student assistants providing support, whenever a popular congregational library contained a full-time, paid professional or clerical staff member, that was unusual.

In further contrast to the congregational libraries, most of the few parochial school and public libraries in these popular library databases had paid staff members, usually full-time, and many of them professionals.[1] Therefore, the number of full-time paid professional and clerical staff members formed only a modest staff proportion in the congregational libraries, but a much larger proportion in parochial school and public libraries. The opening section of this chapter will discuss these matters in detail for professional, clerical, student assistant (volunteer committee), and total staff members, each personnel level being discussed separately.[2] These *American Library Directory* popular library staff members may be contrasted with the CSLA popular library staff members to be discussed in the next chapter.

## Professionals

We can look at the databases for popular libraries starting with professionals in 1988. After an overall survey of the field, we will examine professionals by library type, region, library expenditure, and denomination. Which libraries had the largest numbers of each type of library staff members?

Professionals were found in ninety-five or 15 percent, of the 642 popular North American libraries according to longitudinal table 4.1 for 1988. Five percent of these ninety-five libraries had two or more professionals. In the remaining 85 percent of the cases, the libraries either lacked professionals or failed to mention them in the *ALD* entry. Due to small Ns for parochial school and public libraries most of the professionals were found to work in congregational rather than parochial school or public libraries. The popular libraries having professionals in 1988 averaged 1.6 apiece, compared with four apiece for the 885 (62 percent) scholarly libraries that listed professional librarians.

A 1988 table shows the number of professional staff members sorted by *library type*. The overall means were 1978—1.6 and 1988—1.6 professionals, no longitudinal change. Congregational libraries rose only from 1.6 to 1.7 professionals in this time, or 6 percent. Parochial school and public libraries had numbers that were too small to evaluate. However, these two library types apparently declined in mean number of professionals during the decade, while the number of popular libraries as a whole having professionals rose by 10 percent during that time period.

Tables 4.2 for 1978 and 4.3 for 1988 covered *congregational* libraries in all denominations and showed the specific libraries that led each group.

They showed specific 1978 congregational libraries but contained different sets of libraries. Table 4.3 is led by the LDS Library in Salt Lake City with thirteen or more professionals. Note that the top four libraries come from four different denominations.

Longitudinal table 4.4 shows congregational library professionals by denomination, though the No Response total was high and the active Ns were again small. Only 13 percent (12 percent in 1978) of the libraries in this breakdown had any professionals, eighty (73 in 1978) of them. Leaders for professionals were Baptist, Jewish, and Presbyterian libraries. Please note that the number of libraries with professionals increased 1978 to 1988 by seven persons, or 10 percent.

Which denominations had professionals and which ones had the largest number of them? For congregational libraries, Other Denominations and Baptist denominations had the largest mean number of professionals, 1.7 and 2.2 persons respectively, among those libraries with any professionals at all. However, only two denominations had enough professionals to justify our attention: Jewish and Roman Catholic. Roman Catholic had fourteen professionals altogether, for an average per library of 1.4 professional persons, and Jewish showed forty-nine, to average 1.3 professionals per library. Jewish and Roman Catholic had about half of the 1988 total number of 132 professionals working in congregational libraries, with the Jewish alone registering 37 percent of the total.

Due to the small number of professionals in the congregational libraries, most of the denominational tables of the largest professional staffs, which were made to list specific libraries, were shorter than usual. Even so, the *Baptist* table 4.5 for 1978 had two quite sizeable libraries: the Walnut Street Baptist Church, Louisville, with over thirteen professionals and the First Baptist Church in Murfreesboro, Tennessee with eight of them.

Now let us compare this information with the 1988 Baptist table, table 4.6. The 1988 Baptist table contained only four libraries, the Walnut Street Church being absent, but one library was good-sized—the First Baptist Church in Murfreesboro. This decline represents a considerable change in the staffing of these two leading libraries after a decade. Professional presence in these libraries probably meant that the persons worked there as part-time volunteers. Evidence from the personnel expenditure tables seen later will tell us that some of the professionals in the libraries in this table must have been paid, due to the high salary values found. Whether or not they were full-time or paid, the library had the benefit of their services.

For the 1988 *Christian* churches, one library was located in Indianapolis, and it had one professional. For 1978 *Congregational* church libraries, one library was listed, with two professionals located in Stamford. For 1988 *Churches of Christ*, two libraries had one professional apiece. A table for 1988 *Episcopal/Anglican* listed only three libraries with small numbers of professionals, table 4.7. *Lutheran* libraries in a separate table for 1988 were led by Trinity Lutheran Church in Moorhead, Minnesota, with five professionals, table 4.8. A table for 1988 *Methodist* was short, and its libraries had only two professionals apiece, table 4.9. For *Other Denominations*, five libraries were listed, but only one was especially interesting in this context. It was the Mormon headquarters library in Salt Lake City with over thirteen professionals.

Table 4.10, for 1988 *Presbyterian* churches, contained five leading libraries, all with two or three professionals. The next table in this series, table 4.11 for 1988 and for *Jewish* synagogues, was the largest of them all, with nine libraries listed. It was led by the Stephen S. Wise Temple in Los Angeles, which had five professionals. The last table for 1988, table 4.12 for *Roman Catholic* libraries, was led by Cardinal Ritter parochial school, an outstanding popular library, with three professionals. The next table, 4.13 for 1988, listed four Jewish and four Roman Catholic libraries, making up the entire *parochial school* table. This was a table of small numbers of professionals. A fourth of the libraries were Canadian. Cardinal Ritter School in St. Louis led the table with three professionals.

Now we come to *public* libraries, table 4.14 for 1988. Again the number of professionals was small, and Roman Catholic (5) and Jewish (2) made up the entire table. The Toronto Jewish Congress, the YMWHA, and the Oratoire St. Joseph led with three and two professionals apiece. This picture was similar to that for parochial school libraries. By *region*, the No Response percentage was high, so only a limited number of categories were available for serious consideration. Mean professional staff sizes were in the zero to two range. See table 4.15 for 1988 popular libraries.

If we consider a 1988 table (not shown) showing popular library professional staff members by total annual *library expenditure*, we see that as library expenditure rose the number of professionals rose from 1.3 professionals for those libraries spending less than $1,500 annually to 2.8 professionals for those spending $9,501 to $220,000 annually. We can verify that this is true only for libraries that list some professionals.

In summary, ninety-five popular libraries reported professional librarians in 1988. A few libraries enjoyed the services of over thirteen professionals. The number of professionals rose as total annual expenditure rose. Jewish and Roman Catholic libraries were common in this group. While there were no medium-sized or large libraries by number of professionals in these tables, several libraries had four or more professionals on the staff. The hypothesis that professionals were alien to popular libraries is now refuted. Note, however, that the mean total number of professional staff members remained not quite stationary for the decade. Disappointing! In fact, however, both of the means grew slightly to almost 1.65 and the number of libraries with professionals increased somewhat by 1988.

If we move back to the 1978 Baptist table for a minute, we will see two interesting points. The Walnut Street Baptist Church had over thirteen professionals in that year, a large number, but the Walnut Street Church listed only one professional staff member in the 1988 *ALD* table (not shown). Secondly, the First Baptist Church in Murfreesboro also had more staff members in 1978 than in 1988, eight versus six of them. The author can only wonder what the discrepancies indicated. Perhaps the staff turnover rate was high in many of these congregational libraries.

## Clerical Staff Members

Now we can move on to full and part-time clerical staff members. A set of analyses was made of clerical staff members by library type, region, total annual expenditure, chief librarian's gender, and denomination. Let us start with *library type*. Full-time paid clerks were unusual in congregational but were much more common in parochial school and public libraries. In table 4.16 for 1988 we can see that only sixty-eight, or 11 percent, of the popular libraries had clerks, whereas 858, or 60 percent, of the scholarly libraries had them. We can see further that these sixty-eight libraries averaged three to four clerks apiece and that one percent of the libraries had six or more clerks, a large number, even though most were almost certainly part-time volunteers.

Note that clerks declined in number between 1978 and 1988 by 35 percent, 4.3 to 2.8 per library. Coupled with the nearly stable frequency of professional staff members, this was quite disappointing. The overall mean was 4.3 clerks for the 106 popular libraries that had clerical staff members in 1978, or a total of 456 clerks. Congregational libraries led the popular library group, as usual, and their mean was 4.4 clerks per library.

Parochial school libraries had 1.5 clerks on the average and public libraries had 2.3 on the average, but their Ns were too small to be studied seriously. In 1988 the overall mean was 2.8 clerks for the 68 libraries reporting clerks out of 643 popular libraries, or only 191 clerks—a fall of

58 percent. Congregational libraries averaged three clerks per library for the fifty-five libraries having clerks out of the 593 congregational libraries, 9 percent. Parochial and public libraries averaged 1.7 and 1.6 clerks respectively for the few libraries with clerks.

By type of library, clerical staff members are shown for 1988 *congregational* libraries in longitudinal table 4.17 for all denominations combined. In that same table for 1978 the mean was 4.4 clerks, with Protestant outnumbering Jewish-Catholic. In 1988 the mean was 3.0 clerks per library with Protestant still outnumbering Jewish-Catholic. Apparently, Other Denominations grew in clerical mean values much more than did any other denomination and fell significantly in terms of the number of libraries involved, thirteen to eight.

In tables 4.18 for 1978 and 4.19 for 1988 for congregational libraries combined we have several specific libraries with large clerical staffs. These are the largest of the congregational libraries by clerical staff members. In table 4.18 note that its libraries reached the over thirteen maximum in much larger frequencies than they did in 1988. Three of the first four libraries were Mormon, including the two leaders with over thirteen clerks apiece, large numbers. Other Denominations with four, Jewish with five, and Episcopal/Anglican with three libraries together accounted for more than half of the total.

Now we come to *parochial school* libraries in tables 4.20 and 4.21 for 1988. How many clerical staff members did they report? Only a small number. About a fourth of these libraries had one to three clerks apiece. Two of the libraries in table 4.20 were Jewish and two were Roman Catholic. Finally, the *public* libraries with the highest number of clerical staff members are shown in tables 4.22 for 1978 and 4.21 and 4.23 for 1988. In 1978 the Theosophical Book Association for the Blind led the group with four clerical staff members. In table 4.23 for 1988 the YMWHA Library in New York had three clerks to lead the table. Jewish and Roman Catholic constituted more than half of the total number of libraries. Three of the libraries were located in Ontario and one in Quebec.

We can look at clerks and *regional* differences in table 4.24 for 1978, though its No Response ratios were large and its actual library percentages were small. Regional differences were small, though the Southwest seemed to have the highest mean number of clerks in its libraries with Middle West and Southeast next. As for a*nnual expenditures*, the popular libraries' expenditures were small. None listed expenditures above the $20,001–$95,000 level in 1978 nor above the $95,001–$220,000 level in 1988. Among libraries with clerical staff members, the *chief librar-*

*ian's gender* ratios, female:male, were 1.3:1.0 and 1.8:1.0 for 1978 and 1988. Females increased their dominance in the later year. For clerical staff members, the proportions of libraries reporting these members were about 15 percent and 10.6 percent for 1978 and 1988, small, according to table 4.24 (1978).

Here we can begin a series of discussions by *denomination* of the specific popular libraries with the largest number of clerical staff members. By denomination as a whole in 1978, the largest group was Lutheran with a mean of 7.5 clerks per library for the ten libraries having clerks. Smallest was Other Denominations with only 2.3 clerks per library for the twelve libraries having clerks. For 1988, the largest group by mean number of clerks was Other Denominations having greatly increased its clerical staff mean, and the smallest was Jewish, surprisingly.

Table 4.25 for *Baptist* 1978 libraries showed a large number of clerks to be working in certain ones of them. The three leaders had over thirteen clerks apiece located in three states: the First Baptist Churches in Long Beach and Murfreesboro and the Shiloh Baptist Church in Washington, D.C. Several other libraries in this table reported large numbers of clerks also. A fine showing! The 1988 Baptist table showed only two Albuquerque libraries with five clerks apiece, however. See table 4.26. Seldom have two tables looked as different in terms of size and specific libraries as these two Baptist tables. For *Christian* 1978 libraries, an unreproduced table showed two more libraries with over thirteen clerks apiece in two more states: the Central Christian Church in Lexington and the High Street Christian Church in Akron.

We move on now to *Congregational* 1978 libraries to see another library with over thirteen clerks in yet another state: the First Congregational Church in Stamford, Connecticut. We can look at *Episcopal/Anglican* 1988 libraries also where we find four different libraries in table 4.27 with small clerical totals. However, again we have no way of knowing whether these clerks worked full or part-time or were paid or not. It seems likely, in some instances at least, that they were full-time and paid, or else part-time and paid, while in many instances they must have been unpaid volunteers. And further, the 1978 Episcopal/Anglican table reported tallies for only two different libraries. For *Independent* only one library was listed with one clerk, the Centre for Christian Studies in Toronto.

*Lutheran* in 1978 had four libraries in the top category of over thirteen clerks, as seen in table 4.28. Grace Lutheran Church in La Grange, Illinois, First Lutheran Church in Red Wing, Minnesota, Ascension Lutheran Church and Our Savior's Lutheran Church, both in Milwaukee.

This table showed several other Lutheran libraries to have sizeable clerical staffs also. Table 4.29 for 1988 showed only two libraries with four clerks apiece, however. *Methodist* 1988 libraries listed only a few clerks, table 4.30.

*Other Denominations* 1988 table 4.31 listed six completely different libraries from those listed in the 1978 table (not shown). Three of these new libraries had over thirteen clerks and five of them had Mormon parent institutions—in Mesa, Boca Raton, Ventura, San Diego, and Salt Lake City. *Presbyterian* 1978 libraries in table 4.32 included one library with over thirteen clerks (Presbyterian Church, Tenafly, New Jersey) and seven others also having strong staffs, with at least four clerks apiece. Table 4.33 for 1988 Presbyterians listed two strong libraries, including the First United Presbyterian Church in Albuquerque with nine clerks.

The *United Church of Christ* 1978 table was short and listed only a few clerks. The U.C.C. list for 1988 was even shorter with two libraries. One had five clerks, St. Stephen United Church of Christ, Sandusky, Ohio. We can look at table 4.34 for *Jewish* libraries in 1988 and find again a largely different list from that of 1978 (not shown) with no large libraries included. However, two libraries tied with six clerks apiece to lead that 1978 table. *Roman Catholic* 1988 libraries showed only three libraries with two clerks apiece, table 4.35.

In summary, clerical staff members were used by sixty-eight, or 11 percent, of the popular libraries in 1988. By region, the Southeast led in number of clerks. Lutherans, Baptists, Mormons, Jewish and Other Denominations led by denomination in clerical library staff sizes. For chief librarian's gender, libraries with females led in numbers of clerks. And as the number of clerks rose so did the number of libraries with higher level expenditures. There were fourteen large libraries with more than ten clerks by size of clerical staff. It should be remembered that staff levels were found to be quite dynamic, so prediction of past and future levels was difficult except perhaps in terms of averages.

## Student (Library Committee Volunteer) Staff Members

The third of the three kinds of popular library personnel can be studied now—student assistants—which term, in this context, was given an alternate definition, one more appropriate to popular libraries. These individuals were defined as part-time, generally unpaid adult *volunteer* staff members, usually mature ladies. Among congregational libraries this group often formed a house of worship library committee as a way of carrying out its work and of keeping the library functioning.

Occasionally the library committee included one or more professional librarians or experienced library clerks (often persons working in school libraries elsewhere) among its members. Most of these committees contained three to ten members, but certain of the committees in this series reported many more members providing library service for the congregation. They were performing a "Library Ministry," as some congregations liked to call it. For library committee staff members (student assistants or volunteers), the percentage of libraries so reporting was 14.6 percent for 1978 and 16 percent for 1988. Small. Note, however, that differences in *ALD* reporting procedures seems to account for part of this growth. For the mean student staff group size, among those libraries having any students at all, we have 4.4 members for 1978 and 7.0 members for 1988, a 59 percent decade increase in student or library committee size.

In table 4.36 for 1988 we can see that student (or committee) staff members were not often listed in popular libraries. In 1978 there were one hundred popular libraries with student staff members/committees; and in 1988 103, or 16 percent, of the popular libraries listed student assistants or committee members as compared with 675 and 47 percent of such listings for scholarly libraries. See table 4.37 for 1978 also. The mean for scholarly library student assistants was fifteen per library. For popular libraries, we can study them by congregational libraries only, by type of library, by region, by chief librarian's gender, and then by denomination. The reader should realize that for most popular library entries, no staff at all was shown in the *ALD* beyond the name of the library head, and often not even that, so we are fortunate to find staffing details for any of these libraries.

We can start the library committee analysis with a table summarizing the leading *congregational* libraries. For parochial school and public libraries the staffing data was negligible in both years. Table 4.38 for 1978 shows little more than the "before" for congregational libraries, whereas table 4.39 for 1988 shows the "after" for them. Note, however, that even in 1978 as many as sixteen libraries had thirteen or more committee members.

By *region*, the largest mean committee staff was in the Northeast, with 7.5 members, and the smallest was the West, with 3.2 members for 1978. For 1988, the largest was in the West, with 9.3 members, and the smallest were in the Northeast and Canada, with 2.6 and 3.7 staff members. The

Northeast and West reversed their positions over the decade! The author found also that the libraries *headed by males* averaged 9.2 committee members in 1988 and those headed by females averaged only 6.0 committee members in the same year. So males had the larger committees. There was some evidence that the size of these committees rose with the level of library expenditures.

When we look at the mean size of the committee groups by *denomination*, we see that the largest committees had an average of ten members for Christian, fourteen for Other Denominations, and seventeen for Roman Catholic libraries. Obviously, 1978 produced little on the table, but 1988 produced something more. See longitudinal table 4.39. Table 4.40 for 1988 shows the largest specific *congregational* libraries for student or committee staff members. Four of the first seven libraries were Mormon, and six of the latter reached the scholarly library maximum level of 33.5+ student staff members. Three familiar library names occupied the other three slots among the top seven libraries. This is a table of large libraries that must contain some full-time and paid persons, though we have no positive information on that subject.

Now for the denominational analyses of specific libraries. *Baptists* were leaders in this national field and table 4.41 1988 confirms this statement. The First Baptist Church of Greensboro with 33.5+ committee members had a large staff committee. Two other Baptist libraries had medium-sized committees also. Texas and Florida led the state locations. *Christian* church libraries made up a small table for 1988, but three of its libraries had medium-sized or small staffs, table 4.42.

The short 1988 *Episcopal/Anglican* church list in table 4.43 was good-sized at the top with one medium-sized library but was unusually small at the bottom. Much the same can be said for *Lutherans* for 1988, but two of its libraries had medium-sized staffs, table 4.44. *Methodist* table 4.45 1988 presents a large number of staff members for the table as a whole of which four were above ten in staff size. A good performance. No geographic concentration could be detected.

*Other Denominations* churches in table 4.46 for 1988 present an impressive array of well-staffed libraries, especially the Mormon churches with their genealogical collections, in Mesa, San Diego, Salt Lake City, and Ventura. The top four libraries were large by any standard and all except one Florida library were located in the West. Carmel Presbyterian Church in Glenside, Pennsylvania, was one of the few libraries in this series to reach the scholarly library maximum of 33.5+ committee members. Table 4.47 for 1988 *Presbyterian* presents a list of ten small libraries. A table for 1988 showed a list of small libraries for *United Church of Christ*, also.

*Jewish* libraries in table 4.48 for 1988 include nine typical-sized committee groups plus one large one for the Jewish Community Center in Rockville, Maryland, having 19.5+ staff members. *Roman Catholic* libraries for 1988 contain two large committees, one in the All Saints Catholic Church in Dallas at 33.5+ staff members, and one in the Immaculate Heart of Mary Parish Library in Los Alamos, 15.5 staff members, table 4.49.

In summary, volunteer or student assistant library committee members totaled 4.4 persons in 1978 and 7.0 persons per library in 1988, a 59 percent increase for the decade. One hundred three, or 16 percent, of the 1988 popular libraries listed student assistants. By region, the Northeast and the West had the largest committees. Other Denominations and Baptist had the largest committees by denomination. Male chief librarians and higher expenditures characterized those libraries with the large committees.

Six libraries reached the maximum of 33.5+ volunteer library committee members with half of them being located in Mormon (Other Denominations) churches. Several others had fifteen or more staff members. In total, twenty libraries were above ten committee members, and more than half of them were Baptist, Methodist, or Other Denominations. These libraries must be among the largest in staff size among popular libraries in North America.

## Total Staff Members

Now we have reached the final personnel category, in which we can see the *total staff sizes* for the largest libraries by region and by denomination. They represent the largest popular North American libraries in the *ALD* by personnel and denomination. Total library staff members for 1978 were reported by only a small percentage of the popular libraries, however, 16 percent or 109 libraries and 556 librarians. For 1988 the percentage was 29 percent of the total, or 185 libraries and 1,148 librarians, an improvement. Among these few libraries the mean total staff size was 5.1 in 1978 and 6.2 in 1988. So we have another longitudinal gain and more than twice as many librarians. For the matched pairs the percentages of participation were 23 percent and 21 percent, and the mean staff sizes were 5.2 and 6.8 staff members. What can we make of this?

We have a longitudinal study of total staff members by library type which has an overall mean growth of 22 percent, slightly larger than the corresponding figure for scholarly libraries. Congregational has a percent decade change of 32 percent, but both parochial school ($-50$ percent) and public ($-45$ percent) are on the negative side in decade change, however.

Longitudinal shows mean total staff members for popular libraries and mean percentage change 1978–88 by type of library, region and denomination. The popular library mean grew by almost a fourth, 1978–88. Congregational libraries grew on this variable by one third during the decade, very good. Both parochial school and public libraries shrank in number, but the Ns were small. Note that these percents are somewhat larger than the corresponding one-fifth growth rate of the scholarly libraries. So popular grew somewhat more rapidly than did scholarly library staff membership during the decade.

In table 4.51 for 1978 and table 4.52 for 1988 we see that the spread of staff members listed was more impressive than the advance of the mean. The latter figures can be compared with 945, or 66 percent of the scholarly libraries for a mean of nineteen staff members. In table 4.53 (1988) we can see additional staffing figures for popular libraries. Leaders in this group were the congregational libraries of which 154, or 24 percent, listed staff committees with a mean of six persons. Parochial school and public libraries had much smaller numbers of staff members, the public library group averaging only three persons.

Popular libraries seemed to be generally larger and more fully staffed in 1988 than in 1978. In table 4.54 for 1988 total staff size by *region* we have the problem of large No Responses again. Overall means seemed to be five to six staff members again. These means for staff size are slightly above one-third of the means for scholarly libraries. The Southwest region led the table and the Southeast and West did well also. The Northeast, Canada, and Rocky Mountains did poorly and reflected small staffs.

We can look at total staff members by type of library, region, and denomination. Longitudinal table 4.50 shows mean total staff members for popular libraries and the mean percentage changes for 1978–88. Table 4.55 for 1988 shows total staff members by denomination for popular libraries, but the analysis is plagued by small percentages and large No Response scores. Largest staffs were in the Baptist and Other Denominations groups, with nine and fourteen staff members. Five denominations listed four staff members or more, however. Protestant committees were larger than Jewish and Catholic libraries here also. Table 4.56 shows congregational libraries by denomination. Other Denominations and U.C.C. grew the most in mean size 1978–88.

The *denominational* analysis by specific library can start with the *Baptist* group, which was good-sized and contained two libraries of above twenty total staff members each, table 4.57 (1988). These were the First Baptist Churches of Greensboro and Murfreesboro, familiar names. Five more Baptist libraries had medium-sized staffs.

The popular *Christian* church table for 1988 was short but contained two medium-sized libraries, table 4.58: Central Christian Church in Lexington and the High Street Christian Church in Akron. *Congregational* libraries for 1978 in table 4.59 again provided only a short list, but one library had a medium-sized staff, the First Congregational Church in Stamford. *Episcopal/Anglican* libraries for 1988 were generally small but again two of them were medium-sized, table 4.60; the Church of the Holy Faith, Santa Fe, and St. Thomas Episcopal Church, Sunnyvale, California. *Lutheran* libraries in table 4.61 for 1988 again included two medium-sized staffs: the Ascension Lutheran Church, Milwaukee, and the Grace Lutheran Church, La Grange, Illinois. More than half of this table's libraries were located in Minnesota or Wisconsin.

Leading *Methodist* church libraries are listed in table 4.62 for 1988. The top half of this table's library staffs were medium-sized and were led by the First United Methodist Church in Tulsa. For *Other Denominations*, the chapter prints both 1978 and 1988 tables, 4.63 and 4.64. Although twenty-three libraries appeared on the two tables, only five of them had large staffs. One, the LDS church in Salt Lake City, even reached the highest scholarly library category of over 59.5+ total staff members. Excellent!

Carmel Presbyterian Church again led the *Presbyterian* table of total staff members, table 4.65 for 1988. It had a large staff, over 33.5, one of the largest in the popular library database. And also, incidentally, in 1991 it received a CSLA Level 3 (Advanced) Certificate of Commendation. Two other libraries reported medium-sized staffs also. The largest *United Church of Christ* popular libraries were seen for 1988. One was medium-sized, table 4.66. *Jewish* 1988 popular libraries appear in table 4.67, where they are shown to include two medium-sized libraries: the Jewish Community Center, Rockville, Maryland, and the Stephen S. Wise Temple in Los Angeles. *Roman Catholic* libraries were led again by the All Saints Catholic Church in Dallas with 34.5 staff members and by Immaculate Heart of Mary Parish Church in Los Alamos in 1988, table 4.68.

Another view of the staff members in this study can be obtained in another table for 1988, table 4.69. It shows the ratio of popular library staff members between professional, clerical, student assistant (library committee members), and their total. Many of their Ns are small or nonexistent, and only a subjective impression can be gotten from the tables. Scores for library committee members range from 75 percent to 0 percent in a variety of patterns.

The means for those libraries having such staff members are: popular: 1.0 (professional); 1.2 (clerical); and 4.9 (other committee members). Notice again that both parochial school and public libraries appear to have a much higher percentage of professionals than do congregational libraries. Congregational libraries are staffed primarily by library committee assistants.

In table 4.69 we see popular libraries by type and also by library staff members. Popular libraries may seem to be small in personnel when compared with scholarly libraries, but their personnel group was growing rapidly in size. The percentage of congregational libraries which had professionals was 14 percent, clerks was 17 percent, committee volunteers was 69 percent. Parochial and public libraries had staff members in all categories, also, but with small Ns. Table 4.69 shows staff categories in percentages by denomination. The denomination with the largest percent of professionals was the Jewish, for clerks it was also Jewish and for student (committee) staff it was the Methodists, who led with 87 percent. So again we see that popular libraries reflected the student (committee) employees.

In summary, staff members were found in 109 popular libraries, or 17 percent of the total in 1978 and in 185 or 27 percent in 1988. Total staff sizes were 5.1 and 6.2 for 1978 and 1988. Overall longitudinal growth rate was 24 percent. What can we say about these popular library leaders in total staff size? One of them reached the maximum for scholarly libraries, over 59.5 staff members. In all, thirty-two libraries reached a medium-sized staffing level, in the teens, twenties, or thirties. The West region had the largest mean staff. Of the denominations, Baptist, Methodist and Other Denominations accounted for more than half of the libraries. We can also note that the tables of staffing totals did not always duplicate the breakdowns from earlier variable analyses.

## Chief Librarians

This section will take up another aspect of popular library personnel, the gender of chief librarians (the heads of the library committees) and its implications. In tables 2.7 and 4.70, the dominance of women in congregational library headships was made clear by up to a 7:1 margin. Women were the primary leaders in both parochial school and public libraries, also, but by less one-sided margins, especially for public libraries. We will look at chief librarian's gender by region, by library expenditures, by volume and by denomination.

Among popular libraries as a whole, women led in leadership positions by a 4:1 (1978) and a 6:1 (1988) margin, a considerable contrast to the scholarly library scene, where the two sexes were almost even. Men were strongest (45 percent) in public libraries. Only about an eighth of the popular libraries as a whole were headed by men, however. By region, men were best represented among Rocky Mountains and Canadian libraries in 1978, about a third being men in each region. In 1988 men were best represented among popular libraries in Canada and the Northeast where they made up about a fourth to a third of each total. In table 2.7 for 1978 we see that women were the leaders in popular libraries and were strongest in the following *regions*: Middle Atlantic, Southwest, and Middle West. Women were so dominant that they constituted 87 percent of the Southwestern region chief librarians.

Table 4.70 for 1978 and 1988 enables us to study chief librarian's gender by edition and by its changing proportions. While males made up only 11 percent of the popular library heads, females made up 36 percent of these library heads and 77 percent of the No Response category. Among popular libraries there was almost no change in chief librarian numbers 1978–88 among males, but there was a 53 percent increase among females and a sharp decrease in No Response chief librarians. Two tables for 1978 and 1988 enable us to compare the matched pairs with the newly born and died group of libraries and their chief librarians. The two tables were similar with female growth being somewhat larger in the matched pairs.

Still another table shows another analysis of *chief librarian's gender* for annual expenditure. The male domination here was quite strong for no longer listed and newly listed libraries. Table 4.71 shows popular annual library expenditures for 1978 and 1988 by chief librarian's gender. In each year the libraries with male chief librarians outspent the libraries with female chief librarians, though the gap between the two was smaller in 1988 than it was in 1978. Another table gave a strong hint of what the author has been saying throughout the book: as *library expenditures* rose so did the percentage of male chief librarians among popular libraries. There it is again in tabular form, table 4.72, though this table is full of small Ns.

Now for denominations. Males are so scarce among popular libraries that the tables made with them are often unreproduceable due to small numbers. However, with one useable 1988 table (not shown) we can see that Roman Catholic librarians were relatively strong (32 percent) in males as were Other Denominations libraries (25 percent male). However, Episcopal/Anglicans were 71 percent female and Baptists were 87 percent female. In another table, Episcopal/Anglican were mostly female at 91 percent, but U.C.C. libraries were least female at 69 percent. Still another table, 4.73 for 1988, shows that the mean for libraries headed by males was twice as large as the mean number of volumes held by libraries headed by females. The 1978 figures for this situation were similar.

Table 4.74 for 1988 shows chief librarians' religious order status by library type. The congregational and parochial school portions of the table show few clergy in charge of these libraries. However, a fourth of the public library heads were clergy or nuns. Therefore, public libraries ranked just behind convents/monasteries in the frequency of using "the cloth" as chief librarians. In summary, the dominance of women chief librarians continued in numbers, but the "qualitative" dominance of male chief librarians continued as well. Women were strongest in the Middle Atlantic and men were strongest in Canada and the Northeast. The clergy were chief librarians in only a few libraries, mostly public.

## Library Material Holdings

This section will display and discuss the library material holdings of popular libraries. It will cover volume, periodical title, vertical file, microform, media, map, and art reproduction holdings in that order. Again we are measuring the quantity of each type of material present, not necessarily its quality, for which no specific measure was available.

### Book Volumes

We open with book and bound periodical volume holdings. Again we know that they will be smaller than the corresponding holdings in scholarly libraries, but that fact is immaterial. The material collection carries the same importance for popular as it does for scholarly libraries. We will examine volume holdings in specific libraries for the three types of popular libraries—congregational, parochial school and public—in tables 4.75, 4.76, and 4.77 and other tables. First we will examine the data by type of library, by region, and then by denomination.

An overall view of popular library volume holdings is shown in longitudinal table 4.78. For 1978 and 1988, parochial school libraries were best stocked among popular libraries, with means of 35,560 volumes in 1978 and 20,489 in 1988, and showed also a surprising drop in holdings of 42 percent. For an explanation, we cannot fall back on low Ns or too many No Responses here with only a 22 percent No Response rate in 1988. Public libraries went from 16,553 to 17,800 volumes and congregational from 4,540 to 5,737 volumes, for the means in 1978 and 1988. The median was 2,250 volumes per library. So their order by mean volume holdings was parochial school, public and then congregational libraries.

All *congregational* libraries in table 4.75 for 1988 were large in this specific library table. Any popular library with 35,000 volumes was a large one, and here we have an entire table full of them of that size plus the Salt Lake City Mormon genealogical library with 200,000 volumes! Extraordinary! By denomination and location they were half Jewish and one-fourth Texan. Longitudinal table 4.78 shows congregational library volume holdings by denominations. Gain in volumes was 26 percent in the decade. The Roman Catholic gain was the largest at 175 percent.

*Parochial school* libraries in table 4.76 for 1988 were Jewish and Roman Catholic. They were also Canadian and New York libraries. And a parochial school library with at least 15,000 volumes, as all of them had, was at least medium-sized. This is a table of good-sized parochial school libraries. Table 4.77 for 1988 is another table of large popular libraries. Again they were 80 percent Jewish and Roman Catholic and 60 percent Canadian and New York state libraries. By city three were located in Montreal and two in New York. These were private *public* libraries and the largest one was the Jewish Public Library in Montreal.

Table 4.79 for 1988 shows volume holdings by *region*. Mean holdings in Canada were much larger than those in other regions: 28,890 volumes. Longitudinal table 4.80 shows mean volumes by Canada versus the United States. In 1978 and 1988 the Canadian score was well above the U.S. score, though the Canadian score was based on between twenty-two and twenty-seven libraries. Western region holdings of 4,995 volumes per library were smallest. We can see in a table not shown that Canadian popular libraries were primarily parochial school and public libraries. Holdings for 1978 were similar except that the Southwest occupied second place in holdings. While certainly not clearcut, it seems that volume holdings and annual expenditure correlated positively again in a linear curve, but the lack of active cases makes this result difficult to prove significant.

Mean volume holdings were also measured by chief librarians who were males vs. those who were females. In 1988 (male) 12,650 to (female) 6,143 volumes or a ratio of 2.06:1.00 existed. See table 4.73 for 1978 and 1988. There was also an indication that mean volumes rose as did library expenditures. In 1988, for instance, libraries with expenditures of $1,500 or under averaged 4,061 volumes, while those having expenditures of $20,002–$95,000 had 14,778 mean volumes. It was also true the other way around, that as mean number of volumes rose, so also did mean library expenditure.

By *denomination*, the Roman Catholic mean was highest for 1988 in table 4.81, 17,960 volumes, with Jewish libraries next with 8,340 volumes. Protestant volume totals were significantly smaller than Jewish-Roman Catholic totals, little more than half as large. United Church of Christ libraries were smallest with a mean of only 2,673 volumes, and Episcopal/Anglican libraries were next with 3,844 volumes.

Longitudinal table 4.82 shows overall volume holdings by denomination for popular libraries. Mean number of volumes for 1978 was 6,282 and was held by 505 libraries, or 74 percent of the total. For 1988 the mean was 6,776 volumes held by 618 libraries, or 96 percent. In both years, volume holdings was given for a high percentage of the libraries and was one of the most frequently found variables in the *ALD*. Overall mean growth was 8 percent between 1978 and 1988. Just why this increase was so poor is not clear. Mean Protestant volume holdings were below Jewish-Roman Catholic volume holdings by 29 percent. The denominations leading the table were the Roman Catholic and Jewish in both years. Smallest holdings were those of U.C.C. in both years.

Longitudinal table 4.83 shows volume holdings by denomination for congregational libraries only. Overall again from 1978 to 1988 was 26 percent, modest. Largest longitudinal growth belonged to the Lutheran group with Methodists next, 52 percent and 34 percent. Christian libraries lost ground here. Mean volume leaders in 1988 were Other Denominations and Jewish, both with about 7,000 volumes. Roman Catholics presented a strong picture but for only a small group of eight libraries. Smallest volume collection was in the U.C.C. with 2,673 volumes. The twenty-two tables were more often different than alike.

We have now come to the series of tables showing the volume holdings of specific popular libraries, those 1988 libraries with the largest collections in each denomination. The first one was a table of First *Baptist* churches with good-sized collections. Their collections represented primarily Texas (6) and North Carolina (2) libraries (see table 4.84). *Chris-*

*tian* table 4.85 was smaller in every way and contained three Texas libraries (38 percent). Nor was the *Churches of Christ* list noteworthy, table 4.86. The 1978 *Congregational* list was not made into a table, since it included fifteen libraries tied at the modest number of 2,250 volumes apiece.

Four Texas libraries (40 percent) are featured by number of volumes in table 4.87 for 1988 *Episcopal/Anglican* libraries. Two 15,000-volume libraries led the table, at the St. John the Divine Cathedral in New York and the Church of the Redeemer in Andalusia, Pennsylvania. *Independent* libraries formed a short table. Another short table gave us the *Lutheran* picture in which one library, Grace Lutheran Church, Show Low, Arizona, led all Lutheran libraries with 35,000 volumes, table 4.88. Table 4.89 *Mennonite* popular libraries provided another short table. *Methodist* libraries showed the leader, Christ Church, Louisville, to be an example of a medium-sized congregational library with 35,000 volumes (table 4.90).

The *Other Denominations* group produced unusual and interesting tables in the past, and this one is no exception, table 4.91 for 1988. It was led by a Mormon genealogical library with 200,000 volumes in Salt Lake City. Large! A Swedenborgian and a Friends library followed with 35,000 volumes apiece. *Presbyterian* 1988 libraries could not be made into a table because thirty-three of them were tied at approximately 6,750 volumes apiece. The *United Church of Christ* (table 4.92) is a large one with no noteworthy features except that almost half of the libraries were located in Ohio.

Table 4.93 for 1988 presents another excellent *Jewish* popular library showing. It was led by the Jewish Public Library in Montreal with its 130,000 volume collection. And all other libraries had 35,000 volumes, sizeable collections, several of which were leading Jewish libraries. The *Roman Catholic* table 4.94 for 1988 is another collection of strong libraries. The Petit Seminaire de Québec led with 200,000 volumes followed by the Oratoire St. Joseph Library in Montreal with 75,000 volumes. More than a third of the libraries in this table were Canadian. A fine showing!

Longitudinal table 4.95 shows a special analysis using twenty-three variables that studies gross growth rate related to volume holdings. The variables are listed in the table. Overall growth rate was 36 percent, 8,283 to 11,240 mean volumes. Otherwise results seemed to be similar between the two years. In summary, the overall popular library mean was 6,282 volumes in 1978 and 6,776 in 1988, an 8 percent increase. Jewish and Roman Catholic, New York and Canada libraries excelled in volume holdings. By region Canada again excelled and the West was smallest. Males again led females in size of holdings, and volume holdings rose as expenditure rose. The most significant finding was that the longitudinal volume gain was modest.

In summary for specific libraries, three belonged in the large volume category, one each for Jewish, Other Denominations, and Roman Catholic. Forty-five libraries in seven denominations belonged in the medium-sized category and almost two-thirds of them were Baptist, Jewish or Roman Catholic.

## Periodical Title Subscriptions

We can study the number of popular library religious periodical title subscriptions from five contrasting viewpoints—by type of library, by region, by total expenditures, by chief librarian's gender, and by denomination. Longitudinal table 4.96 shows the mean number of periodical titles subscribed to by each popular library type. Please remember that the mean includes only the 144 (1978) and 242 (1988) congregational libraries (38 percent) which had periodical subscriptions.

Congregational libraries averaged sixty-three titles for 1988, parochial school seventy-five, and public fifty-six titles. It is surprising how small this 1978–88 gain is. Parochial school holdings were largest, but they moved from 133 to 75 titles, a loss of 44 percent for the decade. Congregational libraries had sixty-one titles in 1978 and sixty-three in 1988 to show a small net gain of 3.3 percent. Public libraries had fifty-seven titles in 1978 and fifty-six in 1988 to show a small loss, −1.8 percent. Overall increase was only 2 percent. So change on periodical title subscriptions was small at best and sometimes negative.

Longitudinal table 4.97 shows the congregational library periodical holdings by denomination. Overall mean number of periodical titles was sixty-one for 1978 and sixty-three for 1988, while median number of titles was fifty! In other words, a small number of large libraries held many more periodical subscriptions than sixty-three, while the remaining libraries were quite modest. By *type of library*, table 4.98 for 1988 shows the largest *congregational* library subscription totals and contains five large libraries led by the LDS Headquarters Library in Salt Lake City.

We should remember that the number of subscriptions in the typical congregational library out in the field was small, between one and three, so even twenty titles is a large collection in this context. And seventeen hundred or even nine hundred titles, as we see in table 4.98, is quite large. Notice that the five libraries represent five different denominations, but also that three fifths of the libraries were located in Dallas, where even congregational libraries may grow to be large! Below the top five congregational libraries were 170 more at the fifty-title level!

The *parochial school* libraries seen in table 4.99 for 1988 are represented by four relatively large collections at 150-titles apiece. All of the institutions were Roman Catholic (except one) and all were also Canadian. *Public* libraries included one at the 150-title level—the Friends Free Library of Germantown in Philadelphia—and sixteen more libraries with scores of fifty titles apiece.

From a *regional* viewpoint, we can look at table 4.100 for 1988. It shows that all of the regions were about the same with a mean of sixty-three titles for those libraries having periodical titles. Canada and the Southwest led with ninety and seventy titles in this table, however. Forty-three percent of the libraries had one or more subscriptions, so obviously 57 percent had none. Analyzed by total *library expenditure* the expected result was obtained, the number of periodical subscriptions rose as the expenditure level rose, though not with classic regularity. And, of course, the expenditure levels of the popular libraries were low. Number of periodicals by *chief librarian's gender* showed that libraries headed by males had almost twice as many periodical titles per library as those headed by females, in spite of the much larger number of libraries headed by females.

We can now examine popular library periodical subscription totals from a *denominational* viewpoint though several denominational tables are omitted from this section. Periodical title subscriptions by denomination reveals Other Denominations libraries to have led the list with a large mean of 159 titles in 1978 and 126 in 1988. It was followed by Episcopal/Anglican libraries with 111 titles. Seven denominations with approximately fifty titles for each library holding periodicals fell into the bottom rank.

Now we can take up the periodical title subscriptions for each denomination by specific library. *Baptist* had twenty-eight libraries with fifty titles each, so no table was made. At the top of that unmade table, however, one library had 150 titles, the First Baptist Church in Dallas. Table 4.101 for 1988 shows *Christian* denomination libraries with the largest number of periodical subscriptions for the denomination. All seven libraries had fifty subscriptions. *Churches of Christ* listed only two libraries so no table was made for it.

*Congregational* libraries in table 4.102 for 1978 showed that each library had fifty subscriptions also. In another table for 1978 we see that the *Episcopal/Anglican* picture is the same as that for previous denominations, fifty titles apiece. However, in the 1988 printout, too long for a table, St. John the Divine Cathedral in New York had nine hundred titles! The *Independent* group listed only two libraries, one of which had 150 titles, the Protestant School Board of Montreal. *Lutherans* listed eighteen small libraries, too many for a table. The *Mennonite* group listed only one library, however.

*Methodist* libraries in table 4.103 for 1978 again showed fifty titles per library, and so did their 1988 printout, but one 1988 library with five hundred titles was listed also, Highland Park United Methodist Church, Dallas. *Other Denominations* listed twenty-seven small libraries in 1988 plus one with 150 titles and one with seventeen hundred—the Church of Jesus Christ of Latter-day Saints! *Presbyterian* libraries had no table, since the 1988 group included thirty-eight small libraries tied for the lead.

The *United Church of Christ* libraries in a table for 1988 showed again fifty titles for each library. Three of the four libraries were located in Ohio; see table 4.104. The *Jewish* list included one hundred small libraries so no table was made. When we come to *Roman Catholic* libraries in table 4.105 for 1988 we see a different picture, however. Each library in this table subscribed to 150 titles. Three of the table's four libraries were located in Canada.

In summary, most of the libraries in these tables showed only modest numbers of periodical titles. Longitudinal gain was quite small, also, only a 2 percent increase. The exception was table 4.98 for congregational libraries as a whole where the number of titles was large for a few leading libraries. By region, Canada and the Southwest led the other areas. Library expenditure also increased as the number of subscriptions increased. Libraries headed by males had almost twice as many periodical titles as libraries headed by females! Other Denominations and Episcopal/Anglican libraries led other denominations by mean number of titles held, 159 and 111 titles.

## Vertical File Holdings

The next type of library material to be examined is vertical file material. We may look at vertical file drawer holdings in popular libraries by first studying several tables by type of library. Then we will study regions, total expenditure, and denomination. Again we can expect popular to have much smaller VF collections than did scholarly libraries. Popular libraries averaged 6.1 files in 1978 and 7.5 in 1988, meaning an average gain of 23.7 percent for the decade. Largest decade gain was 99 percent by the parochial school libraries, congregational was next with 18 percent and public was smallest with 0.6 percent.

Vertical files are seen in detail for *type of library* in longitudinal table 4.106. We can see that 19 percent or 131 of the libraries, had these files and that these libraries averaged only 2.5 VF drawers per library in 1978. In 1988 the percent rose to 21 percent. Most of these vertical files were located in *congregational* libraries that averaged 6.5 drawers. Table 4.107 shows the leading congregational libraries and is led by the forty-eight file drawers of Temple Emanu-el in Tucson and the Eastminster Presbyterian Church in Indialantic, Florida. These are large collections.

One-seventh of the parochial schools had vertical files in 1978 increasing to one-fourth by 1988. They averaged seven and fourteen drawers in these two editions. For public libraries the corresponding figures were 23 percent and 40 percent in 1978 and 1988, and they averaged sixteen files in each year. The relevant no longer listed and newly listed libraries table (not shown) showed an average increase between databases of 78 percent, which was much higher than the scholarly libraries increase of 23 percent and the popular library increase of 25 percent.

For *parochial school* libraries we see the Miami Jewish Central Education Agency in the lead with forty-eight files in table 4.108 for 1988. Next is the Jewish Educational Association in Louisville. Table 4.109 for 1988 shows the picture for *public* libraries. The Minnie Cobey Library in Columbus led with ninety-three files followed by the National Council of Jewish Women in Montreal with twenty-five. Half of the libraries were Roman Catholic and the rest were divided between Jewish and Other Denominations. This large table also gave us an illustration of the variety of kinds of libraries which were classified as popular public libraries.

By *region* we were again troubled by small Ns. However, certain observations can be made about popular library vertical file drawers by region. The largest 1988 region had a mean of eleven files in the Southwest and the smallest had a mean of four files in the West. We can look at the number of vertical file drawers by *total annual expenditure* also. We see a positive correlation between total expenditure and files, subject to the limitations mentioned above. Those libraries averaging $1,500 or less annual expenditures averaged 5.6 drawers while those libraries averaging $95,001–$220,000 expenditure averaged 27.0 drawers apiece.

Next comes an introductory study of vertical files by *denomination*. The leading denomination in 1988 was Jewish with 11.0 files and the Other Denominations group was second with 9.6 files. Smallest were the Churches of Christ and Mennonite with 0 files. We can see the specific popular library vertical file holdings by denomination in a series of tables numbered from 4.110 to 4.118, mostly for 1988 but skipping a few numbers. *Baptist* table 4.110 for 1988 shows five libraries of which two have medium-sized numbers of vertical files: the First Baptist Churches in West Terre Haute and in Dallas. Table 4.111 for 1988 *Christian* libraries is another small table of vertical files, but one library held a medium-sized collection: the First Christian Church in Columbia, Missouri. *Congregational* libraries can be studied for 1978 where we find small libraries again—four libraries altogether on two coasts.

The *Episcopal/Anglican* and *Independent* groups listed only one library apiece, in each case Canadian: the Church Army Library in Toronto and the Protestant School Board of Montreal, each one with 2.5 files. *Lutheran* vertical file holdings are shown in table 4.112 for 1988. Three Minnesota and three Wisconsin made up more than half of this table's libraries. Holdings were small.

*Methodist* libraries are shown in table 4.113 for 1988. One library, the First United Methodist Church in Tulsa, had twenty-six files, a large church collection. Two medium-sized collections were located in table 4.114 *Other Denominations* libraries for 1988, with 15.5 drawers apiece. One was the United Church of Religious Science Library in Los Angeles and the other was the Crumbaugh Memorial Public Church Library in Illinois. Three libraries from California led this table's state and province locations. The *Presbyterian* table for 1988 was small but contained one large VF collection, the Eastminster Presbyterian Church in Indialantic, Florida, with forty-eight drawers, table 4.115. A table for 1988 had two small collections for *United Church of Christ* libraries, table 4.116.

*Jewish* popular libraries can be seen in table 4.117 for 1988. This is the best display of VF holdings which we have seen. It was led by Minnie Cobey in Columbus, then Temple Emanu-el in Tucson and the Central Agency of Jewish Education in Miami with forty-eight drawers apiece. The four other libraries in this table had unusually large collections also. Lastly we have the *Roman Catholic* picture in table 4.118 for 1988, which featured Rhode Island and New York libraries and was led by the Union St. Jean Baptiste Library in Woonsocket with sixteen files.

In summary, the means for 1978 and 1988 were 6.1 and 7.5 vertical file drawers. Largest library was Minnie Cobey with ninety-three files.

Several other libraries contained approximately forty-eight files. The Southwest had the largest and the West the smallest collections of files. We found a positive correlation between library expenditure and number of files. Fifteen popular libraries had medium-sized VF collections, and almost half of them were Jewish. None had especially large collections, but we can see that certain of these popular library collections were as large as many scholarly library VF collections.

## Microform Holdings

Since few popular libraries felt the need to collect files of old periodicals and newspapers, manuscripts or rare books in any form, we can hardly expect to see as many microforms in popular as in scholarly libraries. However, a few collections of microforms were found, especially in Mormon genealogical libraries. Popular libraries averaged 49,386 microforms in 1978 and 44,019 in 1988, an 11 percent mean decline. This represented one percent of the libraries in the 1978 database and 2 percent of those in the 1988 database. We will look at them by type of library, chief librarian's gender, and then denomination.

We have a longitudinal table, 4.119, for microform holdings by *library type*. Overall mean decade change was minus 11 percent, which can be compared with the 24 percent for periodical title subscriptions. Largest change was for congregational libraries at 40 percent. Public and parochial school libraries held almost no microforms. Congregational libraries averaged 40,950 microforms in 1978 and 57,160 microforms in 1988, but this represented only six and ten libraries, too small a sample to be depended on. If we compare the scholarly libraries on this variable, we see that they scored strongly on the positive side while the popular libraries tended not to list microforms as a holding at all.

See table 4.120 (1988), which shows the leading *congregational* libraries by microform holdings. There we find two large collections listed, both Mormon, one in Mesa and one in Salt Lake City. These collections were large enough for a university library, 230,000 titles, but focused narrowly on genealogical material. Four more Mormon libraries boasted medium-sized collections. There were two small collections of microforms in 1988 *parochial school* libraries. A predominance of West coast and Florida libraries existed among parochial schools. For *public* libraries only one library was on the "highest" list, the Crumbaugh Memorial Public Church Library with fifty microforms.

Another table of primarily Mormon genealogical material on micro-form can be seen in the Other Denominations table 4.121 for 1988. It has the same two leading libraries as table 4.120. Because of the Mormon ge-nealogy presence, the *Other Denominations* group was the strongest pop-ular library microform denomination and the only one seen here. Two of its libraries had large and four had medium-sized collections. The two largest were the LDS collections in Mesa and Salt Lake City, mentioned before, at 230,000 titles apiece. Microform holdings by *chief librarian's gender* showed the usual heavy weighting in favor of males. Their li-braries averaged 81,683 microforms in 1978 and females' libraries aver-aged only 25,163 microforms. In 1988 males' libraries averaged 118,763 titles and females' libraries averaged only 10,800 titles, in other words 3.25 and 11 times as many for males as for females.

A longitudinal study was made for total microform holdings by *de-nomination*. Its highest mean number of items was 17,940 for Roman Catholics. The largest growth percent was Other Denominations with 58 percent, and the smallest was Roman Catholic with −33 percent, sug-gesting changing patterns of microform usage.

In summary, for microform holdings, only congregational libraries had holdings large enough to merit our study and even they included only six and ten libraries in 1978 and 1988. All of the leading collections were devoted to Mormon genealogy. Popular libraries averaged 44,019 vol-umes in 1988 and represented only 2 percent of the total number of li-braries. Other Denominations and Roman Catholic led the denomina-tions in holdings.

In supplement to the above discussion, several special studies were made, not just of microform holdings, but of the holdings of all four kinds of print (nonmedia) material. We have three tables based not on a single variable but on all four cumulated print-based publications—book vol-umes, periodical titles, vertical files and microforms, illogical as the ag-gregation may seem to some readers. Total scores can be examined for the three types of popular libraries by specific library. For *congregational* libraries the table (not shown) listed only three libraries but all three were LDS libraries, and they included the two largest libraries in this series, the leader reaching 431,700 units of the four combined items.

Table 4.122 for 1988 *parochial schools* listed twelve libraries led by the Petit Seminaire de Québec in Quebec City with 200,000 holdings items. Cardinal Ritter in St. Louis had a large collection to serve only one school library amid the listings for so many central Jewish and Catholic agency libraries each serving several libraries. For *public* libraries, table 4.123 for 1988 shows ten libraries with sizeable collections led by the large Jewish Public Library in Montreal with 130,000 items. For both parochial school and public library tables, Roman Catholic and Jewish constituted the majority of the libraries, and more than a third of them were Canadian.

Several additional tables were made to examine total holdings, that is cumulative book volumes, periodical titles, vertical file drawers, and microforms. But what did they show? Longitudinal table 4.124 shows a net growth of only 11 percent for the decade, small. Other Denominations grew the most, 58 percent, and Roman Catholic least, a loss of 33 percent. If we look at another table, 4.125 (1988), we will see the same collection of print holdings examined by region. Southwest led the regions with a 67 percent decade growth. On the other hand, Canada lost ground, −19 percent.

Total holdings (cumulative) by library type (a longitudinal study of book volumes, periodical titles, VFs, and microforms), longitudinal table 4.126, shows congregational libraries to have gained at the rate of 33 percent with public standing at 13 percent and parochial schools at a poor −50 percent. Seventy-four percent of the 1978 popular libraries were represented in this table, as were 96 percent for 1988.

## Media Holdings

We can open this media discussion with yet another United States versus Canada table. It shows mean cumulative media holdings which favor Canada for both years: 2.3:2.0 for 1978 and 2.0:1.7 for Canada:United States. Table 4.127 for 1978 shows media holdings for popular libraries by type of library. A greater proportion of popular libraries had media holdings in 1988 than in 1978. Popular libraries were stronger in media holdings in 1988 than they were in 1978. For popular libraries as a whole, 35 percent had media holdings, as compared with 20 percent of the scholarly libraries. This gave popular a larger media holdings presence overall than scholarly libraries had.

Tables 4.127 and 4.128 show simply the presence or absence of media in a library for 1978 and 1988 by denomination. That was what the questionnaire asked: Do you hold them or not? Public libraries had the largest percentage of media-holding libraries, 31 percent for 1978 and 40

percent for 1988. Parochial school (1978) and congregational (1988) libraries had the lowest percentages of holdings. However, we note small
Ns in many data cells. Tables 4.129, 4,130, 4,131, and 4.132 show
media-holding libraries by region. Canada was the weakest region in both
4.129 and 4.130 and the Middle West in 1978 and the Southwest in 1988
were largest, at 31 percent and 41 percent. Tables 4.131 and 4.132 for
1978 and 1988 continue the analysis of cumulative media holdings by region. They show only small differences between regions, but in 1978
Canada, the Southwest, and Middle West led, and in 1988 the same three
regions led the table.

By *denomination*, only six denominations contained enough libraries
to be considered, and Lutheran again led the list in both years. In tables
4.133 and 4.134 for 1978 and 1988, we see that Lutherans led in 1978
and again in 1988 with about half of their libraries having media. Finally,
tables 4.135 and 4.136 show media holdings by library expenditure. They
show simply that media holdings were highest for the popular libraries
with small annual expenditure, surprisingly enough.

## Map Holdings

Map holdings can be studied in tables 4.137 and 4.138 for 1978 and 1988.
We can look at library type, region, and denomination. But first we must address the most important map holdings question. We discovered that the percentage of scholarly libraries with maps fell by a third from 1978 to 1988,
from 46 percent to 30 percent. Did the same thing happen among popular
libraries? No! The proportion of libraries having maps remained the same,
16 percent in each year. For congregational libraries the percentage was 16
percent in each year also. So the percent for popular was about the same as
that for seminary and denominational headquarters libraries, but smaller
than that for senior college and university libraries. A fifth of the 1988
parochial school and a sixth of the congregational libraries had maps in 1988
as well. The No Response scores for all popular library types were high,
however, and the parochial school and public library Ns were small.

Tables 4.137 and 4.138 show map holdings by library type. Only congregational library frequencies were large enough to merit consideration,
however. Ninety-two of 593 1988 congregational libraries, or 16 percent,
had maps. This compares with 46 percent for scholarly libraries for 1978
and 30 percent for 1988. For *region*, numbers were often small, and in
most regions one in every six to eight libraries had maps.

## Art Reproduction Holdings

Only one twelfth of the popular libraries held art reproductions in their collections. See tables 4.139 and 4.140 for 1978, in which fifty-six of the popular libraries had art reproductions. Table 4.141 for 1988 shows that only one-thirteenth of the congregational libraries had art reproductions for that year, also, forty-four, or 7 percent. Parochial school and public libraries held this type of media in even smaller proportions. Public libraries were a much smaller group and only 2 or 8 percent of them had art reproductions. For the two larger parts of the 1988 database combined, 10 percent of the scholarly and 7 percent of the popular libraries reported art reproductions.

So, for art reproductions only the houses of worship had enough libraries to warrant study. They scored 8 percent and 7 percent of all popular libraries in 1978 and 1988. By *region* the Southwest led in both years. By *annual expenditure*, the libraries with low expenditure had the most art reproductions, surprisingly. By *denomination*, Jewish and Presbyterian ranked higher than the other denominations.

## Cumulative Media Holdings

Several special studies were made of media holdings, and we can describe them now. As tables 4.141 for 1988, longitudinal 4.142, 4.143, and 4.144 show about a third of the congregational libraries, 38 percent of the parochial school, and 40 percent of the public libraries had media holdings. Public libraries led in percentage with media, but congregational libraries led with number of libraries and with reliability of outcome.

Longitudinal tables 4.142 and 4.144 also show cumulative media holdings (media, maps, and art reproductions) by denomination for popular libraries. Which denomination had the highest number of media-holding libraries? Note first that the Protestant libraries were much stronger in media than were Jewish/Roman Catholic libraries in both years. However, Jewish libraries led the group with top-listed scores (1988) and Presbyterian (1978) was next. In most denominations the number of libraries with media was small.

Table 4.141 for 1988 and longitudinal 4.143 show cumulative media holdings (media, maps, and art reproductions) by type of library. The findings are similar from one type to another, but we notice eventually that the scores were higher in 1978 than they were in 1988. Then we see

that three out of the six popular library Ns were too small for consideration. That left only congregational libraries, and we can note that 93 percent of the popular libraries with media were congregational. They averaged 1.7 media categories in 1988, a similar score to that found among
scholarly libraries, table 4.142. Longitudinal table 4.145 shows popular
library media holdings again. Means were 2.0 for 1978 and 1.7 media for
1988.

There was a scholarly:popular library ratio of media holdings of
958:173 or 5.5:1.0 in 1978. This means that 5.5 scholarly libraries had
media for every 1.0 popular library having media. Looked at in another
way, 70 percent of the scholarly and 25 percent of the popular libraries
had media of some kind. In percentage of popular libraries having media
for 1978, public libraries led with 31 percent, then congregational with
25 percent, then parochial school with 15 percent. However, we can note
again that 93 percent of the popular libraries with media were congregational.

Cumulative media holdings by library type, a longitudinal study,
showed a negative mean picture. Overall mean showed a −15 percent
growth with congregational at −15 percent, parochial at −36 percent,
and public leading the group with 0 percent. Again, the parochial school
and public library listings had small Ns and large No Responses. We have
a 1978 and a 1988 table on total cumulative media holdings by region
also. Highest was the Southwest region with 2.2 media and lowest was
the Northeast at 1.4 media. For 1988, the Middle West and Southwest led
with 1.8 media, and the Northeast was smallest with 1.4 media. Variation
between regions was small.

Between 1978 and 1988 no denomination had a positive gain and the
Episcopal/Anglican with the poorest showing of all had a −21 percent
score. Again differences between denominations were small and scores
not very impressive. Overall mean again was 1.7 media. Longitudinal
media holdings by nation showed Canada again leading the United
States.

Now come additional tables for specific libraries (not reproduced
here) by congregational, parochial school and public libraries on total cumulative holdings of media, maps and art reproductions. For congregational libraries in 1988, thirty-five libraries were tied at three listings (all
thirty-five libraries had one or more examples of each one of the three
kinds of media). Four states made up almost half of this group: Florida,
Ohio, Texas, Wisconsin, and four denominations made up three-fourths
of the list's denominations: Jewish, Baptist, Mennonite, and Presbyter-

ian. For parochial schools, five libraries (three of them Jewish) had two kinds of media. For public libraries, two of them had all three kinds of media and one had two kinds.

## Additional Special Studies

As a concluding section for the library materials discussion, several tables were made for the special studies that were carried out. Here are the pertinent discussions. One, by popular library type, additional library activities (cumulative), studied consortium membership, OCLC membership, and local automation projects as a group. It showed that congregational libraries had an average of 1.2 memberships-projects while the scholarly overall mean was 3.7, three times as much.

Other tables were made for extended services and collections (cumulative) involving subject interests, special collections, and publications. By library type, the highest score was that for parochial schools and the lowest that for congregational libraries with 3.1 and 2.1 mean scores. The overall mean was 2.2 as compared with the overall scholarly mean of 2.5 scores. Change was largest for parochial schools.

An attempt was made to perform a growth analysis for specific popular library variables and to make a summary of the longitudinal growth situation for matched pairs. This brought interesting results, which we can examine here in table 4.146 for 1978. This table shows a study of popular library rating points over twenty-three growth variables (see table 4.95 for a list of them) with a minimal No Response rate. By region, for 1978 Canada led with 49,250 growth points with the Southwest second and the Northeast last. Mean score for the entire group was 8,283 points. Public libraries had the largest number of mean points and parochial school libraries were second. Public libraries gained the most points during the decade. However, parochial school and public libraries had quite small scores relative to scholarly library scores. Congregational library scores were small here, also, the smallest of any library type.

For 1988, table 4.147 shows much the same thing as 1978, with Canada leading in points and with the Southeast second. Mean score was 11,240 points. See table 4.148 for 1978 and 1988 by denomination. Roman Catholic led the 1978 group at 20,120 points with Other Denominations next and Presbyterian last. For 1988, the leaders were Jewish with 19,950 points with Other Denominations and Roman Catholic next. Mean group points were 11,240.

So the leading denominations by growth for twenty-three variables were Roman Catholic, Jewish, and Other Denominations. These groups were growing fastest, with Presbyterian trailing. The highest growth figures 1978–88 by region pointed to Canada and the Southeast. On the other hand, the least growth was shown in the West. A varied picture. An extra growth study was made by chief librarian's gender, and it turned out to be the classic case of male advantage. The male:female growth ratio was 2.0:1.0; males excelled here also.

A longitudinal table summarized the findings for total holdings (cumulative) — volumes, periodicals, vertical files, and microforms — by region. In 1988 the overall mean was 7,745 items. Largest region was Canada, with 28,270 items, and smallest was Middle Atlantic, with 5,376 items. Overall growth was 17 percent. Largest in growth rate was the Southwest with 67 percent and smallest was −19 percent for Canada. So Canada started out well here but soon slipped downward.

## Annual Library Expenditure

Annual library expenditure will be treated in a series of four subsections — material, personnel, other, and total expenditures. We should remember that expenditures for these popular libraries were much smaller than those for scholarly libraries, since popular parent institutions provided either small budgets or none at all in a majority of cases. Each subsection will analyze library expenditure by type of library, by region, by chief librarian's gender, by volume holdings, and finally by denomination.

### Annual Material Expenditure

In most congregational libraries the expenditure for library material traditionally constituted almost all of the library's expenditure for any purpose (you see, even the young congregational libraries already have their traditions!). Usually these libraries spent little or nothing on personnel (volunteers did all of the work!) or on administrative expense beyond the limited library supplies connected with new book processing and circulation, since the sponsoring house of worship provided the quarters, utilities, and often the equipment needed, without charge. However, as we proceed we will discover some interesting exceptions to these generalizations. In fact, the contrast of certain library leaders with the "typical" or "traditional" picture is striking.

Longitudinal tables 4.149 and 4.150 show annual popular library material expenditure by library type. Overall 1988 mean expenditure was $4,085 as compared with the 1978 figure of $1,812. Thirty-four percent of the popular libraries were included in these figures, the rest providing no expenditure data. Of course most of these libraries were part of the congregational group which averaged $2,691 spent on material in 1988. Parochial school libraries averaged $17,380 and public averaged $24,290, both with only a few libraries involved.

The matched pairs scores for these variables and categories are either slightly or more than slightly larger than those shown in tables 4.147 and 4.148 for 1988, for instance. The scores for no longer listed were much smaller than those in table 4.147, and those for the newly listed libraries were moderately lower. Finally, the longitudinal information shows an overall popular library increase in material expenditure of 125 percent, well above the corresponding scholarly library figure. Public libraries led the type of library list with a 187 percent increase.

By *type of library*, *congregational* library material expenditures are shown for specific libraries in table 4.151 for 1988. The first five libraries on the list had sizeable annual material expenditures, from approximately $23 thousand to $37.5 thousand. Impressive! The Las Vegas LDS genealogical library was first among these sizeable libraries. For the table as a whole, Jewish and Other Denominations libraries made up half of the total number. By location, Texas listed seven and California four libraries to make up half of the total number of libraries.

We can move to *parochial school* libraries in table 4.152 for 1988. Again we have four leading libraries, ranging in size from $23,000 to $77,500 spent on material. The Hamilton-Wentworth Catholic School led the list. This is another impressive picture for popular libraries. Between Roman Catholic and Jewish libraries we can account for more than three-fourths of the table. Canada made up more than one-third of the table locations as might be expected. *Public* libraries can be seen in table 4.153 for 1988. The Montreal Jewish Public Library and the YMWHA Library in New York were well above the rest in material expenditure level, $23,000 and $99,000. All were Jewish, Roman Catholic, Other Denominations, Canadian, New York, or Pennsylvania libraries.

Largest by far 1988 mean material expenditure was found in the *region* of Canada at $24,000, and next was the West region with $7,147. Smallest was the Middle West with $1,688. Matched pairs were somewhat below the 1978 figure and above the 1988 figures shown in this regional paragraph. Another *chief librarian's gender* study was made for this variable. It showed 1988 material expenditure to be $6,841 for libraries headed by men and $3,880 for libraries headed by women, a ratio of 1.8:1.0—a picture consistent with those which we have seen before. Longitudinal table 4.154 shows annual material expenditures by *volume holdings*. It shows a strong decade's growth in material expenditures, 126 percent, and a strong correlation between the two variables.

Now, in spite of the large No Response percentage and the small Ns in most columns, we can study annual library material expenditures by *denomination*. The denominations spending most on material per library in 1988 were Roman Catholic at $12,600 and Jewish at $6,465. Smallest were the Lutherans at $643 and Presbyterians at $1,564. The longitudinal study showed the Episcopal/Anglican and Independent denominations to have changed the most 1978–88 and Lutherans to have changed the least.

We can now look at table 4.155 for 1988, which is the first one in the series of denominational analyses for specific libraries. The *Baptist* list of leading libraries by annual material expenditures shows the First Baptist Churches in Dallas and Greensboro to have spent more than $10,000 on material apiece, churches which we have seen before in this type of table. Almost half of the table's libraries were located in Texas. Expenditure at this level should build collections rapidly.

The *Christian* libraries in table 4.156 were relatively small for 1988, and the *Churches of Christ* listed only one small library. For *Episcopal/Anglican* the values were small except for one library with a $14,000 expenditure on material: St. Faith Episcopal Church in Havertown, Pennsylvania, table 4.157 for 1988. *Lutheran* libraries in table 4.158 for 1988 were generally of low income, but more than half of them were located in Minnesota and Wisconsin.

A short table for *Mennonite* libraries for 1988 was quite small in material expenditure also, table 4.159. *Methodist* libraries for 1988, table 4.160 listed only one medium-sized expenditure for Christ Church United Methodist Church in Louisville: $23,000. *Other Denominations* in table 4.161 for 1988 had two sizeable library material expenditure totals. Both were Mormon genealogical libraries in the West, Las Vegas and San Diego. *Presbyterian* libraries can be studied in table 4.162 for 1988 for largest annual material expenditure. One library, the First Presbyterian Church in El Paso, went over the $10,000 figure.

Leading *United Church of Christ* libraries are seen in another table for

1988. They were quite small. Leading *Jewish* popular libraries can be seen in table 4.163 for 1988. All of them were large in this context. One institution reached the $99,000 level at the Jewish Public Library, Montreal. Please note that three of the six libraries on the list belonged to parochial schools, two to synagogues, and one to a public library. A fine display! *Roman Catholic* libraries in table 4.164 for 1988 contained three large libraries: Hamilton-Wentworth, Petit Seminaire de Québec and Oratoire St. Joseph. Most of the libraries in this table belonged to parochial schools, and only one represented a church or synagogue. Half of them were Canadian.

In summary for material expenditure, the overall mean 1978 expenditure was $1,812, which rose by 1988 to $4,085. Longitudinal increase was 126 percent, large. Again the LDS genealogical libraries were strong, this time in material expenditure. By region, Canadian libraries ranked lowest. Roman Catholic and Jewish libraries spent the most on material. Male chief librarians led female chief librarians in material expenditures. As a summary of the denominational section on annual material expenditure for specific libraries, we can point out that sixteen of these popular religious libraries exceeded the $10,000 per year mark. More than half of them appeared in the Roman Catholic or Jewish tables. Surely these sixteen libraries had material expenditures that equaled those of many nonreligious school and special libraries in the United States and Canada.

## Annual Personnel Expenditure

We can study personnel expenditure first by type of library, then by total library expenditure, by chief librarian's gender and finally by denomination. Personnel expenditure can be expected to exceed that for library material and for other expenditures but not to equal personnel expenditure for scholarly libraries.

We can see in table 4.165 for 1988 *by type of library* that the congregational personnel expenditure pattern differed from the pattern for material expenditure. The totals in the highest personnel expenditure table were much higher than those in the highest material expenditure table, since they rose to the $145,000 level on personnel for Stephen S. Wise Temple and All Saints Catholic Church. Other libraries ranked high also. More than half of these libraries were Jewish. This was an outstanding table. Several of the libraries in tables 4.165, 4.166, and 4.167 for congregational, parochial school, and public libraries for 1988 must have maintained full-time paid employees, since their personnel expenditures were so large. Five California, six Texas and four New York libraries constituted almost half of these popular tables. Notably absent was more than a single Mormon library, this one in San Diego.

In longitudinal table 4.168, type of library levels of response differed considerably. The 1988 mean congregational library expenditure level was $15,071, a substantial level for a group of libraries that was expected to have no personnel expenditures. In any case it is based on only 12 percent of the congregational libraries. For parochial schools, the level was $28,060 and for public it was $129,375 for personnel expenditures, both representing very few cases. Mean overall personnel expenditures for 1978 were $6,029 and for 1988 were $21,988, a gain of 265 percent, a strong gain for the decade. Congregational libraries led the longitudinal table with a 253 percent growth, and public libraries were second with an increase of 204 percent. Smallest increase was that of parochial school libraries with only 87 percent, still a sizeable increase.

*Parochial school* libraries were seen in table 4.166 for 1988. Each one of the first four libraries and library agencies in this table apparently had several full-time staff members. St. Mary's School for the Deaf led the list with a $75,000 expenditure. Jewish and Roman Catholic libraries were the only ones listed. *Public* libraries seem to have been few in table 4.167 for 1988, only four of them. However, the Jewish Public Library in Montreal must have had a large full-time paid staff with its $325,000 annual personnel expenditure. The YMWHA library followed in New York with a $75,000 expenditure.

In general, mean personnel expenditure registered a strong positive correlation against *total library expenditure*. In 1978 for those libraries with $1,500 or less total expenditure the mean personnel expenditure was $2,500, an apparent impossibility caused by the discrepancy in lowest category size for total and personnel expenditures. For those libraries with total expenditure of $20,000 to $95,000, the mean personnel expenditure was $24,170. In 1988, the lowest mean personnel expenditure was $2,500 and the highest was $71,000. Personnel expenditures by *chief librarian's gender* can be considered here as well. For 1978 the ratio of personnel expenditures for male-female chiefs was 1.8:1.0, males ahead. For 1988 the ratio was 1.1:1.0, placing the two sexes much closer together.

At this point we will start the denominational analysis of specific libraries with the leading *Baptist* 1988 libraries shown in table 4.169. Two of these libraries were seen to be above the $10,000 level, the First Baptist Church libraries in Dallas and Greensboro, again. For *Episcopal/Anglican* we have two libraries at a relatively high 1988 level, the Episcopal Diocese of West Texas Cathedral in San Antonio and the St. Faith Episcopal Church in Havertown. See table 4.170. A few *Lutheran* libraries can be studied for 1978. One of them, Our Savior's Lutheran Church in Milwaukee, spent $115,000 on popular library personnel! So much for the idea that congregational libraries were staffed exclusively with volunteers!

Personnel expenditures for *Methodist* libraries are shown in table 4.171 for 1988. One was large, Christ Church in Louisville, at $75,000. The 1988 *Other Denominations* table 4.172 shows the personnel expenditures for two medium-sized libraries that we have seen before. One was the Friends Free Library of Germantown in Philadelphia, a public library with a $75,000 expenditure, and the other one was the Mormon library in San Diego. Half of the table contained Mormon and one-third contained Friends libraries.

*Jewish* in table 4.173 for 1988 shows both medium-sized and large libraries in an outstanding table.[3] Again the Jewish Public Library in Montreal and the Stephen S. Wise Temple Library in Los Angeles led the way with expenditures in the six figures. Six libraries were located in synagogues, three in parochial schools, and one was a public library. Two California and two Texas libraries led the locations, all with expenditures above $27,000. An excellent showing! School libraries led the *Roman Catholics* in table 4.174 for 1988, and two church libraries filled out the list. Six libraries were medium-sized or large, and they were led by All Saints Catholic Church in Dallas with $145,000 and St. Mary's School for the Deaf at $75,000! Another strong popular library personnel expenditure picture.

In summary for personnel expenditures, based on 12 percent of the 1988 database, overall popular library expenditure was $6,029 for 1978 and $21,988 for 1988, and 1988 congregational libraries spent $15,071 per library. Longitudinal change was 265 percent for popular libraries as a whole. Strong! There was also a strong positive correlation between personnel and total annual expenditure starting in the lowest expenditure categories. Chief librarian's gender favored males again. In summary, for the lists of specific libraries, there were four large libraries spending $100,000 or more for personnel annually, two Jewish, one Roman Catholic, and one Lutheran. Twenty libraries were medium-sized, of which 40 percent were Jewish and 25 percent were Roman Catholic.

## Annual Other Expenditure

Other expenditures (administrative expenses, such as travel, hospitality, repair, utilities, equipment, and supplies) were small in most popular libraries, but not for all of them. We have only two tables for this field by *type of library*. Table 4.175 for 1988 lists the strongest *congregational* libraries on Other expenses. Three libraries were in the medium-sized class—all Jewish. In fact, 70 percent of the table was Jewish. The top two—Sinai Temple in Los Angeles and Temple Emanuel in Dallas—spent the questionnaire maximum even by scholarly library standards, $20,000 per year. All libraries were located in churches or synagogues. For *parochial schools*, Akiba Hebrew Academy at $5,000 was the only library in the "highest" list, so no table could be made.

A table for 1988 shows the *public* libraries with high Other expenditures. Two Jewish libraries constituted the entire table, table 4.176, each one with the scholarly library maximum of a $20,000 expenditure: the YMWHA Association in New York and the Jewish Public Library of Montreal.

We also have a longitudinal change table that shows overall Other expenditure change to be 247 percent, quite strong. Leading the group was congregational libraries with a 1,630 percent change! Such a large change was due to an unusually small 1978 figure, $500, and some large 1988 figures that strongly influenced the 1988 mean. Public libraries were adequate at 33 percent growth, and parochial school libraries were too poorly represented to be considered. By *denomination*, Jewish libraries dominated this section. Several of their libraries were quite strong in this small expenditure category. Certain synagogue leaders in this category were among the topmost popular libraries in North America. In summary, five congregational and public libraries reached the medium-sized level of $20,000, and all of them were Jewish.

## Annual Total Expenditure

Now we have reached the final financial section for annual popular library expenditures. We should see some new names in this discussion because certain libraries listed only their total expenditure in the *ALD*, and so were found nowhere else on other expenditure tables. We will look at type of library first, then at region and at denomination.

Longitudinal table 4.177 shows popular library expenditure by *library type*. We can examine the totals first. They show means of $4,972 for

1978 and $12,591 for 1988, a 153 percent increase, though the No Response rate was high for this category. For the entire popular database, 155 libraries had expenditures in 1978, or 23 percent. For 1988, 252 libraries showed expenditures, 39 percent. In 1978 mean congregational expenditures were $1,998 for 145 congregational libraries, and $7,904 for 235 libraries in 1988. The mean expenditure figures ascend as we move down the table. Eleven parochial school libraries spent a mean total of $39,023 and six public libraries spent a mean $147,708 in 1988.

A similar table can be seen in table 4.178. It differs from 4.177 in that the table marked "cumulative" contains figures that are the sums of the separate figures for material, personnel, and Other expenditures as shown in the *ALD*, while table 4.177 contains only the total expenditure figures as presented by the *ALD*. The two tables' results are quite similar.

Table 4.179 shows a *congregational* table for total expenditure by denomination. The 1978 mean per library was $2,202 and the 1988 mean was $8,963. Several denominations grew rapidly, but Roman Catholic grew most rapidly, by 3,023 percent. Congregational libraries were one of the fastest growing of all ten types of libraries by total expenditure.

Table 4.180 for 1988 shows total library expenditure for congregational libraries. All twenty libraries were in the medium-sized group except for four that were in a higher expenditure category. They were four libraries already familiar from earlier tables: the Stephen S. Wise Temple in Los Angeles, well ahead of any other library, All Saints Catholic Church in Dallas, Sinai Temple in Los Angeles, and Highland Park Presbyterian Church in Dallas. The libraries in this table were primarily Jewish, more than half of them. There were large expenditures for every library in the table!

The total annual expenditures of *parochial school* libraries can be seen in table 4.181 for 1988. Notice that *all* libraries except one were either Jewish or Roman Catholic. One had a large total expenditure, the Central Agency for Jewish Education in Miami, with $127,500. Six libraries were found in the medium-sized category and the rest were below that level. Altogether a satisfying table! *Public* libraries were seen in table 4.182 for 1988. Again Montreal's Jewish Public Library led the table with more than half a million dollars in annual expenditures. The YMWHA in New York ranked higher also. Only three denominations were listed—Jewish, Roman Catholic, and Other Denominations. Another strong table.

Two other tables examined total expenditure by *region*. They found for 1978 that the mean was $4,885 and for 1988 was $13,740, a 181 percent increase. By region, expenditure was highest in the West in 1978 at $5,635 and the Middle Atlantic at $4,125, and lowest in the Middle West at $1,573. For 1988 expenditure was highest in the West again and the Southwest with $27,290 and $16,470 figures and lowest in the Rocky Mountains at $625 and the Northeast at $2,875. Tables 4.183 and 4.184 for 1978 and 1988.

By *denomination*, Jewish-Roman Catholic libraries were far ahead of Protestant libraries in expenditures here. Another longitudinal table, 4.185, shows the same type of total expenditure by denominational analysis but this time for congregational libraries only and with many small Ns and large No Responses. Overall mean growth rate was 271 percent during the decade, a strong growth. Notice that for the Jewish (and the small Roman Catholic group) the mean was much larger than the Protestant library mean. Largest mean expenditure was shown by Jewish libraries at $14,980 per library with Baptists' total annual expenditures second at $6,509. The lowest was for Lutheran at $824 per library. Largest change was the 592 percent of the Presbyterians which advanced rapidly!

Now for denominational lists of specific libraries in several tables, all for 1988 expenditures, except one. *Baptist* libraries can be seen in table 4.186. This is a short table of sizeable libraries, every one being medium-sized or larger. The largest, the First Baptist Church in Longview, Texas, had a six-figure total expenditure, and the First Baptist Church in Dallas spent $70,000. The *Christian* table (4.187) was longer, but it had only one medium-sized library, the Christian Church in Indianapolis. The *Congregational* church list was seen in table 4.188 for 1978, and it had quite small totals.

*Episcopal/Anglican* libraries are seen in table 4.189, and the table contained two medium-sized libraries: St. Faith Episcopal Church in Havertown and the Episcopal Diocese of West Texas Cathedral in San Antonio. The small *Lutheran* libraries can be seen in table 4.190. Again more than half of these libraries were located in Wisconsin or Minnesota. Another table was a short one of small *Mennonite* libraries. Next was *Methodist* table 4.191. Two of the Methodist libraries were medium-sized, including Christ Church in Indianapolis and the First United Methodist Church in Tulsa. *Other Denominations* libraries are seen in table 4.192. Four of them were medium-sized, including three Mormon and one Friends Library: Friends Free Library of Germantown, Philadelphia, and the LDS genealogical centers in San Diego, Las Vegas, and Mesa.

*Presbyterian* church libraries can be seen in table 4.193. The leaders included one large library and one medium-sized one. Highland Park Presbyterian Church in Dallas was the six-figure leader, and the First Presbyterian Church in El Paso was the medium-sized one. The *United*

*Church of Christ* report was short and dealt with small numbers. *Jewish* libraries produced only a modest-sized expenditure list in table 4.194, but it contained five large and two medium-sized expenditure institutions. The Jewish Public Library in Montreal led the table. Three of these libraries served synagogues, three served schools or school systems, and one served a public library. A fine picture!

We conclude this section by looking at another strong showing by the *Roman Catholic* group, table 4.195. This group included seven medium-sized libraries: St. Mary's School for the Deaf, St. Matthew's and St. Timothy's Neighborhood Center, Hamilton-Wentworth School, the Diocese of St. Cloud Bureau of Education, All Saints Catholic Church, the Edmonton Catholic Schools, and the Church of the Incarnation. Two libraries in New York and two in Texas led the table by state and province. It contained five parochial school, four church, and two public libraries.

In summary for total popular library expenditure, there were seven large expenditure (over $100,000 annually) and twenty-three medium-sized expenditure ($10,000 to $100,000 annually) libraries. Most of the first group were Jewish, and most of the second group were Baptist, Roman Catholic, and Other Denominations. A surprisingly good showing in the midst of many modest performances.

## Analyses of Expenditure, Cumulation, and Growth

### Library Expenditure Analysis

In another study, we have examined matched pairs for popular libraries. Tables 4.196 and 4.197 for 1978 and 1988 show total annual library expenditure by region. For 1978 the mean expenditure was $4,509 and for 1988 it was $10,720. Both figures were heavily influenced by the high expenditure of Canadian libraries. In 1988 Canada was highest with $282,000, then the Southeast with $10,900. Rocky Mountains was smallest in expenditure and had only a few popular libraries. Notable was the increase in expenditures over the decade.

Longitudinal table 4.198 shows a study over time of matched pair expenditures. Let us see what it tells us. Mean popular library expenditure growth equaled 138 percent, which was almost twice the growth rate of the scholarly libraries. Highest growth rate among the popular libraries was 394 percent for the parochial school libraries, with public libraries not far behind at 349 percent. The mean total expenditure for 1988 was $10,720.

For matched pairs the popular library volunteers (student assistants) averaged 4.6 in 1978 and 8.7 in number in 1988, larger than the numbers for the entire databases. For the no longer listed and newly listed libraries we have the usual picture of lower scores for both 1978 and 1988. Additional information on the no longer listed and the newly listed suggests that these two groups do not differ substantially in their regional distribution and had lower expenditures than the database as a whole.

Another longitudinal study was done for annual popular library total expenditure by denomination. Longitudinal table 4.199 shows these results. It shows an overall mean of $12,591 and a 153 percent growth. Largest mean expenditure denomination was Roman Catholic at $30,110. Which denomination changed most during the decade of the study? Presbyterian library expenditures increased 592 percent and Methodist increased 258 percent. Lutherans decreased by 46 percent. Protestant libraries increased by less than Jewish-Roman Catholic libraries did. Note also that seven of these denominations increased by more than 100 percent.

And yet another longitudinal table, 4.200, tells us that popular libraries as a whole grew by 64 percent during the decade in volunteer staff members. Public libraries grew by only 22 percent during that period, however. Table 4.201 for 1988 shows the breakdown of library expenditure categories in percentages by denomination. Largest material expenditure percentage as a proportion of all expenditure was Lutheran—100 percent for seventeen libraries. Largest for personnel salaries was 68 percent for Jewish, and largest percentage for Other was 7 percent for Jewish again. However, the Ns were often small.

We also have a longitudinal study of total library expenditures by type of library. The overall mean change was 153 percent from 1978 to 1988, twice the scholarly library change figure. Congregational libraries led this change with a sizeable 296 percent change, a remarkable growth. Parochial schools and public libraries showed sizeable growth scores, also from 140 to 150 percent.

We can conclude this discussion of longitudinal expenditure with a picture of the library expenditure categories in percentages by denomination. See table 4.202 for 1978 and table 4.201 for 1988. We have cell-size problems here, too, but a few conclusions can be drawn about the situation. In 1978, Presbyterian and Baptist are heavy on material expenditure, Jewish and Roman Catholic on personnel. No denomination was heavy on Other expenditures. Overall figures were 47 percent spent on material, 49 percent on personnel, and 4 percent on Other.

For 1988 Baptist again and Lutheran were heaviest on material, Jewish and Roman Catholic again in personnel expenditures, and Jewish in Other expenditures. Overall 1988 figures were 32 percent spent for material, 63 percent for personnel, and 5 percent for Other expenditures. This statement reveals the mistake in our assumption earlier in the chapter, that nearly 100 percent of library income was spent on material and close to nothing on personnel. It reveals also that between 1978 and 1988 there was both a drop of 15 percent in material expenditure and an increase of 14 percent in personnel expenditure.

It reveals further that personnel spending was higher than material spending in both 1978 and 1988, in the same manner as that for scholarly libraries. It must be remembered, however, that for most small libraries material spending consumed almost all the budget. It was only large libraries with paid personnel that ran up the total personnel spending sum and quickly overtook the sum of spending for all libraries on material.

## Highest Cumulative Tables

This section attempts to show the library qualitative level by ascertaining the library quantitative level. We have a series of 1988 tables that show the result of counting the number of times each popular library appeared in one of the many "highest" tables for its own denomination. The libraries at the top are the specific libraries that were listed in the largest number of these "highest" tables. They are the North American leaders among popular libraries. The best of the best. Most of them are congregational libraries.

We will look at these elite libraries by denomination. We should point out that the maximum number of table listings in this particular analysis was twenty tables. So a library with fourteen listings out of twenty was listed in 70 percent of these tables, a good score. The method used to determine the number of table listings for each library was to calculate the top fifteen or twenty libraries for each denomination on each of twenty numerical variables.

Therefore although many of these tables have not been included in the text, and many of the rest have been shortened significantly, there was a total of thirteen denominations times twenty variables, which equals 260 possible tables. However, it was almost impossible for any individual library to achieve a score of over nineteen since there were four dichotomous variables on the list of twenty-three popular numerical and dichotomous growth variables, and popular libraries were almost never involved in OCLC activities. There were no specific library tables produced for art reproductions, map holdings, or media holdings as separate variables.

Table 4.203 shows *Baptist* libraries with the highest number of table listings. The leader is the First Baptist Church in Murfreesboro, Tennessee. *Christian* churches listed ten leaders in table 4.204, with the High Street Christian Church in Akron in front. *Churches of Christ* leaders are few in number in table 4.205 and their table scores are modest. *Episcopal/Anglican* libraries have nine churches listed, which are led by St. Thomas Episcopal Church, Sunnyvale, in table 4.206.

*Independent* listings are few, but the Protestant School Board in Montreal was listed in eleven tables, table 4.207. *Lutheran* libraries provided a large table of fourteen libraries, table 4.208 was led by the English Lutheran Church in LaCrosse. Of these leaders four were located in Wisconsin and four in Minnesota, totaling more than half of the table. *Mennonite* libraries in table 4.209 had only four libraries listed, and their leader, the Zion Mennonite Church in Souderton, Pennsylvania had only five listings. *Methodist* libraries were both large in number and high in listings, table 4.210. Twelve libraries from eleven states were led by the First United Methodist Church in Tulsa.

*Other Denominations* produced nine table listings. A third of them were located in California and about half of them were LDS churches. The LDS headquarters in Salt Lake City led table 4.211. *Presbyterians* listed eleven libraries in ten states, table 4.212. The leader was the Westwood First Presbyterian Church in Cincinnati with fifteen listings. *United Church of Christ* libraries included a leader, the U.C.C. church in Vermilion, Ohio, with fourteen listings. A third of these libraries were located in Ohio. See table 4.213. *Jewish* libraries were led by the Sinai Temple in Los Angeles with sixteen (80 percent) listings, a high number. California, Florida, and New York constituted 60 percent of the library locations, table 4.214. The *Roman Catholic* table 4.215 listed six libraries with ten or more table listings. All Saints Catholic Church in Dallas was the leader. Canada, New York, Texas led by location.

A second "highest of the highest" analysis was set up calculating which of the popular libraries, regardless of denomination, were listed in terms of the twenty-three numerical variables used on the questionnaire. Again a total possible score per library was probably nineteen or twenty. However, since all libraries were thrown into the same calculation, only twenty tables were produced (instead of 260). Since each table included only fifteen or twenty libraries (as a rule), only a very few libraries could count as being among the "highest of the highest."

Analysis of the high-profile libraries, those appearing on the largest number of "highest" tables, disclosed that their regional breakdown in growth for 1988 was Middle West −29 percent, Southwest −24 percent, with Northeast and Canada producing a total of only 7 percent. These negative "growth" rates for certain regions suggests that libraries which accumulated high scores in 1978 achieved somewhat lower scores in 1988. The conclusions to be gained from this area were that either a larger number of libraries in these regions were competing for laurels in 1988 than in 1978 or that many strong libraries in 1978 had not managed to maintain their position for an entire decade.

Table 4.216 shows the highest and most active popular libraries by region and is laid out in terms of the number of table references. The important column is that of active libraries, the one on the right, which shows the Middle West leading the table, with the Southwest second. By region, and by another method of calculation, most of the best libraries seemed to be located in the South and West. As far as denomination went they were led by Jewish and Other Denominations. Three denominations had no libraries in the final group: Churches of Christ, Independent, and Mennonite.

A further analysis was made of the number of "highest" tables each library was on. For 1988 it showed that forty-five congregational libraries (8 percent), six parochial school (25 percent), and two public libraries (8 percent) were on ten or more tables. It showed further that ten Jewish (5 percent of all Jewish), seven Baptist (10 percent of all Baptist), and seven Presbyterian (7 percent of all Presbyterian) libraries were on ten or more "highest" tables. No Churches of Christ or Mennonite libraries appeared on ten or more tables in this analysis.

Table 4.217 for 1988 shows another version of the "highest of the highest" popular library listings, the libraries that were listed most often on the chapter's "best of the best" tables. One third of them were Jewish and 37 percent were Baptist and Other Denominations. Forty-one percent of them were located in Texas and California. In this analysis, none was Canadian. Table 4.218 provides an additional cumulative table by denomination showing libraries frequently ahead on the "largest" tables.

## Special Analyses

The special analyses of the growth rates of the twenty-seven variables discussed earlier may be examined again. This was a composite longitudinal study of twenty-seven variables relating to growth, but for popular libraries only twenty-three of these variables could be studied. Which libraries scored the highest scores? Table 4.141 shows by region that Canada was the highest scorer on growth with the Southwest next. The Rocky Mountains Ns were too small for serious consideration. Smallest was the Northeast region. This is the 1978 scene.

For 1988 table 4.147 shows that again Canada and this time the Southeast led the way. Smallest score was earned by the West, however. The similarity between scholarly and popular scores was small. All of these scores were made for matched pairs. Note the No Response scores in these tables and remember that in these cases No Response referred to all the weaker libraries, not those that did not respond. There were no libraries with no score at all for this analysis! Table 4.148 shows a final longitudinal study by denomination of the rating points earned and the percentage change. Which denomination was most growth oriented on this important table? Jewish, Other Denominations, and Roman Catholic were the leaders here. They were growing most rapidly over the decade. Please note that the Mennonite and Churches of Christ had 0 percent scores, also, indicating a static or stable status.

With libraries like those in Table 4.181 we see expenditures commensurate with those of nonreligious libraries. Roman Catholic and Jewish led parochial school libraries. Among public libraries, Jewish, Roman Catholic, and Other Denominations libraries led. Popular library total expenditures included seven libraries with over $100,000 spent annually.

## A Projection of Future Development

By the use of simple statistical techniques we can project future development among popular religious library variables. In this section we will discuss specific aspects of the field as they may be expected to develop in coming years, or at least up to the year 1998.

Tables 4.219 and 4.220 give these 1998 figures. For the most part these extrapolations show steady but modest advances for the variables. Among the strongest advances for popular libraries were the total library expenditure and the expenditures in each subdivision of that variable. Readers will note that certain variables are projected as reducing their scores, such as number of library clerks and microform holdings. In the Canada versus United States tables, U.S. volume holdings were predicted to rise strongly. Average U.S. projected 1988–98 change was expected to be 16.2 percent for the whole. For Canada total staff size as well as volume holdings were predicted to drop. Canadian average projected change was predicted to be about −12.2 percent.

## Suggested Search and Research Projects

1. A comparison should be made between a sample of popular religious parochial school libraries and a sample of private nonreligious school libraries on library material selection policies, material holdings, and material expenditure.

2. By mail questionnaire, demographical information should be assembled for comparison on private religious parochial school chief librarians and private nonreligious school chief librarians.

3. A checklist should be developed of good-quality books suitable for a religious parochial school library in a specific denomination. Than one hundred parochial school libraries of that denomination should be evaluated for their holdings from this list.

4. Per parochial and Sunday school student, total expenditure figures should be developed for popular congregational and parochial school libraries and then compared with such figures for selected private school and special libraries.

5. A checklist of the common library characteristics should be made for nonreligious school and special libraries, each one separately. Then the checklist should be applied to congregational libraries and a decision made about their essential nature. Do they possess more school library characteristics or more special library characteristics? Or, are they essentially unique? How are they essentially unique?

6. Take a census of current popular library local automation projects to see for what activities these libraries are now using computers.

7. Develop an instrument to use in examining the book collections of one hundred congregational libraries in one denomination in order to learn the size of the collection in terms of minor and major subject emphases. Compare these findings with a similar study of one hundred scholarly libraries of the same denomination.

8. Compile and analyze by subject a list of the reference questions asked in each one of thirty house of worship libraries. Compare the resulting frequency chart with that made for ten other denominations.

9. Examine the technical processing policies and practices of one hundred congregational libraries and categorize them according to maturity or professionalism level.

10. Compare book collections by title between two groups of congregational libraries: (1) the charismatic or Pentecostal group and (2) the conservative or middle-of-the-road Protestant group. Compare the titles by degree of Bible orientation, fiction versus nonfiction, exhortational versus factual.

11. Prepare twenty-five case studies of large congregational libraries. Assess their strengths and weaknesses and their ability to meet professional library standards.

12. Develop a questionnaire to examine the degree to which the Sunday school/library service relationship approximates that of the elementary school/library service relationship in twenty private schools versus twenty large congregational libraries.

13. Prepare twenty-five case studies of private religious public libraries. Categorize them by denomination and compare them with tax-supported public libraries. Attempt to refine the focus on their role which is available in this study.

14. Attempt to prepare a history of the popular library development in three denominations. Trace it back to its nineteenth-century beginning (or earlier). Note the periods in which popular development changed the library's objectives, when the attachment to the Sunday school began to be strengthened, the period when modern library science ideas began to be used, and the period when the library found a place in the house of worship's administrative structure and budget, if it even did so. Cite outstanding examples. Show library relationships to the house of worship leadership, to denominational seminaries, and to women's groups development.

15. Study the public library services of twenty-five congregational libraries offering services to the general public, often with special weekday opening hours. To what extent is this service a significant part of their library service? Of local public library service?

## Chapter Summary

This chapter concludes our survey and discussion of popular *American Library Directory* libraries. However, Chapters 5–6 supplement chapters 2, 3, and 4 on popular libraries and describe (1) the Church and Synagogue Library Association 1986 internal survey and (2) an analysis of four surveys of popular libraries. They will extend the reader's understanding of the popular library scene.

Chapter 4 started with personnel and examined professional, clerical, student assistant (committees of volunteers) and total staff members. Professionals were found in 15 percent of the popular libraries, and 5 percent of them had two or more professionals. A few libraries had thirteen or more professionals, believe it or not! Jewish and Roman Catholic libraries were numerous, especially in the parochial school group. The denominational tables of several groups showed more than 1 professional in each one of the leading libraries.

For clerks, 12 percent of the popular libraries reported them (whereas 60 percent of the scholarly libraries had them). Eleven percent of the congregational libraries had clerks. Leading denominations were Other Denominations, Jewish, and Episcopal/Anglican. A fourth of the parochial school libraries had clerks, and 28 percent of the public libraries had clerks. Leaders in the denominational tables included Baptist, Lutheran, and Other Denominations. Middle Atlantic led among the regions.

Student staff members (house of worship volunteer library committee members) were used by 16 percent of the popular libraries, as compared with 46 percent of the scholarly libraries. Northeast libraries were best endowed and West libraries least here. In size these groups ranged from nine to six persons for the male versus female averages. Committee size varied directly by expenditure size. Several Mormon genealogical libraries led the tables in this area. By denomination, Other Denominations, Baptists, and Methodists led.

For the total personnel, staff members were reported to exist by 17 percent of the popular libraries in 1978 and 27 percent in 1988 as compared with 66 percent of the scholarly libraries. Mean staff sizes were five to six staff members. Largest staffs were found in the Other Denominations and the Baptist groups. Thirty-two libraries were medium-sized, from ten to thirty-nine staff members. Baptist, Methodist, and Other Denominations led in total staff members. As far as chief librarians went, males had the advantage everywhere, with larger variable scores than were obtained by females.

The second major chapter section was library material holdings, covering book volumes, periodical titles, vertical files, microforms, media, maps, and art reproductions. Book collections ranged from 200,000 down to a few hundred volumes. Parochial school and public libraries were again Jewish, Roman Catholic, and Canadian. By denomination, Other Denominations, Jewish, and Roman Catholic again led the listings with Baptist being strong also. For periodical titles, congregational libraries led. We had strong Roman Catholic libraries in periodical title holdings. Vertical files were found in 20 percent of the popular libraries, and they averaged 7.6 drawers per library. One-sixth of the parochial schools and one-fourth of the public libraries reported them, too. Jewish libraries were especially important here. A few popular library collections were as large as some scholarly library collections.

Microforms were most important in Mormon genealogical collections. The West and Southeast regions were strongest here. Other Denominations was the most important denominational group. For media, 70 percent of the scholarly and 25 percent of the popular libraries had media in 1978 and 35 percent of the popular libraries had media in 1988. Thirty-one percent of the public libraries had media. Maps were held by 16 percent of the popular libraries, 20 percent of the parochial school, and 18 percent of the congregational libraries. Art reproductions were held by 7 percent of the popular libraries—44 libraries in all.

The third major part of chapter 4 dealt first with library expenditure on material, and Jewish and Roman Catholic libraries were leaders in this area. Sixteen libraries had expenditures exceeding $10,000 annually. For annual personnel expenditures, Jewish and Roman Catholic were strong. Certain popular libraries had personnel expenditures of as much as $325,000. Annual other expenditures was strong in many libraries; Jewish libraries were especially strong here. Total expenditure library leaders were primarily Baptist, Jewish, and Presbyterian.

Several special analyses were made to illuminate total expenditures further. These analyses involved a variety of approaches. Matched pairs, longitudinal studies, growth studies and attempts to ascertain quality by studying quantity were involved. Certain studies highlighted the few leading libraries by denomination and region. In certain cases popular library scores equaled those of many school and special libraries. Future development was projected to 1998, and additional analyses and research projects were suggested as well.

# Notes

1. For this study's congregational libraries and for the sake of comparability with scholarly libraries, the unpaid part-time adult staff members or volunteers who carried out most of the library's work were coded as "student assistants." This group formed the house of worship's library committee in

each denomination's congregations. Few congregational libraries had genuine teenage student assistants on the staff. On the other hand, if we can count the Protestant Sunday school students as such students, then in certain libraries these students worked in the congregational libraries on Sunday or the day of the religious service, without pay and without being counted in the *ALD* report. Of course, many parochial school libraries had school students working in the library, also, sometimes for pay and sometimes not. Whether or not they were counted in the *ALD* staff totals is not known.

2. Unfortunately, many of the tables in this popular library section were short and contained only two to three listings because those were the only libraries available in a small sample; other tables in the series were the usual length. Large denominations often produced long listings that needed to be truncated. Therefore, the cutoff point often varied by denomination as the author attempted to average fifteen libraries per table.

3. The Blumenthal Library of Sinai Temple in Los Angeles was a well-known synagogue library with a $75,000 personnel expenditure. As an additional bit of relevant information, the Bank Adult Library of Temple Beth El in Boca Raton, Florida, and the Blumenthal Library in Sinai Temple were accredited by the Association of Jewish Libraries in 1992, Blumenthal at the advanced level and Bank at the basic level.

TABLE 4.1

1978 and 1988 *American Library Directory* Longitudinal Study
Popular Library Professional Staff Members[a]

| | --------------1978-------------- | | | | --------------1988-------------- | | | | Percentage |
| Library Type | Number of Libraries | No Response | Total Libraries | Mean Members | Number of Libraries | No Response | Total Libraries | Mean Members | Change 1978–88 |
|---|---|---|---|---|---|---|---|---|---|
| Popular Congregational | 80 | 607 | 687 | 1.7 | 95 | 548 | 643 | 1.7 | 0.0 |
| Parochial | 73 | 561 | 634 | 1.6 | 80 | 513 | 593 | 1.7 | 6.3 |
| | 2 | 25 | 27 | 3.5 | 8 | 17 | 25 | 1.4 | −60.0 |
| Public | 5 | 21 | 26 | 1.8 | 7 | 18 | 25 | 1.6 | −11.0 |

[a] The high No Response percentage in this table (85–88%) suggests that the true mean number of professionals for all congregational type libraries is probably well below 1.0 persons.

TABLE 4.2

1978 *American Library Directory* Congregational (Type) Libraries
with the Largest Number of Professional Staff Members

| Library | Denomination | Number of Professionals |
|---|---|---|
| Walnut Street Baptist Church, Louisville, KY | Baptist | 13 |
| First Baptist Church, Murfreesboro, TN | Baptist | 8 |
| Trinity Lutheran Church, Moorhead, MN | Lutheran | 6 |
| First United Methodist Church, Tulsa, OK | Methodist | 4 |
| First United Presbyterian Church, Albuquerque, NM | Presbyterian | 3 |
| Emmaus Lutheran Church, Denver, CO | Lutheran | 2 |
| First Congregational Church, Stamford, CT | Congregational | 2 |
| Shiloh Baptist Church, Washington, DC | Baptist | 2 |
| Memorial Presbyterian Church, Midland, MI | Presbyterian | 2 |
| Trinity United Presbyterian Church, Cherry Hill, NJ | Presbyterian | 2 |
| First United Presbyterian Church, Mansfield, OH | Presbyterian | 2 |
| Epworth United Methodist Church, Toledo, OH | Methodist | 2 |
| Holy Trinity Lutheran Church, Abington, PA | Lutheran | 2 |
| Congregation Rodeph Shalom Philadelphia, PA | Jewish | 2 |
| Church of the Incarnation, Dallas, TX | Roman Catholic | 2 |
| First Presbyterian Church, El Paso, TX | Presbyterian | 2 |
| First Baptist Church, San Antonio, TX | Baptist | 2 |

TABLE 4.3

1988 *American Library Directory* Congregational (Type) Libraries
with the Largest Number of Professional Staff Members

| Library | Denomination | Number of Professionals |
|---|---|---|
| Church of Jesus Christ of Latter-day Saints, Salt Lake City, UT | Other Denominations | 13 |
| First Baptist Church, Murfreesboro, TN | Baptist | 6 |
| Stephen S. Wise Temple, Los Angeles, CA | Jewish | 5 |
| Trinity Lutheran Church, Moorhead, MN | Lutheran | 5 |
| First Baptist Church, Gainesville, FL | Baptist | 3 |
| Calvary Episcopal Church, Columbia, MO | Episcopal/Anglican | 3 |
| First Presbyterian Church, Albuquerque, NM | Presbyterian | 3 |
| Hoffmantown Baptist Church, Albuquerque, NM | Baptist | 3 |
| Westwood First Presbyterian Church, Cincinnati, OH | Presbyterian | 3 |
| First Baptist Church, Abilene, TX | Baptist | 3 |
| Sinai Temple, Los Angeles, CA | Jewish | 2 |
| Trinity Episcopal Church, Santa Barbara, CA | Episcopal/Anglican | 2 |
| Pasadena Presbyterian Church, St. Petersburg, FL | Presbyterian | 2 |
| Northside United Methodist Church, Atlanta, GA | Methodist | 2 |
| North Suburban Synagogue Beth El, Highland Park, IL | Jewish | 2 |
| Saul Bradsky Jewish Community, St. Louis, MO | Jewish | 2 |
| St. Paul's United Methodist Church, Las Cruces, NM | Methodist | 2 |
| St. Stephen United Church of Christ, Sandusky, OH | United Church of Christ | 2 |
| Holy Trinity Lutheran Church, Abington, PA | Lutheran | 2 |
| St. Faith Episcopal Church, Havertown, PA | Episcopal/Anglican | 2 |
| Westminster Presbyterian Church, Pittsburgh, PA | Presbyterian | 2 |
| Jewish Temple, Nashville, TN | Jewish | 2 |
| Church of the Incarnation, Dallas, TX | Roman Catholic | 2 |
| First Presbyterian Church, El Paso, TX | Presbyterian | 2 |
| Congregation Beth Jeshurun, Houston, TX | Jewish | 2 |

TABLE 4.4
1978 and 1988 *American Library Directory* Longitudinal Study Congregational (Type) Library Staff Professionals by Denomination

| Denomination | 1978 | | | | 1988 | | | | Percentage Change 1978–88 |
|---|---|---|---|---|---|---|---|---|---|
| | Number of Libraries | No Response | Total Libraries | Mean Members | Number of Libraries | No Response | Total Libraries | Mean Members | |
| Baptist | 9 | 74 | 83 | 3.0 | 9 | 62 | 71 | 2.0 | −33.0 |
| Christian | 2 | 16 | 18 | 1.0 | 1 | 16 | 17 | 1.0 | 0.0 |
| Churches of Christ | 0 | 0 | 0 | 0.0 | 2 | 0 | 2 | 1.0 | N/A |
| Episcopal/Anglican | 1 | 40 | 41 | 1.0 | 4 | 29 | 33 | 2.0 | 100.0 |
| Independent | 0 | 3 | 3 | 0.0 | 0 | 1 | 1 | 0.0 | 0.0 |
| Lutheran | 8 | 45 | 53 | 1.5 | 6 | 36 | 42 | 1.5 | N/A |
| Mennonite | 0 | 3 | 3 | 0.0 | 0 | 4 | 4 | 0.0 | 0.0 |
| Methodist | 6 | 49 | 55 | 1.5 | 8 | 56 | 64 | 1.1 | −24.0 |
| Other Denominations | 8 | 78 | 86 | 1.0 | 4 | 67 | 71 | 3.6 | 264.0 |
| Presbyterian | 15 | 100 | 115 | 1.0 | 9 | 88 | 97 | 1.8 | 79.0 |
| U.C.C. | 0 | 13 | 13 | 0.0 | 3 | 10 | 13 | 1.0 | N/A |
| Summary | | | | | | | | | |
| Jewish | 23 | 127 | 150 | 1.0 | 32 | 138 | 170 | 1.3 | 30.0 |
| Roman Catholic | 1 | 13 | 14 | 2.0 | 2 | 6 | 8 | 1.5 | −25.0 |
| All Protestant | 49 | 421 | 470 | 1.5 | 46 | 369 | 415 | 1.7 | 11.0 |
| Total | 73 | 561 | 634 | 1.6 | 80 | 513 | 593 | 1.7 | 6.3 |

TABLE 4.5
1978 *American Library Directory* Popular Baptist Libraries with the Largest Number of Professional Staff Members

| Library | Number of Professionals |
| --- | --- |
| Walnut Street Baptist Church, Louisville, KY | 13 |
| First Baptist Church, Murfreesboro, TN | 8 |
| Shiloh Baptist Church, Washington, DC | 2 |
| First Baptist Church, San Antonio, TX | 2 |

TABLE 4.6
1988 *American Library Directory* Popular Baptist Libraries with the Largest Number of Professional Staff Members

| Library | Number of Professionals |
| --- | --- |
| First Baptist Church, Murfreesboro, TN | 6 |
| First Baptist Church, Gainesville, FL | 3 |
| Hoffmantown Baptist Church, Albuquerque, NM | 3 |
| First Baptist Church, Abilene, TX | 3 |

TABLE 4.7
1988 *American Library Directory* Popular Episcopal/Anglican Libraries with the Largest Number of Professional Staff Members

| Library | Number of Professionals |
| --- | --- |
| Calvary Episcopal Church, Columbia, MO | 3 |
| Trinity Episcopal Church, Santa Barbara, CA | 2 |
| St. Faith Episcopal Church, Havertown, PA | 2 |

TABLE 4.8
1988 *American Library Directory* Popular Lutheran Libraries with the Largest Number of Professional Staff Members

| Library | Number of Professionals |
| --- | --- |
| Trinity Lutheran Church, Moorhead, MN | 5 |
| Holy Trinity Lutheran Church, Abington, PA | 2 |

TABLE 4.9
1988 *American Library Directory* Popular Methodist Libraries with the
Largest Number of Professional Staff Members

| Library | Number of Professionals |
| --- | --- |
| Northside United Methodist Church, Atlanta, GA | 2 |
| St. Paul's United Methodist Church, Las Cruces, NM | 2 |

TABLE 4.10
1988 *American Library Directory* Popular Presbyterian Libraries with
the Largest Number of Professional Staff Members

| Library | Number of Professionals |
| --- | --- |
| First United Presbyterian Church, Albuquerque, NM | 3 |
| Westwood First Presbyterian Church, Cincinnati, OH | 3 |
| Pasadena Presbyterian Church, St. Petersburg, FL | 2 |
| Westminster Presbyterian Church, Pittsburgh, PA | 2 |
| First Presbyterian Church, El Paso, TX | 2 |

TABLE 4.11
1988 *American Library Directory* Popular Jewish Libraries with the
Largest Number of Professional Staff Members

| Library | Number of Professionals |
| --- | --- |
| Stephen S. Wise Temple, Los Angeles, CA | 5 |
| Toronto Jewish Congress, Willowdale, ON | 3 |
| Sinai Temple, Los Angeles, CA | 2 |
| Central Agency for Jewish Education, Miami, FL | 2 |
| North Suburban Synagogue Beth El, Highland Park, IL | 2 |
| Saul Bradsky Jewish Community Center, St. Louis, MO | 2 |
| Young Men's and Women's Hebrew Association, New York, NY | 2 |
| Temple Library, Nashville, TN | 2 |
| Congregation Beth Yeshurun, Houston, TX | 2 |

TABLE 4.12
1988 *American Library Directory* Popular Roman Catholic Libraries
with the Largest Number of Professional Staff Members

| Library | Number of Professionals |
| --- | --- |
| Cardinal Ritter, St. Louis, MO | 3 |
| Church of the Incarnation, Dallas, TX | 2 |
| Oratoire St. Joseph, Montréal, PQ | 2 |

TABLE 4.13

1988 *American Library Directory* Parochial School Libraries with the Largest Number of Professional Staff Members

| Library | Denomination | Number of Professionals |
|---|---|---|
| Cardinal Ritter, St. Louis, MO | Roman Catholic | 3 |
| Central Agency for Jewish Education, Miami, FL | Jewish | 2 |
| Niles Township Jewish Congregation, Skokie, IL | Jewish | 1 |
| Congregation Beth-el Zedeck, Indianapolis, IN | Jewish | 1 |
| Jewish Education Association, Louisville, KY | Jewish | 1 |
| Portsmouth Abbey School, Portsmouth, RI | Roman Catholic | 1 |
| Edmonton Catholic Schools, Edmonton, AB | Roman Catholic | 1 |
| Commission des Écoles Catholiques, Montréal, PQ | Roman Catholic | 1 |

TABLE 4.14

1988 *American Library Directory* Public Libraries with the Largest Number of Professional Staff Members

| Library | Denomination | Number of Professionals |
|---|---|---|
| Toronto Jewish Congress, Willowdale, ON | Jewish | 3 |
| Young Men's and Women's Hebrew Association, New York, NY | Jewish | 2 |
| Oratoire St. Joseph, Montréal, PQ | Roman Catholic | 2 |
| Stamford Catholic Library, Stamford, CT | Roman Catholic | 1 |
| Slovak Catholic Culture Center, Oak Forest, IL | Roman Catholic | 1 |
| St. Matthew's and St. Timothy's Neighborhood, New York, NY | Roman Catholic | 1 |
| Union St. Jean Baptiste, Woonsocket, RI | Roman Catholic | 1 |

TABLE 4.15

1988 *American Library Directory* Percentage of Popular Libraries by Region for Professional Staff Members

| Region | ---------------Percentage of Popular Libraries--------------- | | | | | | | |
| | 1 Staff Member | 2–3 Staff Members | 4-5 Staff Members | 6+Staff Members | No Response | Total | Number | Mean |
|---|---|---|---|---|---|---|---|---|
| Northeast | 11 | 0 | 0 | 0 | 89 | 100 | 35 | 1 |
| Middle Atlantic | 10 | 3 | 0 | 0 | 88 | 100 | 156 | 1 |
| Southeast | 10 | 5 | 0 | 1 | 84 | 100 | 93 | 2 |
| Southwest | 9 | 9 | 0 | 0 | 83 | 100 | 82 | 2 |
| West | 10 | 4 | 2 | 0 | 84 | 100 | 50 | 2 |
| Rocky Mountains | 0 | 0 | 0 | 13 | 88 | 100 | 8 | 7 |
| Middle West | 12 | 3 | 1 | 0 | 85 | 100 | 197 | 1 |
| Canada | 10 | 10 | 0 | 0 | 81 | 100 | 22 | 2 |
| Mean | 10 | 4 | 0.5 | 0 | 85 | 100 | 643 | 2 |

TABLE 4.16

1988 *American Library Directory* Popular Libraries Clerical Staff Size

| Type of Library | 1 Staff Member | | 2–3 Staff Members | | 4–5 Staff Members | | 6+ Staff Members | | No Response | | Total | Mean Members |
| | Number | % | Number | % | Number | % | Number | % | Number | % | | |
|---|---|---|---|---|---|---|---|---|---|---|---|---|
| Popular | 31 | 5 | 20 | 3 | 10 | 2 | 7 | 1 | 574 | 89 | 642 | 3 |

TABLE 4.17
1978 and 1988 *American Library Directory* Longitudinal Study of Congregational (Type) Library Clerical Staff Members by Denomination

| Denomination | 1978 | | | | 1988 | | | | Percentage Change 1978–88 |
|---|---|---|---|---|---|---|---|---|---|
| | Number of Libraries | No Response | Total Libraries | Mean Members | Number of Libraries | No Response | Total Libraries | Mean Members | |
| Baptist | 11 | 72 | 83 | 6 | 5 | 66 | 71 | 3 | −59 |
| Christian | 4 | 14 | 18 | 8 | 0 | 17 | 17 | 0 | −100 |
| Churches of Christ | 0 | 0 | 0 | 0 | 0 | 2 | 2 | 0 | 0 |
| Episcopal/Anglican | 4 | 37 | 41 | 4 | 5 | 28 | 33 | 3 | −35 |
| Independent | 0 | 3 | 3 | 0 | 0 | 1 | 1 | 0 | 0 |
| Lutheran | 10 | 43 | 53 | 8 | 3 | 39 | 42 | 3 | −60 |
| Mennonite | 0 | 3 | 3 | 0 | 0 | 4 | 4 | 0 | 0 |
| Methodist | 6 | 49 | 55 | 4 | 3 | 61 | 64 | 2 | −49 |
| Other Denominations | 13 | 73 | 86 | 3 | 8 | 63 | 71 | 7 | 117 |
| Presbyterian | 20 | 95 | 115 | 4 | 3 | 94 | 97 | 5 | 25 |
| U.C.C. | 2 | 11 | 13 | 2 | 2 | 11 | 13 | 3 | 50 |
| Summary | | | | | | | | | |
| Jewish | 26 | 124 | 150 | 3 | 26 | 144 | 170 | 2 | −29 |
| Roman Catholic | 2 | 12 | 14 | 13 | 0 | 8 | 8 | 0 | −100 |
| All Protestant | 70 | 400 | 470 | 5 | 29 | 386 | 415 | 4 | −18 |
| Total | 98 | 536 | 634 | 4 | 55 | 538 | 593 | 3 | −32 |

TABLE 4.18

1978 *American Library Directory* Congregational (Type) Libraries
with the Highest Numbers of Clerical Staff Members

| Library | Denomination | Number of Clerks |
|---|---|---|
| First Baptist Church of Lakewood, Long Beach, CA | Baptist | 13 |
| First Congregational Church, Stamford, CT | Congregational | 13 |
| Shiloh Baptist Church, Washington, DC | Baptist | 13 |
| Congregation Solel, Highland Park, IL | Jewish | 13 |
| Grace Lutheran Church, La Grange, IL | Lutheran | 13 |
| Central Christian Church, Lexington, KY | Christian | 13 |
| Jewish Community Center, Rockville, MD | Jewish | 13 |
| First Lutheran Church, Red Wing, MN | Lutheran | 13 |
| Presbyterian Church, Tenafly, NJ | Presbyterian | 13 |
| Immaculate Heart of Mary Church, Los Alamos, NM | Roman Catholic | 13 |
| Church of the Holy Faith, Santa Fe, NM | Episcopal/Anglican | 13 |
| First Baptist Church, Murfreesboro, TN | Baptist | 13 |
| Church of the Incarnation, Dallas, TX | Roman Catholic | 13 |
| Ascension Lutheran Church, Milwaukee, WI | Lutheran | 13 |
| Our Savior's Lutheran Church, Milwaukee, WI | Lutheran | 13 |
| First United Presbyterian Church, Albuquerque, NM | Presbyterian | 9 |
| Westwood First Presbyterian Church, Cincinnati, OH | Presbyterian | 8 |
| First United Methodist Church, Tulsa, OK | Methodist | 8 |
| First Baptist Church, San Antonio, TX | Baptist | 8 |

TABLE 4.19

1988 *American Library Directory* Congregational (Type) Libraries
with the Highest Numbers of Clerical Staff Members

| Library | Denomination | Number of Clerks |
|---|---|---|
| Church of Jesus Christ of Latter-day Saints, Mesa, AZ | Other Denominations | 13 |
| Church of Jesus Christ of Latter-day Saints, Boca Raton, FL | Other Denominations | 13 |
| First Presbyterian Church, Albuquerque, NM | Presbyterian | 9 |
| Church of Jesus Christ of Latter-day Saints, Ventura, CA | Other Denominations | 6 |
| Temple Israel, Binghampton, NY | Jewish | 6 |
| Congregation Beth Yeshurun, Houston, TX | Jewish | 6 |
| Congregation Kins, Chicago, IL | Jewish | 5 |
| First Presbyterian Church, Hastings, NE | Presbyterian | 5 |
| First Baptist Church, Albuquerque, NM | Baptist | 5 |
| Hoffmantown Baptist Church, Albuquerque, NM | Baptist | 5 |
| St. Stephen United Church of Christ, Sandusky, OH | United Church of Christ | 5 |
| Sinai Temple, Los Angeles, CA | Jewish | 4 |
| St. Thomas Episcopal Church, Sunnyvale, CA | Episcopal/Anglican | 4 |
| Trinity Lutheran Church, Moorhead, MN | Lutheran | 4 |
| Holy Trinity Lutheran Church, Abington, PA | Lutheran | 4 |
| Congregation Adath Jeshurun, Elkins Park, PA | Jewish | 4 |
| Church of Jesus Christ of Latter-day Saints, San Diego, CA | Other Denominations | 3 |
| Northside United Methodist Church, Atlanta, GA | Methodist | 3 |
| St. Michael in the Hills Episcopal Church, Toledo, OH | Episcopal/Anglican | 3 |
| St. Faith Episcopal Church, Havertown, PA | Episcopal/Anglican | 3 |

TABLE 4.20
1988 *American Library Directory* Parochial School Libraries with the
Highest Number of Clerical Staff Members

| Library | Denomination | Number of Clerks |
|---|---|---|
| Central Agency for Jewish Education, Miami, FL | Jewish | 2 |
| Jewish Education Association, Louisville, KY | Jewish | 2 |
| Edmonton Catholic Schools, Edmonton, AB | Roman Catholic | 2 |
| Commission des Écoles Catholique, Montréal, PQ | Roman Catholic | 2 |
| Portsmouth Abbey School, Portsmouth, RI | Roman Catholic | 1 |

TABLE 4.21
1988 *American Library Directory* Popular Library Clerical
Staff Members by Library Type

| Type of Library | 1 Staff Member | % | 2–3 Staff Members | % | 4–5 Staff Members | % | 6+ Staff Members | % | No Response | % | Number of Libraries | Mean Clerks per Library |
|---|---|---|---|---|---|---|---|---|---|---|---|---|
| Popular Congregational | 31 | 5 | 20 | 3 | 10 | 2 | 7 | 1 | 574 | 89 | 642 | 3 |
|  | 25 | 4 | 13 | 2 | 10 | 2 | 7 | 1 | 538 | 91 | 593 | 3 |
| Parochial | 2 | 8 | 4 | 17 | 0 | 0 | 0 | 0 | 18 | 75 | 24 | 2 |
| Public | 4 | 16 | 3 | 12 | 0 | 0 | 0 | 0 | 18 | 72 | 25 | 2 |

TABLE 4.22
1978 *American Library Directory* Public Libraries with the Highest
Number of Clerical Staff Members

| Library | Denomination | Number of Clerks |
|---|---|---|
| Theosophical Book Association for the Blind, Ojai, CA | Other Denominations | 4 |
| Friends Free Library of Germantown, Philadelphia, PA | Other Denominations | 3 |
| Minnie Cobey, Columbus, OH | Jewish | 2 |
| Church of England Institute, St. John, NB | Episcopal/Anglican | 2 |
| Toronto Jewish Congress, Toronto, ON | Jewish | 2 |
| Flint Newman Center, Flint, MI | Roman Catholic | 1 |

TABLE 4.23
1988 *American Library Directory* Public Libraries with the Highest
Number of Clerical Staff Members

| Library | Denomination | Number of Clerks |
|---|---|---|
| Young Men's and Women's Hebrew Association, New York, NY | Jewish | 3 |
| Toronto Jewish Congress, Willowdale, ON | Jewish | 2 |
| Oratoire St. Joseph, Montréal, PQ | Roman Catholic | 2 |
| Crumbaugh Memorial Public Church Library, Le Roy, IL | Other Denominations | 1 |
| Flint Newman Center, Flint, MI | Roman Catholic | 1 |
| Centre for Christian Studies, Toronto, ON | Independent | 1 |
| Church Army in Canada, Toronto, ON | Episcopal/Anglican | 1 |

TABLE 4.24
1978 *American Library Directory* Popular Library Clerical Staff
Members by Region

| Region | 1–2 | % | 3–4 | % | 5–6 | % | 7 & over | % | No Response | % | Number of Libraries | Mean Members |
|---|---|---|---|---|---|---|---|---|---|---|---|---|
| Northeast | 0 | 0 | 0 | 0 | 0 | 0 | 1 | 3 | 37 | 97 | 38 | 13 |
| Middle Atlantic | 11 | 7 | 9 | 5 | 2 | 1 | 3 | 2 | 143 | 85 | 168 | 4 |
| Southeast | 6 | 7 | 2 | 2 | 3 | 3 | 2 | 2 | 78 | 86 | 91 | 4 |
| Southwest | 7 | 9 | 3 | 4 | 1 | 1 | 6 | 8 | 60 | 78 | 77 | 5 |
| West | 7 | 11 | 1 | 2 | 0 | 0 | 1 | 2 | 54 | 86 | 63 | 3 |
| Rocky Mountains | 0 | 0 | 1 | 10 | 0 | 0 | 0 | 0 | 9 | 90 | 10 | 3 |
| Middle West | 18 | 8 | 7 | 3 | 6 | 3 | 7 | 3 | 175 | 82 | 213 | 4 |
| Canada | 2 | 7 | 0 | 0 | 0 | 0 | 0 | 0 | 25 | 93 | 27 | 2 |
| Total | 51 | 7 | 23 | 3 | 12 | 2 | 20 | 3 | 581 | 85 | 687 | 4 |

TABLE 4.25

1978 *American Library Directory* Popular Baptist Libraries with the Largest Number of Clerical Staff Members

| Library | Number of Clerks |
| --- | --- |
| First Baptist Church of Lakewood, Long Beach, CA | 13 |
| Shiloh Baptist Church, Washington, DC | 13 |
| First Baptist Church, Murfreesboro, TN | 13 |
| First Baptist Church, San Antonio, TX | 8 |
| First Baptist Church, Kennett, MO | 6 |
| Oak Grove Baptist Church, Carrolton, GA | 5 |
| First Baptist Church, Fairmont, NC | 4 |
| North Park Baptist Church, Sherman, TX | 3 |
| First Baptist Church, West Terre Haute, IN | 2 |
| Walnut Street Baptist Church, Louisville, KY | 2 |

TABLE 4.26

1988 *American Library Directory* Popular Baptist Libraries with the Largest Number of Clerical Staff Members

| Library | Number of Clerks |
| --- | --- |
| First Baptist Church, Albuquerque, NM | 5 |
| Hoffmantown Baptist Church, Albuquerque, NM | 5 |

TABLE 4.27

1988 *American Library Directory* Popular Episcopal/Anglican Libraries with the Largest Number of Clerical Staff Members

| Library | Number of Clerks |
| --- | --- |
| St. Thomas Episcopal Church, Sunnyvale, CA | 4 |
| St. Michael's Episcopal Church, Toledo, OH | 3 |
| St. Faith Episcopal Church, Havertown, PA | 3 |
| Episcopal Diocese of West Texas, San Antonio, TX | 2 |

TABLE 4.28
1978 *American Library Directory* Popular Lutheran Libraries with the
Largest Number of Clerical Staff Members

| Library | Number of Clerks |
|---|---|
| Grace Lutheran Church, La Grange, IL | 13 |
| First Lutheran Church, Red Wing, MN | 13 |
| Ascension Lutheran Church, Milwaukee, WI | 13 |
| Our Savior's Lutheran Church, Milwaukee, WI | 13 |
| Trinity Lutheran Parish, St. Peter, MN | 6 |
| Bethlehem Evangelical Lutheran Church, St. Charles, IL | 5 |
| Holy Trinity Lutheran Church, Abington, PA | 5 |
| Emmaus Lutheran Church, Denver, CO | 3 |
| Trinity Lutheran Church, Moorhead, MN | 3 |

TABLE 4.29
1988 *American Library Directory* Popular Lutheran Libraries with the
Largest Number of Clerical Staff Members

| Library | Number of Clerks |
|---|---|
| Trinity Lutheran Church, Moorhead, MN | 4 |
| Holy Trinity Lutheran Church, Abington, PA | 4 |

TABLE 4.30
1988 *American Library Directory* Popular Methodist Libraries with the
Largest Number of Clerical Staff Members

| Library | Number of Clerks |
|---|---|
| Northside United Methodist Church, Atlanta, GA | 3 |
| Methodist Church, Maplewood, NJ | 2 |

TABLE 4.31

1988 *American Library Directory* Popular Other Denominations
Libraries with the Largest Number of Clerical Staff Members

| Library | Number of Clerks |
| --- | --- |
| Church of Jesus Christ of Latter-day Saints, Mesa, AZ | 13 |
| Church of Jesus Christ of Latter-day Saints, Boca Raton, FL | 13 |
| Church of Jesus Christ of Latter-day Saints, Salt Lake City, UT | 13 |
| Church of Jesus Christ of Latter-day Saints, Ventura, CA | 6 |
| Church of Jesus Christ of Latter-day Saints, San Diego, CA | 3 |
| Pilgrim Congregational Church, Duluth, MN | 2 |

TABLE 4.32

1978 *American Library Directory* Popular Presbyterian Libraries with
the Largest Number of Clerical Staff Members

| Library | Number of Clerks |
| --- | --- |
| Presbyterian Church, Tenafly, NJ | 13 |
| First United Presbyterian Church, Albuquerque, NM | 9 |
| Westwood First Presbyterian Church, Cincinnati, OH | 8 |
| Eastminister Presbyterian Church, Indialantic, FL | 5 |
| New Providence Presbyterian Church, Maryville, TN | 5 |
| Central Presbyterian Church, Houston, TX | 5 |
| First Presbyterian Church, Evanston, IL | 4 |
| Trinity United Presbyterian Church, Cherry Hill, NJ | 4 |

TABLE 4.33

1988 *American Library Directory* Popular Presbyterian Libraries with
the Largest Number of Clerical Staff Members

| Library | Number of Clerks |
| --- | --- |
| First United Presbyterian Church, Albuquerque, NM | 9 |
| First Presbyterian Church, Hastings, NE | 5 |

TABLE 4.34
1988 *American Library Directory* Popular Jewish Libraries with the
Largest Number of Clerical Staff Members

| Library | Number of Clerks |
| --- | --- |
| Temple Israel, Binghampton, NY | 6 |
| Congregation Beth Yeshurun, Houston, TX | 6 |
| Congregation Kins of West Rogers Park, Chicago, IL | 5 |
| Sinai Temple, Los Angeles, CA | 4 |
| Congregation Adath Jeshurun, Elkins Park, PA | 4 |
| Young Men's and Women's Hebrew Association, New York, NY | 3 |

TABLE 4.35
1988 *American Library Directory* Popular Roman Catholic Libraries
with the Largest Number of Clerical Staff Members

| Library | Number of Clerks |
| --- | --- |
| Edmonton Catholic Schools, Edmonton, AB | 2 |
| Commission des Écoles Catholiques, Montréal, PQ | 2 |
| Oratoire St. Joseph, Montréal, PQ | 2 |

TABLE 4.36
1988 *American Library Directory* Popular Library Size of Student
Assistant Staff (or Volunteers)

| Type of Library | 1-4 Staff Members Number | % | 5–8 Staff Members Number | % | 9–12 Staff Members Number | % | 13+ Staff Members Number | % | No Response Number | % | Total | Mean |
| --- | --- | --- | --- | --- | --- | --- | --- | --- | --- | --- | --- | --- |
| Popular | 51 | 8 | 26 | 4 | 13 | 2 | 13 | 2 | 539 | 84 | 642 | 7 |

TABLE 4.37

1988 *American Library Directory* Popular Student Library Assistants
(Committee Members) by Library Type

| Library Type | 1–4 | % | 5–8 | % | 9–12 | % | 13 & over | % | No Response | % | Number of Libraries | Mean Members |
|---|---|---|---|---|---|---|---|---|---|---|---|---|
| Popular | 51 | 8 | 26 | 4 | 13 | 2 | 13 | 2 | 539 | 84 | 642 | 7.2 |
| Congrega-tional | 50 | 8 | 25 | 4 | 13 | 2 | 13 | 2 | 492 | 83 | 593 | 7.3 |
| Parochial | 1 | 4 | 0 | 0 | 0 | 0 | 0 | 0 | 23 | 96 | 24 | 1.5 |
| Public | 0 | 0 | 1 | 4 | 0 | 0 | 0 | 0 | 24 | 96 | 25 | 5.5 |

TABLE 4.38

1978 *American Library Directory* Popular Student Library Assistants
(Committee Members) by Library Type

| Library Type | 1–4 | % | 5–8 | % | 9–12 | % | 13 & over | % | No Response | % | Number of Libraries | Mean Members |
|---|---|---|---|---|---|---|---|---|---|---|---|---|
| Popular | 67 | 10 | 16 | 2 | 1 | 0 | 16 | 2 | 587 | 85 | 687 | 4.4 |
| Congrega-tional | 66 | 10 | 15 | 2 | 1 | 0 | 16 | 3 | 536 | 85 | 634 | 4.4 |
| Parochial | 0 | 0 | 0 | 0 | 0 | 0 | 0 | 0 | 27 | 100 | 27 | 0 |
| Public | 1 | 4 | 1 | 4 | 0 | 0 | 0 | 0 | 24 | 92 | 26 | 4.5 |

TABLE 4.39

1988 *American Library Directory* Longitudinal Study Congregational
(Type) Library Student Assistants (Committee Members)
by Denomination

| Denomination | Number of Libraries | No Response | Total Libraries | Mean Members |
|---|---|---|---|---|
| Baptist | 17 | 54 | 71 | 9 |
| Christian | 3 | 14 | 17 | 10 |
| Churches of Christ | 1 | 1 | 2 | 4 |
| Episcopal/Anglican | 4 | 29 | 33 | 6 |
| Independent | 0 | 1 | 1 | 0 |
| Lutheran | 6 | 36 | 42 | 8 |
| Mennonite | 0 | 4 | 4 | 0 |
| Methodist | 18 | 46 | 64 | 6 |
| Other Denominations | 11 | 60 | 71 | 14 |
| Presbyterian | 12 | 85 | 97 | 7 |
| U.C.C. | 3 | 10 | 13 | 5 |
| Summary | | | | |
| Jewish | 23 | 147 | 170 | 3 |
| Roman Catholic | 3 | 5 | 8 | 17 |
| All Protestant | 75 | 340 | 415 | 8 |
| Total | 101 | 492 | 593 | 7 |

TABLE 4.40

1988 *American Library Directory* Congregational (Type) Libraries
with the Largest Number of Student Assistants (Committee Members)
Staff Members

| Library | Denomination | Number of Committee Members |
|---|---|---|
| Church of Jesus Christ of Latter-day Saints, Mesa, AZ | Other Denominations | 33.5 |
| Church of Jesus Christ of Latter-day Saints, San Diego, CA | Other Denominations | 33.5 |
| First Baptist Church, Greensboro, NC | Baptist | 33.5 |
| Carmel Presbyterian Church, Glenside, PA | Presbyterian | 33.5 |
| All Saints Catholic Church, Dallas, TX | Roman Catholic | 33.5 |
| Church of Jesus Christ of Latter-day Saints, Salt Lake City, UT | Other Denominations | 33.5 |
| Church of Jesus Christ of Latter-day Saints, Ventura, CA | Other Denominations | 21.5 |
| Jewish Community Center, Rockville, MD | Jewish | 19.5 |
| First Baptist Church, Murfreesboro, TN | Baptist | 17.5 |
| Immaculate Heart of Mary, Los Alamos, NM | Roman Catholic | 15.5 |
| Ascension Lutheran Church, Milwaukee, WI | Lutheran | 15.5 |
| First United Methodist Church, Tulsa, OK | Methodist | 13.5 |
| First Baptist Church, Abilene, TX | Baptist | 13.5 |
| Pasadena Community United Methodist Church, St. Petersburg, FL | Methodist | 11.5 |
| First United Methodist Church, Athens, GA | Methodist | 11.5 |
| Grace Lutheran Church, La Grange, IL | Lutheran | 11.5 |
| Central Christian Church, Lexington, KY | Christian | 11.5 |
| Church of the Holy Faith, Santa Fe, NM | Episcopal/Anglican | 11.5 |
| High Street Christian Church, Akron, OH | Christian | 11.5 |
| Highland Park United Methodist Church, Dallas, TX | Methodist | 11.5 |

TABLE 4.41

1988 *American Library Directory* Popular Baptist Libraries with the Largest Number of Student Staff Members (Committee Members)

| Library | Number of Committee Members |
|---|---|
| First Baptist Church, Greensboro, NC | 33.5 |
| First Baptist Church, Murfreesboro, TN | 17.5 |
| First Baptist Church, Abilene, TX | 13.5 |
| First Baptist Church, Gainesville, FL | 9.5 |
| North Central Baptist Media, Gainesville, FL | 9.5 |
| First Baptist Church, San Antonio, TX | 9.5 |
| First Baptist Church, Ashland, KY | 7.5 |
| Hoffmantown Baptist Church, Albuquerque, NM | 7.5 |
| First Baptist Church, Waco, TX | 7.5 |

TABLE 4.42

1988 *American Library Directory* Popular Christian Libraries with the Largest Number of Student Staff Members (Committee Members)

| Library | Number of Committee Members |
|---|---|
| Central Christian Church, Lexington, KY | 11.5 |
| High Street Christian Church, Akron, OH | 11.5 |
| First Christian Church, New Castle, PA | 5.5 |

TABLE 4.43

1988 *American Library Directory* Popular Episcopal/Anglican Libraries with the Largest Number of Student Staff Members (Committee Members)

| Library | Number of Committee Members |
|---|---|
| Church of the Holy Faith, Santa Fe, NM | 11.5 |
| St. Thomas Episcopal Church, Sunnyvale, CA | 5.5 |
| St. Michael's Episcopal Church, Toledo, OH | 3.5 |
| St. Faith Episcopal Church, Havertown, PA | 1.5 |

TABLE 4.44
1988 *American Library Directory* Popular Lutheran Libraries with the
Largest Number of Student Staff Members (Committee Members)

| Library | Number of Committee Members |
|---------|-----------------------------|
| Ascension Lutheran Church, Milwaukee, WI | 15.5 |
| Grace Lutheran Church, La Grange, IL | 11.5 |
| First Lutheran Church, Red Wing, MN | 9.5 |
| Oak Grove Lutheran Church, Richfield, MN | 5.5 |
| Christ Lutheran Church, Bethesda, MD | 3.5 |
| St. Johns Evangelical Lutheran Church, Springfield, OH | 1.5 |

TABLE 4.45
1988 *American Library Directory* Popular Methodist Libraries with the
Largest Number of Student Staff Members (Committee Members)

| Library | Number of Committee Members |
|---------|-----------------------------|
| First United Methodist Church, Tulsa, OK | 13.5 |
| Pasadena Community United Methodist Church, St. Petersburg, FL | 11.5 |
| Athens First United Methodist Church, Athens, GA | 11.5 |
| Highland Park United Methodist Church, Dallas, TX | 11.5 |
| First United Methodist Church, Glen Ellyn, IL | 7.5 |
| Christ Church United Methodist Church, Akron, OH | 7.5 |
| St. Luke's United Methodist Church, Oklahoma City, OK | 7.5 |
| Northside United Methodist Church, Atlanta, GA | 5.5 |
| Wesley United Methodist Church, LaCrosse, WI | 5.5 |

TABLE 4.46

1988 *American Library Directory* Popular Other Denominations
Libraries with the Largest Number of Student Staff Members
(Committee Members)

| Library | Number of Committee Members |
|---|---|
| Church of Jesus Christ of Latter-day Saints, Mesa, AZ | 33.5 |
| Church of Jesus Christ of Latter-day Saints, San Diego, CA | 33.5 |
| Church of Jesus Christ of Latter-day Saints, Salt Lake City, UT | 33.5 |
| Church of Jesus Christ of Latter-day Saints, Ventura, CA | 21.5 |
| Church of Jesus Christ of Latter-day Saints, Boca Raton, FL | 9.5 |
| Church of the Atonement, Silver Spring, MD | 9.5 |
| Friends Meeting, Washington, DC | 3.5 |
| United Church of Los Alamos, Los Alamos, NM | 3.5 |
| Marble Collegiate Church, New York, NY | 3.5 |
| Knox-Metropolitan United Church, Edmonton, AB | 3.5 |

TABLE 4.47

1988 *American Library Directory* Popular Presbyterian Libraries with
Largest Number of Student Staff Members (Committee Members)

| Library | Number of Committee Members |
|---|---|
| Carmel Presbyterian Church, Glenside, PA | 33.5 |
| Westwood First Presbyterian Church, Cincinnati, OH | 7.5 |
| Trinity United Presbyterian Church, Cherry Hill, NJ | 5.5 |
| Neshaminy-Warwick Presbyterian Church, Warminster, PA | 5.5 |
| First Presbyterian Church, Houston, TX | 5.5 |
| First Presbyterian Church, Gadsden, AL | 3.5 |
| Pasadena Presbyterian Church, St. Petersburg, FL | 3.5 |
| First Presbyterian Church, Perth Amboy, NJ | 3.5 |
| Crescent Avenue Presbyterian Church, Plainfield, NJ | 3.5 |
| Providence Presbyterian Church, Virginia Beach, VA | 3.5 |

TABLE 4.48

1988 *American Library Directory* Popular Jewish Libraries with the Largest Number of Student Staff Members (Committee Members)

| Library | Number of Committee Members |
| --- | --- |
| Jewish Community Center, Rockville, MD | 19.5 |
| Stephen Wise Temple, Los Angeles, CA | 5.5 |
| Temple Israel, Lawrence, NY | 5.5 |
| Jewish Community Center, Staten Island, NY | 5.5 |
| Temple Israel, Dayton, OH | 5.5 |
| Morristown Jewish Community Center, Morristown, NJ | 3.5 |
| Temple Sinai, Rochester, NY | 3.5 |
| Temple Israel, Columbus, OH | 3.5 |
| Congregation B'nai Jacob, Phoenixville, PA | 3.5 |
| Congregation Shalom, Milwaukee, WI | 3.5 |

ªThe term *student* refers to library committee members in this table.

TABLE 4.49

1988 *American Library Directory* Popular Roman Catholic Libraries with the Largest Number of Student Staff Members (Committee Members)

| Library | Number of Committee Members |
| --- | --- |
| All Saints Catholic Church, Dallas, TX | 33.5 |
| Immaculate Heart of Mary Parish, Los Alamos, NM | 15.5 |
| Stamford Catholic Library, Stamford, CT | 5.5 |
| Church of the Incarnation, Dallas, TX | 1.5 |

TABLE 4.50
1978 and 1988 *American Library Directory* Longitudinal Study
Popular Library Total Staff Membership by Library Type

| Library Type | Number of Libraries | No Response | Total Libraries | Mean Members | Number of Libraries | No Response | Total Libraries | Mean Members | Percentage Change 1978–88 |
|---|---|---|---|---|---|---|---|---|---|
| | ------------------1 9 7 8------------------ | | | | ------------------1 9 8 8------------------ | | | | |
| Popular | 117 | 570 | 687 | 5.1 | 174 | 469 | 643 | 6.2 | 22 |
| Congregational | 108 | 526 | 634 | 5.1 | 154 | 439 | 593 | 6.8 | 33 |
| Parochial | 2 | 25 | 27 | 5.0 | 9 | 16 | 25 | 2.5 | −50 |
| Public | 7 | 19 | 26 | 4.6 | 11 | 14 | 25 | 2.5 | −46 |

TABLE 4.51
1978 *American Library Directory* Popular Library Total Staff Members

| Library Type | 1–4 Staff Members | % | 5–8 Staff Members | % | 9–12 Staff Members | % | 13+ Staff Members | % | No Response | % | Number of Libraries | Mean Staff per Library |
|---|---|---|---|---|---|---|---|---|---|---|---|---|
| Popular | 70 | 10 | 24 | 3 | 6 | 1 | 17 | 2 | 570 | 83 | 687 | 5.1 |

TABLE 4.52
1988 *American Library Directory* Popular Library Total Staff Members

| Library Type | 1–4 Staff Members | % | 5–8 Staff Members | % | 9–12 Staff Members | % | 13+ Staff Members | % | No Response | % | Number of Libraries | Mean Staff per Library |
|---|---|---|---|---|---|---|---|---|---|---|---|---|
| Popular | 97 | 15 | 41 | 6 | 17 | 3 | 19 | 3 | 468 | 73 | 642 | 6.2 |

TABLE 4.53

1988 *American Library Directory* Popular Library Total Library Committee Size

| Library Type | 1–4 | % | 5–8 | % | 9–12 | % | 13 & over | % | No Response | % | Number of Libraries | Mean Members |
|---|---|---|---|---|---|---|---|---|---|---|---|---|
| | | | Number of Staff Members | | | | | | | | | |
| Popular | 97 | 15 | 41 | 6 | 17 | 3 | 19 | 3 | 468 | 73 | 642 | 6.2 |
| Congrega-tional | 80 | 13 | 38 | 6 | 17 | 3 | 19 | 3 | 439 | 74 | 593 | 7 |
| Parochial | 9 | 38 | 0 | 0 | 0 | 0 | 0 | 0 | 15 | 63 | 24 | 3 |
| Public | 8 | 32 | 3 | 12 | 0 | 0 | 0 | 0 | 14 | 56 | 25 | 3 |

TABLE 4.54

1988 *American Library Directory* Popular Library Staff Members by Region

| Region | 1–2 | % | 3–4 | % | 5–6 | % | 7 & over | % | No Response | % | Number of Libraries | Mean Members |
|---|---|---|---|---|---|---|---|---|---|---|---|---|
| | | | Number of Staff Members | | | | | | | | | |
| Northeast | 4 | 11 | 1 | 3 | 0 | 0 | 1 | 3 | 29 | 83 | 35 | 2.6 |
| Middle Atlantic | 18 | 12 | 9 | 6 | 10 | 6 | 8 | 5 | 111 | 71 | 156 | 4.6 |
| Southeast | 5 | 5 | 6 | 6 | 3 | 3 | 10 | 11 | 69 | 74 | 93 | 8.2 |
| Southwest | 9 | 11 | 5 | 6 | 3 | 4 | 14 | 17 | 51 | 62 | 82 | 8.7 |
| West | 5 | 10 | 1 | 2 | 0 | 0 | 5 | 10 | 39 | 78 | 50 | 9.3 |
| Rocky Mountains | 0 | 0 | 0 | 0 | 0 | 0 | 1 | 13 | 7 | 88 | 8 | 60.0 |
| Middle West | 17 | 9 | 9 | 5 | 9 | 5 | 12 | 6 | 150 | 76 | 197 | 4.6 |
| Canada | 4 | 18 | 4 | 18 | 1 | 5 | 0 | 0 | 13 | 59 | 22 | 2.7 |
| Total | 62 | 10 | 35 | 5 | 26 | 4 | 51 | 8 | 469 | 73 | 643 | 6.2 |

TABLE 4.55

1988 *American Library Directory* Total Popular Library Committee Size by Demonination.[a]

| Denomination | 1–4 Staff Members | % | 5–8 Staff Members | % | 9–12 Staff Members | % | 13+ Staff Members | % | No Response | % | Number of Libraries | Mean Members |
|---|---|---|---|---|---|---|---|---|---|---|---|---|
| Baptist | 5 | 7 | 8 | 11 | 3 | 4 | 5 | 7 | 50 | 70 | 71 | 9 |
| Christian | 1 | 6 | 1 | 6 | 2 | 12 | 0 | 0 | 13 | 76 | 17 | N/A |
| Churches of Christ | 1 | 50 | 1 | 50 | 0 | 0 | 0 | 0 | 0 | 0 | 2 | N/A |
| Episcopal/ Anglican | 4 | 12 | 2 | 6 | 2 | 6 | 0 | 0 | 26 | 76 | 34 | N/A |
| Independent | 2 | 67 | 0 | 0 | 0 | 0 | 0 | 0 | 1 | 33 | 3 | N/A |
| Lutheran | 3 | 7 | 2 | 5 | 2 | 5 | 2 | 5 | 33 | 79 | 42 | N/A |
| Mennonite | 0 | 0 | 0 | 0 | 0 | 0 | 0 | 0 | 4 | 100 | 4 | N/A |
| Methodist | 6 | 9 | 6 | 9 | 4 | 6 | 2 | 3 | 46 | 72 | 64 | 7 |
| Other Denominations | 9 | 12 | 1 | 1 | 1 | 1 | 5 | 6 | 61 | 79 | 77 | 14 |
| Presbyterian | 7 | 7 | 6 | 6 | 2 | 2 | 1 | 1 | 81 | 84 | 97 | 7 |
| U.C.C. | 1 | 8 | 2 | 15 | 0 | 0 | 1 | 8 | 9 | 69 | 13 | N/A |
| Summary | | | | | | | | | | | | |
| Jewish | 49 | 26 | 11 | 6 | 1 | 1 | 1 | 1 | 125 | 67 | 187 | 3 |
| Roman Catholic | 9 | 29 | 1 | 3 | 0 | 0 | 2 | 6 | 19 | 61 | 31 | 7 |
| All Protestant | 39 | 9 | 29 | 7 | 16 | 4 | 16 | 4 | 324 | 76 | 424 | 8 |
| Total | 97 | 15 | 41 | 6 | 17 | 3 | 19 | 3 | 468 | 73 | 642 | 6.2 |

[a] Means have been deleted for denominations with fewer than ten responses as they were misleading.

TABLE 4.56
1978 and 1988 *American Library Directory* Longitudinal Study Congregational (Type) Libraries All Staff Members by Denomination

| Denomination | 1978 | | | | 1988 | | | | Percentage Change 1978–88 |
|---|---|---|---|---|---|---|---|---|---|
| | Number of Libraries | No Response | Total Libraries | Mean Members | Number of Libraries | No Response | Total Libraries | Mean Members | |
| Baptist | 13 | 70 | 83 | 8 | 21 | 50 | 71 | 9 | 13 |
| Christian | 4 | 14 | 18 | 8 | 4 | 13 | 17 | 7 | –11 |
| Churches of Christ | 0 | 0 | 0 | 0 | 2 | 0 | 2 | 3 | 0 |
| Episcopal/Anglican | 4 | 37 | 41 | 4 | 7 | 26 | 33 | 6 | 42 |
| Independent | 0 | 3 | 3 | 0 | 0 | 1 | 1 | 0 | 0 |
| Lutheran | 10 | 43 | 53 | 9 | 9 | 33 | 42 | 7 | –18 |
| Mennonite | 0 | 3 | 3 | 0 | 0 | 4 | 4 | 0 | 0 |
| Methodist | 7 | 48 | 55 | 5 | 18 | 46 | 64 | 7 | 42 |
| Other Denominations | 13 | 73 | 86 | 4 | 14 | 57 | 71 | 16 | 332 |
| Presbyterian | 21 | 94 | 115 | 5 | 16 | 81 | 97 | 7 | 44 |
| U.C.C. | 2 | 11 | 13 | 2 | 4 | 9 | 13 | 6 | 205 |
| Summary | | | | | | | | | |
| Jewish | 32 | 118 | 150 | 3 | 56 | 114 | 170 | 3 | 3.3 |
| Roman Catholic | 2 | 12 | 14 | 14 | 3 | 5 | 8 | 18 | 29 |
| All Protestant | 74 | 396 | 470 | 6 | 95 | 320 | 415 | 9 | 47 |
| Total | 108 | 526 | 634 | 5 | 154 | 439 | 593 | 7 | 33 |

TABLE 4.57

1988 *American Library Directory* Popular Baptist Libraries with the
Largest Total Number of Staff Members

| Library | Number of Staff Members |
| --- | --- |
| First Baptist Church, Greensboro, NC | 34.5 |
| First Baptist Church, Murfreesboro, TN | 23.5 |
| First Baptist Church, Abilene, TX | 16.5 |
| Hoffmantown Baptist Church, Albuquerque, NM | 15.5 |
| First Baptist Church, Gainesville, FL | 12.5 |
| First Baptist Church, Albuquerque, NM | 10.5 |
| First Baptist Church, San Antonio, TX | 10.5 |
| North Central Baptist Media, Gainesville, FL | 9.5 |
| First Baptist Church, Ashland, KY | 7.5 |
| First Baptist Church, Waco, TX | 7.5 |

TABLE 4.58

1988 *American Library Directory* Popular Christian Libraries with the
Largest Total Number of Staff Members

| Library | Number of Staff Members |
| --- | --- |
| Central Christian Church, Lexington, KY | 11.5 |
| High Street Christian Church, Akron, OH | 11.5 |
| First Christian Church, New Castle, PA | 5.5 |

TABLE 4.59

1978 *American Library Directory* Popular Congregational Libraries
with the Largest Total Number of Staff Members

| Library | Number of Staff Members |
| --- | --- |
| First Congregational Church, Stamford, CT | 15 |
| Union Congregational Church, Upper Montclair, NJ | 3 |
| First Congregational Church, Palo Alto, CA | 1 |

TABLE 4.60

1988 *American Library Directory* Popular Episcopal/Anglican
Libraries with the Largest Total Number of Staff Members

| Library | Number of Staff Members |
| --- | --- |
| Church of the Holy Faith, Santa Fe, NM | 11.5 |
| St. Thomas Episcopal Church, Sunnyvale, CA | 10.5 |
| St. Michael's Episcopal Church, Toledo, OH | 6.5 |
| St. Faith Episcopal Church, Havertown, PA | 6.5 |
| Trinity Episcopal Church, Santa Barbara, CA | 3.0 |
| Calvary Episcopal Church, Columbia, MO | 3.0 |
| Episcopal Diocese of West Texas, San Antonio, TX | 2.0 |

TABLE 4.61

1988 *American Library Directory* Popular Lutheran Libraries with the
Largest Total Number of Staff Members

| Library | Number of Staff Members |
| --- | --- |
| Ascension Lutheran Church, Milwaukee, WI | 15.5 |
| Grace Lutheran Church, La Grange, IL | 12.5 |
| First Lutheran Church, Red Wing, MN | 9.5 |
| Trinity Lutheran Church, Moorhead, MN | 9.0 |
| Oak Grove Lutheran Church, Richfield, MN | 6.5 |
| Holy Trinity Lutheran Church, Abington, PA | 6.0 |
| Christ Lutheran Church, Bethesda, MD | 3.5 |
| St. John's Evangelical Lutheran Church, Springfield, OH | 2.5 |
| English Lutheran Church, LaCrosse, WI | 2.0 |

TABLE 4.62

1988 *American Library Directory* Popular Methodist Libraries with the
Largest Total Number of Staff Members

| Library | Number of Staff Members |
| --- | --- |
| First United Methodist Church, Tulsa, OK | 14.5 |
| Highland Park United Methodist Church, Dallas, TX | 12.5 |
| Pasadena Community United Methodist Church, St. Petersburg, FL | 11.5 |
| Athens First United Methodist Church, Athens, GA | 11.5 |
| Northside United Methodist Church, Atlanta, GA | 10.5 |
| Christ Church United Methodist Church, Akron, OH | 8.5 |
| First United Methodist Church, Glen Ellyn, IL | 7.5 |
| St. Luke's United Methodist Church, Oklahoma City, OK | 7.5 |
| Methodist Church, Maplewood, NJ | 6.5 |
| Wesley United Methodist Church, LaCrosse, WI | 6.5 |

TABLE 4.63

1978 *American Library Directory* Popular Other Denominations
Libraries with the Largest Total Number of Staff Members

| Library | Number of Staff Members |
| --- | --- |
| Friends Free Library of Germantown, Philadelphia, PA | 9.5 |
| First Christian Reformed Church, Zeeland, MI | 6.0 |
| Theosophical Book Association for the Blind, Ojai, CA | 4.0 |
| First Church of the Brethren, York, PA | 4.0 |
| Church of Jesus Christ of Latter-day Saints, Los Angeles, CA | 3.0 |
| Friends Meeting, Washington, DC | 3.0 |
| United Church of Los Alamos, Los Alamos, NM | 3.0 |
| United Church of Religious Science, Los Angeles, CA | 2.0 |
| First Christian Reformed Church, Kalamazoo, MI | 2.0 |
| Evangelical Covenant Church, Muskegon, MI | 2.0 |
| Salvation Army Church, Las Vegas, NV | 2.0 |

TABLE 4.64

1988 *American Library Directory* Popular Other Denominations
Libraries with the Largest Total Number of Staff Members

| Library | Number of Staff Members |
| --- | --- |
| Church of Jesus Christ of Latter-day Saints, Salt Lake City, UT | 59.5 |
| Church of Jesus Christ of Latter-day Saints, Mesa, AZ | 46.5 |
| Church of Jesus Christ of Latter-day Saints, San Diego, CA | 36.5 |
| Church of Jesus Christ of Latter-day Saints, Ventura, CA | 28.5 |
| Church of Jesus Christ of Latter-day Saints, Boca Raton, FL | 22.5 |
| Church of the Atonement, Silver Spring, MD | 9.5 |
| Pilgrim Congregational Church, Duluth, MN | 4.5 |
| Friends Meeting, Washington, DC | 3.5 |
| United Church, Los Alamos, NM | 3.5 |
| Marble Collegiate Church, New York, NY | 3.5 |
| Knox-Metropolitan United Church, Edmonton, AB | 3.5 |

TABLE 4.65

1988 *American Library Directory* Popular Presbyterian Libraries with the Largest Total Number of Staff Members

| Library | Number of Staff Members |
|---|---|
| Carmel Presbyterian Church, Glenside, PA | 33.5 |
| First United Presbyterian Church, Albuquerque, NM | 12.0 |
| Westwood First Presbyterian Church, Cincinnati, OH | 10.5 |
| Trinity United Presbyterian Church, Cherry Hill, NJ | 6.5 |
| First Presbyterian Church, Hastings, NE | 6.0 |
| Pasadena Presbyterian Church, St. Petersburg, FL | 5.5 |
| Neshaminy-Warwick Presbyterian Church, Warminster, PA | 5.5 |
| First Presbyterian Church, Houston, TX | 5.5 |
| First Presbyterian Church, Perth Amboy, NJ | 4.5 |

TABLE 4.66

1988 *American Library Directory* Popular United Church of Christ Libraries with the Largest Total Number of Staff Members

| Library | Number of Staff Members |
|---|---|
| St. Stephen United Church of Christ, Sandusky, OH | 14.5 |
| United Church of Christ, Maple Shade, NJ | 4.5 |
| Zion United Church of Christ, North Canton, OH | 4.5 |

TABLE 4.67

1988 *American Library Directory* Popular Jewish Libraries with the
Largest Total Number of Staff Members

| Library | Number of Staff Members |
| --- | --- |
| Jewish Community Center, Rockville, MD | 20.5 |
| Stephen Wise Temple, Los Angeles, CA | 11.5 |
| Congregation Beth Yeshurun, Houston, TX | 8.0 |
| Sinai Temple, Los Angeles, CA | 7.5 |
| Temple Israel, Binghampton, NY | 7.0 |
| Temple Israel, Lawrence, NY | 6.5 |
| Congregation Kins of West Rogers Park, Chicago, IL | 6.0 |
| Jewish Community Center, Staten Island, NY | 5.5 |
| Temple Israel, Dayton, OH | 5.5 |

TABLE 4.68

1988 *American Library Directory* Popular Roman Catholic Libraries
with the Largest Total Number of Staff Members

| Library | Number of Staff Members |
| --- | --- |
| All Saints Catholic Church, Dallas, TX | 34.5 |
| Immaculate Heart of Mary Parish, Los Alamos, NM | 15.5 |
| Stamford Catholic Library, Stamford, CT | 6.5 |
| Cardinal Ritter, St. Louis, MO | 4.0 |
| Oratoire St. Joseph, Montréal, PQ | 4.0 |
| Church of the Incarnation, Dallas, TX | 3.5 |
| Edmonton Catholic Schools, Edmonton, AB | 3.0 |
| Commission des Écoles Catholiques, Montréal, PQ | 3.0 |

TABLE 4.69

1988 *American Library Directory* Popular Library Staff Categories in Percentages by Denomination

| Denomination | Professionals | Clerks | Committee Members | Total Staff | Cumulative Staff Members | Number of Libraries |
|---|---|---|---|---|---|---|
| Baptist | 11% | 7% | 82% | 100% | 186.5 | 71 |
| Valid Responses | 9 | 5 | 17 | 21 | | |
| Christian | 3% | 0% | 97% | 100% | 29.5 | 17 |
| Valid Responses | 1 | 0 | 3 | 4 | | |
| Churches of Christ | 36% | 0% | 64% | 100% | 5.5 | 2 |
| Valid Responses | 2 | 0 | 1 | 2 | | |
| Episcopal/Anglican | 18% | 32% | 50% | 100% | 44.0 | 34 |
| Valid Responses | 4 | 6 | 4 | 8 | | |
| Independent | 0% | 40% | 60% | 100% | 2.5 | 3 |
| Valid Responses | 0 | 1 | 1 | 2 | | |
| Lutheran | 16% | 13% | 70% | 100% | 67.0 | 42 |
| Valid Responses | 6 | 3 | 6 | 9 | | |
| Mennonite | 0% | 0% | 0% | 0% | 1.0 | 4 |
| Valid Responses | 0 | 0 | 0 | 0 | | |
| Methodist | 8% | 5% | 87% | 100% | 121.0 | 64 |
| Valid Responses | 8 | 3 | 18 | 18 | | |
| Other Denominations | 7% | 24% | 69% | 100% | 227.5 | 77 |
| Valid Responses | 5 | 10 | 11 | 16 | | |
| Presbyterian | 15% | 14% | 72% | 100% | 109.0 | 97 |
| Valid Responses | 9 | 3 | 12 | 16 | | |
| United Churches of Christ | 16% | 24% | 59% | 100% | 24.5 | 13 |
| Valid Responses | 3 | 2 | 3 | 4 | | |
| Summary | | | | | | |
| Jewish | 27% | 32% | 41% | 100% | 190.5 | 187 |
| Valid Responses | 38 | 30 | 23 | 62 | | |
| Roman Catholic | 18% | 10% | 72% | 100% | 78.0 | 31 |
| Valid Responses | 10 | 5 | 4 | 12 | | |
| All Protestant | 11% | 14% | 75% | 100% | 817.0 | 424 |
| Valid Responses | 47 | 33 | 76 | 100 | | |
| Total | 14% | 17% | 69% | 100% | 1085.5 | 642 |
| Valid Responses | 95 | 68 | 103 | 174 | | |

TABLE 4.70

1978 and 1988 *American Library Directory* Demographics:
Chief Popular Librarian's Gender by Edition and Showing
Percentage Change

| | 1978 | % of Sample | 1988 | % of Sample | % Change |
|---|---|---|---|---|---|
| Male | 85 | 12 | 82 | 13 | −4 |
| Female | 330 | 48 | 506 | 79 | 53 |
| No Response | 272 | 40 | 54 | 8 | −80 |
| Total | 687 | 100 | 642 | 100 | −7 |

TABLE 4.71

1978 and 1988 *American Library Directory* Total Annual Popular
Library Expenditure by Chief Librarian's Gender

| Librarian's Gender | 1–7,500 | % | 7,501–95,000 | % | 95,001 220,000 | % | 220,001 & over | % | No Response | % | No. of Libraries | Mean Dollars |
|---|---|---|---|---|---|---|---|---|---|---|---|---|
| | --------1978 Total Annual Library Expenditure-------- | | | | | | | | | | | |
| Male | 22 | 26 | 6 | 7 | 0 | 0 | 1 | 1 | 56 | 66 | 85 | 14,580 |
| Female | 113 | 34 | 6 | 2 | 0 | 0 | 0 | 0 | 211 | 64 | 330 | 2,878 |
| No Response | 7 | 3 | 0 | 0 | 0 | 0 | 0 | 0 | 265 | 97 | 272 | 786 |
| Total | 142 | 21 | 12 | 2 | 0 | 0 | 1 | 0 | 532 | 77 | 687 | 4,973 |
| | --------1988 Total Annual Library Expenditure-------- | | | | | | | | | | | |
| Male | 22 | 27 | 5 | 6 | 2 | 2 | 0 | 0 | 53 | 65 | 82 | 14,970 |
| Female | 162 | 32 | 45 | 9 | 3 | 1 | 1 | 0 | 295 | 58 | 506 | 12,210 |
| No Response | 11 | 20 | 1 | 2 | 0 | 0 | 0 | 0 | 42 | 78 | 54 | 4,125 |
| Total | 195 | 30 | 51 | 8 | 5 | 1 | 1 | 0 | 390 | 61 | 642 | 12,140 |

314 Popular Religious Libraries in North America

TABLE 4.72

1978 *American Library Directory* Chief Librarian's Gender by Total Annual Expenditures for Popular Libraries

| Library Expenditures | Male | % | Female | % | No Response | % | Number of Libraries |
|---|---|---|---|---|---|---|---|
| Under $1,500 | 15 | 14 | 89 | 81 | 6 | 5 | 110 |
| $1,501–$20,000 | 11 | 28 | 28 | 70 | 1 | 3 | 40 |
| $20,001–$95,000 | 2 | 50 | 2 | 50 | 0 | 0 | 4 |
| $95,001 and over | 1 | 100 | 0 | 0 | 0 | 0 | 1 |
| No Response | 56 | 11 | 211 | 40 | 265 | 50 | 532 |
| Total | 85 | 12 | 330 | 48 | 272 | 40 | 687 |

TABLE 4.73

1978 and 1988 *American Library Directory* Popular Library Volume Holdings by Chief Librarian's Gender

| Librarian's Gender | 1– 10,000 | % | 10,001– 100,000 | % | 100,001 240,000 | % | 240,001 & over | % | No Response | % | No. of Libraries | Mean Volumes |
|---|---|---|---|---|---|---|---|---|---|---|---|---|
| ------1978 Total Annual Library Expenditure------ | | | | | | | | | | | | |
| Male | 64 | 75 | 4 | 5 | 2 | 2 | 0 | 0 | 15 | 18 | 85 | 12,710 |
| Female | 271 | 82 | 9 | 3 | 0 | 0 | 0 | 0 | 50 | 15 | 330 | 5,830 |
| No Response | 151 | 56 | 4 | 1 | 0 | 0 | 0 | 0 | 117 | 43 | 272 | 4,194 |
| Total | 486 | 71 | 17 | 2 | 2 | 0 | 0 | 0 | 182 | 26 | 687 | 6,282 |
| ------1988 Total Annual Library Expenditure------ | | | | | | | | | | | | |
| Male | 68 | 83 | 3 | 4 | 2 | 2 | 0 | 0 | 9 | 11 | 82 | 12,650 |
| Female | 476 | 94 | 14 | 3 | 1 | 0 | 0 | 0 | 15 | 3 | 506 | 6,143 |
| No Response | 52 | 96 | 1 | 2 | 0 | 0 | 0 | 0 | 1 | 2 | 54 | 4,552 |
| Total | 596 | 93 | 18 | 3 | 3 | 0 | 0 | 0 | 25 | 4 | 642 | 6,776 |

TABLE 4.74
1988 *American Library Directory* Popular Chief Librarian's Religious
Order Status by Library Type

| Type of Library | Priest or Brother | % | Nun or Sister | % | No Religious Order Status | % | Number of Libraries |
|---|---|---|---|---|---|---|---|
| Popular | 4 | 1 | 5 | 1 | 633 | 99 | 642 |
| Congregational | 1 | 0 | 1 | 0 | 591 | 100 | 593 |
| Parochial | 0 | 0 | 1 | 4 | 23 | 96 | 24 |
| Public | 3 | 12 | 3 | 12 | 19 | 76 | 25 |

TABLE 4.75
1988 *American Library Directory* Congregational (Type) Libraries
with the Largest Number of Volumes

| Library | Denomination | Number of Volumes |
|---|---|---|
| Church of Jesus Christ of Latter-day Saints Genealogical Library, Salt Lake City, UT | Other Denominations | 200,000 |
| Grace Lutheran Church, Show Low, AZ | Lutheran | 35,000 |
| Immanuel Church of the Swedenborgian, Glenview, IL | Other Denominations | 35,000 |
| Christ Church United Methodist Church, Louisville, KY | Methodist | 35,000 |
| Congregation Shaarey Zedek Library and Audio-Visual Centre, Southfield, MI | Jewish | 35,000 |
| World Jewish Genealogy Organization, Brooklyn, NY | Jewish | 35,000 |
| Fairmont Temple, Cleveland, OH | Jewish | 35,000 |
| The Temple, Cleveland, OH | Jewish | 35,000 |
| Temple Beth-El Congregation, Providence, RI | Jewish | 35,000 |
| First Baptist Church, Dallas, TX | Baptist | 35,000 |
| Congregation Beth Yeshurun, Houston, TX | Jewish | 35,000 |
| First Baptist Church, Luling, TX | Baptist | 35,000 |

TABLE 4.76

1988 *American Library Directory* Parochial School Libraries with the Largest Number of Volumes

| Library | Denomination | Number of Volumes |
|---|---|---|
| Petit Seminaire de Québec, Québec, PQ | Roman Catholic | 200,000 |
| Central Agency for Jewish Education, Miami, FL | Jewish | 35,000 |
| Cardinal Ritter, St. Louis, MO | Roman Catholic | 35,000 |
| Commission des Écoles Catholiques, Montréal, PQ | Roman Catholic | 35,000 |
| Bureau of Jewish Education, San Francisco, CA | Jewish | 15,000 |
| Talmudical Academy, Baltimore, MD | Jewish | 15,000 |
| St. Mary's School for the Deaf, Buffalo, NY | Roman Catholic | 15,000 |
| Bureau of Jewish Education, Getzville, NY | Jewish | 15,000 |
| Board of Jewish Education, New York, NY | Jewish | 15,000 |
| Portsmouth Abbey School, Portsmouth, RI | Roman Catholic | 15,000 |
| École Secondaire St. Sacrement, Terrebonne, PQ | Roman Catholic | 15,000 |

TABLE 4.77

1988 *American Library Directory* Public Libraries with the Largest Number of Volumes

| Library | Denomination | Number of Volumes |
|---|---|---|
| Jewish Public Library, Montreal, PQ | Jewish | 130,000 |
| Oratoire St. Joseph, Montréal, PQ | Roman Catholic | 75,000 |
| Young Men's and Women's Hebrew Association, New York, NY | Jewish | 35,000 |
| Friends Free Library of Germantown, Philadelphia, PA | Other Denominations | 35,000 |
| Toronto Jewish Congress, Willowdale, ON | Jewish | 35,000 |
| Catholic Lending Library, Hartford, CT | Roman Catholic | 15,000 |
| Crumbaugh Memorial Public Church, Le Roy, IL | Other Denominations | 15,000 |
| St. Matthew's and St. Timothy's Neighborhood Center, New York, NY | Roman Catholic | 15,000 |
| St. Francis Monastery and Chapel, Providence, RI | Roman Catholic | 15,000 |
| National Council of Jewish Women, Montreal, PQ | Jewish | 15,000 |

TABLE 4.78
1978 and 1988 *American Library Directory* Longitudinal Study Congregational (Type) Library Volume Holdings by Denomination

| Denomination | 1978 | | | | 1988 | | | | Percentage Change 1978–88 |
|---|---|---|---|---|---|---|---|---|---|
| | Number of Libraries | No Response | Total Libraries | Mean Volumes | Number of Libraries | No Response | Total Libraries | Mean Volumes | |
| Baptist | 69 | 14 | 83 | 5,196 | 70 | 1 | 71 | 6,664 | 28 |
| Christian | 13 | 5 | 18 | 6,231 | 17 | 0 | 17 | 4,059 | −35 |
| Churches of Christ | 0 | 0 | 0 | 0 | 2 | 0 | 2 | 1,375 | N/A |
| Episcopal/Anglican | 31 | 10 | 41 | 3,250 | 31 | 2 | 33 | 3,952 | 22 |
| Independent | 2 | 1 | 3 | 2,250 | 1 | 0 | 1 | 2,250 | 0 |
| Lutheran | 38 | 15 | 53 | 3,724 | 40 | 2 | 42 | 5,669 | 52 |
| Mennonite | 2 | 1 | 3 | 4,500 | 4 | 0 | 4 | 4,500 | 0 |
| Methodist | 35 | 20 | 55 | 3,421 | 59 | 5 | 64 | 4,576 | 34 |
| Other Denoms. | 57 | 29 | 86 | 5,382 | 66 | 5 | 71 | 7,144 | 33 |
| Presbyterian | 88 | 27 | 115 | 3,068 | 94 | 3 | 97 | 3,878 | 26 |
| U.C.C. | 10 | 3 | 13 | 2,175 | 13 | 0 | 13 | 2,673 | 23 |
| Summary | | | | | | | | | |
| Jewish | 112 | 38 | 150 | 6,045 | 164 | 6 | 170 | 7,067 | 17 |
| Roman Catholic | 8 | 6 | 14 | 2,594 | 8 | 0 | 8 | 7,125 | 175 |
| All Protestant | 345 | 125 | 470 | 4,097 | 397 | 18 | 415 | 5,160 | 26 |
| Total | 465 | 169 | 634 | 4,540 | 569 | 24 | 593 | 5,737 | 26 |

TABLE 4.79

1988 *American Library Directory* Popular Library Volume Holdings by Region

| Region | 1– 20,000 | % | 20,001– 100,000 | % | 100,001 240,000 | % | 240,001 & over | % | No Response | % | No. of Libraries | Mean Volumes |
|---|---|---|---|---|---|---|---|---|---|---|---|---|
| Northeast | 33 | 94 | 1 | 3 | 0 | 0 | 0 | 0 | 1 | 3 | 35 | 6,301 |
| Middle Atlantic | 145 | 93 | 3 | 2 | 0 | 0 | 0 | 0 | 8 | 5 | 156 | 5,343 |
| Southeast | 90 | 97 | 2 | 2 | 0 | 0 | 0 | 0 | 1 | 1 | 93 | 5,293 |
| Southwest | 73 | 89 | 4 | 5 | 0 | 0 | 0 | 0 | 5 | 6 | 82 | 7,727 |
| West | 48 | 96 | 0 | 0 | 0 | 0 | 0 | 0 | 2 | 4 | 50 | 4,995 |
| Rocky Mountains | 7 | 88 | 0 | 0 | 1 | 13 | 0 | 0 | 0 | 0 | 8 | 28,090 |
| Middle West | 185 | 94 | 5 | 3 | 0 | 0 | 0 | 0 | 7 | 4 | 197 | 5,534 |
| Canada | 15 | 71 | 3 | 14 | 2 | 10 | 0 | 0 | 1 | 5 | 21 | 28,890 |
| Total | 596 | 93 | 18 | 3 | 3 | 0 | 0 | 0 | 25 | 4 | 642 | 6,776 |

TABLE 4.80

1978 and 1988 *American Library Directory* Longitudinal Study Popular Library Volume Holdings for Canada and the United States

| | 1978 | | | | 1988 | | | | |
|---|---|---|---|---|---|---|---|---|---|
| Region | Number of Libraries | No Response | Total Libraries | Mean Volumes | Number of Libraries | No Response | Total Libraries | Mean Volumes | Percentage Change 1978–88 |
| Canada | 21 | 6 | 27 | 36,640 | 21 | 1 | 22 | 28,230 | −23 |
| U.S.A. | 484 | 176 | 660 | 4,965 | 597 | 24 | 621 | 6,035 | 22 |
| Total | 505 | 182 | 687 | 6,282 | 618 | 25 | 643 | 6,789 | 8 |

TABLE 4.81
1988 *American Library Directory* Popular Library Volume Holdings
by Denomination

| Denomination | 1–20,000 | % | 20,001–100,000 | % | 100,001 & over | % | No Response | % | No. of Libraries | Mean Volumes |
|---|---|---|---|---|---|---|---|---|---|---|
| Baptist | 68 | 96 | 2 | 3 | 0 | 0 | 1 | 1 | 71 | 6,664 |
| Christian | 17 | 100 | 0 | 0 | 0 | 0 | 0 | 0 | 17 | 4,059 |
| Churches of Christ | 2 | 100 | 0 | 0 | 0 | 0 | 0 | 0 | 2 | 1,375 |
| Episcopal/Anglican | 32 | 94 | 0 | 0 | 0 | 0 | 2 | 6 | 34 | 3,844 |
| Independent | 3 | 100 | 0 | 0 | 0 | 0 | 0 | 0 | 3 | 5,250 |
| Lutheran | 39 | 93 | 1 | 2 | 0 | 0 | 2 | 5 | 42 | 5,669 |
| Mennonite | 4 | 100 | 0 | 0 | 0 | 0 | 0 | 0 | 4 | 4,500 |
| Methodist | 58 | 91 | 1 | 2 | 0 | 0 | 5 | 8 | 64 | 4,576 |
| Other Denominations | 69 | 90 | 2 | 3 | 1 | 1 | 5 | 6 | 77 | 7,521 |
| Presbyterian | 94 | 97 | 0 | 0 | 0 | 0 | 3 | 3 | 97 | 3,878 |
| U.C.C. | 13 | 100 | 0 | 0 | 0 | 0 | 0 | 0 | 13 | 2,673 |
| Summary | | | | | | | | | | |
| Jewish | 171 | 91 | 9 | 5 | 1 | 1 | 6 | 3 | 187 | 8,340 |
| Roman Catholic | 26 | 84 | 3 | 10 | 1 | 3 | 1 | 3 | 31 | 17,960 |
| All Protestant | 399 | 94 | 6 | 1 | 1 | 0 | 18 | 4 | 424 | 5,252 |
| Total | 596 | 93 | 18 | 3 | 3 | 0 | 25 | 4 | 642 | 6,776 |

TABLE 4.82
1978 and 1988 *American Library Directory* Longitudinal Study Popular Library Volume Holdings by Denomination

| Denomination | 1978 | | | | 1988 | | | | Percentage Change 1978–88 |
|---|---|---|---|---|---|---|---|---|---|
| | Number of Libraries | No Response | Total Libraries | Mean Volumes | Number of Libraries | No Response | Total Libraries | Mean Volumes | |
| Baptist | 69 | 14 | 83 | 5,196 | 70 | 1 | 71 | 6,664 | 28 |
| Christian | 14 | 5 | 19 | 5,946 | 17 | 0 | 17 | 4,059 | –32 |
| Churches of Christ | 0 | 0 | 0 | 0 | 2 | 0 | 2 | 1,375 | 0 |
| Episcopal/Anglican | 31 | 11 | 42 | 3,250 | 32 | 2 | 34 | 3,844 | 18 |
| Independent | 2 | 3 | 5 | 2,250 | 3 | 0 | 3 | 5,250 | 133 |
| Lutheran | 38 | 15 | 53 | 3,724 | 40 | 2 | 42 | 5,669 | 52 |
| Mennonite | 2 | 1 | 3 | 4,500 | 4 | 0 | 4 | 4,500 | 0 |
| Methodist | 35 | 20 | 55 | 3,421 | 59 | 5 | 64 | 4,576 | 34 |
| Other Denoms. | 61 | 31 | 92 | 5,730 | 72 | 5 | 77 | 7,521 | 31 |
| Presbyterian | 88 | 27 | 115 | 3,068 | 94 | 3 | 97 | 3,878 | 26 |
| U.C.C. | 10 | 3 | 13 | 2,175 | 13 | 0 | 13 | 2,673 | 23 |
| Summary | | | | | | | | | |
| Jewish | 122 | 41 | 163 | 7,619 | 181 | 6 | 187 | 8,340 | 9.5 |
| Roman Catholic | 33 | 11 | 44 | 23,770 | 31 | 1 | 32 | 17,860 | –25 |
| All Protestant | 350 | 130 | 480 | 4,167 | 406 | 18 | 424 | 5,252 | 26 |
| Total | 505 | 182 | 687 | 6,282 | 618 | 25 | 643 | 6,789 | 8 |

TABLE 4.83
1978 and 1988 *American Library Directory* Longitudinal Study Popular Library Volume Holdings by Denomination (Congregational Type Libraries Only)

| Denomination | 1978 | | | | 1988 | | | | Percentage Change 1978–88 |
|---|---|---|---|---|---|---|---|---|---|
| | Number of Libraries | No Response | Total Libraries | Mean Volumes | Number of Libraries | No Response | Total Libraries | Mean Volumes | |
| Baptist | 69 | 14 | 83 | 5,196 | 70 | 1 | 71 | 6,664 | 28 |
| Christian | 13 | 5 | 18 | 6,231 | 17 | 0 | 17 | 4,059 | −35 |
| Churches of Christ | 0 | 0 | 0 | 0 | 2 | 0 | 2 | 1,375 | 0 |
| Episcopal/Anglican | 31 | 10 | 41 | 3,250 | 31 | 2 | 33 | 3,952 | 22 |
| Independent | 2 | 1 | 3 | 2,250 | 1 | 0 | 1 | 2,250 | 0 |
| Lutheran | 38 | 15 | 53 | 3,724 | 40 | 2 | 42 | 5,669 | 52 |
| Mennonite | 2 | 1 | 3 | 4,500 | 4 | 0 | 4 | 4,500 | 0 |
| Methodist | 35 | 20 | 55 | 3,421 | 59 | 5 | 64 | 4,576 | 34 |
| Other Denoms. | 57 | 29 | 86 | 5,382 | 66 | 5 | 71 | 7,144 | 33 |
| Presbyterian | 88 | 27 | 115 | 3,068 | 94 | 3 | 97 | 3,878 | 26 |
| U.C.C. | 10 | 3 | 13 | 2,175 | 13 | 0 | 13 | 2,673 | 23 |
| Summary | | | | | | | | | |
| Jewish | 112 | 38 | 150 | 6,045 | 164 | 6 | 170 | 7,067 | 17 |
| Roman Catholic | 8 | 6 | 14 | 2,594 | 8 | 0 | 8 | 7,125 | 175 |
| All Protestant | 345 | 125 | 470 | 4,097 | 397 | 18 | 415 | 5,160 | 26 |
| Total | 465 | 169 | 634 | 4,540 | 569 | 24 | 593 | 5,737 | 26 |

TABLE 4.84
1988 *American Library Directory* Popular Baptist Libraries with the Largest Number of Volumes

| Library | Number of Volumes |
|---|---|
| First Baptist Church, Dallas, TX | 35,000 |
| First Baptist Church, Luling, TX | 35,000 |
| First Baptist Church, Van Nuys, CA | 15,000 |
| Flint-Groves Baptist Church, Gastonia, NC | 15,000 |
| First Baptist Church, Greensboro, NC | 15,000 |
| First Baptist Church, Murfreesboro, TN | 15,000 |
| First Baptist Church, Abilene, TX | 15,000 |
| First Baptist Church, Longview, TX | 15,000 |
| First Baptist Church, San Antonio, TX | 15,000 |
| First Baptist Church, Waco, TX | 15,000 |

TABLE 4.85
1988 *American Library Directory* Popular Christian Libraries with the Largest Number of Volumes

| Library | Number of Volumes |
|---|---|
| Christian Church, Indianapolis, IN | 6,750 |
| Englewood Christian Church, Indianapolis, IN | 6,750 |
| Central Christian Church, Lexington, KY | 6,750 |
| First Christian Church, Columbia, MO | 6,750 |
| High Street Christian Church, Akron, OH | 6,750 |
| East Dallas Christian Church, Dallas, TX | 6,750 |
| Pleasant Grove Christian Church, Dallas, TX | 6,750 |
| First Christian Church, Lubbock, TX | 6,750 |

TABLE 4.86
1988 *American Library Directory* Popular Churches of Christ Libraries with the Largest Number of Volumes

| Library | Number of Volumes |
|---|---|
| University Church of Christ, Murray, KY | 2,250 |
| Roanoke Church of Christ, Roanoke, VA | 500 |

TABLE 4.87

1988 *American Library Directory* Popular Episcopal/Anglican
Libraries with the Largest Number of Volumes

| Library | Number of Volumes |
| --- | --- |
| St. John the Divine Cathedral, New York, NY | 15,000 |
| Church of the Redeemer, Andalusia, PA | 15,000 |
| Trinity Episcopal Church, Newtown, CT | 6,750 |
| Church of the Holy Faith, Santa Fe, NM | 6,750 |
| Trinity Church, New York, NY | 6,750 |
| St. Michael and All Angels Episcopal Church, Dallas, TX | 6,750 |
| St. Martin's Episcopal Church, Houston, TX | 6,750 |
| Episcopal Diocese of West Texas, San Antonio, TX | 6,750 |
| St. Mark's Episcopal Church, San Antonio, TX | 6,750 |
| Episcopal Church Center, Burlington, VT | 6,750 |

TABLE 4.88

1988 *American Library Directory* Popular Lutheran Libraries with the
Largest Number of Volumes

| Library | Number of Volumes |
| --- | --- |
| Grace Lutheran Church, Show Low, AZ | 35,000 |
| St. Paul's Lutheran Church, Skokie, IL | 15,000 |
| Ascension Lutheran Church, Milwaukee, WI | 15,000 |

TABLE 4.89

1988 *American Library Directory* Popular Mennonite Libraries with
the Largest Number of Volumes

| Library | Number of Volumes |
| --- | --- |
| Bethesda Mennonite Church, Henderson, NE | 6,750 |
| Zion Mennonite Church, Souderton, PA | 6,750 |
| First Mennonite Church, Reedley, CA | 2,250 |
| Freeport Mennonite Church, Freeport, IL | 2,250 |

TABLE 4.90

1988 *American Library Directory* Popular Methodist Libraries with the Largest Number of Volumes

| Library | Number of Volumes |
|---|---|
| Christ Church, Louisville, KY | 35,000 |
| First Methodist Church, Shreveport, LA | 15,000 |
| First United Methodist Church, Tulsa, OK | 15,000 |
| Highland Park United Methodist Church, Dallas, TX | 15,000 |
| Reveille United Methodist Church, Richmond, VA | 15,000 |

TABLE 4.91

1988 *American Library Directory* Popular Other Denominations Libraries with the Largest Number of Volumes

| Library | Number of Volumes |
|---|---|
| Church of Jesus Christ of Latter-day Saints, Salt Lake City, UT | 200,000 |
| Immanuel Church of the Swedenborgian, Glenview, IL | 35,000 |
| Friends Free Library of Germantown, Philadelphia, PA | 35,000 |
| Church of Jesus Christ of Latter-day Saints, Mesa, AZ | 15,000 |
| Church of Jesus Christ of Latter-day Saints, San Diego, CA | 15,000 |
| Crumbaugh Memorial Public Church, Le Roy, IL | 15,000 |

TABLE 4.92

1988 *American Library Directory* Popular United Church of Christ Libraries with the Largest Number of Volumes

| Library | Number of Volumes |
|---|---|
| St. John's Evangelical United Church of Christ, Collinsville, IL | 6,750 |
| United Church of Christ (Evangelical and Reformed), Vermilion, OH | 6,750 |
| Trinity United Church of Christ, St. Louis, MO | 2,250 |
| United Church of Christ, Keene, NH | 2,250 |
| United Church of Christ, Maple Shade, NJ | 2,250 |
| Middleburg Heights Community Church, Middleburg Heights, OH | 2,250 |
| Zion United Church of Christ, North Canton, OH | 2,250 |
| St. Stephen United Church of Christ, Sandusky, OH | 2,250 |
| Pilgrim Church, Toledo, OH | 2,250 |
| Christ United Church of Christ, Bethlehem, PA | 2,250 |
| Plymouth Congregational United Church of Christ, Burlington, WI | 2,250 |

TABLE 4.93

1988 *American Library Directory* Popular Jewish Libraries with the Largest Number of Volumes

| Library | Number of Volumes |
|---|---|
| Jewish Public Library, Montreal, PQ | 130,000 |
| Central Agency for Jewish Education, Miami, FL | 35,000 |
| Congregation Shaarey Zadek, Southfield, MI | 35,000 |
| World Jewish Genealogy Organization, Brooklyn, NY | 35,000 |
| Young Men's and Women's Hebrew Association, New York, NY | 35,000 |
| Fairmont Temple, Cleveland, OH | 35,000 |
| The Temple, Cleveland, OH | 35,000 |
| Temple Beth-el Congregation, Providence, RI | 35,000 |
| Congregation Beth Yeshurun, Houston, TX | 35,000 |
| Toronto Jewish Congress, Willowdale, ON | 35,000 |

TABLE 4.94

1988 *American Library Directory* Popular Roman Catholic Libraries with the Largest Number of Volumes

| Library | Number of Volumes |
|---|---|
| Petit Seminaire de Québec, Québec, PQ | 200,000 |
| Oratoire St. Joseph, Montréal, PQ | 75,000 |
| Cardinal Ritter, St. Louis, MO | 35,000 |
| Commission des Écoles Catholiques, Montréal, PQ | 35,000 |
| Catholic Lending Library, Hartford, CT | 15,000 |
| Old Cathedral Parish Church, Vincennes, IN | 15,000 |
| St. Mary's School for the Deaf, Buffalo, NY | 15,000 |
| St. Matthew's and St. Timothy's Neighborhood Center, New York, NY | 15,000 |
| Portsmouth Abbey School, Portsmouth, RI | 15,000 |
| St. Francis Chapel, Providence, RI | 15,000 |
| Church of the Incarnation, Dallas, TX | 15,000 |
| École Secondaire St.-Sacrement, Terrebonne, PQ | 15,000 |

TABLE 4.95
1978 and 1988 *American Library Directory* Longitudinal Study Popular Library Composite Variable (27 Questions) Scores by Volume Holdings[a]

| Number of Volumes | 1978 | | | | 1988 | | | | Percentage Change 1978–88 |
|---|---|---|---|---|---|---|---|---|---|
| | Number of Libraries | No Response | Total Libraries | Mean Scores | Number of Libraries | No Response | Total Libraries | Mean Scores | |
| Under 3,500 volumes | 254 | 52 | 306 | 2,406 | 200 | 107 | 307 | 2,327 | –3.2% |
| 3,501–20,000 | 154 | 26 | 180 | 9,498 | 217 | 73 | 290 | 10,690 | 13 |
| 20,001–100,000 | 14 | 3 | 17 | 83,360 | 13 | 5 | 18 | 66,940 | –20 |
| 100,001–240,000 | 1 | 1 | 2 | 361,700 | 2 | 1 | 3 | 610,400 | 69 |
| 240,001 and over | 0 | 0 | 0 | 0 | 0 | 0 | 0 | 0 | 0 |
| No Response | 12 | 170 | 182 | 37 | 2 | 23 | 25 | 33 | –11 |
| Total | 435 | 252 | 687 | 8,283 | 434 | 209 | 643 | 11,240 | 36 |

[a] 1. Growth Variables     S = Scholarly Libraries     P = Popular Libraries

The following twenty-seven variables took either numeric or boolean values that could be compared from one *ALD* edition to another and hence indicate "growth." Only twenty-three of them apply to popular libraries. These twenty-three variables are accordingly tagged with the letter *P*.

1. Total staff (S) (P)
2. Professional staff (S) (P)
3. Clerical staff (S) (P)
4. Student assistants or volunteers (S) (P)
5. Volume holdings (S) (P)
6. Periodical holdings(S) (P)
7. Vertical file holdings (S) (P)
8. Microforms (S) (P)
9. Material expenditures (S) (P)
10. Personnel expenditures(S) (P)
11. Other expenditures (S) (P)
12. Total expenditures (S) (P)
13. Consortium memberships (S) (P)
14. OCLC memberships (S) (P)
15. Media (S) (P)
16. Maps (S) (P)
17. Art reproductions (S) (P)
18. Automation projects (S) (P)
19. Number of subject interests (S) (P)
20. Number of special collections (S) (P)
21. Number of publications (S) (P)
22. Age (S) (P)
23. Institutional accreditations (S)
24. Institutional degree years awarded (S)
25. Students enrolled (S)
26. Faculty members (S)
27. Religious subject interests (S) (P)

TABLE 4.96
1978 and 1988 *American Library Directory* Longitudinal Study
Popular Library Periodical Holdings by Library Type

| Library Type | --------------------1 9 7 8------------------ | | | | --------------------1 9 8 8------------------ | | | | Percentage |
|---|---|---|---|---|---|---|---|---|---|
| | Number of Libraries | No Response | Total Libraries | Mean 1978 | Number of Libraries | No Response | Total Libraries | Mean 1988 | Change 1978–88 |
| Popular | 161 | 526 | 687 | 62 | 275 | 367 | 642 | 63 | 2 |
| Congregational | 144 | 490 | 634 | 61 | 242 | 351 | 593 | 63 | 3 |
| Parochial | 3 | 24 | 27 | 133 | 16 | 8 | 24 | 75 | −44 |
| Public | 14 | 12 | 26 | 57 | 17 | 8 | 25 | 56 | −2 |

TABLE 4.97
1978 and 1988 *American Library Directory* Longitudinal Study Congregational (Type) Library Periodical Subscriptions by Denomination

| Denomination | 1978 | | | | 1988 | | | | Percentage Change 1978–88 |
|---|---|---|---|---|---|---|---|---|---|
| | Number of Libraries | No Response | Total Libraries | Mean Periods | Number of Libraries | No Response | Total Libraries | Mean Periods. | |
| Baptist | 16 | 67 | 83 | 50 | 29 | 42 | 71 | 53 | 6 |
| Christian | 4 | 14 | 18 | 50 | 7 | 10 | 17 | 50 | 0 |
| Churches of Christ | 0 | 0 | 0 | 0 | 1 | 1 | 2 | 50 | N/A |
| Episcopal/Anglican | 4 | 37 | 41 | 50 | 13 | 20 | 33 | 115 | 130 |
| Independent | 0 | 3 | 3 | 0 | 0 | 1 | 1 | 0 | N/A |
| Lutheran | 15 | 38 | 53 | 50 | 18 | 24 | 42 | 50 | 0 |
| Mennonite | 0 | 3 | 3 | 0 | 1 | 3 | 4 | 50 | N/A |
| Methodist | 6 | 49 | 55 | 50 | 13 | 51 | 64 | 85 | 70 |
| Other Denoms. | 17 | 69 | 86 | 147 | 20 | 51 | 71 | 133 | –10 |
| Presbyterian | 29 | 86 | 115 | 50 | 38 | 59 | 97 | 50 | 0 |
| U.C.C. | 4 | 9 | 13 | 50 | 4 | 9 | 13 | 50 | 0 |
| Summary | | | | | | | | | |
| Jewish | 47 | 103 | 150 | 50 | 95 | 75 | 170 | 50 | 0 |
| Roman Catholic | 2 | 12 | 14 | 50 | 3 | 5 | 8 | 83 | 66 |
| All Protestant | 95 | 375 | 470 | 67 | 144 | 271 | 415 | 71 | 6 |
| Total | 144 | 490 | 634 | 61 | 242 | 351 | 593 | 63 | 3.3 |

TABLE 4.98
1988 *American Library Directory* Congregational (Type) Libraries
with the Largest Number of Periodical Subscriptions

| Library | Denomination | Number of Periodical Subscriptions |
|---|---|---|
| Church of Jesus Christ of Latter-day Saints, Salt Lake City, UT | Other Denominations | 1,700 |
| St. John the Divine Cathedral, New York, NY | Episcopal/Anglican | 900 |
| Highland Park United Methodist Church, Dallas, TX | Methodist | 500 |
| All Saints Catholic Church, Dallas, TX | Roman Catholic | 150 |
| First Baptist Church, Dallas, TX | Baptist | 150 |

TABLE 4.99
1988 *American Library Directory* Parochial School Libraries with the
Largest Number of Periodical Subscriptions

| Library | Denomination | Number of Periodical Subscriptions |
|---|---|---|
| Edmonton Catholic Schools, Edmonton, AB | Roman Catholic | 150 |
| Hamilton-Wentworth Catholic Schools, Hamilton, ON | Roman Catholic | 150 |
| Commission des Écoles Catholiques, Montréal, PQ | Roman Catholic | 150 |
| Protestant School Board, Montreal, PQ | Independent | 150 |

TABLE 4.100

1988 *American Library Directory* Popular Library Periodical
Subscriptions by Region

| Region | 1–100 | % | 101–300 | % | 301–450 | % | 451 & over | % | No Response | % | No. of Libraries | Mean Subscriptions |
|---|---|---|---|---|---|---|---|---|---|---|---|---|
| Northeast | 23 | 66 | 0 | 0 | 0 | 0 | 0 | 0 | 12 | 34 | 35 | 50 |
| Middle Atlantic | 63 | 40 | 1 | 1 | 0 | 0 | 1 | 1 | 91 | 58 | 156 | 65 |
| Southeast | 34 | 37 | 0 | 0 | 0 | 0 | 0 | 0 | 59 | 63 | 93 | 50 |
| Southwest | 30 | 37 | 2 | 2 | 0 | 0 | 1 | 1 | 49 | 60 | 82 | 70 |
| West | 21 | 42 | 0 | 0 | 0 | 0 | 0 | 0 | 29 | 58 | 50 | 50 |
| Rocky Mountains | 3 | 38 | 0 | 0 | 0 | 0 | 1 | 13 | 4 | 50 | 8 | 463 |
| Middle West | 85 | 43 | 0 | 0 | 0 | 0 | 0 | 0 | 112 | 57 | 197 | 50 |
| Canada | 6 | 27 | 4 | 18 | 0 | 0 | 0 | 0 | 12 | 55 | 22 | 90 |
| Total | 265 | 41 | 7 | 1 | 0 | 0 | 3 | 0 | 368 | 57 | 643 | 63 |

TABLE 4.101

1988 *American Library Directory* Popular Christian Libraries with the
Largest Number of Periodical Subscriptions

| Library | Number of Periodical Subscriptions |
|---|---|
| Christian Church, Indianapolis, IN | 50 |
| Central Christian Church, Lexington, KY | 50 |
| Douglass Boulevard Christian Church, Louisville, KY | 50 |
| First Christian Church, St. Joseph, MO | 50 |
| High Street Christian Church, Akron, OH | 50 |
| First Christian Church, New Castle, PA | 50 |
| First Christian Church, Alexandria, VA | 50 |

TABLE 4.102
1978 *American Library Directory* Popular Congregational Libraries
with the Largest Number of Periodical Subscriptions

| Library | Number of Periodical Subscriptions |
|---|---|
| First Congregational Church, Palo Alto, CA | 50 |
| First Congregational Church, Stamford, CT | 50 |
| First Congregational Church, Auburn, MA | 50 |
| Plymouth Congregational Church, Seattle, WA | 50 |

TABLE 4.103
1978 *American Library Directory* Popular Methodist Libraries with the
Largest Number of Periodical Subscriptions

| Library | Number of Periodical Subscriptions |
|---|---|
| Lowman United Methodist Church, Topeka, KS | 50 |
| Bethesda United Methodist Church, Bethesda, MD | 50 |
| First United Methodist Church, Tulsa, OK | 50 |
| Highland Park United Methodist Church, Dallas, TX | 50 |
| Harlandale United Methodist Church, San Antonio, TX | 50 |
| First United Methodist Church, Green Bay, WI | 50 |

TABLE 4.104
1988 *American Library Directory* Popular United Church of Christ
Libraries with the Largest Number of Periodical Subscriptions

| Library | Number of Periodical Subscriptions |
|---|---|
| St. Paul's United Church of Christ, Evansville, IN | 50 |
| Zion United Church of Christ, North Canton, OH | 50 |
| St. Stephen United Church of Christ, Sandusky, OH | 50 |
| United Church of Christ (Evangelical and Reformed), Vermilion, OH | 50 |

TABLE 4.105

1988 *American Library Directory* Popular Roman Catholic Libraries
with the Largest Number of Periodical Subscriptions

| Library | Number of Periodical Subscriptions |
| --- | --- |
| All Saints Catholic Church, Dallas, TX | 150 |
| Edmonton Catholic Schools, Edmonton, AB | 150 |
| Hamilton-Wentworth Roman Catholic Library, Hamilton, ON | 150 |
| Commission des Écoles Catholiques, Montréal, PQ | 150 |

TABLE 4.106

1978 and 1988 *American Library Directory* Longitudinal Study
Popular Library Vertical File Drawer Holdings by Library Type

| | --------------------1 9 7 8-------------------- | | | | --------------------1 9 8 8-------------------- | | | | |
| --- | --- | --- | --- | --- | --- | --- | --- | --- | --- |
| Library Type | Number of Libraries | No Response | Total Libraries | Mean Drawers | Number of Libraries | No Response | Total Libraries | Mean Drawers | Percentage Change 1978–88 |
| Popular | 131 | 556 | 687 | 6.1 | 139 | 504 | 643 | 7.6 | 25.0 |
| Congregational | 121 | 513 | 634 | 5.6 | 123 | 470 | 593 | 6.5 | 16.0 |
| Parochial | 4 | 23 | 27 | 7.1 | 6 | 19 | 25 | 14.0 | 97.0 |
| Public | 6 | 20 | 26 | 16.0 | 10 | 15 | 25 | 16.0 | 0.0 |

TABLE 4.107

1988 *American Library Directory* Congregational (Type) Libraries
with the Largest Number of Vertical File Drawers

| Library | Vertical Files |
| --- | --- |
| Temple Emanu-el, Tucson, AZ | 48 |
| Eastminster Presbyterian Church, Indialantic, FL | 48 |
| Temple Emanu-el, Birmingham, AL | 26 |
| Temple Beth Israel, Phoenix, AZ | 26 |
| Stephen S. Wise, Temple, Los Angeles, CA | 26 |
| First United Methodist Church, Tulsa, OK | 26 |

TABLE 4.108

1988 *American Library Directory* Parochial School Libraries with the
Largest Number of Vertical File Drawers

| Library | Denomination | Number of Vertical File Drawers |
|---|---|---|
| Central Agency for Jewish Education, Miami, FL | Jewish | 48 |
| Jewish Education Association, Louisville, KY | Jewish | 16 |
| Cardinal Ritter, St. Louis, MO | Roman Catholic | 8 |
| Bureau of Jewish Education, Getzville, NY | Jewish | 8 |
| St. Mary's School for the Deaf, Buffalo, NY | Roman Catholic | 3 |
| Protestant School Board, Montreal, PQ | Independent | 3 |

TABLE 4.109

1988 *American Library Directory* Public Libraries with the Largest
Number of Vertical File Drawers

| Library | Denomination | Number of Vertical File Drawers |
|---|---|---|
| Minnie Cobey Memorial, Columbus, OH | Jewish | 93 |
| National Council of Jewish Women, Montreal, PQ | Jewish | 26 |
| Crumbaugh Memorial Public Church, Le Roy, IL | Other Denominations | 16 |
| Union St. Jean Baptiste, Woonsocket, RI | Roman Catholic | 16 |
| Old St. Mary's Church, San Francisco, CA | Roman Catholic | 3 |
| Flint Newman Center, Flint, MI | Roman Catholic | 3 |
| St. Matthew's and St. Timothy's Neighborhood Center, New York, NY | Roman Catholic | 3 |
| Cecil Harding Jones, Jenkintown, PA | Other Denominations | 3 |
| St. Francis Monastery and Chapel, Providence, RI | Roman Catholic | 3 |
| Church Army in Canada, Toronto, ON | Episcopal/Anglican | 3 |

TABLE 4.110
1988 *American Library Directory* Popular Baptist Libraries with the
Largest Number of Vertical File Drawers

| Library | Number of Vertical File Drawers |
|---|---|
| First Baptist Church, West Terre Haute, IN | 16 |
| First Baptist Church, Dallas, TX | 16 |
| First Baptist Church, Van Nuys, CA | 8 |
| First Baptist Church, Melrose, MA | 8 |
| First Baptist Church, San Antonio, TX | 8 |

TABLE 4.111
1988 *American Library Directory* Popular Christian Libraries with the
Largest Number of Vertical File Drawers

| Library | Number of Vertical File Drawers |
|---|---|
| First Christian Church, Columbia, MO | 16 |
| First Christian Church, Alexandria, VA | 8 |
| Douglass Boulevard Christian Church, Louisville, KY | 3 |
| First Christian Church, St. Joseph, MO | 3 |
| High Street Christian Church, Akron, OH | 3 |
| First Christian Church, New Castle, PA | 3 |

TABLE 4.112
1988 *American Library Directory* Popular Lutheran Libraries with the
Largest Number of Vertical File Drawers

| Library | Number of Vertical File Drawers |
|---|---|
| Augustana Lutheran Church, Denver, CO | 8 |
| Ascension Lutheran Church, Milwaukee, WI | 8 |
| Grace Lutheran Church, La Grange, IL | 3 |
| First Lutheran Church, Red Wing, MN | 3 |
| Trinity Lutheran Parish, St. Peter, MN | 3 |
| Grace Lutheran Church, Wayzata, MN | 3 |
| Holy Trinity Lutheran Church, Abington, PA | 3 |
| First Lutheran Church, Sioux Falls, SD | 3 |
| St. Martin's Evangelical Lutheran Church, Austin,TX | 3 |
| English Lutheran Church, LaCrosse, WI | 3 |
| Mount Carmel Lutheran Church, Milwaukee, WI | 3 |

TABLE 4.113

1988 *American Library Directory* Popular Methodist Libraries with the Largest Number of Vertical File Drawers

| Library | Number of Vertical File Drawers |
|---|---|
| First United Methodist Church, Tulsa, OK | 26 |
| Christ Church United Methodist Church, Akron, OH | 8 |
| Highland Park United Methodist Church, Dallas, TX | 8 |
| Mount Vernon Place United Methodist Church, Washington, DC | 3 |
| First United Methodist Church, Gainesville, FL | 3 |
| Bethesda United Methodist Church, Bethesda, MD | 3 |
| St. Paul United Methodist Church, Springfield, MO | 3 |
| First United Methodist Church, Green Bay, WI | 3 |
| Wesley United Methodist Church, LaCrosse, WI | 3 |

TABLE 4.114

1988 *American Library Directory* Popular Other Denominations Libraries with the Largest Number of Vertical File Drawers

| Library | Number of Vertical File Drawers |
|---|---|
| United Church of Religious Science, Los Angeles, CA | 16 |
| Crumbaugh Memorial Public Church, Le Roy, IL | 16 |
| First Congregational Church, Palo Alto, CA | 8 |
| Church of Jesus Christ of Latter-day Saints, Tampa, FL | 8 |
| First Congregational Church, Auburn, MA | 8 |
| Westgate Friends Meeting, Columbus, OH | 8 |
| Davis Community Church, Davis, CA | 3 |
| Church of the Atonement, Silver Spring, MD | 3 |
| New Church Union Swedenborgian, Boston, MA | 3 |
| Union Congregational Church, Upper Montclair, NJ | 3 |
| Cecil Harding Jones, Jenkintown, PA | 3 |

TABLE 4.115
1988 *American Library Directory* Popular Presbyterian Libraries with
the Largest Number of Vertical File Drawers

| Library | Number of Vertical File Drawers |
|---|---|
| Eastminister Presbyterian Church, Indialantic, FL | 48 |
| Central Presbyterian Church, Kansas City, MO | 8 |

TABLE 4.116
1988 *American Library Directory* Popular United Church of Christ
Libraries with the Largest Number of Vertical File Drawers

| Library | Number of Vertical File Drawers |
|---|---|
| Trinity United Church of Christ, St. Louis, MO | 8 |
| United Church of Christ (Evangelical and Reformed), Vermilion, OH | 8 |

TABLE 4.117
1988 *American Library Directory* Popular Jewish Libraries with the
Largest Number of Vertical File Drawers

| Library | Number of Vertical File Drawers |
|---|---|
| Minnie Cobey Memorial, Columbus, OH | 93 |
| Temple Emanu-el, Tucson, AZ | 48 |
| Central Agency for Jewish Education, Miami, FL | 48 |
| Temple Emanu-el, Birmingham, AL | 26 |
| Temple Beth Israel, Phoenix, AZ | 26 |
| Stephen S. Wise Temple, Los Angeles, CA | 26 |
| National Council of Jewish Women, Montreal, PQ | 26 |

TABLE 4.118
1988 *American Library Directory* Popular Roman Catholic Libraries
with the Largest Number of Vertical File Drawers

| Library | Number of Vertical File Drawers |
|---|---|
| Union St. Jean Baptiste, Woonsocket, RI | 16 |
| Cardinal Ritter, St. Louis, MO | 8 |
| Old St. Mary's Church, San Francisco, CA | 3 |
| Flint Newman Center, Flint, MI | 3 |
| St. Mary's School for the Deaf, Buffalo, NY | 3 |
| St. Matthew's and St. Timothy's Neighborhood Center, New York, NY | 3 |
| St. Francis Chapel, Providence, RI | 3 |

TABLE 4.119
1978 and 1988 *American Library Directory* Longitudinal Study
Popular Library Microform Holdings by Library Type

| Library Type | Number of Libraries | No Response | Total Libraries | Mean 1978 | Number of Libraries | No Response | Total Libraries | Mean 1988 | Percentage Change 1978–88 |
|---|---|---|---|---|---|---|---|---|---|
| Popular | 7 | 680 | 687 | 49,386 | 13 | 629 | 642 | 44,019 | −11 |
| Congregational | 6 | 628 | 634 | 40,950 | 10 | 583 | 593 | 57,160 | 40 |
| Parochial | 1 | 26 | 27 | 100,000 | 2 | 22 | 24 | 300 | −100 |
| Public | 0 | 26 | 26 | 0 | 1 | 24 | 25 | 50 | N/A |

TABLE 4.120

1988 *American Library Directory* Congregational (Type) Libraries
with the Largest Number of Microforms

| Library | Denomination | Number of Microforms |
|---|---|---|
| Church of Jesus Christ of Latter-day Saints, Mesa, AZ | Other Denominations | 230,000 |
| Church of Jesus Christ of Latter-day Saints, Salt Lake City, UT | Other Denominations | 230,000 |
| Church of Jesus Christ of Latter-day Saints, San Diego, CA | Other Denominations | 30,000 |
| Church of Jesus Christ of Latter-day Saints, Ventura, CA | Other Denominations | 30,000 |
| Church of Jesus Christ of Latter-day Saints, Boca Raton, FL | Other Denominations | 30,000 |
| Las Vegas Family History Center, Las Vegas, NV | Other Denominations | 15,000 |
| Church of Jesus Christ of Latter-day Saints, Jacksonville, FL | Other Denominations | 3,000 |
| Church of Jesus Christ of Latter-day Saints, Tampa, FL | Other Denominations | 3,000 |
| All Saints Catholic Church, Dallas, TX | Roman Catholic | 550 |
| Beth Shalom Congregation, Elkins Park, PA | Jewish | 50 |
| Crumbaugh Memorial Public Church, Le Roy, IL | Other Denominations | 50 |

TABLE 4.121

1988 *American Library Directory* Popular Other Denominations
Libraries with the Largest Number of Microforms

| Library | Number of Microforms |
|---|---|
| Church of Jesus Christ of Latter-day Saints, Mesa, AZ | 230,000 |
| Church of Jesus Christ of Latter-day Saints, Salt Lake City, UT | 230,000 |
| Church of Jesus Christ of Latter-day Saints, San Diego, CA | 30,000 |
| Church of Jesus Christ of Latter-day Saints, Ventura, CA | 30,000 |
| Church of Jesus Christ of Latter-day Saints, Boca Raton, FL | 30,000 |
| Las Vegas Family History Center, Las Vegas, NV | 15,000 |
| Church of Jesus Christ of Latter-day Saints, Jacksonville, FL | 3,000 |
| Church of Jesus Christ of Latter-day Saints, Tampa, FL | 3,000 |
| Crumbaugh Memorial Public Church, Le Roy, IL | 50 |

TABLE 4.122
1988 *American Library Directory* Highest Cumulative Library
Holdings for Parochial School Libraries[a]

| Library | Denomination | Holdings in Items |
|---|---|---|
| Petit Seminaire de Québec, Québec, PQ | Roman Catholic | 200,000 |
| Commission des Écoles Catholiques, Montréal, PQ | Roman Catholic | 35,150 |
| Central Agency for Jewish Education, Miami, FL | Jewish | 35,098 |
| Cardinal Ritter, St. Louis, MO | Roman Catholic | 35,058 |
| St. Mary's School for the Deaf, Buffalo, NY | Roman Catholic | 15,603 |
| Bureau of Jewish Education, Getzville, NY | Jewish | 15,058 |
| Bureau of Jewish Education, San Francisco, CA | Jewish | 15,050 |
| Talmudical Academy, Baltimore, MD | Jewish | 15,050 |
| Board of Jewish Education, New York, NY | Jewish | 15,000 |
| Portsmouth Abbey School, Portsmouth, RI | Roman Catholic | 15,000 |
| Seminaire des Pères Marists, Sillery, PQ | Roman Catholic | 15,000 |
| École Secondaire St. Sacrement, Terrebonne, PQ | Roman Catholic | 15,000 |

[a] Holdings include book volumes, periodical titles, vertical files, and microforms.

TABLE 4.123
1988 *American Library Directory* Highest Cumulative Library
Holdings for Public Libraries[a]

| Library | Denomination | Holdings in Items |
|---|---|---|
| Jewish Public Library, Montreal, PQ | Jewish | 130,000 |
| Oratoire St. Joseph, Montréal, PQ | Roman Catholic | 75,000 |
| Friends Free Library of Germantown, Philadelphia, PA | Other Denominations | 35,150 |
| Young Men's and Women's Hebrew Association, New York, NY | Jewish | 35,050 |
| Toronto Jewish Congress, Willowdale, ON | Jewish | 35,050 |
| Crumbaugh Memorial Public Church, Le Roy, IL | Other Denominations | 15,115 |
| St. Matthew's and St. Timothy's Neighborhood Center, New York, NY | Roman Catholic | 15,053 |
| St. Francis Monastery and Chapel, Providence, RI | Roman Catholic | 15,053 |
| National Council of Jewish Women, Montreal, PQ | Jewish | 15,026 |
| Catholic Lending Library, Hartford, CT | Roman Catholic | 15,000 |

[a] Holdings include book volumes, periodical titles, vertical files, and microforms.

TABLE 4.124

1978 and 1988 *American Library Directory* Longitudinal Study Popular Library Total Material Holdings (Cumulative) by Denomination[a]

| Denomination | 1978 | | | | 1988 | | | | Percentage Change 1978–88 |
|---|---|---|---|---|---|---|---|---|---|
| | Number of Libraries | No Response | Total Libraries | Mean Items | Number of Libraries | No Response | Total Libraries | Mean Items | |
| Baptist | 69 | 14 | 83 | 5,209 | 70 | 1 | 71 | 6,688 | 28 |
| Christian | 14 | 5 | 19 | 5,971 | 17 | 0 | 17 | 4,081 | −32 |
| Churches of Christ | 0 | 0 | 0 | 0 | 2 | 0 | 2 | 1,400 | 0 |
| Episcopal/Anglican | 31 | 11 | 42 | 3,256 | 32 | 2 | 34 | 3,892 | 20 |
| Independent | 3 | 2 | 5 | 1,517 | 3 | 0 | 3 | 5,334 | 252 |
| Lutheran | 38 | 15 | 53 | 3,746 | 40 | 2 | 42 | 5,692 | 52 |
| Mennonite | 2 | 1 | 3 | 4,500 | 4 | 0 | 4 | 4,513 | .3 |
| Methodist | 35 | 20 | 55 | 3,431 | 59 | 5 | 64 | 4,596 | 34 |
| Other Denoms. | 61 | 31 | 92 | 9,792 | 72 | 5 | 77 | 15,490 | 58 |
| Presbyterian | 88 | 27 | 115 | 3,085 | 94 | 3 | 97 | 3,899 | 26 |
| U.C.C. | 10 | 3 | 13 | 2,197 | 13 | 0 | 13 | 2,690 | 22 |
| Summary | | | | | | | | | |
| Jewish | 122 | 41 | 163 | 7,648 | 181 | 6 | 187 | 8,373 | 9.5 |
| Roman Catholic | 33 | 11 | 44 | 26,830 | 31 | 1 | 32 | 17,940 | −33 |
| All Protestant | 351 | 129 | 480 | 4,874 | 406 | 18 | 424 | 6,687 | 37 |
| Total | 506 | 181 | 687 | 6,974 | 618 | 25 | 643 | 7,745 | 11 |

[a] Cumulative material holdings include book volumes, periodical subscriptions, microforms, and vertical file drawers.

TABLE 4.125

1988 *American Library Directory* Popular Library Total Material
Holdings (Cumulative) by Region[a]

| Region | 1– 10,000 | % | 10,001– 100,000 | % | 100,001 300,000 | % | 300,001 & over | % | No Response | % | No. of Libraries | Mean Items |
|---|---|---|---|---|---|---|---|---|---|---|---|---|
| Northeast | 30 | 86 | 4 | 11 | 0 | 0 | 0 | 0 | 1 | 3 | 35 | 6,338 |
| Middle Atlantic | 134 | 86 | 14 | 9 | 0 | 0 | 0 | 0 | 8 | 5 | 156 | 5,376 |
| Southeast | 84 | 90 | 8 | 9 | 0 | 0 | 0 | 0 | 1 | 1 | 93 | 5,705 |
| Southwest | 62 | 76 | 14 | 17 | 1 | 1 | 0 | 0 | 5 | 6 | 82 | 10,750 |
| West | 40 | 80 | 8 | 16 | 0 | 0 | 0 | 0 | 2 | 4 | 50 | 6,581 |
| Rocky Mountains | 7 | 88 | 0 | 0 | 0 | 0 | 1 | 13 | 0 | 0 | 8 | 57,080 |
| Middle West | 171 | 87 | 19 | 10 | 0 | 0 | 0 | 0 | 7 | 4 | 197 | 5,559 |
| Canada | 12 | 55 | 7 | 32 | 2 | 9 | 0 | 0 | 1 | 5 | 22 | 28,270 |
| Total | 540 | 84 | 74 | 12 | 3 | 0 | 1 | 0 | 25 | 4 | 643 | 7,745 |

[a] Holdings include book volumes, periodical titles, vertical files, and microforms.

TABLE 4.126

1978 and 1988 *American Library Directory* Longitudinal Study
Popular Library Total Holdings (Cumulative) by Library Type

| Library Type | --------------------1 9 7 8-------------------- | | | | --------------------1 9 8 8-------------------- | | | | Percentage Change 1978–88 |
|---|---|---|---|---|---|---|---|---|---|
| | Number of Libraries | No Response | Total Libraries | Mean Items | Number of Libraries | No Response | Total Libraries | Mean Items | |
| Popular | 506 | 181 | 687 | 6,974 | 618 | 25 | 643 | 7,745 | 11 |
| Congregational | 465 | 169 | 634 | 5,089 | 569 | 24 | 593 | 6,770 | 33 |
| Parochial | 21 | 6 | 27 | 40,340 | 24 | 1 | 25 | 20,340 | −50 |
| Public | 20 | 6 | 26 | 15,770 | 25 | 0 | 25 | 17,850 | 13 |

TABLE 4.127

1978 *American Library Directory* Popular Libraries with Media
Holdings by Library Type

| Type of Library | Libraries with Media Holdings | % | Libraries with No Media Holdings | % | Number of Libraries |
|---|---|---|---|---|---|
| Popular | 172 | 25 | 515 | 75 | 687 |
| Congregational | 160 | 25 | 474 | 75 | 634 |
| Parochial | 4 | 15 | 23 | 85 | 27 |
| Public | 8 | 31 | 18 | 69 | 26 |

TABLE 4.128

1988 *American Library Directory* Popular Libraries Media Holdings by Library Type

| Library Type | Libraries with Media Holdings | % | No Media Holdings or No Response | % | Number of Libraries |
|---|---|---|---|---|---|
| Popular | 224 | 35 | 418 | 65 | 642 |
| Congregational | 205 | 35 | 388 | 65 | 593 |
| Parochial | 9 | 38 | 15 | 63 | 24 |
| Public | 10 | 40 | 15 | 60 | 25 |

TABLE 4.129

1978 *American Library Directory* Popular Libraries with Media Holdings by Region

| Region | Libraries with Media Holdings | % | No Media Holdings or No Response | % | Number of Libraries |
|---|---|---|---|---|---|
| Northeast | 10 | 26 | 28 | 74 | 38 |
| Middle Atlantic | 35 | 21 | 133 | 79 | 168 |
| Southeast | 22 | 24 | 69 | 76 | 91 |
| Southwest | 20 | 26 | 57 | 74 | 77 |
| West | 13 | 21 | 50 | 79 | 63 |
| Rocky Mountains | 4 | 40 | 6 | 60 | 10 |
| Middle West | 65 | 31 | 148 | 69 | 213 |
| Canada | 3 | 11 | 24 | 89 | 27 |
| Total | 172 | 25 | 515 | 75 | 687 |

TABLE 4.130

1988 *American Library Directory* Popular Libraries with Media Holdings by Region

| Region | Libraries with Media Holdings | % | No Media Holdings or No Response | % | Number of Libraries |
|---|---|---|---|---|---|
| Northeast | 11 | 31 | 24 | 69 | 35 |
| Middle Atlantic | 50 | 32 | 106 | 68 | 156 |
| Southeast | 30 | 32 | 63 | 68 | 93 |
| Southwest | 34 | 41 | 48 | 59 | 82 |
| West | 17 | 34 | 33 | 66 | 50 |
| Rocky Mountains | 3 | 38 | 5 | 63 | 8 |
| Middle West | 74 | 38 | 123 | 62 | 197 |
| Canada | 5 | 24 | 16 | 76 | 21 |
| Total | 224 | 35 | 418 | 65 | 642 |

TABLE 4.131
1978 *American Library Directory* Popular Library Total Media
Holdings (Cumulative) by Region[a]

| Region | 1 | % | 2 | % | 3 | % | 4 & over | % | No Response | % | Number of Libraries | Mean Categories |
|---|---|---|---|---|---|---|---|---|---|---|---|---|
| | | | | Media, Maps and Art Reproductions | | | | | | | | |
| Northeast | 6 | 16 | 4 | 11 | 0 | 0 | 0 | 0 | 28 | 74 | 38 | 1.4 |
| Middle Atlantic | | | | | | | | | | | | |
| | 14 | 8 | 12 | 7 | 10 | 6 | 0 | 0 | 132 | 79 | 168 | 1.9 |
| Southeast | 8 | 9 | 8 | 9 | 6 | 7 | 0 | 0 | 69 | 76 | 91 | 1.9 |
| Southwest | 4 | 5 | 8 | 10 | 8 | 10 | 0 | 0 | 57 | 74 | 77 | 2.2 |
| West | 6 | 10 | 6 | 10 | 1 | 2 | 0 | 0 | 50 | 79 | 63 | 1.7 |
| Rocky Mountains | | | | | | | | | | | | |
| | 1 | 10 | 2 | 20 | 1 | 10 | 0 | 0 | 6 | 60 | 10 | 2.0 |
| Middle West | | | | | | | | | | | | |
| | 16 | 8 | 29 | 14 | 20 | 9 | 0 | 0 | 148 | 69 | 213 | 2.1 |
| Canada | 1 | 4 | 0 | 0 | 2 | 7 | 0 | 0 | 24 | 89 | 27 | 2.3 |
| Total | 56 | 8 | 69 | 10 | 48 | 7 | 0 | 0 | 514 | 75 | 687 | 2.0 |

[a] Cumulative media holdings represents the sum of dichotomous variables art
reproductions, map holdings and media holdings.

TABLE 4.132
1988 *American Library Directory* Popular Library Total Media
Holdings (Cumulative) by Region

| Region | 1 | % | 2 | % | 3 | % | 4 & over | % | No Response | % | Number of Libraries | Mean Categories |
|---|---|---|---|---|---|---|---|---|---|---|---|---|
| | | | | Media, Maps and Art Reproductions | | | | | | | | |
| Northeast | 8 | 23 | 2 | 6 | 1 | 3 | 0 | 0 | 24 | 69 | 35 | 1.4 |
| Middle Atlantic | | | | | | | | | | | | |
| | 31 | 20 | 13 | 8 | 6 | 4 | 0 | 0 | 106 | 68 | 156 | 1.5 |
| Southeast | 16 | 17 | 9 | 10 | 5 | 5 | 0 | 0 | 63 | 68 | 93 | 1.7 |
| Southwest | 15 | 18 | 12 | 15 | 7 | 9 | 0 | 0 | 48 | 59 | 82 | 1.8 |
| West | 8 | 16 | 9 | 18 | 0 | 0 | 0 | 0 | 33 | 66 | 50 | 1.6 |
| Rocky Mountains | | | | | | | | | | | | |
| | 1 | 13 | 2 | 25 | 0 | 0 | 0 | 0 | 5 | 63 | 8 | 1.7 |
| Middle West | | | | | | | | | | | | |
| | 34 | 17 | 24 | 12 | 16 | 8 | 0 | 0 | 123 | 62 | 197 | 1.8 |
| Canada | 2 | 9 | 1 | 5 | 2 | 9 | 0 | 0 | 17 | 77 | 22 | 2.0 |
| Total | 115 | 18 | 72 | 11 | 37 | 6 | 0 | 0 | 419 | 65 | 643 | 1.7 |

TABLE 4.133

1978 *American Library Directory* Popular Library Media Holdings by Denomination

| Denomination | Libraries with Media Holdings | % | No Media Holdings or No Response | % | Number of Libraries |
|---|---|---|---|---|---|
| Baptist | 25 | 30 | 58 | 70 | 83 |
| Christian | 5 | 26 | 14 | 74 | 19 |
| Churches of Christ | 0 | 0 | 0 | 0 | 0 |
| Congregational/ | 2 | 7 | 26 | 93 | 28 |
| Episcopal/Anglican | 5 | 12 | 37 | 88 | 42 |
| Independent | 0 | 0 | 5 | 100 | 5 |
| Lutheran | 18 | 34 | 35 | 66 | 53 |
| Methodist | 13 | 24 | 42 | 76 | 55 |
| Other Denominations | 18 | 27 | 49 | 73 | 67 |
| Presbyterian | 26 | 23 | 89 | 77 | 115 |
| U.C.C. | 5 | 38 | 8 | 62 | 13 |
| Summary | | | | | |
| Jewish | 48 | 29 | 115 | 71 | 163 |
| Roman Catholic | 7 | 16 | 37 | 84 | 44 |
| All Protestant | 117 | 24 | 363 | 76 | 480 |
| Total | 172 | 25 | 515 | 75 | 687 |

TABLE 4.134

1988 *American Library Directory* Popular Library Media Holdings by Denomination

| Denomination | Libraries with Media Holdings | % | No Media Holdings or No Response | % | Number of Libraries |
|---|---|---|---|---|---|
| Baptist | 35 | 49 | 36 | 51 | 71 |
| Christian | 6 | 35 | 11 | 65 | 17 |
| Churches of Christ | 1 | 50 | 1 | 50 | 2 |
| Episcopal/Anglican | 8 | 24 | 26 | 76 | 34 |
| Independent | 1 | 33 | 2 | 67 | 3 |
| Lutheran | 23 | 55 | 19 | 45 | 42 |
| Mennonite | 0 | 0 | 4 | 100 | 4 |
| Methodist | 22 | 34 | 42 | 66 | 64 |
| Other Denominations | 17 | 22 | 60 | 78 | 77 |
| Presbyterian | 27 | 28 | 70 | 72 | 97 |
| U.C.C. | 5 | 38 | 8 | 62 | 13 |
| Summary | | | | | |
| Jewish | 70 | 37 | 117 | 63 | 187 |
| Roman Catholic | 9 | 29 | 22 | 71 | 31 |
| All Protestant | 145 | 34 | 279 | 66 | 424 |
| Total | 224 | 35 | 418 | 65 | 642 |

TABLE 4.135

1978 *American Library Directory* Popular Library Media Holdings by Total Annual Expenditure

| Library Expenditures | Libraries with Media Holdings | % | No Media Holdings or No Response | % | Number of Libraries |
|---|---|---|---|---|---|
| Under $1,500 | 74 | 67 | 36 | 33 | 110 |
| $1,501–$20,000 | 34 | 85 | 6 | 15 | 40 |
| $20,001–$95,000 | 2 | 50 | 2 | 50 | 4 |
| $95,001 and over | 0 | 0 | 1 | 100 | 1 |
| No Response | 62 | 12 | 470 | 88 | 532 |
| Total | 172 | 25 | 515 | 75 | 687 |

TABLE 4.136
1988 *American Library Directory* Popular Library Media Holdings by
Total Annual Expenditure

| Library Expenditures | Libraries with Media Holdings | % | No Media Holdings or No Response | % | Number of Libraries |
|---|---|---|---|---|---|
| Under $1,500 | 62 | 45 | 77 | 55 | 139 |
| $1,501–$20,000 | 49 | 58 | 35 | 42 | 84 |
| $20,001–$95,000 | 12 | 52 | 11 | 48 | 23 |
| $95,001–$220,000 | 3 | 60 | 2 | 40 | 5 |
| $220,001 and over | 0 | 0 | 1 | 100 | 1 |
| No Response | 98 | 25 | 292 | 75 | 390 |
| Total | 224 | 35 | 418 | 65 | 642 |

TABLE 4.137
1978 *American Library Directory* Popular Libraries with Map
Holdings by Type

| Type of Library | Libraries with Map Holdings | % | No Response | % | Number of Libraries |
|---|---|---|---|---|---|
| Popular | 110 | 16 | 577 | 84 | 687 |
| Congregational | 103 | 16 | 531 | 84 | 634 |
| Parochial | 4 | 15 | 23 | 85 | 27 |
| Public | 3 | 12 | 23 | 88 | 26 |

TABLE 4.138
1988 *American Library Directory* Popular Libraries with Map
Holdings by Type

| Type of Library | Libraries with Map Holdings | % | No Response | % | Number of Libraries |
|---|---|---|---|---|---|
| Popular | 100 | 16 | 542 | 84 | 642 |
| Congregational | 92 | 16 | 501 | 84 | 593 |
| Parochial | 5 | 21 | 19 | 79 | 24 |
| Public | 3 | 12 | 22 | 88 | 25 |

TABLE 4.139
1978 *American Library Directory* Popular Libraries with Art
Reproductions by Type

| Type of Library | Libraries with Art Reproductions | % | No Response | % | Number of Libraries |
|---|---|---|---|---|---|
| Popular | 56 | 8 | 631 | 92 | 687 |
| Congregational | 53 | 8 | 581 | 92 | 634 |
| Parochial | 2 | 7 | 25 | 93 | 27 |
| Public | 1 | 4 | 25 | 96 | 26 |

TABLE 4.140
1988 *American Library Directory* Popular Libraries with Art
Reproductions by Type

| Type of Library | Libraries with Art Reproductions | % | No Response | % | Number of Libraries |
|---|---|---|---|---|---|
| Popular | 46 | 7 | 596 | 93 | 642 |
| Congregational | 44 | 7 | 549 | 93 | 593 |
| Parochial | 0 | 0 | 24 | 100 | 24 |
| Public | 2 | 8 | 23 | 92 | 25 |

TABLE 4.141
1988 *American Library Directory* Popular Libraries with Any Kind of
Media Holdings—Media, Maps, and Art Reproductions—by Type

| Type of Library | Libraries with Any Kind of Media Holdings | % | No Response | % | Number of Libraries |
|---|---|---|---|---|---|
| Popular | 224 | 35 | 418 | 65 | 642 |
| Congregational | 205 | 35 | 388 | 65 | 593 |
| Parochial | 9 | 38 | 15 | 63 | 24 |
| Public | 10 | 40 | 15 | 60 | 25 |

TABLE 4.142
1978 and 1988 *American Library Directory* Longitudinal Study Popular Congregational (Type) Library All Media Holdings—Media, Maps, and Art Reproductions—by Denomination

| Denomination | 1978 | | | | 1988 | | | | Percentage Change 1978–88 |
|---|---|---|---|---|---|---|---|---|---|
| | Number of Libraries | No Response | Total Libraries | Mean Categories | Number of Libraries | No Response | Total Libraries | Mean Categories | |
| Baptist | 25 | 58 | 83 | 2.0 | 35 | 36 | 71 | 1.7 | –15 |
| Christian | 4 | 14 | 18 | 2.3 | 6 | 11 | 17 | 1.9 | –17 |
| Churches of Christ | 0 | 0 | 0 | 0.0 | 1 | 1 | 2 | 1.0 | N/A |
| Episcopal/Anglican | 5 | 36 | 41 | 1.4 | 7 | 26 | 33 | 1.1 | –21 |
| Independent | 0 | 3 | 3 | 0.0 | 0 | 1 | 1 | 0.0 | 0 |
| Lutheran | 18 | 35 | 53 | 2.2 | 23 | 19 | 42 | 1.8 | –18 |
| Mennonite | 0 | 3 | 3 | 0.0 | 0 | 4 | 4 | 0.0 | N/A |
| Methodist | 13 | 42 | 55 | 2.2 | 22 | 42 | 64 | 1.8 | –18 |
| Other Denominations | 16 | 70 | 86 | 1.7 | 14 | 57 | 71 | 1.6 | –5.9 |
| Presbyterian | 26 | 89 | 115 | 2.0 | 27 | 70 | 97 | 1.7 | –15 |
| U.C.C. | 5 | 8 | 13 | 2.2 | 5 | 8 | 13 | 2.2 | 0 |
| Summary | | | | | | | | | |
| Jewish | 46 | 104 | 150 | 1.9 | 62 | 108 | 170 | 1.7 | –11 |
| Roman Catholic | 3 | 11 | 14 | 1.7 | 3 | 5 | 8 | 2.0 | 18 |
| All Protestant | 112 | 358 | 470 | 2.0 | 140 | 275 | 415 | 1.7 | –15 |
| Total | 161 | 473 | 634 | 2.0 | 205 | 388 | 593 | 1.7 | –15 |

TABLE 4.143
1978 and 1988 *American Library Directory* Longitudinal Study Total
Media Holdings (Cumulative) by Library Type[a]

| Library Type | Number of Libraries | No Response | Total Libraries | Mean Categories | Number of Libraries | No Response | Total Libraries | Mean Categories | Percentage Change 1978–88 |
|---|---|---|---|---|---|---|---|---|---|
| | ----1 9 7 8---- | | | | ----1 9 8 8---- | | | | |
| Popular | 173 | 514 | 687 | 2.0 | 224 | 419 | 643 | 1.7 | −15 |
| Congregational | 161 | 473 | 634 | 2.0 | 205 | 388 | 593 | 1.7 | −15 |
| Parochial | 4 | 23 | 27 | 2.5 | 9 | 16 | 25 | 1.6 | −36 |
| Public | 8 | 18 | 26 | 1.5 | 10 | 15 | 25 | 1.5 | 0 |

[a] Cumulative media holdings includes media, maps, and art reproductions.

TABLE 4.144
1978 and 1988 *American Library Directory* Longitudinal Study Popular Library Total Media Holdings (Cumulative) by Denomination

| | 1978 | | | | 1988 | | | | Percentage Change 1978–88 |
|---|---|---|---|---|---|---|---|---|---|
| Denomination | Number of Libraries | No Response | Total Libraries | Mean Categories | Number of Libraries | No Response | Total Libraries | Mean Categories | |
| Baptist | 25 | 58 | 83 | 2.0 | 35 | 36 | 71 | 1.7 | −15 |
| Christian | 5 | 14 | 19 | 2.2 | 6 | 11 | 17 | 1.9 | −14 |
| Churches of Christ | 0 | 0 | 0 | 0.0 | 1 | 1 | 2 | 1.0 | N/A |
| Episcopal/Anglican | 5 | 37 | 42 | 1.4 | 8 | 26 | 34 | 1.1 | −21 |
| Independent | 0 | 5 | 5 | 0.0 | 1 | 2 | 3 | 2.0 | N/A |
| Lutheran | 18 | 35 | 53 | 2.2 | 23 | 19 | 42 | 1.8 | −18 |
| Mennonite | 0 | 3 | 3 | 0.0 | 0 | 4 | 4 | 0.0 | N/A |
| Methodist | 13 | 42 | 55 | 2.2 | 22 | 42 | 64 | 1.8 | −18 |
| Other Denoms. | 20 | 72 | 92 | 1.6 | 17 | 60 | 77 | 1.5 | −6.2 |
| Presbyterian | 26 | 89 | 115 | 2.0 | 27 | 70 | 97 | 1.7 | −15 |
| U.C.C. | 5 | 8 | 13 | 2.2 | 5 | 8 | 13 | 2.2 | 0 |
| Summary | | | | | | | | | |
| Jewish | 49 | 114 | 163 | 2.0 | 70 | 117 | 187 | 1.7 | −15 |
| Roman Catholic | 7 | 37 | 44 | 1.8 | 9 | 23 | 32 | 1.7 | −5.6 |
| All Protestant | 117 | 363 | 480 | 2.0 | 145 | 279 | 424 | 1.7 | −15 |
| Total | 173 | 514 | 687 | 2.0 | 224 | 419 | 643 | 1.7 | −15 |

TABLE 4.145
1978 and 1988 *American Library Directory* Longitudinal Study
Popular Total Library Media Holdings (Cumulative) for Canada and
the United States[a]

| | ------------------1 9 7 8------------------ | | | | ------------------1 9 8 8------------------ | | | | Percentage |
| Region | Number of Libraries | No Response | Total Libraries | Mean Categories | Number of Libraries | No Response | Total Libraries | Mean Categories | Change 1978–88 |
|---|---|---|---|---|---|---|---|---|---|
| Canada | 3 | 24 | 27 | 2.3 | 5 | 17 | 22 | 2.0 | −13 |
| U.S.A. | 170 | 490 | 660 | 2.0 | 219 | 402 | 621 | 1.7 | −15 |
| Total | 173 | 514 | 687 | 2.0 | 224 | 419 | 643 | 1.7 | −15 |

[a] "Mean categories" in this case refers to the sum of dichotomous (Boolean) variables art reproductions, map holdings, and media holdings.

TABLE 4.146
1978 *American Library Directory* Gross Popular Library Rating Points
over Twenty-three Growth Variables by Region for Matched Pairs

| | ----------------Gross Library Rating Points---------------- | | | | | | | | No Response | % | Number of Libraries | Mean Points |
| Region | 1– 1,000 | % | 1,001– 10,000 | % | 10,001– 50,000 | % | 50,001 & over | % | | | | |
|---|---|---|---|---|---|---|---|---|---|---|---|---|
| Northeast | 2 | 8 | 20 | 77 | 2 | 8 | 0 | 0 | 2 | 8 | 26 | 4,971 |
| Middle Atlantic | 11 | 10 | 78 | 72 | 11 | 10 | 1 | 1 | 8 | 7 | 109 | 6,020 |
| Southeast | 5 | 7 | 55 | 81 | 3 | 4 | 0 | 0 | 5 | 7 | 68 | 5,250 |
| Southwest | 2 | 3 | 36 | 62 | 15 | 26 | 0 | 0 | 5 | 9 | 58 | 7,953 |
| West | 7 | 18 | 24 | 60 | 4 | 10 | 1 | 3 | 4 | 10 | 40 | 6,739 |
| Rocky Mountains | 1 | 13 | 4 | 50 | 0 | 0 | 1 | 13 | 2 | 25 | 8 | 62,560 |
| Middle West | 17 | 12 | 107 | 73 | 12 | 8 | 1 | 1 | 9 | 6 | 146 | 5,597 |
| Canada | 2 | 13 | 6 | 38 | 3 | 19 | 4 | 25 | 1 | 6 | 16 | 49,250 |
| Total | 47 | 10 | 330 | 70 | 50 | 11 | 8 | 2 | 36 | 8 | 471 | 8,283 |

TABLE 4.147

1988 *American Library Directory* Gross Popular Library Rating Points over Twenty-three Growth Variables by Region for Matched Pairs

| Region | 1–1,000 | % | 1,001–10,000 | % | 10,001–50,000 | % | 50,001 & over | % | No Response | % | Number of Libraries | Mean Points |
|---|---|---|---|---|---|---|---|---|---|---|---|---|
| Northeast | 2 | 8 | 19 | 73 | 3 | 12 | 0 | 0 | 2 | 8 | 26 | 6,096 |
| Middle Atlantic | 9 | 8 | 76 | 70 | 16 | 15 | 1 | 1 | 7 | 6 | 109 | 8,258 |
| Southeast | 4 | 6 | 50 | 74 | 8 | 12 | 1 | 1 | 5 | 7 | 68 | 10,820 |
| Southwest | 2 | 3 | 33 | 57 | 18 | 31 | 0 | 0 | 5 | 9 | 58 | 10,410 |
| West | 6 | 15 | 26 | 65 | 4 | 10 | 0 | 0 | 4 | 10 | 40 | 5,031 |
| Rocky Mountains | 1 | 13 | 4 | 50 | 0 | 0 | 1 | 13 | 2 | 25 | 8 | 75,000 |
| Middle West | 13 | 9 | 104 | 71 | 18 | 12 | 2 | 1 | 9 | 6 | 146 | 7,226 |
| Canada | 2 | 14 | 2 | 14 | 7 | 50 | 2 | 14 | 1 | 7 | 14 | 79,490 |
| Total | 39 | 8 | 314 | 67 | 74 | 16 | 7 | 1 | 35 | 7 | 469 | 11,240 |

TABLE 4.148

1978 and 1988 *American Library Directory* Longitudinal Study Gross Popular Library Rating Points over Twenty-three Growth Variables by Denomination for Matched Pairs[a]

| Denomination | 1978 | | | | 1988 | | | | Percentage Change 1978–88 |
|---|---|---|---|---|---|---|---|---|---|
| | Number of Libraries | No Response | Total Libraries | Mean Points | Number of Libraries | No Response | Total Libraries | Mean Points | |
| Baptist | 60 | 1 | 61 | 6,242 | 60 | 1 | 61 | 7,896 | 26 |
| Christian | 13 | 0 | 13 | 7,364 | 13 | 0 | 13 | 8,037 | 9 |
| Churches of Christ | 0 | 0 | 0 | 0 | 0 | 0 | 0 | 0 | N/A |
| Episcopal/Anglican | 24 | 3 | 27 | 4,134 | 24 | 3 | 27 | 5,842 | 41 |
| Independent | 1 | 0 | 1 | 2,250 | 2 | 0 | 2 | 4,525 | 101 |
| Lutheran | 34 | 1 | 35 | 4,419 | 34 | 1 | 35 | 5,602 | 27 |
| Mennonite | 2 | 1 | 3 | 4,500 | 2 | 1 | 3 | 4,500 | 0 |
| Methodist | 34 | 5 | 39 | 3,555 | 34 | 5 | 39 | 6,084 | 71 |
| Other Denominations | 46 | 7 | 53 | 14,470 | 46 | 7 | 53 | 18,060 | 25 |
| Presbyterian | 80 | 6 | 86 | 3,428 | 80 | 6 | 86 | 4,610 | 34 |
| U.C.C. | 9 | 1 | 10 | 2,443 | 9 | 1 | 10 | 2,943 | 20 |
| Summary | | | | | | | | | |
| Jewish | 110 | 10 | 120 | 12,240 | 110 | 9 | 119 | 19,950 | 63 |
| Roman Catholic | 22 | 1 | 23 | 20,120 | 20 | 1 | 21 | 16,120 | −20 |
| All Protestant | 303 | 25 | 328 | 5,986 | 304 | 25 | 329 | 7,762 | 30 |
| Total | 435 | 36 | 471 | 8,283 | 434 | 35 | 469 | 11,240 | 36 |

[a] Note on this table the single declining growth rate registered by Roman Catholic libraries. The 20 percent fall appears to be substantial and may in fact be so. However, it is necessary to notice that the number of active Roman Catholic libraries in the sample for 1988 was only twenty and that the years 1978 to 1988 was a period of controlled expenditure for many religious institutions in Canada (which is where most of these Roman Catholic parochial school libraries were found). See table 4.184.

TABLE 4.149

1978 and 1988 *American Library Directory* Longitudinal Study Annual Popular Expenditures on Material by Library Type

| Library Type | Number of Libraries | No Response | Total Libraries | Mean 1978 | Number of Libraries | No Response | Total Libraries | Mean 1988 | Percentage Change 1978–88 |
|---|---|---|---|---|---|---|---|---|---|
| | -----1978----- | | | | -----1988----- | | | | |
| Popular | 110 | 577 | 687 | 1,812 | 230 | 412 | 642 | 4,085 | 125 |
| Congregational | 100 | 534 | 634 | 1,128 | 211 | 382 | 593 | 2,691 | 139 |
| Parochial | 3 | 24 | 27 | 9,083 | 13 | 11 | 24 | 17,385 | 91 |
| Public | 7 | 19 | 26 | 8,464 | 6 | 19 | 25 | 24,292 | 187 |

TABLE 4.150

1988 *American Library Directory* Annual Popular Material Expenditure by Library Type

| Library Type | 1–18,000 | % | 18,001–67,000 | % | 67,001–122,000 | % | No Response | % | Number of Libraries | Mean Dollars |
|---|---|---|---|---|---|---|---|---|---|---|
| | ----Material Expenditure---- | | | | | | | | | |
| Popular | 219 | 34 | 9 | 1 | 2 | 0 | 412 | 64 | 642 | 4,085 |
| Congregational | 206 | 35 | 5 | 1 | 0 | 0 | 382 | 64 | 593 | 2,691 |
| Parochial | 9 | 38 | 3 | 13 | 1 | 4 | 11 | 46 | 24 | 17,385 |
| Public | 4 | 16 | 1 | 4 | 1 | 4 | 19 | 76 | 25 | 24,292 |

TABLE 4.151

1988 *American Library Directory* Congregational (Type) Libraries
with the Highest Annual Expenditure on Material

| Library | Denomination | Expenditure on Material |
|---|---|---|
| Church of Jesus Christ of Latter-day Saints, Las Vegas, NV | Other Denominations | $37,500 |
| Stephen S. Wise Temple, Los Angeles, CA | Jewish | 23,000 |
| Church of Jesus Christ of Latter-day Saints, San Diego, CA | Other Denominations | 23,000 |
| Christ Church, Louisville, KY | Methodist | 23,000 |
| First Baptist Church, Dallas, TX | Baptist | 23,000 |
| First Baptist Church, Greensboro, NC | Baptist | 14,000 |
| St. Faith Episcopal Church, Havertown, PA | Episcopal/Anglican | 14,000 |
| First Presbyterian Church, El Paso, TX | Presbyterian | 14,000 |
| Congregation Beth Yeshurun, Houston, TX | Jewish | 14,000 |
| Church of Jesus Christ of Latter-day Saints, Mesa, AZ | Other Denominations | 8,000 |
| Sinai Temple, Los Angeles, CA | Jewish | 8,000 |
| Jewish Community Center, San Diego, CA | Jewish | 8,000 |
| Congregation Solel, Highland Park, IL | Jewish | 8,000 |
| Christian Church, Indianapolis, IN | Christian | 8,000 |
| Congregation Beth Achim, Southfield, MI | Jewish | 8,000 |
| Beth Israel Synagogue, Vineland, NJ | Jewish | 8,000 |
| First Baptist Church, Murfreesboro, TN | Baptist | 8,000 |
| All Saints Catholic Church, Dallas, TX | Roman Catholic | 8,000 |
| Temple Emanuel, Dallas, TX | Jewish | 8,000 |
| First Baptist Church, Longview, TX | Baptist | 8,000 |
| Episcopal Diocese of West Texas, San Antonio, TX | Episcopal/Anglican | 8,000 |

TABLE 4.152

1988 *American Library Directory* Parochial School Libraries with the Highest Annual Expenditure on Material

| Library | Denomination | Expenditure on Material |
|---|---|---|
| Hamilton-Wentworth Catholic School, Hamilton, ON | Roman Catholic | $77,500 |
| Central Agency for Jewish Education, Miami, FL | Jewish | 57,000 |
| Petit Seminaire de Québec, Québec, PQ | Roman Catholic | 37,500 |
| Akiba Hebrew Academy, Merion, PA | Jewish | 23,000 |
| College of Mount St. Vincent, Buffalo, NY | Roman Catholic | 8,000 |
| Jewish Education Association, Louisville, KY | Jewish | 4,000 |
| Diocese of St. Cloud, St. Cloud, MN | Roman Catholic | 4,000 |
| Edmonton Catholic Schools, Edmonton, AB | Roman Catholic | 4,000 |
| Protestant School Board, Montreal, PQ | Independent | 4,000 |
| Westminster Presbyterian Church, Oklahoma City, OK | Presbyterian | 1,500 |
| Commission des Écoles Catholiques, Québec, PQ | Roman Catholic | 1,500 |
| Niles Township Jewish Congregation, Skokie, IL | Jewish | 750 |
| Congregation Beth-El Zedek, Indianapolis, IN | Jewish | 750 |
| Chevy Chase Baptist Church, Washington, DC | Baptist | 250 |

TABLE 4.153

1988 *American Library Directory* Public Libraries with the Highest Annual Expenditure on Material

| Library | Denomination | Expenditure on Material |
|---|---|---|
| Jewish Public Library, Montreal, PQ | Jewish | $99,000 |
| Young Men's and Women's Hebrew Association, New York, NY | Jewish | 23,000 |
| Oratoire St. Joseph, Montréal, PQ | Roman Catholic | 14,000 |
| Friends Free Library of Germantown, Philadelphia, PA | Other Denominations | 8,000 |
| St. Matthew's and St. Timothy's Neighborhood Center, New York, NY | Roman Catholic | 1,500 |
| Cecil Harding Jones, Jenkintown, PA | Other Denominations | 250 |

TABLE 4.154
1978 and 1988 *American Library Directory* Longitudinal Study Popular Annual Library Material Expenditures by Volume Holdings

| Number of Volumes | 1978 | | | | 1988 | | | | Percentage Change 1978–88 |
|---|---|---|---|---|---|---|---|---|---|
| | Number of Libraries | No Response | Total Libraries | Mean Dollars | Number of Libraries | No Response | Total Libraries | Mean Dollars | |
| Under 3,500 | 58 | 248 | 306 | 664 | 80 | 227 | 307 | 1,063 | 60 |
| 3,501–20,000 | 44 | 136 | 180 | 1,767 | 136 | 154 | 290 | 4,042 | 129 |
| 20,001–100,000 | 4 | 13 | 17 | 12,750 | 8 | 10 | 18 | 20,750 | 63 |
| 100,001 and over | 1 | 1 | 2 | 23,000 | 2 | 1 | 3 | 68,250 | 197 |
| No Response | 3 | 179 | 182 | 3,000 | 4 | 21 | 25 | 563 | –81 |
| Total | 110 | 577 | 687 | 1,811 | 230 | 413 | 643 | 4,085 | 126 |

TABLE 4.155

1988 *American Library Directory* Popular Baptist Libraries with the Highest Annual Expenditure on Material

| Library | Expenditure on Material |
| --- | --- |
| First Baptist Church, Dallas, TX | $23,000 |
| First Baptist Church, Greensboro, NC | 14,000 |
| First Baptist Church, Murfreesboro, TN | 8,000 |
| First Baptist Church, Longview, TX | 8,000 |
| First Baptist Church, Van Nuys, CA | 4,000 |
| North Central Baptist Media, Gainesville, FL | 4,000 |
| First Baptist Church, Ashland, KY | 4,000 |
| Hoffmantown Baptist Church, Albuquerque, NM | 4,000 |
| First Baptist Church, Abilene, TX | 4,000 |
| First Baptist Church, San Antonio, TX | 4,000 |
| First Baptist Church, Waco, TX | 4,000 |

TABLE 4.156

1988 *American Library Directory* Popular Christian Libraries with the Highest Annual Expenditure on Material

| Library | Expenditure on Material |
| --- | --- |
| Christian Church, Indianapolis, IN | $8,000 |
| High Street Christian Church, Akron, OH | 4,000 |
| First Christian Church, Alexandria, VA | 4,000 |
| Englewood Christian Church, Indianapolis, IN | 750 |
| First Christian Church, Knoxville, TN | 750 |
| Douglass Boulevard Christian Church, Louisville, KY | 250 |
| East Dallas Christian Church, Dallas, TX | 250 |
| University Christian Church, Seattle, WA | 250 |

TABLE 4.157

1988 *American Library Directory* Popular Episcopal/Anglican Libraries with the Highest Annual Expenditure on Material

| Library | Expenditure on Material |
| --- | --- |
| St. Faith Episcopal Church, Havertown, PA | $14,000 |
| Episcopal Diocese of West Texas, San Antonio, TX | 8,000 |
| St. Thomas Episcopal Church, Sunnyvale, CA | 1,500 |
| Trinity Episcopal Church, Newtown, CT | 1,500 |
| Church of the Holy Faith, Santa Fe, NM | 1,500 |
| Trinity Church, New York, NY | 1,500 |
| St. Mark's Episcopal Church, San Antonio, TX | 1,500 |
| Calvary Episcopal Church, Columbia, MO | 750 |

TABLE 4.158

1988 *American Library Directory* Popular Lutheran Libraries with the Highest Annual Expenditure on Material

| Library | Expenditure on Material |
| --- | --- |
| Ascension Lutheran Church, Milwaukee, WI | $1,500 |
| Our Savior's Lutheran Church, Milwaukee, WI | 1,500 |
| Bethlehem Lutheran Church, St. Charles, IL | 750 |
| First Lutheran Church, Cedar Rapids, IA | 750 |
| First Lutheran Church, Red Wing, MN | 750 |
| Oak Grove Lutheran Church, Richfield, MN | 750 |
| St. Martin's Evangelical Lutheran Church, Austin, TX | 750 |
| Trinity Lutheran Church, Madison, WI | 750 |

TABLE 4.159

1988 *American Library Directory* Popular Mennonite Libraries with the Highest Annual Expenditure on Material

| Library | Expenditure on Material |
| --- | --- |
| Bethesda Mennonite Church, Henderson, NE | $750 |
| First Mennonite Church, Reedley, CA | 250 |
| Freeport Mennonite Church, Freeport, IL | 250 |

TABLE 4.160

1988 *American Library Directory* Popular Methodist Libraries with the Highest Annual Expenditure on Material

| Library | Expenditure on Material |
| --- | --- |
| Christ Church United Methodist Church, Louisville, KY | $23,000 |
| First United Methodist Church, Tulsa, OK | 4,000 |
| Reveille United Methodist Church, Richmond, VA | 4,000 |
| Pasadena Community United Methodist Church, St. Petersburg, FL | 1,500 |
| Bethesda United Methodist Church, Bethesda, MD | 1,500 |
| First United Methodist Church, Gulfport, MS | 1,500 |
| St. Paul United Methodist Church, Springfield, MO | 1,500 |
| Aldersgate United Methodist Church, Rochester, NY | 1,500 |
| Asbury First United Methodist Church, Rochester, NY | 1,500 |

TABLE 4.161

1988 *American Library Directory* Popular Other Denominations
Libraries with the Highest Annual Expenditure on Material

| Library | Expenditure on Material |
| --- | --- |
| Las Vegas Family History Center, Las Vegas, NV | $37,500 |
| Church of Jesus Christ of Latter-day Saints, San Diego, CA | 23,000 |
| Church of Jesus Christ of Latter-day Saints, Mesa, AZ | 8,000 |
| Friends Free Library of Germantown, Philadelphia, PA | 8,000 |
| Church of Jesus Christ of Latter-day Saints, Boca Raton, FL | 4,000 |
| New Church Union Swedenborgian, Boston, MA | 4,000 |
| Church of Jesus Christ of Latter-day Saints, Tampa, FL | 1,500 |
| United Church of Los Alamos, Los Alamos, NM | 1,500 |

TABLE 4.162

1988 *American Library Directory* Popular Presbyterian Libraries with
the Highest Annual Expenditure on Material

| Library | Expenditure on Material |
| --- | --- |
| First Presbyterian Church, El Paso, TX | $14,000 |
| Trinity United Presbyterian Church, Santa Ana, CA | 4,000 |
| Pasadena Presbyterian Church, St. Petersburg, FL | 4,000 |
| First Presbyterian Church, Norwalk, OH | 4,000 |
| Carmel Presbyterian Church, Glenside, PA | 4,000 |

TABLE 4.163

1988 *American Library Directory* Popular Jewish Libraries with the
Highest Annual Expenditure on Material

| Library | Expenditure on Material |
| --- | --- |
| Jewish Public Library, Montreal, PQ | $99,000 |
| Central Agency for Jewish Education, Miami, FL | 57,000 |
| Stephen Wise Temple, Los Angeles, CA | 23,000 |
| Young Men's and Women's Hebrew Association, New York, NY | 23,000 |
| Akiba Hebrew Academy, Merion, PA | 23,000 |
| Congregation Beth Yeshurun, Houston, TX | 14,000 |

TABLE 4.164

1988 *American Library Directory* Popular Roman Catholic Libraries
with the Highest Annual Expenditure on Material

| Library | Expenditure on Material |
|---|---|
| Hamilton-Wentworth Roman Catholic Library, Hamilton, ON | $77,500 |
| Petit Seminaire de Québec, Québec, PQ | 37,500 |
| Oratoire St. Joseph, Montréal, PQ | 14,000 |
| St. Mary's School for the Deaf, Buffalo, NY | 8,000 |
| All Saints Catholic Church, Dallas, TX | 8,000 |
| Diocese of St. Cloud Bureau of Education, St. Cloud, MN | 4,000 |
| Cardinal Ritter, St. Louis, MO | 4,000 |
| Edmonton Catholic Schools, Edmonton, AB | 4,000 |

TABLE 4.165

1988 *American Library Directory* Congregational (Type) Libraries
with the Highest Expenditure on Personnel

| Library | Denomination | Expenditure in 000s |
|---|---|---|
| Stephen S. Wise Temple, Los Angeles, CA | Jewish | $145.0 |
| All Saints Catholic Church, Dallas, TX | Roman Catholic | 145.0 |
| Sinai Temple, Los Angeles, CA | Jewish | 75.0 |
| Congregation Solel, Highland Park, IL | Jewish | 75.0 |
| Christ Church, Louisville, KY | Methodist | 75.0 |
| Congregation Beth Yeshurun, Houston, TX | Jewish | 57.5 |
| Trinity United Presbyterian Church, Santa Ana, CA | Presbyterian | 27.5 |
| Temple Sinai, Washington, DC | Jewish | 27.5 |
| First Baptist Church, Dallas, TX | Baptist | 27.5 |
| Jewish Community Center, Dallas, TX | Jewish | 27.5 |
| Episcopal Diocese of West Texas, San Antonio, TX | Episcopal/Anglican | 27.5 |
| Church of Jesus Christ of Latter-day Saints, San Diego, CA | Other Denominations | 15.0 |
| Jewish Community Center, San Diego, CA | Jewish | 15.0 |
| Temple Israel, Minneapolis, MN | Jewish | 15.0 |
| Temple Beth Zion, Buffalo, NY | Jewish | 15.0 |
| Shalom Park Speizman Jewish Center, Charlotte, NC | Jewish | 15.0 |
| First Baptist Church, Greensboro, NC | Baptist | 15.0 |
| Westwood First Presbyterian Church, Cincinnati, OH | Presbyterian | 15.0 |
| St. Faith Episcopal Church, Havertown, PA | Episcopal/Anglican | 15.0 |
| Temple Emanuel, Dallas, TX | Jewish | 15.0 |

TABLE 4.166

1988 *American Library Directory* Parochial School Libraries with the Highest Expenditure on Personnel

| Library | Denomination | Expenditure in 000s |
|---|---|---|
| St. Mary's School for the Deaf, Buffalo, NY | Roman Catholic | $75.0 |
| Central Agency for Jewish Education, Miami, FL | Jewish | 57.5 |
| Akiba Hebrew Academy, Merion, PA | Jewish | 42.5 |
| Edmonton Catholic Schools, Edmonton, AB | Roman Catholic | 27.5 |
| Jewish Education Association, Louisville, KY | Jewish | 15.0 |
| Diocese of St. Cloud, St. Cloud, MN | Roman Catholic | 15.0 |
| Hamilton-Wentworth Roman Catholic School, Hamilton, ON | Roman Catholic | 15.0 |
| Niles Township Jewish Congregation, Skokie, IL | Jewish | 2.5 |

TABLE 4.167

1988 *American Library Directory* Public Libraries with the Highest Expenditure on Personnel

| Library | Denomination | Expenditure in 000s |
|---|---|---|
| Jewish Public Library, Montreal, PQ | Jewish | $325.0 |
| Young Men's and Women's Hebrew Association, New York, NY | Jewish | 75.0 |
| Friends Free Library of Germantown, Philadelphia, PA | Other Denominations | 75.0 |
| St. Matthew's and St. Timothy's Neighborhood Center, New York, NY | Roman Catholic | 42.5 |

TABLE 4.168
1978 and 1988 *American Library Directory* Longitudinal Study
Popular Annual Expenditures on Personnel by Library Type

| Library Type | Number of Libraries | No Response | Total Libraries | Mean 1978 | Number of Libraries | No Response | Total Libraries | Mean 1988 | Percentage Change 1978–88 |
|---|---|---|---|---|---|---|---|---|---|
| | -------------------1 9 7 8------------------- | | | | -------------------1 9 8 8------------------- | | | | |
| Popular Congregational | 34 | 653 | 687 | $6,029 | 83 | 559 | 642 | $21,988 | 264.7 |
| | 31 | 603 | 634 | 4,274 | 70 | 523 | 593 | 15,071 | 252.6 |
| Parochial | 2 | 25 | 27 | 15,000 | 9 | 15 | 24 | 28,056 | 87.0 |
| Public | 1 | 25 | 26 | 42,500 | 4 | 21 | 25 | 129,375 | 204.4 |

TABLE 4.169
1988 *American Library Directory* Popular Baptist Libraries with the
Highest Annual Expenditure on Personnel

| Library | Expenditure on Personnel |
|---|---|
| First Baptist Church, Dallas, TX | $27,500 |
| First Baptist Church, Greensboro, NC | 15,000 |
| First Baptist Church, Waco, TX | 7,500 |
| Hoffmantown Baptist Church, Albuquerque, NM | 2,500 |
| First Baptist Church, Murfreesboro, TN | 2,500 |
| First Baptist Church, Longview, TX | 2,500 |

TABLE 4.170
1988 *American Library Directory* Popular Episcopal/Anglican
Libraries with the Highest Annual Expenditure on Personnel

| Library | Expenditure on Personnel |
|---|---|
| Episcopal Diocese of West Texas, San Antonio, TX | $27,500 |
| St. Faith Episcopal Church, Havertown, PA | 15,000 |
| Church of the Holy Faith, Santa Fe, NM | 2,500 |
| St. Mark's Episcopal Church, San Antonio, TX | 2,500 |

TABLE 4.171

1988 *American Library Directory* Popular Methodist Libraries with the Highest Annual Expenditure on Personnel

| Library | Expenditure on Personnel |
| --- | --- |
| Christ Church, Louisville, KY | $75,000 |
| First United Methodist Church, Tulsa, OK | 7,500 |
| Bethesda United Methodist Church, Bethesda, MD | 2,500 |
| University United Methodist Church, Las Cruces, NM | 2,500 |
| Christ Church United Methodist Church, Akron, OH | 2,500 |
| First United Methodist Church, Austin, TX | 2,500 |

TABLE 4.172

1988 *American Library Directory* Popular Other Denominations Libraries with the Highest Annual Expenditure on Personnel

| Library | Expenditure on Personnel |
| --- | --- |
| Friends Free Library of Germantown, Philadelphia, PA | $75,000 |
| Church of Jesus Christ of Latter-day Saints, San Diego, CA | 15,000 |
| Church of Jesus Christ of Latter-day Saints, Mesa, AZ | 2,500 |
| Las Vegas Family History Center, Las Vegas, NV | 2,500 |
| Plymouth Congregational Church, Seattle, WA | 2,500 |
| Friends House, Toronto, ON | 2,500 |

TABLE 4.173

1988 *American Library Directory* Popular Jewish Libraries with the Highest Annual Expenditure on Personnel

| Library | Expenditure on Personnel |
| --- | --- |
| Jewish Public Library, Montreal, PQ | $325,000 |
| Stephen S. Wise Temple, Los Angeles, CA | 145,000 |
| Sinai Temple, Los Angeles, CA | 75,000 |
| Congregation Solel, Highland Park, IL | 75,000 |
| Young Men's and Women's Hebrew Association, New York, NY | 75,000 |
| Central Agency for Jewish Education, Miami, FL | 57,500 |
| Congregation Beth Yeshurun, Houston, TX | 57,500 |
| Akiba Hebrew Academy, Merion, PA | 42,500 |
| Temple Sinai, Washington, DC | 27,500 |
| Jewish Community Center, Dallas, TX | 27,500 |

TABLE 4.174

1988 *American Library Directory* Popular Roman Catholic Libraries with the Highest Annual Expenditure on Personnel

| Library | Expenditure on Personnel |
|---|---|
| All Saints Catholic Church, Dallas, TX | $145,000 |
| St. Mary's School for the Deaf, Buffalo, NY | 75,000 |
| St. Matthew's and St. Timothy's Neighborhood Center, New York, NY | 42,500 |
| Edmonton Catholic Schools, Edmonton, AB | 27,500 |
| Diocese of St. Cloud Bureau of Education, St. Cloud, MN | 15,000 |
| Hamilton-Wentworth Roman Catholic Library, Hamilton, ON | 15,000 |
| Church of the Incarnation, Dallas, TX | 7,500 |
| Cardinal Ritter, St. Louis, MO | 2,500 |

TABLE 4.175

1988 *American Library Directory* Congregational (Type) Libraries with the Highest Annual Other Expenditures

| Library | Denomination | Other Expenditures |
|---|---|---|
| Sinai Temple, Los Angeles, CA | Jewish | $20,000 |
| Temple Emanuel, Dallas, TX | Jewish | 20,000 |
| Park Synagogue, Cleveland, OH | Jewish | 13,000 |
| Highland Park Presbyterian Church, Dallas, TX | Presbyterian | 9,000 |
| Congregation Beth Yeshurun, Houston, TX | Jewish | 9,000 |
| Temple Israel, Minneapolis, MN | Jewish | 7,000 |
| Jewish Community Center, Rochester, NY | Jewish | 7,000 |
| Temple Emanu-el, Tucson, AZ | Jewish | 500 |
| Central Presbyterian Church, Terre Haute, IN | Presbyterian | 500 |
| First Congregational Church, Wellesley Hills, MA | Other Denominations | 500 |

TABLE 4.176

1988 *American Library Directory* Public Libraries with the Highest Annual Other Expenditures

| Library | Denomination | Other Expenditures |
|---|---|---|
| Young Men's and Women's Hebrew Association, New York, NY | Jewish | $20,000 |
| Jewish Public Library, Montreal, PQ | Jewish | 20,000 |

TABLE 4.177
1978 and 1988 *American Library Directory* Longitudinal Study
Popular Total Annual Expenditure by Library Type

| Library Type | Number of Libraries | 1978 No Response | Total Libraries | Mean 1978 | Number of Libraries | 1988 No Response | Total Libraries | Mean 1988 | Percentage Change 1978–88 |
|---|---|---|---|---|---|---|---|---|---|
| Popular Congregational | 155 | 532 | 687 | $4,972 | 252 | 390 | 642 | $12,591 | 153 |
|  | 145 | 489 | 634 | 1,998 | 235 | 358 | 593 | 7,904 | 296 |
| Parochial | 3 | 24 | 27 | 15,500 | 11 | 13 | 24 | 39,023 | 152 |
| Public | 7 | 19 | 26 | 62,071 | 6 | 19 | 25 | 147,708 | 138 |

| | |
|---|---|
| Range (material): | $0–$182,000+ |
| Range (personnel): | $0–$350,000+ |
| Range (other): | $0–22,000+ |
| Range (total P.A. expenditure): | $0–610,000+ |

TABLE 4.178
1978 and 1988 *American Library Directory* Longitudinal Study
Popular Total Annual Expenditure (Cumulative) by Library Type

| Library Type | Number of Libraries | 1978 No Response | Total Libraries | Mean Dollars | Number of Libraries | 1988 No Response | Total Libraries | Mean Dollars | Percentage Change 1978–88 |
|---|---|---|---|---|---|---|---|---|---|
| Popular Congregational | 176 | 511 | 687 | 4,885 | 260 | 383 | 643 | 13,740 | 181 |
|  | 163 | 471 | 634 | 2,202 | 239 | 354 | 593 | 8,963 | 307 |
| Parochial | 3 | 24 | 27 | 19,080 | 14 | 11 | 25 | 36,860 | 93 |
| Public | 10 | 16 | 26 | 44,350 | 7 | 18 | 25 | 130,500 | 194 |

TABLE 4.179
1978 and 1988 *American Library Directory* Longitudinal Study Congregational (Type) Library Total Annual Expenditure (Cumulative) by Denomination[a]

| Denomination | 1978 | | | | 1988 | | | | Percentage Change 1978–88 |
|---|---|---|---|---|---|---|---|---|---|
| | Number of Libraries | No Response | Total Libraries | Mean Dollars | Number of Libraries | No Response | Total Libraries | Mean Dollars | |
| Baptist | 20 | 63 | 83 | 2,213 | 29 | 42 | 71 | 6,629 | 200 |
| Christian | 6 | 12 | 18 | 1,667 | 9 | 8 | 17 | 3,444 | 107 |
| Churches of Christ | 0 | 0 | 0 | 0 | 2 | 0 | 2 | 625 | N/A |
| Episcopal/Anglican | 10 | 31 | 41 | 2,075 | 15 | 18 | 33 | 5,750 | 177 |
| Independent | 0 | 3 | 3 | 0 | 0 | 1 | 1 | 0 | N/A |
| Lutheran | 19 | 34 | 53 | 1,737 | 17 | 25 | 42 | 882 | –49 |
| Mennonite | 0 | 3 | 3 | 0 | 3 | 1 | 4 | 500 | N/A |
| Methodist | 15 | 40 | 55 | 1,583 | 29 | 35 | 64 | 5,198 | 228 |
| Other Denoms. | 18 | 68 | 86 | 2,819 | 21 | 50 | 71 | 5,679 | 101 |
| Presbyterian | 30 | 85 | 115 | 842 | 39 | 58 | 97 | 5,814 | 590 |
| U.C.C. | 5 | 8 | 13 | 250 | 3 | 10 | 13 | 500 | 100 |
| Summary | | | | | | | | | |
| Jewish | 36 | 114 | 150 | 4,014 | 68 | 102 | 170 | 16,840 | 320 |
| Roman Catholic | 4 | 10 | 14 | 1,375 | 4 | 4 | 8 | 42,940 | 3,023 |
| All Protestant | 123 | 347 | 470 | 1,699 | 167 | 248 | 415 | 4,943 | 191 |
| Total | 163 | 471 | 634 | 2,202 | 239 | 354 | 593 | 8,963 | 307 |

a The means for this table differ somewhat (but not significantly) from the means for table 4.177 because the total annual expenditure (cumulative) figure is the sum of material + personnel + other expenditure and *not* the total annual library expenditure figure as declared by each of the libraries. In some cases the discrepancy was quite substantial and could not be explained on the basis of information given in the questionnaires. Occasionally it contained items such as building or other extraordinary expenses not usually included in the term "running expenses." Note that the cumulative mean for 1988 outstrips its counterpart by 13.4 percent.

TABLE 4.180

1988 *American Library Directory* Congregational (Type) Libraries
with the Highest Total Annual Expenditure

| Library | Denomination | Total Expenditures |
|---|---|---|
| Stephen S. Wise Temple, Los Angeles, CA | Jewish | $185,000 |
| All Saints Catholic Church, Dallas, TX | Roman Catholic | 153,000 |
| Sinai Temple, Los Angeles, CA | Jewish | 127,500 |
| Highland Park Presbyterian Church, Dallas, TX | Presbyterian | 127,500 |
| Christ Church United Methodist Church, Louisville, KY | Methodist | 98,000 |
| Congregation Solel, Highland Park, IL | Jewish | 83,000 |
| Congregation Beth Yeshurun, Houston, TX | Jewish | 80,500 |
| First Baptist Church, Dallas, TX | Baptist | 70,000 |
| Temple Emanuel, Dallas, TX | Jewish | 43,000 |
| Las Vegas Family History Center, Las Vegas, NV | Other Denominations | 40,000 |
| Church of Jesus Christ of Latter-day Saints, San Diego, CA | Other Denominations | 38,000 |
| Jewish Community Center, San Diego, CA | Jewish | 32,500 |
| Temple Israel, Minneapolis, MN | Jewish | 32,500 |
| World Jewish Genealogy Organisation, Brooklyn, NY | Jewish | 32,500 |
| First Baptist Church, Greensboro, NC | Baptist | 32,500 |
| Isaac M. Wise Temple, Cincinnati, OH | Jewish | 32,500 |
| Park Synagogue, Cleveland, OH | Jewish | 32,500 |
| Congregation Adath Jeshurun, Elkins Park, PA | Jewish | 32,500 |
| St. Faith Episcopal Church, Havertown, PA | Episcopal/Anglican | 32,500 |
| Episcopal Diocese of West Texas, San Antonio, TX | Episcopal/Anglican | 32,500 |

TABLE 4.181

1988 *American Library Directory* Parochial School Libraries with the Highest Total Annual Expenditure

| Library | Denomination | Total Expenditures |
|---|---|---|
| Central Agency for Jewish Education, Miami, FL | Jewish | $127,500 |
| Hamilton-Wentworth Catholic Schools, Hamilton, ON | Roman Catholic | 92,500 |
| St. Mary's School for the Deaf, Buffalo, NY | Roman Catholic | 83,000 |
| Akiba Hebrew Academy, Merion, PA | Jewish | 70,500 |
| Petit Seminaire de Québec, Québec, PQ | Roman Catholic | 37,500 |
| Diocese of St. Cloud, St. Cloud, MN | Roman Catholic | 32,500 |
| Edmonton Catholic Schools, Edmonton, AB | Roman Catholic | 32,500 |
| Jewish Education Association, Louisville, KY | Jewish | 19,000 |
| Cardinal Ritter, St. Louis, MO | Roman Catholic | 6,500 |
| Niles Township Jewish Congregation, Skokie, IL | Jewish | 4,000 |
| Board of Jewish Education, New York, NY | Jewish | 4,000 |
| Protestant School Board, Montreal, PQ | Independent | 4,000 |

TABLE 4.182

1988 *American Library Directory* Public Libraries with the Highest Total Annual Expenditure

| Library | Denomination | Total Expenditures |
|---|---|---|
| Jewish Public Library, Montreal, PQ | Jewish | $560,000 |
| Young Men's and Women's Hebrew Association, New York, NY | Jewish | 185,000 |
| Friends Free Library of Germantown, Philadelphia, PA | Other Denominations | 83,000 |
| St. Matthew's and St. Timothy's Neighborhood Center, New York, NY | Roman Catholic | 70,000 |
| Oratoire St. Joseph, Montréal, PQ | Roman Catholic | 14,000 |
| Slovak Catholic Cultural Center, Oak Forest, IL | Roman Catholic | 1,000 |

TABLE 4.183

1978 *American Library Directory* Popular Library Total Annual
Expenditure (Cumulative) by Region

| Region | Material, Personnel, and Other Expenditures | | | | | | | | Number of Libraries | Mean Dollars |
|---|---|---|---|---|---|---|---|---|---|---|
| | 1–70,000 | % | 70,001–220,000 | % | 220,001–410,000 | % | No Response | % | | |
| Northeast | 10 | 26 | 0 | 0 | 0 | 0 | 28 | 74 | 38 | $2,825 |
| Middle Atlantic | 38 | 23 | 0 | 0 | 0 | 0 | 130 | 77 | 168 | 4,125 |
| Southeast | 23 | 25 | 0 | 0 | 0 | 0 | 68 | 75 | 91 | 2,728 |
| Southwest | 23 | 30 | 0 | 0 | 0 | 0 | 54 | 70 | 77 | 2,217 |
| West | 13 | 21 | 0 | 0 | 0 | 0 | 50 | 79 | 63 | 5,635 |
| Rocky Mountains | 2 | 20 | 0 | 0 | 0 | 0 | 8 | 80 | 10 | 4,125 |
| Middle West | 62 | 29 | 0 | 0 | 0 | 0 | 151 | 71 | 213 | 1,573 |
| Canada | 4 | 15 | 0 | 0 | 1 | 4 | 22 | 81 | 27 | 76,400 |
| Total | 175 | 25 | 0 | 0 | 1 | 0 | 511 | 74 | 687 | 4,885 |

TABLE 4.184
1988 *American Library Directory* Popular Library Total Annual Expenditure (Cumulative) by Region

| Region | 1–70,000 | % | 70,001–220,000 | % | 220,001–410,000 | % | 410,001 & over | % | No Response | % | Number of Libraries | Mean Dollars | Percent Change 1978–88 |
|---|---|---|---|---|---|---|---|---|---|---|---|---|---|
| Northeast | 8 | 23 | 0 | 0 | 0 | 0 | 0 | 0 | 27 | 77 | 35 | 2,875 | 2 |
| Middle Atlantic | 60 | 38 | 4 | 3 | 0 | 0 | 0 | 0 | 92 | 59 | 156 | 12,670 | 207 |
| Southeast | 39 | 42 | 2 | 2 | 0 | 0 | 0 | 0 | 52 | 56 | 93 | 9,622 | 253 |
| Southwest | 39 | 48 | 3 | 4 | 0 | 0 | 0 | 0 | 40 | 49 | 82 | 16,470 | 643 |
| West | 16 | 32 | 2 | 4 | 0 | 0 | 0 | 0 | 32 | 64 | 50 | 27,290 | 384 |
| Rocky Mountains | 2 | 25 | 0 | 0 | 0 | 0 | 0 | 0 | 6 | 75 | 8 | 625 | –85 |
| Middle West | 74 | 38 | 1 | 1 | 0 | 0 | 0 | 0 | 122 | 62 | 197 | 5,447 | 246 |
| Canada | 8 | 36 | 1 | 5 | 0 | 0 | 1 | 5 | 12 | 55 | 22 | 75,030 | –2 |
| Total | 246 | 38 | 13 | 2 | 0 | 0 | 1 | 0 | 383 | 60 | 643 | 13,740 | 181 |

TABLE 4.185

1978 and 1988 *American Library Directory* Longitudinal Study Total Annual Expenditure by Denomination (for Congregational Type Libraries Only)

| Denomination | 1978 | | | | 1988 | | | | Percentage Change 1978–88 |
|---|---|---|---|---|---|---|---|---|---|
| | Number of Libraries | No Response | Total Libraries | Mean Dollars | Number of Libraries | No Response | Total Libraries | Mean Dollars | |
| Baptist | 17 | 66 | 83 | 2,412 | 29 | 42 | 71 | 6,509 | 170 |
| Christian | 6 | 12 | 18 | 1,125 | 9 | 8 | 17 | 3,167 | 182 |
| Churches of Christ | 0 | 0 | 0 | 0 | 2 | 0 | 2 | 625 | N/A |
| Episcopal/Anglican | 8 | 33 | 41 | 2,125 | 15 | 18 | 33 | 5,450 | 156 |
| Independent | 0 | 3 | 3 | 0 | 0 | 1 | 1 | 0 | N/A |
| Lutheran | 16 | 37 | 53 | 1,516 | 17 | 25 | 42 | 824 | –46 |
| Mennonite | 0 | 3 | 3 | 0 | 3 | 1 | 4 | 500 | N/A |
| Methodist | 12 | 43 | 55 | 1,125 | 29 | 35 | 64 | 4,026 | 258 |
| Other Denoms. | 18 | 68 | 86 | 2,792 | 21 | 50 | 71 | 5,000 | 79 |
| Presbyterian | 27 | 88 | 115 | 722 | 39 | 58 | 97 | 4,994 | 592 |
| U.C.C. | 5 | 8 | 13 | 250 | 3 | 10 | 13 | 500 | 100 |
| Summary | | | | | | | | | |
| Jewish | 33 | 117 | 150 | 3,364 | 64 | 106 | 170 | 14,980 | 345 |
| Roman Catholic | 3 | 11 | 14 | 1,750 | 4 | 4 | 8 | 12,810 | 632 |
| All Protestant | 109 | 361 | 470 | 1,592 | 167 | 248 | 415 | 4,394 | 176 |
| Total | 145 | 489 | 634 | 1,998 | 235 | 358 | 593 | 7,420 | 271 |

TABLE 4.186

1988 *American Library Directory* Popular Baptist Libraries with the
Highest Total Annual Expenditure

| Library | Total Expenditures |
| --- | --- |
| First Baptist Church, Longview, TX | $122,500 |
| First Baptist Church, Dallas, TX | 70,000 |
| First Baptist Church, Greensboro, NC | 32,500 |
| First Baptist Church, Murfreesboro, TN | 13,750 |
| First Baptist Church, Waco, TX | 13,750 |

TABLE 4.187

1988 *American Library Directory* Popular Christian Libraries with the
Highest Total Annual Expenditure

| Library | Total Expenditures |
| --- | --- |
| Christian Church, Indianapolis, IN | $13,750 |
| Central Christian Church, Lexington, KY | 4,000 |
| High Street Christian Church, Akron, OH | 4,000 |
| First Christian Church, Alexandria, VA | 4,000 |
| Englewood Christian Church, Indianapolis, IN | 1,000 |
| First Christian Church, Knoxville, TN | 1,000 |
| Douglass Boulevard Christian Church, Louisville, KY | 250 |
| East Dallas Christian Church, Dallas, TX | 250 |
| University Christian Church, Seattle, WA | 250 |

TABLE 4.188

1978 *American Library Directory* Popular Congregational Libraries
with the Highest Total Annual Expenditure

| Library | Total Expenditures |
| --- | --- |
| First Congregational Church, Stamford, CT | $1,000 |
| First Congregational Church, Palo Alto, CA | 250 |
| Bushnell Congregational Church, Detroit, MI | 250 |
| Union Congregational Church, Upper Montclair, NJ | 250 |

TABLE 4.189

1988 *American Library Directory* Popular Episcopal/Anglican Libraries with the Highest Total Annual Expenditure

| Library | Total Expenditures |
|---|---|
| St. Faith Episcopal Church, Havertown, PA | $32,500 |
| Episcopal Diocese of West Texas, San Antonio, TX | 32,500 |
| St. Thomas Episcopal Church, Sunnyvale, CA | 4,000 |
| Church of the Holy Faith, Santa Fe, NM | 4,000 |
| St. Mark's Episcopal Church, San Antonio, TX | 4,000 |
| Trinity Episcopal Church, Newtown, CT | 1,000 |
| Trinity Church, New York, NY | 1,000 |
| Christ Episcopal Church, Charlotte, NC | 1,000 |

TABLE 4.190

1988 *American Library Directory* Popular Lutheran Libraries with the Highest Total Annual Expenditure

| Library | Total Expenditures |
|---|---|
| Our Savior's Lutheran Church, Milwaukee, WI | $4,000 |
| Bethlehem Lutheran Church, St. Charles, IL | 1,000 |
| Christ Lutheran Church, Bethesda, MD | 1,000 |
| First Lutheran Church, Red Wing, MN | 1,000 |
| Oak Grove Lutheran Church, Richfield, MN | 1,000 |
| St. Martin's Evangelical Lutheran Church, Austin, TX | 1,000 |
| Trinity Lutheran Church, Madison, WI | 1,000 |
| Ascension Lutheran Church, Milwaukee, WI | 1,000 |
| Holy Trinity Lutheran Church, West Allis, WI | 1,000 |

TABLE 4.191

1988 *American Library Directory* Popular Methodist Libraries with the Highest Total Annual Expenditure

| Library | Total Expenditures |
|---|---|
| Christ Church, Louisville, KY | $70,000 |
| First United Methodist Church, Tulsa, OK | 13,750 |
| Pasadena Community United Methodist Church, St. Petersburg, FL | 4,000 |
| Bethesda United Methodist Church, Bethesda, MD | 4,000 |
| Asbury First United Methodist Church, Rochester, NY | 4,000 |
| First United Methodist Church, Austin, TX | 4,000 |
| Reveille United Methodist Church, Richmond, VA | 4,000 |

TABLE 4.192

1988 *American Library Directory* Popular Other Denominations Libraries with the Highest Total Annual Expenditure

| Library | Total Expenditures |
| --- | --- |
| Friends Free Library of Germantown, Philadelphia, PA | $70,000 |
| Church of Jesus Christ of Latter-day Saints, San Diego, CA | 32,500 |
| Las Vegas Family History Center, Las Vegas, NV | 32,500 |
| Church of Jesus Christ of Latter-day Saints, Mesa, AZ | 13,750 |
| Church of Jesus Christ of Latter-day Saints, Boca Raton, FL | 4,000 |
| Swedenborgian New Church Union, Boston, MA | 4,000 |
| Plymouth Congregational Church, Seattle, WA | 4,000 |
| Friends House, Toronto, ON | 4,000 |

TABLE 4.193

1988 *American Library Directory* Popular Presbyterian Libraries with the Highest Total Annual Expenditure

| Library | Total Expenditures |
| --- | --- |
| Highland Park Presbyterian Church, Dallas, TX | $127,500 |
| First Presbyterian Church, El Paso, TX | 13,750 |
| Trinity United Presbyterian Church, Santa Ana, CA | 4,000 |
| National Presbyterian Church, Washington, DC | 4,000 |
| Pasadena Presbyterian Church, St. Petersburg, FL | 4,000 |
| Peachtree Presbyterian Church, Atlanta, GA | 4,000 |
| Presbyterian Church of the Atonement, Silver Spring, MD | 4,000 |
| First United Presbyterian Church, Norwalk, OH | 4,000 |
| Carmel Presbyterian Church, Glenside, PA | 4,000 |
| Northminster United Presbyterian Church, New Castle, PA | 4,000 |

TABLE 4.194

1988 *American Library Directory* Popular Jewish Libraries with the Highest Total Annual Expenditure

| Library | Total Expenditures |
|---|---|
| Jewish Public Library, Montreal, PQ | $560,000 |
| Stephen S. Wise Temple, Los Angeles, CA | 185,000 |
| Young Men's and Women's Hebrew Association, New York, NY | 185,000 |
| Sinai Temple, Los Angeles, CA | 127,500 |
| Central Agency for Jewish Education, Miami, FL | 127,500 |
| Akiba Hebrew Academy, Merion, PA | 70,000 |
| Congregation Beth Yeshurun, Houston, TX | 70,000 |

TABLE 4.195

1988 *American Library Directory* Popular Roman Catholic Libraries with the Highest Total Annual Expenditure

| Library | Total Expenditures |
|---|---|
| St. Mary's School for the Deaf, Buffalo, NY | $70,000 |
| St. Matthew's and St. Timothy's Neighborhood Center, New York, NY | 70,000 |
| Hamilton-Wentworth Roman Catholic Library, Hamilton, ON | 70,000 |
| Diocese of St. Cloud Bureau of Education, St. Cloud, MN | 32,500 |
| All Saints Catholic Church, Dallas, TX | 32,500 |
| Edmonton Catholic Schools, Edmonton, AB | 32,500 |
| Church of the Incarnation, Dallas, TX | 13,750 |
| Cardinal Ritter, St. Louis, MO | 4,000 |
| Immaculate Heart of Mary Church, Los Alamos, NM | 4,000 |
| Slovak Catholic Cultural Center, Oak Forest, IL | 1,000 |
| Our Lady Queen of Martyrs Church, Birmingham, MI | 1,000 |

TABLE 4.196

1978 *American Library Directory* Total Annual Popular Library
Expenditure by Region for Matched Pairs

| Region | 1–7,500 | % | 7,501–95,000 | % | 95,001 220,000 | % | 220,001 & over | % | No Response | % | No. of Libraries | Mean Dollars |
|---|---|---|---|---|---|---|---|---|---|---|---|---|
| Northeast | 5 | 19 | 1 | 4 | 0 | 0 | 0 | 0 | 20 | 77 | 26 | $3,625 |
| Middle Atlantic | 27 | 25 | 3 | 3 | 0 | 0 | 0 | 0 | 79 | 72 | 109 | 4,600 |
| Southeast | 16 | 24 | 2 | 3 | 0 | 0 | 0 | 0 | 50 | 74 | 68 | 2,583 |
| Southwest | 20 | 34 | 0 | 0 | 0 | 0 | 0 | 0 | 38 | 66 | 58 | 1,863 |
| West | 8 | 20 | 1 | 3 | 0 | 0 | 0 | 0 | 31 | 78 | 40 | 2,750 |
| Rocky Mountains | 0 | 0 | 0 | 0 | 0 | 0 | 0 | 0 | 8 | 100 | 8 | 0 |
| Middle West | 48 | 33 | 1 | 1 | 0 | 0 | 0 | 0 | 97 | 66 | 146 | 1,429 |
| Canada | 1 | 6 | 0 | 0 | 0 | 0 | 1 | 6 | 14 | 88 | 16 | 133,000 |
| Total | 125 | 27 | 8 | 2 | 0 | 0 | 1 | 0 | 337 | 72 | 471 | 4,509 |

Column headers (spanning "-------1978 Total Annual Library Expenditure-------"): 1–7,500 | 7,501–95,000 | 95,001 220,000 | 220,001 & over

TABLE 4.197

1988 *American Library Directory* Total Annual Popular Library
Expenditure by Region for Matched Pairs

| Region | 1–7,500 | % | 7,501–95,000 | % | 95,001 220,000 | % | 220,001 & over | % | No Response | % | No. of Libraries | Mean Dollars |
|---|---|---|---|---|---|---|---|---|---|---|---|---|
| Northeast | 6 | 23 | 0 | 0 | 0 | 0 | 0 | 0 | 20 | 77 | 26 | $1,250 |
| Middle Atlantic | 31 | 28 | 12 | 11 | 0 | 0 | 0 | 0 | 66 | 61 | 109 | 10,140 |
| Southeast | 22 | 32 | 5 | 7 | 1 | 1 | 0 | 0 | 40 | 59 | 68 | 10,900 |
| Southwest | 19 | 33 | 10 | 17 | 0 | 0 | 0 | 0 | 29 | 50 | 58 | 9,250 |
| West | 11 | 28 | 2 | 5 | 0 | 0 | 0 | 0 | 27 | 68 | 40 | 6,769 |
| Rocky Mountains | 2 | 25 | 0 | 0 | 0 | 0 | 0 | 0 | 6 | 75 | 8 | 625 |
| Middle West | 46 | 32 | 7 | 5 | 0 | 0 | 0 | 0 | 93 | 64 | 146 | 4,071 |
| Canada | 1 | 8 | 0 | 0 | 0 | 0 | 1 | 8 | 11 | 85 | 13 | 282,000 |
| Total | 138 | 29 | 36 | 8 | 1 | 0 | 1 | 0 | 292 | 62 | 468 | 10,720 |

Column headers (spanning "-------1978 Total Annual Library Expenditure-------"): 1–7,500 | 7,501–95,000 | 95,001 220,000 | 220,001 & over

TABLE 4.198
1978 and 1988 *American Library Directory* Longitudinal Study Total
Annual Popular Library Expenditure for Matched Pairs

| Library Type | Number of Libraries | No Response | Total Libraries | Mean Dollars | Number of Libraries | No Response | Total Libraries | Mean Dollars | Percentage Change 1978–88 |
|---|---|---|---|---|---|---|---|---|---|
| Popular | 134 | 337 | 471 | 4,509 | 176 | 292 | 468 | 10,720 | 138 |
| Congregational | 128 | 312 | 440 | 1,873 | 170 | 270 | 440 | 5,791 | 209 |
| Parochial | 1 | 15 | 16 | 13,750 | 4 | 9 | 13 | 67,880 | 394 |
| Public | 5 | 10 | 15 | 70,150 | 2 | 13 | 15 | 315,000 | 349 |

TABLE 4.199
1978 and 1988 *American Library Directory* Longitudinal Study Total Annual Popular Library Expenditure by Denomination

| Denomination | 1978 | | | | 1988 | | | | Percentage Change 1978–88 |
|---|---|---|---|---|---|---|---|---|---|
| | Number of Libraries | No Response | Total Libraries | Mean Dollars | Number of Libraries | No Response | Total Libraries | Mean Dollars | |
| Baptist | 17 | 66 | 83 | 2,412 | 29 | 42 | 71 | 6,509 | 170 |
| Christian | 7 | 12 | 19 | 1,000 | 9 | 8 | 17 | 3,167 | 217 |
| Churches of Christ | 0 | 0 | 0 | 0 | 2 | 0 | 2 | 625 | – |
| Episcopal/Anglican | 8 | 34 | 42 | 2,125 | 15 | 19 | 34 | 5,450 | 156 |
| Independent | 0 | 5 | 5 | 0 | 0 | 3 | 3 | 0 | 0 |
| Lutheran | 16 | 37 | 53 | 1,516 | 17 | 25 | 42 | 824 | –46 |
| Mennonite | 0 | 3 | 3 | 0 | 3 | 1 | 4 | 500 | – |
| Methodist | 12 | 43 | 55 | 1,125 | 29 | 35 | 64 | 4,026 | 258 |
| Other Denominations | 20 | 72 | 92 | 6,700 | 23 | 54 | 77 | 7,620 | 14 |
| Presbyterian | 27 | 88 | 115 | 722 | 39 | 58 | 97 | 4,994 | 592 |
| U.C.C. | 5 | 8 | 13 | 250 | 3 | 10 | 13 | 500 | 100 |
| Summary | | | | | | | | | |
| Jewish | 36 | 127 | 163 | 10,850 | 72 | 115 | 187 | 26,720 | 146 |
| Roman Catholic | 7 | 37 | 44 | 17,500 | 11 | 20 | 31 | 30,110 | 72 |
| All Protestant | 112 | 368 | 480 | 2,299 | 169 | 255 | 424 | 4,757 | 107 |
| Total | 155 | 532 | 687 | 4,972 | 252 | 390 | 642 | 12,591 | 153 |

TABLE 4.200
1978 and 1988 *American Library Directory* Longitudinal Study
Popular Library Student Assistants (Volunteers Committee Members)

| Library Type | --------------------1 9 7 8-------------------- | | | | --------------------1 9 8 8-------------------- | | | | Percentage Change 1978–88 |
|---|---|---|---|---|---|---|---|---|---|
| | Number of Libraries | No Response | Total Libraries | Mean Members | Number of Libraries | No Response | Total Libraries | Mean Members | |
| Popular | 100 | 587 | 687 | 4.4 | 103 | 539 | 642 | 7.2 | 64 |
| Congrega- tional | 98 | 536 | 634 | 4.4 | 101 | 492 | 593 | 7.3 | 66 |
| Parochial | 0 | 27 | 27 | 0 | 1 | 23 | 24 | 1.5 | 0 |
| Public | 2 | 24 | 26 | 4.5 | 1 | 24 | 25 | 5.5 | 22 |

TABLE 4.201

1988 *American Library Directory* Breakdown of Expenditure
Categories in Percentages by Denomination for Popular Libraries[a]

| Denomination | Material | Personnel | Other | Cumulative Total Annual Spending | Cumulative in Dollars | Number of Libraries |
|---|---|---|---|---|---|---|
| Baptist | 62% | 38% | 0% | 125% | $150,750 | 71 |
| Active Libraries | 27 | 6 | 0 | 29 | | |
| Christian | 78% | 22% | 0% | 123% | 23,250 | 17 |
| Active Libraries | 8 | 2 | 0 | 9 | | |
| Churches of Christ | 100% | 0% | 0% | 500% | 250 | 2 |
| Active Libraries | 1 | 0 | 0 | 2 | | |
| Episcopal/Anglican | 40% | 60% | 0% | 103% | 79,000 | 34 |
| Active Libraries | 13 | 4 | 0 | 15 | | |
| Independent | 100% | 0% | 0% | 0% | 4,000 | 3 |
| Active Libraries | 1 | 0 | 0 | 0 | | |
| Lutheran | 100% | 0% | 0% | 156% | 9,000 | 42 |
| Active Libraries | 14 | 0 | 0 | 17 | | |
| Mennonite | 100% | 0% | 0% | 120% | 1,250 | 4 |
| Active Libraries | 3 | 0 | 0 | 3 | | |
| Methodist | 34% | 66% | 0% | 83% | 140,750 | 64 |
| Active Libraries | 28 | 6 | 0 | 29 | | |
| Other Denominations | 48% | 51% | 0% | 90% | 194,250 | 77 |
| Active Libraries | 19 | 6 | 1 | 23 | | |
| Presbyterian | 58% | 32% | 10% | 207% | 94,250 | 97 |
| Active Libraries | 35 | 2 | 2 | 39 | | |
| United Ch. of Christ | 100% | 0% | 0% | 120% | 1,250 | 13 |
| Active Libraries | 3 | 0 | 0 | 3 | | |
| Jewish | 25% | 68% | 7% | 113% | 1,704,250 | 187 |
| Active Libraries | 65 | 49 | 10 | 72 | | |

TABLE 4.201 (continued)

1988 *American Library Directory* Breakdown of Expenditure
Categories in Percentages by Denomination for Popular Libraries[a]

| Denomination | Material | Personnel | Other | Cumulative Total Annual Spending | Cumulative in Dollars | Number of Libraries |
|---|---|---|---|---|---|---|
| Roman Catholic | 33% | 67% | 0% | 67% | 493,750 | 31 |
| Active Libraries | 13 | 8 | 0 | 11 | | |
| All Protestant | 51% | 48% | 1% | 115% | 698,000 | 424 |
| Active Libraries | 152 | 26 | 3 | 169 | | |
| Total | 32% | 63% | 5% | 106% | 2,896,000 | 642 |
| Active Libraries | 230 | 83 | 13 | 252 | | |

[a] Cumulative total annual spending on this table represents the sum of material +
personnel + Other expenditures relative to the figure given as total annual library
expenditure. For example:

| | |
|---|---|
| Material | $4,000 |
| Personnel | $4,000 |
| Other | $1,500 |
| Total annual library expenditure | $8,500 |
| Cumulative total annual spending    = | 1.12% |

The next column, cumulated in dollars, shows the cumulative of "cumulative total annual library expenditure" for all libraries represented in the preceding columns.
Dividing the grand total at the bottom of the page by the number of reporting libraries,
or 252, will not produce an accurate mean due both to rounding errors and the fact that
although 252 libraries reported total annual library expenditure, a slightly smaller
number reported the component parts, i.e., material, personnel, and other expenditures.
Finally, the questionnaire categorization system also created small distortions that
should more or less balance out over 200+ cases. The gross effect of the figures is to
suggest that many of these libraries exceeded their budgets substantially through gifts
or fund-raising.

TABLE 4.202

1978 *American Library Directory* Breakdown of Expenditure
Categories in Percentages by Denomination for Popular Libraries

| Denomination | Material | Personnel | Other | Cumulative Total Annual Spending | Cumulative in Dollars | Number of Libraries |
|---|---|---|---|---|---|---|
| Baptist | 65% | 35% | 0% | 143% | $28,750 | 83 |
| Active Libraries | 15 | 2 | 0 | 17 | | |
| Christian | 45% | 50% | 5% | 70% | 10,000 | 19 |
| Active Libraries | 6 | 2 | 1 | 7 | | |
| Churches of Christ | 0% | 0% | 0% | 0% | 0 | 0 |
| Active Libraries | 0 | 0 | 0 | 0 | | |
| Congregational | 100% | 0% | 0% | 117% | 1,500 | 28 |
| Active Libraries | 1 | 0 | 0 | 4 | | |
| Episcopal/Anglican | 43% | 48% | 10% | 342% | 5,250 | 42 |
| Active Libraries | 5 | 1 | 1 | 8 | | |
| Independent | 100% | 0% | 0% | 0% | 750 | 5 |
| Active Libraries | 1 | 0 | 0 | 0 | | |
| Lutheran | 29% | 71% | 0% | 87% | 28,000 | 53 |
| Active Libraries | 9 | 3 | 0 | 16 | | |
| Methodist | 30% | 70% | 0% | 76% | 17,750 | 55 |
| Active Libraries | 9 | 3 | 0 | 12 | | |
| Other Denominations | 12% | 70% | 18% | 155% | 85,500 | 67 |
| Active Libraries | 8 | 3 | 2 | 16 | | |
| Presbyterian | 79% | 17% | 3% | 134% | 14,500 | 115 |
| Active Libraries | 18 | 1 | 1 | 27 | | |
| United Ch. of Christ | 100% | 0% | 0% | 167% | 750 | 13 |
| Active Libraries | 3 | 0 | 0 | 5 | | |
| Jewish | 55% | 44% | 0% | 232% | 168,750 | 163 |
| Active Libraries | 26 | 17 | 1 | 36 | | |
| Roman Catholic | 71% | 29% | 0% | 203% | 60,250 | 44 |
| Active Libraries | 9 | 2 | 0 | 7 | | |
| All Protestant | 33% | 58% | 9% | 134% | 192,750 | 480 |
| Active Libraries | 75 | 15 | 5 | 112 | | |
| Total | 47% | 49% | 4% | 183% | 421,750 | 687 |
| Active Libraries | 110 | 34 | 6 | 155 | | |

TABLE 4.203

1988 *American Library Directory* Popular Libraries Most Often Listed
in Baptist Tables

| Library | Listings |
|---|---|
| First Baptist Church, Murfreesboro, TN | 13 |
| Hoffmantown Baptist Church, Albuquerque, NM | 12 |
| First Baptist Church, Greensboro, NC | 12 |
| First Baptist Church, Abilene, TX | 12 |
| First Baptist Church, San Antonio, TX | 11 |
| First Baptist Church, Waco, TX | 11 |
| North Central Baptist Media, Gainesville, FL | 10 |
| First Baptist Church, Van Nuys, CA | 9 |
| First Baptist Church, Gainesville, FL | 9 |
| Third Baptist Church, St. Louis, MO | 9 |
| First Baptist Church, Dallas, TX | 9 |

TABLE 4.204

1988 *American Library Directory* Popular Libraries Most Often Listed
in Christian Tables

| Library | Listings |
|---|---|
| High Street Christian Church, Akron, OH | 12 |
| Douglass Boulevard Christian Church, Louisville, KY | 10 |
| First Christian Church, Alexandria, VA | 9 |
| First Christian Church, St. Joseph, MO | 7 |
| First Christian Church, New Castle, PA | 7 |
| University Christian Church, Seattle, WA | 7 |
| Christian Church, Indianapolis, IN | 6 |
| Eaglewood Christian Church, Indianapolis, IN | 6 |
| Central Christian Church, Lexington, KY | 6 |
| First Christian Church, Columbia, MO | 6 |

TABLE 4.205

1988 *American Library Directory* Popular Libraries Most Often Listed
in Churches of Christ Tables

| Library | Listings |
|---|---|
| Roanoke Church of Christ, Roanoke, VA | 9 |
| University Church of Christ, Murray, KY | 7 |

TABLE 4.206

1988 *American Library Directory* Popular Libraries Most Often Listed in Episcopal/Anglican Tables

| Library | Listings |
| --- | --- |
| St. Thomas Episcopal Church, Sunnyvale, CA | 12 |
| St. Michael's in the Hills, Toledo, OH | 11 |
| Episcopal Diocese of West Texas, San Antonio, TX | 11 |
| Church of the Holy Faith, Santa Fe, NM | 10 |
| St. Faith Episcopal Church, Havertown, PA | 10 |
| Calvary Episcopal Church, Columbia, MO | 9 |
| Church Army in Canada, Toronto, ON | 7 |
| Trinity Episcopal Church, Newtown, CT | 6 |
| St. Paul's Episcopal Church, Maumee, OH | 6 |

TABLE 4.207

1988 *American Library Directory* Popular Libraries Most Often Listed in Independent Tables

| Library | Listings |
| --- | --- |
| Protestant School Board, Montreal, PQ | 11 |
| Centre for Christian Studies, Toronto, ON | 4 |
| Wayzata Community Church, Wayzata, MN | 1 |

TABLE 4.208

1988 *American Library Directory* Popular Libraries Most Often Listed in Lutheran Tables

| Library | Listings |
|---|---|
| English Lutheran Church, LaCrosse, WI | 12 |
| Ascension Lutheran Church, Milwaukee, WI | 11 |
| First Lutheran Church, Red Wing, MN | 10 |
| Christ Lutheran Church, Bethesda, MD | 9 |
| Oak Grove Lutheran Church, Richfield, MN | 9 |
| St. Martin's Evangelical Lutheran Church, Austin, TX | 9 |
| Grace Lutheran Church, La Grange, IL | 8 |
| Trinity Lutheran Church, Moorhead, MN | 8 |
| St. John's Evangelical Lutheran Church, Springfield, OH | 8 |
| Augustana Lutheran Church, Denver, CO | 7 |
| Bethlehem Lutheran Church, St. Charles, IL | 7 |
| Trinity Lutheran Parish, St. Peter, MN | 7 |
| Trinity Lutheran Church, Madison, WI | 7 |
| Our Savior's Lutheran Church, Milwaukee, WI | 7 |

TABLE 4.209

1988 *American Library Directory* Popular Libraries Most Often Listed in Mennonite Tables

| Library | Listings |
|---|---|
| Zion Mennonite Church, Souderton, PA | 5 |
| Freeport Mennonite Church, Freeport, IL | 4 |
| First Mennonite Church, Reedley, CA | 3 |
| Bethesda Mennonite Church, Henderson, NE | 3 |

TABLE 4.210

1988 *American Library Directory* Popular Libraries Most Often Listed in Methodist Tables

| Library | Listings |
| --- | --- |
| First United Methodist Church, Tulsa, OK | 14 |
| Bethesda United Methodist Church, Bethesda, MD | 11 |
| Northside United Methodist Church, Atlanta, GA | 10 |
| Methodist Church, Maplewood, NJ | 10 |
| Highland Park United Methodist Church, Dallas, TX | 10 |
| Christ Church United Methodist Church, Akron, OH | 8 |
| Pasadena Community United Methodist Church, St. Petersburg, FL | 7 |
| First United Methodist Church, Glen Ellyn, IL | 7 |
| St. Paul's United Methodist Church, Springfield, MO | 7 |
| St. Paul's United Methodist Church, Las Cruces, NM | 7 |
| Epworth United Methodist Church, Toledo, OH | 7 |
| Wesley United Methodist Church, LaCrosse, WI | 7 |

TABLE 4.211

1988 *American Library Directory* Popular Libraries Most Often Listed in Other Denominations Tables

| Library | Listings |
| --- | --- |
| Church of Jesus Christ of Latter-day Saints, Salt Lake City, UT | 12 |
| Church of the Atonement, Silver Spring, MD | 11 |
| Pilgrim Congregational Church, Duluth, MN | 11 |
| Church of Jesus Christ of Latter-day Saints, Mesa, AZ | 10 |
| Church of Jesus Christ of Latter-day Saints, San Diego, CA | 10 |
| Crumbaugh Memorial Public Church, Le Roy, IL | 10 |
| New Church Union Swedenborgian, Boston, MA | 9 |
| United Church of Religious Science, Los Angeles, CA | 8 |
| Church of Jesus Christ of Latter-day Saints, Ventura, CA | 8 |

TABLE 4.212

1988 *American Library Directory* Popular Libraries Most Often Listed in Presbyterian Tables

| Library | Listings |
|---|---|
| Westwood First Presbyterian Church, Cincinnati, OH | 15 |
| Pasadena Presbyterian Church, St. Petersburg, FL | 13 |
| First Presbyterian Church, Perth Amboy, NJ | 12 |
| First Presbyterian Church, Albuquerque, NM | 12 |
| First Presbyterian Church, El Paso, TX | 12 |
| Neshaminy-Warwick Presbyterian Church, Warminster, PA | 11 |
| First Presbyterian Church, Shreveport, LA | 10 |
| Central Presbyterian Church, Kansas City, MO | 9 |
| Carmel Presbyterian Church, Glenside, PA | 9 |
| First Presbyterian Church, Colorado Springs, CO | 8 |
| First Presbyterian Church, Hastings, NE | 8 |

TABLE 4.213

1988 *American Library Directory* Popular Libraries Most Often Listed in United Church of Christ Tables

| Library | Listings |
|---|---|
| United Church of Christ, Vermilion, OH | 14 |
| United Church of Christ, Maple Shade, NJ | 9 |
| St. Stephen United Church of Christ, Sandusky, OH | 8 |
| St. John Evangelical United Church of Christ, Collinsville, IL | 6 |
| Trinity United Church of Christ, St. Louis, MO | 6 |
| St. Paul's United Church of Christ, Evansville, IN | 5 |
| Zion United Church of Christ, North Canton, OH | 5 |

TABLE 4.214

1988 *American Library Directory* Popular Libraries Most Often Listed in Jewish Tables

| Library | Listings |
| --- | --- |
| Sinai Temple, Los Angeles, CA | 16 |
| Stephen S. Wise Temple, Los Angeles, CA | 13 |
| Central Agency for Jewish Education, Miami, FL | 13 |
| Temple Israel, Minneapolis, MN | 12 |
| Jewish Education Association, Louisville, KY | 11 |
| Temple Beth Zion, Buffalo, NY | 11 |
| Congregation Beth Yeshurun, Houston, TX | 11 |
| Temple Emanu-el, Miami Beach, FL | 10 |
| Congregation Solel, Highland Park, IL | 10 |
| Young Men's and Women's Hebrew Association Library, New York, NY | 10 |

TABLE 4.215

1988 *American Library Directory* Popular Libraries Most Often Listed in Roman Catholic Tables

| Library | Listings |
| --- | --- |
| All Saints Catholic Church, Dallas, TX | 13 |
| Cardinal Ritter, St. Louis, MO | 12 |
| Immaculate Heart of Mary, Los Alamos, NM | 11 |
| Church of the Incarnation, Dallas, TX | 11 |
| St. Mary's School for the Deaf, Buffalo, NY | 10 |
| Edmonton Catholic Schools, Edmonton, AB | 10 |
| Union St. Jean Baptiste, Woonsocket, RI | 9 |
| Oratoire St. Joseph, Montréal, PQ | 9 |
| Stamford Catholic Library, Stamford, CT | 8 |
| St. Matthew's and St. Timothy's Neighborhood Center, New York, NY | 8 |

TABLE 4.216

1988 *American Library Directory:* The Very Highest Popular Libraries (5 References and Over) by Region[a]

| Region | -------Number of Table References ------- | | | | | | | | No Response | % | Number of Libraries | Mean Refs. | Active Libraries |
|---|---|---|---|---|---|---|---|---|---|---|---|---|---|
| | 5–7 | % | 8–9 | % | 10–11 | % | 12 & over | % | | | | | |
| Northeast | 2 | 6 | 0 | 0 | 0 | 0 | 0 | 0 | 33 | 94 | 35 | 5.5 | 2 |
| Middle Atlantic | 6 | 4 | 1 | 1 | 0 | 0 | 0 | 0 | 149 | 96 | 156 | 5.8 | 7 |
| Southeast | 6 | 6 | 0 | 0 | 1 | 1 | 0 | 0 | 86 | 92 | 93 | 6.4 | 7 |
| Southwest | 10 | 12 | 2 | 2 | 1 | 1 | 0 | 0 | 69 | 84 | 82 | 6.9 | 13 |
| West | 5 | 10 | 2 | 4 | 0 | 0 | 0 | 0 | 43 | 86 | 50 | 6.9 | 7 |
| Rocky Mountains | 0 | 0 | 0 | 0 | 0 | 0 | 1 | 13 | 7 | 88 | 8 | 12.0 | 1 |
| Middle West | 16 | 8 | 0 | 0 | 0 | 0 | 0 | 0 | 181 | 92 | 197 | 5.3 | 16 |
| Canada | 2 | 10 | 0 | 0 | 0 | 0 | 0 | 0 | 19 | 90 | 21 | 5.0 | 2 |
| Total | 47 | 7 | 5 | 1 | 2 | 0 | 1 | 0 | 587 | 91 | 642 | 6.2 | 55 |

[a] There are fifty-five "highest of the highest" libraries represented here.

TABLE 4.217

1988 *American Library Directory* Popular Libraries with the Highest
Number of Specific Table Listings (the "Highest of the Highest")

| Library | Denomination | Tables |
|---|---|---|
| Church of Jesus Christ of Latter-day Saints, Salt Lake City, UT | Other Denominations | 12 |
| Central Agency for Jewish Education, Miami, FL | Jewish | 11 |
| All Saints Catholic Church, Dallas, TX | Roman Catholic | 10 |
| Sinai Temple, Los Angeles, CA | Jewish | 9 |
| Stephen S. Wise Temple, Los Angeles, CA | Jewish | 9 |
| First Baptist Church, Dallas, TX | Baptist | 9 |
| Congregation Beth Yeshurun, Houston, TX | Jewish | 9 |
| Young Men's and Women's Hebrew Association Library, New York, NY | Jewish | 8 |
| Church of Jesus Christ of Latter-day Saints, San Diego, CA | Other Denominations | 7 |
| Church of Jesus Christ of Latter-day Saints, Ventura, CA | Other Denominations | 7 |
| First Presbyterian Church, Albuquerque, NM | Presbyterian | 7 |
| First Baptist Church, Greensboro, NC | Baptist | 7 |
| Temple-Congregation Shomer Emunim, Sylvania, OH | Jewish | 7 |
| First United Methodist Church, Tulsa, OK | Methodist | 7 |
| First Baptist Church, Murfreesboro, TN | Baptist | 7 |
| First Baptist Church, Abilene, TX | Baptist | 7 |
| Temple Emanu-el, Tucson, AZ | Jewish | 6 |
| United Church of Religious Science, Los Angeles, CA | Other Denominations | 6 |
| Hoffmantown Baptist Church, Albuquerque, NM | Baptist | 6 |
| Immaculate Heart of Mary, Los Alamos, NM | Roman Catholic | 6 |
| St. Mary's School for the Deaf, Buffalo, NY | Roman Catholic | 6 |
| Westwood First Presbyterian Church, Cincinnati, OH | Presbyterian | 6 |
| Fairmount Temple, Cleveland, OH | Jewish | 6 |
| Friends Free Library of Germantown, Philadelphia, PA | Other Denominations | 6 |
| Temple Beth-el Congregation, Providence, RI | Jewish | 6 |
| First Presbyterian Church, El Paso, TX | Presbyterian | 6 |
| Episcopal Diocese of West Texas, San Antonio, TX | Episcopal/Anglican | 6 |

Variables added into the highest popular libraries by denomination calculation (i.e., those
on the largest number of specific library listing tables):

1. Total staff
2. Professional staff
3. Clerical staff
4. Student assistants (Committee Members)
5. Volume holdings
6. Periodical holdings
7. Vertical file holdings

TABLE 4.217 (continued)
1988 *American Library Directory* Popular Libraries with the Highest
Number of Specific Table Listings (the "Highest of the Highest")

---

  8. Microforms
  9. Material expenditures
10. Personnel expenditures
11. Other expenditures
12. Total expenditure
13. Consortium memberships
14. OCLC membership
15. Maps
16. Art reproductions
17. Media
18. Automation projects
19. Subject interests
20. Special collections
21. Publications
22. Age
23. Institutional accreditation
Total Variables = 23
Total numerical variables = 17
Total dichotomous or Boolean variables = 6

---

TABLE 4.218
1988 *American Library Directory* Analysis of Popular Libraries
Ranking Highest for Numerical Variables by denomination[a]

| Denom-ination | Library, City, and State/Province | Number of Listings | Denominational Totals | % of All Libraries in This Study |
|---|---|---|---|---|
| Baptist | First Baptist Church, Murfreesboro, TN | 4 | | |
| | First Baptist Church, Abilene, TX | 4 | | |
| | First Baptist Church, Dallas, TX | 4 | | |
| | North Central Baptist Media Center, Gainesville, FL | 3 | | |
| | Third Baptist Church, St. Louis, MO | 3 | | |
| | First Baptist Church, Fairmont, NC | 3 | 21 | 10 |
| Christian | Douglass Boulevard Christian Church, Louisville, KY | 3 | | |
| | First Christian Church, Columbia, MO | 3 | | |
| | High Street Christian Church, Akron, OH | 3 | | |
| | First Christian Church, Alexandria, VA | 3 | 12 | 6 |
| Churches of Christ | University Church of Christ, Murray, KY | 2 | | |
| | Roanoke Church of Christ, Roanoke, VA | 2 | 4 | 2 |
| Episcopal/ Anglican | St. Faith Episcopal Church, Havertown, PA | 5 | | |
| | Episcopal Diocese of West Texas, San Antonio, TX | 5 | | |
| | St. Thomas Episcopal Church, Sunnyvale, CA | 4 | | |
| | St. Michael's in the Hills Episcopal Church, Toledo, OH | 3 | 17 | 8 |
| Lutheran | Trinity Lutheran Parish Library, St. Peter, MN | 3 | | |
| | St. Martin's Evangelical Lutheran Church, Austin, TX | 3 | | |
| | English Lutheran Church, LaCrosse, WI | 3 | | |
| | Holy Trinity Lutheran Church, West Allis, WI | 3 | 12 | 6 |

TABLE 4.218 (continued)
1988 *American Library Directory* Analysis of Popular Libraries
Ranking Highest for Numerical Variables[a]

| Denom-ination | Library, City, and State | Number of Listings | Denomination Totals | % of All Libraries in This Study |
|---|---|---|---|---|
| Mennonite | No Listings | | 0 | 0 |
| Methodist | Bethesda United Methodist Church, Bethesda, MD | 3 | | |
| | Morrow Memorial United Methodist Church, Maplewood, NJ | 3 | | |
| | Epworth United Methodist Church, Toledo, OH | 3 | | |
| | First United Methodist Church, Green Bay, WI | 3 | 12 | 6 |
| Other Denominations | Church of Jesus Christ of Latter-day Saints, Salt Lake City, UT | 8 | | |
| | Church of Jesus Christ of Latter-day Saints, San Diego, CA | 4 | | |
| | Church of Jesus Christ of Latter-day Saints, Ventura, CA | 4 | | |
| | Church of Jesus Christ of Latter-day Saints, Mesa, AZ | 3 | | |
| | Church of the Atonement, Silver Spring, MD | 3 | | |
| | Pilgrim Congregational Church, Duluth, MN | 3 | 25 | 12 |
| Presbyterian | Pasadena Presbyterian Church, St. Petersburg, FL | 3 | | |
| | First Presbyterian Church, Shreveport, LA | 3 | | |
| | Memorial Presbyterian Church, Midland, MI | 3 | | |
| | First Presbyterian Church, Albuquerque, NM | 3 | | |
| | Westwood First Presbyterian Church, Cincinnati, OH | 3 | | |
| | First Presbyterian Church, Mansfield, OH | 3 | | |
| | First Presbyterian Church, El Paso, TX | 3 | 21 | 10 |
| United Church of Christ | Trinity United Church of Christ, St. Louis, MO | 4 | | |
| | United Church of Christ (Evangelical and Reformed), Vermilion, OH | 4 | | |

TABLE 4.218 (continued)
1988 *American Library Directory* Analysis of Popular Libraries
Ranking Highest for Numerical Variables[a]

| Denom-ination | Library, City, and State | Number of Listings | Denomination Totals | % of All Libraries in This Study |
|---|---|---|---|---|
| | St. Stephen United Church of Christ, Sandusky, OH | 3 | 11 | 5 |
| Jewish | Stephen S. Wise Temple, Los Angeles, CA | 8 | | |
| | Sinai Temple, Los Angeles, CA | 7 | | |
| | Central Agency for Jewish Education, Miami, FL | 6 | | |
| | Young Men's & Women's Hebrew Association, New York, NY | 6 | | |
| | Congregation Beth Yeshurun, Houston, TX | 6 | | |
| | Temple Emanu-el, Tucson, AZ | 5 | | |
| | Temple-Congregation Shomer Emunim, Sylvania, OH | 5 | | |
| | Jewish Public Library, Montreal, PQ | 5 | | |
| | National Council of Jewish Women, Montreal, PQ | 5 | | |
| | Congregational Solel, Highland Park, IL | 4 | | |
| | Jewish Community Center, West Bloomfield, MI | 4 | | |
| | Akiba Hebrew Academy, Merion, PA | 4 | 65 | 31 |
| Roman Catholic | Immaculate Heart of Mary, Los Alamos, NM | 3 | | |
| | Union of St. Jean Baptiste, Woonsocket, RI | 3 | | |
| | All Saints Catholic Church, Dallas, TX | 3 | 9 | 4 |
| Totals | | | 209 | 100 |

[a] This table studies only popular libraries that were registered as ranking *highest for popular libraries* on numerical variables such as volume or microform holdings, consortium memberships, etc., regardless of denominational affiliation. There are fifty-five libraries shown on this table.

TABLE 4.219

*American Library Directory* Statistical Information and Projections on All Major Numerical Variables: 1978, 1988, and 1998[a] (Profile of Means and Mean Deviations for All Popular Libraries)

| | ±1.65 Standard Deviations (90% Accur.) | Percentage Growth (Ten Yrs.) | Projected Growth (1st Year) | P.A. Projected Unit Change | 1998 Projected Variable Minimum | 1998 Projected Variable Maximum | Actual 1978 Mean | Actual 1988 Mean | Extrapolated 1998 Mean |
|---|---|---|---|---|---|---|---|---|---|
| Library age | 40 | -7.3 | -.7 | -.30 | 35 | 41 | 44 | 41 | 38 |
| Library city population size | 1,038,173 | -1.5 | -.2 | -530.00 | 289,994 | 411,606 | 361,400 | 356,100 | 350,800 |
| Institutional degree years offered | 0 | .0 | .0 | .00 | 0 | 1 | 4 | 0 | 0 |
| Total library staff size | 7.3 | 17.7 | 1.8 | .11 | 5.7 | 8.9 | 5.1 | 6.2 | 7.3 |
| Library professionals | 2.8 | .0 | .0 | .00 | .9 | 2.5 | 1.7 | 1.7 | 1.7 |
| Library clerks | 6.7 | -53.6 | -5.4 | -.15 | .0 | 2.6 | 4.3 | 2.8 | 1.3 |
| Library student assistants | 1.6 | 37.5 | 3.8 | .27 | 7.8 | 12.0 | 4.5 | 7.2 | 9.9 |
| Faculty size | 99.0 | -75.0 | -7.5 | -3.00 | .0 | 81.4 | 70.0 | 40.0 | 10.0 |
| Students enrolled | 233 | 16.7 | 1.7 | 5.00 | 129 | 571 | 250 | 300 | 350 |
| Total annual library expenditure | 37,574 | 59.0 | 5.9 | 717.00 | 13,957 | 24,657 | 4,973 | 12,140 | 19,307 |
| Annual expenditure on material | 7,134 | 55.7 | 5.6 | 227.00 | 5,056 | 7,662 | 1,811 | 4,085 | 6,359 |
| Annual expenditure on personnel | 12,500 | 72.6 | 7.3 | 1,596.0 | 29,717 | 46,185 | 6,029 | 21,990 | 37,951 |
| Annual expenditure on "other" | 8,916 | 71.2 | 7.1 | 720.00 | 12,330 | 22,316 | 2,917 | 10,120 | 17,323 |
| Library volume holdings | 21,198 | 7.5 | .8 | 51.00 | 5,977 | 8,615 | 6,282 | 6,789 | 7,296 |
| Library periodical subscriptions | 216 | 1.6 | .2 | .10 | 43 | 85 | 62 | 63 | 64 |
| Library microform holdings | 133,832 | -12.2 | -1.2 | -537.00 | 0 | 101,138 | 49,390 | 44,020 | 38,650 |
| Library vertical file drawers | 13 | 19.7 | 2.0 | .15 | 7 | 11 | 6 | 8 | 9 |
| Library consortium memberships | 0 | 16.7 | 1.7 | .02 | 1 | 2 | 1 | 1 | 1 |

| | | | | | | | | |
|---|---|---|---|---|---|---|---|---|
| Library subject interests | 2 | -5.3 | -.5 | -.01 | 1 | 2 | 2 | 2 | 2 |
| Library special collections | 2 | -14.3 | -1.4 | -.02 | 1 | 2 | 2 | 1 | 1 |
| Library publications | 0 | .0 | .0 | .00 | 0 | 1 | 0 | 2 | 2 |
| Totals | 1,259,952 | 207 | 21 | 2,246 | 357,262 | 623,002 | 433,258 | 455,720 | 478,183 |
| Averages | 59,998 | 10 | 1 | 107 | 17,012 | 29,667 | 20,631 | 21,701 | 22,771 |

a The proportion of missing data makes some of the figures in the above table highly unreliable. Some, however, such as volume holdings and periodical subscriptions, are much firmer. See individual variable analyses to determine which can be trusted furthest.

TABLE 4.220

*American Library Directory* Statistical Information and Projections on All Major Numerical Variables: 1978, 1988, and 1998ᵃ (Profile of Means and Mean Deviations for All Popular Libraries: Matched Pairs)

| | ±1.65 Standard Deviations (90% Accur.) | Percentage Growth (Ten Yrs.) | Projected Growth (1st Year) | P.A. Projected Unit Change | 1998 Projected Variable Minimum | 1998 Projected Variable Maximum | Actual 1978 Mean | Actual 1988 Mean | Extrapolated 1998 Mean |
|---|---|---|---|---|---|---|---|---|---|
| Library age | 38 | .0 | .0 | .00 | 39 | 47 | 43 | 43 | 43 |
| Library city population size | 982,805 | 2.1 | .2 | 680.00 | 270,890 | 405,110 | 324,400 | 311,200 | 338,000 |
| Institutional degree years offered | 0 | .0 | .0 | .00 | 0 | 1 | 4 | 0 | 0 |
| Total library staff size | 7.4 | 24.6 | 2.5 | .17 | 6.5 | 10.7 | 5.2 | 6.9 | 8.6 |
| Library professionals | 3.0 | 10.5 | 1.1 | .02 | 1.2 | 3.0 | 1.7 | 1.9 | 2.1 |
| Library clerks | 6.7 | −76.0 | −7.6 | −.19 | .0 | 2.0 | 4.4 | 2.5 | .6 |
| Library student assistants | 1.6 | 48.3 | 4.8 | .42 | 10.3 | 15.5 | 4.5 | 8.7 | 12.9 |
| Faculty size | 99.0 | −40.0 | −4.0 | −2.00 | .0 | 100.4 | 70.0 | 50.0 | 30.0 |
| Students enrolled | 233 | 44.4 | 4.4 | 20.00 | 515 | 785 | 250 | 450 | 650 |
| Total annual library expenditure | 38,836 | 57.9 | 5.8 | 621.00 | 10,453 | 23,410 | 4,509 | 10,720 | 16,931 |
| Annual expenditure on material | 6,691 | 61.3 | 6.1 | 256.00 | 5,239 | 8,211 | 93 | 163 | 6,725 |
| Annual expenditure on personnel | 12,644 | 70.5 | 7.1 | 1,351.00 | 22,669 | 42,717 | 5,667 | 19,180 | 32,693 |
| Annual expenditure on "other" | 8,916 | 64.3 | 6.4 | 525.00 | 7,957 | 18,877 | 2,917 | 8,167 | 13,417 |
| Library volume holdings | 18,951 | 16.4 | 1.6 | 119.00 | 6,905 | 9,923 | 6,040 | 7,227 | 8,414 |
| Library periodical subscriptions | 232 | 3.0 | .3 | .20 | 43 | 93 | 64 | 66 | 68 |
| Library microform holdings | 142,374 | 19.9 | 2.0 | 1,368.00 | 0 | 168,674 | 55,120 | 68,800 | 82,480 |
| Library vertical file drawers | 14 | 16.9 | 1.7 | .13 | 6 | 12 | 6 | 8 | 9 |
| Library consortium memberships | 0 | 9.1 | .9 | .01 | 1 | 2 | 1 | 1 | 1 |

| | | | | | | | | |
|---|---|---|---|---|---|---|---|---|
| Library subject interests | 2 | .0 | .0 | .00 | 1 | 3 | 2 | 2 | 2 |
| Library special collections | 2 | −23.1 | −2.3 | −.03 | 0 | 2 | 2 | 1 | 1 |
| Library publications | 0 | .0 | .0 | .00 | 0 | 1 | 0 | 2 | 2 |
| Totals | 1,211,856 | 310 | 31 | 4,939 | 324,736 | 677,996 | 399,204 | 426,100 | 499,490 |
| Averages | 57,707 | 15 | 1 | 235 | 15,464 | 32,286 | 19,010 | 20,290 | 23,785 |

a Although the size of the matched pairs samples is even smaller than the samples represented in the previous table, the 1998 projections given in the above table probably exceed them in reliability as the matched pairs analysis is the record of how real-life libraries actually changed over a decade, whereas the whole popular library subsample included values for an unstable group of no longer listed libraries and an unpredicted (uncontrolled) group of newly listed institutions.

# 5

# POPULAR RELIGIOUS LIBRARIES: THE 1985–86 CHURCH AND SYNAGOGUE LIBRARY ASSOCIATION SURVEY

In the first major North American congregational library survey in 1975, Joyce White found at least three libraries that are so old as to have been started in the later nineteenth century.[1] After such an early start, perhaps it is not surprising that development of the North American popular religious library field was moving ahead rapidly by the late 1940s, or soon after World War II. The 1940s, the 1950s, and the 1960s saw a dramatic growth in the number and size of these libraries, which continues to this day but at a reduced rate in more recent years.

By 1960 the number of popular libraries had increased to the point that several major religious denominations had developed either a popular central North American or U.S. library office or a denominational library association dispensing advice and publications helpful to member libraries. Each national U.S. association had active local chapters and annual regional or national conferences. In Canada, also, were operating several small popular provincial religious library associations.

Just which of these offices and associations were active earliest is difficult to ascertain, but the Southern Baptist Convention headquarters service started in a small way in Nashville about 1934. By the year 1970, eighteen thousand Southern Baptist church libraries had registered with the Nashville office. The forerunner of the Association of Jewish Libraries started work in 1946, but the first national association serving synagogue libraries got going in 1962.[2] Probably the oldest of all the religious library associations, however, is the Catholic Library Association. It began in 1921 as a section of the National Catholic Educational Association and was established as an independent organization by 1931. The Parish/Community Libraries Section for congregational librarians started in 1957, the Association of Christian Librarians started work in 1956, and the Lutheran Church Library Association started soon after, in 1958.

By the mid-1960s, library associations could be identified in the United States and to a smaller extent in Canada for Catholic, Christian, Jewish, and Lutheran librarians, and modest national headquarters service existed for Baptist, Mormon, Presbyterian, Christian Science, and Episcopal/Anglican libraries. Not all major and almost no minor denominations were included among these religious groups, and even a brief study of the field revealed that all of the existing library groups were denominational in spite of the recent development toward a strong international ecumenical movement.

The author was working at Drexel University in Philadelphia in 1960 when he realized that (1) the popular religious library field was surprisingly large in terms of the number of libraries and people involved, (2) it was quite diverse in several regards, and (3) it was essentially unserved by the American Library Association-accredited schools of library and information science. After offering an elective synagogue librarianship course in 1961, Drexel soon began sponsoring a one-day church and synagogue library conference at which annual attendance soon exceeded two hundred persons.

Upon the success of these conferences and of popular Drexel religious library publications and other activities, the author then developed the idea of founding a national popular and ecumenical religious library association. So he began to collect a group that eventually became the Church and Synagogue Library Association (CSLA). A preliminary meeting to test the idea was held during the 1966 American Library Association Conference in New York, and a favorable reception there encouraged the author to proceed with the project.[3]

In the years after World War II, establishment of a specialized library association was part of a professional push to provide better service and to encourage increased respect for the popular religious library field in the eyes of leading congregational librarians. Popular religious library service displayed many of the aspects of a new field at that time, a new library service frontier (in 1966 half of the libraries in Hannaford's CSLA

1985–86 study did not yet exist), and its leaders, many of whom were capable professional librarians, were aware that they were pioneers in an exciting religious, library-oriented innovation. They were eager to see new activity centers develop and prosper.

The 1955–65 decade had seen several new popular religious library associations begin work, and CSLA was yet another and less narrowly restrictive organization. As the culmination of the author's efforts, CSLA had its inaugural board of directors meeting and luncheon at the Bellvue-Stratford Hotel in downtown Philadelphia in July 1967 with its newly elected officers, board, and committee chairpersons present. It was the last of the existing national popular North American religious library associations and advisory offices to be established, the end of the "boom" in the establishment of such groups in North America.

Soon after CSLA started work, certain of its members developed an interest in collecting survey information on congregational libraries. They felt that more information was needed on popular religious libraries before even the most experienced religious librarians could feel confident about making decisions and statements about the field. Joyce White's 1975 survey (see chap. 6) was the most notable result of this interest, but it was only seven years later that the author prepared a proposal for an annual CSLA data collection and analysis program that would regularly bring in information on the libraries from a substantial membership sample. However, the CSLA board of directors did not approve this proposed popular library project.

By 1986, almost two decades after its founding, CSLA was well established with a full-time secretariat and nearly nineteen hundred dues-paying members. The association was organized with the usual set of officers and an executive board. By this time, its annual budget totaled $65,000, and these funds were spent on its publication series, bimonthly bulletin, and headquarters staff personnel. Membership covered most of the fifty states and several Canadian provinces and was relatively heavy in such states as Pennsylvania, Ohio, Michigan, Illinois, and Texas. The denominations best represented were the Presbyterian, Methodist, and Episcopal/Anglican though many other major and minor religious groups were also included.

Certain large congregations with full-time paid librarians were represented in the membership as were a few small ones with no more than one hundred members. In general, the membership represented libraries that were average or above in size and service. Its twenty-nine regional chapters took CSLA activities into many areas of the country. Headquarters was in Bryn Mawr in suburban Philadelphia until 1987, when it moved to Portland, Oregon. The hard work and good judgment of its two successive executive directors, Dorothy Rodda and Lorraine Burson, was vital to its continuing existence and prosperity.

In 1985 the CSLA executive board wished to develop a continuing education program for members and asked Claudia Hannaford, a former association bulletin editor, later president, then an honorary life member, and now deceased, to head a committee to develop it. She appointed the committee and requested the author's participation. Hannaford believed that the committee needed to know the status and condition of association member libraries before it could meet its responsibilities properly, so she developed a questionnaire to be sent to the entire membership. The executive board agreed.

The questionnaire sought to discover essential information on member libraries in terms of collection size and character, staffing, financial support and sources, service and library use. It was duplicated and mailed from the Bryn Mawr office with replies to be sent to Hannaford's home address in Toledo. Returns were still being received more than four years later!

Regrettably, no arrangement was made to recontact the large proportion of libraries that did not reply to the initial mailing. Hannaford followed up on all cases for which there was some problem about the information returned: she sent out notes and postcards to at least fifty of the reporting librarians. For instance, church and synagogue budget figures were sometimes hard to obtain. With the survey information in hand, Ms. Hannaford prepared a series of tables and summaries that were distributed to CSLA officers and committee members and to all respondents. In addition, an early and brief summary was written for in house publication.[4] The original questionnaire reports were then mailed to the present author in Nicosia (Lefkosia), Cyprus, for detailed computer analysis and eventual preparation for the present chapter and book.

The 1986 CSLA survey (also called the Hannaford study) represented both a further attempt to push back the boundaries of ignorance about this little-known field and also an attempt to collect information which would be useful to the continuing education committee. To the extent that its 411 respondents were representative of the large CSLA group, they provided information that was useful for several purposes. Since the breadth of topics covered made it the most comprehensive of the questionnaires encountered in this book, a special effort was made to analyze as many component data factors as possible.

The author edited the questionnaires and then turned them over for keyboarding and analysis to Jo Ann Mouridou, formerly of the Southern Baptist Convention Foreign Missions Board Office for the Middle East and North Africa and later of the American Academy (originally Reformed Presbyterian), both in Nicosia. Results were presented in the form of both text and seven hundred tables. The tables were edited and the most useful ones were selected for publication in this chapter. A consistent limitation in the data analysis, however, was the small size of the useable database, only 411 cases. Thus many of the more complex and potentially interesting data breakdowns were of limited value because of the small number of cases in each one of the tabular data cells. This limitation occurred principally for state-by-state and interdenominational analysis, where the large numbers of states and denominations excessively subdivided the total sample size and effectively annihilated their usefulness. In order to overcome the problem, a system of regional classification and partial aggregation of the denominations into somewhat larger groups was devised.

Following the sections on geography and demography below, the data are presented in roughly the order in which the questions were listed on the CSLA questionnaire, which is reproduced in appendix E. Note that the denominational breakdown for this study included eleven denominational groups, not the fourteen used in the *American Library Directory* studies described in previous chapters. The Churches of Christ, Independent, and Mennonite groups were omitted from the separate CSLA analysis. A small number of Independents and Mennonites were present, however, in the Other Denominations group. The Other Denominations group was repeated here but included fewer denominations than it did in earlier chapters. However, it was developed in the same manner as for the previous Other Denominations group and included libraries from the numerically smaller denominations. In this case it was led in frequencies by the Mennonite, Reformed and Independent denominations.

To the extent possible, this discussion of results attempts to draw a detailed profile of a sample of CSLA membership libraries. Perhaps it should be pointed out that there was no deliberate overlap between the CSLA and the *ALD* databases, but several libraries were included in both sets, for example, the Temple Library in Cleveland. Note further that the CSLA database included only one type of popular religious library—congregational.

Of course, what the reader might like to know about these libraries and what could reasonably be asked on the CSLA questionnaire often differed. Therefore, as far as possible, after analysis of the questionnaire data had been completed, a major effort was made to investigate areas of interest through secondary, combined, or indirect data analysis. However, the status of data exploration, and hence the corresponding data exposition, are descriptive rather than purely analytic in nature, and necessarily so due both to sample characteristics and the current formative stage of our knowledge about popular religious libraries.

Comparisons are made in chapter 6 between this Hannaford study, the White study, and the two *American Library Directory* studies, where similar questions on popular religious libraries drew response data that was similar and in some cases comparable. This chapter's sections and subsections are the following:

I. Introduction
II. Introduction to congregational library statistical information
III. CSLA congregational library study—geography
    A. National and regional comparison
    B. State and provincial comparison
    C. City comparison
IV. The CSLA congregational library study—demography
    A. Library age
    B. Denomination
    C. Congregation membership size
    D. Other variables
    E. Summary of findings
V. The significance of this book's geographic and demographic findings
VI. Personnel
    A. Introduction
    B. Library committee members
    C. Job titles, experience, and chief librarian's gender
    D. Professional librarians and paid committee members
    E. Summary
VII. Library collection
    A. Introduction
    B. Book volumes
    C. Periodical titles
    D. Media
    E. Collection focus and distinctive material
    F. Summary
VIII. Finance
    A. Introduction
    B. Congregation income
    C. Library income

# Introduction to Congregational Library Statistical Information

The reader will notice that the CSLA chapter is organized in somewhat different fashion from that of the earlier book chapters. This chapter covers all aspects of the CSLA database and its first-level analysis. Its organization is based on the questionnaire used for the study and the lack of availability of information which could be used in the analysis. The reader will notice further that this chapter is divided into two parts: (1) an analysis of the CSLA findings and (2) a statement of the book's statistical findings, calculations, and significance for the entire popular library field.

We may begin this discussion with certain interesting gross statistical comparisons based on the data available elsewhere for Canada and the United States. In 1987 there were about 370,800 houses of worship in the United States and Canada, of which 346,000 (93 percent) were in the U.S.[5] A majority of all Canadian and U.S. citizens, adult and child, came within the definition of house of worship members, 62 percent in fact. Apparently, almost no other social and noncommercial institution was as pervasive in North America, certainly not the public and private schools—even when combined.

Most North American hamlets had one or more houses of worship. The number in a large city may have approached many hundreds of either formally or informally organized institutions representing many different denominations and faiths. The existence of so many houses of worship brought this level and kind of religious service within easy reach of the vast majority of the North American population. In Canada and the U.S. most of these houses of worship were Christian organizations, 96 percent, with Jewish organizations equaling 3 percent, and the remaining one percent being distributed among the many other religious faiths.

There were also about 106,000 U.S. public and private elementary, secondary, and tertiary level schools, colleges and universities of all kinds (no figures were available for Canadian schools), so obviously there were more than 3.25 times as many separate religious congregations as separate schools and colleges in the United States.[6] Since the Canadian ratio can be assumed to have been roughly equivalent to the U.S. ratio, these figures show the ubiquity of religious institutions in North America.

At least 3.3 times as many U.S. house of worship members existed as there were elementary, secondary, and tertiary level school students, 159,414,000 to 47,745,000.[7,8] The pervasiveness of religion is further demonstrated through these figures. By examining congregation membership and the number of congregations we can easily calculate the mean congregation size. This was approximately 461 members per house of worship, rather small, but see another section of this chapter for another mean congregation size figure.

It is likely, however, that the 461 membership figure is a closer estimate of the population mean than are any of the sample means, since it is unlikely that congregations with active libraries are typical congregations. The sample means found in this book are probably typical, too, but in the sense that they represent the mean congregation size for houses of worship with slightly more active than average libraries.

While a typical North American hamlet may have maintained one or more congregations, in probability it had no tax-supported public library or public school. The ratio of existing religious houses of worship to non-religious public libraries (only 16,700 of them) was about 22.2:1.0. So community penetration was higher for North American religious congregations than for tax-supported public libraries, at least as far as members go. In view of the ubiquitousness of these private institutions, the potential for carrying library service to the general public was greater for congregational than for public libraries, if eventually every congregation were to develop a library and to make it available for general public use.

A comparison of house of worship members with public library members would add interest to this section. However, while we have a figure for the former, 370,800 North American houses of worship, we have no accurate figure for the number of registered Canadian and U.S. public library members or borrowers. By broad estimate, however, we can guess that the 16,700 public libraries had about 50 million members in 1988, at the rate of 20 percent of the North American population being public library members and 80 percent remaining "unreached." The ratio of about 159,414,000 plus 20 percent for Canada equals 191,296,800 house of worship members to about 50 million public library registered members (the margin of error here must be high!) gives a final ratio of 3.8:1.0. Therefore, the congregational members would seem to greatly outnumber the public library members.

We may raise a new question here, What percentage of these North American churches and synagogues had congregational libraries? Again, the answer to that question can only be estimated, since figures in this study for the national number of popular religious libraries are only general estimations or extrapolations. However, in rough figures, if there were 346,000 congregations in the U.S. and there were estimated to be 29,080 popular religious (omitting parochial school) libraries (see table 5.1), then on the average there existed one congregational library for every 11.9 congregations, or, in other words, 8.4 percent of these congregations had libraries.

Perhaps it is surprising that so few congregations had libraries, but the mean congregation size suggests that many of them may have been too small to justify supporting what many may have regarded as an expensive and perhaps even (in some members' minds) superfluous religious education service. In any case, it is clear that though numerous, congregational libraries were far from penetrating North American communities with their service in the way that their parent congregations do.

The religious library world represents only a small part of the entire religious world, in numbers of people involved, for instance. By putting three sets of estimated figures together, we can approximate the North American religious world ratio of lay religious persons (house of worship members) to house of worship librarians and library assistants. This estimated ratio is about 159,414,000 persons (members) to 87,240 persons (librarians), or 1,827 house of worship members to one house of worship librarian, library assistant, or volunteer.[9–11]

Therefore, in principle, each one of the 87,240 congregational library staff members served 1,827 house of worship members spread over 11.9 congregations, on the average! This large ratio included many houses of worship that had no library staff members and where library service was a priority activity neither among house of worship members nor among their clergy. If there were 29,080 congregational religious (omitting parochial school) libraries, they can be estimated to have averaged three staff members per library, yielding the 87,240 figure (but see elsewhere in this chapter for another staff member figure).

Since house of worship members and their children and young adults participated in a part-time educational program, however, especially if they attended Sunday or synagogue school classes, then they needed library service just as academic and other school students did, at least on a basis of one morning per week for Christian students and several afternoons a week for Jewish students. No one would claim, of course, that these house of worship members needed as much library service as did college, university, and school students, but they required some service, perhaps roughly 10 to 20 percent as much for Christian and 25 to 35 percent as much for Jewish students. Calculating just how much service these congregation members needed would have been a complex and frustrating project even to produce a gross figure that would in turn have varied from denomination to denomination because of religious curriculum differences.

The ratio of 1,827 parishioners to 1 seems especially large when we realize that this congregational staff member usually filled only a part-time position and worked less than one-quarter time. It also seems large in comparison with the somewhat comparable ratio in certain North American universities, colleges, and schools. In a small sample of North American college and university campuses studied for comparison with congregational libraries, the ratio of full-time equivalent (FTE) students to FTE library staff members averaged 214 to 1.[12] The ratio of 1,827 congregation members to 214 higher education students, or 8.5:1.0, suggests that many house of worship members may have been receiving proportionately less service (at least in terms of the number of library staff members) than were most college and university students. They received only 11.7 percent as much service as that rendered for FTE higher education students per student in this small study.

In other words, proportionately, higher education students had access to more library staff members per person than did congregational members, and probably these staff members were both better educated and more professional as well. In addition, this curious ratio between higher educational and congregational library staff members becomes even greater when we remember that the higher education library staff member's work week was from four to twenty times longer than that of the house of worship library staff member.

## The CSLA Congregational Library Study—Geography

The 411 returned CSLA questionnaires represented a self-selected sample of 21 percent of the CSLA membership of about 1,990 libraries. No information is available to tell us the extent to which this group of libraries was representative of the entire membership or the dimensions along which it was or was not representative. Nor can we assess the representativeness of this database relative to the population of all U.S. and Canadian congregational libraries. The author assumes that the CSLA database was sufficiently representative of both larger groups to be helpful in deriving a partial understanding of each one of the others. And furthermore, the author assumes that this sample is interesting enough to justify an intensive questionnaire analysis.

From subjective examination of the data, however, the author estimates that congregational libraries which were larger in collection and staff size, better organized, better financed, and more active than the average were to some unknown extent overrepresented in this sample, but he has no proof with which to support this statement. Certain tables presented later, however, suggest the qualitative superiority of these sample cases, as we shall see.

Further, the author assumes that libraries joining any library association are often superior in certain ways on the average to those not joining. In addition, many social science surveyors would agree that those groups of personnel returning such questionnaires are likely to be somewhat more active than groups or persons who do not return them.

### National and Regional Comparison

A basic geographic questionnaire for congregational libraries can be seen in table 5.2.[13,14] By nation, clearly the United States dominated the table, 401, or almost 97.6 percent, of the libraries replying being American versus 10, or 2.4 percent, from Canada. This result can be compared with the national U.S.-Canadian population ratio of 9.4:1.0, or 90.4 percent American, a ratio of 40.7:1.0, not greatly different from the 1978 *ALD* national ratio. So, density of congregational libraries both without and within the sample was much higher for the U.S. than for Canada.[15] The Canadian comparison provides only a small international element in this analysis. We can now look at a series of CSLA library studies made on a regional basis. Table 5.3 provides a summary of the scores on six regional tables and should be studied carefully in order to facilitate understanding of regional differences. We will examine it in detail. By geographic region, table 5.4 shows the Middle West to have led in questionnaire return, with the Middle Atlantic area coming second.[16] When combined, these two regions produced more than half of the entire number of questionnaires. In contrast, when four other regions—the Northwest, West, the Rocky Mountains, and Canada—were combined, we see that they submitted only one-sixth of the questionnaires.

Table 5.4 shows the most popular denominations by region in much the same fashion that table 5.2 shows the most popular denominations by state and province. The totals show unequal distribution among both denominations and regions. Many of the most popular table 5.2 denominational designations are for the Methodist and Presbyterian denominations. Specific denominational concentrations can be seen in terms of the regional or even statewide focus of certain localized congregations in restricted localities, for example, the Congregational churches in the Northeast.

Table 5.5 shows the results of analyzing three variables by region. The oldest libraries were found in the Northeast and surprisingly in the West and Rocky Mountains areas, and the youngest were found in the Canadian and Southeast areas. The relatively new Canadian libraries were less than half as old as the Northwest libraries. In contrast, the analysis of years of librarian work experience by region showed that Middle Atlantic and Southeast librarians led and Canadian, Northeast, and Southwest librarians, all from regions of great occupational mobility trailed all the rest of the regions on this variable. However, the differences among the regions were small, the largest being only one-third again as large as the smallest.

We can describe the regions in detail as follows. The *Northeast* region was led by Connecticut with fourteen libraries, more than half of the total. Next came Massachusetts and finally Maine. In the *Middle Atlantic* we can see one major leader, Pennsylvania with thirty-seven libraries and three secondary leaders—Maryland with thirteen, Virginia with twelve, and New York with ten libraries. New Jersey, Washington, D.C. and Delaware followed with the last 19 percent of the region. The *Southeast* contained Florida and Georgia, constituting 61 percent of the region. Following are five states for the remaining 39 percent of the Southeast region.

The *Southwest* contained Texas (65 percent) and New Mexico (24 percent) plus four other states for a good-sized region. The *West* was dominated by California with Oregon and Washington completing only the final third of this small region. The *Rocky Mountains* region contained only a small number of states, with Colorado dominating the group. The *Middle West*, the largest region, contained eleven states, led by Ohio with one-third of the total. If we add Illinois, Indiana, Michigan, and Missouri, we have raised the Middle West number to four-fifths of the total. In *Canada* we had Ontario with 70 percent plus three provinces contributing the remainder of the total. The Middle West and Middle Atlantic regions contained more than half of the total both here and in the *ALD* popular library databases. Table 5.6 shows another list of leading denominations for the states and provinces. The table shows Methodist and Presbyterian to lead the other groups.

Regional congregational church and synagogue incomes are displayed in table 5.7. The small Rocky Mountains group showed the highest congregational income mean, $607,000, and the Middle Atlantic group had the smallest, $77,000. This table also shows library income by region. The West and Southwest led this column and the Northwest and Middle Atlantic brought up the rear. Table 5.7 shows a per congregation member income approach by region, also, yet another view of library income. The West was far ahead of the other regions on this measure with a $2.80 figure in contrast to the second ranking region, Canada, with a $2.10 figure. Lowest of the regions this time was the Rocky Mountains, 90 cents per member, earlier found to be the highest in gross congregational (not library) income.

Thus, we have discovered that a library's financial support is influenced by the region in which it is located, there being a 4.3:1.0 difference between support per member in the West and in the Middle Atlantic regions, for instance. We have discovered also that considerable variation existed in the status of the eight regions from variable to variable, for reasons which are often hard to explain.

Table 5.8 shows the denominational breakdown of the regions and the regional breakdown of the denominations. Certain denominations concentrated in a few regions. Christians were found mostly in the Middle West, Congregationalists primarily in the Northeast, Lutherans in the Middle West, Methodists in the Middle West, Other Denominations in the Middle Atlantic and Middle West, Presbyterians the same, and U.C.C. in the Middle West. Or we may look at it the other way round, the Northeast containing primarily the Congregational and Episcopal/Anglican denominations, the Middle Atlantic primarily the Methodists and Presbyterians, the Southeast primarily the Methodists and Presbyterians, as did the Southwest, and the West the Other Denominations and Presbyterians. These regional and denominational relationships were similar to those found for *ADL* popular libraries.

Table 5.9 shows us the mean income by region. Highest was the West with $4,556 per library and lowest was Northeast at $740 per library. Another table shows that annual circulation charges varied by region, with Northwest and Middle Atlantic ranking highest. Table 5.10 shows total expenditures by type and setting—rural, suburban, and urban. Urban led with 45 percent and rural was last with 18 percent of the total expenditures. Another regional table showed library age by region, table 5.11. The oldest means were those in the Northeast, West, and Rocky Mountains, and the youngest was that for the Canadian libraries. Table 5.12 showed congregation membership size by region. The largest membership mean was seen in the Southwest and the smallest was that in the Northeast.

Table 5.13 shows the mean book collection sizes by region. Clearly the Southwest and the West had the largest collection mean and the Northeast had the smallest. This finding continues the trend to find Northeast libraries often to be the smallest and weakest on average and to find Western libraries often to be the largest. Table 5.5 shows the concentration of newspaper and periodical titles by region. The Southwest and Middle Atlantic regions had the largest collections of titles on the average, while the Northeast and Canada tended toward the smallest collections. There was almost a 3:1 ratio between the largest and the smallest regions here.

Table 5.14 shows city population size by region for these congregational libraries. The Southwest showed the largest mean, at 311,865 persons, and the Northeast was smallest, with only 85,125 persons in the cities having congregational libraries. Monthly book circulation was examined by region in table 5.15 also. In part, it showed a familiar pattern. The region with the heaviest circulation was the West with Canada second, and the region with the smallest circulation was the Northeast with the Middle Atlantic next. Circulation in the West was 6.6 times as heavy per library as circulation in the Northeast.

Finally, the last column in table 5.3 shows a summary ranking for all regions and all ten columns in six tables. Ranking highest was the West with the Southwest second. Ranking lowest were the Northeast and Canada. Careful study of this series of tables will reveal regional strengths and weakness. The size differences between regions accounted for some of the other differences among them, but strong support in the West and Southwest should be noticed.

## State and Provincial Comparison

Of the fifty U.S. states and twelve Canadian provinces, the questionnaires were returned from thirty-eight states (73 percent) and four provinces (36 percent). Therefore, a fairly good American state but poorer Canadian provincial coverage was obtained. Concerning number of questionnaires returned, the states of Ohio, Texas, Pennsylvania, Michigan, and California led and together contained two-fifths of the entire sample. This pattern of leading states was predictable, since in general it followed CSLA membership distribution: more than one CSLA chapter existed in each one of these five states. Aside from containing large numbers of religious libraries, the five ranked among the largest North American states and provinces in total population.

Let us look at table 5.2 again in order to see the states and the leading denominations by region. Fragmentation is the theme of this table with few strong concentrations of denominations. But see the Other Denominations focus in Michigan and the Methodists in Indiana. Congregationals were heavy in Connecticut and Massachusetts, Lutherans in Iowa, Wisconsin, and Minnesota, Reformed in Michigan, United Church of Canada in Canada, and Mennonites in Kansas. On the other hand, Baptists, Methodists, Other Denominations, and Presbyterians were found in large numbers in many states and regions, and Christian and Episcopal/Anglican libraries were found in several regions.

Twenty-seven states and provinces (64 percent of the states and provinces) contributed only one questionnaire each or none to the database, thereby constituting less than 2 percent of the total 411 libraries. Among Canadian provinces, Ontario was clearly the leader, since it was the location of seven libraries. When the two national groups were combined, Ontario ranked among the eighteen most productive of the forty-two states and provinces returning congregational library questionnaires.

## City Comparison

Now let us turn to another geographic variable for the CSLA congregational libraries. What was the library distribution among city and rural locations? Certain popular religious librarians have said that the post-World War II rise in congregational librarianship occurred primarily on the outskirts of the large U.S. cities and in their suburban areas.[17] Only one-seventh of the libraries in this study's table 5.16 were located in small towns or rural areas, while the rest were located in cities (39 percent) or metropolitan (suburban) areas, 45 percent. These results were not surprising in view of the CSLA membership profile and the existing library population level. They suggest that we are dealing with a middle class and urbanized group of library committee (staff) members (volunteers). Our approach to CSLA city location is somewhat fuller than the approach used with *ALD* popular libraries, however.

Were any denominations strong in rural areas? Only the small Mennonite group (not shown separately) had a rural focus: somewhat over half of its libraries were located there. The small group of Reformed churches, on the other hand, was found primarily in cities in the state of Michigan, two-thirds being located there. Overall, the suburban was the most popular of the three possible locations. Baptists, in more than two-thirds of the cases, were located in suburban settings, and Roman Catholics almost as often, whereas only one in eight Christian churches were located there.

In a study of mean book volumes per library by region and setting, suburban libraries averaged somewhat more volumes than urban and four times more than rural libraries. See table 5.13 for this information. The largest libraries were found in the urban Southwest and the smallest in the rural Northeast. Southwest and Southeast libraries usually ranked high in population, also, and Canadian and Rocky Mountains libraries usually ranked low.

The specific city and town picture of these libraries represented a relatively large amount of dispersion. Half of the table 5.16 list might be considered to be southern U.S. cities and half northern. Ohio and Texas contained almost half of this total. Together the eleven leading cities provided one-sixth of the total number of libraries. Albuquerque and Kalamazoo led the list of cities that contributed the largest number of libraries.

All of these cities (except Findlay) ranked high in general population, with Houston being the largest among them. Albuquerque was the center of the active New Mexico CSLA chapter area, which may have accounted for its strong questionnaire return, at least in part. Kalamazoo's libraries were primarily from the Reformed Church denomination. These cities contrast with the list of the most popular libraries for the *ALD* popular libraries in being Middle Western instead of eastern and in being smaller cities than those leading in the *ALD*.

The large eastern U.S. and Canadian cities, such as Washington, D.C., Baltimore, Philadelphia, New York, Boston, and Montreal were traditionally thought to be the major centers of North American book collections and of the reading population. This study does not necessarily find that view to be accurate for the location of North American congregational libraries in the 1980s, however, at least not within the city limits of these cities. Southern, western, and middle western cities were more prominent than eastern cities on this list. Only Washington and Cleveland among the large eastern cities were found to contain large numbers of these libraries. Several of the leading congregational library centers were not only located in places like Texas and Ohio but were found in medium-sized cities, rather than large ones.

In another view of cities and denominations, table 5.17 shows the mean city population of the congregational libraries. To some extent it confirms certain findings mentioned above. In any case, the cities with Jewish libraries were over thirteen times the size of the cities in which Congregational churches were located and United Church of Christ library cities were five times larger than Congregational cities, on the average. Mean population level of 411 cities and towns was 152,805, the equivalent of a small city, and much smaller than the mean 1988 *ALD* library city of 356,600 people.

As a supplement to table 5.17, two additional analyses were made for city size. First was an analysis by congregation income. In general, larger city congregations had larger incomes and smaller city congregations had smaller incomes. Second, city size was analyzed by region in table 5.14. Southwestern region library cities were 3.7 times as large as northeastern cities, on the average.

Table 5.18 shows the correlation between congregation membership size and city population. The two variables showed a strong positive correlation in which the congregation membership size rose regularly as city population rose. See also table 5.19 for cities with more than one library, a list of major and minor city centers. See tables 5.20 and 5.21 for large and small city concentrations of CSLA libraries arranged by state. By state, are the library concentrations in large or in small cities? Note that Texas is heavy on large cities, while Pennsylvania concentrates on small cities.

Which denominations were located in the largest cities? See table 5.17. Both Jewish and Roman Catholic libraries were located in large cities and both originated in small library groups. Smallest cities were those in which the Congregational and Lutheran libraries were located. And finally, which denominations were located primarily in rural or else in suburban settings? Roman Catholic, Baptist, and Congregational were located primarily in suburban locations, while Jewish, Episcopal/Anglican and

Christian were strong in urban locations. Only 14 percent of the CSLA libraries were located in rural areas, and Other Denominations, Methodist, and United Church of Christ were the leading groups there (table 5.22).

Table 5.23 shows how congregation library income sources were divided by setting. Note that $1,999 of the total congregation incomes was the mean urban income figure, and $1,582 was the suburban mean income figure. Departures from these amounts were unusual, but rural values exceeded income expectations.

## The CSLA Congregational Library Study — Demography

This section will take up such topics as the congregational library age, denomination, congregational membership size, and other related variables. In moving to a different subject, the demography of congregational libraries, we may begin by asking, What were the characteristics of the congregational and library names? Certain congregations were named after saints, for example, St. Paul and St. Catherine. Roman Catholic, Episcopal/Anglican, Lutheran, and other denominations often used the names of saints for their congregations. Sixty-one congregations did so in this CSLA study, 15 percent.

In a few cases, the library itself was named for a living or recently deceased person. In several of these cases the word "memorial" was part of the name, such as the Northside United Methodist Church McDonald Memorial Library, Atlanta. Instead of using the word "library," a half dozen of the libraries followed a more recent trend and were named "media center" or "learning resources center."

### Library Age

Relatively few congregational libraries were founded before World War II. This study's typical library was two decades old and was founded as part of the postwar upsurge of the North American congregational library movement.[18] While a third of the present libraries were at least twenty-one years old and an eighth of them were thirty or more years old, two-sevenths of them were only a decade or less old. The oldest individual libraries were three dating from the nineteenth century, which are listed in table 5.24. Michigan and Ohio produced almost half of this short list of old congregational libraries, and more than half of them were Methodist, Congregational, or Reformed.

By denomination, table 5.25 shows that the oldest libraries were Jewish and Congregational and the youngest were Roman Catholic. For the Jewish libraries, clearly half were founded before or during World War II and half after the war due to the resurgence of Hebrew school education after the war. The synagogue libraries were significantly older than the church libraries in this study. Just why the Roman Catholic libraries should have been by far the youngest is unclear, since the Catholic parish library movement began about the same time as the Protestant congregational library movement.[19] Is it possibly because the older Roman Catholic libraries would hardly join an ecumenical CSLA?

Several analyses were made for this chapter of the largest libraries for a specific variables. One of them was an analysis of the twenty-seven oldest libraries in the study. In what ways were these libraries distinctive? Aside from averaging sixty-one years of operation, their congregation memberships were twice as large as the overall average, mean library income was three times as large, and media title holdings size more than twice as large. We can conclude that the oldest libraries were also among the larger on all of the factors tested, but that they were only somewhat larger than the average in the per member analyses. This would occur naturally as large congregations with large incomes would not necessarily spend more per member on the congregation library.

## Denomination

One of the most fundamental characteristics of any congregational library is its denominational affiliation.[20] This section acknowledges that variable by analyzing the relevant data. The denominational composition of the CSLA libraries is shown in table 5.26. Presbyterian and Methodist led in number of libraries and constituted two-fifths of the entire sample. If Episcopal/Anglican and Lutheran libraries, and also mainstream denominations, are added, the four groups accounted for three-fifths of the sample. These four established denominations made up a consistent two-thirds of the 1988 U.S. National Council of (Protestant) Churches memberships.[21]

The reader will note the splintering of the religious world by the many denominations represented with small frequencies in the sample. The Other Denominations group, which collects diverse units and small clusters from many of the minor Protestant denominations, was led by the

Mennonite, Reformed, Independent, Pentecostal, and Churches of God subgroups, which constituted somewhat over half of its total number (in similar fashion to the Other Denominations group from the *American Library Directory* analyses).

Not only is the sample fragmented, but it is also, in certain ways, poorly representative of the congregational library universe. Jews and Roman Catholics, two large and popular national congregational library groups, were weakly represented in this database, nor were the Church of Jesus Christ of Latter-day Saints (LDS) (Mormons) or the Christian Scientists represented at all, even though they maintained large numbers of congregational libraries. Probably Baptists and Lutherans, large library groups, were somewhat underrepresented here also.[22] Probably only the Jewish group, however, suffered statistically due to small sample size (six libraries only).

The table 5.26 pattern, however, is a reasonably accurate reflection of the CSLA membership picture. CSLA has always been largely Christian and Protestant; this sample is 98.5 percent Christian and 95.6 percent Protestant. Presumably many Jewish and Roman Catholic librarians preferred to participate primarily in the associations focused exclusively on their own faiths, the AJL and the Cath LA, and so did not join CSLA in any numbers.

While modest, the Lutheran and Baptist showings were acceptable in the CSLA sample (10 percent and 6 percent, respectively, of the returns) in view of the competitive but friendly activity of the LCLA and the Southern Baptist Convention. We can say the same thing for the Christian libraries (5 percent) in view of their relationship to the ACL. For Presbyterian, Methodist, Episcopal/Anglican, Congregational, and United Church of Christ libraries as well as for all of the Other Denominations groups, no denominational association vied with CSLA for their attention, so that factor cannot be used to explain any shortage or shortfall of representation.

How were the denominations distributed by region? Table 5.4 accents regional concentrations. The Middle West dominated the regional picture for most denominations, but certain groups departed from this pattern. Episcopal/Anglican libraries were found more often in four other regions, while Baptist libraries were found slightly more often in the Middle Atlantic region. Congregational libraries were more often located in the Northeast and Roman Catholic in the Southwest. The extensiveness of Presbyterian and Methodist coverage was noteworthy. While Christian, United Church of Christ (or at least the Churches of Christ portion of it) and Lutheran libraries were concentrated heavily within a single region, Baptist, Episcopal/Anglican, and Presbyterian libraries were not.

In the final paragraph of this section we can look at a set of three tables — 5.27, 5.28, and 5.29, which compare denominational expenditures by type of expenditure and by setting — urban, suburban, and rural. In general, urban libraries spent more money on salaries than did rural libraries. Other comparisons can be made between and among the various groups in these tables.

## Congregation Membership Size

Let us study congregation membership size now. Are we dealing with large or small congregations? Table 5.30 shows a mean CSLA house of worship membership of 1,379 persons, which suggests again that we are dealing with a group of congregations that is larger (3.0:1.0) and therefore more prosperous than the national average of 461 members per congregation described in a previous section. This table shows the relative membership size focus of each denomination: were most of these congregations large or small for each denomination? The table shows that two-thirds of the United Church of Christ congregations fell into the medium-sized or small membership category, for instance.

Mennonite congregations (not shown separately in table 5.30) were even more concentrated within small groups, and Other Denominations and Congregational congregations were small also. In contrast, both the Jewish and Roman Catholic congregations were weighted heavily on the side of large congregation memberships and were much larger than the average Protestant denomination congregation membership. The Roman Catholic and Jewish membership sizes were ten times larger than the 632 members per house of worship of the United Church of Christ; and the Baptist, Lutheran, and Methodist churches, which led the Protestants in membership size, were more than double that small size. Table 5.18 shows that mean congregation size increased as city population size increased. This suggests that most of the larger congregations were located in larger cities and the smaller ones were located in smaller cities. Neat, if always true.

In all, fifty-nine (14.4 percent) house of worship congregations had two thousand or more members. Five congregations were tied for the lead in membership size with fifteen thousand members apiece, in table 5.31 listing large institutions. Five of the table's fourteen large churches and synagogues were in the large state of Texas, and five Roman Catholic congregations appeared on the list. Most of the congregations were located in metropolitan areas, providing a large population base from which to draw. We will see several of these congregational names again when we list those congregations with the largest collections and income. In a separate analysis with this data, the author discovered that larger tended to be somewhat older, up to a certain point, than smaller congregations, the apparent inverse of an earlier finding.

## Other Variables

Several other variables could have been included in this demographic presentation for congregational libraries, but instead, their discussion was located in other sections of this chapter in order to place them with discussions of closely related variables. They include discussions of library personnel, the chief librarian gender ratio, and library finance. In addition, in most demographic discussions in other fields the topics of births, deaths, and migrations, are given some space. See the chapter 2 discussion for *ALD* popular libraries, for example. However, in this non-longitudinal database we have no evidence to present on these topics. Surely certain libraries were born while others died and still others moved, but we have no evidence of this in the CSLA database and little enough evidence of it in the *American Library Directory* (*ALD*) databases.

North American church and synagogue migration has been mostly from inner city core areas to the city's outskirts, or to suburban locations, and certainly some of this migration occurred between 1978 and 1988. However, migration was noted in only a few instances in the CSLA database, and in these few instances which we could identify, the move was one of some distance, from one city to another.

## Summary of Findings

We should summarize the information learned in this section on popular library geography and demography. After an introductory discussion, the chapter moved on to bring out the extensiveness of religious congregations and their congregational members in North America. The study found on average that the ratio of congregation library staff members to congregation membership could be estimated as 1,827 to 1. This was a much less favorable ratio than that found to exist between the academic library staff members and students in any one U.S. state.

In the Hannaford (CSLA) study, 21 percent of CSLA's 1986 members returned questionnaires in useable form, a good return for this group. The majority of the congregational libraries were American, and California, Michigan, Ohio, Pennsylvania, and Texas led the states and provinces in responses. Among the regions, the Middle West and the Middle Atlantic were the two largest, and most libraries were located in metropolitan rather than rural areas. Albuquerque and Kalamazoo led the individual cities in returns.

Congregations often used the names of saints and libraries often used the word "memorial" in their names. The typical CSLA library was twenty years old, with Jewish typically being forty-two and Roman Catholic libraries only twelve years old. Presbyterians and Methodists led the denominations in responses, and five specific house of worship congregations were largest with fifteen thousand members apiece. Jewish, Roman Catholic, and Baptist churches and synagogues tended to be large and urban or suburban, while Mennonite and United Church of Christ churches were generally small and Mennonite were rural. There was a positive correlation between congregation size, city size, and library age. Naturally, some cities and their congregations have grown up together.

## The Significance of This Book's Geographic and Demographic Findings

The section will discuss (1) the frequencies of North American libraries, (2) their division between religious and nonreligious, and as a result of (1) and (2), we have (3) the numerical importance of religious libraries and (4) its consequences. In this discussion the figures come from a variety of sources: (1) the 1988 *ALD*; (2) the intrapolations and extrapolations from earlier congregational library surveys and studies; (3) the U.S. National Center for Education Statistics, and (4) Church of Christ, Scientist and Church of Jesus Christ of Latter-day Saints headquarters offices.[23–25]

The statistical definitions employed are (1) those used by *ALD*, which are explained in the preface of each edition of that reference source, and (2) definitions proposed by this author for common use when referring to both popular and scholarly religious libraries but have not yet been subjected to extensive discussion or have not obtained full agreement. The latter definitions are discussed in the text, appendix B, and in certain of the author's previous publications. For the most part, the religiously affiliated or sponsored libraries can be classified as "religious," through formal and official or else informal connections of various degrees and kinds of past and present identification closeness with a large variety of church and synagogue groups. This criterion is both practical and easy to apply.[26]

*American Library Directory* data represented a count of questionnaires returned along with the data they contained. Presumably certain libraries existed for which no questionnaire was sent or received, usually small ones, though this situation may be changing. In certain cases, the Canadian figures were based on an estimate. Canadian libraries were estimated to be about 12 percent as frequent as occurred in the United States since the *ALD* national total numbers of libraries and the frequencies in the present study represented approximately 0.084:1.000 ratios between the two countries (11.9 percent), and furthermore, no other Canadian figures were available.[23]

While basing estimates on a general 12 percent ratio is acceptable in many situations, hopefully including this one, certainly in many other situations this method of arriving at a Canadian figure is inadequate. In spite of the weakness of given estimates, perhaps the reader will forgive the author for proceeding without further discussion, since he is not aware that any more accurate figures are either available or feasible to obtain at the present time.[27]

Totals for all types of popular libraries are given in table 5.1. The assumptions on which the table 5.1 figures are presented include the following: that (1) the *ALD* figures are acceptable and substantially accurate, in spite of a few obvious omissions, errors, and duplications; (2) the author's extrapolations and estimates are a provisional but acceptable way of arriving at an approximation of popular religious library totals; (3) the Christian Science and LDS headquarters library estimates are substantially accurate, and (4) the author's estimate of the number of school libraries is reasonably accurate.[28] All comprehensive religious library figures have been separated from nonreligious library figures. Incidentally, these calculations grew out of the author's attempt to estimate the total number of North American congregational libraries several years ago.

Certain generalizations about these table 5.1 North American library figures seem to be fairly obvious:

1. The grand total number of Canadian and United States popular (congregational, school, and public) libraries was estimated to be 141,080 of which 42,980 or about *30.5 percent* were religiously connected or sponsored, closely or distantly. Perhaps it should be noted that a substantial portion of the

house of worship libraries, 67 percent to 85 percent as a range estimate, are not listed in any national or North American library directory. Probably in most cases they are not listed in any library directory of any kind, old or new. Such is the current status of North American religious library demography!

2. The ratio of popular to scholarly religious libraries was 41,280 to 2,180, or almost exactly 19:1, 95 percent popular.[10,25] See table 5.32 for the world figures of popular libraries. Based on intrapolations there were at least 25,300 congregational libraries in the U.S. and 500 in Canada. Perhaps as many as sixty thousand popular religious libraries existed in the U.S. and one thousand in Canada; various estimates exist but the true values are unknown.[10]

   Perhaps it should be noted that the calculation on which the 25,300 congregational library figure is based was made before the author had widened his popular library definition to include Christian Science reading rooms and before he possessed any figures for the approximately thirty-two hundred popular LDS libraries. The extrapolation in question was explained in one of his previous books, but briefly, it was based on exact counts of house of worship and a very few religious public libraries in the states of Maryland and New Mexico and from which a national U.S. figure was projected.[10,29]

3. The ratio of public and private nonreligious school libraries to private religious and parochial school libraries was about 6.7 to 181,400 to 12,200 libraries, 87 percent nonreligious.[28,30]

4. The ratio of nonreligious to religious public libraries (including branches and those of Roman Catholic and other denominations plus Christian Science reading rooms) was about 16,700 to 1,630, 10.2:1.0, or 91.1 percent nonreligious.

5. The ratio of nonreligious to religious special libraries (including religious organization administrative office, convent, monastery, religious history, and archive libraries) was 11,950 to 400, a ratio of 30:1, or 97 percent nonreligious.

In view of the figures in table 5.1, we can make the following points with some confidence concerning certain aspects of this study's significance for North American religious libraries:

1. With more than a fourth of all North American libraries having religious connections, obviously this group formed a significant

portion of the whole. Few other distinctive library groups were as large.

2. It is clear that there were more religiously connected or sponsored libraries than all of the public, academic, and special nonreligious libraries combined. Perhaps we should point out further that there were more *popular* religiously connected or sponsored libraries than all of the public, academic and special nonreligious libraries combined.

3. While popular religious libraries were vastly larger in total number, of course the material collection, expenditures and personnel size of most individual popular religious libraries were much smaller than those of most nonreligious public, academic, and special libraries, and also of most other scholarly religious libraries, as earlier chapters show.

4. The total number of persons working full-time or part-time, paid or volunteer, in North American religious scholarly and popular libraries can be estimated as being about 136,920.[31] Based on 1987 population figures, this means that 1 of every 1,972 Canadian and U.S. citizens worked in a religious library!

5. In spite of the numbers shown above, the religious library field is little known and seldom studied by American and Canadian library and information field students.[32] It deserves more respect and attention from the library and information service world than it has received in the past. The religious library field has its own distinctive organization and service patterns and subpatterns, which should be identified, described, and studied. At the least, it is an intriguing field and deserves further investigation.

6. This study describes and analyzes an extensive list of factors in order to fill certain information gaps in the geography, demography, personnel, finance, collection, service, accreditation, age, management, and other aspects of religious libraries.

7. This book should enable students of the religious library subfields both to understand them better and to evaluate their importance in the larger information world.

8. In analyzing about thirteen hundred popular libraries, apparently this book constitutes one of only a few systematic analyses of significant groups of popular religious libraries.

9. In (1) analyzing 1,329 popular religious libraries in two segments a decade apart in the *ALD*, (2) analyzing the CSLA membership survey of 411 libraries and (3) reanalyzing 1,822 White

survey libraries, this book constitutes only the second systematic analysis of a significant group of general popular religious libraries.[33]

10. The study provides an introductory guide to the significant literature of the popular religious library field, its acronyms and vocabulary, attempts to stimulate thinking thereon and to suggest subject areas for further study.

# Personnel

## Introduction

One of the most interesting aspects of congregational librarianship is its personnel. It is unfortunate that we know so little about the persons who work in these libraries, that there was no space on the CSLA questionnaire for more questions about them. Congregational librarians differed from the personnel of other library fields because (1) most of them were volunteers, (2) only a modest percentage of them had any library education and many lacked a college educational, as we have mentioned above, and (3) most of them belonged to the religious denomination of the library in which they were working.

While congregational libraries share many personnel opportunities and problems with other kinds of libraries, for the most part they have few (1) salary, wage, and social benefit problems, few (2) previous work experience problems, and few (3) educational requirements for potential employees, since most of the employees are volunteers without previous library experience. Personnel standards do not yet exist for most of them, but such standards need to be developed in the next few years. Many congregational libraries have the problem that several people must carry out any particular task, such as charging out books or making book displays, since they must often work at different times of the day or week, and this may create confusion. They may also suffer from too frequent staff turnover and the consequent reduction in committee effectiveness.

In most congregations, the library work is carried out by an institutionally appointed committee. Library committee members need certain personality and occupational characteristics, most of them similar to those of the more traditional librarians, for example, the quiet type of temperament suited to library work and the maturity needed to take responsibility for carrying out specific library routines. They should maintain a high level of interest in their tasks, have an interest in religious library material, have at least a secondary school diploma, preferably a college degree, and if possible a library and information science degree, be neat in their work habits, be well organized, be effective computer operators, preferably belong to the library's religious denomination or sect (clear-cut religious discrimination!), and be willing to contribute their labors for several years.

The library must depend on the strength of the potential staff member's religious and cultural interests to provide good service. New committee members must be recruited from the congregational membership and be available for part-time, usually unpaid work. In some cases, the pool of candidates possessing all of these various characteristics is a small one indeed!

## Library Committee Members

The author had several questions about the library committee and its members. As a start, we need to know the size of the committee and the number of service hours provided. Size information is shown in table 5.33. The typical, relatively small committee had six members, and this size limited the work which could be accomplished. Roman Catholic and Baptist committees were largest and United Church of Christ committees smallest, half as large. In addition, the data showed that twenty committees (5 percent) from a variety of denominations had fifteen or more members. Denomination, then, was a strong influence on library committee size.

Another influence on committee size was congregation size. Table 5.34 shows that committee size rose consistently with congregation size. Probably congregation size and denomination were primary determinants of committee size. Table 5.35 shows the largest committee to have had fifty-two volunteer members at the All Saints Catholic Parish in Dallas. Half of the largest committees were Presbyterian or Baptist and were located in Pennsylvania or Minnesota. In other cases, however, the committees consisted of only one person who did everything. Obviously, the large committee could carry out more projects, provide more opportunities to substitute for an absent member, and be more likely to include a professional or at least an experienced library assistant to guide library development. We can suggest to the field that each committee should have at least ten members in order to get all its work done properly.

Parenthetically we may note the comparison between the three library committee members estimated in chapter 1 to be the national average and the six found in this chapter to be the average for the CSLA sample. The two figures arose from possibly different sampling populations, so their divergence is not surprising. The larger CSLA figure is to be expected, since the present sample is an atypically prosperous one. These CSLA members were involved and interested enough to answer questionnaires, and this suggests that they had enough worker hours to do it. So this sample is probably skewed in the direction of larger committees.

An additional study was made of the number of committee members. How were the libraries with the largest committees or staffs distinctive? First, in the largest group the mean committee size was 20.8 members, large. On every variable checked—congregation size, library age, income size, income size per member, number of media titles, media titles per member, circulation size, and circulation per member—this group was significantly higher than the sample mean. Apparently, if the library group was significantly larger than the overall mean on one variable, then it was larger than the overall mean on all other variables checked.

We need to know the average number of hours worked per week by the typical committee member. Apparently, this member worked about 2.0 hours per week, again a modicum. However, table 5.36 shows that Other Denominations and Roman Catholic committee members worked more hours than that. Therefore, they were presumably able to accomplish more than the committee members of the Christian and Lutheran denominations who averaged less than one hour per week. Again the author would like to suggest to the field an upgrading of the weekly hours worked, perhaps to four or five hours per week per committee member, if possible, in order to accomplish more within the aims of the library. The reader should note that the findings of this table were based on a much less than normal response rate, since no response to this question was obtained from 46 percent of the libraries.

The next logical question was how many committee hours in total were available for work per week. Eight hours per week was the committee mean, equaling at least 20 percent of one full-time staff member, according to table 5.37, again small. The committee hours per week values for the Roman Catholic and Baptist groups were high and represented in total the full-time equivalent of a half- or three-quarters-time staff member. At the opposite extreme, Christian church committees with only four hours of work per week could accomplish less; significantly, most of their libraries were small.

Just what this finding meant in terms of applied work schedules is not clear, since we do not know the frequency of various work schedule patterns. Presumably most committees were able to carry out both technical and reader services at any time that a committee member worked in the library. Probably every library was open for one or more hours per week on each Sunday morning or else on the congregation's religious service day. Usually this was its primary readers' service day when certain libraries were quite busy with users who needed reference, circulation, and browsing service.

In most cases, the library was open for use about eight hours per week, more than for just a religious service morning to use. We assume that most libraries were open for one or more additional days during which the six (on the average) committee members were carrying out technical service for library material as well as serving an occasional user. Certain of these committee hours may have been worked as a group on one day per week in order to allow one staff member to teach others, or, the hours and staff members may have been spread over several weekdays. Notice, in table 5.37, incidentally, that the Jewish-Roman Catholic combination worked 11 percent more hours per week than did all Protestant groups combined.

A qualification must be made of table 5.37 findings. They were based on an even smaller number of cases than were those of most other tables. Forty-seven percent of the libraries made no reply to this question. Therefore, the findings on staffing hours were less reliable than those for most other subjects and also were less satisfactory in that they left several questions unanswered. Table 5.38 shows committee size in terms of the total number of staffed hours per week by specific library. Two strong congregational libraries led the table—the First Baptist Church, La Crescenta, California, and The Temple, Cleveland. Baptist and Jewish congregations made up more than half of the total at forty hours and above, and half of these large libraries were located in either California or Texas.

Table 5.39 shows the number of congregation members existing per library committee member for specific libraries. Obviously, the smaller the number of congregation members which each library staff member must serve, the better the service which can be provided. In other words, the higher the user-librarian ratio, the more difficult the librarian's job becomes. Table 5.39 is heavily Mennonite with Reformed and Presbyterian churches being well represented also. Ohio, Oregon, Michigan and Missouri have two libraries each in this table. Two libraries led table 5.39, the First Christian Church in San Lorenzo, California, and Trinity Lutheran Church in Canton.

Service can also be examined in terms of the number of hours or minutes the library is open per congregation member. Obviously, the larger the number of minutes open the better the service which is offered. Trinity Bible Church in Los Alamos was far ahead of any other library here, since it was open at the rate of eighteen minutes per week for each congregation member. Table 5.40 shows this picture.

## Job Titles, Experience, and Chief Librarian's Gender

What were the job titles of these library assistants? According to table 5.41 more than three-fifths of these libraries called the head of the committee (and perhaps each committee member also) the "librarian." No other title was nearly as popular. "Chairperson" was the second title in frequency of use and was used by 10 percent of the congregational libraries. The designation "church librarian" was used by 10 percent of the Episcopal/Anglican libraries. Presumably, for 9 percent of the libraries no response meant that no title at all was used!

Were these experienced or inexperienced librarians? The number of years of congregational library experience per librarian turned out to be a large value, a mean of ten years with a range from zero to forty years. This means that, on the average, the present librarian had worked in the library for half of its lifetime. Table 5.42 shows that while the librarian's years of experience may have averaged ten years, there was some variation by denomination. Baptist and Lutheran librarians reported the most experience and United Church of Christ and Congregational librarians the least, little more than half as much as Baptist librarians.

In further study of the librarian's experience, the author found that committee size rose with the librarian's years of congregational library experience. This finding may suggest that the librarian's recruiting of committee members was more successful after some years of experience than when new at the job. Table 5.43 shows that three persons with forty years of experience apiece headed the "most years of experience" list, which also shows great variety by geographic location if not by denomination: Elinor Burnham, Edmond Headler (the only male on this list), and Agnes Harnett. More than half of the fifteen librarians belonged to the Baptist, Lutheran, or Methodist denominations.

What about gender? The vast majority of CSLA questionnaire respondents were female.[34] However, in the Christian, Congregational, and Episcopal/Anglican denominations the incidence of male library committee members was somewhat higher than the average, as table 5.44 shows. We can analyze this situation by region and denomination. Table 5.45 shows the West to have the largest percentage of men and the Rocky Mountains region to have the largest percentage of women chief librarians. Table 5.46 shows the largest percentage of men to be found in the Christian denomination, while the largest percentage of women was found in the Jewish and Roman Catholic groups.

Further analysis in another direction revealed that in all but a few cases, the questionnaire listed the library head by name, since this was the person who filled it out. The number of these librarians who belonged to a religious order of nuns or priests was zero. The number who were ministers or directors of religious education was very small, perhaps one percent of the total.

## Professional Librarians and Paid Committee Members

How many libraries had a professional librarian on the committee? The author does not wish to imply that having a professional librarian on the committee solves all problems, since many nonprofessionals have become quite skillful religious library staff members. However, the formal education and experience of the typical professional can be assumed normally to add some useful capabilities to those of most congregational library committees.

Table 5.47 reveals that professionals were surprisingly common in this sample. Many libraries had no professionals, but at the other extreme almost a fifth of these CSLA libraries reported three or more of them! Even the smaller denominations in the Other Denominations group had a ratio of one professional for every other library, while the Roman Catholic and Presbyterian groups averaged more than one professional per library, a significant accomplishment. A dozen Methodist libraries (15 percent) and twenty-three Presbyterian libraries (24 percent) had two or more professionals. While Jewish libraries averaged 1.5 professionals per library, their total of six libraries was too small to be considered statistically reliable.

From table 5.47 we can estimate that there was a total of 343 professionals working in the 411 libraries in this database. Thus, many libraries were receiving professional guidance and service, which should have influenced their performance positively. By subtracting the number of professionals (table 5.47) from the total number of committee members (table

5.33), the reader can obtain the number of nonprofessionals on each committee. By region, table 5.48 shows the largest number of professionals to have been located in the Southeast and Southwest regions. Table 5.49 shows the same thing for the entire committee, except that the two regions with the best mean figures were the West and again the Southwest.

This finding for professional staff members may also suggest that the sample was biased toward better staffed libraries.[35] The libraries listed in tables 5.50 and 4.54 had the largest number of professional staff members, strongly led by the Sinai Temple in Los Angeles, which could have staffed a large public library with its twenty professionals. Half of the librarians on table 5.50 were Methodist or Presbyterian.

No information was provided on the full versus part-time status of the librarians, but the author assumes that the majority of them worked only part-time and were probably paid at modest rates or were unpaid. In table 5.51 we see that almost one-third of the Jewish staff members were professional, from only six libraries, however, whereas only 11 percent were professional in four other denominations. We can see evidence here that congregational libraries have been evolving to become more like school and special libraries in that large numbers of them now have professional librarians working on the staff. If the author were to suggest a standard for this ratio, it would be just what the Jewish group nearly attained, one-third of all staff members should be professional.

Were any of these committee members paid? Though the data were often unclear on this point and the questionnaire asked no direct questions about it, table 5.52 shows the libraries that apparently had one or more paid staff members. In certain cases, the paid person(s) was a committee member, in others was the committee head, and in still others was not a professional but was a part-time paid clerical assistant rather than a regular committee member.

Just how much these staff members were paid was unclear or indeterminate, but when identifiable it seemed usually to be an amount well below the salary level for a comparable library position outside religious librarianship. Similarly, just what they were paid to do was seldom revealed, but in certain cases the paid staff members did much of the library's work, in other cases they provided professional service, and in still others they provided skilled clerical service. Synagogue, Methodist, and Presbyterian libraries were well represented on this list. Five Texas and three California libraries led the states and provinces in values. The reader may wish to see how many of these twenty-four libraries were covered in the ALD study.

## Summary

We may summarize the picture for congregational library personnel that was revealed in the CSLA database as follows. Typically, the library assistant served on a committee of six members, all volunteers, who worked eight hours a week altogether; typically had the job title of librarian, was female, had ten years of congregational library experience, was named on the questionnaire, and was not a minister, priest, or rabbi. This committee member worked an average of two hours per week. In addition, typical committee members were neither professionals nor paid workers, but a surprisingly large minority of them were either one or the other, or both.

# The Library Collection

## Introduction

Congregational library collections of books, newspapers, periodicals, and media were quite small when compared with those of other kinds of religious libraries. That was their first and foremost characteristic. Certain house of worship collections were large enough to fill only one or two shelving sections (75–200 volumes), but others could have filled one hundred or more sections (up to ten thousand volumes). The media collections were the most distinctive and occasionally the largest of the four types of library material collections.

While much of the house of worship collection was often aimed at children and youth, this emphasis varied greatly. Most of the collection content was religious, but this proportion varied, too. Often part of the content was denominational, purchased from denominational publishers, such as the Fortress Press (Lutheran) in Philadelphia. In certain denominations, such as the Baptist, many new or recent library publications were integrated with and supported the church school curriculum directly and so were clearly desirable purchases.

## Book Volumes

In carrying the significant ideas of the institution's faith as well as those of related groups, the library's book collection became the chief medium for communication with its clientele—the house of worship congregation. What should we attempt to learn about it in this statistical analysis? We need information about the book collection's size, subject coverage, and emphasis, and about the congregations that had the largest collections. Close study of the questionnaire replies will give us at least partial answers to these and other questions. While we might like to know the answers to many other questions, also, limitations within the data preclude many possibilities.

House of worship book collections are shown in table 5.53. They ranged in size from a few hundred to ten thousand volumes. As a matter of fact, probably a few were well above ten thousand volumes. The mean was 2,824 volumes (with a median of 2,712 volumes), a relatively large congregational library collection. The total cumulated number of volumes in all 411 CSLA libraries was about 1,149,400 volumes. At this rate, incidentally, the entire CSLA membership of about 1,950 or so libraries must have possessed about 5,506,800 volumes!

And by denomination? The denominations with the largest numbers of volumes were the Jewish (but for only a small sample) and Baptist. The per synagogue figure of 7,750 volumes was particularly large, and intriguing, almost twice as large as that for any other denomination. The Baptist group was well ahead of other Protestant denominations. Table 5.54 shows book holdings by denomination, also, but in a somewhat different format. It shows Jewish, Baptist, and Roman Catholic to lead the table while U.C.C. was last.

Table 5.55 shows volume holdings per congregation member by denomination. Other Denominations and Christian libraries led the table, while Roman Catholic libraries were at the bottom of the list, laid low by the per member analysis as a direct result of their large congregation sizes. The largest individual book collections are shown in table 5.56. All checked the highest category of volumes and so are listed at the twelve-thousand-plus level. Texas, California, and Georgia led this list, and Presbyterian and Jewish libraries represented half of the total. In a special substudy, the mean number of volume holdings was found to rise as the congregation size rose.

Three additional analyses were made of volume holdings by denomination, in each case with one or two additional variables being studied. What effect did years of library operation have on number of volumes per congregation member? Table 5.57 shows this picture. As age increased, so did number of volumes held. This shows that the older libraries had well used the additional time to increase in volume and holdings size. Other Denominations, Christian, and Baptist libraries led, while Roman

Catholic and Jewish libraries brought up the rear this time. In another analysis of the number of volumes per congregation member by years of operation, we see that all means rose in parallel. This suggests that the growth cycle for all libraries tends to be similar.

In another analysis, number of volumes was analyzed per library staff member. As the number of staff members rose in table 5.58, the number of volumes per library also rose. Those libraries with four or more staff members had more than twice as many volumes as those libraries with up to two staff members. Just why this should have been true was not entirely clear, but perhaps the richer libraries in volumes had also the larger incomes and the larger numbers of years of operation as well as the larger number of staff members. Baptists and Jewish (still with only six libraries) led this table, while United Church of Christ and Congregational churches were at the bottom. Also for volumes per staff member, table 5.59 shows volume holdings to rise regularly as the numbers of library staff members increased.

The number of books held per congregation member is a valid means of evaluating library service. The larger the collection of suitable books per member, the better. Table 5.60 shows eight libraries to be tied for the lead in size of book collection per congregation member. Three of them were in Mennonite churches and two were in Christian churches. The ratio of 22.5 books per member compares favorably with those ratios found per student in many public and private school libraries.

A further study was made of the largest libraries by number of volumes. What were their characteristics when compared with the other libraries in this study? The sixteen large libraries studied were larger than most other libraries on all of the eleven variables studied, even on the per member analyses. Congregation membership size, library income, library age, and region seemed to be fundamentally important in correlating with library size in volumes, perhaps with region, age, and congregation size in being most influential.

## Periodical Titles

Newspaper and periodical collections came up next for consideration. The mean number of newspaper titles received was small. A cumulative total of only 219 titles was received by all libraries. No library received more than ten titles and most received none. Table 5.61 shows the libraries with the largest newspaper collections. Jewish and Presbyterian,

Texas and New Mexico congregations led the list. Trinity Evangelical Lutheran Church in Perkasie, Pennsylvania, and All Saints Catholic Parish in Dallas led the list of specific libraries. Table 5.62 shows the libraries having newspaper subscriptions by denomination. Jewish and Roman Catholic libraries led.

The CSLA libraries were weak in periodicals, also, the mean number being only eight titles per library. However, Roman Catholic, Jewish and Baptist libraries were strongest with twelve and twenty-five titles received apiece, as shown in tables 5.63 and 5.64. For periodical subscriptions only table 5.64 shows Jews, Roman Catholic, and Baptists to have had the largest subscription lists. The total number of periodical titles in all libraries was 3,179. Like many scholarly religious libraries, these popular religious libraries were much more book than serial oriented. Of at least three thousand religious serial titles worldwide, these libraries held a remarkably small number. Certain useful free or moderately priced titles were available to supplement the existing subscriptions if the libraries had only looked for and requested them.

Which specific libraries received the largest number of periodical titles? Table 5.65 shows that All Saints Church in Dallas received 108 titles to lead the list. By denomination, most of the libraries in table 5.65 were Roman Catholic, Jewish, or Baptist, and several were located in Illinois or Texas. This analysis shows that a few congregational libraries were as large as certain private school or special libraries in holdings of book and periodical titles.

Which libraries received the largest number of periodical and newspaper titles per congregation member? Each library wishes to provide as many newspaper and periodical titles for congregational member use as possible. Table 5.66 shows the libraries that were most successful in doing this. Obviously, the more newspaper and periodical titles available per member the better the service being provided. Mennonite, Baptist, Pennsylvania, and Oregon churches were dominant in this table.

## Media

In most libraries, the last two decades have witnessed a steady rise in media (audiovisual or nonbook) holdings and use. CSLA congregational libraries were no exception to this trend, and certain of them were strong in media holdings. One-twelfth of them had one thousand or more media titles, one-third of that media-oriented group being Methodist. On the other hand, a fourth of the libraries had two or fewer titles. The mean holding was 375 media titles per library. We can see the mean title holdings per library by denomination in table 5.67. Baptist and Roman Catholic led in holdings per library, while United Church of Christ and Episcopal/Anglican had the smallest number of titles.

Thus, for the entire database, the mean library's figures were 2,824 book volumes, 8 newspaper and periodical titles, and 375 media titles, for a total of 3,207 volumes/titles. An extrapolation of this total shows that the 1,950 North American CSLA members together must have had about 6,253,650 volumes/titles.

Table 5.68 points up the contrast in numbers of media titles among the denominations. For instance, half of the Episcopal/Anglican and Lutheran libraries had no more than fifty titles each, yet two-fifths of the Methodist libraries reported more than 350 media titles. The ratio of the largest to the smallest denominational means was 5.9:1.0, a large disparity between the more and the less media oriented. This ratio reflected not only the contrast in emphasis on media material between the congregations and denominations but also the amount of denominationally tailored material available for the congregations to purchase.

Table 5.69 shows what kinds of media we are talking about. Clearly, cassette tapes led the long list, with picture and clipping files second in number of titles or items. Together they constituted more than half of the total, with pamphlet files and filmstrips adding another 25 percent. The largest media collections are shown in table 5.70. The Interchurch Center in Portland (serving several houses of worship) led the libraries. The Baptist and Methodist groups constituted half of the total number on the list, as did Texas and Georgia by state. Table 5.71 shows the filmstrip holdings by denomination. Baptists led with Other Denominations next.

If we may consider table 5.70 on a per-member basis, we will see not just which congregations made the largest effort but which ones made the largest effort per member. Table 5.72 shows that the Burlingame Baptist Church in Portland, Oregon, was well ahead of other congregations in this respect. Baptists and Mennonites lead the denominations in this table of libraries with strong media collections per member. In a special study, the author found that the number of media titles available rose regularly as the number of book volumes rose, and further, that the number of media titles available in suburban locations was equal to the number of media titles available in urban and rural locations combined.

We should obtain an interesting result if we put all four kinds of library material together with their per-member scores, and so let's do that. Table 5.73 shows the result. The mean total number of titles/volumes per library per member was 5.2, one of which books constituted the largest proportion. Other Denominations, Christian, and Baptist denominations led the list with Roman Catholic and Jewish at the bottom on a per-member basis. So we see that while the latter two denominations excelled in absolute numbers based on large congregations, their per-member ratios were the poorest of all for material collections. And conversely, the denominations that lead this table were doing better per member than earlier tables might have led the reader to believe. Note the superiority of the Protestant libraries reflected in the Jewish-Roman Catholic versus Protestant score. Presumably there comes a point at which even a large congregation's library is large enough.

## Collection Focus and Distinctive Material

One of the questionnaire's open-ended questions asked for a description of the collection's subject focus. This question proved difficult for the librarians to deal with, but it had little to do with the matters discussed in our chapter 1 discussion of religious library and librarian focus. It was almost true that we received 411 different answers and that each librarian used a somewhat different interpretation of the question in formulating a response. The frequent use of vague terms increased the difficulty of understanding also. Table 5.74 attempts to categorize these replies in two different formulations. The upper part of the table shows Mouridou's summary categories, which were listed when the questionnaires were examined directly. The lower part shows the author's library-type characterization of the summary. Neither one is satisfactory, but here they are.

Perhaps the best way to characterize this information is to say that it showed much scatter. In addition, children's and young adult material made up a significant part of many collections, as we noticed above. Recreational and fiction reading material were important as well as devotional and inspirational material. A certain amount of reference material was found in most libraries. Theology and philosophy material was present in many cases, and personal and community social problems accounted for part of the collection. Denominational authors and subjects were important in certain places as well. In a third of the cases the librarian said the congregational library had no main focus or was a multifocused collection, probably a generalization that applied to most of them.

While many collections contained no more than material routinely useful for that particular denomination, time, and location, a few of the librarians considered certain of their material to be unique or at least

distinctive and perhaps even rare. The terms that were used to characterize these collections are listed in table 5.75. Special denominational material and archives constituted a third of the collection while other libraries listed nonprint and large-print material collections as being
distinctive.

. Table 5.76 shows these holdings in detail because a variety of material is available that has a reference usefulness for study or even possible
interlibrary loan to other libraries. Certain other congregational libraries
once had unusual material but recognized its research or archive value
and sent it to a regional or national denominational or university archive
or history collection depository for safekeeping. While the table 5.76 material was doubtless unusual and some of it quite distinctive in the library's locality, probably not all of it was valuable on a national basis.
The reader should note that almost two-thirds of the libraries had nothing to contribute to this list.

## Summary

What have we learned about the library collections in this section? The collections varied in size but generally were of modest proportions, 2,824 volumes being the mean book collection size. Jewish and Roman Catholic
congregation libraries were the largest per library. Newspaper and periodical title holdings were small, also, eight periodical titles being the average
figure. Certain libraries had more than one thousand media titles, and Baptist and Roman Catholic libraries led the media holdings list. The mean library contained 375 media titles. Cassette tapes and picture and clipping
files were the most popular types of media held. Library collection subject
focus was difficult to pin down with many libraries being multifocused and
having much variety. A comprehensive list of distinctive material concluded the section, table 5.76.

## Finance

### Introduction

A small library that often lacks a well established funding source, the
congregational library and the financial support it receives deserve close
analysis. Generally, its support is quite modest, even in the present above

average database, but not always. As a rule this support must be obtained from a variety of sources both inside and outside the institution, thereby complicating the situation. For many libraries, obtaining a regular annual institutional budget allotment may still be an unfulfilled objective, sometimes just a dream.

Usually the congregation office or budgetary source is less dependable than administrative sources for other kinds of libraries and therefore the library committee members must spend much time and energy on various kinds of aggressive and low-level fund-raising activities. Further, there are no generally recognized financial standards for these libraries, either as a percentage of the congregational budget or per congregation member. While policies, practices, and sources are often similar among them, this does not mean that their financial management is necessarily either sophisticated or productive. Income and expenditures were treated as being the same here since presumably the libraries spent approximately their full incomes each year.

We are discussing the financial management of an organization that may receive only a few hundred dollars or less, annually. Sometimes its funds are received primarily in gift and memorial book "income" form (either a check earmarked for books or else a physical book). If any supplies are purchased in the smallest of these libraries, they may be paid for by the house of worship petty cash box or by the librarian! Few of the organization's staff members are accustomed to preparing or even reading the kinds of financial requests and reports that constitute everyday reading in scholarly religious libraries. Obviously, it is time that more of them started to learn modern popular library financial management!

In addition to the above problems, congregational libraries share financial problems experienced by other kinds of libraries. Often they have insufficient funds to purchase the material needed to provide good-quality service for the congregation and its Sunday or synagogue school, and they must also keep up with inflation affecting library material, equipment, and supply costs. Most of these organizations have one financial advantage, however: their nonexistent or at least modest personnel expenditures. Whatever the library's income, most of it can be spent for library material, equipment, and supplies.

In several subject areas the questionnaire replies were difficult to interpret. Finance was one of them. While one question asked the librarian about the library's budget allocation from the church/synagogue officials, a more useful approach to understanding the financial picture required combining the budget allocation information obtained with the information about allocations from church/synagogue departments or other groups as well as the income received from gifts, memorials, and other fund-raising activities. Expenditure statements for material, supplies, and equipment were also useful.

Only when the entire list of sources was considered could any useful income or expenditure totals be obtained. We will look also at the subcategories of library expenditures and at per congregation member figures. First, however, to provide background for the analysis, we will examine the house of worship's own income from which part of the library allocation came.

## Congregation Income

Table 5.77 compares income ranges within congregational and other library groups and also between congregational denominations. There was a wide range of annual congregation income levels. We can see that the Episcopal/Anglican and Roman Catholic denominations showed the lowest congregational income values, and Other Denominations and Baptist had the highest income scores.

Twenty-seven congregations (7 percent) led with million-dollar incomes, the entire table annual income range progressing from $0 to $6 million. Perhaps the most surprising aspect of the situation is that 7 percent of the congregations also had annual incomes of $70,000 or less. Also surprising, when we think about it, is these librarians' full disclosure of both congregational and library incomes rather than the confidentiality (even secrecy!) of the figures that would have been expected in earlier years. Perhaps not quite as surprising is the finding in a separate analysis that older libraries had a somewhat larger mean congregational income than younger libraries. Jewish libraries were again too few to be relied upon statistically.

Table 5.78 analyzes congregation library expenditures size by denomination and shows Other Denominations and Baptist income to have been the largest, the latter averaging $750,000 annually and the former averaging $369,000 per annum.[36] United Church of Christ and Congregational churches had only $170,000 and $150,000 annual incomes on average, small.[37,38] There was a comparative income ratio between Baptist and Congregational institutions of 4.8:1.0. The mean annual income figure for all congregations was somewhat over a third of a million dollars, $370,000.

A further analysis was made for congregational income, this time by region. In which regions were located the congregations with the largest and smallest incomes? The overall picture was not surprising. Rocky Mountains (with its few libraries) led in congregational income along with Southwest libraries, while Northeast and Middle West libraries brought up the rear. The performance of the Southwest and Northeast was as expected, but that of the other two regions was surprising. Later parts of this chapter show regional support patterns with which the present findings are consistent, however. The causes of these patterns are not fully known to the author. At least one major cause is standard of personal income in the U.S. as it varies by state and region. A second cause of regional dispersion is no doubt the tendency toward larger and smaller congregations. Therefore, regions with larger cities also produce larger congregational incomes.

Which specific churches and synagogues had the largest congregational incomes? They are shown in table 5.79. The Mt. Paran Union Church of God in Atlanta led with a $6 million annual budget. Georgia, California, and Maryland were the locales, and Baptist, Presbyterian, and Jewish were the denominations of half of the table's congregations. Table 5.80 shows the congregations with the largest incomes *per congregation member*, the Bethel (Interdenominational) Church in San Jose leading with a $2,000 figure. Note that four of the eleven churches were Mennonite and that California and Pennsylvania were the leading states in this table. Note further that only one church appeared on both tables 5.79 and 5.80, quite an accomplishment for the Bethel Church. Apparently this was a situation in which the church was both large in membership and in per member church income! Congratulations!

## Library Income

Let us return to table 5.77 to study the library income range. The lowest library income low value was as low as zero dollars in the Lutheran, Methodist, and Presbyterian denominations. Highest of the highs was the Other Denominations denomination, since the Jewish figure could not be accepted as typical of Jewish synagogue libraries as a group. Certainly for this table, however, as individual libraries produce the range values, the Jewish high is extraordinary.

Annual library income is shown also in table 5.81. Which ones of all of the denominational groups were best supported? The leading denomination was the Roman Catholic, if we can depend on a figure representing twelve cases only. The $21,048 mean figure for Jewish libraries was very large and would surely have decreased with a larger sample. The mean annual library income for all congregations was $1,651. Among Protestants the Baptists led by a large margin in income size, while the Lutherans were on the bottom with about $800 devoted to each library. The specific libraries with the largest incomes are shown in table 5.82. The Sinai Temple Library in Los Angeles led the list, with the Temple Library in Cleveland second. Jewish and Baptist libraries constituted half of this table as did those from California, Georgia, and Illinois.

Which libraries spent the largest percentage of the congregation's income? This calculation provides one way of ascertaining the congregation's interest in library service: those congregations that were most determined to build up the library allocated it a comparatively large slice of the congregational income "pie." The mean percentage of the CSLA congregation income going to the library was 0.49 percent, disappointingly small.

Table 5.83 shows library income as a percentage of congregation income by denomination. The United Church of Christ and Roman Catholic groups led this table, with the Lutheran group on the bottom. This is an important finding and shows which denominations were trying hardest to provide superior service. All six Jewish synagogues were strong.

Those denominations scoring below 0.49 percent had some distance to go before they could be said to be making a sustained effort to support their libraries. These are low percentages, so apparently the standard for the percentage of total congregation income going to the library should be set at about 1.0 percent. In a further analysis, library income as a percentage of congregational income was found to rise as congregational income rose. Perhaps this reflected greater leeway to support the library within the budgets of the larger congregations.

Two specific libraries led by wide margins in percentage of congregational income going to the library, those of the St. Elias Eastern Orthodox Church in Battle Creek and the St. Charles Borromeo Catholic Church in Bloomington with at least 13 percent of the congregation income. The thirteen libraries in table 5.84 came primarily from three states—California, Texas, and Indiana—and from United Church of Christ and Presbyterian churches.

Table 5.85 shows another denominational approach to library income. Mean library income per congregation member was $1.53. The Jewish (far ahead but of questionable validity) and Other Denominations congregations led this important table with the Methodist, Lutheran, and Roman

Catholic churches ranking lowest. No doubt the Mennonite, Churches of God, and Interdenominational church libraries were exerting strong upward pressure on the Other Denominations group!

Another table also takes the analysis a step forward by studying the congregational income per membership. Certain results were similar to those of the previous analysis, but others differed. Congregational congregations were low while Baptist and Other Denominations congregations ranked high in both columns. Mennonites were surprisingly high in both columns. The Roman Catholic, Jewish, and Methodist groups suffered most from the per member analysis due to large memberships. That is, their large total income was impressive, but their per member income level sank significantly. Annual mean congregation income per member showed Other Denominations to lead at $523. However, in interpreting these figures that compare among the denominations, it is necessary to remember that some denominations count children as members and others, such as many Anglican churches, count mainly couples or only members of the electoral roll.

Table 5.86 proves a rather obvious point. When we allow congregation membership level to rise, library income level rises with it. In a separate analysis, the author found again that there was a relationship between library age and library income. Older libraries tended to have larger incomes than younger libraries.

The annual library income per congregation member can be seen in table 5.87 for the leading thirteen congregations. The University Avenue Church of Christ in Austin led by a large margin, spending almost $32 per member on the library. By denomination, the libraries on this list were led by the Baptists and Mennonites, and by state they were led by Pennsylvania, California, and Michigan. In considering a standard for annual library income per congregation member, probably any figure above $3 would be too high, but $3 would be fair enough.

Table 5.88 analyzes the situation by denomination to tell us the sources of the libraries' funds. All denominations received more than half of their funds from the official congregation allocation. However, certain denominations—Jewish, Roman Catholic, and Baptist—derived much more from this source than did other denominations—Congregational and Lutheran, for instance. Those denominational libraries receiving more than others from congregational organizations and departments, the second category, were Other Denominations and Methodist, but none of them received very much from this source.

Denominations obtaining the most from gifts and memorials were the Jewish and Roman Catholic. The United Church of Christ profited most from fund-raising programs, and Roman Catholic and Baptist got the most from Other Sources. It should be noted that certain denominations seemed to benefit greatly from a few large congregational donations that could not necessarily be expected to recur annually.

Table 5.89 shows in more detail library income sources exclusive of congregational income. Book fairs and sales, gifts and memorials made up almost two-fifths of the total, with the rest scattered among a considerable variety of sources. Note that almost half of the libraries listed no such sources, however, which suggests that we may have recorded an incomplete set of answers. Or does this mean that those libraries reporting nothing had no outside income? Perhaps, but no evidence is available on that question.

Several special analyses were made also. The libraries that had the highest income from gifts were the First Congregational Church in Kalamazoo and the Sinai Temple in Los Angeles. Table 5.90 shows the libraries with the highest income from congregational sources. Leaders were the Fourth Presbyterian Media Center in Bethesda and the Central Schwenkfelder Church in Worcester. Further, table 5.91 shows the libraries with the highest income from the proceeds of various activities. Leader was St. James Roman Catholic Church in Arlington Heights. Table 5.92 shows the leaders with income from other sources. Mt. Paran Union Church of God in Atlanta was highest here.

Table 5.93 shows total library expenditures in the operating budgets for all types by denominations. The leaders again were the Jewish synagogues for their six-library group, and next came the Roman Catholic and Baptist groups. Another table dealt with the relationship between total income and church congregation size. It showed library income rising with the size of their congregation. See table 5.94 for a technical comparison.

Table 5.95 shows the percentage of total library income accounted for by each one of five income categories. Notice how heavily Jews depended on the basic budget allocation, Congregationals on gifts, Methodists on the congregation, Roman Catholic on proceedings, and U.C.C. on Other. Table 5.96 shows chief librarian's gender and annual library budget. The congregational libraries supervised by women had an average annual income of $1,045, whereas those supervised by men had an average annual income of $339, thereby providing a ratio of 3.1:1.0. This finding is quite different from the one for *ALD* libraries, but the number of male librarians here is small, too. Table 5.97 shows library salary expenditures by denomination. Notice that the table confirms the earlier findings on this variable and its relationship.

## Large and Small Library Incomes

A study was made of the twenty-one largest libraries by library income. Were these libraries distinctive with regard to other variables also? Not surprisingly, if the library was unusually large on one factor, then it tended to be larger than average on most of the other variables checked. As an interesting sidelight, an analysis was made of the fifteen congregations with the smallest incomes to see what sort of picture they projected. The main point of this exercise was to examine congregations for which it was a hardship to support the library, therefore congregations which apparently had a strong belief in its importance.

The congregation incomes of this group ranged from $35,000 down to $3,500 per year (St. Victor School and Church, Monroe, Wisconsin), as compared with the overall mean annual income of about $370,000. For these libraries with small incomes, annual per member library income ranged from $20.50 down to $0.46. It averaged $4.56 per library as compared with the overall library income per member of $1.53, so these financially poor congregations were apparently more library oriented in terms of providing funds than most richer congregations. Mean percentage of the congregational income going to the library in this small income group was 4 percent per library, again well above the 0.49 percent average.

In addition, and in much the same spirit of adventure, an analysis was made of the twelve smallest annual library incomes per congregation member. Yes, certain libraries listed no income at all: five of them. All were relatively small congregations, 350 to 750 members apiece. Several large congregations numbering fifteen hundred to fifteen thousand members, had small library incomes, also, ranging from $0.46 to $0.80 per member. The five largest congregations in this group had a total of 44,500 members but provided only an annual mean of $0.06 worth of library service per member for them! Note that this amounts to $2,670 spread over five libraries.

## Library Expenditure Analysis

The preceding subsections have described and analyzed the data reported on the questionnaire for congregation and library income and follow Hannaford's original analysis of this data. In addition to her analysis, the author reexamined the questionnaire, since the financial data was difficult to locate and interpret, in the hope both of creating new breakdowns and of identifying income items that might previously have been over-looked.

The second analysis was successful in achieving the former but not the latter purpose. The expenditure values by denomination using the author's figures were almost exactly the same as those for library income using Hannaford's figures. To separate the author's analysis from Hannaford's, the author's is referred to as an analysis of library *expenditure*, while hers is referred to as an analysis of library *income*. All of the tables described in this subsection were made from the same library expenditure information.

The new breakdowns available with the new data analysis enable us to see expenditure for salaries, books and periodicals, media, supplies, and equipment. Table 5.98 shows the personnel expenditures by denomination and enables us to answer such questions as which denominations spent the largest amounts on personnel and how much was spent. Table 5.98 shows the salary breakdown. Generally, the Ns are small, too small among Jewish libraries for consideration. Roman Catholic and U.C.C. lead the means column.

Table 5.98 shows that Jewish congregations spent much more than any other denomination on personnel, $7,026 per library, but this expenditure covered only six libraries. Roman Catholic and Baptist denominations came next in their emphasis on personnel. Perhaps those libraries with paid staff members came predominantly from these three groups? Mean annual personnel expenditure for all denominations was only $331 per library, however. Tables 5.99 and 5.100 provide additional information on the financial situation.

A question which table 5.98 does not answer is which specific libraries spent the most money on personnel. Table 5.101 lists the ten largest libraries by salary expenditure and shows that two synagogue libraries led the list with $15,000 annual expenditures. This table shows that Roman Catholic, Presbyterian, and Jewish libraries accounted for half of the table. These findings show again the importance of salaries in libraries thought previously to have almost none at all.

Books, newspapers, and periodicals remain the primary expenditure categories for congregational libraries. Table 5.102 shows that the mean library spent $942 per year for this material, with Jewish, Baptist, and Roman Catholic libraries leading the denominations. Table 5.103 shows which congregational libraries spent the largest amounts annually on material, with the Sinai Temple Library leading by a wide margin through a $52,000 expenditure. This time the first three libraries were Jewish. Baptist libraries clearly dominated the rest of the list. California, Georgia, and Texas libraries led the list by state.

Media was a major expenditure category also, the libraries spending a mean of $215 on it annually. The same three denominations as before led denominational table 5.104. Table 5.105 shows that four libraries spent $5,000 per year on media, two of them being Baptist and two being located in Georgia. Annual expenditures for supplies and equipment were small, averaging $74 for supplies and $60 for equipment. The same two denominations as before led tables 5.106 and 5.107.

In certain cases, the figures for specific churches and synagogues were high because they represented special purchases, but we have no way of knowing how often this kind of purchasing occurred. Tables 5.108 and 5.109 show the libraries scoring high on supply and equipment expenditures. In table 5.108, Sinai Temple and Chapelwood United Church led and in table 5.109 the Central Schwenkfelder Church spent $3,000 on equipment. There is much overlap between these tables. Both tables show much scatter among denominations, but synagogues were important in each one.

At this point we need to examine the allocation of expenditures among all five categories. Table 5.110 provides a summary and shows that 58 percent of the expenditures were for books, newspapers, and periodicals. Another 13 percent went to media, and supplies and equipment took up 9 percent of the total, leaving 20 percent for salaries. Certain notable exceptions are shown in these tables, for instance for salaries, in which the Jewish and Roman Catholic (plus U.C.C.) denominations ranked far ahead of the rest. For media, Lutheran spent a higher proportion of its funds than did the other denominations. For books, the Episcopal/Anglican libraries spent almost three-fourths of their money on purchasing.

Finally, in this special series of analyses, we were able to introduce an additional element to the expenditure factor, one of unusual interest. For this examination, the various denominations and faiths were divided roughly into four groups by religious philosophy: (1) nonbiblical Asians, (2) the liberal, or mainstream, mostly Christian denominational group, (3) the charismatic and Pentecostal Christian denominational group, and (4) evangelical Christians. The latter two groups included denominations that were largely more active than the rest in proselytizing and converting new members, in missionary work, in "miracles," and in outreach generally, while the two former groups seemed to have a more balanced and conservative cycle of activities that was less dedicated to single-minded evangelizing. See table 5.111. How did these two contrasting denominational groups compare on library expenditures? Which one seemed to be the more "library-minded" — spending more on the library? The bottom line of table 5.112 figures told the story clearly. The evangelical and charismatic group was more library-minded and spent more on library service than did the mainstream group, on the average, in spite of the presence of the well-funded Jewish libraries in the latter group. So apparently library service was a conscious or unconscious part of the evangelical program of the denominations in the lower part of the table. They spent 37.7 percent more than the mean figure on their libraries, according to table 5.112. The difference was especially noticeable for salaries, media, and equipment. So perhaps the activities of the latter two groups were better balanced and more rounded than they appear to the average layperson!

Additional analyses were made to contrast these two groups of denominations. Did they confirm this preliminary analysis? For the most part they did. Table 5.113 shows these figures. The separation can be seen most clearly in the number of media titles held, with the evangelical and charismatic group having half again as many titles as the mainstream group. Of course, media use could be expected to separate these groups, since it was an evidence of the use of "modern" teaching techniques. Next most distinctive was library age. The evangelical and charismatic group was 38 percent younger than the mainstream group, though it is not entirely clear whether youthfulness was an asset or a liability for any denomination (although youth is often a sign of greater vigor).

Staff hours worked per week and library cost per circulation charge could be considered to demonstrate library efficiency. If so, for the former, the charismatic group could be said to be the harder working while for the latter, the mainstream, was the more efficient group. Efficient library management was a strongly positive asset for any library. In addition, the number of library committee members was 26 percent more for the evangelical and charismatic than for the mainstream group. On the other hand, the mainstream group libraries had somewhat more books per library than did the evangelical and charismatic group.

## Summary

What have we learned about congregational library finance in this long and concentrated discussion? Congregational and library income (expenditure) ranged respectively from zero to $6 million and $0 to $69,000 annually. Mean annual congregational income was $370,000 and per congregational member income was $360 annually. Twenty-seven congregations had million-dollar incomes. Synagogue and Baptist congregations were the largest and United Church of Christ and Congregational the smallest. Baptist and Other Denominations incomes were largest and Roman Catholic smallest on a per member basis. The largest congregation spent $2,000 on library service for each member. In terms of regions, Rocky Mountains, Southwest, and West led in congregational income, while the West led in library income per member.

Among the denominations, the Jewish, Roman Catholic, and Baptist had the highest mean annual library incomes. The Sinai Temple Library in Los Angeles was the richest library. One Eastern Orthodox and one Roman Catholic church library spent the largest percentages of congregation funds, both above 13 percent. Mean percentage of the congregational income reflected in the library income was 0.49 percent, very small. Mean annual library income per member was $1.53, with Jewish, Roman Catholic, and Baptist having the largest amounts. In addition to the congregation income source, which was of primary importance, other library income sources were led by gifts, memorials, and book fairs.

As an interesting sidelight, the congregations with the smallest gross support and the libraries with the smallest per member support were examined. Support of library service by these small congregations was surprisingly strong, while the opposite was naturally true of the libraries with the smallest support per member. In general, as congregational membership level rose, so did library income level. The West, Southeast, and Southwest regions led the rest of North America in congregational library support.

A special analysis was made of these libraries' expenditures. It highlighted their spending on salaries, books, media, supplies, and equipment. A final analysis divided the denominations between the evangelical and charismatic on the one hand and the mainstream groups on the other, and showed the extent to which the former group seemed to be more library-minded than the latter.

# Readers Service

## Introduction

Many of the congregational libraries in this study were at some point in the process of leaving an amateur and unsystematic status and becoming professionalized or at least systematized—of offering fully professional service. They were in the process of establishing a card catalog, using professional cataloging rules and a standard classification system, ordering from nationally recognized book, library furniture, equipment, and supply dealers, using a standard charging system, and using modern policies, practices, and forms in all work areas. The goal of many of these librarians was to achieve a status in which the library was professionally organized and operated in every way. Certainly the influx of experienced library professionals and clerical staff members in the last decade or two has moved many of these libraries closer to professional status. Probably only a modest percentage of the libraries had fully achieved that status, but the more active ones were moving resolutely in that direction.

As an emerging field, probably congregational librarianship was younger than secondary school librarianship and special librarianship, and even younger than elementary school librarianship. Just how old it was and what event would normally be used as an inauguration benchmark from which to date the field are unclear to this author beyond the information already provided. Many of the libraries were only a decade or two old and could find few role models and little well-informed professional advice available locally. If congregational librarianship was viewed as an emerging professional or semiprofessional field, one that in the 1970s was still trying to find its proper role in the modern religious and library worlds, then its showing was understandable.

This field can be expected to become more stabilized and professionalized in the future, at least in part, and its libraries increasingly should resemble small but typical school or special libraries. While the number of congregational libraries with library work experience and education requirements for new personnel must be small, we can hope that this number is growing, since it would introduce more professionalism into the field.

Congregational libraries battle the problem that many professional readers' service librarians in other libraries did not regard them as being part of the professional information service world due to their small size and part-time services. Hence, these librarians did not necessarily look to them for service of any kind, even though in some cases their collections and staff competence would have supported certain kinds of service to other libraries, primarily in the religious and childrens' fields. This situation should change slowly as their librarians participate more actively in local, state, and provincial information world activities and gain increased respect. Probably more congregational libraries will be listed in regional databases in the future as their collections grow, their relations with other libraries become closer, and their staff members include more professionals and experienced paraprofessionals.

Congregational library service is similar to service in special or school libraries, with differences usually relating to size and budget and often to professionalism. Most of these religious libraries were open only a few hours per week. They had small material collections and small part-time staffs without college or library education and so could provide only limited circulation and reference service. Usually the library committee members worked closely with the church school instructors to provide appropriate material and answer reference questions. Little is known about congregational library reference work, and no CSLA survey question was asked about it. Of course, a few of the best libraries listed in the chapter's tables must have provided models in this area for others to follow.

## Catalogs

Presumably, selecting and preparing the material collection and its catalogs for public service use consumed most of the library committee's time, or at least most of the library committee's library processing time. The survey instrument asked two questions about cataloging and classification: Which types of catalogs were available? Which book classification system was used? A third of the libraries, according to table 5.114, had available all six of the catalogs or headings listed and another third had five of the six available, usually omitting the subject headings or perhaps the accession record.

Shelf lists and author catalogs were available in almost all libraries, and title and media catalogs in most of them. This table shows almost all of these libraries to be providing good card catalog service as far as we can tell except that almost half of them provided no subject headings for their users. Roman Catholic and Jewish had the highest percentages of the full set of catalogs, and United Church of Christ had the lowest.

The classification situation emphasized the extensive popularity of the Dewey Decimal Classification (DDC). Three-fourths of the libraries used it; DDC is the most popular classification system in the world in all kinds of libraries. While 10 percent of the libraries listed a local classification system, the remaining 15 percent used a considerable variety of systems, most of them more or less adapted for use in religious libraries, as seen in table 5.115.

Several denominations had their own classification adaptations—Roman Catholic, Jewish, Lutheran, Methodist, and Presbyterian. In certain libraries two or more systems were used for different kinds of material, for instance, books and pamphlets. Probably the most sophisticated systems were those which expanded the Dewey 200s, for example, the Roman Catholic list, and those which combined a denominational classification with a list of appropriate subject headings, for example, the Weine classification for Jewish material.

## Library Use

Not all libraries gave access to material to outside users. One-fifth of the libraries were not available and another two-fifths were available to outsiders only with restrictions. Only the final two-fifths of the libraries were completely open to outsiders' use. Table 5.116 shows the restrictions put on outside use. In many cases introduction by a congregation member or obtaining the librarian's permission was the only requirement, though a considerable variety of restrictions was listed by the remaining libraries. For *ALD* popular libraries, the main characteristic of those libraries restricting use was their small size.

The times and staffing of service are shown in table 5.117. Many of these libraries were available even when no staff member was present and others were open part of the time with a self-service arrangement, whenever the building was open. Certain closed libraries could be opened during normal working hours by the director of religious education, the minister, the congregation secretary, or the building janitor.

Circulation and use were small when compared with other kinds of libraries. See table 5.118. This is understandable in a library open no more than 20 percent as long as the typical special or school library and usually serving primarily a one to four hour-a-week school. Circulation charges went approximately 50–55 percent to adults and the rest to children. Many libraries did not keep accurate figures to distinguish between adult and children's circulation, so the total could not be obtained merely by adding the two together. The reader should notice, however, that while only three-fifths of the libraries replied to the question for adult and children's use, the total circulation question reply percentage rose to three-fourths of the libraries suggesting that 15 percent of all CSLA librarians simply did not separate adult from children's circulation.

We should not say that the nonreporting libraries had no circulation, merely that we have no information on their circulation. In some cases these figures represented circulation only in the weekly religious service period. Certain libraries kept no written circulation record so could report nothing to CSLA. In other cases, the person who kept the records, sometimes without prior experience or aptitude for this kind of work, was unable to calculate the use figures accurately or to maintain them consistently and so reported nothing.

Circulation reports for adults and children by region and denomination are shown in tables 5.119, 5.120, 5.121 and 5.122. For table 5.119, adult book circulation by region showed the West to lead with a mean monthly circulation of 115 per month. The Northeast was smallest here. Table 5.120 shows monthly adult circulation by denomination. Baptists and Presbyterians led, while Congregationals were last on the table. Table 5.121, monthly children's circulation by region, showed Canada to lead the table and the Northeast to bring up the rear, and to produce an 8.8:1.0 ratio between them. Finally, table 5.122 showed children's monthly circulation by denomination. Aside from the large Jewish figure representing only six cases, the Other Denominations group led, while the United Church of Christ and Episcopal/Anglican denominations brought up the rear.

The libraries with the largest adult, children's, and total circulation are listed in tables 5.123, 5.124, and 5.125. Certain of the libraries were quite busy and circulated large numbers of books. Table 5.123 shows that two libraries led in adult circulation: University Presbyterian Church, Seattle, and the Fourth Presbyterian Church, Bethesda, each one with at least 185 charges per week. Texas, Presbyterian, and Baptist libraries led the table; note that all three of the top leaders were Presbyterian churches. Children's circulation was somewhat smaller than adult but still strong for the nine busy libraries listed in table 5.124, more than ninety charges per week for the top five libraries. Note also that only two of the libraries that led in adult circulation were among the children's circulation leaders, indicating a degree of specialization. Methodist and Baptist churches were most numerous here.

Which libraries excelled in total circulation? Table 5.125 shows the total circulation for the twelve leading libraries. One library dominated this table, the First Baptist Church Library, La Crescenta, California. Circulation there averaged *105 charges* calculated *for each one of the 365 days of the year*, thirty-two hundred per month! That hardly suggests a limited Sunday morning reader service period. Among tables 5.123, 5.124, and 5.125 overlap was small. Seven libraries appeared in table 5.125 from the total of thirty-two that appeared in all three tables. Only one library, the Pleasant Grove Presbyterian Church in Youngstown, appeared in all three tables. The Presbyterian, Baptist, and Methodist churches constituted more than half of the total, and California and Georgia were the leading states.

When we analyze total circulation by denomination, table 5.126 shows a mean circulation of 115 charges per month, or 29 per week. It shows also that the Baptist and Jewish circulation were highest and Congregational and United Church of Christ were lowest per library per month. A major difference was made to synagogue libraries when a library served the synagogue school as well as the congregation. Nevertheless there were too few synagogue libraries in this table to give them much weight.

What will happen when we analyze monthly circulation per house of worship member and by denomination? Table 5.127 shows the results. That circulation per member is small, a mean of only fourteen per month per one hundred members. The mean showed one book to be circulated for every seven congregation members per month, or about one and two-thirds volumes per member per year. With such a low total, we can understand why a congregation member might question the value to the congregation of such a little used service. Perhaps one reason for the small volume of book circulation in certain libraries was the fact that most of it occurred in the church school on the morning of the religious service day and did not necessarily require taking the book out of the building or even recording a circulation charge, since in most cases it was returned to the library that same morning. This would particularly be true for supplementary volumes used for Sunday school and Bible study classes.

Of course two denominations were well above the average, the Other Denominations and the Baptist. They ranged from 3.24 to 4.92 charges per member per year. Just what level should be set as a standard for this circulation is only a guess, but a higher standard is easier to defend than a low one. No response constituted almost a quarter of the total, however. Notice that Protestant was slightly higher than Jewish-Roman Catholic circulation, possibly because Jewish and Roman Catholic infants sometimes are listed as church or synagogue members but borrow no books.

When we push the analysis further and ask which libraries had the largest circulation per congregation member, we have come to one of the prime output measures. The results should be gratifying for the churches listed in table 5.128, more than half of which are Mennonite and Baptist located in California, Ohio, Oregon, and Pennsylvania. These are the libraries with the highest annual circulation per congregation member. Several old favorite libraries headed this list. The Lombard Mennonite Church lead with a circulation of 2.4 books per member per month, or 28.8 per member per year, a heavy reading congregation! For all of these libraries the output was high in terms of circulation. Perhaps it should be explained further that most of the libraries in the table were medium-sized or small, with a mean congregation size of only 411 members.

And finally, let us see what happens when we calculate the cost of circulating each item for each denomination. Presumably each library had two objectives: (1) maximizing circulation of material titles/items to members, and (2) minimizing annual library cost. This, then, is a simple cost/benefit analysis, with the circulation being the benefit and the total library expenditure figure representing the cost. Table 5.129 shows a denominational picture that is almost the opposite of most of the preceding tables.

Lutherans, Christians, and Presbyterians had low (favorable income dollars) circulation per library ratios while Jewish, Roman Catholic and Congregational had relatively high ratios (unfavorable). Note, however, that 22 percent of the libraries did not reply to this question. Perhaps a desirable cost/benefit ratio for these libraries would not be greater than $1.50 per circulation charge. Of course, the libraries with high expense/circulation ratios may have been providing more service to their users than were other libraries, such as large material collections and a paid part-time assistant and so provided more service than just book browsing and circulation.

In a further analysis, the author discovered that circulation per member rose as library income rose, supporting the argument in favor of greater library efforts. Circulation per member rose from 58.9 charges per month, for a monthly library income of $0.00 to $0.50, to 109 charges per month, for an income of $0.51 to $1.00, and then to 153 charges per month for an income of $1.00+ per month. This suggests a justification for increasing the library budget in order to increase library use! Note also that increase in expenditure produced an almost exactly proportional increase in circulation, a one-on-one growth rate.

A further examination of library income and circulation reveals that there were great differences in these ratios. Table 5.130 shows that one library had an income (expenditure) of $20.83 per charge while eight libraries in table 5.131 received no income at all but continued circulation. Therefore the libraries in table 5.131 are to be congratulated on their ability to provide a circulation service at minimum cost, while the libraries in table 5.130 are only to be wondered at since their congregations were providing a large amount of input or money and reaping only a relatively modest reward in terms of measurable output or circulation. Or, in other terms, this cost/benefit analysis favors the table 5.131 libraries and not the table 5.130 libraries.

Of course, we have only an incomplete picture of each group's expenditures. Since our knowledge of these libraries' situations is so superficial, such easy conclusions as these should be regarded with caution. A more careful look at these two tables is needed. The library cost being examined here was spent only indirectly on circulation; presumably it went primarily for library material, with smaller amounts being spent on salaries, supplies, and equipment. This fact does not compromise the analysis but must be clearly understood within the nature of this cost/benefit study.

Further, before the reader criticizes the table 5.130 libraries too severely, we must realize that circulation is only one output or benefit measure for a religious library, and that reference service, including reference questions answered, and other kinds of circulation service, such as reserve book service and browsing service, which may not be recorded in many house of worship libraries, as well as publicity for new publications and media availability, may be quite important in others. In additional libraries, circulation of media and periodicals either may not be permitted or else not be recorded since it may have constituted in-house use. Consequently, these tables should be viewed primarily as examples of specialized kinds of analyses that may represent all or only part of the usage picture. In conclusion, we may note that table 5.131's libraries were primarily Presbyterian and Lutheran from Ohio.

## Summary

Congregational staffing and use figures were small when compared with other kinds of libraries. Normally service was provided for one to a few hours each week. Circulation was a self-service activity part of the time and a staffed activity at other times. Many librarians worked with house of worhip school teachers to provide reference service. Several kinds of catalogs were widely available: only subject headings seemed to be missing from many of them. The libraries used the DDC primarily, though a variety of other religious classification systems was found to be in use.

Use was available to outsiders in most cases, sometimes with modest restrictions. Mean circulation was twenty-seven charges per week, but in one library it reached 105 charges daily! Baptist and Jewish circulation means were highest among the denominations. Monthly circulation per member was low, but Other Denominations and Baptist groups led it. The West and Canada led circulation by region, and the Lombard Mennonite Church led circulation per member per month. A final cost/benefit analysis showed each circulation charge to cost a mean $1.85, with Lutherans and Christians spending must less than that per year.

## Management

Organization and supervision should have been simple to carry out in such small libraries, but certain factors complicated the situation. Few congregational library committee heads had had any library or religious management experience, so most of them had a poor background for congregational library management. Obviously, the lack of funds and the small committee size and inexperienced nature of the staff members were problems. Of course, most experienced congregational library professionals and subprofessionals could handle library management adequately and were doing that, but the other chief librarians were forced to struggle with it.

### Schools, Quarters, Computers, and Publications

In addition to the congregational membership and church and synagogue school students, fifty-five libraries (13.4 percent) were found to serve a special school, often one housed in the congregational building. Table 5.132 suggests the nature of that school. In many cases, this was a day care center, a preschool, or a kindergarten with limited access to the congregational library. No information was available on the amount of use derived from these schools.

No specific question was asked about library quarters, but remarks were culled about them from various open-ended question replies. Favorable and unfavorable comments often counterbalanced each other, for instance, in comments on the library location as shown in table 5.133. Among the unfavorable comments, crowded and divided quarters occurred more than once. Overall, there were somewhat more unfavorable than favorable comments. Again we should note that a large proportion of the respondents, in this case three-fourths, made no comment at all. Each library needed a central and heavy traffic location, usually near the church or synagogue school area, with attractive decor and furnishings and much growth space. In this, as in so many other aspects of congregational library service, the principles and policies of good special and school library service applied here as well.

Computer use was just beginning for a few of these libraries that were keeping records in a small database. A variety of uses was made of the computer, as shown in table 5.134. Bibliographic recordkeeping was common among them. Commodores and IBM PCs were the two most common makes, and the Church Administrative Program system was the program most commonly used. Usually the church or synagogue office computer was the one used by these pioneering libraries.

The survey publication questions asked to what extent the library had its own publications or else was mentioned in congregational publications. Table 5.135 shows the results. Other Denominations and Jewish congregations had their own library publications most often, but an average of only one in eleven libraries of all kinds had such a publication. As far as inclusion in the congregation's newsletter or leaflet, the former occurred frequently but the latter did not. Jewish and Congregational (they were leaders here!) libraries led the newsletter group, while Roman Catholic and Jewish libraries led the leaflet group. Library newsletter publication frequently was monthly, for the most part, as table 5.136 shows. Certain congregations were doing well in the publication area, but most of them still had much room for improvement.

## Strengths and Weaknesses

Another open-ended question dealt with the librarians' concepts of their libraries' strengths. These replies were difficult to categorize, as were the replies to other open-ended questions. Aside from the difficulty of summarizing, any sort of categorization of replies would reduce the reader's understanding of the librarian's meaning. Many librarians at either end of the membership size scale were happy with their libraries and the support received and said so in detail. Of course, libraries had different strengths. Suffice it to say that almost every major or minor aspect of library operation was listed by someone as a strength (or a weakness).

The last of the questionnaire's open-ended questions asked the librarian to list the areas in which outside help or information was needed. This was a roundabout way of asking about unsuccessful or weak facets of libraries or librarians. Again there was difficulty in interpreting the results, but first to be noted is the fact that a fourth of the libraries listed no area in which help or information was needed. Was this self-confidence or capability or innocence or laziness or fatigue?

However, another quarter of the group requested help with publicity and use stimulation. Another fifth's questions related to the library's material collection and another sixth to the need for better location and staffing. The last three categories accounted for more than two-thirds of the total. The remaining categories accounted for most of the remaining library activity areas with considerable spread among them. Table 5.137 provides the reader with the entire gamut of replies to this question, which demonstrates the difficulty of summarizing such disparate answers and also takes the reader closer to the problems existing in the librarian's real world.

## A Study of Effort and Benefit

A further attempt was made to divide the denominations and the congregations between the more and the less effective and efficient in providing library facilities and promoting their use. A set (cluster) of varied analyses was made to identify denominations that had made a strong effort to provide good library facilities (effort) and to compare them with the results obtained in terms of circulation (benefit). All scores were expressed in per-member terms and were obtained for each responding congregation and denomination. This is a summary of the results obtained with some difficulty in the most revealing evaluations of effectiveness.

The analysis involved developing a per-member effort or input score based on the six variables that are listed in table 5.138. These variables were thought to be those most indicative of a strong congregational effort to provide good library service. In addition, the monthly circulation per member figure was calculated for each congregation. Then the effort score was divided into the circulation score (charges) to yield a benefit cost or circulation/effort ratio or score. This result told us whether a congregation or denomination had gotten a high circulation/low effort score (desirable) or the opposite (undesirable), or more likely something in between.

Note that this was not simply a cost analysis but that effort was a complex of varied factors expressed in terms of persons, hours, dollars, and volumes. Note further that this result was expressed in terms of a benefit/effort, not a cost/benefit score. The variables involved in this measure of per-member congregational emphasis on library service were the following: library income, library committee size, cumulative material collection size total (book volumes, newspapers, periodicals, and media), committee hours worked per week, number of professionals on the committee, and library income as a percentage of congregational income.

What were the results of this study? The initial part of the study dealt with library effort alone. It found that basically only two denominations had made a substantial effort to give libraries strong support—the Jewish and the Roman Catholic. The other denominational scores fell well below these two. Weakest in effort to support the library were the Methodists and the Lutherans.

For the second part of the study, benefit and effort were compared. For this part, table 5.138 shows that Lutheran libraries were far ahead of the other denominations in this comparison, surprisingly enough. Why is that? Apparently, while Lutheran libraries had only average use scores, usually they had made only minimal effort, so their benefit/effort ratio was relatively high. The per-member analysis hit the denominations with large congregations hard, the synagogues and Roman Catholic churches. Of course, we may notice that 29 percent of the 411 libraries did not provide information for all parts of this analysis, also, thereby weakening the correlation of the results to that extent. The facts that 29 percent did not respond and that we still have clear-cut results shows that the original correlation was very strong indeed! Following the Lutherans, Baptist and Presbyterian churches were next in strength on this ratio, with the Congregational and Roman Catholic churches being weakest. For the latter churches with poor circulation/effort ratios, either their circulation was low or their effort was high (costly) per member.

In the third part of this analysis, the author attempted to refine effort by identifying factors that seemed to correlate most closely with circulation. In this study, the three best predictors of a library's circulation score were media holdings, committee membership size, and total number of staff hours worked per week. In general, the same specific congregations which excelled on many previous tables excelled in this analysis also. Mennonite churches led this parade, with several Baptist churches following them closely. The Mennonite churches were noteworthy for quite modest library support efforts but high per member circulation figures, small congregation size and quite acceptable effort scores per congregation member.

In conclusion and as a supplementary observation, certain information for this series of analyses suggested that in some cases a minimum circulation level was obtained with little effort by a congregation or denomination, and when a strong attempt was made to improve the circulation the result obtained was only somewhat better. In other words, evidence supported the idea that considerable input was required to improve circulation significantly over a minimum level.

## Standards

A set of suggested congregational library performance standards is shown in table 5.139. Probably an excellent library should meet all ten of these standards, a superior library should meet at least two-thirds of them, and an acceptable library should meet at least one-third of them. Each congregational library should attempt to improve its standing relative to these standards.

## Summary

There was little in the small library to manage, but management experience was usually small. Lack of funds and staff often limited what could be done. Fifty-five libraries provided service to a daily private preschool or primary school in or near the house of worship building. Some of the comments about quarters were unfavorable and seemed to relate primarily to location and space. Computer use had begun in several libraries for a variety of purposes, and various manufacturer brands and programs were being used.

The areas in which the libraries needed help were primarily publicity and increasing usage, by material collection, location, and quarters. A series of analyses was made—benefit/cost and circulation/effort analyses—to discover and discuss indications of input and output. The chapter concluded by suggesting a series of minimum standards for the libraries in this new field.

## Table Summaries and Denominational Library Characterizations

### Two Denominational Table Summaries

If we take a backward look over certain of the tables of this chapter, we can identify denominational standings on them in terms of mean, median, or total figures. Table 5.140 summarizes the net rank of each denomination on twenty-two CSLA tables. Which denominations ranked consistently high or low on these tables and therefore were providing the best or poorest overall service among them?

Apparently the best service in this formulation was being given by three denominations—Jewish, Baptist, and Roman Catholic—since their average table rank was highest. All three groups were prominent within the population and stood at or near the top of most of the tables in which they appeared.[39] The Association of Jewish Libraries deserves some credit for this fine Jewish showing. We may note further that denominations with either a national denominational library office or a denominational association ranked first, second, third, sixth, and eighth out of eleven denominations on the table, an above average showing of four points relative to a median of six.

A similar and supplementary analysis was made that summarized the denominational findings on tables that contained *per-member* analyses. The results are shown in table 5.141. This per-member examination is in some ways a truer analysis of support and service than gross analyses of raw scores that give an advantage to the large institutions. Here, the results for certain denominations are quite different from those shown for the raw scores in table 5.140. Table 5.141 shows Other Denominations, Baptist, and Christian to have led while Roman Catholic, Methodist, and Lutheran brought up the rear. Notice that the Baptist group does well in many circumstances. Generally, the leading denominations on this table had small churches but were supporting them and their libraries well per member.

## An Individual Library Table Summary

Table 5.142 ranks the specific libraries on the number of "top 10" tables in which they were represented. It shows that more of these leading libraries were from the West and Middle West than from any other region, with Canada and the Rocky Mountains regions coming in last. This table includes many of the outstanding congregational libraries in North America. Both the First Baptist Church in La Crescenta, near Los Angeles, and the Sinai Temple Library in Los Angeles deserve congratulations for their fine showing on this chapter's tables.

These two libraries led table 5.142 with fourteen and thirteen listings, respectively, on twenty-five previous tables. However, this left almost half of the tables on which they were not represented, though they may have ranked just below the leaders on certain lists. More than half of the twenty-five libraries on table 5.142 belonged to the Baptist, Jewish, Roman Catholic, and Presbyterian denominations, and more than a third of them were located in Texas, California, Pennsylvania, and Georgia, four leading states.

## An Individual Library Table Summary per Member

In a similar fashion, table 5.143 lists the nine individual libraries that were leaders on the eight special per-member tables. Two libraries lead this small group: the Burlingame Baptist Church in Portland and the Perkasie (Pennsylvania) Mennonite Church. Each one was listed on five previous per-member tables. Four Mennonite and two Baptist libraries constituted two-thirds of the total number of libraries on this table. Another table 5.144, lists outstanding CSLA libraries and librarians.[40]

## Denominational Library Characteristics

A brief characterization will be given of the libraries for each denomination in this sample to show their strengths and weaknesses on the study's variables, both for raw scores and for per-member scores. *Baptist* libraries ranked second among eleven denominations on twenty-five raw score tables and second among eleven denominations on eight per-member tables. Geographically they were well spread out over the country and preferred suburban locations in medium-sized cities. They were somewhat older than the average library. Their table rankings were among the top four for every raw score and per-member table but two, in which they stood seventh and eighth. An excellent record! Baptists were also evangelicals.

*Christian* church libraries were generally located near the middle of most raw score tables and their overall ranking was eighth, just below the middle. They were stronger than that in certain variables, such as cost of circulation, and weaker than that in others, such as staffing hours. On per-member tables, on the other hand, Christian church libraries ranked third with a per-table range from second to tenth. These libraries were also among the youngest by denomination. Christian church libraries were located in the Middle West in urban locations of above average population.

*Congregational* church libraries were eleventh and last in overall raw score ranking and eighth in per-member ranking. They were found primarily in the Northeast and the Middle West, in both urban and suburban locations, and often in smaller cities. On most tables they ranked in the bottom group or near it. They were among the oldest library groups. Only in library income as a percentage of congregational income and volumes per member and in library age did they rank at an average level.

*Episcopal/Anglican* church libraries were only one step up from the bottom in the overall raw score ranking, tenth of eleven denominations, but approached the middle on per-member ranking, seventh of eleven denominations. Their libraries were spread over several regions, in both urban and suburban locations, and often in middle-sized cities. Their ranks were average on only two tables—library newsletters and congregational income by denomination. On the other tables they were usually in the below average or the bottom groupings. This group of libraries was one of the youngest in the study.

*Jewish* synagogues were well spread out over the geographic regions and were found in both urban and suburban locations but usually in large cities. Their performance on the raw score tables was usually excellent, but only average on the per-member tables. On nineteen raw score tables, and one per-member table, they ranked first or second. However, in three instances their rank was well below average. They were also much older than all other groups. Their overall raw score rank was in the first position, while their per-member rank was in the sixth position. It is unfortunate that the Jewish library sample was so small, but this small group produced a very good record!

*Lutheran* libraries were near the middle in overall raw score ranking, seventh, and near the bottom in per-member ranking, tenth. Such a modest showing should have been disappointing to the LCLA. They were among the younger groups in average age also. They were found primarily in the Middle West in both urban and suburban cities of below average size. On most tables they ranked in the middle or the bottom group of denominations, for example, on library income. On one table, however, they were well above average—cost per circulation.

The *Methodist* libraries were one notch up from Lutheran in overall raw score ranking, sixth, at the midpoint. However, they were only ninth on per-member tables. These libraries were above average on media collection size. On the other tables, Methodist libraries ranked somewhat above or below the raw score average and were below average on per-member analyses. On library income as a percentage of congregational income they ranked very low. In age they were average and in geographic location they were well spread out over the country, with libraries in all three types of settings but mostly in smaller cities. This group was the second largest in the study.

A heterogeneous group, the *Other Denominations*, was of average age, was well spread over the continent geographically, existed in some numbers in all three types of settings, and usually was found in smaller cities. They were strong on the raw score tables in library newsletters and circulation but weak in numbers of professionals. They ranked around the middle on most raw score lists and they ranked first on four of six per-member tables. Their overall rank was fifth on raw score and first on per-member analyses. In summary, a superior performance.

In order to learn more about the individual denominations within the Other Denominations group, a separate analysis was made of each one of them. The *Church of God* group was the strongest in this collection of denominations with small representation. It was relatively strong on congregation size, congregation income per member, years of operation, library income per member, percentage of hours open that were staffed, media titles per member, and periodical titles per library, but less strong on book circulation per member.

The *Pentecostal* group was relatively strong on several variables: percentage of the congregation income going to the library, number of hours staffed per week, congregation income per member, and book and media holdings per member, but less so on library income per member and circulation per member. The *Interdenominational* group was relatively strong on congregational income per member, hours staffed per week, and percentage of congregational income going to the library, but less so on media titles, book circulation, and library income per member.

The *Reformed* church group of libraries was known primarily for being centered in cities (64 percent) rather than suburban or rural locations, and it was relatively strong also in number of years of operation, size of library committee, percentage of congregational income going to the library, congregational size, and library income per member but less so for circulation per month. *Mennonite* churches were relatively strong in congregational income per member, number of committee members, books per member, and years of operation. They appeared on several of the "top 12" tables, and it was clear that several of them were relatively strong in both library financial support and usage per member.

Back to the major denominations now. The *Presbyterian* church library group was the largest in the study. It was among the oldest denominational groups and was located primarily in the Middle West and Middle Atlantic regions. Its libraries were spread out among the three types of settings in average-sized cities. For both raw score and per-member analyses Presbyterian libraries ranked low on no table, most of their rankings being average or above. They ranked third or fourth on thirteen variables but also ninth on one. Overall ranking was fourth of eleven denominations on raw scores and fifth on per member analyses. Consistent!

Now we have come to the *Roman Catholic* church libraries, only twelve of them, the second smallest denominational group in the sample. Again it is regrettable that this group was so small because it ranked in third place overall on raw scores but in eleventh and last place on per-member analyses. A similarity with the Jewish group was the Catholic library pattern of raw score table rankings—almost a complete reversal of their per-member rankings. On seventeen raw score tables this group ranked first, second or third. On three tables, however, it ranked near the bottom, including cost of circulation. On five of six per-member tables it ranked last. An excellent record was marred by the scores on three raw score tables with nothing to redeem it on per-member tables. Catholic parish libraries were the youngest in the study. They were located primarily in the Middle West and Southwest and in large suburban and city areas.

Last alphabetically comes the *United Church of Christ*, which ranked low on thirteen raw score tables, at a middle level on another nine, and in the upper portion of two—library income and library income as a percentage of congregation income. Ranking on four per-member tables was above average, on the other hand. These churches were located primarily in the Middle West, in both large cities and suburban locations, and they were younger than the average. Overall ranking was ninth of eleven denominations in twenty-five raw score tables and fourth of eleven denominations in six per-member tables.

In conclusion, we can see that overall rank of these denominations was approximately the following: Baptist, Other Denominations, Jewish, Presbyterian, Christian, United Church of Christ, Roman Catholic, Methodist, Episcopal/Anglican, Lutheran, and Congregational.

## Significant Findings

This section will address the question, What have we learned about 411 CSLA member congregational libraries which is particularly significant?

We have accumulated a mass of facts and generalizations about them, but which ones of these facts are the most significant?

1. The database seemed to be approximately representative of the CSLA membership on distribution by state, province, and region, as well as by denomination.
2. While the questionnaire database was representative of the CSLA membership and was clearly a national database, probably it was not very representative of the North American congregational library world. Chapter 6 has more information on this topic.
3. Membership and questionnaire return were widely distributed in the United States as a whole, but the Northeast, West, Rocky Mountains, and Canadian areas were poorly represented.
4. In an international comparison, Canada looked both small and poor. Apparently congregational libraries were more sparsely distributed there and were less prosperous, for the most part, than they were in the U.S. Alternatively, the CSLA had little power to attract Canadian libraries.
5. The Middle West and Middle Atlantic regions had the highest concentration of both membership and questionnaire return.
6. Suburban and city locations were the primary geographic focus of congregational libraries.
7. There were no major concentrations of these CSLA libraries in any specific North American cities.
8. There were major differences by denomination and per library in mean city size.
9. Congregation size rose as city population size rose.
10. Though congregational librarianship was basically a post-World War II development, it began in the nineteenth and early twentieth centuries.
11. While mean library age was two decades, Jewish and Roman Catholic libraries contrasted with that figure by being much older and much younger, respectively.
12. While Presbyterian and Methodist were the most numerous denominations, denominational fragmentation was another feature of this sample.
13. House of worship membership size differed in certain cases by

as much as a 43:1 ratio, but the typical congregation had about 1,380 members.

14. Generally, library committees were small, four to ten members, though the range was from one to fifty.

15. The sample seriously underrepresented the large number of congregational libraries that were operated by only one volunteer.

16. Total library committee work hours were also small, most of them two to ten hours per week, and the mean per person was only 2.0 hours per week.

17. The typical library committee head had the title of Librarian.

18. Females dominated library personnel.

19. The typical librarian had had ten years of congregational library experience.

20. One or more professional librarians were found on many library committees, making professional guidance readily available.

21. Certain libraries had paid staff members, so congregational funds were sometimes available for wages or salaries.

22. A surprisingly large number of professional and paid library assistants were found in these libraries, both encouraging signs. It would be useful to learn the trends existing for these two characteristics. Were the recent proportions of libraries with professionals and paid staff members rising?

23. The mean congregation had an annual income of about $370,000.

24. Mean library income was about 0.49 percent of mean congregational income per member.

25. On the other hand, a few congregations were supporting the library with substantial percentages of the congregational income, for example, above 5 percent.

26. Mean library income was $1,640, or $1.53 per congregation member.

27. While the church and synagogue's official budget was the primary source of library funds in this sample, the percentage of congregation funds going to the library was small. The library must have been one of the least-well-supported aspects of the institution's operation.

28. The West and Northeast supported the library best on a per-member basis.

29. Library income rose as congregation income rose.
30. When library expenditures were examined by type, the ratios were the following: salaries, 20 percent; books, newspapers, and periodicals, 58 percent; media, 13 percent; supplies and equipment, 9 percent.
31. Apparently the evangelical and charismatic denominations spent more for library service than did the mainstream denominations, at least a third more on the average.
32. The study suggested that certain house of worship officials regarded libraries as useful for the active congregation which is trying to build up its educational service program and perhaps even that certain of these officials regarded the library as being useful in the evangelizing or missionary programs.
33. Library book holdings averaged twenty-five hundred to three thousand volumes per library, probably representing an increase of about 140 volumes per year since founding.
34. Apparently certain large libraries had collections of at least fifteen to twenty thousand volumes.
35. Apparently the top 5 to 10 percent of these libraries had collections (and in certain cases incomes) that rivaled those of many full-time school and special libraries. This finding shows the steady rise of congregational libraries in size and service.
36. Newspaper and periodical holdings were quite small. Just why the majority of these libraries subscribed to so few newspapers and periodicals is not clear. Further study of this phenomenon is needed.
37. Media holdings varied greatly by denomination.
38. A dozen libraries had several thousand media titles per library.
39. The average library had a total of four titles/volumes of material per congregation member.
40. A few libraries had distinctive book, archive, and media collections, which were particularized.
41. Apparently, cataloging and classification were performed well, and a variety of religious library classification systems was used.
42. Circulation, a library benefit, was small, somewhat over one hundred volumes per month per library on the average, though there were some notable exceptions.

43. Circulation per member averaged 1.68 volumes per year.
44. A few libraries were active in publishing their own bulletins.
45. When total circulation was divided by total library cost, the mean was $11.85 per charge, which was expensive.
46. Among denominations, Jewish, Baptist, and Roman Catholic were the leaders on most raw score tables.
47. On the per-member tables, the Other Denominations, Baptist, and United Church of Christ denominations led all others.
48. A per-member circulation/effort analysis showed Lutheran libraries to have led the rest.
49. The West and Southwest led many regional tables in library service.
50. Twenty-five specific libraries were cited for outstanding records on many raw score tables, and they were led by the First Baptist Church in La Crescenta, California, and the Sinai Temple, Los Angeles, California.
51. Nine specific libraries were cited for outstanding records on per-member tables. They were led by the Burlingame Baptist Church Library, Portland, Oregon and the Perkasie Mennonite Church Library in Perkasie, Pennsylvania.
52. A set of ten objective standards was recommended for consideration in the field.

## Summary

Table summaries were shown for the eleven denominations on twenty-three to twenty-five raw score tables. Jewish, Baptist, and Roman Catholics scored high and Congregational libraries scored low on these tables. On the per-member analyses, Other Denominations, Baptist, and Christian libraries scored high and Roman Catholic libraries scored low. The specific leading libraries on these tables were shown in tables 5.142 and 5.143 which included some overlap. The subsection concluded with a brief characterization of the libraries in each denomination. In conclusion, a list of the fifty-three most significant findings was given.

# Notes

1. Joyce L. White, "The Demography of American Church and Synagogue Libraries," in *Church and Synagogue Libraries*, ed. John F. Harvey (Metuchen, N.J.: Scarecrow, 1980), pp. 19–33.

2. See chapters 11 and 19 of Harvey's *Church and Synagogue Libraries*, (2) "Church and Synagogue Libraries," *Drexel Library Quarterly* 6 (April 1970): 147–53; (3) Catholic Library Association, *Handbook and Membership Directory* (Haverford: CLA; 1989), pp. 4, 5; and Mancil Ezell, "The Church Media Library Going for the Gold," *Church Media Library Magazine* 8 (October/December 1992): 6–7.

3. Dorothy J. Rodda, "The Church and Synagogue Library Association," In *Church and Synagogue Libraries*, pp. 241–64.

4. Claudia Hannaford, "CSLA Survey of Librarians Tabulated," *Church and Synagogue Libraries* (Bulletin) 119 (November/December 1985): 1, 5.

5. *Yearbook of American and Canadian Churches 1993*, ed. Kenneth B. Bedell (Nashville: Abingdon 1993), pp. 257–58.

6. *Statistical Abstract of the United States* (Washington, D.C.: Government Printing Office, 1984), pp. 134–36.

7. *Yearbook of American and Canadian Churches*, pp. 253, 257.

8. *World Almanac 1988* (New York: Pharos Books, 1988), pp. 227, 229.

9. *American Library Directory* (New York: R. R. Bowker Company, annual).

10. Harvey, *Church and Synagogue Libraries*.

11. *Yearbook of American and Canadian Churches*, pp. 253, 257.

12. *American Library Directory*, 1988, s.v. "Alabama."

13. The denominations shown in table 5.2 represent those in each state or province with the largest numbers of libraries. In certain cases, two or more denominations were tied in number of libraries, so only the first one listed alphabetically was shown in the table, due to space limitations.

14. The reader should note that a large number of tables is used herein to show findings. The book's discussion is often strongly influenced by its statistical findings. The discussion is oriented primarily around the book's topics and ideas and the libraries' services, and its tables and statistics provide a convenient and succinct way of displaying information and expressing the degree to which topics or services are present or absent, strong or weak. Tables show more data than can easily be given in a prose discussion. Further, it should be noted that certain percentage columns in specific tables add up to a figure that is only approximately 100 percent, due to the function of rounding off, a necessary process to avoid the appearance of spurious accuracy.

15. *Canadian Library Yearbook* (Toronto: Micromedia, 1987).

16. In table 5.4 the first line for each domination shows the raw score or N for each region under each denomination. The table's second line can be read from left to right to learn the regional percentage distribution of the libraries in each denomination. Under each denomination the table can be read from top to bottom to learn the denominational percentage distribution of the libraries in each region. Thus for Lutherans under NE, the figures show two libraries, that 5 percent of the Lutheran libraries were found in the Northeast and that Lutherans constituted 10 percent of all Northeast libraries.

17. Harvey, *Church and Synagogue Libraries*, pp. x–xi.

18. The author believes that the upsurge in congregational library inauguration had leveled off or even started to decline by 1986, but only guesswork is available to support that belief.

19. The age differential may be just an accident of this particular small sample. However, there are many findings in this study that the author can only describe, not explain. The primary function of the study is to describe in a relatively new and unresearched field rather than to probe deeply into details. The data available will not support such intensive analysis. Perhaps later studies by other students will be able to ascertain causes, influences, relationships, and histories to a much fuller extent than this one can.

20. The author used a simplified denominational breakdown by placing all separate but related groups with the same basic name into one major denominational category. For instance, all separate Lutheran groups—Lutheran Church-Missouri Synod, Evangelical Lutheran Church, Wisconsin Evangelical Lutheran Church, and so on—were placed in one all-inclusive Lutheran denominational category.

21. *Yearbook of American and Canadian Churches*, p. 264.

22. *Ibid.*, p. 259.

23. The *ALD* grand scholarly and popular totals (p. xi) were 30,717 libraries in the United States and 3,649 libraries in Canada, giving Canada 11.9 percent of the total.

24. ". . . Christian Science Reading Rooms," *Christian Science Journal* 106 (May 1988): 9–30.

25. See John F. Harvey, "An Introductory World Survey of Popular Church and Synagogue Libraries," *International Library Review* 18 (October 1986): 350. See especially footnote 2 and David M. Mayfield, "The Genealogical Library of the Church of Jesus Christ of Latter-day Saints," *Library Trends* 32 (Summer 1983): 111–27.

26. Personal letters dated October 20, 1988, and December 9, 1988, from Dean Hollister, director, Informational Databases, R. R. Bowker, 245 West 17th Street, New York, NY 10011. Perhaps it should be noted that the author offered Hollister the 1988 CSLA membership address list of two thousand names as a way of increasing *ALD* coverage of popular religious libraries. However, Hollister refused the offer and said that "while we do not exclude libraries based on size or type if they wish to be in *ALD*, I think these libraries are too small and specialized for us to make a special effort to include (them)."

27. The author will be grateful to any person who sends him more accurate information to improve these figures which, in certain instances, are merely estimates that have neither been proven to be accurate nor inaccurate.

28. *Statistical Abstract*, pp. 156–57.

29. See *Directory of Church and Synagogue Libraries in Maryland*, ed. Joyce White (Bryn Mawr, Pa.: Church and Synagogue Library Association, 1973)

and *New Mexico Church and Synagogue Library Directory*, ed. L. Martin Ruoss and Marilyn M. Ruoss (Albuquerque: University of New Mexico Zimmerman Library, 1973).

30. L. Jones Milbrey, "NCES Survey of Private School Library Media Centers 1979," *Bowker Annual* (New York: R. R. Bowker, 1983), pp. 352–55. The 1979 U.S. National Center for Education Services survey found about 14,200 private school libraries with 28,400 employees @ 2.0 employees per library. In this study, incidentally, Milbrey found that Roman Catholic schools were most likely to have libraries (97 percent), schools with another religious affiliation were next most likely to have libraries (68 percent), and schools without religious affiliation were least likely to have them (62 percent).

31. This estimate assumes that there are 41,280 popular and 2,180 scholarly religious libraries in the United States. If we can arbitrarily assume an average of three (part-time) staff members in each popular and six full-time staff members in each scholarly religious library (see chaps. 2, 3, and 4), these figures will give us totals of 123,840 popular and 13,080 scholarly library staff members, or a grand total of 136,920 staff members, part-time and full-time.

32. This is essentially a negative comment on the size and character of the library research component of each country, and not on the inadequacy of the religious library field. On the other hand, critics of the religious library field who conceive it to be a derivative one with little to recommend it as unique or creative within the larger library world have made a valid, if diffuse, point. Probably this argument is largely valid for religious scholarly but less so for popular libraries, however.

House of worship libraries, constituting the bulk of the popular religious library field, are unique in both their institutional setting and the character of their work. No other type of library serves houses of worship directly as their institutional library, and the character of their work is that of a hybrid. In type, they are either (1) special libraries serving an institutional program for part-time schools and religious congregations, (2) part-time private religious school libraries, or (3) neither of the above but instead a unique and distinctive combination of school and special library constituting a separate form or type of library in their own right. This author recommends (3).

33. See White,"The Demography of American Church and Synagogue Libraries," pp. 19–33.

34. Of course, a half hour's attendance at any annual CSLA or LCLA conference or chapter meeting would have told the reader the answer to that question. All of these groups, including AJL and Cath LA were primarily female organizations. Although the personal age question was not asked on the questionnaire, again based on conference observation and library visits, the author believes that the typical female congregational librarian was well into middle age, perhaps in her middle or late 50s.

35. Harvey, *Church and Synagogue Libraries*, p. viii.

36. This study's means were often influenced by the atypically high values of a few superlative libraries. In such cases the means were skewed toward the high end. As a result their calculation was carried out in such a way as to partly compensate for this complication. The author and statistician were aware of the nature of the skew and deliberately designed category systems to minimize the distortion of the mean and mode. No distortion of this sort ever affected the median, however. Median values were always 100 percent accurate.

37. The author recognizes the problems of mixing U.S. and Canadian dollars in these tables, two currencies with not quite the same value. But he believes that the separate currencies purchased about the same amount of congregational library service. He recognizes further that he is mixing various groups that may count their memberships differently. Certain groups count heads while other groups count families. The reader should bear these differences in mind when comparing denominational membership figures.

38. See Lyle Schaller, "UMC: What's the Future of the Small-Church Denomination?" *Circuit Rider* 11 (December/January, 1987): 8–10 and David A. Roozen and Adair T. Lummis, *Leadership and Theological Education in the Episcopal Church* (Hartford: Hartford Seminary Center for Social and Religious Education, 1987). Schaller reported that in 1984, 10,117 Methodist congregations (about 27 percent of the U.S. total) had an average attendance of thirty-five or fewer persons at regular Sunday morning services and that about 7 percent of the Lutheran churches had attendance at the same low level. The figure for Episcopal/Anglican churches at this attendance level was 38 percent of the whole group. These figures make it easier to understand denominational groups with low annual congregational expenditures.

39. The author has greater confidence in the general usefulness of this ranking for Baptist than for Jewish and Roman Catholic libraries, however, due to the larger size of the Baptist subsample than those of the Jewish and Roman Catholic groups here.

40. As of December 1994, the list of member libraries that had reached level 3 (the top level) of the CSLA self-assessment program was the following:

## Self-Assessment Completed - Level 3

| Date | Church/Address | Librarian |
|------|----------------|-----------|
| 03/05/87 | Reformed Presbyterian Church of Atonement 10613 Georgia Street Wheaton, MD 20902 | Vicky Hess |
| 04/28/92 | Babylon United Methodist Church 21 James Street Babylon, NY 11702 | Deborah K. Morris |

| | | |
|---|---|---|
| 02/14/88 | Bakerview Mennonite Brethren Church 2285 Clearbrook Road Clearbrook, BC Canada V2T 2X4 | Betty Giesbrecht |
| 10/28/91 | Belmont United Methodist Church P.O. Box 1200098 Nashville, TN 37212 | Christine Brown |
| 05/01/91 | Carmel Presbyterian Church Carmel Memorial Library 100 Edge Hill Road Glenside, PA 19038 | Margaret Eaton |
| 06/29/89 | Castleview Baptist Church 8601 Hague Road Indianapolis, IN 46256 | Lillian Koppin |
| 03/09/92 | Central United Methodist Church 616 Jackson Street S.E. Decatur, AL 35601 | Kitty DeFreese |
| 12/13/93 | Christ The Good Shepherd Catholic Church 18511 Klein Church Road Spring, TX 77379 | Jane Arnholt |
| 11/16/89 | Corpus Christi Church Corpus Christi Library 234 Southern Boulevard Chatham, NJ 07928 | Lottie Kula |
| 02/28/88 | Clear Lake United Methodist Church Library 16335 El Camino Road Houston, TX 77062 | Betty Burghduff |
| 07/18/91 | Epeworth United Methodist Church Library 9008 Rosemont Drive Gaitherburg, IN 20877 | Lois Seyfrit |
| 10/26/92 | First Baptist Church 2025 Sonoma Boulevard Vallejo, CA 94590 | Anita Flaten-Falltrick |
| 02/19/90 | First Baptist Shawnee Church 11400 Johnson Drive Shawnee, KS 66203 | Jean Miller |
| 01/19/93 | First Baptist Church 175 Allen's Creek Road Rochester, NY 14618 | Ms. Henderson |
| 01/15/92 | First Church of God 4300 Lansing Avenue Jackson, MI 49201 | Dianne Barnum |

| 08/08/87 | First Church of the Nazarene<br>1200 North Liberty Road<br>Boise, ID 83704 | Betty Waller |
|---|---|---|
| 07/22/91 | First Congregational Church<br>535 Forest Avenue<br>Glen Ellyn, IL 60137 | Virginia Less |
| 10/26/86 | First Presbyterian Church<br>106 East Church Street<br>Orlando, FL 32801 | Suzanne Sugiuchi |
| 05/23/94 | First Presbyterian Church<br>One Symphony Circle<br>Buffalo, NY 14201 | El Schneiderman |
| 09/19/93 | First United Methodist Church<br>474 E. Main Street<br>Springville, NY 14141 | Helen R. Shearer |
| 11/27/86 | First United Methodist Church<br>1016 Sam Houston Avenue<br>Huntsville, TX 77340 | Janelle Paris |
| 03/12/89 | Fourth Presbyterian Church<br>Grace Churchill, Media<br>    Services Administrator<br>5500 River Road<br>Bethesda, MD 20816 | Robert Klassen |
| 05/08/90 | Grace United Methodist Church<br>306 W. 30th Street<br>Marion, IN 46953 | Margaret Perin |
| 10/27/92 | Highland Christian Church<br>3384 West 119 Street<br>Cleveland, OH 44111 | Shirley Berndsen |
| 04/20/93 | Highlands United Church Library<br>3255 Edgemont Boulevard<br>North Vancouver, BC<br>    Canada V7R 2P1 | Elizabeth Glavin |
| 02/06/92 | Hyde Park Community United<br>    Methodist Church<br>1345 Grace Avenue<br>Cincinnati, OH 45208 | Shirley Joy |
| 02/01/91 | Jarvis Memorial United Methodist<br>    Church<br>510 S. Washington Street<br>Greenville, NC 27858 | Lois G. Patterson |
| 10/01/86 | Mt. Paran Church of God<br>2055 Mt. Paran Road N.W.<br>Atlanta, GA 30327 | Sally Bruce McClatchey |

| | | |
|---|---|---|
| 07/15/91 | Martin Reformed Church<br>1073 West Allegan St Rd 192<br>Martin, MI 49070 | Leona Schipper |
| 06/06/88 | Oak Hill Presbyterian Church<br>2406 Ardwell Avenue<br>Akron, OH 44312 | Zelma Myers |
| 10/30/94 | Penfield United Methodist Church<br>1795 Baird Road<br>Penfield, NY 14526 | Thelma Twiss |
| 02/16/90 | Pleasant Valley Church of Brethren<br>Rt. 1, Box 204<br>Weyers Cave, VA 24486 | Nellie Flora |
| 01/14/92 | Plymouth Congregational Church<br>2001 E. Grand River Street<br>Lansing, MI 48912 | Helen Elliot |
| 11/26/93 | Ryerson United Church<br>2195 W. 45th Avenue<br>Vancouver, BC Canada V6M 2J2 | Carol Sloan |
| 10/10/88 | St. Charles Borromeo Church<br>2224 E. Third Street<br>Bloomington, IN 47401 | Ruth Gleason |
| 05/08/90 | St. Matthew's United Methodist<br>Church<br>P.O. Box 10026<br>Houston, TX 77206 | Dorothy Lofton |
| 05/24/93 | Shiloh United Church of Christ<br>5300 Philadelphia Drive<br>Dayton, OH 45415 | Phyllis Banta |
| 05/25/94 | Temple Baptist Church<br>807 W. Chapel Hill Street<br>Durham, NC 27701-3112 | Mary Beth Conover |
| 07/22/91 | Third Reformed Church<br>2345 N. 10th Street<br>Kalamazoo, MI 49009 | Lora LaNae Hess |
| 06/29/92 | Triumphant Love Lutheran Church<br>9508 Great Hills Trails<br>Austin, TX 78759 | Eleanor Erchinger |
| 10/21/91 | Wayne Presbyterian Church<br>125 East Lancaster Avenue<br>Wayne, PA 19087 | Mary Augusterfer |
| 02/04/92 | Westwood First Presbyterian<br>Church<br>3011 Harrison Avenue<br>Cincinnati, OH 45211 | Marian McNair |

Personal Letter from Lorraine E. Burson, Church and Synagogue Library Association, Portland, OR 97280-0357, dated December 11, 1992, plus a supplementary list from Judy Janzen, CSLA, dated January 25, 1995.

TABLE 5.1

1988 Estimate of the Number of North American Popular Religious
and Nonreligious Libraries

| Kind of Library | Number of Libraries | Source of Information: Chapter 5, Note: |
|---|---|---|
| NONRELIGIOUS | | |
| Canadian | | |
| Public school | 7,100 | 6 |
| Private school | 300 | 6 |
| Public | 1,700[a] | 9, 15 |
| American | | |
| Public school | 71,000 | 6 |
| Private school | 3,000 | 6, 30 |
| Public | 15,000 | 9 |
| Total | 98,100 | |
| POPULAR RELIGIOUS | | |
| Canadian | | |
| House of worship | 500 | 1, 10, 15 |
| Parochial and private school | 1,000 | 1, 6, 8, 10, 15, 30 |
| Public | 20 | 10 |
| Christian Science reading room | 70 | 10, 15, 24 |
| Church of Jesus Christ of Latter-day Saints | 150 | 10, 15, 25 |
| American | | |
| House of worship | 25,300 | 1, 10 |
| Parochial and private school | 11,200 | 1, 6, 8, 10, 30 |
| Public | 40 | 1, 10 |
| Christian Science reading room | 1,500 | 34 |
| Church of Jesus Christ of Latter-day Saints | 3,200 | 10, 25 |
| Total | 42,980 | |
| GRAND TOTAL | 141,080 | |

[a]Includes branches.

TABLE 5.2
Church and Synagogue Library Association Major Denominations by
Region — The Most Common Denominations in Each State/Province

| Region | Name of State | Major Denominations | Number of Libraries | % of State Totals | State Totals |
|---|---|---|---|---|---|
| Northeast | Connecticut | Congregational | 6 | | |
| | | Episcopal/Anglican | 5 | 11 | 79 | 14 |
| | Massachusetts | Congregational | 2 | | |
| | | Episcopal/Anglican | 1 | | |
| | | Other Denominations | 1 | 4 | 100 | 4 |
| | Maine | Congregational | 1 | | |
| | | Episcopal/Anglican | 1 | 2 | 100 | 2 |
| Middle Atlantic | District of Columbia | Baptist | 1 | | |
| | | Episcopal/Anglican | 1 | | |
| | | Presbyterian | 3 | 5 | 100 | 5 |
| | Delaware | Methodist | 2 | | |
| | | Other Denominations | 1 | 3 | 100 | 3 |
| | Maryland | Methodist | 4 | | |
| | | Other Denominations | 4 | 8 | 62 | 13 |
| | New Jersey | Methodist | 2 | | |
| | | Other Denominations | 2 | | |
| | | Presbyterian | 2 | 6 | 67 | 9 |
| | New York | Methodist | 3 | | |
| | | Presbyterian | 3 | 6 | 60 | 10 |
| | Pennsylvania | Episcopal/Anglican | 6 | | |
| | | Other Denominations | 7 | | |
| | | Presbyterian | 12 | 25 | 68 | 37 |
| Southeast | Alabama | Presbyterian | 2 | 2 | 100 | 2 |
| | Florida | Methodist | 6 | | |
| | | Presbyterian | 4 | 10 | 56 | 18 |
| | Georgia | Episcopal/Anglican | 4 | | |
| | | Methodist | 2 | | |
| | | Other Denominations | 2 | 8 | 73 | 11 |
| | North Carolina | Episcopal/Anglican | 2 | | |
| | | Presbyterian | 2 | 4 | 57 | 7 |
| | South Carolina | Presbyterian | 1 | 1 | 100 | 1 |
| | Tennessee | Methodist | 3 | | |
| | | United Church of Christ | 1 | 4 | 100 | 4 |
| | Virginia | Methodist | 3 | | |
| | | Other Denominations | 3 | | |
| | | Presbyterian | 4 | 10 | 83 | 12 |

TABLE 5.2 (continued)
Church and Synagogue Library Association Major Denominations by
Region—The Most Common Denominations in Each State/Province

| Region | Name of State | Major Denominations | Number of Libraries | % of State Totals | State Totals |
|--------|---------------|--------------------|--------------------|-------------------|--------------|
| Southeast (cont.) | West Virginia | Baptist | 2 | | |
| | | Lutheran | 1 | | |
| | | Presbyterian | 1 | 4 | 100 | 4 |
| Southwest | Arkansas | Methodist | 1 | 1 | 100 | 1 |
| | Arizona | Methodist | 1 | | |
| | | United Church of Christ | 2 | 3 | 100 | 3 |
| | Louisiana | Baptist | 1 | 1 | 100 | 1 |
| | New Mexico | Methodist | 5 | | |
| | | Presbyterian | 3 | 8 | 53 | 15 |
| | Oklahoma | Episcopal/Anglican | 1 | | |
| | | Methodist | 1 | 2 | 100 | 2 |
| | Texas | Methodist | 10 | | |
| | | Presbyterian | 7 | 17 | 41 | 41 |
| West | California | Methodist | 5 | | |
| | | Other Denominations | 4 | | |
| | | Presbyterian | 5 | 14 | 64 | 22 |
| | Oregon | Other Denominations | 3 | | |
| | | Presbyterian | 2 | 5 | 63 | 8 |
| | Washington | Christian | 1 | | |
| | | Lutheran | 2 | | |
| | | Other Denominations | 1 | | |
| | | Presbyterian | 1 | 5 | 100 | 5 |
| Rocky Mountain | Colorado | Christian | 1 | | |
| | | Congregational | 1 | | |
| | | Presbyterian | 3 | 5 | 100 | 5 |
| | Wyoming | Episcopal/Anglican | 1 | 1 | 100 | 1 |
| Middle West | Iowa | Lutheran | 3 | | |
| | | Methodist | 3 | 6 | 86 | 7 |
| | Illinois | Lutheran | 5 | | |
| | | Methodist | 5 | 10 | 63 | 16 |
| | Indiana | Methodist | 7 | | |
| | | Other Denominations | 2 | | |
| | | Presbyterian | 2 | 11 | 73 | 15 |
| | Kansas | Methodist | 2 | | |
| | | Baptist/Christian (1 each) | 2 | | |
| | | Episcopal/RC/UCC (1 each) | 3 | 7 | 100 | 7 |

TABLE 5.2 (continued)
Church and Synagogue Library Association Major Denominations by
Region — The Most Common Denominations in Each State/Province

| Region | Name of State | Major Denominations | Number of Libraries | % of State Totals | State Totals |
|--------|---------------|---------------------|---------------------|-------------------|--------------|
| | Michigan | Congregational | 3 | | |
| | | Other Denominations | 15 | 18 | 78 | 23 |
| | Minnesota | Congregational | 1 | | |
| | | Lutheran | 5 | | |
| | | Presbyterian | 1 | 7 | 100 | 7 |
| | Missouri | Methodist | 2 | | |
| | | Presbyterian | 4 | | |
| | | United Church of Christ | 2 | 8 | 73 | 11 |
| | Nevada | Christian | 1 | | |
| | | Methodist | 1 | | |
| | | Other Denominations | 1 | 3 | 100 | 3 |
| | Ohio | Christian | 7 | | |
| | | Methodist | 11 | | |
| | | Presbyterian | 11 | 29 | 62 | 47 |
| | South Dakota | Lutheran | 1 | 1 | 100 | 1 |
| | Wisconsin | Congregational | 1 | | |
| | | Lutheran | 1 | | |
| | | Methodist | 1 | | |
| | | Roman Catholic | 1 | 4 | 100 | 4 |
| Canada | Alberta | Other Denominations | 1 | 1 | 100 | 1 |
| | British Colombia | Episcopal/Anglican | 1 | 1 | 100 | 1 |
| | Manitoba | Other Denominations | 1 | 1 | 100 | 1 |
| | Ontario | Baptist | 2 | | |
| | | Other Denominations | 4 | 6 | 86 | 7 |
| Total | | | | 288 | 70 | 411 |

TABLE 5.3
Church and Synagogue Library Association: A Regional Analysis: Table Rankings[a]

| Region | Table V-2 % of Total Libraries | Table V-5 Library Age | Table V-5 Librarian Experience | Table V-7 Congregation Income | Table V-7 Library Income | Table V-7 Library Income per Member | Table V-13 Volumes | Table V-5 Newspaper and Periodical Titles | Table V-15 Circulation | Table V-145 Final Library Summary | Table Ranking Means |
|---|---|---|---|---|---|---|---|---|---|---|---|
| Northeast | 6 | 1 | 6 | 8 | 8 | 2 | 8 | 8 | 8 | 6 | 6.1 |
| Middle Atlantic | 2 | 6 | 1 | 7 | 7 | 5 | 4 | 2 | 7 | 3 | 4.4 |
| Southeast | 4 | 7 | 2 | 4 | 4 | 3 | 3 | 6 | 4 | 5 | 4.2 |
| Southwest | 3 | 5 | 7 | 2 | 2 | 6 | 2 | 1 | 5 | 4 | 3.7 |
| West | 5 | 3 | 3 | 3 | 1 | 1 | 1 | 3 | 1 | 1 | 2.2 |
| Rocky Mountains | 8 | 2 | 5 | 1 | 3 | 8 | 7 | 4 | 3 | 7 | 4.8 |
| Middle West | 1 | 4 | 4 | 6 | 5 | 4 | 5 | 5 | 6 | 2 | 4.2 |
| Canada | 7 | 8 | 8 | 5 | 6 | 7 | 6 | 7 | 2 | 8 | 6.4 |

[a]For this table, regions with the lowest mean scores rank highest, as a "1" represents top place whereas "8" is lowest. Highest overall score is for the western region.

TABLE 5.4

Church and Synagogue Library Association. Congregational Libraries by Denomination and Geographic Region

| Denomination | NE | MA | SE | SW | W | RM | MW | CAN | Number | Percentage |
|---|---|---|---|---|---|---|---|---|---|---|
| Baptist (N) | 0 | 6 | 4 | 5 | 4 | 0 | 5 | 2 | 26 | 100 |
| % (Horizontal) | 0 | 23 | 15 | 19 | 15 | 0 | 19 | 8 | | |
| % (Vertical) | 0 | 8 | 7 | 8 | 11 | 0 | 4 | 20 | | |
| Christian | 0 | 1 | 4 | 1 | 3 | 1 | 11 | 0 | 21 | 100 |
| % (Horizontal) | 0 | 5 | 19 | 5 | 14 | 5 | 52 | 0 | | |
| % (Vertical) | 0 | 1 | 7 | 2 | 9 | 17 | 8 | 0 | | |
| Congregational | 9 | 1 | 0 | 0 | 0 | 1 | 6 | 0 | 17 | 100 |
| % (Horizontal) | 53 | 6 | 0 | 0 | 0 | 6 | 35 | 0 | | |
| % (Vertical) | 45 | 1 | 0 | 0 | 0 | 17 | 4 | 0 | | |
| Episcopal/Anglican | 7 | 10 | 9 | 8 | 3 | 1 | 4 | 1 | 43 | 100 |
| % (Horizontal) | 16 | 23 | 21 | 19 | 7 | 2 | 9 | 2 | | |
| % (Vertical) | 35 | 13 | 15 | 13 | 9 | 17 | 3 | 10 | | |
| Lutheran | 2 | 3 | 3 | 7 | 3 | 0 | 23 | 1 | 42 | 100 |
| % (Horizontal) | 5 | 7 | 7 | 17 | 7 | 0 | 55 | 2 | | |
| % (Vertical) | 10 | 4 | 5 | 11 | 9 | 0 | 16 | 10 | | |
| Methodist | 0 | 14 | 15 | 18 | 4 | 0 | 29 | 0 | 80 | 100 |
| % (Horizontal) | 0 | 18 | 19 | 22 | 5 | 0 | 37 | 0 | | |
| % (Vertical) | 0 | 18 | 25 | 29 | 11 | 0 | 21 | 0 | | |
| Other Denominations | 2 | 12 | 5 | 3 | 9 | 0 | 20 | 6 | 57 | 100 |
| % (Horizontal) | 4 | 21 | 9 | 5 | 16 | 0 | 35 | 11 | | |
| % (Vertical) | 10 | 16 | 8 | 5 | 26 | 0 | 14 | 60 | | |
| Presbyterian | 0 | 24 | 15 | 10 | 8 | 3 | 25 | 0 | 85 | 100 |
| % (Horizontal) | 0 | 28 | 18 | 12 | 9 | 4 | 29 | 0 | | |
| % (Vertical) | 0 | 31 | 25 | 16 | 23 | 50 | 18 | 0 | | |
| United Church of Christ | 0 | 3 | 2 | 5 | 0 | 0 | 12 | 0 | 22 | 100 |
| % (Horizontal) | 0 | 14 | 9 | 23 | 0 | 0 | 55 | 0 | | |
| % (Vertical) | 0 | 4 | 3 | 8 | 0 | 0 | 9 | 0 | | |
| Summary | | | | | | | | | | |
| Jewish | 0 | 1 | 1 | 1 | 1 | 0 | 2 | 0 | 6 | 100 |
| % (Horizontal) | 0 | 17 | 17 | 17 | 17 | 0 | 33 | 0 | | |
| % (Vertical) | 0 | 1 | 2 | 2 | 3 | 0 | 1 | 0 | | |
| Roman Catholic | 0 | 2 | 1 | 5 | 0 | 0 | 4 | 0 | 12 | 100 |
| % (Horizontal) | 0 | 17 | 8 | 42 | 0 | 0 | 33 | 0 | | |
| % (Vertical) | 0 | 3 | 2 | 8 | 0 | 0 | 3 | 0 | | |
| All Protestant | 20 | 74 | 57 | 57 | 34 | 6 | 135 | 10 | 393 | 100 |
| % (Horizontal) | 5 | 19 | 15 | 15 | 9 | 2 | 34 | 3 | | |
| % (Vertical) | 100 | 96 | 97 | 90 | 97 | 100 | 96 | 100 | | |
| Total | 20 | 77 | 59 | 63 | 35 | 6 | 141 | 10 | 411 | 100 |
| % (Horizontal) | 5 | 19 | 14 | 15 | 9 | 1 | 34 | 2 | | |
| % (Vertical) | 100% | 100% | 100% | 100% | 100% | 100% | 100% | 100% | | |

TABLE 5.5

Church and Synagogue Library Association: Three Variables Analyzed by Region[a]

| Region | Mean Library Age (Years) | Rank | Mean Years of Librarian Experience | Rank | Mean Number of Newspaper and Periodical Titles | Rank | Cumulative Gross Rank | Rank |
|---|---|---|---|---|---|---|---|---|
| Northeast | 25.7 | 1 | 9.3 | 6 | 4.1 | 8 | 15 | 2 |
| Middle Atlantic | 18.3 | 6 | 11.2 | 1 | 9.8 | 2 | 9 | 5 |
| Southeast | 18.1 | 7 | 10.8 | 2 | 6.7 | 6 | 15 | 2 |
| Southwest | 18.8 | 5 | 8.9 | 7 | 11.9 | 1 | 13 | 3 |
| West | 25.1 | 3 | 10.4 | 3 | 9.4 | 3 | 9 | 5 |
| Rocky Mountains | 25.6 | 2 | 9.7 | 5 | 7.5 | 4 | 11 | 4 |
| Middle West | 20.8 | 4 | 9.8 | 4 | 7.3 | 5 | 13 | 3 |
| Canada | 12.1 | 8 | 8.4 | 8 | 5.6 | 7 | 23 | 1 |
| Total | 20.0 | | 10.0 | | 8.4 | | | |

[a]Gross rank in this table shows libraries with the highest scores, e.g., 23, to take top rank, e.g., 1.

TABLE 5.6

Church and Synagogue Library Association: List of Denominations for Either Leading States or Those in Second Position

| Denomination | Leading Position | % | Second Position | % | Total Libraries | % |
|---|---|---|---|---|---|---|
| Baptist | 2 | 3 | 3 | 7 | 5 | 5 |
| Christian | 1 | 2 | 4 | 10 | 5 | 5 |
| Congregational | 4 | 7 | 3 | 7 | 7 | 7 |
| Episcopal/Anglican | 6 | 10 | 5 | 13 | 11 | 11 |
| Lutheran | 6 | 10 | 1 | 3 | 7 | 7 |
| Methodist | 17 | 29 | 4 | 10 | 21 | 21 |
| Other Denominations | 7 | 12 | 8 | 20 | 15 | 15 |
| Presbyterian | 14 | 24 | 8 | 20 | 22 | 23 |
| U.C.C. | 1 | 2 | 3 | 7 | 4 | 4 |
| Summary | | | | | | |
| Jewish | 0 | 0 | 0 | 0 | 0 | 0 |
| Roman Catholic | 1 | 2 | 1 | 3 | 2 | 2 |
| All Protestant | 58 | 99 | 39 | 97 | 98 | 98 |
| Total | 59 | 100 | 40 | 100 | 100 | 100 |

TABLE 5.7

Church and Synagogue Library Association: Annual Congregational
and Library Income per Congregation and per Congregation Member
by Region

| Region | Number of Congregations/ Libraries | Mean Congregational Income | Budget per Library | Library Income per Congregation Member |
|---|---|---|---|---|
| Northeast | 20 | $199,742 | $ 740 | $1.70 |
| Middle Atlantic | 77 | 77,273 | 1,087 | 1.40 |
| Southeast | 59 | 424,584 | 1,818 | 1.50 |
| Southwest | 63 | 396,141 | 1,961 | 1.70 |
| West | 35 | 401,686 | 4,556 | 2.80 |
| Rocky Mountains | 6 | 606,763 | 1,649 | 0.90 |
| Middle West | 141 | 106,950 | 1,200 | 1.20 |
| Canada | 10 | 330,439 | 1,092 | 2.10 |
| Total | 411 | 233,665 | 1,654 | 1.50 |

TABLE 5.8
Church and Synagogue Library Association: Denominational Breakdown by Region

| Region | Baptist | Christian | Congregational | Episcopal/ Anglican | Lutheran | Methodist | Other Denoms | Presbyterian | UCC | Jewish | Roman Catholic | All Libraries |
|---|---|---|---|---|---|---|---|---|---|---|---|---|
| NE | 0 | 0 | 9 | 7 | 2 | 0 | 2 | 0 | 0 | 0 | 0 | 20 |
| MA | 6 | 1 | 1 | 10 | 3 | 14 | 12 | 24 | 3 | 1 | 2 | 77 |
| SE | 4 | 4 | 0 | 9 | 3 | 15 | 5 | 15 | 2 | 1 | 1 | 59 |
| SW | 5 | 1 | 0 | 8 | 7 | 18 | 3 | 10 | 5 | 1 | 5 | 63 |
| WEST | 4 | 3 | 0 | 3 | 3 | 4 | 9 | 8 | 0 | 1 | 0 | 35 |
| RM | 0 | 1 | 1 | 1 | 0 | 0 | 0 | 3 | 0 | 0 | 0 | 6 |
| MW | 5 | 11 | 6 | 4 | 23 | 29 | 20 | 25 | 12 | 2 | 4 | 141 |
| CAN | 2 | 0 | 0 | 1 | 1 | 0 | 6 | 0 | 0 | 0 | 0 | 10 |
| TOTAL | 26 | 21 | 17 | 43 | 42 | 80 | 57 | 85 | 22 | 6 | 12 | 411 |

TABLE 5.9
Church and Synagogue Library Association: Total Library Income by Region

| Region | $1–500 | % | $501–1,000 | % | $1,001–10,000 | % | $10,001 & over | % | No Response | % | All Libraries | Mean |
|---|---|---|---|---|---|---|---|---|---|---|---|---|
| NE | 12 | 60 | 5 | 25 | 3 | 15 | 0 | 0 | 0 | 0 | 20 | $740 |
| MA | 32 | 42 | 25 | 32 | 18 | 23 | 1 | 1 | 1 | 1 | 77 | 1,087 |
| SE | 20 | 34 | 19 | 32 | 17 | 29 | 2 | 3 | 1 | 2 | 59 | 1,818 |
| SW | 24 | 38 | 11 | 17 | 26 | 41 | 2 | 3 | 0 | 0 | 63 | 1,961 |
| WEST | 11 | 31 | 9 | 26 | 11 | 31 | 4 | 11 | 0 | 0 | 35 | 4,556 |
| RM | 3 | 50 | 2 | 33 | 1 | 17 | 0 | 0 | 0 | 0 | 6 | 1,649 |
| MW | 68 | 48 | 42 | 30 | 26 | 18 | 4 | 3 | 1 | 1 | 141 | 1,200 |
| CAN | 2 | 20 | 5 | 50 | 3 | 30 | 0 | 0 | 0 | 0 | 10 | 1,092 |
| TOTAL | 172 | 42 | 118 | 29 | 105 | 26 | 13 | 3 | 3 | 1 | 411 | 1,654 |

TABLE 5.10
Church and Synagogue Library Association: Means and Percentages of Total Expenditures Accounted for by Each of Five Expenditure Categories by Setting[a]

| | Books | % | Media Purchases | % | Equipment | % | Supplies | % | Salaries | % | Total Expenditure | Expend % |
|---|---|---|---|---|---|---|---|---|---|---|---|---|---|
| Urban | $1,090 | 56 | $234 | 12 | $53 | 3 | $75 | 4 | $506 | 26 | $1,958 | 45 |
| Rural | 557 | 70 | 96 | 12 | 29 | 4 | 51 | 6 | 64 | 8 | 797 | 18 |
| Suburban | 941 | 59 | 235 | 15 | 76 | 5 | 78 | 5 | 268 | 17 | 1,598 | 37 |
| Total | 944 | 58 | 215 | 13 | 60 | 4 | 73 | 5 | 332 | 20 | 1,619 | 100 |

[a]Number of cases in this study was 410. One library could not be placed by setting.

TABLE 5.11

Church and Synagogue Library Association: Library Age by Region

| Region | 1–5 | % | 6–9 | % | 11–25 | % | 26 & over | % | No Response | % | All Libraries | Mean Years |
|--------|-----|---|-----|---|-------|---|-----------|---|-------------|---|---------------|------------|
| NE | 5 | 25 | 1 | 5 | 5 | 25 | 4 | 20 | 5 | 25 | 20 | 25 |
| MA | 9 | 12 | 13 | 17 | 32 | 42 | 21 | 27 | 2 | 3 | 77 | 18 |
| SE | 10 | 17 | 11 | 19 | 24 | 41 | 12 | 20 | 2 | 3 | 59 | 18 |
| SW | 11 | 17 | 12 | 19 | 18 | 29 | 15 | 24 | 7 | 11 | 63 | 19 |
| WEST | 2 | 6 | 3 | 9 | 14 | 40 | 12 | 34 | 4 | 11 | 35 | 25 |
| RM | 0 | 0 | 0 | 0 | 3 | 50 | 2 | 33 | 1 | 17 | 6 | 25 |
| MW | 18 | 13 | 16 | 11 | 59 | 42 | 35 | 25 | 13 | 9 | 141 | 21 |
| CAN | 2 | 20 | 4 | 40 | 2 | 20 | 1 | 10 | 1 | 10 | 10 | 12 |
| TOTAL | 57 | 14 | 60 | 15 | 157 | 38 | 102 | 25 | 35 | 9 | 411 | 20 |

The "Years" spanning header covers the columns 1–5, %, 6–9, %, 11–25, %, 26 & over, %.

TABLE 5.12
Church and Synagogue Library Association: Church Congregation Membership Size by Region

| Region | 1–499 | % | 500–999 | % | 1000–1999 | % | 2000– & over | % | No Response | % | All Libraries | Mean Persons |
|---|---|---|---|---|---|---|---|---|---|---|---|---|
| NE | 12 | 60 | 4 | 20 | 3 | 15 | 0 | 0 | 1 | 5 | 20 | 589 |
| MA | 29 | 38 | 25 | 32 | 14 | 18 | 7 | 9 | 2 | 3 | 77 | 1,185 |
| SE | 19 | 32 | 11 | 19 | 16 | 27 | 13 | 22 | 0 | 0 | 59 | 1,498 |
| SW | 20 | 32 | 15 | 24 | 11 | 17 | 16 | 25 | 1 | 2 | 63 | 2,145 |
| WEST | 13 | 37 | 7 | 20 | 9 | 26 | 4 | 11 | 2 | 6 | 35 | 1,108 |
| RM | 3 | 50 | 1 | 17 | 0 | 0 | 2 | 33 | 0 | 0 | 6 | 2,133 |
| MW | 51 | 36 | 41 | 29 | 33 | 23 | 15 | 11 | 1 | 1 | 141 | 1,253 |
| CAN | 3 | 30 | 3 | 30 | 2 | 20 | 2 | 20 | 0 | 0 | 10 | 1,305 |
| TOTAL | 150 | 37 | 107 | 26 | 88 | 21 | 59 | 14 | 7 | 2 | 411 | 1,384 |

TABLE 5.13

Church and Synagogue Library Association: Mean Book Volumes per
Library by Region and Setting

| Region | Mean Urban Book Volumes | Mean Rural Book Volumes | Mean Suburban Book Volumes | Mean Volumes by Region | Total Libraries |
|---|---|---|---|---|---|
| Northeast | 2,220 | 950 | 1,609 | 1,666 | 20 |
| Middle Atlantic | 2,165 | 1,805 | 2,814 | 2,540 | 77 |
| Southeast | 3,585 | 2,375 | 3,142 | 3,192 | 59 |
| Southwest | 3,986 | 3,643 | 3,256 | 3,641 | 63 |
| West | 3,827 | 2,250 | 3,891 | 3,586 | 35 |
| Rocky Mountains | 2,333 | 2,250 | 2,250 | 2,292 | 6 |
| Middle West | 2,831 | 1,946 | 2,362 | 2,498 | 141 |
| Canada | 2,800 | 2,250 | 1,738 | 2,320 | 10 |
| Total | 3,137 | 2,166 | 2,781 | 2,824 | 411 |
| No. of libraries | 160 | 59 | 191 | | |
| Missing | | | | 1 | |

TABLE 5.14
Church and Synagogue Library Association: Library City Population Size by Region[a]

| Region | City Population | | | | | | | | | | All Libraries | Mean |
|---|---|---|---|---|---|---|---|---|---|---|---|---|
| | 1–30,000 | % | 30,001–200,000 | % | 200,001–800,000 | % | 800,001 & over | % | No Response | % | | |
| Northeast | 13 | 65.0 | 5 | 25.0 | 2 | 10.0 | 0 | 0.0 | 0 | 0.0 | 20 | 85,125 |
| Middle Atlantic | 50 | 64.9 | 11 | 14.3 | 12 | 15.6 | 3 | 3.9 | 1 | 1.3 | 77 | 118,750 |
| Southeast | 20 | 33.9 | 23 | 39.0 | 16 | 27.1 | 0 | 0.0 | 0 | 0.0 | 59 | 132,246 |
| Southwest | 21 | 33.3 | 14 | 22.2 | 18 | 28.6 | 10 | 15.9 | 0 | 0.0 | 63 | 311,865 |
| West | 11 | 31.4 | 16 | 45.7 | 7 | 20.0 | 1 | 2.9 | 0 | 0.0 | 35 | 170,786 |
| Rocky Mountains | 3 | 50.0 | 1 | 16.7 | 2 | 33.3 | 0 | 0.0 | 0 | 0.0 | 6 | 158,333 |
| Middle West | 53 | 37.6 | 65 | 46.1 | 22 | 15.6 | 1 | 0.7 | 0 | 0.0 | 141 | 112,234 |
| Canada | 3 | 30.0 | 5 | 50.0 | 2 | 20.0 | 0 | 0.0 | 0 | 0.0 | 10 | 172,000 |
| Total | 174 | 42.3 | 140 | 34.1 | 81 | 19.7 | 15 | 3.6 | 1 | 0.2 | 411 | 152,805 |

[a]There was only one library in the CSLA sample that could not be recorded accurately by city population size. This library was registered as No Response.

TABLE 5.15
Church and Synagogue Library Association: Monthly Library
Circulation by Region by Descending Order of the Means

| Region | ----Monthly Circulation---- | | | Number of Libraries | No Response | Mean |
|---|---|---|---|---|---|---|
| | 0–50 | 51–100 | 101+ | | | |
| West | 11 | 7 | 13 | 35 | 4 | 259 |
| Canada | 3 | 0 | 5 | 10 | 2 | 217 |
| Rocky Mountains | 2 | 0 | 2 | 6 | 2 | 163 |
| Southeast | 18 | 15 | 11 | 59 | 15 | 125 |
| Southwest | 20 | 11 | 16 | 63 | 16 | 121 |
| Middle West | 63 | 19 | 26 | 141 | 33 | 88 |
| Middle Atlantic | 39 | 16 | 11 | 77 | 11 | 77 |
| Northeast | 10 | 1 | 1 | 20 | 8 | 40 |
| Total | 166 | 69 | 85 | 411 | 91 | 115 |

TABLE 5.16
Church and Synagogue Library Association: Cities with the Largest
Numbers of Congregational Libraries

| City | Number of Libraries | % |
|---|---|---|
| Kalamazoo, MI | 8 | 2 |
| Albuquerque, NM | 8 | 2 |
| Atlanta, GA | 7 | 2 |
| Austin, TX | 7 | 2 |
| Houston, TX | 7 | 2 |
| Washington, DC | 5 | 1 |
| Rochester, NY | 4 | 1 |
| Cleveland, OH | 4 | 1 |
| Findlay, OH | 4 | 1 |
| Toledo, OH | 4 | 1 |
| Other cities | 353 | 86 |
| Total | 411 | 100 |

TABLE 5.17
Church and Synagogue Library Association: City Population Size by Denomination

| Denomination | 0–30,000 | % | 30,001–200,000 | % | 200,001–500,000 | % | 500,001 & over | % | No Response | % | Total | Mean |
|---|---|---|---|---|---|---|---|---|---|---|---|---|
| Baptist | 11 | 42.3 | 8 | 30.8 | 7 | 26.9 | 0 | 0.0 | 0 | 0.0 | 26 | 126,250 |
| Christian | 7 | 33.3 | 6 | 28.6 | 8 | 38.1 | 0 | 0.0 | 0 | 0.0 | 21 | 190,119 |
| Congregational | 10 | 58.8 | 7 | 41.2 | 0 | 0.0 | 0 | 0.0 | 0 | 0.0 | 17 | 42,353 |
| Episcopal/Anglican | 13 | 30.2 | 15 | 34.9 | 10 | 23.3 | 4 | 9.3 | 1 | 2.3 | 43 | 226,012 |
| Lutheran | 20 | 47.6 | 15 | 35.7 | 7 | 16.7 | 0 | 0.0 | 0 | 0.0 | 42 | 99,524 |
| Methodist | 40 | 50.0 | 26 | 32.5 | 12 | 15.0 | 2 | 2.5 | 0 | 0.0 | 80 | 123,625 |
| Other Denominations | 29 | 50.9 | 20 | 35.1 | 8 | 14.0 | 0 | 0.0 | 0 | 0.0 | 57 | 105,658 |
| Presbyterian | 31 | 36.5 | 34 | 40.0 | 17 | 20.0 | 3 | 3.5 | 0 | 0.0 | 85 | 154,206 |
| U.C.C. | 9 | 40.9 | 3 | 13.6 | 8 | 36.4 | 2 | 9.0 | 0 | 0.0 | 22 | 240,114 |
| Summary | | | | | | | | | | | | |
| Jewish | 0 | 0.0 | 2 | 33.3 | 2 | 33.3 | 2 | 33.3 | 0 | 0.0 | 6 | 563,333 |
| Roman Catholic | 4 | 33.3 | 4 | 33.3 | 2 | 16.7 | 2 | 16.7 | 0 | 0.0 | 12 | 275,000 |
| All Protestant | 170 | 43.3 | 134 | 34.1 | 77 | 19.6 | 11 | 2.8 | 1 | 0.3 | 393 | 142,781 |
| Total | 174 | 42.3 | 140 | 34.1 | 81 | 19.7 | 15 | 3.6 | 1 | 0.2 | 411 | 152,805 |

TABLE 5.18
Church and Synagogue Library Association: Congregation Membership Size by City Population Size

| City Population Size | Congregation Membership Size | | | | | | | | | | Total | Mean |
|---|---|---|---|---|---|---|---|---|---|---|---|---|
| | 1–999 | % | 1,000–2,499 | % | 2,500–4,999 | % | 5,000–& over | % | No Response | % | | |
| Under 30,000 | 127 | 72.6 | 35 | 20.0 | 9 | 5.1 | 2 | 1.1 | 2 | 1.1 | 175 | 1,022 |
| 30,001–200,000 | 82 | 58.6 | 33 | 23.6 | 19 | 13.6 | 3 | 2.1 | 3 | 2.1 | 140 | 1,343 |
| 200,001–500,000 | 34 | 52.3 | 15 | 23.1 | 10 | 15.4 | 5 | 7.7 | 1 | 1.5 | 65 | 1,742 |
| 500,001–750,000 | 9 | 52.9 | 4 | 23.5 | 3 | 17.6 | 1 | 5.9 | 0 | 0.0 | 17 | 2,056 |
| 750,001 & over | 5 | 35.7 | 1 | 7.1 | 3 | 21.4 | 4 | 28.6 | 1 | 7.1 | 14 | 4,004 |
| Total | 257 | 62.5 | 88 | 21.4 | 44 | 10.7 | 15 | 3.6 | 7 | 1.7 | 411 | 1,384 |

TABLE 5.19
Church and Synagogue Library Association: Cities with More Than One Library: Most Common Denomination Shown If More Than One per City

| Region | State | City Name | Number of Libraries | Most Common Denominations | | State Totals |
|---|---|---|---|---|---|---|
| Northeast | Massachusetts | Boston | 2 | | | 2 |
| Middle Atlantic | District of Columbia | Washington | 5 | Presbyterian | 3 | 5 |
| | Maryland | Baltimore | 3 | Episcopal/Anglican | 2 | |
| | | Bethesda | 2 | | | 5 |
| | New York | Rochester | 4 | | | 4 |
| | Pennsylvania | Beaver | 2 | | | |
| | | Glenside | 2 | | | |
| | | Jenkintown | 2 | | | |
| | | Perkasie | 2 | | | |
| | | Pittsburgh | 3 | Presbyterian | 2 | |
| | | State College | 2 | | | 13 |
| Southeast | Florida | Clearwater | 3 | Methodist | 2 | |
| | | St. Petersburg | 3 | Episcopal/Anglican | 2 | 6 |
| | Georgia | Atlanta | 7 | Episcopal/Anglican | 3 | 7 |
| | North Carolina | Durham | 3 | | | 3 |
| | Virginia | Harrisonburg | 2 | Other Denominations | 2 | |
| | | Richmond | 3 | | | 5 |
| Southwest | New Mexico | Albuquerque | 8 | Methodist | 2 | |
| | | | | Presbyterian | 2 | |
| | | Los Alamos | 3 | | | |
| | Texas | Austin | 7 | Baptist | 2 | 11 |
| | | | | Lutheran | 2 | |
| | | | | United Church of Christ | 2 | |
| | | Dallas | 3 | Presbyterian | 2 | |
| | | Fort Worth | 2 | | | |
| | | Houston | 7 | Methodist | 3 | 19 |
| | | | | Presbyterian | 3 | |

TABLE 5.19 (continued)
Church and Synagogue Library Association: Cities with More Than One Library: Most Common Denomination Shown
If More Than One per City

| Region | State | City Name | Number of Libraries | Most Common Denominations | | State Totals |
|---|---|---|---|---|---|---|
| West | California | Davis | 2 | | | 2 |
| | Oregon | Portland | 2 | | | 5 |
| | | Salem | 3 | Presbyterian | 2 | 2 |
| | Washington | Seattle | 2 | | | 2 |
| Middle West | Iowa | Cedar Rapids | 2 | | | |
| | Indiana | Bloomington | 2 | | | |
| | | Fort Wayne | 2 | | | 4 |
| | Kansas | Overland Park | 2 | | | |
| | | Wichita | 2 | | | 4 |
| | Michigan | Dearborn Heights | 2 | | | |
| | | Grand Rapids | 3 | Other Denominations | 2 | |
| | | Holland | 2 | Other Denominations | 2 | |
| | | Kalamazoo | 8 | Other Denominations | 6 | |
| | | Lansing | 2 | | | 17 |
| | Missouri | Kansas City | 2 | | | |
| | | St. Louis | 2 | United Church of Christ | 2 | 4 |
| | Nebraska | Omaha | 2 | | | 2 |
| | Ohio | Akron | 3 | | | |
| | | Ashland | 2 | | | |
| | | Canton | 3 | United Church of Christ | 2 | |
| | | Cleveland | 4 | | | |
| | | Coshocton | 2 | | | |
| | | Findlay | 4 | Methodist | 2 | |
| | | North Omstead | 2 | | | |
| | | Toledo | 4 | | | |
| | | Youngstown | 2 | Presbyterian | 2 | 26 |
| Total | | | 148 | | | 148 |

TABLE 5.20
Church and Synagogue Library Association: List of States and
Provinces with Libraries in Cities of 600,000 Persons and Over

| State Name | --------------------Number in Cities--------------------| | | |
| | 1,500,000 Person Category | 850,000 Person Category | 600,000 Person Catagory | Total |
|---|---|---|---|---|
| Texas | 5 | 4 | 0 | 9 |
| District of Columbia | 0 | 0 | 5 | 5 |
| Ohio | 0 | 0 | 4 | 4 |
| Maryland | 0 | 3 | 0 | 3 |
| Massachusetts | 0 | 0 | 2 | 2 |
| California | 1 | 0 | 1 | 2 |
| Oregon | 0 | 0 | 1 | 1 |
| Colorado | 0 | 0 | 1 | 1 |
| Wisconsin | 0 | 0 | 1 | 1 |
| Alberta | 0 | 0 | 1 | 1 |
| Manitoba | 0 | 0 | 1 | 1 |
| Arizona | 0 | 1 | 0 | 1 |
| Indiana | 0 | 1 | 0 | 1 |
| Total | 6 | 9 | 17 | 32 |

TABLE 5.21
Church and Synagogue Library Association: List of States and
Provinces with Libraries in the Two Smallest City Population Size
Categories

| State Name | 2,500 Person Category | 7,500 Person Category | Total in State |
|---|---|---|---|
| Pennsylvania | 13 | 9 | 22 |
| Connecticut | 3 | 2 | 5 |
| New York | 2 | 3 | 5 |
| Indiana | 1 | 2 | 3 |
| Michigan | 3 | 0 | 3 |
| Texas | 2 | 1 | 3 |
| Colorado | 2 | 0 | 2 |
| Delaware | 1 | 1 | 2 |
| Florida | 2 | 0 | 2 |
| Iowa | 0 | 2 | 2 |
| Maine | 1 | 1 | 2 |
| Maryland | 2 | 0 | 2 |
| Massachusetts | 1 | 1 | 2 |
| Minnesota | 0 | 2 | 2 |
| Missouri | 0 | 2 | 2 |
| Ohio | 1 | 1 | 2 |

TABLE 5.21 (continued)
Church and Synagogue Library Association: List of States and
Provinces with Libraries in the Two Smallest City Population Size
Categories

| State Name | 2,500 Person Category | 7,500 Person Category | Total in State |
|---|---|---|---|
| Ontario | 1 | 1 | 2 |
| Oregon | 2 | 0 | 2 |
| Virginia | 1 | 1 | 2 |
| Arkansas | 1 | 0 | 1 |
| California | 0 | 1 | 1 |
| Georgia | 1 | 0 | 1 |
| Nevada | 1 | 0 | 1 |
| New Jersey | 0 | 1 | 1 |
| New Mexico | 1 | 0 | 1 |
| Wisconsin | 0 | 1 | 1 |
| Total | 42 | 32 | 74 |

TABLE 5.22
Church and Synagogue Library Association: Library Setting by
Denomination

| Denomination | Urban | % | Rural | % | Suburban | % | Unknown | % | Total |
|---|---|---|---|---|---|---|---|---|---|
| Baptist | 7 | 27 | 1 | 4 | 18 | 69 | 0 | 0 | 26 |
| Christian | 14 | 67 | 2 | 10 | 5 | 24 | 0 | 0 | 21 |
| Congregational | 7 | 41 | 1 | 6 | 9 | 53 | 0 | 0 | 17 |
| Episcopal/Anglican | 21 | 49 | 4 | 9 | 17 | 40 | 1 | 2 | 43 |
| Lutheran | 17 | 40 | 7 | 17 | 18 | 43 | 0 | 0 | 42 |
| Methodist | 26 | 33 | 15 | 19 | 39 | 49 | 0 | 0 | 80 |
| Other Denominations | 19 | 33 | 14 | 25 | 24 | 42 | 0 | 0 | 57 |
| Presbyterian | 35 | 41 | 9 | 11 | 41 | 48 | 0 | 0 | 85 |
| U.C.C. | 8 | 36 | 4 | 18 | 10 | 45 | 0 | 0 | 22 |
| Summary | | | | | | | | | |
| Jewish | 4 | 67 | 0 | 0 | 2 | 33 | 0 | 0 | 6 |
| Roman Catholic | 2 | 17 | 2 | 17 | 8 | 67 | 0 | 0 | 12 |
| All Protestant | 154 | 39 | 57 | 15 | 181 | 46 | 1 | 0 | 393 |
| Total | 160 | 39 | 59 | 14 | 191 | 46 | 1 | 0 | 411 |

TABLE 5.23

Church and Synagogue Library Association: Means and Percentages of Total Library Incomes Accounted for by Each of Five Expenditure Categories by Setting[a]

| Setting | Library Budget | % | Gifts | % | Congre- gational Income | % | Proceeds from Activities | % | Other Income | % | Total | Total Income % |
|---------|------|----|------|----|------|---|------|---|------|----|------|----|
| Urban | $1,302 | 65 | $267 | 13 | $45 | 2 | $68 | 3 | $318 | 16 | $1,999 | 48 |
| Rural | 466 | 58 | 191 | 24 | 51 | 6 | 15 | 2 | 85 | 10 | 808 | 7 |
| Suburban | 906 | 57 | 238 | 15 | 84 | 5 | 102 | 6 | 252 | 16 | 1,582 | 45 |
| Total | 998 | 60 | 243 | 15 | 64 | 4 | 76 | 5 | 254 | 15 | 1,654 | 100 |

[a]Number of cases in this study was 410. One library could not be placed by setting.

TABLE 5.24

Church and Synagogue Library Association: Oldest Congregational Libraries

| Library | Founding Year |
|---------|---------------|
| Trinity Church, Boston, MA | 1827 |
| The Temple, Cleveland, OH | 1850 |
| First Congregational Church, Kalamazoo, MI | 1883 |
| St. Luke's Episcopal Church, Atlanta, GA | 1904 |
| Immanuel Reformed Church, Grand Rapids, MI | 1908 |
| First United Methodist Church, Pasadena, CA | 1911 |
| Third Reformed Church, Kalamazoo, MI | 1916 |
| First Centenary United Methodist Church, Chattanooga, TN | 1921 |
| Washington Street United Methodist Church, Tiffin, OH | 1922 |
| University Presbyterian Church, Seattle, WA | 1923 |
| Park Congregational Church, Norwich, CT | 1931 |
| Hyde Park Baptist Church, Austin, TX | 1931 |

TABLE 5.25
Church and Synagogue Library Association: Library Age by
Denomination in Descending Order by Age

| Denomination | | --Library Age in Years-- | | | | | | Mean Age | Number of Libraries | | No Response | |
|---|---|---|---|---|---|---|---|---|---|---|---|---|
| | | 1–10 | | 11–20 | | 21+ | | | | | | |
| Congregational | 4 | | | 3 | | 7 | | 26 | 17 | | 3 | |
| Baptist | 6 | | | 6 | | 13 | | 24 | 26 | | 1 | |
| Other Denominations | 16 | | | 16 | | 18 | | 20 | 57 | | 7 | |
| Presbyterian | 18 | | | 27 | | 34 | | 20 | 85 | | 6 | |
| Methodist | 23 | | | 20 | | 32 | | 20 | 80 | | 5 | |
| Episcopal/Anglican | 18 | | | 13 | | 10 | | 19 | 43 | | 2 | |
| Christian | 3 | | | 6 | | 8 | | 18 | 21 | | 4 | |
| Lutheran | 13 | | | 9 | | 16 | | 17 | 42 | | 4 | |
| United Church of Christ | 7 | | | 6 | | 8 | | 17 | 22 | | 1 | |
| Summary | | % | | % | | % | | | % | | % | |
| Jewish | 2 | 33 | 1 | 17 | 1 | 17 | 41 | 6 | 100 | 2 | 33 | |
| Roman Catholic | 7 | 58 | 2 | 17 | 3 | 25 | 12 | 12 | 100 | 0 | 0 | |
| All Protestant | 108 | 28 | 106 | 27 | 146 | 37 | 20 | 393 | 100 | 33 | 8 | |
| Total | 117 | 29 | 109 | 27 | 150 | 36 | 20 | 411 | 100 | 35 | 9 | |

TABLE 5.26
Church and Synagogue Library Association: Number of
Congregational Libraries by Denomination

| Denomination | Number of Libraries | % |
|---|---|---|
| Baptist | 26 | 6 |
| Christian | 21 | 5 |
| Congregational | 17 | 4 |
| Episcopal/Anglican | 43 | 11 |
| Jewish | 6 | 1 |
| Lutheran | 42 | 10 |
| Methodist | 80 | 19 |
| Presbyterian | 85 | 21 |
| Roman Catholic | 12 | 3 |
| United Church of Christ | 22 | 6 |
| Other Denominations | 57 | 14 |
|   Adventist | 1 | 0.2 |
|   Brethren | 4 | 1 |
|   Church of God | 5 | 1 |
|   Friends | 4 | 1 |
|   Mennonite | 11 | 3 |
|   Orthodox | 1 | 0.2 |
|   Pentecostal | 5 | 1 |
|   Reformed | 11 | 3 |
|   Schwenkfelder | 1 | 0.2 |
|   Unitarian-Universalist | 1 | 0.2 |
|   United Church of Canada | 3 | 1 |
|   Unity | 1 | 0.2 |
|   Independent or Interdisciplinary | 9 | 2 |
| Total | 411 | 100 |

TABLE 5.27

Church and Synagogue Library Association: Means and Percentages of
Total Expenditures Accounted for by Each of Five Expenditure
Categories—Urban Only

| Denomination | Books | % | Media Purchases | % | Equip- ment | % | Supplies | % | Salaries | % | Total Expenditure |
|---|---|---|---|---|---|---|---|---|---|---|---|
| Baptist | $641 | 48 | $93 | 7 | $43 | 3 | $50 | 4 | $514 | 38 | $1,341 |
| Christian | 485 | 75 | 84 | 13 | 16 | 3 | 59 | 9 | 0 | 0 | 644 |
| Congregational | 595 | 85 | 21 | 3 | 14 | 2 | 66 | 9 | 0 | 0 | 696 |
| Episcopal/ Anglican | 655 | 73 | 70 | 8 | 10 | 1 | 48 | 5 | 119 | 13 | 901 |
| Lutheran | 626 | 71 | 175 | 20 | 28 | 3 | 54 | 6 | 0 | 0 | 882 |
| Methodist | 551 | 51 | 264 | 24 | 31 | 3 | 55 | 5 | 185 | 17 | 1,085 |
| Other Denomi- nations | 577 | 43 | 281 | 21 | 122 | 9 | 62 | 5 | 316 | 23 | 1,357 |
| Presbyterian | 861 | 58 | 255 | 17 | 71 | 5 | 79 | 5 | 229 | 15 | 1,495 |
| U.C.C. | 1,400 | 38 | 375 | 10 | 44 | 1 | 100 | 3 | 1,750 | 48 | 3,668 |
| Summary | | | | | | | | | | | |
| Jewish | 16,208 | 61 | 1,463 | 6 | 175 | 1 | 495 | 2 | 8,033 | 30 | 26,373 |
| Roman Catholic | 1,550 | 0 | 550 | 0 | 200 | 0 | 150 | 0 | 5,000 | 0 | 7,450 |
| All Protestant | 691 | 21 | 198 | 7 | 41 | 3 | 63 | 2 | 258 | 67 | 1,253 |
| Total | 1,090 | 56 | 234 | 12 | 52 | 3 | 75 | 4 | 506 | 26 | 1,958 |

TABLE 5.28

Church and Synagogue Library Association: Means and Percentages of
Total Expenditures Accounted for by Each of Five Expenditure
Categories—Suburban Only

| Denomination | Books | % | Media Purchases | % | Equip- ment | % | Supplies | % | Salaries | % | Total Expenditure |
|---|---|---|---|---|---|---|---|---|---|---|---|
| Baptist | $2,378 | 56 | $772 | 18 | $84 | 2 | $141 | 3 | $889 | 21 | $4,265 |
| Christian | 1,401 | 71 | 376 | 19 | 100 | 5 | 83 | 4 | 0 | 0 | 1,960 |
| Congregational | 420 | 64 | 111 | 17 | 78 | 12 | 52 | 8 | 0 | 0 | 662 |
| Episcopal/ Anglican | 697 | 75 | 150 | 16 | 24 | 3 | 61 | 7 | 0 | 0 | 931 |
| Lutheran | 411 | 63 | 153 | 23 | 39 | 6 | 54 | 8 | 0 | 0 | 656 |
| Methodist | 623 | 62 | 189 | 19 | 63 | 6 | 82 | 8 | 51 | 5 | 1,008 |
| Other De- nominations | 1,009 | 49 | 292 | 14 | 194 | 9 | 66 | 3 | 506 | 24 | 2,067 |
| Presbyterian | 643 | 67 | 93 | 10 | 39 | 4 | 62 | 6 | 122 | 13 | 959 |
| U.C.C. | 310 | 87 | 5 | 1 | 10 | 3 | 30 | 8 | 0 | 0 | 355 |

TABLE 5.28 (continued)
Church and Synagogue Library Association: Means and Percentages of
Total Expenditures Accounted for by Each of Five Expenditure
Categories — Suburban Only

| Denomination | Books | % | Media Purchases | % | Equip-ment | % | Supplies | % | Salaries | % | Total Expenditure |
|---|---|---|---|---|---|---|---|---|---|---|---|
| Summary | | | | | | | | | | | |
| Jewish | 8,100 | 78 | 100 | 1 | 350 | 3 | 350 | 3 | 1,500 | 14 | 10,400 |
| Roman Catholic | 1,602 | 39 | 554 | 14 | 131 | 3 | 149 | 4 | 1,625 | 40 | 4,061 |
| All Protestant | 833 | 60 | 221 | 16 | 70 | 5 | 72 | 5 | 194 | 14 | 1,392 |
| Total | 942 | 59 | 235 | 15 | 75 | 5 | 78 | 5 | 268 | 17 | 1,598 |

TABLE 5.29
Church and Synagogue Library Association: Means and Percentages of
Total Expenditures Accounted for by Each of Five Expenditure
Categories — Rural Only

| Denomination | Books | % | Media Purchases | % | Equip-ment | % | Supplies | % | Salaries | % | Total Expenditure |
|---|---|---|---|---|---|---|---|---|---|---|---|
| Baptist | 185 | 62 | 100 | 33 | 0 | 0 | 15 | 5 | 0 | 0 | 300 |
| Christian | 218 | 76 | 50 | 17 | 0 | 0 | 20 | 7 | 0 | 0 | 288 |
| Congregational | 310 | 67 | 100 | 22 | 0 | 0 | 50 | 11 | 0 | 0 | 460 |
| Episcopal/ Anglican | 274 | 71 | 75 | 19 | 13 | 3 | 26 | 7 | 0 | 0 | 388 |
| Lutheran | 593 | 63 | 153 | 16 | 29 | 3 | 53 | 6 | 107 | 11 | 934 |
| Methodist | 713 | 82 | 63 | 7 | 30 | 3 | 65 | 7 | 0 | 0 | 872 |
| Other Denomi-nations | 409 | 73 | 96 | 17 | 7 | 1 | 45 | 8 | 3 | 1 | 560 |
| Presbyterian | 768 | 59 | 67 | 5 | 70 | 5 | 54 | 4 | 333 | 26 | 1,293 |
| U.C.C. | 568 | 73 | 118 | 15 | 50 | 6 | 48 | 6 | 0 | 0 | 783 |
| Summary | | | | | | | | | | | |
| Jewish | 0 | 0 | 0 | 0 | 0 | 0 | 0 | 0 | 0 | 0 | 0 |
| Roman Catholic | 538 | 0 | 325 | 0 | 50 | 0 | 50 | 0 | 0 | 0 | 963 |
| All Protestant | 558 | 56 | 88 | 34 | 29 | 5 | 50 | 5 | 67 | 0 | 791 |
| Total | 557 | 70 | 96 | 12 | 29 | 4 | 50 | 6 | 64 | 8 | 797 |

TABLE 5.30

Church and Synagogue Library Association: Congregational
Membership Size by Denomination

| Denomination | -Membership Size- | | | Mean Membership Size | Number of Libraries | No Response |
|---|---|---|---|---|---|---|
| | 0–500 | 501–1,000 | 1,001+ | | | |
| Baptist | 10 | 7 | 8 | 1,470 | 26 | 1 |
| Lutheran | 9 | 11 | 22 | 1,432 | 42 | 0 |
| Methodist | 21 | 19 | 40 | 1,400 | 80 | 0 |
| Presbyterian | 27 | 26 | 32 | 1,196 | 85 | 0 |
| Episcopal/Anglican | 17 | 15 | 10 | 1,124 | 43 | 1 |
| Christian | 9 | 8 | 3 | 845 | 21 | 1 |
| Other Denominations | 35 | 11 | 9 | 741 | 57 | 2 |
| Congregational | 8 | 4 | 3 | 670 | 17 | 2 |
| U.C.C. | 14 | 6 | 2 | 632 | 22 | 0 |

| Summary | | % | | % | | % | | % | | | % |
|---|---|---|---|---|---|---|---|---|---|---|---|
| Jewish | 0 | 0 | 0 | 0 | 6 | 100 | 6,333 | 100 | 6 | 0 | 0 |
| Roman Catholic | 0 | 0 | 1 | 8 | 11 | 92 | 6,646 | 100 | 12 | 0 | 0 |
| All Protestant | 150 | 38 | 107 | 27 | 129 | 33 | 1,138 | 100 | 393 | 7 | 2 |
| Total | 150 | 36 | 108 | 26 | 146 | 36 | 1,379 | 100 | 411 | 7 | 2 |

TABLE 5.31

Church and Synagogue Library Association: Congregations with the
Largest Memberships

| Congregation | Members |
|---|---|
| St. James Roman Catholic Church, Arlington Heights, IL | 15,000 |
| The Temple, Cleveland, OH | 15,000 |
| Shepherd of the Hills Church, Bechtelsville, PA | 15,000 |
| All Saints Catholic Church, Dallas, TX | 15,000 |
| Christ the Good Shepherd Church, Spring, TX | 15,000 |
| First Presbyterian Church, Colorado Springs, CO | 7,500 |
| Mt. Paran Union Church of God, Atlanta, GA | 7,500 |
| Queen of the Holy Rosary Church, Overland Park, KS | 7,500 |
| Broadmoor Baptist Church, Shreveport, LA | 7,500 |
| Baltimore Hebrew Congregation, Baltimore, MD | 7,500 |
| First United Methodist Church, Tulsa, OK | 7,500 |
| Hyde Park Baptist Church, Austin, TX | 7,500 |
| Catholic Community of St. Luke the Evangelist Church, Houston, TX | 7,500 |
| Chapelwood United Methodist Church, Houston, TX | 7,500 |

TABLE 5.32

Seminary, Congregational, and Public Religious Library Distribution by Continent

| | Seminary Libraries (Ruoss) | | Congregational and Public Libraries (Harvey)[a] | |
|---|---|---|---|---|
| | No. | % | No. | % |
| Europe | 658 | 37.0 | North America | 26,245 | 63.0 |
| North America | 478 | 26.9 | Europe | 8,867 | 21.4 |
| Asia | 232 | 13.0 | Asia | 4,517 | 10.8 |
| South America | 186 | 10.5 | South America | 1,302 | 3.1 |
| Africa | 174 | 9.8 | Oceania | 531 | 1.3 |
| Oceania | 50 | 2.8 | Africa | 182 | 0.4 |
| Totals | 1,778 | 100.0 | | 41,644 | 100.0 |

[a]Excludes Christian Science reading rooms.
*Sources:* John F. Harvey, ed., *Church and Synagogue Libraries* (Metuchen, N.J.: Scarecrow, 1980). John F. Harvey, "An Introductory World Survey of Popular Church and Synagogue Libraries," *International Library Review* 18 (October 1986): 347–72. G. Martin Ruoss, *A World Directory of Theological Libraries* (Metuchen, N.J.: Scarecrow, 1968). *Source:* John F. Harvey, "Scholarly and Popular Religious Libraries," *International Library Review* 19 (October 1987): 359–86.

TABLE 5.33

Church and Synagogue Library Association: Library Committee Members by Denomination

| | Number of Committee Members | | | | | |
|---|---|---|---|---|---|---|
| Denomination | 1–3 | 4–8 | 9+ | Mean per Library | No. of Libraries | No Response |
| Baptist | 9 | 10 | 7 | 7.8 | 26 | 0 |
| Lutheran | 11 | 16 | 15 | 7.1 | 42 | 0 |
| Christian | 4 | 12 | 5 | 6.6 | 21 | 0 |
| Presbyterian | 38 | 31 | 16 | 6.1 | 85 | 0 |
| Methodist | 33 | 34 | 13 | 5.1 | 80 | 0 |
| Other Denominations | 26 | 25 | 5 | 4.9 | 57 | 1 |
| Episcopal/Anglican | 19 | 17 | 7 | 4.7 | 43 | 0 |
| Congregational | 6 | 7 | 3 | 4.4 | 17 | 1 |
| U.C.C. | 12 | 9 | 1 | 4.1 | 22 | 0 |
| Summary | | | | | | |
| Jewish | 3 | 2 | 1 | 5.2 | 6 | 0 |
| Roman Catholic | 4 | 4 | 4 | 10.7 | 12 | 0 |
| All Protestant | 158 | 161 | 72 | 5.7 | 393 | 2 |
| Total | 165 | 167 | 77 | 5.8 | 411 | 2 |

TABLE 5.34

Church and Synagogue Library Association: Congregational
Membership Size by Library Committee Size

| | Library Committee ----Members---- | | | Mean | Number | No |
| Congregation Members | 0–2 | 3–5 | 6+ | Committee Size | Libraries | Response |
| --- | --- | --- | --- | --- | --- | --- |
| 5,000+ | 3 | 2 | 10 | 11.1 | 15 | 0 |
| 2,001–5,000 | 3 | 11 | 30 | 9.7 | 44 | 0 |
| 1,001–2,000 | 22 | 22 | 44 | 7.4 | 88 | 0 |
| 501–1,000 | 23 | 43 | 41 | 5.1 | 107 | 0 |
| 201–500 | 50 | 43 | 27 | 3.9 | 122 | 2 |
| 0–200 | 13 | 16 | 6 | 3.3 | 35 | 0 |
| Total | 114 | 137 | 158 | 5.8 | 411 | 2 |

TABLE 5.35

Church and Synagogue Library Association: Libraries with the Largest
Number of Volunteer Committee Members by Denomination

| Library | Denomination | Number of Volunteers |
| --- | --- | --- |
| All Saints Catholic Parish, Dallas, TX | Roman Catholic | 52 |
| Carmel Presbyterian Church, Glenside, PA | Presbyterian | 40 |
| Westminster Presbyterian Church, Minneapolis, MN | Presbyterian | 30 |
| University Presbyterian Church, Seattle, WA | Presbyterian | 30 |
| Northwest Baptist Church, Fresno, CA | Baptist | 25 |
| Briarlake Baptist Church, Decatur, GA | Baptist | 25 |
| High Street Christian Church, Akron, OH | Christian | 21 |
| First Presbyterian Church, Kalamazoo, MI | Presbyterian | 18 |
| Burlingame Baptist Church, Portland, OR | Baptist | 18 |
| Seymour Christian Reformed Church, Grand Rapids, MI | Other Denominations | 17 |
| Gloria Dei Lutheran Church, Downers Grove, IL | Lutheran | 16 |
| Community United Methodist Church, Naperville, IL | Methodist | 16 |
| Fourth Presbyterian Church, Bethesda, MD | Presbyterian | 16 |
| United Methodist Church, Bethesda, MD | Methodist | 16 |
| Davisville Baptist Church, Southampton, PA | Baptist | 16 |
| First Baptist Church, La Crescenta, CA | Baptist | 15 |
| Christiania Lutheran Church, Lakeville, MN | Lutheran | 15 |
| Bethel Lutheran Church, Rochester, MN | Lutheran | 15 |
| Shepherd of the Hills Episcopal Church, Bechtelsville, PA | Episcopal/Anglican | 15 |

TABLE 5.36

Church and Synagogue Library Association: Number of Hours Worked per Library Committee Member by Denomination

| Denomination | Mean Number of Hours Worked per Week Per Member | Number of Libraries | Number of Libraries Responding | No Response |
|---|---|---|---|---|
| Other Denominations | 3.0 | 57 | 25 | 32 |
| U.C.C. | 2.1 | 22 | 11 | 11 |
| Methodist | 1.8 | 80 | 51 | 29 |
| Episcopal/Anglican | 1.8 | 43 | 21 | 22 |
| Baptist | 1.6 | 26 | 13 | 13 |
| Congregational | 1.5 | 17 | 9 | 8 |
| Presbyterian | 1.4 | 85 | 44 | 41 |
| Christian | 0.9 | 21 | 10 | 11 |
| Lutheran | 0.9 | 42 | 22 | 20 |
| Summary | | | | |
| Jewish | 5.9 | 6 | 5 | 1 |
| Roman Catholic | 3.8 | 12 | 9 | 3 |
| All Protestant | 1.7 | 393 | 206 | 187 |
| Total | 1.9 | 411 | 220 | 191 |

TABLE 5.37

Church and Synagogue Library Association: Library Staff Hours Worked by Denomination

| Denomination | -Total Weekly Staff Hours Worked- | | | Mean | Number of Libraries | No Response |
|---|---|---|---|---|---|---|
| | 1–5 | 6–10 | 11+ | | | |
| Baptist | 4 | 4 | 5 | 18.6 | 26 | 13 |
| Other Denominations | 14 | 4 | 7 | 8.9 | 57 | 32 |
| U.C.C. | 8 | 2 | 1 | 8.1 | 22 | 11 |
| Presbyterian | 23 | 15 | 6 | 7.6 | 85 | 41 |
| Methodist | 31 | 12 | 8 | 6.8 | 80 | 29 |
| Episcopal/Anglican | 12 | 7 | 2 | 5.9 | 43 | 22 |
| Lutheran | 15 | 3 | 4 | 5.5 | 42 | 20 |
| Congregational | 4 | 5 | 0 | 4.9 | 17 | 8 |
| Christian | 9 | 0 | 1 | 4.2 | 21 | 11 |

| Summary | | % | | % | | % | Mean | | % | | % |
|---|---|---|---|---|---|---|---|---|---|---|---|
| Jewish | 1 | 17 | 0 | 0 | 4 | 67 | 26.4 | 6 | 100 | 1 | 17 |
| Roman Catholic | 1 | 8 | 2 | 17 | 6 | 50 | 17.6 | 12 | 100 | 3 | 25 |
| All Protestant | 120 | 31 | 52 | 13 | 34 | 9 | 7.6 | 393 | 100 | 187 | 48 |
| Total | 122 | 30 | 54 | 13 | 44 | 11 | 8.4 | 411 | 100 | 191 | 47 |

TABLE 5.38

Church and Synagogue Library Association: Libraries with the Largest
Number of Staff Hours Worked

| Library | Number of Staff Hours Worked Per Week |
|---|---|
| First Baptist Church, La Crescenta, CA | 50 |
| The Temple, Cleveland, OH | 50 |
| Fourth Presbyterian Church, Bethesda, MD | 48 |
| University Avenue Church of Christ, Austin, TX | 48 |
| Mt. Paran Union Church of God, Atlanta, GA | 46 |
| Davisville Baptist Church, Southampton, PA | 44 |
| Sinai Temple, Los Angeles, CA | 40 |
| St. Charles Borromeo Catholic Church, Bloomington, IN | 40 |
| Hyde Park Baptist Church, Austin, TX | 40 |

TABLE 5.39

Church and Synagogue Library Association: Congregation Members
per Library Staff Member

| Library | Congregation Members Per Library Staff Member |
|---|---|
| First Christian Church, San Lorenzo, CA | 17 |
| Trinity Lutheran Church, Canton, OH | 17 |
| Zion Mennonite Church, Hubbard, OR | 19 |
| Faith United Presbyterian Church, Lakewood, OH | 20 |
| Burlingame Baptist Church, Portland, OR | 20 |
| Immanuel Reformed Church, Grand Rapids, MI | 25 |
| Lombard Mennonite Church, Lombard, IL | 29 |
| Martin Reformed Church, Martin, MI | 32 |
| Harrisonville Mennonite Church, Harrisonville, MO | 32 |
| First Presbyterian Church, St. Joseph, MO | 32 |
| First Deaf Mennonite Church, Lancaster, PA | 32 |

TABLE 5.40

Church and Synagogue Library Association: Number of Minutes
Library Open per Member per Week

| Library | Number of Minutes Library Open per Member per Week |
|---|---|
| Trinity Bible Church, Los Alamos, NM | 18 |
| University Avenue United Church of Christ, Austin, TX | 4 |
| Trinity United Methodist Church, Chico, CA | 3 |
| Broad Street Christian Church, Tampa, FL | 3 |
| Harrisonville Mennonite Church, Harrisonville, MO | 3 |
| Christ Church Unity, Rochester, NY | 3 |
| Davisville Baptist Church, Southampton, PA | 3 |

TABLE 5.41

Church and Synagogue Library Association: Librarians' Job Titles

| Title | Number of Libraries | % |
|---|---|---|
| Librarian | 254 | 62 |
| Chairperson, library committee | 43 | 10 |
| Church Librarian | 24 | 6 |
| Director | 16 | 4 |
| Head or chief librarian | 7 | 2 |
| Coordinator | 7 | 2 |
| Other | 21 | 5 |
| No response | 39 | 9 |
| Total | 411 | 100 |

TABLE 5.42

Church and Synagogue Library Association: Chief Librarians' Years of
Congregational Library Experience by Denomination

| Denomination | -Years of Experience- | | | Mean Years | Number of Libraries | No Response |
|---|---|---|---|---|---|---|
| | 1–5 | 6–10 | 11+ | | | |
| Baptist | 6 | 7 | 12 | 13.3 | 26 | 1 |
| Lutheran | 9 | 17 | 13 | 11.7 | 42 | 3 |
| Other Denominations | 16 | 15 | 22 | 10.8 | 57 | 4 |
| Episcopal/Anglican | 17 | 7 | 16 | 10.1 | 43 | 3 |
| Presbyterian | 30 | 20 | 29 | 9.9 | 85 | 6 |
| Methodist | 28 | 23 | 28 | 9.7 | 80 | 1 |
| Christian | 10 | 3 | 4 | 7.4 | 21 | 4 |
| Congregational | 7 | 4 | 2 | 7.0 | 17 | 4 |
| U.C.C. | 9 | 7 | 3 | 6.9 | 22 | 3 |
| Summary | | | | | | |
| Jewish | 2 | 1 | 2 | 11.8 | 6 | 1 |
| Roman Catholic | 5 | 5 | 2 | 8.4 | 12 | 0 |
| All Protestant | 132 | 103 | 129 | 10.1 | 393 | 29 |
| Total | 139 | 109 | 133 | 10.0 | 411 | 30 |

TABLE 5.43

Church and Synagogue Library Association: Librarians with the Most
Years of Congregational Library Experience

| Name and Congregation | Years |
|---|---|
| Elinor Burnham, Calvary Episcopal Church, Suffield, CT | 40 |
| Edmund Henderer, Takoma Park Presbyterian Church, Takoma Park, MD | 40 |
| Agnes Harnett, Garfield-Trinity Baptist Church, Garfield Heights, OH | 40 |
| Opal Ziemer, Littlefield Presbyterian Church, Dearborn Heights, MI | 36 |
| Ruth Wolfe, Downtown United Presbyterian Church, Rochester, NY | 36 |
| Kathryn L. Buck, First Christian Church, Omaha, NE | 35 |
| Mercedes Gugisberg, First Baptist Church, Albuquerque, NM | 32 |
| Betty Hollibaugh, Lamb of God Lutheran Church, Humble, TX | 32 |
| Lorraine Pike, Ascension Lutheran Church, Milwaukee, WI | 32 |
| Elizabeth Newton, United Methodist Church, Roswell, GA | 30 |
| Mary A. Starlie, Christiania Lutheran Church, Lakeville, MN | 30 |
| Claudia M. Fechter, The Temple, Cleveland, OH | 30 |
| Lorraine Burson, Burlingame Baptist Church, Portland, OR | 30 |
| Gwen N. Hartzel, Ruthfred Lutheran Church, Bethel Park, PA | 30 |
| Janelle Paris, First United Methodist Church, Stephenville, TX | 30 |

TABLE 5.44
Church and Synagogue Library Association: Chief Librarians' Gender by Denomination

| Gender | Denominational Total | Number | % |
|---|---|---|---|
| Female | – | 384 | 93 |
| Male | – | 24 | 6 |
| No Response | – | 3 | 1 |
| Total | 411 | 411 | 100 |
| **Males in Selected Denominations** | | | |
| Christian | 21 | 3 | 14 |
| Congregational | 17 | 2 | 12 |
| Episcopal/Anglican | 43 | 4 | 9 |
| Total | 81 | 9 | 11 |

TABLE 5.45
Church and Synagogue Library Association: Chief Librarian's Gender by Region

| Denomination | Male | % | Female | % | No Response | % | All Libraries |
|---|---|---|---|---|---|---|---|
| Northeast | 1 | 5 | 18 | 90 | 1 | 5 | 20 |
| Middle Atlantic | 6 | 8 | 71 | 92 | 0 | 0 | 77 |
| Southeast | 3 | 5 | 55 | 93 | 1 | 2 | 59 |
| Southwest | 2 | 3 | 61 | 97 | 0 | 0 | 63 |
| West | 5 | 14 | 30 | 86 | 0 | 0 | 35 |
| Rocky Mountains | 0 | 0 | 6 | 100 | 0 | 0 | 6 |
| Middle West | 6 | 4 | 134 | 95 | 1 | 1 | 141 |
| Canada | 1 | 10 | 9 | 90 | 0 | 0 | 10 |
| Total | 24 | 6 | 384 | 93 | 3 | 1 | 411 |

TABLE 5.46

Church and Synagogue Library Association: Chief Librarian's Gender by Denomination

| Denomination | Male | % | Female | % | No Response | % | All Libraries |
|---|---|---|---|---|---|---|---|
| Baptist | 1 | 4 | 25 | 96 | 0 | 0 | 26 |
| Christian | 3 | 14 | 18 | 86 | 0 | 0 | 21 |
| Congregational | 2 | 12 | 14 | 82 | 1 | 6 | 17 |
| Episcopal/Anglican | 4 | 9 | 39 | 91 | 0 | 0 | 43 |
| Lutheran | 1 | 2 | 41 | 98 | 0 | 0 | 42 |
| Methodist | 2 | 3 | 78 | 98 | 0 | 0 | 80 |
| Other Denominations | 4 | 7 | 51 | 89 | 2 | 4 | 57 |
| Presbyterian | 6 | 7 | 79 | 93 | 0 | 0 | 85 |
| U.C.C. | 1 | 5 | 21 | 95 | 0 | 0 | 22 |
| Summary |  |  |  |  |  |  |  |
| Jewish | 0 | 0 | 6 | 100 | 0 | 0 | 6 |
| Roman Catholic | 0 | 0 | 12 | 100 | 0 | 0 | 12 |
| All Protestant | 24 | 6 | 366 | 93 | 3 | 1 | 393 |
| Total | 24 | 6 | 384 | 93 | 3 | 1 | 411 |

TABLE 5.47

Church and Synagogue Library Association: Number of Library Professionals by Denomination

| Denomination | -Library Professionals- 0 | 1 | 2 or more | Mean Professionals per Library | Number of Libraries | No Response |
|---|---|---|---|---|---|---|
| Presbyterian | 31 | 31 | 23 | 1.1 | 85 | 0 |
| Baptist | 11 | 11 | 4 | 0.9 | 26 | 0 |
| U.C.C. | 9 | 9 | 4 | 0.9 | 22 | 0 |
| Episcopal/Anglican | 18 | 18 | 7 | 0.9 | 43 | 0 |
| Lutheran | 22 | 13 | 7 | 0.8 | 42 | 0 |
| Christian | 11 | 7 | 3 | 0.7 | 21 | 0 |
| Methodist | 35 | 32 | 13 | 0.7 | 80 | 0 |
| Congregational | 7 | 8 | 1 | 0.6 | 17 | 1 |
| Other Denominations | 34 | 16 | 6 | 0.5 | 57 | 1 |
| Summary |  | % | % | % |  | % | % |
| Jewish | 0 | 0 | 4 | 67 | 2 | 33 | 1.5 | 6 | 100 | 0 | 0 |
| Roman Catholic | 2 | 17 | 6 | 50 | 4 | 33 | 1.2 | 12 | 100 | 0 | 0 |
| All Protestant | 178 | 45 | 145 | 37 | 68 | 17 | 0.8 | 393 | 100 | 2 | 1 |
| Total | 180 | 44 | 155 | 38 | 74 | 18 | 0.8 | 411 | 100 | 2 | 0 |

TABLE 5.48

Church and Synagogue Library Association: Total Number of Library Professionals by Region[a]

| Region | ------Committee Professionals------ | | | | | | | | No Response | % | Total | Mean |
|---|---|---|---|---|---|---|---|---|---|---|---|---|
| | 0 | % | 1 | % | 2 | % | ≥3 | % | | | | |
| Northeast | 9 | 45 | 10 | 50 | 0 | 0 | 0 | 0 | 1 | 5 | 20 | 1.0/0.5 |
| Middle Atlantic | 32 | 42 | 31 | 40 | 10 | 13 | 4 | 5 | 0 | 0 | 77 | 1.5/0.9 |
| Southeast | 15 | 25 | 28 | 47 | 6 | 10 | 9 | 15 | 1 | 2 | 59 | 1.8/1.3 |
| Southwest | 28 | 44 | 20 | 32 | 7 | 11 | 8 | 13 | 0 | 0 | 63 | 1.9/1.0 |
| West | 12 | 34 | 16 | 46 | 4 | 11 | 3 | 9 | 0 | 0 | 35 | 1.6/1.0 |
| Rocky Mountains | 3 | 50 | 2 | 33 | 0 | 0 | 1 | 17 | 0 | 0 | 6 | 2.0/1.0 |
| Middle West | 78 | 55 | 42 | 30 | 15 | 11 | 6 | 4 | 0 | 0 | 141 | 1.5/0.7 |
| Canada | 3 | 30 | 6 | 60 | 0 | 0 | 1 | 10 | 0 | 0 | 10 | 1.4/1.0 |
| Total | 180 | 44 | 155 | 38 | 42 | 10 | 32 | 8 | 2 | 0 | 411 | 1.6/0.9 |

[a]For this table and due to the large proportion of them, libraries with no professional committee members were not added into the means but were considered, as for the *ALD* studies, to be No Response. The means for professionals calculated using all except the two No Response libraries were 0.5, 0.9, 1.3, 1.0, 1.0, 1.0, 0.7, 1.0, and 0.9 for the total sample.

TABLE 5.49

Church and Synagogue Library Association: Total Library Committee Size by Region

| Region | -Committee Membership Size- | | | | | | No Response | % | Total | Mean |
|---|---|---|---|---|---|---|---|---|---|---|
| | 1–2 | % | 3–4 | % | 5 & over | % | | | | |
| Northeast | 10 | 50 | 3 | 15 | 6 | 30 | 1 | 5 | 20 | 3.8 |
| Middle Atlantic | 23 | 30 | 23 | 30 | 31 | 40 | 0 | 0 | 77 | 5.5 |
| Southeast | 10 | 17 | 16 | 27 | 32 | 54 | 1 | 2 | 59 | 6.0 |
| Southwest | 15 | 24 | 12 | 19 | 36 | 57 | 0 | 0 | 63 | 6.8 |
| West | 7 | 20 | 3 | 9 | 25 | 71 | 0 | 0 | 35 | 8.0 |
| Rocky Mountains | 1 | 17 | 2 | 33 | 3 | 50 | 0 | 0 | 6 | 4.5 |
| Middle West | 44 | 31 | 39 | 28 | 58 | 41 | 0 | 0 | 141 | 5.3 |
| Canada | 3 | 30 | 2 | 20 | 5 | 50 | 0 | 0 | 10 | 5.9 |
| Total | 113 | 28 | 100 | 24 | 196 | 48 | 2 | 0 | 411 | 5.8 |

TABLE 5.50

Church and Synagogue Library Association: Libraries with the Largest
Number of Professional Staff Members

| Library | Professional Staff Members |
|---|---|
| Sinai Temple, Los Angeles, CA | 20 |
| Velda Rose United Methodist Church, Mesa, AZ | 9 |
| St. Elias Eastern Orthodox Church, Battle Creek, MI | 6 |
| Independent Presbyterian Church, Birmingham, AL | 5 |
| First United Methodist Church, Wabash, IN | 5 |
| St. Luke's Episcopal Church, Atlanta, GA | 4 |
| Stone Mountain Community Church, Stone Mountain, GA | 4 |
| Asbury United Methodist Church, Prairie Village, KS | 4 |
| Redeemer Lutheran Church, Austintown, OH | 4 |
| Grace United Methodist Church, Perrysburg, OH | 4 |
| Park Presbyterian Church, Beaver, PA | 4 |

TABLE 5.51

Church and Synagogue Library Association: Ratio of Nonprofessional
to Professional Staff Members by Denomination

| Denomination | ---Ratio: Nonprofessionals to Professionals--- | | | | | | | | | | | Mean Ratio Nonprof to Prof |
|---|---|---|---|---|---|---|---|---|---|---|---|---|
| | 0.1–0.9 | % | 1.0–1.9 | % | 2.0–2.9 | % | 3.0 & over | % | No Response | % | Total | |
| Baptist | 2 | 7.7 | 3 | 11.5 | 4 | 15.4 | 6 | 23.1 | 11 | 42.3 | 26 | 4.2 |
| Christian | 0 | 0.0 | 3 | 14.3 | 1 | 4.8 | 6 | 28.6 | 11 | 52.4 | 21 | 4.0 |
| Congregational | 1 | 5.9 | 3 | 17.6 | 1 | 5.9 | 4 | 23.5 | 8 | 47.1 | 17 | 2.8 |
| Episcopal/ Anglican | 5 | 11.6 | 5 | 11.6 | 3 | 7.0 | 12 | 27.9 | 18 | 41.9 | 43 | 2.9 |
| Lutheran | 1 | 2.4 | 0 | 0.0 | 2 | 4.8 | 17 | 40.5 | 22 | 52.4 | 42 | 5.6 |
| Methodist | 9 | 11.3 | 3 | 3.8 | 7 | 8.8 | 26 | 32.5 | 35 | 43.8 | 80 | 3.9 |
| Other Denominations | 6 | 10.5 | 2 | 3.5 | 5 | 8.8 | 9 | 15.8 | 35 | 61.4 | 57 | 2.6 |
| Presbyterian | 9 | 10.6 | 11 | 12.9 | 7 | 8.2 | 27 | 31.8 | 31 | 36.5 | 85 | 3.6 |
| U.C.C. | 5 | 22.7 | 1 | 4.5 | 3 | 13.6 | 4 | 18.2 | 9 | 40.9 | 22 | 2.4 |
| Summary | | | | | | | | | | | | |
| Jewish | 1 | 16.7 | 2 | 33.3 | 1 | 16.7 | 2 | 33.3 | 0 | 0.0 | 6 | 2.9 |
| Roman Catholic | 1 | 8.3 | 2 | 16.7 | 1 | 8.3 | 6 | 50.0 | 2 | 16.7 | 12 | 7.7 |
| All Protestant | 38 | 9.7 | 31 | 7.9 | 33 | 8.4 | 111 | 28.2 | 180 | 45.8 | 393 | 3.6 |
| Total | 40 | 9.7 | 35 | 8.5 | 35 | 8.5 | 119 | 29.0 | 182 | 44.3 | 411 | 3.8 |

TABLE 5.52

Church and Synagogue Library Association: Libraries Reporting Paid
Staff Members[a]

---

Library

---

First Baptist Church, La Crescenta, CA
Sinai Temple, Los Angeles, CA
First United Methodist Church, Pasadena, CA
National Presbyterian Church, Washington, DC
Temple Beth El, Boca Raton, FL
Briarlake Baptist Church, Decatur, GA
St. James Roman Catholic Church, Arlington Heights, IL
Beth El Synagogue, Highland Park, IL
St. Charles Borromeo, Bloomington, IN
First Lutheran Church, Newton, IA
Broadmoor Baptist Church, Shreveport, LA
Baltimore Hebrew Congregation, Baltimore, MD
Fourth Presbyterian Church, Bethesda, MD
The Temple, Cleveland, OH
First United Methodist Church, Tulsa, OK
Interchurch Center, Portland, OR
First United Methodist Church, Oak Ridge, TN
University Avenue Church of Christ, Austin, TX
All Saints Catholic Church, Dallas, TX
Clear Lake United Methodist Church, Houston, TX
Episcopal Diocese of Texas, Houston, TX
St. Mark's Episcopal Church, San Antonio, TX
First Presbyterian Church, Martinsville, VA
University Presbyterian Church, Seattle, WA

---

[a]There were twenty-four libraries altogether reporting paid staff members.

TABLE 5.53

Church and Synagogue Library Association: Library Book Volume Holdings by Denomination

| Denomination | Library Book Volumes 0–1,000 | 1001–3,000 | 3,001+ | Mean Volumes per Library | Number of Libraries | No Response |
|---|---|---|---|---|---|---|
| Baptist | 6 | 8 | 12 | 4,287 | 26 | 0 |
| Presbyterian | 14 | 40 | 29 | 3,193 | 85 | 2 |
| Methodist | 17 | 39 | 22 | 2,763 | 80 | 2 |
| Other Denominations | 15 | 24 | 17 | 2,458 | 57 | 1 |
| Christian | 4 | 12 | 5 | 2,457 | 21 | 0 |
| Lutheran | 14 | 19 | 9 | 2,324 | 42 | 0 |
| Episcopal/ Anglican | 17 | 18 | 8 | 2,241 | 43 | 0 |
| Congregational | 3 | 10 | 3 | 2,147 | 17 | 1 |
| U.C.C. | 7 | 13 | 2 | 1,841 | 22 | 0 |

| Summary | | % | | % | | % | | | % | | % |
|---|---|---|---|---|---|---|---|---|---|---|---|
| Jewish | 1 | 17 | 1 | 17 | 4 | 67 | 7,750 | 6 | 100 | 0 | 0 |
| Roman Catholic | 2 | 17 | 4 | 33 | 6 | 50 | 3,958 | 12 | 100 | 0 | 0 |
| All Protestant | 97 | 25 | 183 | 47 | 107 | 27 | 2,713 | 393 | 100 | 6 | 2 |
| Total | 100 | 25 | 188 | 46 | 117 | 28 | 2,824 | 411 | 100 | 6 | 1 |

TABLE 5.54
Church and Synagogue Library Association: Library Book Volume Holdings by Denomination

| Denomination | Volume Holdings | | | | | | | | | | Total Libraries | Mean Volumes |
| | 0–500 | % | 501–1,000 | % | 1,001–3,000 | % | 3,001 & over | % | No Response | % | | |
|---|---|---|---|---|---|---|---|---|---|---|---|---|
| Baptist | 2 | 8 | 4 | 15 | 8 | 31 | 12 | 46 | 0 | 0 | 26 | 4,287 |
| Christian | 1 | 5 | 3 | 14 | 12 | 57 | 5 | 24 | 0 | 0 | 21 | 2,457 |
| Congregational | 1 | 6 | 2 | 12 | 10 | 59 | 3 | 18 | 1 | 6 | 17 | 2,147 |
| Episcopal/Anglican | 6 | 14 | 11 | 26 | 18 | 42 | 8 | 19 | 0 | 0 | 43 | 2,241 |
| Lutheran | 6 | 14 | 8 | 19 | 19 | 45 | 9 | 21 | 0 | 0 | 42 | 2,324 |
| Methodist | 7 | 9 | 10 | 13 | 39 | 49 | 22 | 28 | 2 | 3 | 80 | 2,763 |
| Other Denominations | 4 | 7 | 11 | 19 | 24 | 42 | 17 | 30 | 1 | 2 | 57 | 2,458 |
| Presbyterian | 4 | 5 | 10 | 12 | 40 | 47 | 29 | 34 | 2 | 2 | 85 | 3,193 |
| U.C.C. | 5 | 23 | 2 | 9 | 13 | 59 | 2 | 9 | 0 | 0 | 22 | 1,841 |
| Summary | | | | | | | | | | | | |
| Jewish | 0 | 0 | 1 | 17 | 1 | 17 | 4 | 67 | 0 | 0 | 6 | 7,750 |
| Roman Catholic | 0 | 0 | 2 | 17 | 4 | 33 | 6 | 50 | 0 | 0 | 12 | 3,958 |
| All Protestant | 36 | 9 | 61 | 16 | 183 | 47 | 107 | 27 | 6 | 2 | 393 | 2,713 |
| Total | 36 | 9 | 64 | 16 | 188 | 46 | 117 | 28 | 6 | 1 | 411 | 2,824 |

TABLE 5.55
Church and Synagogue Library Association: Library Book Holdings per Congregation Member by Denomination

| Denomination | Book Holdings per Member | | | | | | | | | | Total Libraries | Mean Volumes |
|---|---|---|---|---|---|---|---|---|---|---|---|---|
| | 0–.5 | % | .51–.75 | % | .76–1 | % | 1.1– & over | % | No Response | % | | |
| Baptist | 2 | 7.7 | 0 | 0.0 | 4 | 15.4 | 19 | 73.1 | 1 | 3.8 | 26 | 4.6 |
| Christian | 0 | 0.0 | 1 | 4.8 | 1 | 4.8 | 18 | 85.7 | 1 | 4.8 | 21 | 5.4 |
| Congregational | 0 | 0.0 | 0 | 0.0 | 1 | 5.9 | 13 | 76.5 | 3 | 17.6 | 17 | 3.6 |
| Episcopal/Anglican | 3 | 7.0 | 0 | 0.0 | 7 | 16.3 | 32 | 74.4 | 1 | 2.3 | 43 | 3.2 |
| Lutheran | 6 | 14.3 | 2 | 4.8 | 5 | 11.9 | 29 | 69.0 | 0 | 0.0 | 42 | 2.3 |
| Methodist | 5 | 6.3 | 1 | 1.3 | 13 | 16.3 | 59 | 73.8 | 2 | 2.5 | 80 | 2.5 |
| Other Denominations | 1 | 1.8 | 1 | 1.8 | 7 | 12.3 | 45 | 78.9 | 3 | 5.3 | 57 | 7.1 |
| Presbyterian | 3 | 3.5 | 1 | 1.2 | 5 | 5.9 | 74 | 87.1 | 2 | 2.4 | 85 | 4.0 |
| U.C.C. | 1 | 4.5 | 0 | 0.0 | 5 | 22.7 | 16 | 72.7 | 0 | 0.0 | 22 | 4.2 |
| Summary | | | | | | | | | | | | |
| Jewish | 1 | 16.7 | 1 | 16.7 | 1 | 16.7 | 3 | 50.0 | 0 | 0.0 | 6 | 1.7 |
| Roman Catholic | 5 | 41.7 | 3 | 25.0 | 1 | 8.3 | 3 | 25.0 | 0 | 0.0 | 12 | 1.0 |
| All Protestant | 21 | 5.3 | 6 | 1.5 | 48 | 12.2 | 305 | 77.6 | 13 | 3.3 | 393 | 4.0 |
| Total | 27 | 6.6 | 10 | 2.4 | 50 | 12.2 | 311 | 75.7 | 13 | 3.2 | 411 | 3.8 |

TABLE 5.56

Church and Synagogue Library Association: Largest Libraries by
Number of Book Volumes Held

| Library | Volumes |
|---|---|
| First Baptist Church, La Crescenta, CA | 12,000+ |
| Sinai Temple, Los Angeles, CA | 12,000+ |
| Pasadena Community United Methodist Church, St. Petersburg, FL | 12,000+ |
| St. Phillip's Episcopal Church, Atlanta, GA | 12,000+ |
| Briarlake Baptist Church, Decatur, GA | 12,000+ |
| Beth El Synagogue, Highland Park, IL | 12,000+ |
| Church of the Nativity, Baltimore, MD | 12,000+ |
| Ghost Ranch United Presbyterian Church, Abiquiu, NM | 12,000+ |
| The Temple, Cleveland, OH | 12,000+ |
| First United Methodist Church, Tulsa, OK | 12,000+ |
| Carmel Presbyterian Church, Glenside, PA | 12,000+ |
| Hyde Park Baptist Church, Austin, TX | 12,000+ |
| University Avenue Church of Christ, Austin, TX | 12,000+ |
| Preston Hollow Presbyterian Church, Dallas, TX | 12,000+ |
| First Presbyterian Church, Charleston, WV | 12,000+ |
| Ascension Lutheran Church, Milwaukee, WI | 12,000+ |

TABLE 5.57

Church and Synagogue Library Association: Mean Number of
Volumes per Congregation Member by Years of Library Operation

| Denomination | Mean Volumes for --Years of Library Operation-- | | | Overall Mean Volumes | Number of Libraries | No Response |
|---|---|---|---|---|---|---|
| | 1–10 | 11–25 | 26+ | | | |
| Other Denominations | 4.8 | 8.4 | 8.5 | 7.2 | 57 | 10 |
| Christian | 1.8 | 5.7 | 12.1 | 5.8 | 21 | 5 |
| Baptist | 2.3 | 4.4 | 6.6 | 4.8 | 26 | 2 |
| Presbyterian | 3.4 | 4.7 | 3.7 | 4.1 | 85 | 8 |
| Congregational | 5.1 | 3.2 | 3.8 | 4.0 | 17 | 5 |
| U.C.C. | 2.0 | 3.1 | 7.2 | 3.3 | 22 | 1 |
| Episcopal/Anglican | 2.5 | 4.1 | 3.5 | 3.3 | 43 | 3 |
| Methodist | 2.0 | 2.5 | 3.2 | 2.5 | 80 | 7 |
| Lutheran | 1.9 | 3.0 | 1.9 | 2.4 | 42 | 4 |
| Summary | | | | | | |
| Jewish | 1.1 | 3.4 | 0.8 | 1.6 | 6 | 2 |
| Roman Catholic | 0.5 | 0.9 | 5.0 | 1.0 | 12 | 0 |
| All Protestant | 2.8 | 4.3 | 4.7 | 4.0 | 393 | 45 |
| Total | 2.7 | 4.2 | 4.7 | 3.9 | 411 | 47 |

TABLE 5.58

Church and Synagogue Library Association: Mean Number of
Volumes per Library Staff Member by Denomination

| Denomination | Mean Volumes per -- Library Staff Member-- | | | Overall Mean No. of Volumes per Library Staff Member | Number of Libraries | No Response |
|---|---|---|---|---|---|---|
| | 0–2 | 3–4 | 5+ | | | |
| Baptist | 1,158 | 875 | 6,313 | 4,287 | 26 | 0 |
| Presbyterian | 2,293 | 2,609 | 4,128 | 3,193 | 85 | 2 |
| Methodist | 1,538 | 1,775 | 4,074 | 2,763 | 80 | 2 |
| Christian | 1,375 | 1,833 | 2,900 | 2,457 | 21 | 0 |
| Other Denominations | 1,567 | 1,669 | 3,510 | 2,458 | 57 | 1 |
| Lutheran | 1,517 | 1,183 | 2,846 | 2,324 | 42 | 0 |
| Episcopal/ Anglican | 1,372 | 1,872 | 3,197 | 2,241 | 43 | 0 |
| Congregational | 1,808 | 3,125 | 1,833 | 2,147 | 17 | 1 |
| U.C.C. | 1,183 | 1,217 | 3,207 | 1,841 | 22 | 0 |
| Summary | | | | | | |
| Jewish | 750 | 12,000 | 7,250 | 7,750 | 6 | 0 |
| Roman Catholic | 1,000 | 5,313 | 4,042 | 3,958 | 12 | 0 |
| All Protestant | 1,623 | 1,941 | 3,741 | 2,713 | 393 | 6 |
| Total | 1,604 | 2,280 | 3,805 | 2,824 | 411 | 6 |

TABLE 5.59

Church and Synagogue Library Association: Library Volume Holdings
by Library Staff Membership

| Staff Members | ------------Volume Holdings------------ | | | | | | | | | | Total Libraries | Mean |
|---|---|---|---|---|---|---|---|---|---|---|---|---|
| | 0– 1,000 | % | 1,001– 3,000 | % | 3,001– 10,000 | % | 10,001 & over | % | No Response | % | | |
| 1 | 22 | 37 | 28 | 48 | 8 | 14 | 0 | 0 | 1 | 2 | 59 | 1,672 |
| 2 | 20 | 37 | 29 | 54 | 5 | 9 | 0 | 0 | 0 | 0 | 54 | 1,532 |
| 3 | 16 | 31 | 27 | 52 | 6 | 12 | 2 | 4 | 1 | 2 | 52 | 2,193 |
| 4–5 | 22 | 26 | 43 | 51 | 19 | 22 | 1 | 1 | 0 | 0 | 85 | 2,381 |
| 6–7 | 9 | 14 | 30 | 48 | 18 | 29 | 3 | 5 | 3 | 5 | 63 | 3,288 |
| 8+ | 11 | 11 | 31 | 32 | 45 | 46 | 10 | 10 | 1 | 1 | 98 | 4,667 |
| Total | 100 | 24 | 188 | 46 | 101 | 25 | 16 | 4 | 6 | 2 | 411 | 2,824 |

TABLE 5.60
Church and Synagogue Library Association: Libraries with the Largest
Number of Book Volumes per Congregation Member

| Library | Number of Book Volumes Held per Congregation Member |
| --- | --- |
| First Christian Church, San Lorenzo, CA | 22.5 |
| Lombard Mennonite Church, Lombard, IL | 22.5 |
| Church of the Open Door, Wyoming, MI | 22.5 |
| Christ Church Unity, Rochester, NY | 22.5 |
| Brecksville United Church of Christ, Brecksville, OH | 22.5 |
| Highland Christian Church, Cleveland, OH | 22.5 |
| Perkasie Mennonite Church, Perkasie, PA | 22.5 |
| Weavers Mennonite Church, Harrisonburg, VA | 22.5 |
| Westwood Church of God, Kalamazoo, MI | 21.4 |
| Central Presbyterian Church, Kansas City, MO | 21.4 |
| Burlingame Baptist Church, Portland, OR | 21.4 |
| St. Matthew's United Methodist Church, Houston, TX | 21.4 |

TABLE 5.61
Church and Synagogue Library Association: Libraries with the Largest
Number of Newspaper Titles

| Library | Number of Titles |
| --- | --- |
| Trinity Evangelical Lutheran Church, Perkasie, PA | 10 |
| All Saints Catholic Parish, Dallas, TX | 10 |
| The Temple, Cleveland, OH | 7 |
| University Presbyterian Church, Seattle, WA | 6 |
| Temple Beth-El, Boca Raton, FL | 5 |
| Beth El Synagogue, Highland Park, IL | 5 |
| Forest Park United Methodist Church, Fort Wayne, IN | 5 |
| Fourth Presbyterian Church, Bethesda, MD | 5 |
| Monte Vista Christian Church, Albuquerque, NM | 5 |
| Congregation Ahavath Shalom, Fort Worth, TX | 5 |
| Church of the Presentation, Upper Saddle River, NJ | 4 |
| Ghost Ranch United Presbyterian Church, Abiquiu, NM | 4 |
| St. John's Lutheran Church, Waterloo, ON | 4 |

TABLE 5.62

Church and Synagogue Library Association: Library Newspaper
Subscriptions by Denomination[a]

| Denomination | 1–5 | % | 6 & over | % | No Response | % | Total | Mean |
|---|---|---|---|---|---|---|---|---|
| | -Number of Newspaper- Subscriptions | | | | | | | |
| Baptist | 5 | 19.2 | 0 | 0.0 | 21 | 80.8 | 26 | 1.8 |
| Christian | 3 | 14.3 | 0 | 0.0 | 18 | 85.7 | 21 | 2.7 |
| Congregational | 5 | 29.4 | 0 | 0.0 | 12 | 70.6 | 17 | 1.4 |
| Episcopal/Anglican | 16 | 37.2 | 0 | 0.0 | 27 | 62.8 | 43 | 1.7 |
| Lutheran | 7 | 16.7 | 1 | 2.4 | 34 | 81.0 | 42 | 2.9 |
| Methodist | 34 | 42.5 | 0 | 0.0 | 46 | 57.5 | 80 | 1.3 |
| Other Denominations | 2 | 3.5 | 0 | 0.0 | 55 | 96.5 | 57 | 1.5 |
| Presbyterian | 24 | 28.2 | 1 | 1.2 | 60 | 70.6 | 85 | 1.9 |
| U.C.C. | 3 | 13.6 | 0 | 0.0 | 19 | 86.4 | 22 | 2.3 |
| Summary | | | | | | | | |
| Jewish | 3 | 50.0 | 1 | 16.7 | 2 | 33.3 | 6 | 5.5 |
| Roman Catholic | 5 | 41.7 | 1 | 8.3 | 6 | 50.0 | 12 | 4.0 |
| All Protestant | 99 | 25.2 | 2 | 0.5 | 292 | 74.3 | 393 | 1.8 |
| Total | 107 | 26.0 | 4 | 1.0 | 300 | 73.0 | 411 | 2.0 |

[a]The means here exclude all libraries reporting no newspaper subscriptions. This
produces results that are comparable with *ALD* procedures and increases mean holdings
significantly. Note the large No Response proportion of 73 percent.

TABLE 5.63

Church and Synagogue Library Association: Library Periodical and
Newspaper Titles by Denomination[a]

| Denomination | 0 | % | 1–5 | % | 6–20 | % | 21 & over | % | No Response | % | Total | Mean |
|---|---|---|---|---|---|---|---|---|---|---|---|---|
| | --------Periodical and Newspaper Titles-------- | | | | | | | | | | | |
| Baptist | 3 | 11.5 | 7 | 26.9 | 12 | 46.2 | 4 | 15.4 | 0 | 0.0 | 26 | 12.5 |
| Christian | 2 | 9.5 | 6 | 28.6 | 11 | 52.4 | 1 | 4.8 | 1 | 4.8 | 21 | 7.9 |
| Congregational | 0 | 0.0 | 11 | 64.7 | 4 | 23.5 | 1 | 5.9 | 1 | 5.9 | 17 | 6.0 |
| Episcopal/Anglican | 9 | 20.9 | 16 | 37.2 | 15 | 34.9 | 2 | 4.7 | 1 | 2.3 | 43 | 6.8 |
| Lutheran | 10 | 23.8 | 13 | 31.0 | 17 | 40.5 | 2 | 4.8 | 0 | 0.0 | 42 | 7.6 |
| Methodist | 11 | 13.8 | 30 | 37.5 | 38 | 47.5 | 1 | 1.3 | 0 | 0.0 | 80 | 6.3 |
| Other Denomi- nations | 14 | 24.6 | 22 | 38.6 | 17 | 29.8 | 3 | 5.3 | 1 | 1.8 | 57 | 6.2 |
| Presbyterian | 11 | 12.9 | 38 | 44.7 | 27 | 31.8 | 9 | 10.6 | 0 | 0.0 | 85 | 9.3 |
| U.C.C. | 8 | 36.4 | 8 | 36.4 | 4 | 18.2 | 2 | 9.1 | 0 | 0.0 | 22 | 7.0 |

TABLE 5.63 (continued)
Church and Synagogue Library Association: Library Periodical and
Newspaper Titles by Denomination[a]

| Denomination | 0 | % | 1–5 | % | 6–20 | % | 21 & over | % | No Response | % | Total | Mean |
|---|---|---|---|---|---|---|---|---|---|---|---|---|
| Summary |
| Jewish | 2 | 33.3 | 0 | 0.0 | 2 | 33.3 | 2 | 33.3 | 0 | 0.0 | 6 | 23.5 |
| Roman Catholic | 2 | 16.7 | 2 | 16.7 | 4 | 33.3 | 4 | 33.3 | 0 | 0.0 | 12 | 24.7 |
| All Protestant | 68 | 17.3 | 151 | 38.4 | 145 | 36.9 | 25 | 6.4 | 4 | 1.0 | 393 | 7.6 |
| Total | 72 | 17.5 | 153 | 37.2 | 151 | 36.7 | 31 | 7.5 | 4 | 1.0 | 411 | 8.4 |

[a]This table includes all zero responses as added to the means. The results are therefore more accurate than for the two *ALD* edition calculations but are noncomparable, as for the *ALD* data we cannot distinguish between libraries with no holdings and libraries providing no response to the question. For the CSLA we can do this easily. The means, however, are reduced.

TABLE 5.64
Church and Synagogue Library Association: Library Periodical and
Newspaper Titles by Denomination[a]

| Denomination | 1–5 | % | 6–20 | % | 21–50 | % | 51 & over | % | Zero Subscriptions or No Response | % | Total | Mean |
|---|---|---|---|---|---|---|---|---|---|---|---|---|
| Baptist | 7 | 26.9 | 12 | 46.2 | 3 | 11.5 | 1 | 3.8 | 3 | 11.5 | 26 | 14.1 |
| Christian | 6 | 28.6 | 11 | 52.4 | 1 | 4.8 | 0 | 0.0 | 3 | 14.3 | 21 | 8.8 |
| Congregational | 11 | 64.7 | 4 | 23.5 | 1 | 5.9 | 0 | 0.0 | 1 | 5.9 | 17 | 6.0 |
| Episcopal/Anglican | 16 | 37.2 | 15 | 34.9 | 2 | 4.7 | 0 | 0.0 | 10 | 23.3 | 43 | 8.6 |
| Lutheran | 13 | 31.0 | 17 | 40.5 | 1 | 2.4 | 1 | 2.4 | 10 | 23.8 | 42 | 10.0 |
| Methodist | 30 | 37.5 | 38 | 47.5 | 1 | 1.3 | 0 | 0.0 | 11 | 13.8 | 80 | 7.3 |
| Other Denominations | 22 | 38.6 | 17 | 29.8 | 3 | 5.3 | 0 | 0.0 | 15 | 26.3 | 57 | 8.2 |
| Presbyterian | 38 | 44.7 | 27 | 31.8 | 7 | 8.2 | 2 | 2.4 | 11 | 12.9 | 85 | 10.6 |
| U.C.C. | 8 | 36.4 | 4 | 18.2 | 1 | 4.5 | 1 | 4.5 | 8 | 36.4 | 22 | 11.1 |
| Summary |
| Jewish | 0 | 0.0 | 2 | 33.3 | 1 | 16.7 | 1 | 16.7 | 2 | 33.3 | 6 | 35.3 |
| Roman Catholic | 2 | 16.7 | 4 | 33.3 | 2 | 16.7 | 2 | 16.7 | 2 | 16.7 | 12 | 29.6 |
| All Protestant | 151 | 38.4 | 145 | 36.9 | 20 | 5.1 | 5 | 1.3 | 72 | 18.3 | 393 | 9.3 |
| Total | 153 | 37.2 | 151 | 36.7 | 23 | 5.6 | 8 | 1.9 | 76 | 18.5 | 411 | 10.2 |

[a]All no holdings libraries were recorded as No Response and were not added to the means, thus increasing the size of the means significantly.

TABLE 5.65

Church and Synagogue Library Association: Libraries with the Largest
Number of Periodical Subscriptions

| Library | Number of Titles |
| --- | --- |
| All Saints Catholic Parish, Dallas, TX | 108 |
| Fourth Presbyterian Church, Bethesda, MD | 90 |
| Trinity Evangelical Lutheran Church, Perkasie, PA | 75 |
| University Avenue United Church of Christ, Austin, TX | 70 |
| Central Presbyterian Church, Kansas City, MO | 53 |
| St. John's Free Will Baptist Church, Washington, DC | 50 |
| St. James Roman Catholic Church, Arlington Heights, IL | 50 |
| The Temple, Cleveland, OH | 50 |
| First Baptist Church, La Crescenta, CA | 45 |
| Beth El Synagogue, Highland Park, IL | 45 |
| Burlingame Baptist Church, Portland, OR | 42 |

TABLE 5.66

Church and Synagogue Library Association: Congregation Members
per Newspaper or Periodical Title

| Library | Congregation Members for each Newspaper or Periodical Title |
| --- | --- |
| Perkasie Mennonite Church, Perkasie, PA | 3 |
| Presbyterian Church of the Good Shepherd, Melbourne, FL | 5 |
| Central Presbyterian Church, Kansas City, MO | 6 |
| Davis Friends Meeting, Davis, CA | 7 |
| St. John's Free Will Baptist Church, Washington, DC | 7 |
| Lombard Mennonite Church, Lombard, IL | 7 |
| Burlingame Baptist Church, Portland, OR | 8 |
| Trinity Evangelical Lutheran Church, Perkasie, PA | 9 |
| Highland Christian Church, Cleveland, OH | 10 |
| St. Mark's Episcopal Church, Madras, OR | 10 |

TABLE 5.67

Church and Synagogue Library Association: Number of Media Titles Held by Denomination[a,b]

| | --------------Media Titles-------------- | | | | | | | | | | |
| Denomination | 1–10 | % | 11–100 | % | 101–500 | % | 500 & over | % | Zero Holdings or No Response | % | Total | Mean |
|---|---|---|---|---|---|---|---|---|---|---|---|---|
| Baptist | 3 | 11.5 | 4 | 15.4 | 6 | 23.1 | 6 | 23.1 | 7 | 26.9 | 26 | 777.3 |
| Christian | 3 | 14.3 | 6 | 28.6 | 4 | 19.0 | 1 | 4.8 | 7 | 33.3 | 21 | 282.1 |
| Congregational | 1 | 5.9 | 4 | 23.5 | 6 | 35.3 | 0 | 0.0 | 6 | 35.3 | 17 | 131.8 |
| Episcopal/ Anglican | 6 | 14.0 | 12 | 27.9 | 8 | 18.6 | 3 | 7.0 | 14 | 32.6 | 43 | 139.7 |
| Lutheran | 2 | 4.8 | 14 | 33.3 | 15 | 35.7 | 5 | 11.9 | 6 | 14.3 | 42 | 223.0 |
| Methodist | 5 | 6.3 | 19 | 23.8 | 25 | 31.3 | 7 | 8.8 | 24 | 30.0 | 80 | 237.1 |
| Other Denomi- nations | 6 | 10.5 | 13 | 22.8 | 16 | 28.1 | 6 | 10.5 | 16 | 28.1 | 57 | 271.5 |
| Presbyterian | 11 | 12.9 | 30 | 35.3 | 19 | 22.4 | 7 | 8.2 | 18 | 21.2 | 85 | 200.8 |
| U.C.C. | 2 | 9.1 | 6 | 27.3 | 2 | 9.1 | 1 | 4.5 | 11 | 50.0 | 22 | 141.3 |
| Summary | | | | | | | | | | | | |
| Jewish | 0 | 0.0 | 1 | 16.7 | 3 | 50.0 | 0 | 0.0 | 2 | 33.3 | 6 | 180.0 |
| Roman Catholic | 0 | 0.0 | 1 | 8.3 | 2 | 16.7 | 5 | 41.7 | 4 | 33.3 | 12 | 579.1 |
| All Protestant | 39 | 9.9 | 108 | 27.5 | 101 | 25.7 | 36 | 9.2 | 109 | 27.7 | 393 | 252.3 |
| Total | 39 | 9.5 | 110 | 26.8 | 106 | 25.8 | 41 | 10.0 | 115 | 28.0 | 411 | 260.2 |

[a]All libraries registering zero media holdings were recategorized to register No Response; therefore, only those libraries with media holdings have been included in the denominational means.
[b]See table 5.69 for holdings of *all* media.

TABLE 5.68

Church and Synagogue Library Association: All Media Holdings by Denomination[a, b]

| | -----------All Media Holdings---------- | | | | | | | | | | |
| Denomination | 1–100 | % | 101–500 | % | 501–750 | % | 751 & over | % | Zero Holdings or No Response | % | Total | Mean |
|---|---|---|---|---|---|---|---|---|---|---|---|---|
| Baptist | 8 | 30.8 | 7 | 26.9 | 0 | 0.0 | 8 | 30.8 | 3 | 11.5 | 26 | 964.8 |
| Christian | 9 | 42.9 | 5 | 23.8 | 1 | 4.8 | 3 | 14.3 | 3 | 14.3 | 21 | 365.3 |
| Congregational | 10 | 58.8 | 5 | 29.4 | 1 | 5.9 | 1 | 5.9 | 0 | 0.0 | 17 | 198.8 |
| Episcopal/ Anglican | 28 | 65.1 | 9 | 20.9 | 2 | 4.7 | 3 | 7.0 | 1 | 2.3 | 43 | 162.2 |
| Lutheran | 13 | 31.0 | 18 | 42.9 | 6 | 14.3 | 4 | 9.5 | 1 | 2.4 | 42 | 312.3 |
| Methodist | 29 | 36.3 | 22 | 27.5 | 9 | 11.3 | 13 | 16.3 | 7 | 8.8 | 80 | 476.8 |
| Other Denomi- nations | 27 | 47.4 | 17 | 29.8 | 6 | 10.5 | 4 | 7.0 | 3 | 5.3 | 57 | 387.4 |

TABLE 5.68 (continued)
Church and Synagogue Library Association: All Media Holdings by
Denomination[a, b]

| Denomination | 1–100 | % | 101–500 | % | 501–750 | % | 751 & over | % | No Response | % | Total | Mean |
|---|---|---|---|---|---|---|---|---|---|---|---|---|
| Presbyterian | 38 | 44.7 | 27 | 31.8 | 8 | 9.3 | 5 | 5.9 | 7 | 8.2 | 85 | 267.9 |
| U.C.C. | 14 | 63.6 | 2 | 9.1 | 2 | 9.1 | 1 | 4.5 | 3 | 13.6 | 22 | 146.2 |
| Summary | | | | | | | | | | | | |
| Jewish | 2 | 33.3 | 3 | 50.0 | 0 | 0.0 | 1 | 16.7 | 0 | 0.0 | 6 | 670.8 |
| Roman Catholic | 3 | 25.0 | 3 | 25.0 | 1 | 8.3 | 5 | 41.7 | 0 | 0.0 | 12 | 739.9 |
| All Protestant | 176 | 44.8 | 112 | 28.5 | 35 | 8.9 | 42 | 10.7 | 28 | 7.1 | 393 | 359.4 |
| Total | 181 | 44.0 | 118 | 28.7 | 36 | 8.8 | 48 | 11.7 | 28 | 6.8 | 411 | 376.2 |

[a]All libraries registering zero media holdings were recategorized to register No Response; therefore, only those libraries with media holdings have been included in the denominational means. The means here are quite substantial.
[b]This table includes all library material except books and periodicals.

TABLE 5.69
Church and Synagogue Library Association: Grand Total Number of
Media Titles Held by Category

| Media Titles | Number | % |
|---|---|---|
| Cassette tapes | 44,829 | 32 |
| Picture and clipping files (in drawers) | 34,510 | 25 |
| Pamphlet file | 18,360 | 13 |
| Filmstrips | 16,168 | 12 |
| Recordings | 13,092 | 9 |
| Kits | 3,793 | 3 |
| Maps | 2,832 | 2 |
| Paintings | 1,588 | 1 |
| Games | 1,408 | 1 |
| Videotapes | 1,159 | 1 |
| Slides | 807 | 1 |
| Flannelgraphs | 392 | 0 |
| Transparencies | 101 | 0 |
| Music (book or sheet) | 100 | 0 |
| AV equipment | 97 | 0 |
| Visual aids | 67 | 0 |
| Posters | 55 | 0 |
| Color prints | 50 | 0 |
| Visual stories | 50 | 0 |
| Show-and-tell sets | 39 | 0 |

TABLE 5.69 (continued)
Church and Synagogue Library Association: Grand Total Number of
Media Titles Held by Category

| Media Titles | Number | % |
|---|---|---|
| Sculpture | 33 | 0 |
| Banners | 18 | 0 |
| Puppets | 15 | 0 |
| Models | 12 | 0 |
| Charts | 7 | 0 |
| Sewing patterns | 4 | 0 |
| Other | 36 | 0 |
| Total | 139,622 | 100 |

TABLE 5.70
Church and Synagogue Library Association: Largest Libraries by
Number of Media Titles Held

| Library | Number of Media Titles |
|---|---|
| Interchurch Center, Portland, OR | 8,560 |
| First Baptist Church, La Crescenta, CA | 7,023 |
| Briarlake Baptist Church, Decatur, GA | 5,425 |
| First United Methodist Church, Tulsa, OK | 3,891 |
| Clear Lake United Methodist Church, Houston, TX | 3,506 |
| First United Methodist Church, Lufkin, TX | 3,325 |
| The Temple, Cleveland, OH | 3,315 |
| All Saints Catholic Church, Dallas, TX | 3,310 |
| Fourth Presbyterian Church, Bethesda, MD | 2,875 |
| Burlingame Baptist Church, Portland, OR | 2,638 |
| First Christian Church, Ft. Collins, CO | 2,500 |
| University Presbyterian Church, Seattle, WA | 2,395 |
| Mt. Paran Union Church of God, Atlanta, GA | 2,018 |

TABLE 5.71
Church and Synagogue Library Association Library Filmstrip Holdings by Denomination[a]

| | ------------Filmstrips------------ | | | | | | | | | |
|---|---|---|---|---|---|---|---|---|---|---|
| Denomination | 1–5 | % | 51–100 | % | 101 & over | % | Zero Holdings or No Response | % | Total Libraries | Mean |
| Baptist | 4 | 15 | 0 | 0 | 6 | 23 | 16 | 62 | 26 | 268 |
| Christian | 2 | 10 | 2 | 10 | 1 | 5 | 16 | 76 | 21 | 65 |
| Congregational | 3 | 18 | 2 | 12 | 2 | 12 | 10 | 59 | 17 | 89 |
| Episcopal/Anglican | 7 | 16 | 1 | 2 | 2 | 5 | 33 | 77 | 43 | 67 |
| Lutheran | 11 | 26 | 6 | 14 | 2 | 5 | 23 | 55 | 42 | 66 |
| Methodist | 17 | 21 | 5 | 6 | 18 | 23 | 40 | 50 | 80 | 116 |
| Other Denominations | 11 | 19 | 3 | 5 | 3 | 5 | 40 | 70 | 57 | 133 |
| Presbyterian | 27 | 32 | 4 | 5 | 8 | 9 | 46 | 54 | 85 | 62 |
| U.C.C. | 5 | 23 | 1 | 5 | 0 | 0 | 16 | 73 | 22 | 22 |
| Summary | | | | | | | | | | |
| Jewish | 0 | 0 | 2 | 33 | 1 | 17 | 3 | 50 | 6 | 120 |
| Roman Catholic | 3 | 25 | 1 | 8 | 2 | 17 | 6 | 50 | 12 | 86 |
| All Protestant | 87 | 22 | 24 | 6 | 42 | 11 | 240 | 61 | 393 | 98 |
| Total | 90 | 22 | 27 | 7 | 45 | 11 | 249 | 61 | 411 | 98 |

[a]Means for this table were calculated on the basis of all libraries showing filmstrip holdings of >0. All zero entries were reregistered as No Response.

TABLE 5.72
Church and Synagogue Library Association: Libraries with the Largest Number of Media Titles Held per Congregation Member

| Library | Number of Media Titles Held per Congregation Member |
|---|---|
| Burlingame Baptist Church, Portland, OR | 7.5 |
| Church of the Open Door, Wyoming, MI | 5.8 |
| First Baptist Church, La Crescenta, CA | 4.7 |
| Zion Mennonite Church, Hubbard, OR | 2.9 |
| St. Matthew's United Methodist Church, Houston, TX | 2.9 |
| Presbyterian Church of the Good Shepherd, Melbourne, FL | 2.8 |
| Lutheran Church of the Living Christ, Chanhassen, MN | 2.8 |
| Perkasie Mennonite Church, Perkasie, PA | 2.8 |
| Trinity Parish Episcopal Church, Newton, CT | 2.7 |
| Highland Christian Church, Cleveland, OH | 2.5 |

TABLE 5.73

Church and Synagogue Library Association: Books, Serials, and Media Held per Congregation Member and per One Hundred Members[a]

| Denomination | Number of Libraries | Mean Number of Book Volumes per Member | Mean Number of Serial Titles per 100 Members | Mean Number of Media Titles per member | Total Items |
|---|---|---|---|---|---|
| Other Denominations | 57 | 7.1 | 2 | 0.6 | 9.7 |
| Christian | 21 | 5.4 | 2 | 0.5 | 7.9 |
| Baptist | 26 | 4.6 | 2 | 1.0 | 7.6 |
| U.C.C. | 22 | 4.2 | 1 | 0.4 | 5.6 |
| Presbyterian | 85 | 4.0 | 1 | 0.3 | 5.3 |
| Congregational | 17 | 3.6 | 1 | 0.4 | 5.0 |
| Episcopal/Anglican | 43 | 3.2 | 1 | 0.2 | 4.4 |
| Methodist | 80 | 2.5 | 1 | 0.4 | 3.9 |
| Lutheran | 42 | 2.3 | 1 | 0.3 | 3.6 |
| Summary | | | | | |
| Jewish | 6 | 1.7 | 0 | 0.1 | 1.8 |
| Roman Catholic | 12 | 1.0 | 1 | 0.2 | 2.2 |
| All Protestant | 393 | 4.0 | 1 | 0.4 | 5.4 |
| Total | 411 | 3.8 | 1 | 0.4 | 5.2 |

[a]Serial titles includes both newspaper and periodical titles.

TABLE 5.74

Church and Synagogue Library Association: Main Collection Subject Focus[a]

| Subject Focus Based on Questionnaires | Number of Libraries | % |
|---|---|---|
| Devotion, worship, religious, Christian living, inspirational, etc. | 139 | 26 |
| No main focus, multifocus, "balanced," etc. | 131 | 25 |
| Reference material | 50 | 9 |
| Children's or young adult's material | 33 | 6 |
| Denominational authors, subjects | 12 | 2 |
| Bible study or emphasis on curriculum material | 8 | 1 |
| Recreational reading, including fiction | 7 | 1 |
| Theology | 5 | 1 |
| Other | 131 | 25 |
| No response | 19 | 4 |
| Total | 535 | 100 |

TABLE 5.74 (continued)
Church and Synagogue Library Association: Main Collection Subject
Focus[a]

| Subject Focus Based on Summary | Number of Libraries | % |
|---|---|---|
| Recreational reading and fiction | 13 | 14 |
| Theology and philosophy | 13 | 14 |
| Children's and young adult's material | 11 | 12 |
| Personal problems | 10 | 10 |
| Current social issues | 8 | 9 |
| Bible study | 7 | 8 |
| Devotional material | 6 | 7 |
| Religious education | 6 | 7 |
| Supports ongoing congregational programs | 6 | 7 |
| Denominational authors and reading | 5 | 5 |
| Missions | 4 | 4 |
| Reference material | 3 | 3 |
| Total | 92 | 100 |

[a]Total exceeds 411, since the above categories are not mutually exclusive and each
library may have had more than one focus.

TABLE 5.75
Church and Synagogue Library Association: Distinctive
Congregational Library Holdings

| Distinctive Material | Number of Libraries | % |
|---|---|---|
| Denominational material | 27 | 7 |
| Archives | 20 | 5 |
| Media and large print material | 20 | 5 |
| Local and general history | 12 | 3 |
| Art, great books, and music | 10 | 2 |
| Bibles | 10 | 2 |
| Rare books | 8 | 2 |
| Reference books | 6 | 1 |
| Youth | 5 | 1 |
| Journals | 4 | 1 |
| Martin Luther | 3 | 1 |
| Peace | 3 | 1 |
| Other | 17 | 4 |
| No response | 266 | 65 |
| Total | 411 | 100 |

TABLE 5.76
Church and Synagogue Library Association: Unique or Distinctive
Holdings Questionnaire Replies by Congregation Size

Membership up to 199 members:
1. Broad Street Christian Church, Tampa, FL
    Restoration history and Christian churches
2. Lombard Mennonite Church, Lombard, IL
    Peace literature for all ages
3. St. Elias Eastern Orthodox, Battle Creek, MI
    Some foreign-language Bibles and books
4. Westminster Presbyterian Church, Roswell, NM
    Bequest of Great Books of the Western World
5. Liberty United Presbyterian Church, Youngstown, OH
    Two titles by United Presbyterian Church mission pioneers
    Several out-of-print reference books
    Several books on the work of the Wycliffe translators
6. St. Mark's Episcopal and Third Order of St. Francis, Madras,
    OR
    Large section on St. Francis, and the history and practice of
        Franciscans
7. Perkasie Mennonite Church, Perkasie, PA
    Growing collection of board books for babies
    Members share current periodicals (placed in plastic covers
        for circulation)
8. Arlington Church of the Brethren, Arlington, VA
    With Mennonites and Quakers, a historic peace church,
        books on peace and peacemaking
Membership of 200 to 499:
1. Madera Seventh-Day Adventist Church, Madera, CA
    Nature study guides
2. Trinity United Methodist Church, Chico, CA
    Most California-Nevada annual conference journals from 1904
3. Woodland Hills Presbyterian Church, Woodland Hills, CA
    Novels by a former member
4. First Presbyterian Church of Yuma, Yuma, CO
    Set of the Bible on records; also a set on cassette tapes

TABLE 5.76 (continued)
Church and Synagogue Library Association: Unique or Distinctive
Holdings Questionnaire Replies by Congregation Size

---

5. First Congregational Church, Woodstock, CT
    Various antiquities relating to Woodstock's founding in 1686
    George Washington letter thanking church for chaplain to
    troops
6. Trinity Episcopal Church, Newtown, CT
    Large liturgical collection
    Large collection of material by and about C. S. Lewis
7. St. Paul's Episcopal Church, Rock Creek Parish, Washington, DC
    Old family Bibles with geneaological material
8. Lincolnshire Church of the Brethren, Ft. Wayne, IN
    Magazine exchange among congregation
9. St. Paul's United Methodist Church, Bloomington, IN
    Some volumes date from 1200
10. Zion United Church of Christ, Burlington, IA
    History/archives collection of church
11. Mt. Nebo United Methodist Church, Boonsboro, MD
    Historical materials about predecessors (United Brethren &
    EUB) in county
12. King's Chapel, Boston, MA
    Irreplaceable Unitarian and King's Chapel history titles
13. Pennway Church of God, Lansing, MI
    Out-of-print and historical denominational titles
14. Westwood Church of God, Kalamazoo, MI
    Over 200 volumes written by early denominational leaders
    (all types of books)
15. Central Presbyterian Church, Kansas City, MO
    Autographed titles, denominational history, large print, 53
    periodicals, 3 papers
16. First Presbyterian Church, St. Joseph, MO
    Beautifully illustrated books
17. Sutton Federated Church, Sutton, NE
    Number and quality of reference books considered unusual
    for small library
18. Holy Trinity Lutheran Church, North Canton, OH
    Hymnals from all congregations

---

TABLE 5.76 (continued)
Church and Synagogue Library Association: Unique or Distinctive
Holdings Questionnaire Replies by Congregation Size

19. Olmsted Christian Church, Disciples of Christ, Olmsted Falls, OH
    Bound sets of Biblical archaeological magazines
20. Washington Street United Methodist Church, Tiffin, OH
    Collection of Horatio Alger novels: old religious and religious history books
21. Burlingame Baptist Church, Portland, OR
    Nearly every version and paraphrase of the Bible in print and many on tapes
    Complete Bible in Braille
22. Friendswood Friends Church, Friendswood, TX
    Historical collection of Quaker writings and local history
23. Holy Cross Lutheran Church, Nederland, TX
    Denominational material; works by Martin Luther
24. St. Matthew's United Methodist Church, Houston, TX
    Archival records; portraits of past ministers
25. Central Christian Church, Springfield, VA
    Restoration Movement titles
Membership of 500 to 999:
1. Mabelvale United Methodist Church, Mabelvale, AR
   Collection of conference journals
   Douglott Bible (Welsh & English)
2. St. Luke's Lutheran Church, La Mesa, CA
   Hebrew Old Testament; Greek New Testament, c. 1896
   Bible ABC's in Braille
3. St. Thomas Episcopal Church, Sunnyvale, CA
   1604 copy of "Summa Theologicae" rebound in leather
   Complete set of Classics of Western Spirituality
4. Christ and Holy Trinity Episcopal Church, Westport, CT
   Anchor Bible series
5. St. Catherine Church, Broad Brook, CT
   Record collection; Old and New Testament for the blind
6. St. Vincent's Episcopal Church, St. Petersburg, FL
   Cassette tapes of each (entire) service, lent to shut-ins together with player

TABLE 5.76 (continued)
Church and Synagogue Library Association: Unique or Distinctive
Holdings Questionnaire Replies by Congregation Size

7. Central Presbyterian Church, Terre Haute, IN
   Archival collection
8. First Christian Church, Shelbyville, IN
   Complete set of Braille Bibles
9. Forest Park United Methodist Church, Ft. Wayne, IN
   Old books and Bibles; Methodist portraits
10. First Lutheran Church, Newton, IA
   Collection includes state and local histories, biographies
   and fiction
11. Trinity Lutheran Church, Marshalltown, IA
   Antiques from former church (materials and books)
12. Church of the Nativity Episcopal, Baltimore, MD
   Collection of foreign language prayerbooks
13. Haven Reformed Church, Kalamazoo, MI
   Old commentaries
14. Immanuel Reformed Church, Grand Rapids, MI
   Cassettes of worship services; music, entire Bible
   Denominational Bible and Missionary Conferences,
   books
15. Third Reformed Church, Kalamazoo, MI
   Video tape collection of services and special programs
16. Pilgrim Congregational Church United Church of Christ, Du-
   luth, MN
   Local and denominational works
17. Episcopal Church of the Holy Faith, Santa Fe, NM
   Books about Southwest mission history and architecture
18. First United Methodist Church, Deming, NM
   Games, cassettes
19. First Presbyterian Church, Clarence, NY
   Published in 1835: Battleboro 5-volume set, *Comprehensive Commentary of the Holy Bible,* containing text according to Authorized Version; Matthew Henry's commentary
20. Setauket Presbyterian Church, Setauket, NY
   The only "reserve" bookshelf is devoted to books on and
   related to peacemaking

TABLE 5.76 (continued)
Church and Synagogue Library Association: Unique or Distinctive
Holdings Questionnaire Replies by Congregation Size

21. Monte Vista Christian Church, Disciples of Christ, Albu-
    querque, NMDenominational titles
    Books on the Southwest and New Mexico: history, travel,
        fiction, biography
22. First Presbyterian Church, Warren, OH
    Archival materials
23. Howard United Methodist Church, Findlay, OH
    Color-coded self-service; extensive picture file
24. The Presbyterian Church, Coshocton, OH
    Archival materials; anniversary celebration every five years
25. St. Michael's in the Hills Episcopal Church, Toledo, OH
    60-volume set of *Summa Theologicae* (St. Thomas Aquinas)
26. Court Street Christian Church, Salem, OR
    Collection donated by pioneer missionary woman
27. Newberg Friends Church, Newberg, OR
    Books by and about Quakers
28. Addisville Reformed Church, Richboro, PA
    Videotape library on cartoon Bible stories
29. Beaver United Methodist Church, Beaver, PA
    Large print section
30. Davisville Baptist Church, Southampton, PA
    Archival materials
31. Grace Presbyterian Church, Jenkintown, PA
    Some rare books, including autographed title
32. Myerstown United Church of Christ, Myerstown, PA
    Old volumes belonging to first pastors; historical collec-
        tion of materials
33. St. Andrew's Episcopal Church, State College, PA
    Three shelves for the local Alcoholics Anonymous group
        lending library
34. St. John's Episcopal Church, Huntingdon Valley, PA
    Library of Christian classics
35. Trinity Evangelical Lutheran Church, Perkasie, PA
    Local church, community history; denominational history
36. Zion Mennonite Church, Souderton, PA
    Denominational history books

TABLE 5.76 (continued)
Church and Synagogue Library Association: Unique or Distinctive
Holdings Questionnaire Replies by Congregation Size

37. First Presbyterian Church, Galveston, TX
    Teaching resources
38. Lamb of God Lutheran Church, Humble, TX
    Special emphasis on devotional & spiritual growth; youth
    and juvenile interests
39. University Avenue Church of Christ, Austin, TX
    Restoration history; Bible exegesis
Membership of 1,000 to 1,999:
 1. Davis Community Church Presbyterian, Davis, CA
    Large print titles
 2. First United Methodist Church, Pasadena, CA
    Videocassettes of dramas presented annually by youth un-
    der professional leadership
 3. Northwest Baptist Church, Fresno, CA
    Videocassettes
 4. San Marino Community Church Presbyterian, San Marino, CA
    Large collection of various translations and versions of the
    Bible; commentaries
 5. Heritage United Methodist Church, Clearwater, FL
    Pictures and slides of church history
 6. Shalimar United Methodist Church Library, Shalimar, FL
    Antique books on Methodism
    Webster's dictionary, 2d edition, 1935
 7. Temple Beth El of Boca Raton, FL
    Adult library; *Encyclopaedia Judaica* and *Encyclopaedia
    Brittanica*
 8. Lutheran Church of the Redeemer, Atlanta, GA
    Salzburger Collection (describes history of Lutherans in the
    Southeast)
 9. North Avenue Presbyterian Church, Atlanta, GA
    Large-print collection
10. Northside United Methodist Church, Atlanta, GA
    Bound National Geographics (1913 to present)
11. St. Luke's Episcopal Church, Atlanta, GA
    Rare Bible; church histories and drawings
12. Forest Congregational Church, Glen Ellyn, IL
    Wide range of educational resources

TABLE 5.76 (continued)
Church and Synagogue Library Association: Unique or Distinctive
Holdings Questionnaire Replies by Congregation Size

13. First Presbyterian Church, Deerfield, IL
    Archival collection
14. St. John's Lutheran Church, Bloomington, IL
    Christian videos
15. St. Mark's United Methodist Church, Decatur, IN
    Collection on deafness and sign language (active deaf ministry)
16. The First United Methodist Church, Storm Lake, IA
    Collection of denominational hymnals
17. Valley View United Methodist Church, Overland Park, KS
    Handicapped collection
18. Trinity Church Episcopal, Boston, MA
    Sermons of Phillips Brooks; architecture of H. H. Richardson
19. Plymouth Congregational Church, Lansing, MI
    Collection on aging, death, and grief
20. Trinity Parish Lutheran Church, St. Peter, MN
    Record collection
21. King's Way United Methodist Church, Springfield, MO
    Personal library of former associate pastor (built in 1920s, 1930s)
22. Packanack Community Church, Wayne, NJ
    Storytelling resources
23. Aquinas Newman Center, Albuquerque, NM
    Fathers of the Church series; Ancient Christian Writers series; Anchor Bible
    Classics of Western Spirituality series
    Old Testament and New Testament Message commentary series
24. Downtown United Presbyterian Church, Rochester, NY
    Materials on social issues
25. Jarvis Memorial United Methodist Church, Greenville, NC
    Media Bible
    Materials by and about the denomination for use by a large area of eastern North Carolina
26. First Lutheran Church, Findlay, OH
    Book reproduced from antique book on the beginning of the church college and church mission

TABLE 5.76 (continued)
Church and Synagogue Library Association: Unique or Distinctive
Holdings Questionnaire Replies by Congregation Size

27. High Street Christian Church, Akron, OH
    Archival collection in separate room
28. United Methodist Church, Berea, OH
    Memorial room of science material (books, microscope)
    Photo album of a pipe organ from another church being re-
    built for our use
29. Carmel Presbyterian Church, Glenside, PA
    Sectional bookcase and contents gift of men's Bible class to
    memorialize its teacher
30. Central Schwenkfelder Church, Worcester, PA
    Archival collection
31. Neshaminy-Warwick Presbyterian Church, Warminster,
    PA
    Local history, particularly area denominational history
32. Salem Baptist Church, Jenkintown, PA
    Black studies books
33. Episcopal Church of the Advent, Stafford, TX
    Extensive tape library
34. First United Methodist Church, Lufkin, TX
    Filmstrip and equipment collection; listening stations provided
35. First United Methodist Church, Stephenville, TX
    Denominational history
36. St. Mark's Episcopal Church, San Antonio, TX
    Fifty-eight books written by a parishioner
37. First Presbyterian Church, Richmond, VA
    Denominational history
38. Longview Community Church, Longview, WA
    Collection of Bibles in other languages; reference section
Membership of 2,000 to 4,999:
1. St. John's Lutheran Church, Waterloo, Ontario, Canada
   Works on Martin Luther
2. Independent Presbyterian Church, Birmingham, AL
   Oversized books in fine arts (music and art)
3. Velda Rose United Methodist Church, Mesa, AZ
   Various versions and editions of the Bible
   Talking Bible; Large-print collection
   Archival collection of songs and hymns

TABLE 5.76 (continued)
Church and Synagogue Library Association: Unique or Distinctive
Holdings Questionnaire Replies by Congregation Size

4. Sinai Temple, Los Angeles, CA
   Some rare books c. 1600s, polyglot Bibles
5. St. Paul's United Methodist Church, Wilmington, DE
   Archival collection
6. Pasadena Community United Methodist Church, St. Petersburg, FL
   Missionary oriented wood carvings
   Antique religious diorama in plaster
7. Temple Beth El, Boca Raton, FL
   Youth library; display case of Jewish ritual items, which
   teachers may use with lessons
   "Stay Here" books (small, spiral bound, pop-up) for the
   youngest children
8. Beth El Synagogue, Highland Park, IL
   Hebrew, Yiddish holdings
9. St. Charles Borromeo, Bloomington, IN
   Replicas of archaeological materials (coins, lamps, etc.)
10. First Lutheran Church, Cedar Rapids, IA
    Complete volumes of Luther's works
    Over 100 pictures to be checked out (art shows often sponsored)
11. St. John the Baptist Catholic Church, Silver Spring, MD
    Catholic authors on subjects for adults
    Titles for preschoolers (others use school library)
12. Church of the Presentation, Upper Saddle River, NJ
    Catholic college catalogs
13. First Baptist Church, Albuquerque, NM
    One hundred years of our own church history
14. Olivet Lutheran Church, Sylvania, OH
    Luther and Lutheran materials
15. First-Century United Methodist Church, Chattanooga, TN
    Small collection of books unique because of age
16. First United Methodist Church, Oak Ridge, TN
    Holston Conference archives (local conference journals from
    1834)
17. Clear Lake United Methodist Church, Houston, TX
    Collection of Bible versions, translations, modern narratives

TABLE 5.76 (continued)
Church and Synagogue Library Association: Unique or Distinctive
Holdings Questionnaire Replies by Congregation Size

<table>
<tr><td colspan="2">Five hundred books recommended for the United Methodist Women's Reading Program<br>Children's juvenile biographies<br>Current college catalogs for 150 Texas colleges</td></tr>
<tr><td>18.</td><td>Congregation Ahavath Sholom, Ft. Worth, TX<br>Complete collection of hand-painted plates on the Old Testament stories (3 dozen plates, all numbered)</td></tr>
<tr><td>19.</td><td>University Presbyterian Church, Seattle, WA<br>Extensive collection on women and the church<br>Large collection of teaching audio cassettes</td></tr>
<tr><td>20.</td><td>Ascension Lutheran Church, Milwaukee, WI<br>Library includes Spanish section<br>Extensive library of organ music loaned to community organists, including nuns</td></tr>
</table>

Membership of 5,000 to 9,999:

1. Mt. Paran Church of God, Atlanta, GA
   Large Pentecostal reference section
   Book placed in library for each infant, dedicated with plaque
2. Broadmoor Baptist Church, Shreveport, LA
   Commentaries, theological literature
3. First United Methodist Church, Tulsa, OK
   Wesley collection (many rare); Methodist collection
4. Catholic Community of St. Luke the Evangelist, Houston, TX
   Titles by local author

Membership over 10,000:

1. The Temple, Cleveland, OH
   Rabbi Abba Hillel Silver Archives
2. All Saints Catholic Church, Dallas, TX
   Audio and video cassette collections
3. Christ the Good Shepherd Church, Spring, TX
   Large audiotape collection; reference books

Size not indicated:

First Church of Christ Congregational, Middletown, CT
Outstanding Bible story collection (used by teachers)

TABLE 5.76 (continued)
Church and Synagogue Library Association: Unique or Distinctive
Holdings Questionnaire Replies by Congregation Size

> Ecumenical Music and Liturgy Resource Library, Lincoln, NE
> Needs and contributions of minority persons in the worship
> setting (i.e., Asians, Hispanics, blacks, Native Americans,
> aging, disabled, singles, women)
> Ghost Ranch Library, Abiquiu, NM
> Southwest collection: history, archaeology
> Interchurch Center Media Resource Library, Portland, OR
> Ministers' burnout library
> Health and healing, women's language
> Youth workers' library
> Biblical reference library
> Peacemaking library
> Episcopal Diocese of Texas, Department of Christian Educa-
> tion, Houston, TX
> Reading program offered through mail

TABLE 5.77
Church and Synagogue Library Association: Annual Congregation and
Library Income Ranges by Denomination

| Denomination | Number | Congregation Income Minimum | Congregation Income Maximum | No Response | Library Income Minimum | Library Income Maximum | No Response |
|---|---|---|---|---|---|---|---|
| Baptist | 26 | $85,000 | $4,550,000 | 2 | $75 | $23,500 | 0 |
| Christian | 21 | 30,000 | 1,500,000 | 3 | 115 | 7,556 | 1 |
| Congregational | 17 | 24,387 | 329,100 | 2 | 150 | 4,800 | 0 |
| Episcopal/ Anglican | 43 | 0 | 900,000 | 5 | 50 | 5,000 | 0 |
| Lutheran | 42 | 66,000 | 1,000,000 | 1 | 0 | 2,900 | 0 |
| Methodist | 80 | 26,400 | 1,720,000 | 5 | 0 | 4,590 | 1 |
| Other Denomi- nations | 57 | 9,360 | 6,000,000 | 9 | 115 | 25,200 | 1 |
| Presbyterian | 85 | 37,000 | 2,000,000 | 6 | 0 | 16,804 | 0 |
| U.C.C. | 22 | 46,500 | 675,000 | 3 | 80 | 23,900 | 0 |
| Summary | | | | | | | |
| Jewish | 6 | 400,000 | 1,625,000 | 2 | 1,950 | 69,380 | 0 |
| Roman Catholic | 12 | 3,500 | 1,120,000 | 3 | 200 | 13,050 | 0 |
| All Protestant | 393 | 0 | 6,000,000 | 3 | 0 | 25,200 | 3 |
| Total | 411 | 0 | 6,000,000 | 41 | 0 | 69,380 | 3 |

TABLE 5.78

Church and Synagogue Library Association: Annual Library Operating Expenditures by Denomination[a]

| Denomination | $0 100 | % | $101– 250 | % | $251– 500 | % | $501 & over | % | No Response | % | Total | Mean |
|---|---|---|---|---|---|---|---|---|---|---|---|---|
| Baptist | 9 | 35 | 4 | 15 | 2 | 8 | 11 | 42 | 0 | 0 | 26 | $1,837 |
| Christian | 5 | 24 | 3 | 14 | 6 | 29 | 6 | 29 | 1 | 5 | 21 | 667 |
| Congregational | 3 | 18 | 6 | 35 | 3 | 18 | 4 | 24 | 1 | 6 | 17 | 411 |
| Episcopal/ Anglican | 17 | 40 | 4 | 9 | 10 | 23 | 12 | 28 | 0 | 0 | 43 | 520 |
| Lutheran | 9 | 21 | 7 | 17 | 15 | 36 | 11 | 26 | 0 | 0 | 42 | 477 |
| Methodist | 22 | 28 | 13 | 16 | 19 | 24 | 25 | 31 | 1 | 1 | 80 | 552 |
| Other Denomi- nations | 8 | 14 | 10 | 18 | 24 | 42 | 14 | 25 | 1 | 2 | 57 | 800 |
| Presbyterian | 12 | 14 | 14 | 16 | 29 | 34 | 30 | 35 | 0 | 0 | 85 | 686 |
| U.C.C. | 7 | 32 | 4 | 18 | 8 | 36 | 3 | 14 | 0 | 0 | 22 | 517 |
| Summary |  |  |  |  |  |  |  |  |  |  |  |  |
| Jewish | 0 | 0 | 0 | 0 | 2 | 33 | 4 | 67 | 0 | 0 | 6 | 18,750 |
| Roman Catholic | 1 | 8 | 0 | 0 | 1 | 8 | 10 | 83 | 0 | 0 | 12 | 2,138 |
| All Protestant | 92 | 23 | 65 | 17 | 116 | 30 | 116 | 30 | 4 | 1 | 393 | 689 |
| Total | 93 | 23 | 65 | 16 | 119 | 29 | 130 | 32 | 4 | 1 | 411 | 998 |

[a]All zero dollar budgets are represented in the initial category, as is usual for the Hannaford Study, leaving only four libraries that actually did not respond.

TABLE 5.79

Church and Synagogue Library Association: Congregations with the Largest Incomes

| Congregation | Annual Congregational Income (in 000s) |
|---|---|
| 1. Mt. Paran Union Church of God, Atlanta, GA | $6,000 |
| 2. Hyde Park Baptist Church, Austin, TX | 4,550 |
| 3. Bethel Church, San Jose, CA | 3,000 |
| 4. Broadmoor Baptist Church, Shreveport, LA | 2,900 |
| 5. First Presbyterian Church, Colorado Springs, CO | 2,000 |
| 6. Briarlake Baptist Church, Decatur, GA | 1,902 |
| 7. University Presbyterian Church, Seattle, WA | 1,873 |
| 8. United Methodist Church, Roswell, GA | 1,720 |
| 9. Chapelwood United Methodist Church, Houston, TX | 1,700 |
| 10. Sinai Temple, Los Angeles, CA | 1,625 |
| 11. Baltimore Hebrew Congregation, Baltimore, MD | 1,600 |
| 12. Beth El Synagogue, Highland Park, IL | 1,500 |
| 13. Fourth Presbyterian Church, Bethesda, MD | 1,500 |
| 14. Country Club Christian Church, Kansas City, MO | 1,500 |

TABLE 5.80

Church and Synagogue Library Association: Congregations with the Largest Incomes per Congregation Member

| Library | Annual Income per Congregation Member |
|---|---|
| 1. Bethel Church, San Jose, CA | $2,000 |
| 2. Trinity Lutheran Church, Canton, OH | 1,749 |
| 3. First United Methodist Church, Taft, CA | 1,564 |
| 4. Weaver's Mennonite Church, Harrisonburg, VA | 1,540 |
| 5. Bramalea Baptist Church, Brampton, ON | 1,496 |
| 6. University Baptist Church, Austin, TX | 1,311 |
| 7. First Deaf Mennonite Church, Lancaster, PA | 1,161 |
| 8. Perkasie Mennonite Church, Perkasie, PA | 1,040 |
| 9. King's Chapel, Boston, MA | 1,033 |
| 10. Lombard Mennonite Church, Lombard, IL | 1,000 |
| 11. First Church of God, Edmonton, AB | 1,000 |

TABLE 5.81

Church and Synagogue Library Association: Total Library Income by Denomination[a]

| Denomination | 0–500 | % | 501–1,000 | % | 1,001–2,000 | % | 2,001 & over | % | No Response | % | Total | Mean |
|---|---|---|---|---|---|---|---|---|---|---|---|---|
| Baptist | 12 | 46.2 | 4 | 15.4 | 3 | 11.5 | 7 | 26.9 | 0 | 0.0 | 26 | 3,188.0 |
| Christian | 10 | 47.6 | 7 | 33.3 | 2 | 9.5 | 1 | 4.8 | 1 | 4.8 | 21 | 954.8 |
| Congregational | 8 | 47.1 | 6 | 35.3 | 2 | 11.8 | 1 | 5.9 | 0 | 0.0 | 17 | 899.4 |
| Episcopal/ Anglican | 19 | 44.2 | 13 | 30.2 | 7 | 16.3 | 4 | 9.3 | 0 | 0.0 | 43 | 846.8 |
| Lutheran | 16 | 38.1 | 16 | 38.1 | 6 | 14.3 | 3 | 7.1 | 1 | 2.4 | 42 | 806.4 |
| Methodist | 30 | 37.5 | 25 | 31.3 | 11 | 13.8 | 11 | 13.8 | 3 | 3.8 | 80 | 1,026.2 |
| Other Denominations | 27 | 47.4 | 15 | 26.3 | 8 | 14.0 | 6 | 10.5 | 1 | 1.8 | 57 | 1,476.6 |
| Presbyterian | 30 | 35.3 | 24 | 28.2 | 20 | 23.5 | 9 | 10.6 | 2 | 2.4 | 85 | 1,269.8 |
| U.C.C. | 13 | 59.1 | 4 | 18.2 | 3 | 13.6 | 2 | 9.1 | 0 | 0.0 | 22 | 1,633.0 |
| Summary | | | | | | | | | | | | |
| Jewish | 0 | 0.0 | 0 | 0.0 | 1 | 16.7 | 5 | 83.3 | 0 | 0.0 | 6 | 21,048.3 |
| Roman Catholic | 2 | 16.7 | 3 | 25.0 | 2 | 16.7 | 5 | 41.7 | 0 | 0.0 | 12 | 4,109.2 |
| All Protestant | 165 | 42.0 | 114 | 29.0 | 62 | 15.8 | 44 | 11.2 | 8 | 2.0 | 393 | 1,272.1 |
| Total | 167 | 40.6 | 117 | 28.5 | 65 | 15.8 | 54 | 13.1 | 8 | 1.9 | 411 | 1,651.1 |

[a]For this table all libraries with zero incomes have been added into the means, as was the usual procedure for the CSLA study. This left eight libraries that actually did not respond to the questionnaire query.

TABLE 5.82

Church and Synagogue Library Association: Libraries with the Largest Incomes

| Library | Annual Income |
|---|---|
| Sinai Temple, Los Angeles, CA | $69,380 |
| The Temple, Cleveland, OH | 31,000 |
| Mt. Paran Union Church of God, Atlanta, GA | 25,200 |
| University Avenue United Church of Christ, Austin, TX | 23,900 |
| First Baptist Church, La Crescenta, CA | 23,500 |
| Briarlake Baptist Church, Decatur, GA | 18,369 |
| Bethel Synagogue, Highland Park, IL | 17,000 |
| University Presbyterian Church, Seattle, WA | 16,804 |
| St. James Roman Catholic Church, Arlington Heights, IL | 13,050 |
| St. Charles Borromeo Church, Bloomington, IN | 13,000 |
| Interchurch Center, Portland, OR | 13,000 |
| Addisville Reformed Church, Richboro, PA | 11,000 |
| Hyde Park Baptist Church, Austin, TX | 10,700 |

TABLE 5.83

Church and Synagogue Library Association: Library Income as a Percentage of Congregational Income by Denomination

| Denomination | $0–500 | % | $501 & over | % | No Response | % | Total | Mean Percentage |
|---|---|---|---|---|---|---|---|---|
| Baptist | 12 | 46 | 14 | 54 | 0 | 0 | 26 | 0.41 |
| Christian | 10 | 48 | 10 | 48 | 1 | 5 | 21 | 0.45 |
| Congregational | 8 | 47 | 9 | 53 | 0 | 0 | 17 | 0.42 |
| Episcopal/Anglican | 19 | 44 | 24 | 56 | 0 | 0 | 43 | 0.44 |
| Lutheran | 16 | 38 | 25 | 60 | 1 | 2 | 42 | 0.33 |
| Methodist | 30 | 38 | 47 | 59 | 3 | 4 | 80 | 0.35 |
| Other Denominations | 27 | 47 | 29 | 51 | 1 | 2 | 57 | 0.62 |
| Presbyterian | 30 | 35 | 53 | 62 | 2 | 2 | 85 | 0.38 |
| U.C.C. | 13 | 59 | 9 | 41 | 0 | 0 | 22 | 0.65 |
| Summary | | | | | | | | |
| Jewish | 0 | 0 | 6 | 100 | 0 | 0 | 6 | 0.51 |
| Roman Catholic | 2 | 17 | 10 | 83 | 0 | 0 | 12 | 2.39 |
| All Protestant | 165 | 42 | 220 | 56 | 8 | 2 | 393 | 0.43 |
| Total | 167 | 41 | 236 | 57 | 8 | 2 | 411 | 0.49 |

TABLE 5.84

Church and Synagogue Library Association: Libraries with the Largest
Incomes as a Percentage of Congregation Income

| Library | % |
|---|---|
| St. Elias Eastern Orthodox Church, Battle Creek, MI | 13.7 |
| St. Charles Borromeo Catholic Church, Bloomington, IN | 13.0 |
| St. Victor School and Church, Monroe, WI | 10.0 |
| Lenape Valley Presbyterian Church, New Britain, PA | 5.6 |
| University Avenue Church of Christ, Austin, TX | 5.5 |
| Sinai Temple, Los Angeles, CA | 4.3 |
| Episcopal Diocese of Texas, Houston, TX | 3.8 |
| Addisville Reformed Church, Richboro, PA | 3.5 |
| Broad Street Christian Church, Tampa, FL | 3.3 |
| Davis Friends Meeting, Davis, CA | 3.2 |
| First Baptist Church, La Crescenta, CA | 2.9 |
| North Side Church of Christ, Austin, TX | 2.6 |
| Faith Presbyterian Church, Kokomo, IN | 2.4 |

TABLE 5.85

Church and Synagogue Library Association: Library Income per
Congregation Member by Denomination

| Denomination | $0.00–0.50 | % | $0.51–$1.00 | % | $1.01+ | % | Mean Library Income per Member | Number | No Response | % |
|---|---|---|---|---|---|---|---|---|---|---|
| Other Denominations | 11 | 19 | 10 | 18 | 34 | 60 | $2.82 | 57 | 2 | 4 |
| U.C.C. | 8 | 36 | 4 | 18 | 10 | 45 | 2.59 | 22 | 0 | 0 |
| Baptist | 6 | 23 | 8 | 31 | 11 | 42 | 2.22 | 26 | 1 | 4 |
| Christian | 4 | 19 | 6 | 29 | 9 | 43 | 1.76 | 21 | 2 | 10 |
| Congregational | 3 | 18 | 3 | 18 | 9 | 53 | 1.35 | 17 | 2 | 12 |
| Presbyterian | 15 | 18 | 39 | 46 | 31 | 36 | 1.32 | 85 | 0 | 0 |
| Episcopal/Anglican | 13 | 30 | 11 | 26 | 18 | 42 | 1.16 | 43 | 1 | 2 |
| Methodist | 30 | 38 | 27 | 34 | 22 | 28 | 0.86 | 80 | 1 | 1 |
| Lutheran | 18 | 43 | 14 | 33 | 10 | 24 | 0.85 | 42 | 0 | 0 |
| Summary | | | | | | | | | | |
| Jewish | 1 | 17 | 1 | 17 | 4 | 67 | 4.78 | 6 | 0 | 0 |
| Roman Catholic | 6 | 50 | 4 | 33 | 2 | 17 | 0.78 | 12 | 0 | 0 |
| All Protestant | 108 | 27 | 122 | 31 | 154 | 40 | 1.50 | 393 | 9 | 2 |
| Total | 115 | 28 | 127 | 31 | 160 | 39 | 1.53 | 411 | 9 | 2 |

TABLE 5.86

Church and Synagogue Library Association: Mean Library Income by Congregation Size

| Congregation Size in Members | Mean Annual Library Income | Number of Libraries | % |
|---|---|---|---|
| 5,000+ | $9,100 | 15 | 4 |
| 2,000–4,999 | 4,795 | 43 | 10 |
| 1,000–1,999 | 1,599 | 87 | 21 |
| 500–999 | 1,122 | 107 | 26 |
| 200–499 | 456 | 121 | 30 |
| 0–199 | 1,021 | 34 | 8 |
| No response | – | 4 | 1 |
| Total | 1,654 | 411 | 100 |

TABLE 5.87

Church and Synagogue Library Association: Libraries with the Largest Incomes per Congregation Member

| Library | Annual Library Income per Congregation Member |
|---|---|
| University Avenue Church of Christ, Austin, TX | $31.66 |
| St. Elias Eastern Orthodox Church, Battle Creek, MI | 20.50 |
| Sinai Temple, Los Angeles, CA | 19.82 |
| First Baptist Church, La Crescenta, CA | 15.66 |
| Addisville Reformed Church, Richboro, PA | 14.66 |
| Broad Street Christian Church, Tampa, FL | 10.00 |
| Perkasie Mennonite Church, Perkasie, PA | 8.75 |
| Church of the Open Door, Wyoming, MI | 8.00 |
| Stone Mountain Community Church, Stone Mountain, GA | 7.20 |
| First Deaf Mennonite Church, Lancaster, PA | 7.12 |
| Roxbury Congregational Church, Newtown, CT | 6.04 |
| Oakwood Baptist Church, New Braunfels, TX | 6.00 |
| New Life Assembly, Petrolia, ON | 6.00 |

TABLE 5.88

Church and Synagogue Library Association: Library Financial Income
Sources by Denomination[a,b]

| Denomination | ----------Mean Figures from Financial Sources---------- | | | | | |
| | Budget Allocation | Congregational Organizations | Gifts and Memorials | Fund-raising | Other Sources | Annual Total |
|---|---|---|---|---|---|---|
| Baptist | $1,837 | $32 | $500 | $77 | $742 | $3,188 |
| Methodist | 552 | 85 | 265 | 32 | 60 | 994 |
| Christian | 667 | 31 | 145 | 61 | 51 | 952 |
| Congregational | 387 | 24 | 436 | 26 | 27 | 899 |
| Episcopal/Anglican | 520 | 59 | 134 | 60 | 74 | 847 |
| Lutheran | 477 | 31 | 227 | 20 | 32 | 787 |
| Presbyterian | 686 | 84 | 194 | 30 | 246 | 1,240 |
| Other Denominations | 800 | 98 | 123 | 36 | 420 | 1,477 |
| U.C.C. | 517 | 38 | 183 | 239 | 655 | 1,632 |
| Summary | | | | | | |
| Jewish | 18,750 | 17 | 1,708 | 42 | 532 | 21,048 |
| Roman Catholic | 2,138 | 0 | 125 | 950 | 896 | 4,109 |
| Maximum | 65,000 | 5,000 | 4,200 | 10,000 | 20,200 | 69,380 |
| Minimum | 0 | 0 | 0 | 0 | 0 | 0 |
| Mean | 996 | 64 | 242 | 76 | 253 | 1,651 |
| Median | 364 | 23 | 88 | 28 | 100 | 604 |
| Number of libraries | 411 | 411 | 411 | 411 | 411 | 411 |
| No response | 4 | 4 | 4 | 4 | 4 | 4 |

[a]For smaller denominations, such as Congregational, the means may appear slightly low
due to libraries registering 0 on some source of funds, with this zero then being added
into the means rather than being counted as showing "missing data" or "no response." In
some cases it is difficult to distinguish between data that is null or missing, especially
when a dash is used by questionnaire respondents.

[b]Median figures include all libraries reporting zero income on any given category.
Therefore, all medians appear to be low.

TABLE 5.89

Church and Synagogue Library Association: Comments on
Nonbudgetary Library Income Sources[a]

| Comment | Number of Libraries | % |
|---|---|---|
| 1. Income from book fairs or sales | 71 | 17 |
| 2. Gifts | 61 | 15 |
| 3. Memorials | 20 | 5 |
| 4. Endowments | 8 | 2 |
| 5. Fines and memberships | 8 | 2 |
| 6. Library staff donations | 6 | 1 |
| 7. Women's or men's congregational group contributions | 6 | 1 |
| 8. Discount book purchases | 4 | 1 |
| 9. Friends of the university or the library | 3 | 1 |
| 10. Christmas tree, jewelry, or card sales | 2 | 0.5 |
| 11. Development campaigns | 2 | 0.5 |
| 12. Others | 23 | 6 |
| 13. No response | 197 | 48 |
| 14. Total | 411 | 100 |

[a]The No Response category on this table is actually larger than 197, as the other
categories listed are not mutually exclusive.

TABLE 5.90

Church and Synagogue Library Association: Libraries with the Highest
Dollar Income from Congregational Sources

| Library Name | City | State | Denomination | Income from Other Sources |
|---|---|---|---|---|
| Fourth Presbyterian Media Center | Bethesda | MD | Presbyterian | 5,000 |
| Central Schwenkfelder Church | Worcester | PA | Other Denominations | 4,500 |
| Pasadena Community United Methodist Methodist | St. Petersburg 1,500 | | | FL |
| First United Methodist Church | Stephenville | TX | Methodist | 1,225 |
| National Presbyterian Church | Washington | DC | Presbyterian | 700 |
| Westwood Church of God | Kalamazoo | MI | Other Denominations | 635 |
| St. Mark's United Methodist Church Methodist | Findlay 550 | | | OH |
| Watts Street Baptist Church | Durham | NC | Baptist | 500 |
| First United Methodist Church | Lufkin | TX | Methodist | 500 |
| St. Mark's Episcopal Church | San Antonio | TX | Episcopal/Anglican | 500 |
| St. Luke's Episcopal Church | Atlanta | GA | Episcopal/Anglican | 400 |
| St. Mark's Episcopal Church | Beaumont | TX | Episcopal/Anglican | 400 |

TABLE 5.91

Church and Synagogue Library Association: Libraries with the Highest
Dollar Income from Proceeds of Various Activities

| Library Name | City | State | Denomination | Income from Other Sources |
|---|---|---|---|---|
| St. James Roman Catholic Church | Arlington Heights | IL | Roman Catholic | 10,000 |
| University Avenue United Church of | | Austin | | TX |
| U.C.C. | 4,500 | | | |
| Christ | | | | |
| National Presbyterian Church | Washington | DC | Presbyterian | 1,000 |
| Briarlake Baptist Church | Decatur | GA | Baptist | 1,000 |
| St. Charles Borromeo Church | Bloomington | IN | Roman Catholic | 1,000 |
| Stone Mountain Community Church | | Stone | | GA |
| Other Denominations | 850 | | | |
| | Mountain | | | |
| Court Street Christian Church | Salem | OR | Christian | 750 |
| St. Thomas Episcopal Church | Sunnyvale | CA | Episcopal/Anglican | 550 |

TABLE 5.92

Church and Synagogue Library Association: Libraries with the Highest
Dollar Income from Other Sources

| Library Name | City | State | Denomination | Income from Other Sources |
|---|---|---|---|---|
| Mt. Paran Union Church of God | Atlanta | GA | Other Denominations | 20,200 |
| University Avenue United Church of Christ | Austin | TX | U.C.C. | 14,150 |
| First Baptist Church | La Crescenta | CA | Baptist | 10,000 |
| St. Charles Borromeo Church | Bloomington | IN | Roman Catholic | 10,000 |
| University Presbyterian Church | Seattle | WA | Presbyterian | 8,700 |
| Hyde Park Baptist Church | Austin | TX | Baptist | 5,200 |
| Broadmoor Baptist Church | Shreveport | LA | Baptist | 3,600 |
| First Presbyterian Church | Martinsville | VA | Presbyterian | 3,000 |
| Carmel Presbyterian Church | Glenside | PA | Presbyterian | 2,250 |
| North Avenue Presbyterian Church | Atlanta | GA | Presbyterian | 2,000 |
| Temple Beth-El, Adults & Children | Boca Raton | FL | Jewish | 1,860 |
| Beaver United Methodist Church | Beaver | PA | Methodist | 1,500 |

TABLE 5.93

Church and Synagogue Library Association: Total Library Expenditure of All Types by Denomination[a]

|  | ---------Library Expenditures--------- | | | | | | | | | | |
| Denomination | $0–100 | % | 101–500 | % | 501–1,000 | % | 1,001 & over | % | No Response | % | Total | Mean |
|---|---|---|---|---|---|---|---|---|---|---|---|---|
| Baptist | 2 | 7.7 | 10 | 38.5 | 4 | 15.4 | 10 | 38.5 | 0 | 0.0 | 26 | 3,188.0 |
| Christian | 0 | 0.0 | 10 | 47.6 | 7 | 33.3 | 3 | 14.3 | 1 | 4.8 | 21 | 952.3 |
| Congregational | 0 | 0.0 | 8 | 47.1 | 6 | 35.3 | 3 | 17.6 | 0 | 0.0 | 17 | 899.4 |
| Episcopal/ Anglican | 4 | 9.3 | 15 | 34.9 | 13 | 30.2 | 11 | 25.6 | 0 | 0.0 | 43 | 846.8 |
| Lutheran | 4 | 9.5 | 13 | 31.0 | 16 | 38.1 | 9 | 21.4 | 0 | 0.0 | 42 | 787.2 |
| Methodist | 4 | 5.0 | 28 | 35.0 | 26 | 32.5 | 21 | 26.2 | 1 | 1.3 | 80 | 994.5 |
| Other Denomi- nations | 0 | 0.0 | 27 | 47.4 | 15 | 26.3 | 14 | 24.6 | 1 | 1.8 | 57 | 1,653.4 |
| Presbyterian | 4 | 4.7 | 28 | 32.9 | 24 | 28.2 | 29 | 34.1 | 0 | 0.0 | 85 | 1,239.9 |
| U.C.C. | 3 | 13.6 | 10 | 45.5 | 4 | 18.2 | 5 | 22.7 | 0 | 0.0 | 22 | 1,633.0 |
| Summary |  |  |  |  |  |  |  |  |  |  |  |  |
| Jewish | 0 | 0.0 | 0 | 0.0 | 0 | 0.0 | 6 | 100.0 | 0 | 0.0 | 6 | 21,048.3 |
| Roman Catholic | 0 | 0.0 | 2 | 16.7 | 3 | 25.0 | 7 | 58.3 | 0 | 0.0 | 12 | 4,109.2 |
| All Protestant | 21 | 5.3 | 149 | 37.9 | 115 | 29.3 | 105 | 26.7 | 3 | 0.8 | 393 | 1,279.9 |
| Total | 21 | 5.1 | 151 | 36.7 | 118 | 28.7 | 118 | 28.7 | 3 | 0.7 | 411 | 1,653.9 |

[a]All libraries showing zero expenditure for this study were registered as making no expenditure and not registered as No Response as with the two *ALD* studies. Therefore, these zero expenditure libraries were added into the means thereby reducing their value significantly.

TABLE 5.94

Church and Synagogue Library Association: Library Operating Budget by Denomination: Table for Comparison with Table 5.77 Removing the Effects of Zero Entries[a]

| Denomination | $1–100 | % | $101–250 | % | $251–1,000 | % | $1,001 & over | % | No Response | % | Total | Mean |
|---|---|---|---|---|---|---|---|---|---|---|---|---|
| Baptist | 5 | 19.2 | 4 | 15.4 | 4 | 15.4 | 9 | 34.6 | 4 | 15.4 | 26 | 2,171.3 |
| Christian | 3 | 14.3 | 3 | 14.3 | 11 | 52.4 | 1 | 4.8 | 3 | 14.3 | 21 | 740.6 |
| Congregational | 0 | 0.0 | 6 | 35.3 | 5 | 29.4 | 2 | 11.8 | 4 | 23.5 | 17 | 505.8 |
| Episcopal/ Anglican | 6 | 14.0 | 4 | 9.3 | 17 | 39.5 | 5 | 11.6 | 11 | 25.6 | 43 | 698.1 |
| Lutheran | 5 | 11.9 | 7 | 16.7 | 21 | 50.0 | 5 | 11.9 | 4 | 9.5 | 42 | 527.4 |
| Methodist | 11 | 13.8 | 13 | 16.3 | 35 | 43.8 | 9 | 11.3 | 12 | 15.0 | 80 | 640.8 |
| Other Denomi- nations | 4 | 7.0 | 10 | 17.5 | 32 | 56.1 | 6 | 10.5 | 5 | 8.8 | 57 | 861.0 |
| Presbyterian | 6 | 7.1 | 14 | 16.5 | 45 | 52.9 | 14 | 16.5 | 6 | 7.1 | 85 | 737.9 |
| U.C.C. | 3 | 13.6 | 4 | 18.2 | 9 | 40.9 | 2 | 9.1 | 4 | 18.2 | 22 | 632.2 |

TABLE 5.94 (continued)
Church and Synagogue Library Association: Library Operating Budget
by Denomination: Table for Comparison with Table 5.77: Removing
the Effects of Zero Entries[a]

| Denomination | $1– 100 | % | $101– 250 | % | $251– 1,000 | % | $1,001 & over | % | No Response | % | Total | Mean |
|---|---|---|---|---|---|---|---|---|---|---|---|---|
| Summary | | | | | | | | | | | | |
| Jewish | 0 | 0.0 | 0 | 0.0 | 2 | 33.3 | 4 | 66.7 | 0 | 0.0 | 6 | 18,750.0 |
| Roman Catholic | 0 | 0.0 | 0 | 0.0 | 4 | 33.3 | 7 | 58.3 | 1 | 8.3 | 12 | 2,332.7 |
| All Protestant | 43 | 10.9 | 65 | 16.5 | 179 | 45.5 | 53 | 13.5 | 53 | 13.5 | 393 | ⁻788.5 |
| Total | 43 | 10.5 | 65 | 15.8 | 185 | 45.0 | 64 | 15.6 | 54 | 13.1 | 411 | 1,137.9 |

[a]Means for this table were calculated on the basis of all libraries showing a budget of >0.
All zero entries were re-registered as No Response, raising the mean value.

TABLE 5.95
Church and Synagogue Library Association: Percentage of Total
Library Incomes Accounted for by Each of Five Income Categories

| Denomination Income | Budgetary Income | % | Gifts | % | Congreg- ational Sources | % | Proceedings from Activities | % | Other Income | % | Total |
|---|---|---|---|---|---|---|---|---|---|---|---|---|
| Baptist | 47,769 | 58 | 13,005 | 16 | 825 | 1 | 2,000 | 2 | 19,290 | 23 | 82,889 |
| Christian | 13,330 | 70 | 2,904 | 15 | 624 | 3 | 1,214 | 6 | 1,020 | 5 | 19,092 |
| Congrega- tional | 6,574 | 43 | 7,404 | 48 | 405 | 3 | 440 | | | | |
| | 465 | 3 | 15,289 | | | | | | | | |
| Episcopal/ Anglican | 22,340 | 61 | 4,750 | 16 | 2,558 | 7 | 2,599 | 7 | 3,167 | 9 | 35,414 |
| Lutheran | 20,040 | 61 | 9,528 | 29 | 1,285 | 4 | 855 | 3 | 1,355 | 4 | 33,063 |
| Methodist | 43,574 | 55 | 20,949 | 27 | 6,750 | 9 | 2,537 | 3 | 5,199 | 7 | 79,009 |
| Other Denom- inations | -44,771 | 54 | 6,889 | 8 | 5,504 | 7 | 1,991 | 2 | 23,532 | 28 | 82,687 |
| Presbyterian | 58,294 | 55 | 16,481 | 16 | 7,142 | 7 | 2,548 | 2 | 20,925 | 20 | 105,390 |
| U.C.C. | 11,380 | 32 | 4,035 | 11 | 830 | 2 | 5,262 | 15 | 14,420 | 40 | 35,927 |
| Summary | | | | | | | | | | | |
| Jewish | 112,500 | 89 | 10,250 | 8 | 100 | 0 | 250 | 0 | 3,190 | 3 | 126,290 |
| Roman Catholic | 25,660 | 52 | 1,500 | 3 | 0 | 0 | 11,400 | 23 | 10,750 | 22 | 49,310 |
| All Protestant | 268,072 | 55 | 85,945 | 18 | 25,923 | 5 | 19,446 | 4 | 89,373 | 18 | 488,760 |
| Total | 406,232 | 60 | 97,695 | 15 | 26,023 | 4 | 31,096 | 5 | 103,313 | 15 | 664,360 |

TABLE 5.96

Church and Synagogue Library Association: Annual Library Budget by Chief Librarian's Gender

| Gender | -------Library Budget in Dollars------- | | | | | | | | | | All Libraries | Mean |
|---|---|---|---|---|---|---|---|---|---|---|---|---|
| | $0– 250 | % | 251– 500 | % | 501– 2,000 | % | 2,001 & over | % | No Response | % | | |
| Females | 146 | 38 | 107 | 28 | 102 | 27 | 25 | 7 | 4 | 1 | 384 | 1,045 |
| Males | 11 | 46 | 10 | 42 | 3 | 13 | 0 | 0 | 0 | 0 | 24 | 339 |
| No response | 1 | 33 | 2 | 67 | 0 | 0 | 0 | 0 | 0 | 0 | 3 | 317 |
| Totals | 158 | 38 | 119 | 29 | 105 | 26 | 25 | 6 | 4 | 1 | 411 | 998 |

TABLE 5.97

Church and Synagogue Library Association: Annual Library Expenditure on Personnel by Denomination[a,b]

| Denomination | $0– 1,000 | % | 1,001– 5,000 | % | 5,001– 10,000 | % | 10,001 & over | % | Total | Mean |
|---|---|---|---|---|---|---|---|---|---|---|
| Baptist | 22 | 84.6 | 3 | 11.5 | 1 | 3.8 | 0 | 0.0 | 26 | 754 |
| Christian | 21 | 100.0 | 0 | 0.0 | 0 | 0.0 | 0 | 0.0 | 21 | 0 |
| Congregational | 17 | 100.0 | 0 | 0.0 | 0 | 0.0 | 0 | 0.0 | 17 | 0 |
| Episcopal/Anglican | 42 | 97.7 | 1 | 2.3 | 0 | 0.0 | 0 | 0.0 | 43 | 58 |
| Lutheran | 42 | 100.0 | 0 | 0.0 | 0 | 0.0 | 0 | 0.0 | 42 | 18 |
| Methodist | 77 | 96.3 | 3 | 3.8 | 0 | 0.0 | 0 | 0.0 | 80 | 85 |
| Other Denomina-tions | 54 | 94.7 | 1 | 1.8 | 2 | 3.5 | 0 | 0.0 | 57 | 319 |
| Presbyterian | 81 | 95.3 | 4 | 4.7 | 0 | 0.0 | 0 | 0.0 | 85 | 188 |
| U.C.C. | 21 | 95.5 | 0 | 0.0 | 0 | 0.0 | 1 | 4.5 | 22 | 636 |
| Summary | | | | | | | | | | |
| Jewish | 2 | 33.3 | 2 | 33.3 | 0 | 0.0 | 2 | 33.3 | 6 | 5,855 |
| Roman Catholic | 9 | 75.0 | 1 | 8.3 | 2 | 16.7 | 0 | 0.0 | 12 | 1,917 |
| All Protestant | 377 | 95.9 | 12 | 3.1 | 3 | 0.8 | 1 | 0.3 | 393 | 198 |
| Total | 388 | 94.4 | 15 | 3.6 | 5 | 1.2 | 3 | 0.7 | 411 | 331 |

[a]All libraries with no personnel expenditure have been added into the means. The questionnaire categorization system assumes that if no personnel expenditure figure is provided, then personnel expenditure = 0.

[b]It is interesting to note (see table 5.98) that 383 of the libraries seem to have had no budgets at all for personnel (< $1.00), while 26 of them had budgets over $500. For another picture of the CSLA personnel expenditure means see tables 6.34, 6.37.

TABLE 5.98

Church and Synagogue Library Association: Annual Library
Expenditure on Salaries by Denomination[a]

| Denomination | Annual Expenditure on ---Salaries per Library--- | | | | Number of Libraries | Mean Per Library | --Range-- | |
|---|---|---|---|---|---|---|---|---|
| | No Response or $0 | 1–100 | 101– 500 | 501+ | | | Low | High |
| Baptist | 22 | 0 | 0 | 4 | 26 | $4,900 | $0 | $10,000 |
| U.C.C. | 21 | 0 | 0 | 1 | 22 | 14,000 | 0 | 14,000 |
| Other Denominations | 52 | 1 | 1 | 3 | 57 | 3,638 | 0 | 10,000 |
| Presbyterian | 81 | 0 | 0 | 4 | 85 | 4,000 | 0 | 5,000 |
| Methodist | 77 | 0 | 0 | 3 | 80 | 2,267 | 0 | 2,800 |
| Episcopal/Anglican | 41 | 0 | 0 | 2 | 43 | 1,250 | 0 | 1,500 |
| Lutheran | 41 | 0 | 0 | 1 | 42 | 750 | 0 | 750 |
| Christian | 21 | 0 | 0 | 0 | 21 | 0 | 0 | 0 |
| Congregational | 17 | 0 | 0 | 0 | 17 | 0 | 0 | 0 |
| Summary | | | | | | | | |
| Jewish | 1 | 0 | 0 | 5 | 6 | 7,026 | 0 | 15,000 |
| Roman Catholic | 9 | 0 | 0 | 3 | 12 | 7,667 | 0 | 10,000 |
| All Protestant | 373 | 1 | 1 | 18 | 393 | 3,892 | 0 | 14,000 |
| Total | 383 | 1 | 1 | 26 | 411 | 4,856 | 0 | 15,000 |

[a]All libraries with zero salary expenditure were recategorized to register No Response—
this has produced a tremendous effect on the denominational means. Here the means for
only those libraries with salary expenditures are shown: overall mean = $4,856 versus
$331 when those libraries without salary expenditures are added into the calculations for
the means. The overall effect of the all-inclusive calculation form is that those
denominations with many libraries showing no paid staff have the lowest denominational
means simply because of the large number of zero responses added into the sum used for
generating the mean statistic. And hence $4,856 becomes reduced to $331! An
undesirable outcome.

TABLE 5.99

Church and Synagogue Library Association: Congregational Income by Denomination[a]

| Denomination | $1–10,000 | % | $10,001–50,000 | % | $50,001–250,000 | % | $250,001 & over | % | No Response | % | Total | Mean |
|---|---|---|---|---|---|---|---|---|---|---|---|---|
| Baptist | 2 | 7.7 | 0 | 0.0 | 11 | 42.3 | 13 | 50.0 | 0 | 0.0 | 26 | $626,511 |
| Christian | 3 | 14.3 | 1 | 4.8 | 14 | 66.7 | 3 | 14.3 | 0 | 0.0 | 21 | 98,012 |
| Congregational | 2 | 11.8 | 1 | 5.9 | 11 | 64.7 | 3 | 17.6 | 0 | 0.0 | 17 | 21,784 |
| Episcopal/ Anglican | 6 | 14.0 | 1 | 2.3 | 24 | 55.8 | 11 | 25.6 | 1 | 2.3 | 43 | 108,115 |
| Lutheran | 1 | 2.4 | 0 | 0.0 | 22 | 52.4 | 19 | 45.2 | 0 | 0.0 | 42 | 265,310 |
| Methodist | 5 | 6.3 | 2 | 2.5 | 38 | 47.5 | 35 | 43.8 | 0 | 0.0 | 80 | 264,641 |
| Other Denominations | 10 | 17.5 | 4 | 7.0 | 27 | 47.4 | 16 | 28.1 | 0 | 0.0 | 57 | 153,535 |
| Presbyterian | 6 | 7.1 | 1 | 1.2 | 42 | 49.4 | 36 | 42.4 | 0 | 0.0 | 85 | 314,191 |
| U.C.C. | 3 | 13.6 | 1 | 4.5 | 14 | 63.6 | 4 | 18.2 | 0 | 0.0 | 22 | 15,941 |
| Summary | | | | | | | | | | | | |
| Jewish | 2 | 33.3 | 0 | 0.0 | 0 | 0.0 | 4 | 66.7 | 0 | 0.0 | 6 | 520,833 |
| Roman Catholic | 4 | 33.3 | 0 | 0.0 | 3 | 25.0 | 5 | 41.7 | 0 | 0.0 | 12 | 127,458 |
| All Protestant | 38 | 9.7 | 11 | 2.8 | 203 | 51.7 | 140 | 35.6 | 1 | 0.3 | 393 | 233,116 |
| Total | 44 | 10.7 | 11 | 2.7 | 206 | 50.1 | 149 | 36.3 | 1 | 0.2 | 411 | 234,234 |

[a]All houses of worship showing no budget were recategorized to register No Response— in this case only one Episcopal/Anglican library.

TABLE 5.100

Church and Synagogue Library Association: Annual Library Expenditures by Denomination[a]

| Denomination | $1–100 | % | $101–500 | % | $501–1,000 | % | $1,001 & over | % | No Response | % | Total Libraries | Mean |
|---|---|---|---|---|---|---|---|---|---|---|---|---|
| Baptist | 2 | 8 | 10 | 38 | 3 | 12 | 11 | 42 | 0 | 0 | 26 | $3,325 |
| Christian | 0 | 0 | 10 | 48 | 7 | 33 | 3 | 14 | 1 | 5 | 21 | 970 |
| Congregational | 0 | 0 | 8 | 47 | 7 | 41 | 2 | 12 | 0 | 0 | 17 | 664 |
| Episcopal/ Anglican | 4 | 9 | 15 | 35 | 13 | 30 | 11 | 26 | 0 | 0 | 43 | 847 |
| Lutheran | 3 | 7 | 12 | 29 | 17 | 40 | 9 | 21 | 1 | 2 | 42 | 813 |
| Methodist | 2 | 3 | 29 | 36 | 25 | 31 | 21 | 26 | 3 | 4 | 80 | 1,047 |
| Other Denominations | 0 | 0 | 27 | 47 | 15 | 26 | 14 | 25 | 1 | 2 | 57 | 1,487 |
| Presbyterian | 2 | 2 | 30 | 35 | 23 | 27 | 28 | 33 | 2 | 2 | 85 | 1,245 |
| U.C.C. | 3 | 14 | 10 | 45 | 4 | 18 | 5 | 23 | 0 | 0 | 22 | 1,638 |
| Summary | | | | | | | | | | | | |
| Jewish | 0 | 0 | 0 | 0 | 0 | 0 | 6 | 100 | 0 | 0 | 6 | 21,048 |
| Roman Catholic | 0 | 0 | 2 | 17 | 3 | 25 | 7 | 58 | 0 | 0 | 12 | 4,109 |
| All Protestant | 16 | 4 | 151 | 38 | 114 | 29 | 104 | 26 | 8 | 2 | 393 | 1,273 |
| Total | 16 | 4 | 153 | 37 | 117 | 28 | 117 | 28 | 8 | 2 | 411 | 1,652 |

[a]All libraries with zero library total expenditure were recategorized to register No Response with resulting changes to the means for denominations: Christian, Lutheran, Methodist, Other Denominations, Presbyterian, and the overall total.

TABLE 5.101

Church and Synagogue Library Association: Libraries with the Largest
Annual Expenditure on Personnel

| Library | Annual expenditure on Personnel |
|---|---|
| Sinai Temple, Los Angeles, CA | $15,000 |
| The Temple, Cleveland, OH | 15,000 |
| University Avenue United Church of Christ, Austin, TX | 14,000 |
| First Baptist Church, La Crescenta, CA | 10,000 |
| Mt. Paran Union Church of God, Atlanta, GA | 10,000 |
| St. James Roman Catholic Church, Arlington Heights, IL | 10,000 |
| St. Charles Borromeo Church, Bloomington, IN | 10,000 |
| Interchurch Media Resource Center, Portland, OR | 6,000 |
| Fourth Presbyterian Media Center, Bethesda, MD | 5,000 |
| University Presbyterian Church, Seattle, WA | 5,000 |

TABLE 5.102

Church and Synagogue Library Association: Annual Library
Expenditure on Book Volumes by Denomination[a]

| Denomination | ----Annual Book Expenditure---- | | | | Number of Libraries | Mean per Library | ----Range---- | |
|---|---|---|---|---|---|---|---|---|
| | $0 | 1–100 | 101–500 | 501+ | | | Low | High |
| Baptist | 0 | 3 | 9 | 14 | 26 | $1,826 | $65 | $9,469 |
| Presbyterian | 3 | 2 | 40 | 40 | 85 | (773) 746 | 0 | 9,400 |
| U.C.C. | 0 | 4 | 11 | 7 | 22 | 753 | 50 | 6,250 |
| Other Denominations | 1 | 1 | 38 | 17 | 57 | (731) 718 | 0 | 6,204 |
| Christian | 1 | 1 | 12 | 7 | 21 | (712) 678 | 0 | 5,756 |
| Episcopal/Anglican | 0 | 4 | 23 | 16 | 43 | 623 | 50 | 4,900 |
| Methodist | 3 | 3 | 35 | 39 | 80 | (640) 616 | 0 | 2,520 |
| Lutheran | 1 | 3 | 21 | 17 | 42 | (541) 528 | 0 | 1,750 |
| Congregational | 0 | 0 | 10 | 7 | 17 | 486 | 140 | 1,220 |
| Summary | | | | | | | | |
| Jewish | 0 | 0 | 0 | 6 | 6 | 13,505 | 500 | 52,080 |
| Roman Catholic | 0 | 0 | 2 | 10 | 12 | 1,416 | 150 | 4,350 |
| All Protestant | 9 | 21 | 199 | 164 | 393 | (753) 736 | 0 | 9,469 |
| Total | 9 | 21 | 201 | 180 | 411 | (963) 942 | 0 | 52,080 |

[a]Those denominations showing libraries with no expenditures on book volumes have
means slightly reduced in value, since these zero responses have been added into the
denominational means. Adjusted means are shown in parentheses.

TABLE 5.103

Church and Synagogue Library Association: Libraries with the Largest
Annual Expenditure on Material

| Library | Annual Expenditure on Material |
|---|---|
| Sinai Temple, Los Angeles, CA | $52,080 |
| Beth El Synagogue, Highland Park, IL | 13,100 |
| The Temple, Cleveland, OH | 10,200 |
| Briarlake Baptist Church, Decatur, GA | 9,469 |
| Mt. Paran Union Church of God, Atlanta, GA | 9,400 |
| Hyde Park Baptist Church, Austin, TX | 8,700 |
| First Baptist Church, La Crescenta, CA | 8,500 |
| Northwest Baptist Church, Fresno, CA | 6,300 |
| University Avenue United Church of Christ, Austin, TX | 6,250 |
| University Presbyterian Church, Seattle, WA | 6,204 |

TABLE 5.104

Church and Synagogue Library Association: Library Expenditures on
Media Titles by Denomination[a]

| Denomination | ----Media Expenditures---- | | | | | | No Response or No Media Expenditure | % | Total Libraries | Mean |
|---|---|---|---|---|---|---|---|---|---|---|
| | 1–100 | % | 101–500 | % | 501 & over | % | | | | |
| Baptist | 7 | 27 | 4 | 15 | 5 | 19 | 10 | 38 | 26 | $ 563 |
| Christian | 8 | 38 | 4 | 19 | 1 | 5 | 8 | 38 | 21 | 150 |
| Congregational | 6 | 35 | 1 | 6 | 1 | 6 | 9 | 53 | 17 | 74 |
| Episcopal/Anglican | 9 | 21 | 10 | 23 | 2 | 5 | 22 | 51 | 43 | 101 |
| Lutheran | 10 | 24 | 18 | 43 | 2 | 5 | 12 | 29 | 42 | 162 |
| Methodist | 17 | 21 | 20 | 25 | 9 | 11 | 34 | 43 | 80 | 190 |
| Other Denominations | 13 | 23 | 14 | 26 | 3 | 5 | 27 | 47 | 57 | 240 |
| Presbyterian | 35 | 41 | 14 | 16 | 4 | 5 | 32 | 38 | 85 | 157 |
| U.C.C. | 2 | 9 | 2 | 9 | 1 | 5 | 17 | 77 | 22 | 160 |
| Summary | | | | | | | | | | |
| Jewish | 1 | 17 | 1 | 17 | 2 | 33 | 2 | 33 | 6 | 1,008 |
| Roman Catholic | 1 | 8 | 5 | 42 | 3 | 25 | 3 | 25 | 12 | 515 |
| All Protestant | 107 | 27 | 87 | 22 | 28 | 7 | 171 | 44 | 393 | 193 |
| Total | 109 | 27 | 93 | 23 | 33 | 8 | 176 | 43 | 411 | 215 |

[a]Libraries with no response for this expenditure category were assumed to have no media
expenditures.

TABLE 5.105

Church and Synagogue Library Association: Libraries with the Largest
Annual Expenditure on Media Titles

| Library | Annual Expenditure on Media Titles |
|---|---|
| First Baptist Church, La Crescenta, CA | $5,000 |
| Mt. Paran Union Church of God, Atlanta, GA | 5,000 |
| Briarlake Baptist Church, Decatur, GA | 5,000 |
| The Temple, Cleveland, OH | 5,000 |
| University Presbyterian Church, Seattle, WA | 4,500 |
| Interchurch Media Resource Center, Portland, OR | 3,500 |
| University Avenue United Church of Christ, Austin, TX | 3,000 |
| All Saints Catholic Parish Resource Center, Dallas, TX | 2,500 |
| First Christian Church, Fort Collins, CO | 1,600 |
| First United Methodist Church, Lufkin, TX | 1,500 |
| Fourth Presbyterian Church, Bethesda, MD | 1,200 |

TABLE 5.106

Church and Synagogue Library Association: Annual Library
Expenditure on Supplies by Denomination

| Denomination | --Annual Supplies Expenditure-- | | | | Number of Libraries | Mean per Library | ----Range---- | |
|---|---|---|---|---|---|---|---|---|
| | $0 | 1–100 | 101–500 | 501+ | | | Low | High |
| Baptist | 0 | 19 | 6 | 1 | 26 | $112 | $10 | $700 |
| Methodist | 3 | 69 | 7 | 1 | 80 | 70 | 0 | 1,000 |
| Presbyterian | 4 | 73 | 8 | 0 | 85 | 68 | 0 | 500 |
| Christian | 1 | 18 | 2 | 0 | 21 | 61 | 0 | 300 |
| Other Denominations | 2 | 50 | 5 | 0 | 57 | 59 | 0 | 400 |
| U.C.C. | 0 | 21 | 1 | 0 | 22 | 59 | 10 | 450 |
| Congregational | 0 | 17 | 0 | 0 | 17 | 58 | 10 | 100 |
| Lutheran | 1 | 39 | 2 | 0 | 42 | 54 | 0 | 200 |
| Episcopal/Anglican | 1 | 41 | 1 | 0 | 43 | 50 | 0 | 200 |
| Summary | | | | | | | | |
| Jewish | 0 | 1 | 3 | 2 | 6 | 447 | 80 | 1,000 |
| Roman Catholic | 0 | 7 | 5 | 0 | 12 | 133 | 20 | 350 |
| All Protestant | 12 | 347 | 32 | 2 | 393 | 65 | 0 | 1,000 |
| Total | 12 | 355 | 40 | 4 | 411 | 73 | 0 | 1,000 |

TABLE 5.107

Church and Synagogue Library Association: Annual Library
Expenditure on Equipment by Denomination in Descending Order

| Denomination | Annual Equipment Expenditure | | | | Number of Libraries | Mean Per Library | Range | |
|---|---|---|---|---|---|---|---|---|
| | $0 | 1–100 | 101–500 | 501+ | | | Low | High |
| Other Denomina-tions | 40 | 10 | 3 | 4 | 57 | $124 | $0 | $3,000 |
| Baptist | 15 | 8 | 3 | 0 | 26 | 70 | 0 | 500 |
| Presbyterian | 54 | 20 | 11 | 0 | 85 | 56 | 0 | 500 |
| Congregational | 14 | 1 | 2 | 0 | 17 | 47 | 0 | 500 |
| Methodist | 57 | 15 | 7 | 1 | 80 | 46 | 0 | 1,000 |
| Christian | 17 | 3 | 1 | 0 | 21 | 35 | 0 | 500 |
| Lutheran | 32 | 8 | 1 | 1 | 42 | 33 | 0 | 600 |
| U.C.C. | 15 | 6 | 1 | 0 | 22 | 30 | 0 | 200 |
| Episcopal/Anglican | 36 | 6 | 1 | 0 | 43 | 15 | 0 | 200 |
| Summary | | | | | | | | |
| Jewish | 2 | 0 | 4 | 0 | 6 | 233 | 0 | 500 |
| Roman Catholic | 3 | 5 | 4 | 0 | 12 | 129 | 0 | 300 |
| All Protestant | 280 | 77 | 30 | 6 | 393 | 55 | 0 | 3,000 |
| Total | 285 | 82 | 38 | 6 | 411 | 60 | 0 | 3,000 |

TABLE 5.108

Church and Synagogue Library Association: Libraries with the Largest
Annual Expenditure on Supplies

| Library | Annual Expenditure on Supplies |
|---|---|
| Sinai Temple, Los Angeles, CA | $1,000 |
| Chapelwood United Methodist Church, Houston, TX | 1,000 |
| Hyde Park Baptist Church, Austin, TX | 700 |
| The Temple, Cleveland, OH | 600 |
| University Presbyterian Church, Seattle, WA | 500 |
| University Avenue United Church of Christ, Austin, TX | 450 |
| North Avenue Presbyterian Church, Atlanta, GA | 400 |
| Briarlake Baptist Church, Decatur, GA | 400 |
| Beth El Synagogue, Highland Park, IL | 400 |
| Interchurch Media Resource Center, Portland, OR | 400 |

TABLE 5.109

Church and Synagogue Library Association: Libraries with the Largest
Annual Expenditure on Equipment

| Library | Annual Expenditure on Equipment |
|---|---|
| 1. Central Schwenkfelder Church, Worcester, PA | $3,000 |
| 2. Twin Lakes Reformed Church, Kalamazoo, MI | 1,100 |
| 3. Chapelwood United Methodist Church, Houston, TX | 1,000 |
| 4. Westwood Church of God, Kalamazoo, MI | 635 |
| 5. Newberg Friends Meeting, Newberg, OR | 615 |
| 6. Gloria Dei Lutheran Church, Downers Grove, IL | 600 |
| 7. Sinai Temple, Los Angeles, CA | 500 |
| 8. First Christian Church, Fort Collins, CO | 500 |
| 9. Mt. Paran Union Church of God, Atlanta, GA | 500 |
| 10. Briarlake Baptist Church, Decatur, GA | 500 |
| 11. Beth El Synagogue, Highland Park, IL | 500 |
| 12. Hyde Park Baptist Church, Austin, TX | 500 |
| 13. University Presbyterian Church, Seattle, WA | 500 |
| 14. North Shore Congregational Church, Fox Point, WI | 500 |

TABLE 5.110

Church and Synagogue Library Association: Means and Percentages of
Library Expenditure Spent on Five Categories by Denomination

| Denomination | Salaries | % | Books | % | Media | % | Supplies | % | Equipment | % | Total |
|---|---|---|---|---|---|---|---|---|---|---|---|
| Baptist | 754 | 23 | 1,826 | 55 | 563 | 17 | 112 | 3 | 70 | 2 | 3,325 |
| U.C.C. | 636 | 39 | 753 | 46 | 160 | 10 | 59 | 4 | 30 | 2 | 1,638 |
| Christian | 0 | 0 | 678 | 73 | 150 | 16 | 61 | 7 | 35 | 4 | 924 |
| Episcopal/Anglican | 58 | 7 | 623 | 74 | 101 | 12 | 50 | 6 | 15 | 2 | 847 |
| Lutheran | 18 | 2 | 528 | 67 | 162 | 20 | 54 | 7 | 33 | 4 | 794 |
| Congregational | 0 | 0 | 486 | 73 | 74 | 11 | 58 | 9 | 47 | 7 | 664 |
| Other Denominations | 319 | 22 | 718 | 49 | 240 | 16 | 59 | 4 | 124 | 9 | 1,461 |
| Presbyterian | 188 | 15 | 746 | 61 | 157 | 13 | 68 | 6 | 56 | 5 | 1,215 |
| Methodist | 85 | 8 | 616 | 61 | 190 | 19 | 70 | 7 | 46 | 5 | 1,007 |
| Summary | | | | | | | | | | | |
| Jewish | 5,855 | 28 | 13,505 | 64 | 1,008 | 5 | 447 | 2 | 233 | 1 | 21,048 |
| Roman Catholic | 1,917 | 47 | 1,416 | 34 | 515 | 13 | 133 | 3 | 129 | 3 | 4,109 |
| All Protestant | 198 | 16 | 736 | 59 | 194 | 16 | 65 | 5 | 55 | 4 | 1,247 |
| Total | 331 | 20 | 942 | 58 | 215 | 13 | 73 | 5 | 60 | 4 | 1,620 |

TABLE 5.111
North American Religious Groups[a]

---

**NONBIBLICAL ASIAN**

| | |
|---|---|
| Baha'i | Theosophist |
| Buddhist | TMT |
| Hindu | Unitarian-Universalist |
| Islam | Zoroastrians |
| Rosicrucians | |

**LIBERAL MAINSTREAM, MOSTLY CHRISTIAN** (Middle class, urban, conservative)

| | |
|---|---|
| Amish | Jewish |
| Christian Science | Lutheran |
| Church of Canada | Methodist |
| Congregational | Presbyterian |
| Eastern Orthodox | Reformed |
| Episcopal/Anglican | Roman Catholic |
| Friends or Brethren: conservative | United Church of Christ |
| (relative to outsiders) | |
| Greek Orthodox | |

**CHARISMATIC/ PENTECOSTAL CHRISTIAN** (Healing, emphasis on miracles, God's intervention in life, the Holy Spirit, baptism, speaking in tongues, gifts of the Spirit)

| | |
|---|---|
| Christian | Church of the Nazarene |
| Churches of Christ | Pentecostal |
| Churches of God | Pillar of Fire |

**EVANGELICAL CHRISTIAN** (Witnesses who spread the gospel)

| | |
|---|---|
| Adventists | Mennonites |
| Assemblies of God | Mormons |
| Baptists | Roman Catholic |
| Brethren (evangelical ethnically) | Salvation Army |
| Jehovah's Witnesses | United Church of Christ |

---

[a]The above four groups are clear enough conceptually but disintegrate when strictly applied to any given denomination. Therefore, the categorization is highly subjective and nonexclusive. The author wishes no offense to any group, intending only to identify statistical tendencies.

TABLE 5.112

Church and Synagogue Library Association: Mainstream vs.
Evangelical and Charismatic Denominations by Annual Library
Expenditures[a,b]

| Denomination | ---Raw Means for Liberal, Mainstream Denominations--- | | | | | |
| | Salaries | Books | Media | Supplies | Equipment | Mean |
|---|---|---|---|---|---|---|
| Congregational | $0 | $486 | $74 | $58 | $47 | $665 |
| Episcopal/Anglican | 58 | 623 | 101 | 50 | 15 | 847 |
| Jewish | 5,855 | 13,505 | 1,008 | 447 | 233 | 21,048 |
| Lutheran | 18 | 541 | 166 | 55 | 34 | 814 |
| Methodist | 89 | 637 | 195 | 73 | 47 | 1,041 |
| Presbyterian | 193 | 764 | 161 | 70 | 57 | 1,245 |
| Total | 230 | 940 | 175 | 73 | 47 | 1,465 |

| Denomination | Raw Means for Nonbiblical Asians, Evangelical, --Charismatic, and Pentecostal Christian Denominations-- | | | | | |
| | Salaries | Books | Media | Supplies | Equipment | Mean |
|---|---|---|---|---|---|---|
| Baptist | $754 | 1,826 | 563 | 112 | 70 | 3,325 |
| Christian | 0 | 712 | 158 | 64 | 37 | 971 |
| Other Denominations | 325 | 730 | 244 | 61 | 126 | 1,486 |
| Roman Catholic | 1,917 | 1,416 | 515 | 133 | 129 | 4,110 |
| U.C.C. | 636 | 753 | 160 | 59 | 30 | 1,638 |
| Total | 550 | 1,001 | 303 | 77 | 87 | 2,018 |
| Net difference in $ | 320 | 61 | 128 | 4 | 40 | 553 |
| Net difference between mainstream & evangelical & charismatic denominations in percent | 139% | 6.5% | 73% | 5.5% | 85% | 37.7% |

[a]Means shown above are based on those libraries registering expenditure in each one of the categories listed. Libraries with zero expenditure have been omitted from the means in order to show more accurate rankings between mainstream versus evangelical for each of the five expenditure subcategories (see final row for percentage differences).
[b]Obviously, arbitrary placement of Other Denominations in any one category is an oversimplification.

TABLE 5.113
Church and Synagogue Library Association: Mainstream vs.
Evangelical and Charismatic Denominations: Mean Figures for a
Variety of Variables[a,b]

| Variable | Means | Percentage Difference |
|---|---|---|
| City population (in 000s) | | |
| Mainstream denominations | 109.8 population | |
| Evangelical and charismatic denominations | 96.6 | −12 |
| Library age | | |
| Mainstream denominations | 25.2 years | |
| Evangelical and charismatic denominations | 18.2 | −28 |
| Library committee members | | |
| Mainstream denominations | 5.4 members | |
| Evangelical and charismatic denominations | 6.8 | 26 |
| Library staff hours worked per week | | |
| Mainstream denominations | 9.5 hours | |
| Evangelical and charismatic denominations | 11.5 | 21 |
| Library income as a percentage of congregational income | | |
| Mainstream denominations | 0.568% | |
| Evangelical and charismatic denominations | 0.652 | 15 |
| Book holdings | | |
| Mainstream denominations | 3,293 volumes | |
| Evangelical and charismatic denominations | 2,968 | −10 |
| Media title holdings | | |
| Mainstream denominations | 347 titles | |
| Evangelical and charismatic denominations | 521 | 50 |
| Circulation per month | | |
| Mainstream denominations | 110 volumes | |
| Evangelical and charismatic denominations | 135 | 23 |
| Library cost per circulation charge | | |
| Mainstream denominations | $2.81 | |
| Evangelical and charismatic denominations | 2.02 | −28 |

[a]Liberal mainstream denominations: Congregational, Episcopal/Anglican, Jewish,
Lutheran, Methodist, Presbyterian.
[b]Nonbiblical Asian, evangelical and charismatic denominations: Buddhist, Christian
Science, Islam, Unitarian-Universalist, Baptist, Christian, Other Denominations (some of
them), Roman Catholic, United Church of Christ.

TABLE 5.114
Church and Synagogue Library Association: Library Card Catalogs
Available

| Number of Catalogs Available | Number of Libraries | % |
|---|---|---|
| Six | 145 | 35 |
| Five | 150 | 37 |
| Four | 64 | 16 |
| Three | 23 | 5 |
| Two | 14 | 3 |
| One | 11 | 3 |
| No response | 4 | 1 |
| Total libraries | 411 | 100 |
| Mean number of catalogs per library | 4.9 | |
| Catalogs | | |
| Shelf list | 387 | 94 |
| Author | 386 | 94 |
| Title | 353 | 86 |
| Nonbook material | 353 | 86 |
| Accession record | 279 | 68 |
| Subject | 224 | 55 |
| Mean catalog types per library | 4.9 | 81 |

TABLE 5.115
Church and Synagogue Library Association: Classification Systems
Used[a]

| Classification Systems | Number of Libraries | % |
|---|---|---|
| Dewey Decimal Classification | 333 | 81 |
| Locally designed system | 45 | 11 |
| Library of Congress classification or subject headings | 9 | 2 |
| A–Z Browne system | 5 | 1 |
| Judaic systems | 5 | 1 |
| Weine classification | 3 | |
| Elazar | 1 | |
| Leikind | 1 | |
| Erwin John, Lutheran classification | 3 | 1 |
| Cokesbury system | 3 | 1 |
| Color codes | 3 | 1 |
| Sears list of subject headings | 2 | 0.5 |
| Expanded Dewey 200s | 2 | 0.5 |
| Pamphlets filed alphabetically by subject | 2 | 0.5 |
| Have only main entry (or title) cards | 2 | 0.5 |

TABLE 5.115 (continued)
Church and Synagogue Library Association: Classification Systems
Used[a]

| Classification Systems | Number of Libraries | % |
|---|---|---|
| Dictionary catalog | 2 | 0.5 |
| Age level classification | 2 | 0.5 |
| Westminster, Lavose Newton, Catholic subject headings, Elton Shell, subjects, adults vs. youth, author's last name, church-related, and R. McEwan: one instance of each | 9 | 2 |
| Certain kinds of books not cataloged | 3 | 1 |
| No response | 17 | 4 |
| Total | 447 | 109 |

[a]The above classification systems are not mutually exclusive. They total in excess of the number of cases.

TABLE 5.116
Church and Synagogue Library Association: Library Use Privilege
Availability

| Privilege | Number of Libraries | % |
|---|---|---|
| Open to outside users | 172 | 42 |
| Open to outside users with restrictions | 156 | 38 |
| Identification or address required | 35 | 9 |
| Must be recommended by a member | 21 | 5 |
| Librarian's permission needed | 14 | 3 |
| Only church visitors and students eligible | 12 | 3 |
| Only members of other churches | 7 | 2 |
| Borrowers must be personally known to the Librarian | 7 | 2 |
| Clergy only | 4 | 1 |
| Interlibrary loan service only | 4 | 1 |
| Material must be used in the building only | 3 | 1 |
| Fee required | 1 | 0 |
| Miscellaneous | 48 | 12 |
| Not open to outside users | 83 | 20 |
| Total | 411 | 100 |

TABLE 5.117

Church and Synagogue Library Association: Library Service Provided for Users[a]

| Service | Number of Libraries | % |
|---|---|---|
| Always self-service when building open | 144 | 35 |
| Part-time staff, self-service at other times | 239 | 58 |
| Always staffed when open | 36 | 9 |
| Total | 419 | 102 |

[a]Some overlap among libraries existed since the three service categories were not necessarily mutually exclusive, i.e., some libraries were both "staffed" and "self-service" simultaneously.

TABLE 5.118

Church and Synagogue Library Association: Monthly Library Circulation[a]

| Type | Number of Libraries | % | No Response | % | Mean Monthly Circulation | Total Libraries |
|---|---|---|---|---|---|---|
| Adult | 258 | 63 | 153 | 37 | 55.0 | 411 |
| Children's | 258 | 63 | 153 | 37 | 47.2 | 411 |
| Total | 320 | 78 | 91 | 22 | 114.5 | 411 |

[a]Some libraries reported only a total circulation score, which presumably included both adult and children's circulation. Therefore, the *true* mean adult circulation per month can be calculated as shown below:

Adult circulation mean        =    55.0 monthly circulation

Children's circulation mean   =    47.2

Total for 258 libraries       =    102.2

Adult proportion              =    53.8%

The same proportion for 320 libraries   =   .538 × 114.5 = 61.6 circulation mean.

Finally $((55.0 \times 258) + (61.6 \times 320))/(258 + 320) = 33902/578 = 58.7$ circulation mean.

Therefore, the true value for Adult circulation is probably close to 60 books per month working on the assumption that the division between adult and children's circulation remains roughly constant.

TABLE 5.119

Church and Synagogue Library Association: Library Monthly Adult Book Circulation by Region

| Region | -------Adult Book Circulation------- | | | | | | | | | | Total | |
| | 1–25 | % | 26–50 | % | 51–75 | % | 76 & over | % | No Response | % | Libraries | Mean |
|---|---|---|---|---|---|---|---|---|---|---|---|---|
| Northeast | 9 | 45 | 0 | 0 | 1 | 5 | 1 | 5 | 9 | 45 | 20 | 28 |
| Middle Atlantic | 34 | 44 | 8 | 10 | 6 | 8 | 5 | 6 | 24 | 31 | 77 | 43 |
| Southeast | 12 | 20 | 12 | 20 | 4 | 7 | 4 | 7 | 27 | 46 | 59 | 56 |
| Southwest | 14 | 22 | 9 | 14 | 4 | 6 | 9 | 14 | 27 | 43 | 63 | 72 |
| West | 8 | 23 | 4 | 11 | 3 | 9 | 8 | 23 | 12 | 34 | 35 | 115 |
| Rocky Mountains | 2 | 33 | 0 | 0 | 0 | 0 | 2 | 33 | 2 | 33 | 6 | 131 |
| Middle West | 55 | 39 | 25 | 18 | 2 | 1 | 11 | 8 | 48 | 34 | 141 | 40 |
| Canada | 1 | 10 | 3 | 30 | 0 | 0 | 2 | 20 | 4 | 40 | 10 | 60 |
| Total | 135 | 33 | 61 | 15 | 20 | 5 | 42 | 10 | 153 | 37 | 411 | 55 |

TABLE 5.120

Church and Synagogue Library Association: Library Monthly Adult Book Circulation by Denomination

| Denomination | -------Adult Book Circulation------- | | | | | | | | | | Total | |
| | 0–50 | % | 51–100 | % | 101–250 | % | 251 & over | % | No Response | % | Libraries | Mean |
|---|---|---|---|---|---|---|---|---|---|---|---|---|
| Baptist | 9 | 35 | 5 | 19 | 2 | 8 | 2 | 8 | 8 | 31 | 26 | 83 |
| Christian | 9 | 43 | 4 | 19 | 1 | 5 | 1 | 5 | 6 | 29 | 21 | 68 |
| Congregational | 8 | 47 | 0 | 0 | 0 | 0 | 0 | 0 | 9 | 53 | 17 | 16 |
| Episcopal/ Anglican | 25 | 58 | 4 | 9 | 1 | 2 | 0 | 0 | 13 | 30 | 43 | 32 |
| Lutheran | 23 | 55 | 4 | 10 | 1 | 2 | 0 | 0 | 14 | 33 | 42 | 36 |
| Methodist | 43 | 54 | 4 | 5 | 3 | 4 | 2 | 3 | 28 | 35 | 80 | 47 |
| Other Denomi- nations | 23 | 40 | 6 | 11 | 3 | 5 | 2 | 4 | 23 | 40 | 57 | 69 |
| Presbyterian | 34 | 40 | 10 | 12 | 1 | 1 | 3 | 4 | 37 | 44 | 85 | 80 |
| U.C.C. | 13 | 59 | 0 | 0 | 1 | 5 | 0 | 0 | 8 | 36 | 22 | 29 |
| Summary | | | | | | | | | | | | |
| Jewish | 4 | 67 | 0 | 0 | 0 | 0 | 0 | 0 | 2 | 33 | 6 | 41 |
| Roman Catholic | 5 | 42 | 0 | 0 | 2 | 17 | 0 | 0 | 5 | 42 | 12 | 65 |
| All Protestant | 187 | 48 | 37 | 9 | 13 | 3 | 10 | 3 | 146 | 37 | 393 | 55 |
| Total | 196 | 48 | 37 | 9 | 15 | 4 | 10 | 2 | 153 | 37 | 411 | 55 |

TABLE 5.121

Church and Synagogue Library Association: Library Monthly
Children's Book Circulation by Region

| Region | Children's Book Circulation | | | | | | | | | | | |
|---|---|---|---|---|---|---|---|---|---|---|---|---|
| | 0–50 | % | 51–100 | % | 101–250 | % | 251 & over | % | No Response | % | Total Libraries | Mean |
| Northeast | 11 | 55 | 0 | 0 | 0 | 0 | 0 | 0 | 9 | 45 | 20 | 12 |
| Middle Atlantic | 44 | 57 | 5 | 7 | 4 | 5 | 0 | 0 | 24 | 31 | 77 | 35 |
| Southeast | 20 | 34 | 8 | 14 | 2 | 3 | 2 | 3 | 27 | 46 | 59 | 65 |
| Southwest | 23 | 37 | 7 | 11 | 5 | 8 | 2 | 3 | 26 | 41 | 63 | 70 |
| West | 16 | 46 | 5 | 14 | 2 | 6 | 0 | 0 | 12 | 34 | 35 | 40 |
| Rocky Mountains | 3 | 50 | 1 | 17 | 0 | 0 | 0 | 0 | 2 | 33 | 6 | 33 |
| Middle West | 69 | 49 | 16 | 11 | 4 | 3 | 3 | 2 | 49 | 35 | 141 | 43 |
| Canada | 3 | 30 | 1 | 10 | 1 | 10 | 1 | 10 | 4 | 40 | 10 | 98 |
| Total | 189 | 46 | 43 | 10 | 18 | 4 | 8 | 2 | 153 | 37 | 411 | 47 |

TABLE 5.122

Church and Synagogue Library Association Library Monthly
Children's Book Circulation by Denomination

| Denomination | Children's Book Circulation | | | | | | | | | | | |
|---|---|---|---|---|---|---|---|---|---|---|---|---|
| | 0–50 | % | 51–100 | % | 101–250 | % | 251 & over | % | No Response | % | Total Libraries | Mean |
| Baptist | 11 | 42 | 3 | 12 | 1 | 4 | 2 | 8 | 9 | 35 | 26 | 73 |
| Christian | 13 | 62 | 0 | 0 | 2 | 10 | 0 | 0 | 6 | 0 | 21 | 31 |
| Congregational | 7 | 41 | 1 | 6 | 0 | 0 | 0 | 0 | 9 | 53 | 17 | 21 |
| Episcopal/ Anglican | 27 | 63 | 2 | 5 | 1 | 2 | 0 | 0 | 13 | 30 | 43 | 19 |
| Lutheran | 18 | 43 | 7 | 17 | 2 | 5 | 1 | 2 | 14 | 33 | 42 | 58 |
| Methodist | 38 | 48 | 10 | 13 | 2 | 3 | 2 | 3 | 28 | 35 | 80 | 47 |
| Other Denom- inations | 18 | 32 | 10 | 18 | 4 | 7 | 2 | 4 | 23 | 40 | 57 | 79 |
| Presbyterian | 37 | 44 | 6 | 7 | 4 | 5 | 1 | 1 | 37 | 44 | 85 | 41 |
| U.C.C. | 14 | 64 | 0 | 0 | 0 | 0 | 0 | 0 | 8 | 36 | 22 | 19 |
| Summary | | | | | | | | | | | | |
| Jewish | 0 | 0 | 3 | 50 | 1 | 17 | 0 | 0 | 2 | 33 | 6 | 117 |
| Roman Catholic | 6 | 50 | 1 | 8 | 1 | 8 | 0 | 0 | 4 | 33 | 12 | 47 |
| All Protestant | 183 | 47 | 39 | 10 | 16 | 4 | 8 | 2 | 147 | 37 | 393 | 47 |
| Total | 189 | 46 | 43 | 10 | 18 | 4 | 8 | 2 | 153 | 37 | 411 | 47 |

TABLE 5.123

Church and Synagogue Library Association: Libraries with the Largest Monthly Adult Circulation

| Library | Monthly Adult Circulation |
|---|---|
| University Presbyterian Church, Seattle, WA | 899 |
| Fourth Presbyterian Church, Bethesda, MD | 800 |
| Pleasant Grove Presbyterian Church, Youngstown, OH | 440 |
| First Christian Church, Ft. Collins, CO | 400 |
| Mt. Paran Union Church of God, Atlanta, GA | 400 |
| First United Methodist Church, Tulsa, OK | 400 |
| Bethel Church, San Jose, CA | 375 |
| Hyde Park Baptist Church, Austin, TX | 300 |
| Clear Lake United Methodist Church, Houston, TX | 291 |
| Burlingame Baptist Church, Portland, OR | 275 |
| University Avenue Church of Christ, Austin, TX | 225 |

TABLE 5.124

Church and Synagogue Library Association: Libraries with the Largest Monthly Children's Circulation

| Library | Monthly Children's Circulation |
|---|---|
| Harrisonville Mennonite Church, Harrisonville, MO | 500 |
| Stone Mountain Community Church, Stone Mountain, GA | 400 |
| Broadmoor Baptist Church, Shreveport. LA | 400 |
| First United Methodist Church, Tulsa, OK | 400 |
| Our Savior's Lutheran Church, Sioux Falls, SD | 400 |
| Bramalea Baptist Church, Brampton, ON | 300 |
| Jarvis Memorial United Methodist Church, Greenville, NC | 298 |
| Pleasant Grove Presbyterian Church, Youngstown, OH | 260 |
| Clear Lake United Methodist Church, Houston, TX | 229 |

TABLE 5.125

Church and Synagogue Library Association: Libraries with the Largest Monthly Total Circulation

| Library | Monthly Total Circulation |
|---|---|
| First Baptist Church, La Crescenta, CA | 3,200 |
| University Presbyterian Church, Seattle, WA | 1,034 |
| Fourth Presbyterian Church, Bethesda, MD | 1,000 |
| First United Methodist Church, Tulsa, OK | 800 |
| First United Methodist Church, Oak Ridge, TN | 800 |
| Sinai Temple, Los Angeles, CA | 700 |
| Pleasant Grove Presbyterian Church, Youngstown, OH | 699 |
| Forward Baptist Church, Cambridge, ON | 667 |
| Mt. Paran Union Church of God, Atlanta, GA | 600 |
| Stone Mountain Community Church, Stone Mountain, GA | 600 |
| Harrisonville Mennonite Church, Harrisonville, MO | 600 |
| Our Savior's Lutheran Church, Sioux Falls, SD | 600 |
| Clear Lake United Methodist Church, Houston, TX | 520 |

TABLE 5.126

Church and Synagogue Library Association: Total Monthly Circulation by Denomination

| Denomination | -Total Library Circulation- | | | Mean Circulation | Number of Libraries | No Response |
|---|---|---|---|---|---|---|
| | 0–50 | 51–100 | 101+ | | | |
| Baptist | 10 | 4 | 11 | 277 | 26 | 1 |
| Other Denominations | 20 | 4 | 21 | 143 | 57 | 12 |
| Presbyterian | 28 | 18 | 14 | 112 | 85 | 25 |
| Methodist | 36 | 16 | 13 | 99 | 80 | 15 |
| Lutheran | 17 | 8 | 10 | 99 | 42 | 7 |
| Christian | 7 | 6 | 3 | 98 | 21 | 5 |
| Episcopal/Anglican | 23 | 7 | 4 | 50 | 43 | 9 |
| U.C.C. | 13 | 2 | 1 | 47 | 22 | 6 |
| Congregational | 8 | 2 | 0 | 34 | 17 | 7 |
| Summary | % | % | % | | % | |
| Jewish | 0 | 0    1 | 16    4 | 67    265.0 | 6    1 | 16 |
| Roman Catholic | 4 | 33    1 | 8    4 | 33    111.0 | 12    3 | 25 |
| All Protestant | 162 | 41    67 | 17    77 | 19    112.0 | 393    87 | 22 |
| Total | 166 | 40    69 | 17    85 | 21    114.5 | 411    91 | 22 |

TABLE 5.127

Church and Synagogue Library Association: Total Monthly Circulation per 100 Congregation Members by Denomination

| Denomination | Mean Monthly Circulation per 100 Members | Number of Libraries | % | Total Libraries | No Response |
|---|---|---|---|---|---|
| Other Denominations | 41 | 44 | 77 | 57 | 13 |
| Baptist | 27 | 24 | 92 | 26 | 2 |
| Christian | 15 | 16 | 76 | 21 | 5 |
| Presbyterian | 10 | 60 | 71 | 85 | 25 |
| U.C.C. | 10 | 16 | 73 | 22 | 6 |
| Lutheran | 8 | 35 | 83 | 42 | 7 |
| Episcopal/Anglican | 7 | 34 | 79 | 43 | 9 |
| Methodist | 6 | 65 | 81 | 80 | 15 |
| Congregational | 5 | 9 | 53 | 17 | 8 |
| Summary | | | | | |
| Jewish | 6 | 5 | 83 | 6 | 1 |
| Roman Catholic | 2 | 9 | 75 | 12 | 3 |
| All Protestant | 15 | 303 | 77 | 393 | 90 |
| Total | 14 | 317 | 77 | 411 | 94 |

TABLE 5.128

Church and Synagogue Library Association: Libraries with the Largest Monthly Circulation per Congregation Member

| Library | Denomination | Monthly Circulation per Congregation Member | Annual Circulation per Congregation Member |
|---|---|---|---|
| Lombard Mennonite Church, Lombard, IL | Other Denominations | 2.40 | 29 |
| First Baptist Church, La Crescenta, CA | Baptist | 2.13 | 26 |
| Perkasie Mennonite Church, Perkasie, PA | Other Denominations | 2.05 | 25 |
| Harrisonville Mennonite Church, Harrisonville, MO | Other Denominations | 1.71 | 21 |
| First Deaf Mennonite Church, Lancaster, PA | Other Denominations | 1.45 | 17 |
| Immanuel Reformed Church, Grand Rapids, MI | Other Denominations | 1.14 | 14 |
| Weaver's Mennonite Church, Harrisonburg, VA | Other Denominations | 1.00 | 12 |
| Pleasant Grove Presbyterian Church, Youngstown, OH | Presbyterian | 0.93 | 11 |
| Burlingame Baptist Church, Portland, OR | Baptist | 0.92 | 11 |
| Stone Mountain Community Church, Stone Mountain, GA | Other Denominations | 0.80 | 10 |
| New Life Assembly, Petrolia, ON | Other Denominations | 0.71 | 9 |
| Davis Friends Meeting, Davis, CA | Other Denominations | 0.70 | 8 |
| Highland Christian Church, Cleveland, OH | Christian | 0.70 | 8 |

TABLE 5.129

Church and Synagogue Library Association: Annual Library Income
Divided by Annual Circulation[a]

| Denomination | Annual Library Income over Circulation | Number of Libraries | % | Total Libraries | No Response |
|---|---|---|---|---|---|
| Lutheran | $1.08 | 35 | 83 | 42 | 7 |
| Christian | 1.56 | 15 | 71 | 21 | 6 |
| Presbyterian | 1.60 | 60 | 71 | 85 | 25 |
| Baptist | 1.65 | 25 | 96 | 26 | 1 |
| Methodist | 1.65 | 65 | 81 | 80 | 15 |
| U.C.C. | 1.72 | 16 | 73 | 22 | 6 |
| Episcopal/Anglican | 2.06 | 34 | 79 | 43 | 9 |
| Other Denominations | 2.07 | 45 | 79 | 57 | 12 |
| Congregational | 2.87 | 10 | 59 | 17 | 7 |
| Summary | | | | | |
| Jewish | 7.62 | 5 | 83 | 6 | 1 |
| Roman Catholic | 3.12 | 9 | 75 | 12 | 3 |
| All Protestant | 1.72 | 305 | 78 | 393 | 88 |
| Total | 1.85 | 319 | 78 | 411 | 92 |

[a]The result of dividing annual circulation into annual library income is an estimate of the cost of charging out one volume. This composite value tells us two things: (1) for those libraries that have the least expensive charge costs, it tells us how efficient they are and (2) for those libraries with the more expensive costs, it suggests how generously these libraries are supported by their congregations.

TABLE 5.130

Church and Synagogue Library Association: Annual Library Income
Divided by Annual Library Circulation—The Most Expensive Libraries
per Circulation Charge

| Library | Cost Per Circulation Charge |
|---|---|
| Ebenezer United Methodist Church, Lanham, MD | $20.83 |
| St. Elias Eastern Orthodox Church, Battle Creek, MI | 18.98 |
| The Temple, Cleveland, OH | 17.22 |
| Briarlake Baptist Church, Decatur, GA | 17.00 |
| Addisville Reformed Church, Richboro, PA | 15.28 |
| Central Schwenkfelder Church, Worcester, PA | 13.89 |
| Westminster Presbyterian Church, Dekalb, IL | 10.00 |
| Catholic Community of St. Luke, Houston, TX | 10.00 |
| Beth El Synagogue, Highland Park, IL | 9.44 |
| Sinai Temple, Los Angeles, CA | 8.26 |
| King's Chapel, Boston, MA | 8.21 |

TABLE 5.131
Church and Synagogue Library Association: Annual Library Income
Divided by Annual Library Circulation—The Least Expensive
Libraries per Circulation Charge

| Library | Cost per Circulation Charge |
|---|---|
| Harrisonville Mennonite Church, Harrisonville, MO | 0.03 |
| Pleasant Grove Presbyterian Church, Youngstown, OH | 0.06 |
| Ruthfred Lutheran Church, Bethel Park, PA | 0.11 |
| First Church of Christ, Defiance, OH | 0.13 |
| Lombard Mennonite Church, Lombard, IL | 0.16 |
| Lincolnshire Church of the Brethren, Fort Wayne, IN | 0.16 |
| St. John's Free Will Baptist Church, Washington, DC | 0.17 |
| St. Mark's Lutheran Church, Toledo, OH | 0.17 |

TABLE 5.132
Church and Synagogue Library Association: Explanations from Those
Congregational Libraries "Serving a School Also"

| Explanations | Number of Libraries | % |
|---|---|---|
| Preschool | 22 | 5 |
| Sunday school | 9 | 2 |
| Children's reading program | 7 | 2 |
| Day care center | 5 | 1 |
| Kindergarten | 5 | 1 |
| Adult or teenage users | 3 | 1 |
| College or university library | 3 | 1 |
| Preschool teachers | 3 | 1 |
| Library used as classroom | 2 | 0.5 |
| School has its own library | 2 | 0.5 |
| Others | 3 | 1 |
| No response | 347 | 84 |
| Total | 411 | 100 |

TABLE 5.133
Church and Synagogue Library Association: Summary of Comments
on Library Quarters

| Favorable Comments | Number | % |
|---|---|---|
| Good location | 8 | 2 |
| Will build larger quarters | 7 | 2 |
| New rooms | 4 | 1 |
| Spacious and modern facility in old sanctuary or social area | 4 | 1 |
| Attractive, pleasant room | 3 | 1 |
| Accessible, visible | 2 | 0.5 |
| Favorable quarters | 2 | 0.5 |
| Ideal location but little shelf space | 1 | 0 |
| Separate children's room | 1 | 0 |
| **Unfavorable Comments** | | |
| Crowded, need more space | 28 | 7 |
| Certain material kept elsewhere | 12 | 3 |
| Poor space and location | 5 | 1 |
| Room used primarily for other purposes | 4 | 1 |
| In a separate building | 3 | 1 |
| Nonfunctional quarters | 2 | 0.5 |
| In social hall | 2 | 0.5 |
| No library room | 2 | 0.5 |
| Housed in the narthex | 1 | 0.25 |
| Have one-third wall in a lounge | 1 | 0.25 |
| Library in basement | 1 | 0.25 |
| Glass enclosed shelves | 1 | 0.25 |
| In a hallway | 1 | 0.25 |
| Unfavorable | 1 | 0.25 |
| No response | 315 | 77 |
| Total | 411 | 100 |

TABLE 5.134
Church and Synagogue Library Association: Library Computer Use

| Purpose | Number of Libraries | % |
|---|---|---|
| Bibliographies | 5 | 1 |
| Catalog and shelflist | 2 | 0.5 |
| Book annotations, book labels, pockets, etc. | 2 | 0.5 |
| Other | 2 | 0.5 |
| Only considering use or have one that is unused | 14 | 3 |
| No response | 386 | 94 |
| Total | 411 | 100 |
| Manufacturer of computer used | | |
| Commodore | 6 | 1.5 |
| IBM PC | 6 | 1.5 |
| Atari | 3 | 1 |
| AT&T | 3 | 1 |
| Alto | 2 | 0.5 |
| Apple | 2 | 0.5 |
| Hewlett Packard | 2 | 0.5 |
| Decmate | 1 | 0.25 |
| No response | 386 | 94 |
| Total | 411 | 100 |
| Software used | | |
| Church administrative program system | 6 | 1.5 |
| dBase II or III | 4 | 1 |
| BASIC | 2 | 0.5 |
| Librarian's helper | 2 | 0.5 |
| Other, one per library responding | 12 | 3 |
| No response | 385 | 94 |
| Total | 411 | 100 |

TABLE 5.135
Church and Synagogue Library Association: Congregational Publications and the Library by Denomination[a]

| Denomination | No. of Libraries | Congregation Newsletter Contains Library News | Percentage Yes | Separate Library Newsletter | Percentage Yes | Library Described in Cong. Leaflet | Percentage Yes | All Published Library News and Descriptions | Total Percentage Yes |
|---|---|---|---|---|---|---|---|---|---|
| Baptist | 26 | 23 | 88% | 1 | 4% | 7 | 27% | 31 | 119% |
| Christian | 21 | 13 | 62 | 3 | 14 | 4 | 19 | 20 | 95 |
| Congregational | 17 | 16 | 94 | 0 | 0 | 3 | 18 | 19 | 112 |
| Episcopal/Anglican | 43 | 36 | 84 | 5 | 12 | 9 | 21 | 50 | 117 |
| Lutheran | 42 | 38 | 90 | 5 | 12 | 5 | 12 | 48 | 114 |
| Methodist | 80 | 69 | 86 | 4 | 5 | 14 | 18 | 87 | 109 |
| Other Denominations | 57 | 38 | 67 | 13 | 23 | 8 | 14 | 59 | 104 |
| Presbyterian | 85 | 76 | 89 | 4 | 5 | 12 | 14 | 92 | 108 |
| U.C.C. | 22 | 20 | 91 | 0 | 0 | 2 | 9 | 22 | 100 |
| Summary | | | | | | | | | |
| Jewish | 6 | 6 | 100 | 1 | 17 | 2 | 33 | 9 | 150 |
| Roman Catholic | 12 | 8 | 67 | 1 | 8 | 7 | 58 | 16 | 133 |
| All Protestant | 393 | 329 | 84 | 35 | 9 | 64 | 16 | 428 | 109 |
| Total | 411 | 343 | 83 | 37 | 9 | 73 | 18 | 453 | 110 |

[a]Final two columns exceed total sample size since the three activities listed in previous columns are nonexclusive.

TABLE 5.136
Church and Synagogue Library Association: Library Publication
Frequency Groups

| Frequency | Number of Libraries | Percentage |
|---|---|---|
| Monthly | 98 | 24 |
| Weekly | 29 | 7 |
| Bimonthly | 16 | 4 |
| Quarterly | 11 | 3 |
| Biweekly | 10 | 2 |
| Other | 5 | 1 |
| Irregularly | 22 | 5 |
| No response | 220 | 54 |
| Total | 411 | 100 |

TABLE 5.137

Church and Synagogue Library Association: Areas in Which the
Libraries Needed Help or Information

Funding
Children's librarian needed
Promoting use
Volunteer typists
Catalogers
Use of space (furnishings, arrangement) especially when limited
Development of audiovisual material collection
    videotape collection
    card catalog
    videocassette collection
    awareness of importance of the library, publicity
Recataloging / improving classification
Sources of books on mission work in the United States and abroad
Bibliographies and reviews of books dealing with social problems
    for older elementary and junior high ages
    on sociology and social problems
    on career choices for youth
    on family budgeting
    on family relationships
    single men
    men who are divorced (or widowed)
    children's books that teach Christian living
    devotional books
    adult fiction
    audiocassette tapes
    biographies
    filmstrips
    teaching aids
    the best books on theology
New bulletin board ideas
Weeding
Computer information
Promotional ideas directed toward men, teens, and young women
Information on storage of AV supplies (no details, perhaps humidity, method, etc.)
Archivist needed
Overdues procedures (general, circulation)
Liaison needed to work with teachers and leaders
Recording circulation in self-serve library
Archival material: storage ideas, preservation, accessing
Processing audiovisuals, including storage and display
Sources of audiovisuals (e.g., filmstrip catalogs, Christian listings)
How to get the cooperation of the minister
Dealing with superiors, e.g., education chairman, religious education director
Communication with large institutional staff

TABLE 5.137 (continued)
Church and Synagogue Library Association: Areas in Which the
Libraries Needed Help or Information

---

Subject determination for vertical file (authority list)
Developing policy statements
Computer cataloging programs
Organizing and cataloging nonbook materials
Sources of printed catalog card sets
Subject catalog cross-referencing
Setting goals
Controlling circulation (titles not signed out) in self-serve library
How to organize a working committee
Getting books returned
Increasing use by teachers
Setting up a vertical file
Forming support group (not workers or staff) such as friends of the library
How to get on publishers' lists for mailing
Writing procedures manuals
Training volunteers
How to form a bond with other congregational libraries in community (not a chapter)
Need catalogs of Judaic music to add to collection
How to catalog and classify
How to take inventory
Computerizing the library collection
Computerized database program
Book selection principles
Keeping volunteer workers (organizing tasks effectively)
Accessing titles
Filing rules for catalog cards
Using church's computer for record keeping
Ideas for story hours
Incentives, ideas for adult reading clubs
Ideas for summer reading programs for children
Promotional skits and promotional skills
Ideas for book displays
Formation and duties of a library committee
Need more space (where is ideal location?)
Cataloging audiovisuals
Circulation methods for nonbook materials
How to preserve photos
What to do with old magazines (clipping file, etc.)
How to preserve old books
How to organize interlibrary loans with other local church libraries

---

TABLE 5.138

Church and Synagogue Library Association: Number of Books Circulated per Month in Relation to Library Support Effort by Denomination[a-d]

| Denomination | Mean Raw Score | Denominational Rank | Number of Libraries | No Response |
|---|---|---|---|---|
| Lutheran | 273 | 1 | 42 | 7 |
| Baptist | 77 | 2 | 26 | 3 |
| Presbyterian | 65 | 3 | 85 | 29 |
| Other Denominations | 51 | 4 | 57 | 17 |
| Methodist | 35 | 5 | 80 | 18 |
| Christian | 29 | 7 | 21 | 6 |
| Episcopal/Anglican | 17 | 8 | 43 | 14 |
| U.C.C. | 15 | 9 | 22 | 8 |
| Congregational | 9 | 11 | 17 | 8 |
| Summary | | | | |
| Jewish | 30 | 6 | 6 | 3 |
| Roman Catholic | 10 | 10 | 12 | 6 |
| All Protestant | 72 | – | 393 | 110 |
| Total | 70 | – | 411 | 119 |

[a]This table measures circulation/effort or benefit/effort among congregational libraries. The mean raw score was obtained by dividing circulation per member into effort per member.

[b]Effort was defined to include the scores on the following variables:

Library income

Committee size

Material collection size total

Committee hours worked per week

Number of professionals on committee

Library income as a percentage of congregational income

Congregational size

[c]When data was missing for either of the two main variables, then No Response was registered for that library.

[d]What this table indicates is the mean relative amount of effort or support per member provided by each denomination in order to produce the same number of circulation charges. All was calculated per member in order to neutralize the discrepancies among larger congregations and smaller ones. On the whole it would appear that Congregational, United Church of Christ, and Roman Catholic libraries are very efficient in terms of generating circulation at little cost per member and that Lutherans, Baptists, and Presbyterians produce significant support per member and generate fewer charges per support unit given.

TABLE 5.139

Church and Synagogue Library Association: Suggested Minimum Standards for Congregational Libraries[a,b]

| Variable | Standard |
|---|---|
| Number of hours each library committee member works per week | 4.0 |
| Percentage of library committee members who are professionals | 33.3% |
| Congregation members per library staff member | 50.0 |
| Percent of annual congregational expenditure going to the library | 1.0% |
| Annual library income per congregation member | $2.75 |
| Total cost per circulation charge (annual library income divided by annual circulation) | $1.50 |
| Book volumes available per congregation member | 5.0 |
| Congregation members per newspaper and periodical title | 33.0 |
| Media titles available per congregation member | 1.0 |
| Book circulation per congregation member per month | 0.5 |

[a]The definitions of these terms are those shown in the latest edition of the American Library Association *Glossary* (Chicago: ALA). The definition of congregational libraries is shown in chapter 1 and appendix B.

[b]The standards shown above assume that the library staff members now average two hours of work per week each.

TABLE 5.140

Church and Synagogue Library Association: Mean Ranks of
Aggregated Denominational Means from Previous Tables and in
Descending Order[a-c]

| Denomination | Aggregated Mean Table Rank |
|---|---|
| Jewish | 2.2 |
| Baptist | 3.0 |
| Roman Catholic | 3.8 |
| Presbyterian | 5.4 |
| Other Denominations | 5.8 |
| Methodist | 6.1 |
| Lutheran | 7.0 |
| Christian | 7.1 |
| U.C.C. | 7.6 |
| Episcopal/Anglican | 8.1 |
| Congregational | 10.0 |

[a]This table summarizes findings on 22 previous tables: 5.14, 5.30, 5.34, 5.37, 5.42, 5.47, 5.51, 5.53, 5.58, 5.64, 5.67, 5.71, 5.81, 5.83, 5.98, 5.102, 5.104, 5.106, 5.107, 5.113, 5.129, and 5.135.

[b]The mean rank column shows the aggregated mean table rank of each denomination from all of the tables listed in note 1 above and then divided by 22.

[c]Note that the numbering system works from 1 to approximately 25, with 1 ranking highest and 25 ranking lowest.

TABLE 5.141

Church and Synagogue Library Association: Summary Rankings by
Denomination of per Member Mean Data Found in Selected CSLA
Chapter Tables[a–d]

| Denomination | Mean Rank on Previous per Member Tables |
|---|---|
| Other Denominations | 1.3 |
| Baptist | 3.5 |
| Christian | 4.3 |
| U.C.C. | 4.7 |
| Presbyterian | 5.3 |
| Jewish | 6.3 |
| Episcopal/Anglican | 6.7 |
| Congregational | 7.5 |
| Methodist | 7.8 |
| Lutheran | 8.8 |
| Roman Catholic | 9.7 |
| Mean of the Means | 6.0 |
| Median Rank | 6.3 |

[a]This table summarizes findings on six previous Per Member tables: 5.36, 5.57, 5.60, 5.73, 5.85 and 5.127.

[b]The mean rank column shows the mean value of the aggregated denominational ranks as shown in the tables listed in Note 1 above and then divided by 6.

[c]Denominations with the lowest scores, e.g., 1.3, have the highest ranks.

[d]Libraries with very large congregations are somewhat penalized by this calculation. This phenomenon probably arises as the result of a decision being taken concerning library optimal size before the congregation has reached its maximum size. Hence congregations may continue to grow, especially Roman Catholic, Lutheran, and Jewish ones, even *after* the library no longer continues to expand. The effort made per member then falls relative to effort within smaller congregations.

TABLE 5.142

Church and Synagogue Library Association: Ranks of Specific
Libraries on Previous Tables[a]

| Library | Number of Tables on Which Listed |
|---|---|
| First Baptist Church, La Crescenta, CA | 14 |
| Sinai Temple, Los Angeles, CA | 13 |
| The Temple, Cleveland, OH | 12 |
| University Avenue Church of Christ, Austin, TX | 12 |
| Fourth Presbyterian Church, Bethesda, MD | 11 |
| Mt. Paran Union Church of God, Atlanta, GA | 10 |
| Hyde Park Baptist Church, Austin, TX | 10 |
| University Presbyterian Church, Seattle, WA | 10 |
| Briarlake Baptist Church, Decatur, GA | 9 |
| Beth El Synagogue, Highland Park, IL | 8 |
| First United Methodist Church, Tulsa, OK | 7 |
| Interchurch Center, Portland, OR | 6 |
| All Saints Catholic Church, Dallas, TX | 6 |
| Stone Mountain Community Church, Stone Mountain, GA | 5 |
| St. James Roman Catholic Church, Arlington Heights, IL | 5 |
| St. Charles Borromeo Roman Catholic Church, Bloomington, IN | 5 |
| Pleasant Grove Presbyterian Church, Youngstown, OH | 5 |
| Burlingame Baptist Church, Portland, OR | 5 |
| Clear Lake United Methodist Church, Houston, TX | 5 |
| Bethel Church, San Jose, CA | 4 |
| Broadmoor Baptist Church, Shreveport, LA | 4 |
| St. Elias Eastern Orthodox Church, Battle Creek, MI | 4 |
| Harrisonville Mennonite Church, Harrisonville, MO | 4 |
| Perkasie Mennonite Church, Perkasie, PA | 4 |
| Chapelwood United Methodist Church, Houston, TX | 4 |

[a]This table lists the libraries found on four or more of twenty-five previous tables: 5.24,
5.31, 5.32, 5.34, 5.35, 5.38, 5.50, 5.52, 5.56, 5.65, 5.72, 5.79, 5.80, 5.82, 5.84, 5.87,
5.101, 5.103, 5.105, 5.108, 5.109, 5.123, 5.125, 5.128 and 5.131.

TABLE 5.143

Church and Synagogue Library Association: Ranks of Specific
Libraries on per Congregation Member Tables[a]

| Library | Number of per Congregation Member Tables on Which Listed |
|---|---|
| Burlingame Baptist Church, Portland, OR | 5 |
| Perkasie Mennonite Church, Perkasie, PA | 5 |
| Lombard Mennonite Church, Lombard, IL | 4 |
| Church of the Open Door, Wyoming, MI | 4 |
| Harrisonville Mennonite Church, Harrisonville, MO | 4 |
| Highland Christian Church, Cleveland, OH | 4 |
| First Baptist Church, La Crescenta, CA | 3 |
| Trinity Lutheran Church, Canton, OH | 3 |
| First Deaf Mennonite Church, Lancaster, PA | 3 |

[a]This table lists the libraries found on three or more of eight per congregation member
tables: 5.39, 5.40, 5.60, 5.66, 5.72, 5.80, 5.87, and 5.128.

TABLE 5.144

Church and Synagogue Library Association: Outstanding
Congregational Library Award Winners

| | |
|---|---|
| Temple Israel Library, Sharon, MA: Helen Greif | 1975 |
| Reveille United Methodist Church Library, Richmond, VA: Alma Lowance | 1976 |
| Congregation B'nai Israel Library, Albuquerque, NM: Dr. & Mrs. I. Auerbach | 1977 |
| Temple Emanu-el Library, Dallas, TX: Deanna Kasten | 1978 |
| Church of the Atonement, Silver Spring, MD: Ada P. Jorgensen | 1979 |
| First Christian Church Library, New Castle, PA: Eileen McEwen | 1980 |
| Lutheran Church of the Holy Comforter, Baltimore, MD: Thyra Fischer | 1981 |
| Library, Beth Shalom Congregation, Elkins Park, PA: David J. Salaman | 1982 |
| Monte Vista Christian Church Library, Albuquerque, NM: C. Pelsor | 1983 |
| Champion Forest Baptist Church Library, Houston, TX: J. Hope, A. Hall | 1984 |
| Blumenthal Library, Sinai Temple, Los Angeles, CA: Rita Frischer | 1985 |
| First Baptist Church, La Crescenta, CA: Eleanor Matthews | 1986 |
| Pathfinder's Memorial Resource Library, Chapelwood United Methodist Church, Houston, TX: Dona Badgett | 1988 |
| Applebee Memorial Library, Country Club Christian Church, Kansas City, MO: Mimi McLin | 1989 |
| Velda Rose United Methodist Church, Mesa, AZ: Esther Ayres | 1990 |
| First Presbyterian Church Library, Orlando, FL: Suzanne Sugiuchi | 1992 |
| Clear Lake United Methodist Church Resource Library, Houston, TX: Betty Burghduff | 1993 |
| First Presbyterian Church, Flint, MI: Steven R. Hill | 1994 |

# 6

# POPULAR RELIGIOUS LIBRARIES: FOUR CONGREGATIONAL LIBRARY STUDIES COMPARED

This chapter will summarize and compare four popular congregational library surveys, three of which were prepared, at least in part, for this book. They are (1) the 1971–76 study of 1,822 congregational libraries conducted by Joyce White for the Church and Synagogue Library Association (CSLA) and summarized in a chapter of an earlier book, *Church and Synagogue Libraries* and the 1978 *American Library Directory* (*ALD*) study of congregational libraries carried out by the present author and summarized in chapters 2, 3, and 4 of this book: (3) the 1985–86 study of 411 CSLA congregational libraries supervised by the late Claudia Hannaford and summarized in chapter 5 of this book; and (4) the 1988 *ALD* edition study of congregational libraries carried out by the author and also summarized in chapters 2, 3, and 4 of this book as part of the longitudinal 1978–88 ten-year *ALD* study.[1,2] Thus the studies cover the period from 1971 to 1988, a span of seventeen years. Two of these four studies were CSLA projects and two were the present author's own independent projects. These four studies represent the only major published surveys and analyses of the North American popular religious library field to date.

The following are the section headings of this chapter:

I. Introduction
II. Four Congregational Library Studies Juxtaposed and Compared
   A. Introduction

## Introduction

What do the four studies in this chapter tell us about the status and progress of North American popular religious librarianship in the last three decades of the twentieth century? Dynamic or sluggish? Changing or static? This chapter will compare the four studies, describe their findings, and discuss points of agreement and disagreement. In a longitudinal analysis, the chapter will describe the changes since White's original survey, the variables on which the field moved ahead or backward from the earliest to the latest study. Whenever possible, the relevant trends will be identified and discussed.

In carrying out its discussion and analysis, the chapter will recapitulate certain data and information from the four studies in order to provide a proper background for the reader's understanding. No attempt will be made to repeat the full chapter findings for the two *ALD* and the Hannaford studies, but White's findings will be reported in some detail to provide a proper background since they have not yet been described in this book. This chapter covers congregational libraries only, religious school and public as well as scholarly libraries being omitted from its scope. All of the White material in the present chapter is original, since the previous analyses were incompatible with the remaining three studies. The data was, therefore, redeveloped from scratch using revised categories and more comparable methodology.

The chapter assumes a kind of social science null hypothesis, that no point, idea, or trend has yet been established or is known to be true for the field as a whole in a research sense unless these four studies approach agreement on it and this chapter identifies the areas of conjunction specifically. While certain verities were established about the variables being examined, and agreed to more or less closely among the four studies, and while perhaps certain aspects even showed improvement in later years, other findings neither converged nor did given variables progress and some may even have displayed a downward trend over time. We will see further that several other developments were sufficiently complex that no clear-cut conclusion could be reached about them.

As in all other chapters, the discussion is conceptually oriented and tabular representation of the social survey statistical data expresses the ideas numerically through labels, categories, and values or frequencies. This chapter, like others, is devoted primarily to establishing relatively elementary comparisons and relationships within concepts for the field, matters that have not yet been established as true or functional. More advanced and complex concepts must wait for later research projects. Further, while it is straightforward to describe the situation and establish concepts, ascertaining causes beyond the obvious and drawing conclusions from them is hazardous and in many cases unjustified at the present time.

As a result of these surveys the North American congregational library subfield of the popular religious library field has progressed in the past two decades from the status of having no sets of objective, published interdenominational survey information available to having four overlapping and more or less replicating sets of them available! That, in itself, is progress!

The term definitions used in the four studies were the same or were very similar, and the populations from which the samples were drawn were similar, if not ultimately and replicably the same, except for the passage of time. However, the Hannaford study used only the CSLA paid membership as its population, and both White and Hannaford were weak on certain Protestant denominations, for example, Mormons and Christian Scientists. The choice of main study topics agreed remarkably well among the studies, however.

Undoubtedly many specific libraries appeared in more than one of the four studies and perhaps several libraries appeared in all four of the communal or recurring libraries. No attempt was made to identify more than a few of the communal or recurring libraries. For example, the Temple Library, Cleveland (one of the oldest of them all), led for many years by Mariam Leikind and Claudia Fechter, was an outstanding library at any time; the Bethesda Methodist Church Library in Maryland, begun by Ruth S. Smith of CSLA; the Zion Mennonite Church in Souderton, Pennsylvania, well known for its service to the community; the Immaculate Heart of Mary Roman Catholic Parish Library in Los Alamos, New

Mexico, long a leader; and the famous National Presbyterian Church Library in Washington, D.C.

We should bear in mind also that the Hannaford study was subjectively believed by this author to represent a superior congregational library group, rather than a typical one. This supposition may or may not have been true (and in any case is unprovable) of the White and the two *ALD* reply groups. But if true, the idea may have applied to the other three groups to a somewhat greater or lesser extent than for the Hannaford study, or at least that is this author's subjective impression.

Obviously, in this popular religious library field we are still so ignorant that we have no clear picture of how "typical" or median libraries (the fiftieth percentile in the congregational library population) appear in their statistical profiles. We may guess that only a 20 percent to 25 percent sample of them answer library questionnaires, so we can make only informed guesses about their profiles and about the corresponding profiles of "superior" (seventy-fifth percentile and above) and "inferior" (twenty-fifth percentile and below) libraries. Probably "typical" or average libraries were small and were quite modestly staffed, stocked, and used. And they were not very active (only active librarians answer questionnaires!).

The two CSLA questionnaire forms (White and Hannaford) were aimed at congregational libraries while the single *ALD* questionnaire form (Harvey) addressed all ten types of scholarly and popular religious libraries. The forms differed somewhat in length, topics, and specificity. Probably the Hannaford questionnaire was the most and the White questionnaire the least extensive in covering varied aspects of interests. Further, the Hannaford study was analyzed in considerable detail while the White study could be analyzed only as far as the set of available data allowed.

Therefore, to a large extent, the limited parameters of the White report necessarily established the parameters for this entire chapter. Of course, also, the four studies were conducted by three different persons with three different questionnaire forms at four different dates over a seventeen-year period, so these factors combine to further restrict the four studies' comparability. Due to the inherent survey differences, the statements of conjunction or disjunction among studies must be understood to represent the situation only approximately and sometimes cannot be established to any degree of valid statistical significance. On the other hand, see the footnotes to tables 6.1, 6.2, 6.3, and those concluding this chapter for relevant comments.

# Four Congregational Library Studies Juxtaposed and Compared

## Introduction

This subsection will set the stage for later sections that will compare the four studies. The White study was initiated in 1971 in CSLA's fourth year and stemmed from its interest in discovering what was out there, the exact nature of the huge and little known North American congregational library field which was almost entirely ignored by the professional library associations and library schools. Joyce L. White, then the University of Pennsylvania's chief education librarian, in Philadelphia, the third CSLA president, later an honorary CSLA life member, and now a Denver seminary chief librarian, conducted a comprehensive survey of North American congregational libraries.

She was assisted by a grant from the Council on Library Resources for computer analysis. Hers was the first comprehensive and interdenominational survey and analysis of North American popular religious libraries, and it is still by far the largest survey yet carried out. Unfortunately, of the 1,822 libraries returning questionnaires, it appears that twenty-nine marked no denominational affiliation and were dropped from the computer tallies. For the purposes of this chapter these libraries were reinstituted by including them in the Other Denominations group.

White used twenty-two congregational library mailing lists to compile a master list of 58,358 libraries (that's right, fifty-eight thousand!) from which she drew a more manageable sample of ten thousand libraries, to each of which a questionnaire copy was sent. The early 1975 CSLA membership list of 755 libraries and a 1974 *ALD* list of four hundred congregational libraries were among the mailing lists used. Just what criteria were used in drawing the 5.8:1.0 sample, aside from the avoidance of duplication, which she said was heavy among the original lists, especially among the denominational and the regional lists, is unknown. She may have used random stratified nonsystematic sampling here. Useable replies were received from 1,833 White libraries, as compared with 411 Hannaford libraries (a 4.5:1.0 ratio), and later from 634 *ALD*-1978 libraries and from 593 *ALD*-1988 congregational libraries.

When compared with the other three studies, White's study was much larger both in the number of questionnaire forms mailed out and in the number of replies received. No information is available to establish the precise extent to which the replies were representative of the universe, of the 58,358 mailing list libraries or of the 10,000 library sample. If White's twenty-two mailing lists could be said to represent an approach to tapping the entire North American population or universe of congregational libraries, or a good portion thereof (a claim that she never made, incidentally), then the list of the majority thereof in table 6.4 should be interesting. At any rate, the White sample was certainly more representative of the population than were the CSLA or the *ALD* studies. These latter three studies were probably representative too, but what they were representative of was the American population of libraries that can be classified as intentional joiners or association members, quite a different thing altogether.

Note that well over half of the original White mailing list libraries were either Baptist (mostly Southern Baptist) or Methodist. Note the response column, also, with Jewish, Friends, Lutheran, and Roman Catholic leading the table in reply percentages. Table 6.5 shows the representatives of all four samples by denomination. Four denominations were strong—Lutheran, Methodist, Presbyterian, and Jewish. United Church of Christ was moderate to strong. However, unfortunately, only seven of the fourteen denominations were represented in satisfactory fashion.

In the Hannaford study the mailing list was composed of the CSLA paid membership list, which rose in size steadily with each passing year. Apparently at the time the questionnaire (appendix E) was mailed out the membership stood at 1,650, but by the end of the year the membership total reached 1,950 to 1,980 persons. Table 6.6 shows the ratio of CSLA memberships per denomination by the number of questionnaire responses per denomination. Leading in return percentages were the Congregational, Episcopal/Anglican, and Lutheran denominations. At the bottom in return percentages were Baptists, Jews, and Christians. Overall mean was a 22 percent return, which was acceptable and as high as could be expected. There was a 41 percent difference between the top and bottom denominations in return percentages.

The *ALD*-1978 and *ALD*-1988 studies were planned and carried out in identical manner. There was no mailing involved. Instead, the questionnaire (appendix D) was applied to edition 31 and edition 41 of the *ALD*, and the responses were copied directly from one to the other in each case by the present author. There was no selection of libraries, all congregational libraries in the *ALD* being included. It is obvious, however, that the *ALD* editors used a selective congregational library inclusion criterion of some sort and that the replying librarians were self-selected. So we can conclude that the four studies were organized and their data collection carried out using three different procedures. Two studies mailed out questionnaires directly while the other two did not.

## Geography and Demography

This subsection will examine the data collection by nation, region, state or province, and city. All four studies covered both Canada and the United States to varying degrees. However, in general terms, in each study, at least 90 percent of the libraries were located south of the common border. Table 6.7 shows a comparison of the four studies relative to the populations from which they originated, plus the findings by study in terms of libraries. The notes explain and comment on the table and deal both with matters of the adequacy of the sample size and the density of the library population. Both congregational and Canadian libraries were underrepresented in the samples. Table 6.8 shows what percentages of the total population (not libraries but persons) were located in each state and province. It also shows which geographical areas were over or underrepresented in the samples as well as the library representation and distribution for each study.

Table 6.9 shows population by region for the four studies. Notice that in all four, the Middle Atlantic region was overrepresented, and it was overrepresented quite uniformly in each study. This may be due to the fact that the North American congregational library field apparently originated or else grew most rapidly in its earlier years in the Middle Atlantic region. It certainly got itself organized there rapidly. At least that is the story of the congregational libraries in CSLA, in which the chief center of interest in 1967 seemed to be the Philadelphia area.[3]

Not only was the Middle West region a leader in producing replies, but about half of each survey's total number of libraries were found in the Middle Atlantic and Middle West regions taken together. If the Southeast and Southwest are added to the Middle Atlantic and Middle West, the CSLA libraries' percentage accounted for then rises to 80 percent. There was uniformity in this concentration. The Rocky Mountains and Canadian regions were poorly represented in all four surveys. Canada produced only eight libraries for White (less than one percent) and ten for Hannaford (2 percent) though for the two *ALD* studies it produced larger proportions.

Fifty-three states and provinces were represented in the White study and forty-one in the Hannaford study. Each one of the *ALD* samples contained fifty-six states and provinces, thereby demonstrating their wide coverage, at least of the United States. Leading White states in order were Pennsylvania, Maryland, Minnesota, Washington, New Mexico, California, Wisconsin, and Illinois, which produced three-fifths of her libraries. Leading Hannaford states in order were Ohio, Texas, Pennsylvania, Michigan, California, Florida, Illinois, Indiana, and New Mexico, which produced almost three-fifths of her libraries.

From which states and provinces did the *ALD* studies come? In 1978 they came primarily from Pennsylvania, New York, California, Ohio, Texas, Illinois, Michigan, Missouri, North Carolina, and Tennessee. In 1988 they came primarily from Pennsylvania, New York, Texas, California, Ohio, Illinois, Quebec, Wisconsin, Maryland, and North Carolina. In both cases, the ten states and provinces listed for each edition contained three-fifths of the respective databases. Notice that the White pattern of leading states and provinces differed somewhat from those of the three later studies, at least for the prominence of Maryland and New Mexico libraries. Notice further that Utah produced only one library, even in the midst of so many Mormon stake and meetinghouse libraries.

To some extent this shift in states and provinces from study to study and year to year may have illustrated and may have been produced by the shift in the spread of the congregational library concept. It is more likely that the shift is the result, however, of various sampling procedures, since three different and somewhat inconsistent techniques were used. Some future student should be able to check this movement by state and province and show it to us in a tabular or map presentation. Certainly the spread of popular religious libraries is still in progress, with major portions of both Canada and the U.S. still waiting for more than token popular religious library service.

The list of the least well represented states and provinces—Nevada, Wyoming, Alaska, Idaho, Montana, Utah, New Brunswick, Newfoundland, Northwest Territories, Nova Scotia, Prince Edward Island, Yukon, for instance—differed little between the four surveys. For White, the eighteen least well represented states and provinces produced only eleven libraries (0.6 percent) and for Hannaford the same eighteen plus fourteen more states and provinces produced only fifteen libraries (3.6 percent).

Now we need to ask, how large was the overlap between White and the other three databases in terms of leading states and provinces? About a 35 percent overlap existed between the four lists of ten leading states and provinces, not as high an overlap as might have been expected. For Hannaford it was three states, for *ALD*-1978 it was three states and for

*ALD*-1988 it was four states. However, overlap between Hannaford and the two *ALD* studies was five states in each case. The three leading states that overlapped within all four studies were Pennsylvania, California, and Illinois. With the inclusion of Florida and Texas as leaders only in the more recent surveys, we can guess that these two fast-growing Sun Belt states had only recently grown into a numerical leadership group and can predict that their ranking therein may rise in 1998.

It seems clear that certain and even whole regions were heavily populated with congregational study libraries, while others were much more sparsely represented. In other words, dramatic state and regional differences existed in popular religious library density, not wholly accounted for by general population differences. These demographic differences reflected not only general population density but also the density of those denominations giving strong encouragement to library formation as contrasted with the Bible-centered denominations, which were less sensitive to library growth and development. Differences of congregation and denomination member educational level and financial status may have been influential here also.

City data was found only in the Hannaford and the two *ALD* studies. In Hannaford only three-twentieths of the libraries were located in small town or rural areas while eight-twentieths were located in cities and nine twentieths in suburban areas. The two *ALD* studies showed again that only a small fraction of the libraries were located in small town or rural areas and that the majority of the remaining libraries were divided about equally between city and suburban areas.

As far as leading cities, the specific cities which were most popular in the Hannaford study were Albuquerque and Kalamazoo. For *ALD*-1978 they were Philadelphia and Washington and for *ALD*-1988 they were New York City and Washington. This listing of the leading cities suggests a degree of scatter in primary locations that is accurate up to a point. However, it was true also that there was some overlap between the three studies if we extend the examination to the top ten to fifteen cities, as shown in table 2.39.

As an example of the demographic variations mentioned above, neither New York City nor Chicago nor Los Angeles—the three largest North American cities—has ever had a major CSLA chapter. New York has had neither a CSLA nor a Lutheran Church Library Association chapter, though it showed up well in certain of the *ALD* city studies. Or perhaps that simply tells us something about congregational librarians!

In summary, there was much similarity but by no means complete replication in the geography and demography of the 1976, 1978, 1986, and 1988 libraries. Overlaps among leading states was 35 percent, smaller than expected. All four studies covered the United States fairly well, with the Northeast and Rocky Mountains regions represented much less well and Canada sampled slightly. Much spread existed in library concentration among the leading cities, states, and provinces.

## Library Age

This subsection and tables 6.10 and 6.11 compare the library founding dates among the four studies. While the four sets of libraries showed similar founding dates, one-fourth of the White study libraries, one-eleventh of the Hannaford study libraries, 55 percent of the *ALD*-1978 and 43 percent of the *ALD*-1988 congregational libraries—widely varying percentages—provided no dates at all. The median library founding date for White's survey was 1962, only nine years before her survey was started. The 1986 Hannaford survey median date was 1966 and in the *ALD* studies these dates were 1948 and 1950. It is curious that the two *ALD* studies yielded founding dates that were significantly older than the Hannaford and White founding dates. Just why this happened is unclear, but probably because the CSLA recruits primarily young, new libraries.

The oldest White library was founded in 1882, the oldest Hannaford library in 1827, and the oldest of the two sets of *ALD* libraries in 1808. As long as we are studying library founding dates, we should look at table 6.12, which lists the few oldest libraries for each denomination. It shows a variety of dates and a variety of locations. White listed forty-seven (2.6 percent) libraries from the pre-1931 period, while Hannaford found twelve (2.9 percent) from that period. The two *ALD* studies listed fifty-six (4.6 percent) of them, with some overlap. To explain the disappearances of thirty-five of White's older libraries, which were not listed elsewhere, we can suggest that perhaps some of those not found in the *ALD* and CSLA studies were neither CSLA members nor listed in *ALD,* or had been absorbed into other libraries, or were dormant by that time.

Seventy-three (4 percent) of White's libraries were founded before World War II, three in the nineteenth century, 0.2 percent. Of Hannaford's libraries, six (1.5 percent) were founded before World War II and three in the nineteenth century, 0.7 percent. Of the *ALD* libraries sixty were founded before World War II (4.9 percent) plus an uncounted number that were founded between 1934 and World War II. In addition, nineteen

*ALD* libraries (1.5 percent) were founded in the nineteenth century. Only one of the nineteenth-century libraries was repeated on the four lists, the Temple Library, Cleveland, mentioned earlier.

Table 6.13 is a master list of the sixty-one oldest popular libraries using information combined from the four studies.[4] In this table the Middle Atlantic and Northeast regions dominated the long list of the earliest libraries. The Rocky Mountains, Southeast, and Canadian regions were underrepresented, but of course all had relatively low library population densities in these years. More than half of the libraries on table 6.13 were Presbyterian, Episcopal/Anglican, Methodist, Jewish, or Other Denominations. Two-fifths of these libraries were located in Michigan, Texas, California, Ohio, or Pennsylvania. In summary, founding dates presented patterns that were often similar but not identical between the four studies.

Table 6.14 provides another master table for library ages and shows what happens when the White and Hannaford studies are put into the same table with the entire *ALD*-1978 and *ALD*-1988 samples. Of course, the "total four samples" column puts together in one column figures for studies that are not entirely comparable and must be examined with that in mind. The figures differ somewhat from those in other age tables. The difference in median ages between the White-Hannaford studies and the two *ALD* studies is the major difference to be seen. Table 6.15 shows a Canada-U.S. comparison. Notice that Canadian libraries were always younger than those of the U.S. However, the number of Canadian libraries was so small that this table could be acceptable as suggestive only.

## Denomination

How did the four databases compare by denominational group? Twenty-two denominations were included in each study, White and Hannaford. The 1978 *ALD* study included many more—fifty-three denominations—and the 1988 *ALD* study included fifty-six denominations, thereby demonstrating the greater magnitude of the *ALD* studies. Tables 6.4 and 6.16 showed the denominational breakdowns of the four studies. There were many similarities in the denominational representation in these studies, but certain differences could be noted, also. All of the denominations found in Hannaford were found elsewhere except the Churches of Christ and the Independent groups, and both the Congregational and Mennonite denominations were represented with fifteen or more usable questionnaires. Even Reformed libraries ranking just below the top thirteen denominations in number of libraries in the *ALD* studies were represented here by thirty-three libraries and deserved separate consideration.

Ten percent of the Hannaford libraries were Lutheran, and 5 to 6 percent of the *ALD* libraries combined were Lutheran, also, but almost a third of the White libraries were Lutheran. Certainly this was a case of overrepresentation and a statistically significant difference that had potential implications for the results obtained. Presbyterian libraries were overrepresented in White's study, also, at 16.2 percent, along with 21 percent for Hannaford (even more overrepresented) as opposed to 9 to 10 percent for the two *ALD* studies. The implications were not, however, realized in fact, since both the Lutheran and the Presbyterian denominations tended to be very middle of the road in terms of performance on almost all variables of interest.

Jewish libraries made up 5 percent for White and 10 to 11 percent for *ALD*, twice as much, but only 1 percent for Hannaford, one-fifth as large. This finding shows the long-existing and unintentional CSLA membership underrepresentation of the Jewish libraries. The Roman Catholic group varied greatly between the two *ALD* studies, which were one-fourth Catholic, and the Hannaford and White studies, which were only about one-twenty-fifth Catholic. Again this is due to the influence of the long-existing and unintentional CSLA underrepresentation of Roman Catholics in its membership for Hannaford, but to account for the low White Roman Catholic figure is difficult. Perhaps the lack of easily obtainable lists of Roman Catholic parish libraries was part of the problem here. Otherwise, the percentages of the totals for each one of the four databases were similar in each study.

Table 6.4 shows the percentages by denomination of the original library mailing lists that replied to White's questionnaire. Jewish, Lutheran, Friends, and Roman Catholic libraries responded well, but Baptist, Methodist, Presbyterian, Christian, Mormon, and the evangelical libraries did not. The denominational breakdown of the entire CSLA membership is shown in table 6.6. It corresponds closely to the questionnaire response percentages shown also on this table. The table's final column shows the percentage of each denomination that responded to the questionnaire.

The Episcopal/Anglican, Congregational, and Lutheran denominations responded best and the Baptist, Christian, and Jewish groups most poorly. There was no apparent response rate correlation between the Hannaford and the *ALD* studies on the one hand, and White's denominational response rate on the other. Of course response rate for the *ALD* studies was vicariously 100 percent. Regrettably, all four studies had poor reply representation from several denominations with large numbers of libraries.

The Lutheran, Presbyterian, Methodist, and Baptist denominations accounted for two-thirds of the White study, almost three fifths of the Hannaford study, 37 percent of the *ALD*-1978 group and 36 percent of the *ALD*-1988 group. Thus we see again that the two *ALD* studies differed from the White and Hannaford groups in containing more Jewish and Roman Catholic and fewer Lutheran, Presbyterian, Methodist, and Baptist libraries.

In summary, the White and Hannaford studies presented similar denominational profiles with the same four denominations leading each study, but the Hannaford study was much the better balanced of the two within itself. On the other hand, the *ALD* studies differed from White and Hannaford. Some credit may be given to the influence of Hannaford's mailing sent on CSLA's behalf to CSLA members only; whereas White's mailing sent on CLSA's behalf to a large group of libraries of whom only about 10 percent were CSLA members. Perhaps the White study served to round up the non-CSLA joiners and ended up resembling the Hannaford response group in several ways.

## Service

Relatively little data was available in any study on any kind of service. However, a high percentage of White's libraries responded to the service questions that were asked. All libraries offered service to their own congregations and a fourth of the Mennonite, Roman Catholic, and Jewish libraries offered service to their communities. Most of White's libraries (by a ratio 1.4:1.0) reported the service mode to have been self-service on weekdays whenever the house of worship building was open and staffed service on the holy day. Almost a fourth of the libraries were open before and after group meetings.

Seventy-three percent of the Episcopal/Anglican libraries offered self-service and over 70 percent of the Jewish libraries featured self-service, as did Christian, Congregational, Methodist, Presbyterian, and U.C.C. Baptist featured staffed service, as did Roman Catholic libraries. Although it was difficult to compare White with Hannaford on this matter, this author seemed to detect a trend in the intervening years, 1975 to 1986, to provide more staffed service and less self-service. If true, that showed a service improvement. Eighty-five percent of White's libraries reported service to the entire congregation and 9 percent of them reported service to the entire community, also, a public library function carried out by certain congregational libraries. Neither *ALD* study reported any such information on service because the *ALD* did not address the issue.

The median White survey library charged out 73.5 volumes per month and the median Hannaford survey library charged out 115 volumes per month, a 56 percent increase in eleven years, or a gain of about four volumes per year. See table 6.17. Therefore, this important measure of output or service rendered showed a rising score. That was progress! See Table 6.18. The figures were not sufficiently comparable or detailed to make other circulation comparisons, however. Three percent of White's and 22 percent of Hannaford's librarians failed to reply to this question. Jewish, Roman Catholic, and Baptist libraries led in 1975 circulation and Jewish and Baptist led in 1986 circulation. In summary, the brief comparison possible between White and Hannaford on service suggested that some progress had been made in recent years, but there were no *ALD* figures with which to confirm or refute this statement for the later decade.

The overall mean circulation per library for the White and Hannaford studies was about 111 charges per month, as seen in table 6.18. Note further that the Jewish, Baptist, and Roman Catholic denominations led in overall circulation. Table 6.19 shows circulation per house of worship member by denomination. Obviously the typical house of worship member charged out only about 1.8 pieces of library material per month. The average Other Denominations house of worship member charged out more than one piece every month, however, while the average Roman Catholic member charged out one piece every three months. These frequencies showed considerable variation.

For the two *ALD* studies, but not for the White and Hannaford studies, we have information on the libraries restricting phenomenon use—either circulation or reference service. The Ns were small, but we still see what tables 6.20 to 6.23 tell us. For the 1978 and 1988 circulation restriction phenomenon we see that it was almost entirely Protestant and Jewish, not Roman Catholic. Jewish libraries led the tables. For restrictions on reference use, the Jewish and Presbyterian denomination libraries led the tables.

## Personnel

In general, personnel questions about size, paid, and professional status produced similar replies among the four studies, but for certain of them the results were puzzling, and in others the results were contradictory. Sometimes insufficient data was available on which to base a table, especially for the White study. In other cases, certain large libraries influenced the mean figure considerably. One of the first examples of this confounding inconsistency was that for library (or library committee) staffing. From the author's analysis of White's cumulative staff membership-size table, library staffing had improved in membership by 1986. White showed a mean per-library response of approximately 2.3 committee members (volunteers) per library. On the other hand, by Mouridou's calculations taken directly from the raw data, many libraries responded to not one White personnel category but to two or more of them, distinguished by management versus nonmanagement, paid versus unpaid and professionals versus volunteers. Therefore, her figures show a mean staff per library of 5.7 persons with the Presbyterian, Reformed, and Roman Catholic groups being the largest. The difference between the author's and Mouridou's interpretations results from a lack of clarity in the definitions used for the White study questionnaire.

Hannaford showed a mean of 5.8 committee members per library, a 152 percent increase in eleven years over the 2.3 figure and 2 percent over the 5.7 figure. That was progress! *ALD* figures showed further progress in 1978 and 1988. In 1978, staff size showed a mean of 5.1 staff members, and in 1988 it showed a mean of 6.8 staff members. Thus, by the evidence that we have here, the mean staff size rose from 2.3 (White) to 5.7 (Hannaford) to 6.8 (Harvey) persons, an increase of about 1.1 persons, or 19 percent over eleven years, not very rapid growth. However, seven persons may represent optimal committee size. The denominations with the largest number of library staff committee members were the Reformed, Presbyterian, and Roman Catholic. The smallest were the Mennonite and Christian (Disciples of Christ). The Jewish group was the most stable of the denomination subgroups with its 100 percent response rate.

Though her figures were difficult to understand, White found 247, or 3.0 percent, of the total number of library committee members to have been paid, probably on a part-time basis. That left 7,902, or 97.0 percent, as volunteers. Apparently, most of the paid persons were in charge of their committees. Among the denominations Jewish staff members were most likely to be paid, while twenty-four (6 percent) of Hannaford's libraries apparently had paid assistants, that is all we can say with statistical assurance about these persons.

No data is available on salaries from the *ALD* data studies. Perhaps there was no progress in eleven years concerning the percentage of paid personnel between the White and Hannaford studies, since both of them were at the 6 percent level. This represents an unsatisfactorily static or holding situation and deserves further study. An opposing view would suggest that the library working situation may have improved in other ways between 1975 and 1986, of course, such as through improved working conditions or better equipment being made available.

Out of her 8,149 library committee members, White found 1,189 of them to have been professionals, or 14.6 percent. The remainder, or 6,960, 85.4 percent, were nonprofessional. From her 2,378 committee members, Hannaford found 228 of them to be professionals, or 9.6 percent. This was a drop of 34 percent 1975–86. What could have caused such a drop in the ratio of professionals to other committee members? It appears that the 1975–86 increase in number of committee members per library was primarily an increase in the number of nonprofessionals, or that the word "professional" was understood differently, or the qualifications for professionals were raised in the interim.

However, the author does not know why either the number of committee members may have increased or why the increase was to such an extent nonprofessional. This change remains an unsolved problem and deserves further study. The *ALD* tables showed 95 out of 266 library staff members, or 36 percent, to be professionals in 1988. So the percentage professional continued to rise. *ALD* clerk frequency did not rise proportionately in 1988, however.

While most of the persons in charge of White's library committees were neither paid nor professional, two-thirds of her professionals were in charge of their committees. No evidence was available to identify the Hannaford study committee chairs, nor was it available on the committee chairmen/chairwomen for *ALD* libraries. The overall ratio of White's chairpersons to committee members was one to one in Harvey's analysis, and later 4.7:1.0, therefore many one-person libraries must have existed.

Apparently fewer one-person libraries existed in the Hannaford study than in the White study, however, an improvement. On the other hand, another view says that 48.9 percent of the committees claimed one professional committee member for White and 55.5 percent of the committees claimed one professional committee member for Hannaford, an increase of 13 percent over 1975. Therefore, the number of professionals must have increased slightly for the Hannaford study, by 6.6 percent, an improvement.

While the number of committee members per library increased and the ratio of nonprofessionals to professionals increased between 1975 and 1986, apparently this still left enough professionals to yield a slight increase per library in 1986, though the two sets of data were hardly comparable or easy to interpret. Three of Hannaford's denominations averaged slightly more than one professional per library—Roman Catholic, Baptist, and Presbyterian. That was encouraging but only modest progress. However, the *ALD* studies offered additional progress in the number of professionals working in these libraries.

The ratio of clerks to professionals in *ALD* libraries was 4.4:1.6 in 1978 and 3.0:1.7 in 1988. These totals were then 6.0 for professional and clerical staff members in 1978 and 4.7 in 1988, a loss of 22 percent in the decade. This left us with *ALD* means of 1.6 and 1.7 professionals for those libraries having any professionals at all for 1978 and 1988. To make these *ALD* figures comparable to the White and Hannaford figures, however, we must show the ratio of the number of professionals per library with all libraries counted, for example, professionals + clerks + student assistants. These ratios were 32 percent for 1978 and 24 percent for 1988. The decline was due to increased committee size in 1988 from a mean of five to a new mean of seven members. So much for the trend toward more professionals per library!

One hundred forty-nine paid professionals, or 1.8 percent of the total number of staff members, worked in White's libraries, but no comparable figure existed for Hannaford's paid professionals, though we may guess that it was about 3.7 percent. This section particularly demonstrates the problem of discontinuity between the White and Hannaford studies, not to mention the problems of comparing those two studies with the *ALD* studies, nor the problem of the difficulty of understanding just exactly how to interpret certain of White's figures. For *ALD*-1988 the figures were eighty-five paid professionals and 14 percent, substantial progress in number of paid professionals over previous years. Although only the Hannaford and *ALD* studies analyzed personnel by gender and none of them by age, we can be fairly confident that the vast majority of the staff members in all four studies were females of mature years.

In summary, the personnel comparison between the studies yielded uncertain improvement, but some progress was made in thirteen years, primarily in number of committee members but also in number of paid professional staff members. Other favorable signs included more nonprofessionals, better formal organization structure was implied, greater willingness for crossdenominational communication, and signs of more ecumenical tolerance by the time of the Hannaford and *ALD*-1988 studies. Other forms of improvement were not indicated largely as a result of the limited data gathered by the survey instruments.

## Collection

In this section we will study library book volume, periodical, and media holdings. Tables 6.24 and 6.25 show CSLA (Hannaford) study holdings for book volumes. The mean library had 1,667 book volumes in 1975 (White) and 2,824 volumes in 1986 (Hannaford), a 69 percent increase, or a mean increase of 105 volumes per library per year. Jewish libraries averaged 3,758 volumes and Baptist 1,851 volumes in 1975, whereas in 1986 these groups averaged 7,750 and 4,287 volumes respectively. Four percent of the libraries had collections of five thousand or more volumes in 1975, but in 1986 the same four percent had ten thousand volumes or more, as shown in table 6.26. This represents a definite improvement.

ALD-1978 showed 4,540 mean volumes per library, a figure already above that for Hannaford in 1986. *ALD*-1988 showed yet another increase—to 5,737 volumes per library. *Median ALD* figures were 2,833 and 3,392 volumes for 1978 and 1988. The 5,737 figure mentioned above represented an increase of 244 percent over the White 1975 figure. Just why the White and Hannaford figures were so low and the two *ALD* figures were so high is unclear. How comparable these figures were is equally unclear.

Jewish synagogues led the denominations with a mean of 7,750 book volumes in 1986, a large collection. Baptists and Roman Catholics followed in collection size. United Church of Christ collections were smallest, with only 1,841 volumes on the average. Jewish-Roman Catholic collections were usually somewhat larger than Protestant collections. Longitudinal table 6.26 shows volume holdings for *ALD* by denomination. The rise in holdings shown in the table amounted to 26 percent from 1978 to 1988. Largest 1988 volume collections were those of the Other Denominations, Roman Catholic, and Jewish groups, each one above seven thousand volumes in mean holdings.

Table 6.3 compares library book volume holdings for all four studies by denomination. Overall mean was 3,692 volumes with the Jewish, Other Denominations and Roman Catholics leading the table. The Jewish mean was 6,155 volumes per library. The means of the four studies followed the pattern found previously with the two *ALD* studies both having much higher means than either White or Hannaford. Again, only the libraries reporting holdings are represented here. Further explanation is provided in the table's notes.

Now to the periodical subscriptions of these libraries. See table 6.27 for the White findings. In 1975 thirty-two (1.8 percent) White libraries reported more than one hundred periodical subscriptions whereas in 1986 (Hannaford) only one (0.2 percent) library reported that many. On the other hand, White had a mean of thirty-six titles per library and the *mean* number of subscriptions in the Hannaford study averaged 8 titles per library, small. Jews, Roman Catholics, and Baptists received the largest number of periodical titles.

Were there more periodical subscriptions in the earliest than the later studies? Apparently not, but the 1975 data is incomplete. Presbyterians and United Church of Christ had the largest numbers of periodical titles in 1975, with Congregational, Mennonite, and Reformed at the bottom end. Roman Catholics and Jews led the list in 1986. In 1978 the *ALD* study found the typical congregational library to possess sixty-one periodical titles and in 1988 the typical congregational library to have had sixty-three periodical titles, a gain of only 3.3 percent. Again, the *ALD* figures were much larger than the White and Hannaford figures. Other Denominations, United Church of Christ, and Presbyterian libraries had almost three-fifths of the total number of libraries with periodicals.

Now we can move on to an analysis of library media holdings. The mean White survey library had about thirty-nine films and seventy-six filmstrips combined, yielding a total of 105 items. Mean holdings for phonograph records was forty-eight. Obviously filmstrips were the most popular of these types of media in 1975. Table 6.28 shows the Lutherans, Presbyterians, and Methodists to lead in number of libraries with films. For records, Presbyterians and Lutherans led the table. For total media holding means Lutheran, Methodist, and Presbyterian libraries led the table in holdings, while Mennonite, Reformed, and Congregational denominations were the weakest. The mean Hannaford survey library had 376 media titles of many kinds featuring cassette tapes and picture and clipping files. That was progress, a 258 percent increase, or the addition of about twenty-five media titles to each library per year!

However, for *ALD* media (media, maps and art reproductions), table 4.145 shows the 1988 mean holdings figure to have been 1.7 categories for popular libraries. Again the *ALD* figures were out of sync with the White and Hannaford figures. This time they were much smaller than the White and Hannaford libraries. Perhaps the reason for this is that the *ALD* reports were quite incomplete for media in that they showed no media holdings for most congregational libraries, presumably because the library reported none, or because they were lumped into the volume figure, or because media were now handled by a separate house of worship service office.

Table 6.2 deals with the filmstrip holdings of White and Hannaford. While *ALD* libraries had filmstrips also they were seldom listed separately so could seldom be counted. Table 6.2 showed White to average slightly more filmstrips than Hannaford which is surprising, to say the least. Otherwise the Baptist libraries led the table. Another study of filmstrips in White and Hannaford can be seen in table 6.1, by denomination. Again White had more filmstrips than Hannaford, 101 to 39 in mean figures. Churches of Christ, Jews and Baptists led in nonbook material holdings. Note the remarks at the bottom of this table, and other tabular note remarks in this chapter, which were prepared by Mouridou.

Not only was Hannaford smaller than White in filmstrips but it was smaller than White in media as a whole. For Hannaford's films, mean holdings were much smaller than those for White, as seen in tables 6.28 and 6.29 with an overall mean of only ninety-eight pieces per library. Most of the libraries had no films at all. As we have seen before, the Baptists were leaders in this area, with an average of 268 films. Other Denominations libraries were second at 133 pieces and U.C.C. libraries last at 23 pieces per library. Jewish-Roman Catholic and Protestant libraries were about equal in this table.

Tables 6.30 and 6.31 show the Hannaford library expenditures and holdings for media by denomination, with Jewish and Baptist leading at $1,008 and $563 spent per library. Overall mean annual media expenditures were small, only $215 per library, however. Jews and Roman Catholics were far above Protestants in their mean scores here, and Congregational was smallest at $74 per library. Table 5.68 shows the media holdings of all kinds in the Hannaford study. Overall mean was 260 media pieces per library.

Baptist again led the list with 777 pieces while Congregational was smallest with 132 pieces per library. So at least media holdings were growing in these congregational libraries. Books were much more numerous than films in the Hannaford libraries, 2,824 book volumes to 376 media pieces in overall means, in table 5.69 and table 6.24. For books Jewish led in number, 7,750, and for all media Baptists led in number, 965. The U.C.C. was the smallest group for these tables.

In summary, book and media collections grew rapidly between the

White and Hannaford studies, but the status of periodicals was apparently stationary between White and Hannaford for reasons which obviously need further study. However, these libraries gained in number of titles in *ALD*-1988. Media holdings were quite different for each one of the four studies so little can be made of the numerous inconsistent figures.

## Finance

Congregational library finance was an interesting study but was handled somewhat differently in the White, Hannaford, and *ALD* studies so they were harder to compare than was expected. Table 5.99 shows congregation (not library but congregation) income in the Hannaford study, 1986.[5] Overall mean was an income of $234,234 per year. Leading denominations were the Baptist and Jewish groups at $626,511 and $520,833 per house of worship per year, respectively. The U.C.C. and Congregational incomes at means of $15,941 and $21,784 were smallest. Note that the Jewish-Roman Catholic congregation income was somewhat larger than that of the Protestants.

Table 6.32 shows the annual *library* income breakdowns for all four studies. Median library income was $252 for White and $637 for Hannaford, an increase of 153 percent in eleven years. Of White's annual library incomes only 5.6 percent were above $1,000, whereas 13.5 percent of Hannaford's income levels exceeded $2,000. Almost 30 percent of the libraries had incomes of $100 or less in White's study, whereas the comparable Hannaford figure was only 5 percent. Was this progress or merely price inflation? Apparently it was mostly progress, since inflation seldom caused large increases in the frequency of small incomes. This table showed a net increase of 60 percent without inflation. Good! By denomination, Jewish libraries had the largest budgets with Roman Catholic coming next in both studies.

The two *ALD* financial studies were again out of sync with the White and Hannaford studies, though not so much as to have reflected again the superior nature of the samples obtained. It is clear that library income rose as the years progressed. For the median to have moved from $252 to $1,243 in thirteen years, White to *ALD*-1988, a 4.8:1.0 ratio, is impressive, if we can assume that all four of these median figures were comparable. Again, by denomination, Jewish libraries had the largest *ALD* incomes in these years because of their salary expenditures.

In another view, table 6.33 shows a comparison of annual expenditure among the four studies by denomination. The figures represented only those libraries reporting some expenditures, not those which did not report any expenditures. Clearly Jewish, Roman Catholic and Baptist denominations led in mean expenditures. Note that the mean expenditure rose irregularly as time passed, from $337 in 1975 to $7,420 in 1988. And again, Jewish-Roman Catholic libraries considerably outspent Protestant libraries, the Jewish/Catholic group ratio to Protestant groups being high, 3.5:1.0. The Jewish-Roman Catholic expenditure mean was about $8,500 as compared with the Protestant mean of $1,273 annually, quite a contrast.

We can examine Hannaford library expenditure by denomination gain. Overall mean was $1,652 per library. The Baptists were high; lowest groups were Congregational and Lutheran. To see the Hannaford study expenditures with all 411 libraries included, look at tables 5.78 and 5.100. The overall mean annual Hannaford expenditure appeared to drop from $1,652 to $998 due to two different ways of calculating the means and with Jewish and Roman Catholics still leading the table.

Tables 6.34 and 6.35 compared the four studies on personnel expenditures by denomination. Clearly the two *ALD* studies scored quite differently from the White and Hannaford studies again. On the three-study table 6.35 Jewish and Roman Catholics led the list. Table 6.36 is a kind of summary or reference table showing the score made by each one of the four studies on selected variables that were examined in this chapter.

Table 5.97 shows the Hannaford 1986 personnel expenditure figures by denomination again. They contrast with the *ALD* figures seen below. Overall mean was $331 per library, with Jewish again leading and Roman Catholics coming next. Christian and Congregational had means of $0. Again Jewish and Roman Catholic libraries greatly outdistanced the Protestant libraries by $2,638 to $198 in personnel expenditure! Table 6.37 shows the *ALD* longitudinal study for personnel expenditure by denomination. The mean expenditure rose strongly between 1978 and 1988, by 253 percent. Episcopal/Anglican, Methodist, Presbyterian, Jewish, and Roman Catholic led this rise. Overall mean personnel expenditure was $4,274 in 1978 and $15,070 in 1988. It was $9,672 for the two studies combined. Roman Catholic and Methodist led the list in 1988, but Jewish was not far behind. Jewish and Roman Catholic greatly outdistanced Protestant libraries here again.

In summary, we have looked at several congregational library expenditure tables and found a few surprises and a few disappointments. White and Hannaford seem to be compatible as do the two *ALD* studies. However, the White and Hannaford studies show some degree of discontinuity with the two *ALD* studies. Jewish, Roman Catholic, and Baptist libraries led most tables. The financial comparison showed primarily the effects of substantial expenditure progress and house of worship librarians should take full credit for this rise. However, the effects of some degree of price inflation could be seen also in the seventeen years separating the four studies.

## Conclusion

In a final conclusion for this section of the chapter, in spite of their differences in emphases, presentation and sometimes in content, at least in general terms, the White, Hannaford and the two *ALD* studies agreed on several facets in several subject areas. Though the evidence is unclear, congregational libraries seem generally to have been growing and improving their collections, staffing and service in the 1970s and 1980s and probably in the 1990s also. Almost all of these libraries were small, at least when compared with other kinds of libraries, but there was a large number of them.

Most of the specific variables examined showed improvement for the White through the Hannaford to the *ALD* studies. That was victory of a sort with the congregational library field improving between 1971 and 1988. Specifically, the areas of *improvement* seemed to be: (1) focus in specific states and provinces, (2) circulation and use, (3) total staff size, (4) clerical staff size, (5) number of book volumes, (6) number of periodical titles, (7) size of annual library expenditure, (8) size of personnel expenditure, and (9) media. However, the discontinuity between studies was noticeable and the comparability of studies was open to question, especially between White and Hannaford on the one hand and the two *ALD* studies on the other hand.

Denominational distribution and paid staff member status were variables for which the results were neither particularly encouraging nor particularly discouraging. On the other hand, library age and media holdings were two variables that seemed to be on the negative side, to be moving down instead of up.

Few of these libraries met the types of qualitative library standards that were well known to other library types, but some of them were giving good service anyhow. Change was a constant in this picture, usually in the form of growth but sometimes in the form of unaccountable jumps or drops. Clearly, these conclusions should give us some confidence in thinking that we can now see, to some extent at least, if only for certain variables and for certain groups of libraries, and often rather unclearly— just what is out there.[6]

## The Joys of Replication and Selective Research

A few final words are in order for this short chapter. Reality is harder to find than many readers believe. Future students of congregational library and information service—and this author hopes there will be many of them—should try to replicate as closely as possible the work which has already been carried out in the field in order to help us in developing a more meaningful body of factual survey information. Already the field suffers from the lack of research information following the White study and the discontinuity existing between the four studies described in this chapter. A follow-up on the Hannaford study needs to be done as soon as possible. Another study of the White type, large and comprehensive in coverage of libraries, could greatly enrich the field's scholarly literature.

Much remains to be discovered about congregational religious libraries. No aspect of either their reference service or their book, periodical, and media selection and acquisition policies has been studied. Little is known about their cataloging and classification policies and practices beyond a few basic facts, and those are found only in certain studies. Management policies and practices, including the library's relation to the house of worship minister or pastor, the director of Christian education, the church or synagogue school teachers, and the curriculum are all unexplored areas. For these and other subjects, we must learn what is done now and how, and why it is done under varied circumstances. Then perhaps we can eventually work out reasonable policies to recommend to librarians for the future.

### Possible Research Topics

Many aspects of the popular religious library field should provide intriguing studies. Here is a list of several of these ideas for those persons who are interested in considering a research or survey project:

1.   What are the basic differences and similarities between the libraries of any four Christian religious denominations? And

why do these differences exist? How do they relate to each denomination's history and to its unique theological concepts?

2. What are the detailed characteristics of twenty-five congregations and libraries that manage to achieve a low input or cost level and a high output or monthly circulation level, such as that of the Lombard, Illinois, Mennonite Church Library?

3. The entire area of standards needs study, for instance, for (1) percentage of congregational expenditure going to the library, (2) library income per house of worship member, (3) circulation per member, (4) hours of library staffing per month per member, and (5) number of books, periodicals, and media available per member.

4. Detailed descriptions and analyses are needed of twenty-five case studies of clearly (1) superior or (2) inferior libraries to try to ascertain causes and associated factors.

5. Analyses are needed of the objectives and effectiveness of a dozen specific national popular religious library association local and regional chapters in their service areas.

6. Analyses are needed of the types of congregation library committee job assignments made and the work schedule patterns.

7. A history should be written of national U.S. congregational library development in the nineteenth century to World War I.

8. The international aspect of congregational librarianship should be studied in some detail since several thousand of these libraries exist outside North America, for example, Baptists, and Christian Scientist libraries, not to mention the Seventh-day Adventists and the Jews. Both the (1) locally affiliated libraries and (2) those affiliated with North American religious groups that have houses of worship located abroad should be included.

9. What are the objectives and services of religious public libraries? To what extent do Roman Catholic public libraries and Christian Science reading rooms serve both a congregational and a religious public library function? And are Mormon genealogical libraries more accurately classified as congregational or religious public libraries, or as scholarly religious libraries?

10. We need comprehensive statements of the justification for congregational library existence from (1) a religious viewpoint and (2) a library and information service viewpoint.

11. We need a straightforward and detailed statement of the role

that the library should serve in (1) Christian church school and (2) Jewish synagogue or Hebrew school, statements written with a professional school librarian's understanding and viewpoint.

12. A detailed description and analysis of objectives, organization, and service is needed for each one of the two international systems of popular congregational and public libraries. They are sponsored by the Church of Jesus Christ of Latter-day Saints and by the Church of Christ, Scientist.

13. A practical plan is needed for collecting selective North American interdenominational congregational library statistics annually.

14. A comparative analysis is needed of the influence of the denomination's theological views on each one of five denominations' congregational library services.

15. An extensive analysis is needed of the influence on congregational library service of mean congregation educational level and income level, as well as region and denomination.

## Notes

1. Joyce L. White, "The Demography of American Church and Synagogue Libraries," in *Church and Synagogue Libraries*, ed. John F. Harvey (Metuchen, N.J.: Scarecrow, 1980), pp. 19–33. The survey project was carried out by White for CSLA. The above paper describing and analyzing it was written by Harvey from White's report and with her concurrence. See pp. 32–33 of the paper for the complete list of White's many mailing lists. This summary and analysis was supplemented in 1993 by the opportunity to study and analyze the original computer printouts produced by the University of Pennsylvania Computer Center in 1976 tabulating and analyzing Ms. White's returned questionnaires.

2. For the most part, the two ALD studies will be considered as separate data collections and will not be combined into one study. To distinguish the two CSLA studies, each one will be referred to by the name of the woman who performed most of its work, Joyce White (1975) or Claudia Hannaford (1986).

3. The author should point out, however, that by 1967 (CSLA's founding date), both the Association of Jewish Libraries Synagogue, School and Center Libraries Section, and the Catholic Library Association Parish Libraries Section were well established and had local chapters in operation in certain leading eastern and middle western cities.

4. The White report of founding tables for specific congregations was only partially complete. It was a list of the single earliest library for each denomination reporting. On the other hand, the three other "oldest" library lists displayed the oldest libraries in their databases regardless of denomination.

5. In the four studies at least three different words were used to show financial outlays: budget, income, and expenditures. All three more or less represent the same thing—the library's annual expenditures. However, the separate discussions of the four studies here will try to emphasize the proper word used in each study.

6. Interpretation of results: Before we can discuss the results of the four-study comparison, it is best if we look briefly at the characteristics of an acceptable sample. We can then examine how our four samples varied from the ideal and make some of the necessary corrections or qualifications.

Any sample randomly selected out of a large population needs to be managed in such a way as to obtain representative subsamples of all the major subgroups. When some of them are quite small, a random sample needs to be "beefed up" to cover these smallest elements adequately. Therefore, although a sample of 250 to cover a homogeneous population of 2,500 (i.e., a sample of 1:10) is statistically adequate, subsamples of at least thirty to fifty to cover each subgroup are desirable. If our population were fifty thousand religious libraries, an ideal sample of 10 percent would require five thousand random responses— hard or impossible to obtain and expensive to analyze. Perhaps unfortunately, our population does boast at least fourteen major denominational groups. Hypothetically speaking, obtaining subsamples of fifty of each one of these denominations would demand a minimum of $50 \times 20 = 1,000$ libraries sampled randomly. However, since each denomination varies in size from all of the others, a proportional, random, and representative sample would approximate 1,650 Methodist libraries alone, as, let us say, Jewish libraries in the population = approximately 442 versus 14,547 Methodist libraries, or a ratio of 33:1!

So, if fifty Jewish libraries were to be randomly sampled, a proportionate number of Methodist libraries would need to be sampled too, i.e., about 1,650, or 11.3 percent of both their total populations respectively. It is simple to demonstrate that obtaining a random, representative sample is difficult to achieve and nearly impossible to prove. However, there are small explanations or corrections that can be made to make interpretation of the results more reliable and useful.

In addition to the problem of pure representativeness, our four studies display certain other weaknesses. Two of these are major, and both of them, while troublesome, can be turned to good account:

(1) Though obviously to some extent self-selective, the White sample was probably quite close to being random. The Hannaford sample was a self-selective sample of the entire CSLA membership, while the *ALD* samples overlapped heavily and were self-selective samples of libraries choosing upon request to submit reports to the *American Library Directory*.

(2) The data analysis for the White study was only partial at the time it was performed with arbitrary upper category limits selected (upper limits were a problem in three of the four studies and correspondingly distorted the variable means). This problem did not occur for the Hannaford data as the actual data values for all variables were used giving an absolute and accurate data range for each one: the CSLA study was hand checked for accuracy recording both No Responses and also true zero entries. This fact is crucial to our analysis: the ALD studies showed no zero-values and high No Responses, but many of the latter may have been either low variable values or else the missing zero responses, a conjunction producing inevitable upward distortion of all ALD means.

It is likely for the latter set of libraries (editions ALD-1978 and ALD-1988) that many librarians submitting data for publication did one of two things where No Responses occurred: (1) less well organized or small libraries might have failed to submit data simply because it was not available to them, e.g., volume holdings or accurate expenditure figures, etc., and (2) libraries with low known variable values may have chosen not to submit them simply because the figures would have had poor promotional/publicity value. A third tendency was probably for small libraries not to submit anything to the ALD through lack of staff, lack of interest or even lack of relevance of the ALD to their religious library activities, etc.

In any event, we can make certain small adjustments on the basis of the above shortcomings to assist the analysis. Reference to the final summary table 6.36 shows that the ALD congregational libraries were twice as old as the libraries in either the White or the Hannaford studies. Both of the subsets coincide closely: we will continue to refer to them as sets. The fact of the interset disparity gives us one incontrovertible fact to use. The ALD libraries do not represent the larger population of libraries in the same way in which the Hannaford and White libraries do; they are certainly older and probably also larger, better staffed and better funded. A profile of the average ALD libraries in 1978 and 1988 gives us a good idea of the better religious libraries and their growth over this period.

An examination of book holdings (table 6.3) shows a ten-year congregational library growth rate of 26.5 percent (ALD set) or 30 to 32 percent of the mean variation. This is true for both of the subsets. Although the two sets were not taken at the same periods of time (i.e., they are not within the same time *frames*: 1971–75 → 1986 is not equivalent to 1978 → 1988), we should be able to demonstrate that the two sets still differ or congrue significantly. We can say that the midpoint in time for the first set is approximately 1979.5. The midpoint for the latter set is about 1983: the difference is roughly four years. Therefore, if the growth rate over ten years is 32 percent, the same rate for four years would be 12.8 percent.

The means for the two data sets contain 2,246 and 5,139 volumes. Note that set two is more than twice as well endowed in terms of volumes as is set one. In fact, the *ALD* libraries have a 129 percent advantage over the White and Hannaford sample libraries. This is equivalent to the extra 100 percent in terms of age (38 years versus 18 years) plus at least the extra 12.8 percent growth that would have accrued over the four or five year time disparity between the time frames.

An examination of filmstrip holdings is equally instructive. Only the White and Hannaford studies reported on filmstrips specifically. However, there are two important points here. The first of them is that Hannaford data is demonstrably of better quality than is the data for any of the other three studies. A "0" for a CSLA study variable means precisely "no holdings" for that variable. Therefore, it is probably true that the average CSLA library, and by extension, the average library within the overall congregational population, possessed in 1986 something less than 39.3 filmstrips.

The reason for this situation is that many of these libraries had none at all and the CSLA libraries may be somewhat better off than the real-life average. However, if we look at only those libraries *reporting* filmstrips, we find both the Hannaford and White libraries to have a mean of about one hundred each. The congruence of 101.1 and 98 is too close to be a coincidence. We cannot guess accurately what the population mean might be for those libraries holding filmstrips, but it will certainly be below one hundred filmstrips per library. A third point stands out: library filmstrip holdings did not appear to increase significantly within the ten to thirteen year frame. This conclusion is not validated, unfortunately, by the *ALD* or other results, because they reported almost no values for filmstrips, but it appears to be the case.

Library circulation charges needed no adjustment of zero-responses as the two rates of missing values (White: 13.2 percent and Hannaford: 22.0 percent) were not so different to deal with. Had they been larger, then the reliability of the data would have been correspondingly reduced. Nearly 40 percent of White's libraries reported no filmstrips, as did 60 percent of Hannaford's libraries. Data with large proportions of missing values tends to a certain selective and sometimes unpredictable bias or "skewness." Therefore, the best data in terms of quality is that with no missing values. The next best data has a low proportion of missing cases. High proportions are difficult to deal with; but the worst case of all is intersample comparison or discriminate cluster analysis such as we are doing here in which one sample has a significantly higher proportion of missing values than the other.

In this respect our analysis works out fortuitously, as the last contingency either does not arise or can be adjusted by making the necessary correction to the sample zero-values, i.e., by removing all of the true zero-values from the CSLA data and placing them in the No Response category. This is essentially the same thing as was originally done for the two *ALD* samples through the inability to distinguish a zero-response from a No Response in the *ALD*. Making this one correction to the CSLA data makes the four data sets much more comparable and analyzable. In several details, the configuration of study particulars as found in the four data samples could not have been better arranged. Circulation charges for Hannaford and White are again comparable: monthly means of 108, cf. 114.5 respectively.

This congruence leads to three conclusions: the mean monthly circulation per library was (1) approximately 110 volumes for the first set during their time frame; (2) did not change significantly over the duration of the time frame; (3) was certainly lower than 110 volumes per month for the average population library's circulation; and (4) was probably up to twice as high (or even higher?) for the average *ALD* congregational library. Only the first of these conclusions is certain. However, the other three are strongly implied and are partially validated by the similar analysis of previous variables — library age, volumes, and filmstrip holdings — and will be further validated by the expenditure analysis.

Annual library expenditure on personnel suffered the same problem as for filmstrip holdings. Again, the CSLA (Hannaford) data is certainly the best in quality from a statistician's viewpoint. In 1986 the average CSLA library was paying out annually approximately $331 in personnel salaries. This was the case simply because 93.2 percent of all libraries were paying out nothing at all! As CSLA libraries are likely to be somewhat better than the population average we can state confidently that in 1986 about 95 percent of all North American congregational libraries had no paid personnel. Of those libraries paying annual salaries, we find that the Hannaford (1986) mean personnel expenditure was $4,856; compare the *ALD* means of $4,274 in 1978 and $15,070 in 1988. These three figures tell us several things: (1) about 7 percent of the CSLA libraries had paid personnel; (2) the older *ALD* libraries did not show up much better at the beginning of their ten-year frame; in 1978 only 5 percent of the *ALD* congregational libraries reported personnel expenditure; (3) by 1988 this percentage had risen to 11.8 percent. Let us examine this variable more closely below.

Personnel Expenditures: 3 Studies — Longitudinal Summary

| | -----*ALD*-Hannaford----- | | | -------*ALD*-White------- | | |
| --- | --- | --- | --- | --- | --- | --- |
| | 1978 | 1986 | % Change | 1988 | % Change | Ratio |
| Percentage of libraries with salaries | 4.89% | 6.8% | 39% | 11.8% | 73.5% | 1.91:1 |
| Expenditure | $4,274 | $4,856 | 13.6% | $15,070 | 210% | 15:1 |
| Percentage change in time | | | 10.3% | | 2.3% | 0.22:1 |

The results of the above analysis are apparently, but not in fact, problematic: (1) most congregational libraries did not pay their personnel between 1978 and 1988 (?); (2) this situation changed somewhat over the period of ten years. If the CSLA libraries were within the same subset as the *ALD* libraries, then they would have shown 10.4 percent of all CSLA libraries with paid personnel by 1986 according to the ten-year growth trend and annual personnel expenditures of $12,911 (cf. $4,856) according to the trend for salaries as a variable (the increment compounded of true growth plus inflation). For the *ALD* libraries there is obviously much room for both inflation and growth in the 253 percent change from 1978 to 1988. But again, the CSLA libraries were not within the same set of samples; (3) true growth did occur. The inflation rate for 1978 to 1988 approximated 70 percent according to earlier calculations. Therefore, real growth would have been in the nature of 180 percent for those *ALD* libraries paying salaries. (4) CSLA and the population's libraries as a whole probably also gained on both aspects of the personnel variable.

However, on the basis of the data available we cannot estimate how much growth occurred for either group (White data does not exist for this variable). It is most likely that the change for *number* of libraries paying salaries would be less than the 141 percent growth rate for *ALD* libraries and again less than the 253 percent change in *actual salaries paid*, again for the *ALD* samples. Let us hypothesize that the true value would be about 50 percent of these figures for CSLA libraries over a similar ten-year period and somewhat less than this for the overall population.

The final variable for which we have data is much less complicated to deal with, as: (1) we have four studies to work with and (2) the proportion of missing data was low for the first set (10.3 percent and 1 percent) but high (77 percent and 60.4 percent) for the second set. These figures were as one would expect: neither the White nor the Hannaford sample libraries were using their data submissions for any purpose except to provide study information, and they provided it much more according to the needs of the researcher. Fortunately, we *can* use the resulting values meaningfully.

The mean annual expenditure for set one was $995 (there was significant growth between 1975 and 1986—390 percent). The matching mean for the *ALD* libraries was $4,709 with 271 percent growth. Although the first set covers an additional two or three years, this is not sufficient to account for the marked disparity in growth rates. However, we *do* find that the two sets are quite different again: the *ALD* set is approximately 373 percent better off! This outsized percentage needs to cover a number of components: (1) 70 percent inflation; (2) an unspecified growth in personnel expenditures (*ALD* growth rates versus the Hannaford-White group of libraries' rates); (3) the fact that *ALD* libraries possess more than twice as many volume holdings (129 percent more, and probably more of other types of holdings as well); (4) significant true growth. About the only sure conclusion we can draw from this situation is that the disparity is large enough to cover all four known components:

| | | |
|---|---|---|
| 1. Inflation | 70% ⎫ | |
| 2. Growth (assumed) | 25–30% ⎬ | (See Tables 6.34 and 6.36) |
| 3. Additional volumes | 129% ⎭ | |
| 4. Salary and other additional expenditures | 100% + | |
| Total Disparity | 373% | |

As this large deviation (373 percent) is the difference between the two sets, we know that all four sources of variation probably affect the sets differently, *and* we know that the *ALD* libraries were roughly twice as strong in their showing as were the set one libraries, we should not be surprised to discover a figure in excess of 300 percent. Anything less would be inconsistent with our experiences as the missing values for *ALD* libraries were so high (over 60 percent).

That is, in addition to covering the listed sources of variation, probably we also need to make allowance for a high proportion of lower income libraries within the *ALD* samples failing to report their expenditures at all, thereby driving the *ALD* means artificially high. We cannot estimate the degree of distortion accurately, but, if the relatively reliable CSLA mean is to be believed, then it is reasonable to assume that the *ALD* mean for all sample libraries by 1986 would be twice as high, i.e., $3,300 p.a. (cf. the calculated *ALD*-1988 mean of $7,420) and this figure would include those libraries failing to report.

The remaining problem is that of the large difference between the reported expenditures for the White and Hannaford studies. We would expect over a period of roughly twelve years for this to be 326 percent if we use the two *ALD* studies' growth rate as a base; instead we have 390 percent, which is larger than expected. The incremental difference could be due to any one of four factors: (1) it is possible that as early as 1971–75 few congregational libraries made any expenditures and that the trend to larger expenditures did not start until subsequent to 1975; (2) the White data shows a 10.3 percent No Response rate — could some of the nonrespondents have been somewhat better off? (3) did the White category expenditure maximum fall too low? i.e., was the White mean artificially depressed because the maximum expenditure category limit was *$1,500* compared to no upper limit for CSLA data on expenditures? (4) were the White libraries truly poorer than those responding to the Hannaford CSLA study? Any or all of the above are *possible*, but the most likely one is the third "solution" combined with the first. Probably the White mean is considerably too low due to the artificial, applied maximum ($1,500 — note that of the 1,635 White libraries (a surprisingly large return percentage!) submitting expenditure data, ninety-one were in the top category and forty of these were Jewish! Also, the bottom category for this set of expenditure data started at zero and probably included a high proportion of libraries with no annual expenditure at all) and may have been low anyway due to the small nature of congregational libraries in general, especially in the early 1970s. What is almost certainly the case, however, is that the average population library had expenditures of well under the White-Hannaford mean of $995 p.a.

Although only a few variables can be compared across the four congregational library studies, the effort is far from fruitless. In fact, the divergences and disparities throw light on the larger population of libraries and largely validate the findings of each one of the other studies. Although none of the statistical problems that arose were desirable in themselves, it is doubtful if as much information could have been deduced without them. From this standpoint therefore, the study differences have been rewarding in that it has been possible to build at least partial profiles of all four study samples and also of the larger American congregational library population.

Although the partial analysis of Canada (see tables 6.5, 6.8, 6.9) is hardly satisfactory, neither is it problematic. The best that can be said for this northern region is that it appears to be not very much different from its seven counterpart North American regions and that it needs further, possibly separate, study. The seven U.S. regions are relatively well represented. Although a number of states show up poorly for all of the four studies, none of the larger or more populous areas is sufficiently underrepresented to cause either alarm or major qualification of the results. See table 6.9.

TABLE 6.1
Two-Study Comparison of Library Filmstrip Holdings: White and Hannaford Congregational Library Studies Only[a,b]

| Denomination | White | | | Hannaford | | | 2-Study Total | | | Summary | |
|---|---|---|---|---|---|---|---|---|---|---|---|
| | Number of Libraries | No Response | Mean Filmstrip Holdings | Number of Libraries | No Response | Mean Filmstrip Holdings | Number of Libraries | No Response | Overall Mean Holdings | Difference between Sample Means | Difference as % of Overall Mean |
| Baptist | 136/165 | 29 | 142 | 25/26 | 1 | 107 | 161/191 | 30 | 125 | 35 | 28 |
| Christian | –/0 | – | – | 20/21 | 1 | 16 | 20/21 | 1 | 16 | – | – |
| Churches of Christ | 27/40 | 13 | 96 | –/0 | – | – | 27/40 | 13 | 96 | – | – |
| Congregational | –/15 | 15 | – | 17/17 | 0 | 37 | 17/32 | 15 | 37 | – | – |
| Episcopal/Anglican | 71/118 | 47 | 80 | 42/43 | 1 | 16 | 113/161 | 48 | 48 | 64 | 133 |
| Lutheran | 357/560 | 203 | 92 | 42/42 | 0 | 30 | 399/602 | 203 | 61 | 62 | 102 |
| Mennonite | –/22 | 22 | – | –/0 | – | – | –/22 | 22 | – | – | – |
| Methodist | 161/202 | 41 | 118 | 79/80 | 1 | 59 | 240/282 | 42 | 88 | 59 | 67 |
| Other Denominations | 21/159 | 138 | 74[c] | 57/57 | 0 | 40 | 78/216 | 138 | 57 | 34 | 60 |
| Presbyterian | 195/290 | 95 | 82 | 83/85 | 2 | 29 | 278/375 | 97 | 56 | 53 | 94 |
| U.C.C. | 76/98 | 22 | 82 | 21/22 | 1 | 6 | 97/120 | 23 | 44 | 76 | 172 |

| | | | | | | | | | | | |
|---|---|---|---|---|---|---|---|---|---|---|---|
| Jewish | 55/87 | 32/38 | 130 | 6/6 | 0 | 60 | 61/93 | 32 | 95 | 70 | 74 |
| Roman Catholic | 66 | 28 | 124 | 12/12 | 0 | 43 | 50/78 | 28 | 84 | 81 | 96 |
| Total | 1,137/1,822 | 685 | 101 | 404/411 | 7 | 39 | 1,541/ | 6922/233 | 70 | 62 | 88 |

[a]The surprisingly disparate nature of the Hannaford versus the White results suggests that neither should be trusted too far. It would appear that almost all Hannaford libraries reported film holdings (404/411), whereas only 62 percent of White's respondents so reported. One reason for the disparity possibly lies in the White questionnaire, which seems to have prompted only those libraries with a policy for accumulating filmstrips as a major collection to respond to the question. Although this is a *possibility* it is unlikely to be significant, as two other sources of incomparability definitely did come into play and are great enough to account for the incongruence: (1) in the Hannaford questionnaire all libraries not showing filmstrips were marked as zero, whereas (2) for the White study nonfilmstrip holding libraries were registered as No Response. This has two potential biasing effects: (1) all Hannaford means are *reduced* in size, possibly greatly, and (2) those Hannaford denominations with the largest number of zero entries are reduced most with biasing effect on their denominational ranks. The overall result is that all the White means are higher than for the Hannaford denominations. Therefore, it is probable that the Hannaford means are closer to the actual case for all denominations. It is best, just the same, to assume some means to be higher than those shown for the Hannaford, especially for the smallest denominations, i. e., Congregational, United Church of Christ, Jewish, and Roman Catholic, as these groups are too small to be representative. Similarly, denominations with only one study reporting, e. g., Christian for Hannaford and Churches of Christ for White, ought to be treated with caution.

[b]About the only certain conclusions that can be drawn from the table results are (1) the overall mean for filmstrip holdings, including nonholder libraries, is probably between fifty and seventy-five filmstrips per library and, (2) those denominations with the highest filmstrip holdings using noncomparable evidence are certainly Baptist, Methodist, and Lutheran, possibly joined by Churches of Christ, Jewish, and, Roman Catholic in that order. In other words, the largest traditional Protestant denominations *appear* as groups to possess the largest collections of filmstrips. However, reference to table 5.67 in which all libraries with no media holdings of any kind have been withdrawn from the calculations for the means shows that 115 libraries have no media at all and that the overall mean for all media holdings is 260 items per Hannaford library. The corresponding table for filmstrip holdings is table 6.28. Therefore, see table 6.2 for *comparable* White and Hannaford statistics dealing with filmstrips.

[c] For Reformed only.

**TABLE 6.2**
Two-Study Comparison of Library Filmstrip Holdings: Hannaford Congregational Library Study Results Improved for Comparability[a-e]

| Denomination | White | | | Hannaford | | | 2-Study Total | | | Summary | |
|---|---|---|---|---|---|---|---|---|---|---|---|
| | Number of Libraries | No Response | Mean Filmstrip Holdings | Number of Libraries | No Response | Mean Filmstrip Holdings | Number of Libraries | No Response | Overall Mean Holdings | Difference between Sample Means | Difference as % of Overall Mean |
| Baptist | 136/165 | 29 | 142 | 10/26 | 16 | 268 | 146/191 | 45 | 205 | 126 | 61.0 |
| Christian | -/0 | - | 5/21 | 16 | 65 | 5/21 | 16 | 65 | - | - | - |
| Churches of Christ | 27/40 | 13 | 96 | -/0 | - | - | 27/40 | 13 | 96 | - | - |
| Congregational | -/15 | 15 | - | 7/17 | 10 | 89 | 7/32 | 25 | 89 | - | 18.0 |
| Episcopal/Anglican | 71/118 | 47 | 80 | 10/43 | 33 | 67 | 81/161 | 80 | 74 | 13 | 18.0 |
| Lutheran | 357/560 | 203 | 92 | 19/42 | 23 | 66 | 376/602 | 226 | 79 | 26 | 33.0 |
| Mennonite | -/22 | 22 | - | -/0 | - | - | -/22 | 22 | - | - | - |
| Methodist | 161/202 | 41 | 118 | 40/80 | 40 | 116 | 201/282 | 81 | 117 | 2 | 1.7 |
| Other Denominations | 21/159 | 138 | 74[b] | 17/57 | 40 | 133 | 38/216 | 178 | 104 | 59 | 57.0 |
| Presbyterian | 195/290 | 95 | 82 | 39/85 | 46 | 62 | 234/375 | 141 | 72 | 20 | 28.0 |
| U.C.C. | 76/98 | 22 | 82 | 6/22 | 16 | 22 | 82/120 | 38 | 52 | 60 | 115.0 |
| Jewish | 55/87 | 32 | 130 | 3/6 | 3 | 120 | 58/93 | 35 | 125 | 10 | 8.0 |
| Roman Catholic | 38/66 | 28 | 124 | 6/12 | 6 | 86 | 44/78 | 34 | 105 | 38 | 36.0 |
| Total | 1,137/1,822 | 685 | 101 | 162/411 | 249 | 98 | 1,299/2,233 | 934 | 100 | 3 | 3.1 |

[a]Hannaford libraries showing no filmstrip holdings were removed from the calculations for the denominational means, as was originally done for the White study results.

bBecause of the small number of Hannaford Baptist, United Church of Christ, and Roman Catholic libraries with filmstrips, the difference between sample means is unacceptably large for these denominations (61 percent, 115 percent, and 36 percent respectively). The same argument applies to the Reformed group within the White study (57 percent). In addition, Reformed as a denomination is hardly equivalent to *ALD*'s Other Denominations group. However, in this case there was no cell into which to drop these twenty-one libraries appropriately.

cThe tiny remaining difference (3.1 percent), which applies to the overall means for all denominations, indicates three things: (1) a total of 1,299 libraries makes quite a satisfactory sample; (2) the White and Hannaford library studies are both taken from the same population and definitely replicate each other with the few qualifications mentioned above; (3) there was little *overall change* in filmstrip holdings in the few years between the two studies; the average library with films possessed approximately one hundred of them and Baptists unequivocally led the field with 50 percent to 100 percent above the overall means (for both studies).

dLeading denominations for filmstrip holdings were

1. Baptist
2. Jewish
3. Methodist
4. Roman Catholic
5. Other Denominations
6. Churches of Christ
7. Congregational
8. Lutheran

Note the difference between the order in this list and the rank order in Table 6.1.

eThe *matching list* for total annual library expenditure (see table 6.33) is

1. Jewish
2. Roman Catholic
3. Baptist
4. Other Denominations
5. Episcopal/Anglican
6. Presbyterian
7. Christian
8. Methodist

It is notable and hardly a coincidence that the tops of the two lists include Jewish, Roman Catholic, Baptist, and Other Denominations as leaders. Films cost money. More prosperous libraries can afford to buy films that tend to be short-term investments.

fFor Reformed only.

TABLE 6.3
Four-Study Comparison of Library Book Volume Holdings: Congregational Libraries Only[a-f]

| Denomination | White | | Hannaford | | ALD-1978 | | ALD-1988 | | Summary | | | |
|---|---|---|---|---|---|---|---|---|---|---|---|---|
| | Number of Libraries | Mean | Number of Libraries | Mean | Number of Libraries | Mean | Number of Libraries | Mean | Total Libraries | Overall Mean | Average Difference Among Means | % of Overall Mean |
| Baptist | 164/165 | 1,851 | 26/26 | 4,287 | 69/83 | 5,196 | 70/71 | 6,664 | 329/345 | 4,500 | 1,430 | 32 |
| Christian | –/0 | – | 21/21 | 2,457 | 13/18 | 6,231 | 17/17 | 4,059 | 51/56 | 4,249 | 1,321 | 31 |
| Churches of Christ | –/40 | – | –/0 | – | – | – | 2/2 | 1,375 | 2/42 | 1,375 | – | – |
| Congregational | –/15 | – | 16/17 | 2,147 | –/0 | – | –/0 | – | 16/32 | 2,147 | – | – |
| Episcopal/Anglican | 116/118 | 1,402 | 43/43 | 2,241 | 31/41 | 3,250 | 31/33 | 3,952 | 221/235 | 2,711 | 890 | 33 |
| Independent | –/0 | – | –/0 | – | 2/3 | 2,250 | 1/1 | 2,250 | 3/4 | 2,250 | 0 | 0 |
| Lutheran | 547/560 | 1,141 | 42/42 | 2,324 | 38/53 | 3,724 | 40/42 | 5,669 | 667/697 | 3,215 | 1,482 | 46 |
| Mennonite | –/22 | – | –/0 | – | 2/3 | 4,500 | 4/4 | 4,500 | 6/29 | 4,500 | 0 | 0 |
| Methodist | 199/202 | 1,595 | 78/80 | 2,762 | 35/55 | 3,421 | 59/64 | 4,576 | 371/401 | 3,089 | 910 | 30 |
| Other Denominations | –/159 | – | 56/57 | 2,458 | 57/86 | 5,382 | 66/71 | 7,144 | 179/373 | 4,995 | 1,691 | 34 |
| Presbyterian | 286/290 | 1,670 | 83/85 | 3,192 | 88/115 | 3,068 | 94/97 | 3,878 | 551/587 | 2,952 | 641 | 22 |
| U.C.C. | 94/98 | 1,440 | 22/22 | 1,841 | 10/13 | 2,175 | 13/13 | 2,673 | 139/146 | 2,032 | 392 | 19 |
| Jewish | 84/87 | 3,758 | 6/6 | 7,750 | 112/150 | 6,045 | 164/170 | 7,067 | 366/413 | 6,155 | 1,254 | 20 |
| Roman Catholic | –/66 | – | 12/12 | 3,958 | 8/14 | 2,594 | 8/8 | 7,125 | 28/100 | 4,559 | 1,711 | 38 |
| Total | 1,490/1,822 | 1,667 | 405/411 | 2,824 | 465/634 | 4,540 | 569/593 | 5,737 | 2,929/3,460 | 3,692 | 1,447 | 39 |

[a]The designation 164/165 means 164 active cases out of a possible 165 cases and is used throughout the chapter.

[b]The percentage values in the far right-hand column represent several sources of variation: (1) sampling variations within the four groups; the proportion of the variation that is attributable to sampling fluctuations can be estimated by examining how the rank ordering of denominations within

the four samples varies; (2) random error; (3) natural variation by libraries around the overall denominational mean; (4) variation caused by definitional differences about what constitutes a book or volume, e.g., are periodicals included?; (5) growth over time in library holdings.

It is quite obvious from examining the four sample means, 1,667, 2,824, 4,540 and 5,737, that a large part of the variation is the result of true growth. This is particularly borne out by the fact that 1,640 of the two *ALD* samples are matched pairs using the same sets of definitions and true growth in volumes for these libraries approximated 25 percent of the base of 4,540 (or $5,737-4,540) = 1,197$ units; 1,197 placed over the group mean of 3,692 is almost exactly 32 percent. We can conclude from this that somewhat less than one half of the variance (39 percent) is due to growth, leaving more than one half (including the half contributed by the Hannaford and White studies) unexplained.

[c] The question now becomes, How much variance is contributed by sampling fluctuation either natural or due to bias? Let us put the four samples into rank order:

| White | Hannaford | *ALD* 1978 | *ALD* 1988 |
|---|---|---|---|
| 1. Jewish | Jewish | Christian | Other Denominations |
| 2. Baptist | Baptist | Jewish | Roman Catholic |
| 3. Presbyterian | Roman Catholic | Baptist | Jewish |
| 4. Methodist | Presbyterian | Other Denominations | Baptist |
| 5. U.C.C. | Methodist | Mennonite | Lutheran |
| 6. Episcopal/Anglican | Other Denominations | Lutheran | Methodist |
| 7. Lutheran | Christian | Methodist | Mennonite |

[d] The appropriate test for this type of rank correlation is Spearman's co-efficient of rank-order correlation. However, as Spearman breaks down where growth over time is concerned, it is probably sufficient to calculate the denominational *average of the cumulative rank values* and juxtapose them against the rank values for the overall means. This produces the following results:

TABLE 6.3 (continued)
Four-Study Comparison of Library Book Volume Holdings: Congregational Libraries Only[a-f]

Rank values for overall means with average four-study scores shown on the right:

| Denomination | Overall Mean Rank | Average 4-Study Rank | Absolute Difference | |
|---|---|---|---|---|
| Baptist | 4 | 2 | 2 | The sum of the differences between the mean and the average rank scores = 14; over 14 denominations this works out to a mean difference of 1 each or 1/14 or 7.1%, very reasonable considering the problems and sample sizes. |
| Christian | 5 | 5 | 0 | |
| Churches of Christ | 13 | 13 | 0 | |
| Congregational | 11 | 11 | 0 | |
| Episcopal/Anglican | 9 | 9 | 0 | |
| Independent | 10 | 12 | 2 | The average 4-study rank = the sum of the ranks per denomination for each of the 4 studies and then divided by 4. e. g., for Jewish [see preceding page] the four ranks are 1 + 1 + 2 + 3 = 7/4 = 1st place as no other denomination totaled less than 7/4.) |
| Lutheran | 6 | 8 | 2 | |
| Mennonite | 4 | 7 | 3 | |
| Methodist | 7 | 6 | 1 | |
| Other Denominations | 2 | 3 | 1 | |
| Presbyterian | 8 | 8 | 0 | |
| U.C.C. | 12 | 10 | 2 | |
| Jewish | 1 | 1 | 0 | |
| Roman Catholic | 3 | 4 | 1 | |
| Sum: | | | 14 | |

*e*To sum up: the growth between 1978 and 1988 accounted for 32 percent of the variation for the two *ALD* studies. Another 7.1 percent (for the 4 studies together) is the acceptable variation accounted for by differences between the numerical means and the denominational rank scores. This variation actually helps to validate the mean scores; if they were really out, then the percentage variation would be well over 10 percent. However, it could also be thought of as variation arising from random sampling error or from bias of various types introduced by nonrepresentative samples, poor study design, etc. The total 39 percent mean variation (the average mean difference as a percentage of the overall mean) can now be reduced by 32 percent for two studies and 7.1 percent for four studies, leaving roughly 32 percent variation from the remaining two studies: White and Hannaford. The White study was carried out between 1971 and 1975, approximately ten years before the matching Hannaford CSLA study which was done in 1985–86. Is it therefore reasonable to assume a corresponding "growth" rate of another 30 percent? The total means for White and Hannaford are 1,667.2 and 2,824 volumes. Although there is little overlap between the two studies (certainly not 75 percent as with the two *ALD* studies) they were both taken from the same populations and the percentage change over time = 1,156.8/1,667.2 = 69%. This change value of 1,156.8 volumes divided by the total mean of 3,692 gives us a very interesting figure of 31 percent! It appears that the remaining variation is now explained in full. Statistically this solution is rather too perfect, as there is no variation left for errors due to definitional discrepancies, etc. However, this latter type of error ought to be purely random in its occurrence and *should* balance itself out naturally over a sample as large as 2,929 libraries, assuming that the definitional differences were not actually specified in the questionnaire (as it appears they were not in this case).

*f*We can conclude quite confidently from the above that the leading population denominations for volume holdings are generally as indicated by the overall means column: Jewish, Other Denominations, Roman Catholic, Baptist, Christian, Lutheran, and Methodist. The ten-year growth rate is roughly 30 percent and can be expected to be again roughly 30 percent for congregational libraries in the upcoming decade. The four samples all represent the sample base population, and if they do not represent it without bias, then at least the bias *tends in the same direction in all four cases*. This is true even for the 1978 *ALD* study in which missing data for volume holdings approximated 26 percent, and the White study, on which Other Denominations, a very strong group, was not represented at all on this variable.

TABLE 6.4
Denominational Breakdown for the White Popular Library Survey[a,b]

| Denomination and Area Lists | Number of Libraries on Mailing List | Percentage of Total Respondents | Percentage of Mailing List Responding |
|---|---|---|---|
| Baptist | 20,000 | 37.0 | 0.83 |
| Methodist | 14,547 | 27.0 | 1.4 |
| Presbyterian | 5,040 | 9.0 | 5.8 |
| Mormon | 4,000 | 7.0 | 0.025 |
| U.C.C. | 3,615 | 7.0 | – |
| Christian | 2,658 | 5.0 | 5.2 |
| Lutheran | 2,000 | 4.0 | 28.0 |
| Jewish | 442 | 0.8 | 19.7 |
| Canadian (BC and ON) | 425 | 0.8 | – |
| Evangelical | 370 | 0.7 | 0.4 |
| Roman Catholic | 300 | 0.6 | 22.0 |
| Pacific Northwest | 250 | 0.5 | – |
| Baltimore Libraries | 150 | 0.3 | – |
| Washington, DC Libraries | 125 | 0.2 | – |
| Friends | 102 | 0.2 | 28.4 |
| Total | 54,024 | 100.0 | |

[a]Additional mailing lists brought White's grand total representation of the entire population up to 58,358 libraries.
[b]The last column shows that portion of the 10,000-questionnaire mailing list that responded. Net return was 18.2 percent.

TABLE 6.5
Four Study Comparison of Representativeness by Denomination: Congregational Libraries Only (Source of Estimated Total Library Population Size is Table 6.4)[a,b]

| Denomination | Estimate of Population Size | % of Total | White | Hannaford | ALD-1978 | ALD-1988 | Total | % of All Libraries | Quality of Representation |
|---|---|---|---|---|---|---|---|---|---|
| Baptist | 20,000 | 41.00 | 165 | 26 | 83 | 71 | *345 | 10.0 | Moderate |
| Christian | 2,658 | 5.50 | – | 21 | 18 | 17 | 56 | 1.62 | Weak |
| Churches of Christ | N/A | – | 40 | – | 0 | 2 | 42 | 1.21 | Unknown |
| Congregational | N/A | – | 15 | 17 | – | – | 32 | 0.92 | Unknown and misleading, as combined with Other Denoms for ALD editions |
| Episcopal/Anglican | N/A | – | 118 | 43 | 41 | 33 | *235 | 6.80 | Unknown but acceptable |
| Independent | N/A | – | – | – | 3 | 1 | 4 | 0.12 | Unknown |
| Lutheran | 2,000 | 4.10 | 560 | 42 | 53 | 42 | *697 | 20.00 | Strong |
| Mennonite | N/A | – | 22 | – | 3 | 4 | 29 | 0.84 | Unknown |
| Methodist | 14,547 | 30.00 | 202 | 80 | 55 | 64 | *401 | 11.60 | Strong |
| Other Denominations | N/A | – | 159 | 57 | 86 | 71 | *373 | 10.80 | Unknown and possibly weak |
| Presbyterian | 5,040 | 10.40 | 290 | 85 | 115 | 97 | *587 | 17.00 | Strong |
| U.C.C. | 3,615 | 7.40 | 98 | 22 | 13 | 13 | 146 | 4.20 | Moderate to strong |
| Jewish | 442 | 0.90 | 87 | 6 | 150 | 170 | *413 | 11.90 | Strong |

TABLE 6.5 (continued)
Four Study Comparison of Representativeness by Denomination: Congregational Libraries Only (Source of Estimated Total Library Population Size is Table 6.4)[a,b]

| Denomination | Estimate of Population Size | % of Total | White | Hannaford | ALD-1978 | ALD-1988 | Total | % of All Libraries | Quality of Representation |
|---|---|---|---|---|---|---|---|---|---|
| Roman Catholic | 300 | 0.62 | 66 | 12 | 14 | 8 | 100 | 2.90 | Moderate to weak |
| Total | 48,602 | 100.00 | 1,822 | 411 | 634 | 593 | 3,460 | 100.00 | |

[a]*Total Estimated* congregational libraries = 25,800 (United States and Canada)

*Degree of overlap/duplication* within the lists of denominational estimates = 109 percent, i. e., ([54,024 − 25,800]/25,800)

[b]A satisfactory level of representativeness is found for the following denominations: Baptist, Episcopal, Lutheran, Methodist, Other Denominations, Presbyterian, United Church of Christ, and Jewish. It must be pointed out that this situation is based largely on the size of these denominations in sheer numbers, as the data relating to the *population parameters* for almost all denominations is so inadequate as to make reliable judgments (on the basis of this data) about representative sample size broken down by denomination next to impossible. However, it may be assumed statistically that all those denominations with more than thirty libraries per sample per denomination or type are reasonably, if not adequately, represented, i. e., Baptist, Episcopal/Anglican, Lutheran, Methodist, Other Denominations, Presbyterian, and Jewish. or seven groups out of thirteen—slightly more than one-half. Note that out of the four-sample total of 3,460 these seven denominations account for 3,051, or 88 percent of the whole, and as a group possess most of the essential attributes for sample reliability.

TABLE 6.6
1986 Church and Synagogue Library Association (Hannaford):
Congregational Library Study Responses

| Denomination | CSLA Membership | % | Number Responding | % | Percentage of Membership Responding |
|---|---|---|---|---|---|
| Baptist | 151 | 8 | 26 | 6 | 17 |
| Christian | 120 | 6 | 21 | 5 | 18 |
| Congregational | 65 | 3 | 17 | 4 | 26 |
| Episcopal/Anglican | 157 | 8 | 43 | 11 | 27 |
| Lutheran | 163 | 9 | 42 | 10 | 26 |
| Methodist | 403 | 21 | 80 | 20 | 20 |
| Other Denominations | 233 | 12 | 57 | 14 | 24 |
| Presbyterian | 428 | 23 | 85 | 21 | 20 |
| U.C.C. | 88 | 5 | 22 | 5 | 25 |
| Summary | | | | | |
| Jewish | 34 | 2 | 6 | 1 | 18 |
| Roman Catholic | 60 | 3 | 12 | 3 | 20 |
| All Protestant (mean) | 1,808 | 95 | 393 | 96 | (22) |
| Total (mean) | 1,902 | 100 | 411 | 100 | (22) |

**TABLE 6.7**

Comparison by Sample Size and Representativeness for Four Popular Library Studies, c.f., 1988 U.S. Religious Population Estimates and Canadian Census (1986)[a–f]

| Number of Libraries | White | | Hannaford | | ALD-1978 | | ALD-1988 | | 4-Sample Total | | % of 1988 Estimate Shown on Left |
|---|---|---|---|---|---|---|---|---|---|---|---|
| | Actual | % | Actual | % | Actual | % | Actual | % | Actual | % | |
| **CANADIAN LIBRARIES** | | | | | | | | | | | |
| College and university 150 8.5% | N/A | — | N/A | — | 74 | 59.20 | 120 | 64.50 | 194 | 59.00 | 129 |
| Seminary 20 1.13% | N/A | — | N/A | — | 8 | 6.40 | 25 | 13.40 | 33 | 10.00 | 165 |
| Convent and monastery 50 2.83% | N/A | — | N/A | — | 3 | 2.40 | 4 | 2.20 | 7 | 2.10 | 14 |
| Religious history and archive 10 0.56% | N/A | — | N/A | — | 10 | 8.00 | 9 | 4.80 | 19 | 5.80 | 190 |
| Organization administration office 20 1.13% | N/A | — | N/A | — | 3 | 2.40 | 7 | 3.80 | 10 | 3.00 | 50 |
| Popular: congregational 500 28% | 8 | 100 | 10 | 100 | 4 | 3.20 | 6 | 3.20 | 28 | 8.50 | 5.6 |
| Popular: parochial school 1,000 56.5% | N/A | — | N/A | — | 13 | 10.40 | 8 | 4.30 | 21 | 6.40 | 2.1 |

| | | | | | | | | | | | |
|---|---|---|---|---|---|---|---|---|---|---|---|
| Popular: public 20 1.13% | N/A | – | N/A | – | 10 | 8.00 | 7 | 3.80 | 17 | 5.20 | 85 |
| Canadian total 1,770 or 100% | 8 | 100 | 10 | 100 | 125 | 100 | 186 | 100 | 329 | 100 | 18.6 |
| U.S. Libraries | | | | | | | | | | | |
| College and university 1,500 3.9% | N/A | – | N/A | – | 909 | 46.93 | 882 | 46.70 | 1,791 | 29.65 | 119 |
| Seminary 110 0.28% | N/A | – | N/A | – | 225 | 11.61 | 206 | 10.90 | 431 | 7.10 | 392 |
| Convent and monastery 200 0.52% | N/A | – | N/A | – | 32 | 1.65 | 21 | 1.10 | 53 | 0.88 | 27 |
| Religious history and archive 20 0.5% | N/A | – | N/A | – | 67 | 3.46 | 77 | 4.10 | 144 | 2.40 | 720 |
| Organization administration office 100 0.26% | N/A | – | N/A | – | 44 | 2.30 | 81 | 4.30 | 125 | 2.10 | 125 |
| Popular: congregational 25,300 66% | 1,814 | 100 | 401 | 100 | 630 | 32.50 | 587 | 31.10 | 3,432 | 56.80 | 13.6 |
| parochial school 11,200 29% | N/A | – | N/A | – | 14 | 0.72 | 16 | 0.85 | 30 | 0.50 | 0.27 |
| public 40 0.1% | N/A | – | N/A | – | 16 | 0.83 | 18 | 0.95 | 34 | 0.56 | 85 |

TABLE 6.7 (continued)
Comparison by Sample Size and Representativeness for 4 Popular Library Studies, CF, 1988 U.S. Religious Population Estimates and Canadian Census (1986)[a–f]

| Number of Libraries | White Actual | % | Hannaford Actual | % | ALD-1978 Actual | % | ALD-1988 Actual | % | 4-Sample Total Actual | % | % of 1988 Estimate Shown on Left |
|---|---|---|---|---|---|---|---|---|---|---|---|
| U.S. total 38,470 or 100% | 1,814 | 100 | 401 | 100 | 1,937 | 100 | 1,888 | 100 | 6,040 | 100 | 15.7 |
| Grand total 40,240 | 1,822 | – | 411 | – | 2,062 | – | 2,074 | – | 6,369 | – | 15.8 |

[a]National population data taken from *Whittaker's Almanac 1988*.

[b]*Left-hand* column material taken from *table 6.1: 1988 Estimate of the Number of North American Religious and Nonreligious Libraries.*

[c]Christian Science Reading Rooms and Church of Jesus Christ of Latter-day Saints libraries have been omitted, as these two groups were almost entirely unrepresented by the four samples.

[d]N/A stands here for Not Applicable.

[e]Whereas overrepresentation presents no problem statistically, underrepresentation can prove critical.

[f]Note that with regard to the United States, sample size is inadequate for *public libraries* due to the limited number of cases and for convent/monastery and parochial school libraries for the above reason *and* because of underrepresentation.

For *Canada* the situation is much more serious: only colleges and universities (as a combined group of junior colleges, senior colleges, and universities) and seminaries can be considered as both adequately represented *and* as having a sufficient number of cases each. For seminaries it needs to be pointed out that a 1978 and 1988 total of thirty-three libraries is barely sufficient to ensure representativeness.

In general, a subgroup magnitude of fifty to two hundred cases is considered adequate regardless of the representation percentage. However, even for very large populations a representative sample of *at least 10 percent* is considered desirable. Even the 1988 *ALD* Canadian sample of 186 cases, or 9.9 percent of the U.S. total of 1,888 for *ALD* 1988, just barely meets this minimum and is statistically unbalanced (skewed) compared with the U.S. figures; colleges and universities are overrepresented whereas popular: congregational libraries are badly underrepresented (3.2 percent vs. 31.1 percent). The comparison of U.S.A. versus Canada in the final column is even more markedly unbalanced, partly as a result of the small number of Canadian libraries, partly through inadequacies in the estimated population statistics (from tables 6.1 and 6.5), and partly through sampling bias in all four studies.

The one redeeming element in this table is that both the United States and Canada appear to be represented to the extent of 16 percent to 19 percent of their estimated library populations (15.7 percent for the U.S.A. and 18.6 percent for Canada). This congruence may be a coincidence, given the above mentioned sources of error. However, it is unlikely as aggregated figures derived for totals are generally more reliable than are their constituent substatistics. The estimated totals for the United States and Canada are likely to be quite reliable. Therefore, it can be supposed that whereas Canada's 329 religious libraries do not compare favorably with the 6,040 libraries for the United States (5.4 percent), if we look at them from the standpoint of per capita population, they are not so bad, in fact almost even, in terms of their respective estimated library populations. If we do look at per capital population, we find the following library density estimates:

| ---------Canada--------- | | | ---------------United States--------------- | | |
|---|---|---|---|---|---|
| Population | Estimated Libraries | Sampled Libraries | Population | Estimated Libraries | Sampled Libraries |
| 25,409,000 | 1,770 | 329 | 236,500,000 | 38,470 | 6,040 |

Density Canada: .0697 libraries per 1,000 persons and a sample of .013 libraries per 1,000 persons

Density U.S.A.: .163 libraries per 1,000 persons and a sample of .026 libraries per 1,000 persons

Note from this that the United States has considerably more estimated libraries per 1,000 persons than does Canada: $(.163 - .0697)/.0697 = .0933$ or 134 percent as many. Working on the basis of that statistic then, Canada does not do so badly, as the sample libraries for the U.S.A. cf. Canada are actually only 100 percent in excess relative to the per capital population bases, $(.026 - .013)/.013 = 100$ percent! In any case, Canada is underrepresented, although possibly not as badly as might have been expected.

As the United States and Canada are similar peoples, one would assume that the Canadian library situation would be similar to that for the United States. However, scholarship concerning Canadian religious libraries is rather sparse. It must be assumed, therefore, that Canadian religious library density *may not be similar* to that of the United States and/or that the estimated statistics for Canadian libraries are poorer than those for the United States and/or that the Canadian library scene is inadequately represented by our four studies, as appears to be the case. See John S. Moir (Knox College), "Canadian Religious Historiography: An Overview," American Theological Library Association *Proceedings* (Winter 1991): 101. As shown in the preceding paragraph, it appears from our statistics that Canada possesses fewer religious libraries per capita by more than one half.

TABLE 6.8
Population Size Comparison: From Canadian Census (1986) and U.S. Population Estimates (1988)
Source: *Whittaker's Almanac, 1988* (London: Whittaker)[a-e]

| | Population in 000s | Percentage of Total | White | Hannaford | ALD-1978 | ALD-1988 | Total 4 Studies | Percentage of Total 4 Studies | See Footnote[a] |
|---|---|---|---|---|---|---|---|---|---|
| **CANADA** | | | | | | | | | |
| Province | | | | | | | | | |
| Alberta | 2,366 | 9 | 0 | 1 | 0 | 2 | 3 | 11 | +1.7 |
| British Columbia | 2,883 | 11 | 2 | 1 | 0 | 0 | 3 | 11 | −0.3 |
| Manitoba | 1,063 | 4 | 0 | 1 | 0 | 0 | 1 | 4 | −0.4 |
| New Brunswick | 709 | 3 | 0 | 0 | 0 | 0 | 0 | | −3.0 |
| Newfoundland | 568 | 2 | 0 | 0 | 0 | 0 | 0 | | −2.0 |
| Nova Scotia | 973 | 4 | 0 | 0 | 0 | 0 | 0 | | −4.0 |
| Ontario | 9,102 | 36 | 6 | 7 | 3 | 4 | 20 | 71 | +35.4 |
| Prince Edward Island | 127 | 0 | 0 | 0 | 0 | 0 | 0 | | 0 |
| Quebec | 6,532 | 26 | 0 | 0 | 0 | 0 | 0 | | −26.0 |
| Saskatchewan | 1,010 | 4 | 0 | 0 | 1 | 0 | 1 | 4 | −0.4 |
| Yukon | 24 | 0 | 0 | 0 | 0 | 0 | 0 | | 0 |
| Northwest Territories | 52 | 0 | 0 | 0 | 0 | 0 | 0 | | 0 |
| Total | 25,409 | 100 | 8 | 10 | 4 | 6 | 28 | 100 | |
| **UNITED STATES** | | | | | | | | | |
| State | | | | | | | | | |
| Alabama | 3,989 | 1.7 | 10 | 2 | 13 | 10 | 35 | 1 | −0.70 |
| Alaska | 505 | 0.2 | 1 | 0 | 1 | 0 | 2 | 0 | −0.14 |

| | | | | | | | | | |
|---|---|---|---|---|---|---|---|---|---|
| Arizona | 3,072 | 1.3 | 12 | 3 | 7 | 6 | 28 | 1 | −0.48 |
| Arkansas | 2,346 | 1.0 | 4 | 1 | 3 | 1 | 9 | 0 | −0.74 |
| California | 25,795 | 10.9 | 91 | 22 | 37 | 36 | 186 | 5 | −5.48 |
| Colorado | 3,190 | 1.3 | 14 | 5 | 7 | 6 | 32 | 1 | −0.37 |
| Connecticut | 3,155 | 1.3 | 26 | 14 | 16 | 11 | 67 | 2 | +0.65 |
| Delaware | 614 | 0.3 | 18 | 3 | 3 | 2 | 26 | 1 | +0.46 |
| Florida | 11,050 | 4.7 | 20 | 18 | 18 | 24 | 80 | 2 | −2.37 |
| Georgia | 5,842 | 2.5 | 12 | 11 | 11 | 10 | 44 | 1 | −1.22 |
| Hawaii | 1,037 | 0.4 | 4 | 0 | 6 | 2 | 12 | 0 | −0.05 |
| Idaho | 999 | 0.4 | 2 | 0 | 0 | 0 | 2 | 0 | −0.34 |
| Illinois | 11,522 | 4.9 | 83 | 16 | 24 | 23 | 146 | 4 | −0.65 |
| Indiana | 5,492 | 2.3 | 30 | 15 | 18 | 17 | 80 | 2 | +0.03 |
| Iowa | 2,903 | 1.2 | 32 | 7 | 1 | 4 | 44 | 1 | +0.10 |
| Kansas | 2,440 | 1.0 | 13 | 7 | 2 | 2 | 24 | 1 | −0.30 |
| Kentucky | 3,720 | 1.6 | 11 | 0 | 7 | 8 | 25 | 1 | −0.84 |
| Louisiana | 4,461 | 1.9 | 32 | 1 | 9 | 5 | 47 | 1 | −0.53 |
| Maine | 1,156 | 0.5 | 3 | 2 | 1 | 0 | 6 | 0 | −0.33 |
| Maryland | 4,349 | 1.8 | 155 | 13 | 15 | 15 | 198 | 6 | +4.00 |
| Massachusetts | 5,798 | 2.5 | 29 | 4 | 12 | 14 | 59 | 2 | −0.80 |
| Michigan | 9,058 | 3.8 | 60 | 23 | 45 | 34 | 162 | 5 | +0.90 |
| Minnesota | 4,163 | 1.8 | 136 | 7 | 20 | 20 | 183 | 5 | +3.50 |
| Mississippi | 2,598 | 1.1 | 2 | 0 | 5 | 5 | 12 | 0 | −0.75 |
| Missouri | 5,001 | 2.1 | 21 | 11 | 16 | 17 | 65 | 2 | −0.20 |
| Montana | 823 | 0.3 | 6 | 0 | 1 | 0 | 7 | 0 | −0.10 |
| Nebraska | 1,605 | 0.7 | 19 | 3 | 4 | 5 | 31 | 1 | +0.20 |
| Nevada | 917 | 0.4 | 2 | 0 | 2 | 2 | 6 | 0 | −0.23 |
| New Hampshire | 978 | 0.4 | 3 | 0 | 2 | 2 | 7 | 0 | −0.20 |
| New Jersey | 7,517 | 3.2 | 58 | 9 | 26 | 24 | 117 | 3 | +0.20 |
| New Mexico | 1,426 | 0.6 | 100 | 15 | 10 | 15 | 140 | 4 | +3.50 |

TABLE 6.8 (continued)
Population Size Comparison: From Canadian Census (1986) and U.S. Population Estimates (1988)
Source: *Whittaker's Almanac, 1988* (London: Whittaker)[a-e]

| | Population in 000s | Percentage of Total | White | Hannaford | ALD-1978 | ALD-1988 | Total 4 Studies | Percentage of Total 4 Studies | See Footnote[a] |
|---|---|---|---|---|---|---|---|---|---|
| District of Columbia | 625 | 0.3 | 20 | 5 | 14 | 12 | 51 | 1 | +1.19 |
| New York | 17,746 | 7.5 | 56 | 10 | 35 | 41 | 142 | 4 | -3.36 |
| North Carolina | 6,166 | 2.6 | 28 | 7 | 12 | 12 | 59 | 2 | -0.88 |
| North Dakota | 687 | 0.3 | 14 | 0 | 3 | 2 | 19 | 1 | +0.25 |
| Ohio | 10,740 | 4.5 | 89 | 47 | 49 | 37 | 222 | 6 | +1.97 |
| Oklahoma | 3,310 | 1.4 | 9 | 2 | 4 | 5 | 20 | 1 | -0.82 |
| Oregon | 2,676 | 1.1 | 53 | 8 | 4 | 1 | 66 | 2 | +0.80 |
| Pennsylvania | 11,887 | 5.0 | 206 | 37 | 62 | 51 | 356 | 10 | +5.40 |
| Rhode Island | 962 | 0.4 | 6 | 0 | 3 | 2 | 11 | 0 | -0.08 |
| South Carolina | 3,302 | 1.4 | 4 | 1 | 2 | 1 | 8 | 0 | -1.17 |
| South Dakota | 705 | 0.3 | 8 | 1 | 4 | 4 | 17 | 1 | +0.20 |
| Tennessee | 4,726 | 2.0 | 18 | 4 | 8 | 9 | 39 | 1 | -0.86 |
| Texas | 16,083 | 6.8 | 56 | 41 | 43 | 48 | 188 | 5 | -1.32 |
| Utah | 1,623 | 0.7 | 1 | 0 | 1 | 1 | 3 | 0 | -0.61 |
| Vermont | 530 | 0.2 | 1 | 6 | 1 | 1 | 3 | 0 | -0.11 |
| Virginia | 5,636 | 2.4 | 32 | 12 | 11 | 9 | 64 | 2 | -0.54 |
| Washington | 4,349 | 1.8 | 107 | 5 | 8 | 6 | 126 | 4 | +1.87 |
| West Virginia | 1,951 | 0.8 | 7 | 4 | 2 | 3 | 16 | 0 | -0.34 |
| Wisconsin | 4,762 | 2.0 | 86 | 4 | 22 | 22 | 134 | 4 | +1.90 |
| Wyoming | 513 | 0.2 | 0 | 1 | 0 | 0 | 1 | 0 | -0.17 |

| | | | | | | | | | |
|---|---|---|---|---|---|---|---|---|---|
| Not Reported | 236,500 | 100 | 3 | 0 | 0 | 0 | 3 | 0 | +0.09 |
| Total | 3,451 | | 1,814 | 401 | 630 | 587 | 3,432 | 100 | +0.03 |
| Puerto Rico | | 100 | 1 | 0 | 0 | 0 | 1 | 0 | |

a Deviation from state/province population percentage estimate based on provincial/state population as a percentage of total national population and the four-study total as a percentage of the total national sample of 3,432.

b A regional analysis would have an intensified smoothing effect over the four studies. However, as denominational differences appear more salient by state than by region, the state-by-state analysis is considered equally important.

c Total number of States/Provinces overrepresented = 22 (statistically unimportant)
underrepresented = 40

d Total number of cases of serious underrepresentation (23 percent of total sample required) = 30—see column 2; compare column 8. Of these, fifteen are significantly underrepresented.
Marginal cases = 3

e List of states/provinces seriously underrepresented for congregational libraries
NB, NF, NS, PQ, SK, AL, AK, AZ, AR, CA, FL, GA, ID, KS, KY, ME, MA, MS, MT, NV, NH, NY, NC, OK, SC, TN, UT, VT, WV, WY
Marginally underrepresented
Virginia, Louisiana, Colorado
(Of the above-mentioned states fifteen are poorly represented, but not significantly so; they still contain a considerable number of libraries each, e.g., California with 186 libraries)

TABLE 6.9

Comparison of Four Groups According to Regional Population Estimates 1988: Congregational Libraries Only[a,b]

| | Percent of All North American Population | White | | Hannaford | | ALD-1978 | | ALD-1988 | | 4-Group Total | | Deviation from Population Percentage |
|---|---|---|---|---|---|---|---|---|---|---|---|---|
| | | Actual | % | Actual | % | Actual | % | Actual | % | Actual | % | |
| Northeast | 5 | 68 | 4 | 20 | 5 | 35 | 6 | 30 | 5 | 153 | 4 | -0.4 |
| Middle Atlantic | 16 | 513 | 28 | 77 | 19 | 155 | 24 | 145 | 25 | 890 | 26 | +9.4 |
| Southeast | 19 | 144 | 8 | 59 | 14 | 89 | 14 | 91 | 15 | 383 | 11 | -7.6 |
| Southwest | 12 | 213 | 12 | 63 | 15 | 76 | 12 | 80 | 14 | 432 | 13 | +0.8 |
| West | 14 | 260 | 14 | 35 | 9 | 58 | 9 | 47 | 8 | 400 | 12 | -2.3 |
| Rocky Mountains | 2 | 21 | 1 | 6 | 2 | 9 | 1 | 7 | 1 | 43 | 1 | -1.1 |
| Middle West | 23 | 591 | 33 | 141 | 34 | 208 | 33 | 187 | 32 | 1,127 | 33 | +10.0 |
| Canada | 10 | 8 | 1 | 10 | 2 | 4 | 1 | 6 | 1 | 28 | 1 | -8.9 |
| Unknown or Other | | 4 | | | | | | | | 4 | 0 | |
| Total | 100 | 1,822 | 100 | 411 | 100 | 634 | 100 | 593 | 100 | 3,460 | 100 | |

[a]*Regional representation according to population distribution* is satisfactory for all regions except Rocky Mountains, on the basis of the small sample size and slight underrepresentation, and Canada for the same two reasons. The case for Canada, however, is severe for congregational-type libraries, as has already been remarked on table 6.8 (Canada has a total of only twenty-eight libraries across the four studies).

[b]Otherwise, the sampling vs. population balance is remarkably even. The variation between the two values as represented by the final column never exceeds 10 percent! Ironically, the largest deviation is on the positive side and is for Middle Atlantic. This is an example of how regionally aggregating the individual state/province data tends to smooth subgroup deviations. It also, however, illustrates that the sampling for the four studies nearly adequately covers all of the regional areas of the United States, if not of Canada.

List of compiled regional populations and component states provinces (covers all four library studies):

| Region | States/Provinces | Population |
|---|---|---|
| Northeast | CT, MA, ME, NH, RI, VT | 12,579,000 (4.8%) |
| Middle Atlantic | DC, DE, MD, NJ, NY, PA | 42,738,000 (16.3%) |
| Southeast | AL, FL, GA, KY, MS, NC, SC, TN, VA, WV | 48,980,000 (18.7%) |
| Southwest | AR, AZ, LA, NM, OK, TX | 30,698,000 (11.7%) |
| West | AK, CA, HI, ID, NV, OR, WA | 36,278,000 (13.9%) |
| Rocky Mountains | CO, MT, UT, WY (not in 1978 and 1988 databases) | 6,419,000 (2.3%) |
| Middle West | IA, IL, IN, KS, MI, MN, MO, ND, OH, NE, SD, WI | 59,078,000 (22.6%) |
| Canada, other | BC, AB, MB, NB, NF, NS, ON, PQ, SK, PE (not in 1978 and 1988 databases) | 25,409,000 (9.7%) |

*Puerto Rico* was not added into any of the eight regions as it contributed only one library to the White sample.

*Total population* of United States plus Canada (from 1988 estimates) = 261,909,000

Total Number of States and Provinces = 60

TABLE 6.10

Popular Library Founding Dates for Four Studies: Congregational
Libraries Only

| Years | White 1976 | | ALD 1978 | | Hannaford 1986 | | ALD-1988 | |
|---|---|---|---|---|---|---|---|---|
| | Number | Percentage | Number | Percentage | Number | Percentage | Number | Percentage |
| 0–1800 | 0 | 0 | 0 | 0.0 | 0 | 0 | 0 | 0.0 |
| 1801–1820 | 0 | 0 | 1 | 0.1 | 0 | 0 | 1 | 0.17 |
| 1821–1840 | 0 | 0 | 1 | 0.1 | 1 | 0.25 | 1 | 0.17 |
| 1841–1860 | 0 | 0 | 1 | 0.1 | 1 | 0.25 | 1 | 0.17 |
| 1861–1880 | 0 | 0 | 6 | 1.0 | 0 | 0 | 4 | 0.8 |
| 1881–1900 | 6 | 0 | 4 | 1.0 | 1 | 0.25 | 7 | 1.2 |
| 1901–1920 | 13 | 1 | 8 | 1.2 | 4 | 1 | 8 | 1.3 |
| 1921–1940 | 54 | 3 | 25 | 4.0 | 9 | 2.2 | 29 | 4.9 |
| 1941–1960 | 512 | 28 | 166 | 26.0 | 87 | 21 | 179 | 30.2 |
| 1961–1970 | 588 | 32 | 60 | 9.5 | 100 | 24 | 81 | 13.7 |
| 1971–1980 | 193 | 11 | 11 | 2.0 | 116 | 28 | 25 | 4.2 |
| 1981–1990 | 0 | 0 | 1 | 0.1 | 57 | 14 | 3 | 0.51 |
| No response | 456 | 25 | 350 | 55.0 | 35 | 9 | 254 | 43.0 |
| Total | 1,822 | 100 | 634 | 100.0 | 411 | 100 | 593 | 100.0 |
| Median age | 19 | | 39 | | 17.5 | | 38 | |
| | | | | 1976: 19 | 1990: 39 | | 1985: 17.5 | 1990: 38 |
| Median year | | | | 1957 | 1949 | | 1968 | 1950 |
| Mean age | | | | 17.6 | 44 | | 20 | 41 |
| Mean age if base year = 1990 | | | | 31.5 | 46 | | 24.5 | 43 |
| Mean age for all four studies = 33.2 years | | | | | | | | |

TABLE 6.11

Comparison of Library Ages for Four Popular Library Data Samples:
White, Hannaford, *ALD* 1978 and *ALD* 1988—All Library Types[a-c]

| Age in Years | White | % | Hannaford | % | ALD-1978 | % | ALD-1988 | % | Total 4 Samples | % |
|---|---|---|---|---|---|---|---|---|---|---|
| 1–10 | 193 | 11 | 117 | 28.5 | 1 | 0 | 9 | 0 | 320 | 5 |
| 11–20 | 588 | 32 | 110 | 26.8 | 37 | 2 | 87 | 4 | 822 | 13 |
| 21–30 | 392 | 22 | 94 | 23 | 183 | 9 | 210 | 10 | 879 | 14 |
| 31–50 | 146 | 8 | 43 | 10.5 | 435 | 21 | 422 | 20 | 1,046 | 16 |
| 51–70 | 37 | 2 | 6 | 1.5 | 236 | 11 | 233 | 11 | 512 | 8 |
| 71–90 | 7 | 0 | 3 | 0.75 | 171 | 8 | 163 | 8 | 344 | 5 |
| 91–110 | 3 | 0 | 1 | 0.25 | 180 | 9 | 183 | 9 | 367 | 6 |
| 111–130 | 0 | 0 | 0 | 0 | 124 | 6 | 126 | 6 | 250 | 4 |
| 131–150 | 0 | 0 | 1 | 0.25 | 126 | 6 | 120 | 6 | 247 | 4 |
| 151–170 | 0 | 0 | 1 | 0.25 | 49 | 2 | 59 | 3 | 109 | 2 |
| 171–190 | 0 | 0 | 0 | 0 | 16 | 1 | 17 | 1 | 33 | 1 |
| 191+ | 0 | 0 | 0 | 0 | 13 | 1 | 16 | 1 | 29 | 0 |
| No response | 456 | 25 | 35 | 8.5 | 491 | 24 | 429 | 21 | 1,411 | 22 |
| Total | 1,822 | 100 | 411 | 100 | 2,062 | 100 | 2,074 | 100 | 6,369 | 100 |
| Median age (estimated) | 19.33 | | 17.45 | | 61.98 | | 59.11 | | 39.76 | |

[a]Some rearrangement of categories was necessary to permit the four samples to be fit together. Also, there is some significant percentage of overlap among the four groups. This is particularly the case for the >75 percent overlap between the two *ALD* samples.
[b]The final percentage column indicates, as might be expected, that the age distribution is much smoother for the four groups together than for any of the component groups, i.e., the most recently established libraries make up only 5 percent of the overall group of 6,369 libraries, with the group between eleven and twenty years absorbing approximately 13 percent of the total sample. This proportion then increases to 16 percent for the 31- to 50-year old group, which is also the *modal* group. Over fifty years in operation, the number of libraries slowly decreases to approximately 190 years of age. The obvious problem with doing an accurate comparison of library ages is that the four studies were done at four different times. Therefore, should all the libraries have been surveyed at one benchmark date, e.g., 1980, the results would have been a little different since problems of slight incomparability would be eliminated. It is not to be supposed, however, that the difference would have been statistically significant.
[c]Median ages have been estimated here to illustrate the effect of combining all-congregational with mixed-type samples. Note that the two *ALD* studies vary by less than three years in median age even though their *component types* vary somewhat in terms of sample proportions. The two congregational studies vary even less, however, by less than two years despite categorizational differences in recording ages. This result suggests that the White and Hannaford libraries both belong to the same population and that these two samples, although taken at different times, appear to be unbiased or are biased in the same direction (we *expect* the *ALD* libraries to show the same median ages as the sample overlap between them is so high). It is reasonable for all four studies to expect the bias to work in terms of greater age, as it is the better established libraries that are best equipped and most likely to answer questionnaires.

TABLE 6.12
1978 and 1988 *American Library Directory* Oldest Library for Each
Denomination[a]

| Denomination | Library | Founding Year |
|---|---|---|
| Baptist | First Baptist Church, Dallas, TX | 1888 |
| | First Baptist Church, Albuquerque, NM | 1928 |
| | First Baptist Church, San Antonio, TX | 1928 |
| Christian | Douglass Boulevard Christian Church, | |
| | Louisville, KY | 1928 |
| Churches of Christ | University Church of Christ, Murray, KY | 1948 |
| Congregational | First Congregational Church, Stamford, CT | 1938 |
| | Union Congregational Church, Upper Montclair, NJ | 1938 |
| | First Congregational Church, Auburn, MA | 1938 |
| | First Congregational Church, St. Joseph, MI | 1938 |
| | Plymouth Congregational Church, Seattle, WA | 1938 |
| Episcopal/Anglican | Church of the Redeemer, Andalusia, PA | 1888 |
| | Episcopal Church Center, Burlington, VT | 1888 |
| | Mount Union College, Columbus, OH | 1908 |
| Independent | No information available | |
| Lutheran | Hope Lutheran Church, Milwaukee, WI | 1858 |
| | Oak Grove Lutheran Church, Richfield, MN | 1898 |
| | First Lutheran Church, Sioux Falls, SD | 1898 |
| Mennonite | Zion Mennonite Church, Souderton, PA | 1948 |
| Methodist | Mount Vernon Place United Methodist | |
| | Church, Washington, DC | 1848 |
| | First United Methodist Church, Alhambra, CA | 1928 |
| | Christ Church United Methodist Church, | |
| | Columbus, OH | 1928 |
| | First United Methodist Church, Tulsa, OK | 1928 |
| Other Denominations | Massachusetts New-Church Union | |
| | Swedenborgian, Boston, MA | 1868 |
| | Heritage Christian Reformed Church, Kalamazoo, MI | 1868 |
| Presbyterian | Westminster Church, Detroit, MI | 1908 |
| United Church of | St. John Evangelical United Church of Christ, | 1948 |
| Christ | Collinsville, IL | |
| | St. Paul's United Church of Christ, Evansville, IN | 1948 |
| | Trinity United Church of Christ, St. Louis, MO | 1948 |
| | United Church of Christ Evangelical | |
| | and Reformed, Vermilion, OH | 1948 |
| Jewish | Congregation Rodeph Shalom, Philadelphia, PA | 1808 |
| | Congregation Mishkan Israel, Hamden, CT | 1828 |
| Roman Catholic | St. Ignatius Loyola Church, New York, NY | 1858 |
| | Newman Hall Holy Spirit Parish, Berkeley, CA | 1898 |

[a]All ages are approximate due to the use of category mid-points and estimates.

TABLE 6.13
The Sixty-One Oldest Congregational Libraries in Four Studies[a]

| Library | Founding Date |
|---|---|
| 1. Congregation Rodeph Shalom, Philadelphia, PA | 1808 |
| 2. Trinity Church, Boston, MA | 1827 |
| 3. Congregation Mishkan Israel, Hamden, CT | 1828 |
| 4. Mount Vernon Place United Methodist Church, Washington, DC | 1848 |
| 5. The Temple, Cleveland, OH | 1850 |
| 6. Massachusetts New-Church Union Swedenborgian, Boston, MA | 1868 |
| 7. Temple Beth El, Birmingham, MI | 1868 |
| 8. Heritage Christian Reformed Church, Kalamazoo, MI | 1868 |
| 9. St. Ignatius Loyola Church, New York, NY | 1868 |
| 10. Temple-Congregational Shomer Emunim, Sylvania, OH | 1868 |
| 11. Hope Lutheran Church, Milwaukee, WI | 1868 |
| 12. Church of the Redeemer, Andalusia, PA | 1882 |
| 13. First Congregational Church, Kalamazoo, MI | 1883 |
| 14. Unitarian-Universalist Church, Binghampton, NY | 1888 |
| 15. Temple Beth-El Congregation, Providence, RI | 1888 |
| 16. First Baptist Church, Dallas, TX | 1888 |
| 17. Church of Jesus Christ of Latter-day Saints, Salt Lake City, UT | 1888 |
| 18. Episcopal Church Center, Burlington, VT | 1888 |
| 19. Brooklyn Friends Meeting, Brooklyn, NY | 1890 |
| 20. Byberry Friends Meeting, Philadelphia, PA | 1894 |
| 21. First Church of Christ, Congregational, New Britain, CT | 1900 |
| 22. Woodbrook Baptist Church, Baltimore, MD | 1900 |
| 23. St. Luke's Episcopal Church, Atlanta, GA | 1904 |
| 24. Newman Hall Holy Spirit Parish, Berkeley, CA | 1908 |
| 25. Westminster Church, Detroit, MI | 1908 |
| 26. Immanuel Reformed Church, Grand Rapids, MI | 1908 |
| 27. Pilgrim Congregational Church, Duluth, MN | 1908 |
| 28. Oak Grove Lutheran Church, Richfield, MN | 1908 |
| 29. Trinity Episcopal Church, Columbus, OH | 1908 |
| 30. First Lutheran Church, Sioux Falls, SD | 1908 |
| 31. First United Methodist Church, Pasadena, CA | 1911 |
| 32. First Presbyterian Church, Charlotte, NC | 1912 |
| 33. North and Southampton Reformed Church, Churchville, PA | 1915 |
| 34. Third Reformed Church, Kalamazoo, MI | 1916 |
| 35. Maple Grove Mennonite Church, New Wilmington, PA | 1920 |
| 36. First Centenary United Methodist Church, Chattanooga, TN | 1921 |
| 37. Episcopal Diocese of Texas, Houston, TX | 1921 |
| 38. Washington Street United Methodist Church, Tiffin, OH | 1922 |
| 39. University Presbyterian Church, Seattle, WA | 1923 |
| 40. College Lutheran Church, Tacoma, WA | 1923 |
| 41. Church of Jesus Christ of Latter-day Saints, Mesa, AZ | 1928 |

TABLE 6.13 (continued)
The Sixty-One Oldest Congregational Libraries in Four Studies[a]

| Library | Founding Date |
| --- | --- |
| 42. First United Methodist Church, Alhambra, CA | 1928 |
| 43. First Presbyterian Church, San Diego, CA | 1928 |
| 44. Friends Meeting, Washington, DC | 1928 |
| 45. Second Presbyterian Church, Bloomington, IL | 1928 |
| 46. Christ Church Cathedral, Indianapolis, IN | 1928 |
| 47. Douglass Boulevard Christian Church, Louisville, KY | 1928 |
| 48. St. Thomas Episcopal Church, Battle Creek, MI | 1928 |
| 49. First Baptist Church, Albuquerque, NM | 1928 |
| 50. First Presbyterian Church, Greensboro, NC | 1928 |
| 51. Summit United Methodist Church, Columbus, OH | 1928 |
| 52. Westminster Presbyterian Church, Oklahoma City, OK | 1928 |
| 53. First United Methodist Church, Tulsa, OK | 1928 |
| 54. First Baptist Church, San Antonio, TX | 1928 |
| 55. First Presbyterian Church, Yakima, WA | 1928 |
| 56. Old St. Mary's Church, San Francisco, CA | 1930 |
| 57. First Christian Church, Honolulu, HI | 1930 |
| 58. Park Congregational Church, Norwich, CT | 1931 |
| 59. Hyde Park Baptist Church, Austin, TX | 1931 |
| 60. Catholic Community of St. Luke, Houston, TX | 1931 |
| 61. St. Martin's Lutheran Church, Austin, TX | 1934 |

[a]This information was taken from the 1976 White survey, the 1978 *American Library Directory* survey, the 1986 Hannaford survey, and the 1988 *American Library Directory* survey. Some dates may be adjusted to the nearest decade.

TABLE 6.14

Comparison of Library Ages for Four Data Samples: White, Hannaford, *ALD*-1978 and *ALD*-1988: Congregational Libraries Only[a–d]

| Age in Years | White | % | Hannaford | % | ALD-1978 | % | ALD-1988 | % | Total for 4 Samples | % |
|---|---|---|---|---|---|---|---|---|---|---|
| 1–10 | 193 | 11 | 117 | 29 | 1 | 0 | 3 | 1 | 314 | 9 |
| 11–20 | 588 | 32 | 110 | 27 | 11 | 2 | 25 | 4 | 734 | 21 |
| 21–30 | 392 | 22 | 94 | 23 | 60 | 10 | 81 | 14 | 627 | 18 |
| 31–50 | 146 | 8 | 43 | 10 | 166 | 26 | 179 | 30 | 534 | 15 |
| 51–70 | 37 | 2 | 6 | 1 | 25 | 4 | 29 | 5 | 97 | 3 |
| 71–90 | 7 | 0 | 3 | 1 | 8 | 1 | 8 | 1 | 26 | 1 |
| 91–110 | 3 | 0 | 1 | 0 | 4 | 1 | 7 | 1 | 15 | 1 |
| 111–130 | 0 | 0 | 0 | 0 | 6 | 1 | 4 | 1 | 10 | 0 |
| 131–150 | 0 | 0 | 1 | 0 | 1 | 0 | 1 | 0 | 3 | 0 |
| 151–170 | 0 | 0 | 1 | 0 | 1 | 0 | 1 | 0 | 3 | 0 |
| 171–190 | 0 | 0 | 0 | 0 | 1 | 0 | 1 | 0 | 2 | 0 |
| 191+ | 0 | 0 | 0 | 0 | 0 | 0 | 0 | 0 | 0 | 0 |
| No response | 456 | 25 | 35 | 9 | 350 | 55 | 254 | 43 | 1,095 | 32 |
| Total | 1,822 | 100 | 411 | 100 | 634 | 100 | 593 | 100 | 3,460 | 100 |
| Median age (estimated) | 19 | | 17 | | 39 | | 38 | | 23 | |

[a] Some rearrangement of categories was necessary to permit the four samples to be fitted together. Also, there is a significant percentage of overlap among the four groups. This is particularly the case for the >75 percent overlap between the two *ALD* samples.

[b] The final percentage column indicates, as might be expected, that the age distribution is much smoother for the four groups together than for any of the component groups both because the sample size is correspondingly larger and because fluctuations in the curves for each of the four component subparts occur in somewhat different decades. For example, the modes for the four groups do not always coincide, although they are reasonably close.

[c] Note also for all congregational libraries that the median age is between fifteen and forty years, as opposed to thirty-one to fifty years for the four studies combined, including scholarly, parochial, and public libraries.

[d] The median ages for all four groups of congregational libraries illustrate that (1) White and Hannaford samples are taken from the same population and (2) the *ALD* samples are taken from an older, much better established *subsample* of this same population. White and Hannaford medians differ by less than two years. The *ALD* edition samples also differ by less than two years, but the difference between the two sets is extreme—set two is almost exactly twice as old as set one. We must conclude that the bias in the second set is proportionately pronounced and expect to find it in other variables than age also. We must also expect, however, that the exact degree of *ALD* bias will be difficult to estimate.

TABLE 6.15
Library Age Comparison for Four Studies: United States Versus Canada—Congregational Libraries Only[a-d]

| Approximate Age in Years at Time of Study | White | | Hannaford | | ALD-1978 | | ALD-1988 | | All U.S.A. | | All Canada | | % Difference |
|---|---|---|---|---|---|---|---|---|---|---|---|---|---|
| | U.S.A. | Canada | U.S.A. | Canada | U.S.A. | Canada | U.S.A. | Canada | Actual | % | Actual | % | |
| 1–10 | 193 | N/A | 111 | 6 | 1 | 0 | 3 | 0 | 308 | 9 | 6 | 30 | +21 |
| 11–20 | 588 | N/A | 108 | 2 | 11 | 0 | 25 | 0 | 732 | 21 | 2 | 10 | −11 |
| 21–30 | 392 | N/A | 93 | 1 | 59 | 1 | 80 | 1 | 624 | 18 | 3 | 15 | −3 |
| 31–50 | 146 | N/A | 43 | 0 | 164 | 2 | 176 | 3 | 529 | 15 | 5 | 25 | +10 |
| 51–70 | 37 | N/A | 6 | 0 | 25 | 0 | 29 | 0 | 97 | 4 | 0 | 0 | −4 |
| 71–90 | 7 | N/A | 3 | 0 | 8 | 0 | 8 | 0 | 26 | 1 | 0 | 0 | −1 |
| 91–110 | 3 | N/A | 1 | 0 | 4 | 0 | 7 | 0 | 15 | 0 | 0 | 0 | 0 |
| 111–130 | 0 | N/A | 0 | 0 | 6 | 0 | 4 | 0 | 10 | 0 | 0 | 0 | 0 |
| 131–150 | 0 | N/A | 1 | 0 | 1 | 0 | 1 | 0 | 3 | 0 | 0 | 0 | 0 |
| 151–170 | 0 | N/A | 1 | 0 | 1 | 0 | 1 | 0 | 3 | 0 | 0 | 0 | 0 |
| 171–190 | 0 | N/A | 0 | 0 | 1 | 0 | 1 | 0 | 2 | 0 | 0 | 0 | 0 |
| 191+ | 0 | N/A | 0 | 0 | 0 | 0 | 0 | 0 | 0 | 0 | 0 | 0 | 0 |
| No response | 456 | N/A | 34 | 1 | 349 | 1 | 252 | 2 | 1,091 | 32 | 4 | 20 | −12 |
| Total | 1,822 | N/A (8) | 401 | 10 | 630 | 4 | 587 | 6 | 3,440 | 100 | 20 | 100 | — |
| Median age (estimated) | 19 | – | 18 | 9 | 40 | 36 | 38 | 38 | 23 | – | 21 | – | |

[a]N/A: Not available.

[b]The total number of Canadian libraries in the White study was eight; their ages were not separately tabulated. Total number of Canadian libraries for all four studies was $8 + 10 + 4 + 6 = 28$ *congregational* libraries—highly inadequate as a sample.

[c]The only remarkable deviation is the six Canadian Hannaford libraries of one to ten years of age. This disparity may be at least partly due to slight differences in the library age categorization systems used or to the appeal of the CSLA to younger, newer libraries. In support of this, note that 111 of the 401 U.S. Hannaford libraries are between one and ten years old. This is 27.7 percent of the responding CSLA libraries, much higher than for any of the other three studies for this age group.

[d]Note that median age between U.S.A. and Canada differs significantly only in the Hannaford study. The other two studies and the totals have similar median ages for the two countries, even though the sample size for Canada is trivial. This distinct congruence helps to validate the Canadian samples and illustrates that there is little intrasample or even intersample bias. Presumably the nine-year difference for Hannaford is connected in some way with the nature of CSLA membership versus the actual sampling resulting from the methods used by White and the *ALD*, both of which were much more random.

TABLE 6.16
Returned Questionnaires for Four Popular Library Studies by Denomination[b,c]

| Denomination | 4 Sample Total | % | White | % | Hannaford | % | ALD-1978 | % | ALD-1988 | % |
|---|---|---|---|---|---|---|---|---|---|---|
| Baptist | 286 | 9.2 | 165 | 9 | 26 | 6.0 | 24 | 10 | 71 | 11.0 |
| Christian/Churches of Christ | 86 | 2.8 | 40 | 2 | 21 | 5.0 | 7 | 3 | 18 | 3.0 |
| Congregational | 38 | 1.2 | 15 | 1 | 17 | 4.0 | 6 | 3 | | |
| Episcopal/Anglican | 206 | 6.6 | 118 | 6 | 43 | 10.5 | 11 | 5 | 34 | 5.0 |
| Independent | 4 | 0.1 | | | | | 1 | 0 | 3 | 0.5 |
| Jewish | 341 | 11.0 | 87 | 5 | 6 | 1.5 | 61 | 27 | 187 | 29.0 |
| Lutheran | 664 | 21.4 | 560 | 31 | 42 | 10.0 | 21 | 9 | 41 | 6.0 |
| Mennonite | 26 | 0.84 | 22 | 1 | | | | | 4 | 1.0 |
| Methodist | 366 | 11.8 | 202 | 11 | 80 | 19.5 | 20 | 9 | 64 | 10.0 |
| Other Denominations | 315 | 10.2 | 159 | 9 | 57 | 14.0 | 22 | 10 | 77 | 12.0 |
| Presbyterian | 513 | 16.5 | 290 | 16 | 85 | 21.0 | 42 | 18 | 96 | 15.0 |
| Reformed[a] | (33) | (1.1) | (33) | (2) | | | | | | |
| Roman Catholic | 122 | 3.9 | 66 | 4 | 12 | 3.0 | 13 | 6 | 31 | 5.0 |

| | | | | | | | | | | |
|---|---|---|---|---|---|---|---|---|---|---|
| U.C.C.[a] | 135 | 4.4 | 98 | 5 | 22 | 5.0 | 2 | 1 | 13 | 2.0 |
| Total | 3,102 | 100 | 1,822 | 100 | 411 | 100 | 230 | 100 | 639 | 100 |

[a]Later moved to Other Denominations.

[b]Records shown on this table represent only those popular libraries returning their questionnaires. This was a return of unity for White and Hannaford by definition and then *ALD* returns 230/687 and 639/642, or 33.5 percent and 99.5 percent, for 1978 and 1988. For the *ALD* editions all popular library types are represented.

[c]Comparison of columns 1 and 2 with the denominational percentage breakdown in table 6.5 for all sample congregational libraries (Baptist 10%, Christian/Churches of Christ 2.8%, Congregational 1%, Episcopal/Anglican 7%, Independent 0.1%, Lutheran 20%, Mennonite 1%, Methodist 12%, Other Denominations 11%, Presbyterian 17%, United Church of Christ 4.2%, Jewish 12%, Roman Catholic 3%) shows that despite the poor response rate for *ALD* in 1978 the denominational distribution is almost identical for popular versus congregational libraries and responding versus all sample libraries. The near total correspondence indicates a complete lack of denominational and library-type bias in nonresponse rates for 1978 and suggests, at least, that response rates may not be attached to any particular variable of interest to us. A good sign.

TABLE 6.17
Monthly Library Circulation of Book Volumes for Two Popular
Library Studies

| Monthly Circulation | -------White 1976--------- | | ----Hannaford 1986---- | |
|---|---|---|---|---|
| | Number | Percentage | Number | Percentage |
| 436 and over | 78 | 4.2 | 14 | 3.4 |
| 216–435 | 105 | 5.8 | 20 | 4.9 |
| 111–215 | 355 | 19.5 | 50 | 12.2 |
| 46–110 | 643 | 35.3 | 69 | 16.8 |
| 0–45 | 589 | 32.3 | 167 | 40.6 |
| No response | 52 | 2.9 | 91 | 22.1 |
| Total | 1,822 | 100 | 411 | 100 |
| Median | 73.5 | | 41.2 | |
| Mean | 108.0 | | 115.0 | |

TABLE 6.18
Two-Study Comparison of Monthly Library Circulation Charges by Denomination: White vs. Hannaford Congregational Library Studies Only[a-c]

| Denomination | White | | | Hannaford | | | Two-Study Total | | | Summary—Difference | |
|---|---|---|---|---|---|---|---|---|---|---|---|
| | Number of Libraries | No Response | Mean Monthly Charges | Number of Libraries | No Response | Mean Monthly Charges | Number of Libraries | No Response | Overall Monthly Response Mean | Difference between Sample Means | Difference as % of Overall Mean |
| Baptist | 157/165 | 8 | 112 | 25/26 | 1 | 277 | 182 | 9 | 195 | 165 | 148 |
| Christian | –/0 | 0 | – | 16/21 | 5 | 98 | 16 | 5 | 98 | – | – |
| Churches of Christ | 40/40 | 0 | 106 | – | – | – | 40 | 0 | 106 | – | – |
| Congregational | –/15 | 15 | – | 10/17 | 7 | 34 | 10 | 22 | 34 | – | – |
| Episcopal/Anglican | 117/118 | 1 | 69 | 34/43 | 9 | 50 | 151 | 10 | 60 | 19 | 17 |
| Lutheran | 545/560 | 15 | 100 | 35/42 | 7 | 99 | 580 | 22 | 100 | 1 | 1 |
| Mennonite | –/22 | 22 | – | – | – | –36 | 0 | 22 | – | – | – |
| Methodist | 194/202 | 8 | 87 | 65/80 | 15 | 99 | 259 | 23 | 93 | 12 | 11 |
| Other Denominations | –/159 | 159 | – | 45/57 | 12 | 143 | 45 | 171 | 143 | – | – |
| Presbyterian | 287/290 | 3 | 86 | 60/85 | 25 | 112 | 347 | 28 | 99 | 26 | 23 |
| U.C.C. | 93/98 | 5 | 79 | 16/22 | 6 | 47 | 109 | 11 | 63 | 32 | 29 |

TABLE 6.18 (continued)
Two-Study Comparison of Monthly Library Circulation Charges: White vs. Hannaford Congregational Library Studies Only[a-c]

| | | | | | | | | | | |
|---|---|---|---|---|---|---|---|---|---|---|
| Jewish | 86/87 | 1 | 288 | 5/6 | 1 | 265 | 91 | 2 | 277 | 23 | 21 |
| Roman Catholic | 62/66 | 4 | 206 | 9/12 | 3 | 111 | 71 | 7 | 159 | 95 | 85 |
| Total | 1,581/1,822 | 241 | 108 | 320/411 | 91 | 115 | 1,901/2,233 | 332 | 111 | 7 | 6 |

[a]The designation 157/165 means 157 active cases out of a possible 165 cases.

[b]Interpretation of the far right-hand column: the gross difference between the means for Baptists in the two studies is due to the disproportionately large monthly circulations of several Baptist libraries among a CSLA sample of only twenty-five libraries. Similarly, the large difference between the Roman Catholic means is due to the small CSLA sample size of only nine responding Roman Catholic libraries with moderate circulation figures. The upper circulation category minimum for White was set arbitrarily at 150, whereas for CSLA it was established at 800! The result, as might be expected, is great potential variation between means for each denomination, especially among the libraries in the top category.

[c]It can be assumed from the above and from the very close congruence between the overall CSLA and White study means that the *denominational groups* within the CSLA study with only small sample sizes (especially Baptist and Roman Catholic) might have been less representative of their overall denominations than is the case for the White library respondents, with 157 and 62 responding libraries respectively. Nevertheless, it is also true that the real overall mean for the entire 2,233 libraries is probably closer to 111 circulations per month than it is to either of the component means of 108 or 115. The same argument stipulates that as only two of the denominations (representing only 12 percent of the overall sample) show significant disparities, the two samples can be assumed to be quite close in terms of the populations they represent. By extension then, the monthly circulation means for the *ALD* congregational libraries, had they been sampled, would probably also approximate 111 circulations per month (or rather higher as the *ALD* responding libraries tend to show higher overall means on leading variables than is the case for the White and Hannaford study libraries).

TABLE 6.19
Church and Synagogue Library Association (Hannaford) Study: Monthly Library Circulation per Member by Denomination[a]

| Denomination | Volumes Circulation per Member | | | | | | | | | | All Libraries | Mean |
|---|---|---|---|---|---|---|---|---|---|---|---|---|
| | Less than .11 | % | .11 –.5 | % | .51 –1.5 | % | More than 1.5 | % | No Response | % | | |
| Baptist | 0 | 0.0 | 8 | 30.8 | 7 | 26.9 | 9 | 34.6 | 2 | 7.7 | 26 | 3.3 |
| Christian | 0 | 0.0 | 1 | 4.8 | 10 | 47.6 | 5 | 23.8 | 5 | 23.8 | 21 | 1.8 |
| Congregational | 0 | 0.0 | 4 | 23.5 | 5 | 29.4 | 0 | 0.0 | 8 | 47.1 | 17 | 0.7 |
| Episcopal/Anglican | 1 | 2.3 | 17 | 39.5 | 12 | 27.9 | 4 | 9.3 | 9 | 20.9 | 43 | 0.9 |
| Lutheran | 1 | 2.4 | 9 | 21.4 | 15 | 35.7 | 10 | 23.8 | 7 | 16.7 | 42 | 1.0 |
| Methodist | 3 | 3.8 | 26 | 32.5 | 26 | 32.5 | 10 | 12.5 | 15 | 18.8 | 80 | 0.8 |
| Other Denominations | 0 | 0.0 | 10 | 17.5 | 7 | 12.3 | 27 | 47.4 | 13 | 22.8 | 57 | 5.0 |
| Presbyterian | 0 | 0.0 | 17 | 20.0 | 29 | 34.1 | 14 | 16.5 | 25 | 29.4 | 85 | 1.3 |
| U.C.C. | 0 | 0.0 | 4 | 18.2 | 6 | 27.3 | 6 | 27.3 | 6 | 27.3 | 22 | 1.3 |
| Summary | | | | | | | | | | | | |
| Jewish | 0 | 0.0 | 2 | 33.3 | 2 | 33.3 | 1 | 16.7 | 1 | 16.7 | 6 | 0.8 |
| Roman Catholic | 2 | 16.7 | 5 | 41.7 | 2 | 16.7 | 0 | 0.0 | 3 | 25.0 | 12 | 0.3 |
| All Protestant | 5 | 1.3 | 96 | 24.4 | 117 | 29.8 | 85 | 21.6 | 90 | 22.9 | 393 | 1.8 |
| Total | 7 | 1.7 | 103 | 25.1 | 121 | 29.4 | 86 | 20.9 | 94 | 22.9 | 411 | 1.8 |

[a] Libraries showing no response on either monthly circulation or congregational membership were placed in the No Response column and dropped from the means.

TABLE 6.20

1978 *American Library Directory* Congregational Libraries Restricting Reference Service by Denomination

| Denomination | Yes with Restriction | % | No Response | % | Number of Libraries |
|---|---|---|---|---|---|
| Baptist | 5 | 6 | 78 | 94 | 83 |
| Christian | 1 | 6 | 17 | 94 | 18 |
| Churches of Christ | 0 | 0 | 0 | 0 | 0 |
| Congregational | 1 | 4 | 27 | 96 | 28 |
| Episcopal/Anglican | 0 | 0 | 41 | 100 | 41 |
| Independent | 0 | 0 | 3 | 100 | 3 |
| Lutheran | 2 | 4 | 51 | 96 | 53 |
| Methodist | 4 | 7 | 51 | 93 | 55 |
| Other Denominations | 3 | 5 | 58 | 95 | 61 |
| Presbyterian | 12 | 10 | 103 | 90 | 115 |
| U.C.C. | 3 | 23 | 10 | 77 | 13 |
| Summary | | | | | |
| Jewish | 7 | 5 | 143 | 95 | 150 |
| Roman Catholic | 2 | 14 | 12 | 86 | 14 |
| All Protestant | 31 | 7 | 439 | 93 | 470 |
| Total | 40 | 6 | 594 | 94 | 634 |

TABLE 6.21

1988 *American Library Directory* Congregational Libraries Restricting Reference Service by Denomination

| Denomination | Yes with Restriction | % | No Response | % | Number of Libraries |
|---|---|---|---|---|---|
| Baptist | 9 | 13 | 62 | 87 | 71 |
| Christian | 2 | 12 | 15 | 88 | 17 |
| Churches of Christ | 1 | 50 | 1 | 50 | 2 |
| Episcopal/Anglican | 0 | 0 | 33 | 100 | 33 |
| Independent | 0 | 0 | 1 | 100 | 1 |
| Lutheran | 3 | 7 | 39 | 93 | 42 |
| Mennonite | 0 | 0 | 4 | 100 | 4 |
| Methodist | 6 | 9 | 58 | 91 | 64 |
| Other Denominations | 5 | 7 | 66 | 93 | 71 |
| Presbyterian | 8 | 8 | 89 | 92 | 97 |
| U.C.C. | 4 | 31 | 9 | 69 | 13 |
| Summary | | | | | |
| Jewish | 12 | 7 | 158 | 93 | 170 |
| Roman Catholic | 2 | 25 | 6 | 75 | 8 |
| All Protestant | 38 | 9 | 377 | 91 | 415 |
| Total | 52 | 9 | 541 | 91 | 593 |

TABLE 6.22

1978 *American Library Directory* Congregational Libraries Restricting
Circulation by Denomination

| Denomination | Yes with Restriction | % | No Response | % | Number of Libraries |
|---|---|---|---|---|---|
| Baptist | 6 | 7 | 77 | 93 | 83 |
| Christian | 1 | 6 | 17 | 94 | 18 |
| Churches of Christ | 0 | 0 | 0 | 0 | 0 |
| Congregational | 1 | 4 | 27 | 96 | 28 |
| Episcopal/Anglican | 1 | 2 | 40 | 98 | 41 |
| Independent | 0 | 0 | 3 | 100 | 3 |
| Lutheran | 2 | 4 | 51 | 96 | 53 |
| Methodist | 3 | 5 | 52 | 95 | 55 |
| Other Denominations | 4 | 7 | 57 | 93 | 61 |
| Presbyterian | 14 | 12 | 101 | 88 | 115 |
| U.C.C. | 3 | 23 | 10 | 77 | 13 |
| Summary | | | | | |
| Jewish | 14 | 9 | 136 | 91 | 150 |
| Roman Catholic | 2 | 14 | 12 | 86 | 14 |
| All Protestant | 35 | 7 | 435 | 93 | 470 |
| Total | 51 | 8 | 583 | 92 | 634 |

TABLE 6.23

1988 *American Library Directory* Congregational Libraries Restricting
Circulation by Denomination

| Denomination | Yes with Restriction | % | No Response | % | Number of Libraries |
|---|---|---|---|---|---|
| Baptist | 10 | 14 | 61 | 86 | 71 |
| Christian | 2 | 12 | 15 | 88 | 17 |
| Churches of Christ | 1 | 50 | 1 | 50 | 2 |
| Episcopal/Anglican | 0 | 0 | 33 | 100 | 33 |
| Independent | 0 | 0 | 1 | 100 | 1 |
| Lutheran | 3 | 7 | 39 | 93 | 42 |
| Mennonite | 0 | 0 | 4 | 100 | 4 |
| Methodist | 6 | 9 | 58 | 91 | 64 |
| Other Denominations | 5 | 7 | 66 | 93 | 71 |
| Presbyterian | 9 | 9 | 88 | 91 | 97 |
| U.C.C. | 4 | 31 | 9 | 69 | 13 |
| Summary | | | | | |
| Jewish | 17 | 10 | 153 | 90 | 170 |
| Roman Catholic | 2 | 25 | 6 | 75 | 8 |
| All Protestant | 40 | 10 | 375 | 90 | 415 |
| Total | 59 | 10 | 534 | 90 | 593 |

TABLE 6.24

Church and Synagogue Library Association (Hannaford): Library
Volume Holdings by Denomination

| Denom-ination | 0–250 | % | 251–500 | % | 501 & over | % | No Response | % | Total Libraries | Mean |
|---|---|---|---|---|---|---|---|---|---|---|
| Baptist | 1 | 4 | 1 | 4 | 24 | 92 | 0 | 0 | 26 | 4,287 |
| Christian | 0 | 0 | 1 | 5 | 20 | 95 | 0 | 0 | 21 | 2,457 |
| Congregational | 0 | 0 | 1 | 6 | 15 | 88 | 1 | 6 | 17 | 2,147 |
| Episcopal/ Anglican | 0 | 0 | 6 | 14 | 37 | 86 | 0 | 0 | 43 | 2,241 |
| Lutheran | 1 | 2 | 5 | 12 | 36 | 86 | 0 | 0 | 42 | 2,324 |
| Methodist | 3 | 4 | 4 | 5 | 71 | 89 | 2 | 3 | 80 | 2,762 |
| Other Denom-inations | 0 | 0 | 4 | 7 | 52 | 91 | 1 | 2 | 57 | 2,458 |
| Presbyterian | 0 | 0 | 4 | 5 | 79 | 93 | 2 | 2 | 85 | 3,192 |
| U.C.C. | 0 | 0 | 5 | 23 | 17 | 77 | 0 | 0 | 22 | 1,841 |
| Summary | | | | | | | | | | |
| Jewish | 0 | 0 | 0 | 0 | 6 | 100 | 0 | 0 | 6 | 7,750 |
| Roman Catholic | 0 | 0 | 0 | 0 | 12 | 100 | 0 | 0 | 12 | 3,958 |
| All Protestant | 5 | 1 | 31 | 8 | 351 | 89 | 6 | 2 | 393 | 2,713 |
| Total | 5 | 1 | 31 | 8 | 369 | 90 | 6 | 1 | 411 | 2,824 |

## TABLE 6.25
## Congregational Library Book Volumes for Four Studies[a]

| Book Volumes | ----White 1976---- Number | % | ---ALD-1978--- Number | % | ---Hannaford 1986--- Number | % | ---ALD-1988--- Number | % |
|---|---|---|---|---|---|---|---|---|
| 10,000+ | 0 | 0 | 165 | 26 | 16 | 4 | 274 | 46 |
| 5,000 to 9,999 | 72 | 4 | 253 | 40 | 39 | 10 | 243 | 41 |
| 2,000 to 4,999 | 316 | 17 | | | 188 | 45 | | |
| 1,000 to 1,999 | 315 | 17 | 47 | 7 | 62 | 15 | 52 | 9 |
| 500 to 999 | 486 | 27 | | | 64 | 16 | | |
| 200 to 499 | 294 | 16 | | | 31 | 8 | | |
| 100 to 199 | 242 | 13 | | | 3 | 1 | | |
| 0 to 99 | 57 | 3 | | | 2 | 0 | | |
| No Response | 40 | 2 | 169 | 27 | 6 | 1 | 24 | 4 |
| Total | 1,822 | 100 | 634 | 100 | 411 | 100 | 593 | 100 |
| Mean | 1,473 | | 4,540 | | 2,824 | | 5,737 | |
| Median (est.) | 807 | | 2,833 | | 2,638 | | 3,392 | |

[a]The 1975 White mean of 1,667 found in table 6.3 was based on a sample size of 1,490 in which minor denominations had been dropped during the pre-analysis. For the analysis above the sample size is 1,782/1,822. All minor denominations have been *included* in the mean, producing a somewhat lower overall mean of 1,473. For the original study, Churches of Christ, Congregational, Mennonite, Reformed, and Roman Catholic were not tabulated. However, although 292 libraries (16 percent) were not included in the original mean, the effect on the mean itself was a difference of 194, or 11.6 percent. For the sake of consistency the original calculated mean was retained for the present chapter. Note, however, that both the White mean and the White median are much below the means and medians for the other three samples. This leads to the inescapable conclusion that it is bigger libraries that belong to library organizations and publicize themselves.

TABLE 6.26
1978 and 1988 *American Library Directory* Longitudinal Study Congregational Library Volume Holdings by Denomination

| Denomination | 1978 | | | | 1988 | | | | % Change 1978–88 |
|---|---|---|---|---|---|---|---|---|---|
| | No. of Libraries | No Response | Total Libraries | Mean Volumes | No. of Libraries | No Response | Total Libraries | Mean Volumes | |
| Baptist | 69 | 14 | 83 | 5,196 | 70 | 1 | 71 | 6,664 | 28 |
| Christian | 13 | 5 | 18 | 6,231 | 17 | 0 | 17 | 4,059 | –35 |
| Churches of Christ | 0 | 0 | 0 | | 2 | 0 | 2 | 1,375 | 22 |
| Episcopal/Anglican | 31 | 10 | 41 | 3,250 | 31 | 2 | 33 | 3,952 | 22 |
| Independent | 2 | 1 | 3 | 2,250 | 1 | 0 | 1 | 2,250 | 0 |
| Lutheran | 38 | 15 | 53 | 3,724 | 40 | 2 | 42 | 5,669 | 52 |
| Mennonite | 2 | 1 | 3 | 4,500 | 4 | 0 | 4 | 4,500 | 0 |
| Methodist | 35 | 20 | 55 | 3,421 | 59 | 5 | 64 | 4,576 | 34 |
| Other Denominations | 57 | 29 | 86 | 5,382 | 66 | 5 | 71 | 7,144 | 33 |
| Presbyterian | 88 | 27 | 115 | 3,068 | 94 | 3 | 97 | 3,878 | 26 |
| U.C.C. | 10 | 3 | 13 | 2,175 | 13 | 0 | 13 | 2,673 | 23 |
| Summary | | | | | | | | | |
| Jewish | 112 | 38 | 150 | 6,045 | 164 | 6 | 170 | 7,067 | 17 |
| Roman Catholic | 8 | 6 | 14 | 2,594 | 8 | 0 | 8 | 7,125 | 175 |
| All Protestant | 345 | 125 | 470 | 4,097 | 397 | 18 | 415 | 5,160 | 26 |
| Total | 465 | 169 | 634 | 4,540 | 569 | 24 | 593 | 5,737 | 26 |

TABLE 6.27
1975 White Periodical Holdings by Denomination

| Denomination | Libraries | ---Periodical Titles--- | | | % of Libraries | Mean Number of Titles |
|---|---|---|---|---|---|---|
| | | 0–100 | 100+ | Total | | |
| Baptist | 165 | 135 | 2 | 137 | 7.5 | 24 |
| Christian | 40 | 36 | 1 | 37 | 2.0 | 25 |
| Congregational | 15 | 13 | | 13 | 0.71 | 20 |
| Episcopal/Anglican | 118 | 85 | 5 | 90 | 4.9 | 34 |
| Lutheran | 560 | 444 | 5 | 449 | 24.6 | 35 |
| Mennonite | 22 | 20 | | 20 | 1.1 | 20 |
| Methodist | 202 | 166 | 1 | 167 | 9.2 | 22 |
| Other Denominations | 159 | 75 | 5 | 80 | 4.4 | 38 |
| Presbyterian | 290 | 251 | 8 | 259 | 14.2 | 41 |
| Reformed[a] | (33) | (23) | | (23) | (1.3) | (20) |
| U.C.C. | 98 | 82 | 2 | 84 | 4.6 | 64 |
| Jewish | 87 | 83 | 1 | 84 | 4.6 | 25 |
| Roman Catholic | 66 | 50 | 2 | 52 | 2.9 | 31 |
| No response | 29 | | | 350 | 19.2 | |
| Total | 1,822 | 1,440 | 32 | 1,472 | 100 | 36 |

[a]Later added to Other Denominations.

TABLE 6.28

Church and Synagogue Library Association (Hannaford): Library Film
Holdings by Denomination[a]

| Denomination | 1–25 | % | 26–50 | % | 51–100 | % | 101 & over | % | No Response | % | Total | Mean |
|---|---|---|---|---|---|---|---|---|---|---|---|---|
| Baptist | 4 | 15.4 | 0 | 0.0 | 0 | 0.0 | 6 | 23.1 | 16 | 61.5 | 26 | 268.3 |
| Christian | 1 | 4.8 | 1 | 4.8 | 2 | 9.5 | 1 | 4.8 | 16 | 76.2 | 21 | 65.2 |
| Congregational | 2 | 11.8 | 1 | 5.9 | 2 | 11.8 | 2 | 11.8 | 10 | 58.8 | 17 | 88.7 |
| Episcopal/ Anglican | 4 | 9.3 | 3 | 7.0 | 1 | 2.3 | 2 | 4.7 | 33 | 76.7 | 43 | 67.4 |
| Lutheran | 9 | 21.4 | 2 | 4.8 | 6 | 14.3 | 2 | 4.8 | 23 | 54.8 | 42 | 65.6 |
| Methodist | 11 | 13.8 | 6 | 7.5 | 5 | 6.3 | 18 | 22.5 | 40 | 50.0 | 80 | 116.2 |
| Other Denominations | 6 | 10.5 | 5 | 8.8 | 3 | .5.3 | 3 | 5.3 | 40 | 70.2 | 57 | 133.1 |
| Presbyterian | 19 | 22.4 | 8 | 9.4 | 4 | 4.7 | 8 | 9.4 | 46 | 54.1 | 85 | 62.1 |
| U.C.C. | 3 | 13.6 | 2 | 9.1 | 1 | 4.5 | 0 | 0.0 | 16 | 72.7 | 22 | 21.8 |
| Summary | | | | | | | | | | | | |
| Jewish | 0 | 0.0 | 0 | 0.0 | 2 | 33.3 | 1 | 16.7 | 3 | 50.0 | 6 | 120.0 |
| Roman Catholic | 2 | 16.7 | 1 | 8.3 | 1 | 8.3 | 2 | 16.7 | 6 | 50.0 | 12 | 86.2 |
| All Protestant | 59 | 15.0 | 28 | 7.1 | 24 | 6.1 | 42 | 10.7 | 240 | 61.1 | 393 | 98.1 |
| Total | 61 | 14.8 | 29 | 7.1 | 27 | 6.6 | 45 | 10.9 | 249 | 60.6 | 411 | 98.1 |

[a]Libraries with no films have not been added into the mean.

TABLE 6.29
1975 White Film, Phonograph Record, and Total Media Holdings
by Denomination

| Denomination | Number of Libraries with Films | Number of Libraries with Records | Total Libraries with Media | Mean |
|---|---|---|---|---|
| Baptist | 84 | 136 | 159 | 221 |
| Christian | 21 | 28 | 36 | 137 |
| Congregational | 9 | 11 | 15 | 109 |
| Episcopal/Anglican | 54 | 70 | 92 | 134 |
| Lutheran | 277 | 412 | 479 | 178 |
| Mennonite | 10 | 13 | 18 | 81 |
| Methodist | 107 | 160 | 192 | 158 |
| Other Denominations | 38 | 45 | 73 | 102 |
| Presbyterian | 147 | 200 | 258 | 132 |
| Reformed | 19 | 21 | 27 | 121 |
| U.C.C. | 55 | 72 | 93 | 148 |
| All Protestant | 821 | 1,168 | 1,442 | 159 |
| Jewish | 36 | 64 | 77 | 189 |
| Roman Catholic | 29 | 41 | 52 | 231 |
| Total libraries | 886 | 1,273 | 1,571 | 163 |
| Missing | 936 | 549 | 251 | |
| Grand total | 1,822 | 1,822 | 1,822 | |

Media Holdings

TABLE 6.30

Church and Synagogue Library Association (Hannaford): Library
Expenditures on Media Titles by Denomination[a]

| Denom-ination | No Media Expenditure | % | ---Media Expenditures--- | | | | | | Total | |
| | | | $ 1–100 | % | $101–500 | % | $501 & over | % | Libraries | Mean |
|---|---|---|---|---|---|---|---|---|---|---|
| Baptist | 10 | 38 | 7 | 27 | 4 | 15 | 5 | 19 | 26 | $563 |
| Christian | 8 | 38 | 8 | 38 | 4 | 19 | 1 | 5 | 21 | 150 |
| Congregational | 9 | 53 | 6 | 35 | 1 | 6 | 1 | 6 | 17 | 74 |
| Episcopal/ Anglican | 22 | 51 | 9 | 21 | 10 | 23 | 2 | 5 | 43 | 101 |
| Lutheran | 12 | 29 | 10 | 24 | 18 | 43 | 2 | 5 | 42 | 162 |
| Methodist | 34 | 43 | 17 | 21 | 20 | 25 | 9 | 11 | 80 | 190 |
| Other Denomi-nations | 27 | 47 | 13 | 23 | 14 | 26 | 3 | 5 | 57 | 240 |
| Presbyterian | 32 | 38 | 35 | 41 | 14 | 16 | 4 | 5 | 85 | 157 |
| U.C.C. | 17 | 77 | 2 | 9 | 2 | 9 | 1 | 5 | 22 | 160 |
| Summary | | | | | | | | | | |
| Jewish | 2 | 33 | 1 | 17 | 1 | 17 | 2 | 33 | 6 | 1,008 |
| Roman Catholic | 3 | 25 | 1 | 8 | 5 | 42 | 3 | 25 | 12 | 515 |
| All Protestant | 171 | 44 | 107 | 27 | 87 | 22 | 28 | 7 | 393 | 193 |
| Total | 176 | 43 | 109 | 27 | 93 | 23 | 33 | 8 | 411 | 215 |

[a]Libraries with no media expenditures were added to the nonresponse category and were
not added into the means.

TABLE 6.31
Church and Synagogue Library Association (Hannaford): Library
Media Holdings by Denomination[a,b]

| Denomination | 0–100 | % | 101–200 | % | 201–350 | % | 351 & over | % | No Response | % | Total | Mean |
|---|---|---|---|---|---|---|---|---|---|---|---|---|
| Baptist | 14 | 53.8 | 2 | 7.7 | 3 | 11.5 | 7 | 26.9 | 0 | 0.0 | 26 | 568.0 |
| Christian | 16 | 76.2 | 1 | 4.8 | 2 | 9.5 | 2 | 9.5 | 0 | 0.0 | 21 | 188.1 |
| Congregational | 11 | 64.7 | 3 | 17.6 | 2 | 11.8 | 1 | 5.9 | 0 | 0.0 | 17 | 85.3 |
| Episcopal/ Anglican | 32 | 74.4 | 5 | 11.6 | 3 | 7.0 | 3 | 7.0 | 0 | 0.0 | 43 | 94.2 |
| Lutheran | 22 | 52.4 | 6 | 14.3 | 7 | 16.7 | 7 | 16.7 | 0 | 0.0 | 42 | 191.1 |
| Methodist | 47 | 58.7 | 11 | 13.8 | 6 | 7.5 | 15 | 18.8 | 1 | 1.3 | 80 | 168.1 |
| Other Denominations | 35 | 61.4 | 6 | 10.5 | 6 | 10.5 | 10 | 17.5 | 0 | 0.0 | 57 | 195.3 |
| Presbyterian | 58 | 68.2 | 14 | 16.5 | 3 | 3.5 | 9 | 10.6 | 1 | 1.2 | 85 | 160.1 |
| U.C.C. | 19 | 86.4 | 1 | 4.5 | 0 | 0.0 | 2 | 9.1 | 0 | 0.0 | 22 | 70.6 |
| Summary |  |  |  |  |  |  |  |  |  |  |  |  |
| Jewish | 3 | 50.0 | 2 | 33.3 | 0 | 0.0 | 1 | 16.7 | 0 | 0.0 | 6 | 120.0 |
| Roman Catholic | 5 | 41.7 | 1 | 8.3 | 0 | 0.0 | 6 | 50.0 | 0 | 0.0 | 12 | 386.1 |
| All Protestant | 254 | 64.6 | 49 | 12.5 | 32 | 8.1 | 56 | 14.2 | 2 | 0.5 | 393 | 183.3 |
| Total | 262 | 63.7 | 52 | 12.7 | 32 | 7.8 | 63 | 15.3 | 2 | 0.5 | 411 | 188.3 |

[a]Libraries registering zero media holdings were added into the means, producing a mean significantly lower than would have been the case if they were excluded. For comparison, see table 5.67.
[b]See table 5.68 for holdings of *all* media.

TABLE 6.32
Annual Library Expenditure/Income for Four Studies for Congregational Libraries[a]

| | $0–$100 | % | $101–$500 | % | $501–$1,000 | % | $1,001–$2,000 | % | $2,001–$3,000 | % | $3,001 & over | % | No Response | % | Total | % | Median ($) | Mean ($) |
|---|---|---|---|---|---|---|---|---|---|---|---|---|---|---|---|---|---|---|
| White 1976 | 517 | 28 | 1,009 | 55 | 170 | 9 | 101 | 6 | 0 | 0 | 0 | 0 | 25 | 1 | 1,822 | 100 | 252 | 337 |
| American Library Directory 1978 | – | - | 62 | 10 | 45 | 7 | 38 | 6 | | | | | 489 | 77 | 634 | 100 | 733 | 1,998 |
| Hannaford 1986 | 21 | 5 | 151 | 37 | 118 | 29 | 62 | 15 | 20 | 5 | 36 | 9 | 3 | 1 | 411 | 100 | 637 | 1,652 |
| American Library Directory 1988 | | | 64 | 11 | 72 | 12 | 99 | 17 | | | | | 358 | 60 | 593 | 100 | 1,243 | 7,420 |

[a]Expenditure figures were used for the 2 ALD sets of data as no income data was gathered for the ALD editions.

TABLE 6.33
Four-Study Comparison of Total Annual Library Expenditure by Denomination: Congregational Libraries Only[a-e]

| Denomination | White No. of Libraries | White Mean | Hannaford No. of Libraries | Hannaford Mean | ALD-1978 No. of Libraries | ALD-1978 Mean | ALD-1988 No. of Libraries | ALD-1988 Mean | Summary Total No. of Libraries | Summary Overall Mean | Summary Average Difference Among Means | Summary Overall % of Mean |
|---|---|---|---|---|---|---|---|---|---|---|---|---|
| Baptist | 164/165 | $405 | 26/26 | $3,325 | 17/83 | $2,412 | 29/71 | $6,509 | 236/345 | $3,163 | $1,754 | 55 |
| Christian | –/0 | – | 20/21 | 970 | 6/18 | 1,125 | 9/17 | 3,167 | 35/56 | 1,754 | 942 | 54 |
| Churches of Christ | 39/40 | 300 | –/0 | – | –/0 | – | 2/2 | 625 | 41/42 | 463 | 163 | 35 |
| Congregational | –15 | – | 16/17 | 664 | –/0 | – | –/0 | – | 16/32 | 664 | – | – |
| Episcopal/Anglican | 117/118 | 306 | 43/43 | 847 | 8/41 | 2,125 | 15/33 | 5,450 | 183/235 | 2,182 | 1,634 | 75 |
| Independent | –/0 | – | –/0 | – | –3 | 0 | –1 | 0 | –4 | – | – | – |
| Lutheran | 554/560 | 264 | 42/42 | 813 | 16/53 | 1,516 | 17/42 | 824 | 629/697 | 854 | 331 | 39 |
| Mennonite | –22 | – | –/0 | – | –3 | – | 3/4 | 500 | 3/29 | 500 | – | – |
| Methodist | 198/202 | 288 | 79/80 | 1,047 | 12/55 | 1,125 | 29/64 | 4,026 | 318/401 | 1,622 | 1,202 | 74 |
| Other Denoms. | 29/159 | 236 | 56/57 | 1,487 | 18/86 | 2,792 | 21/71 | 5,000 | 124/373 | 2,379 | 1,517 | 64 |
| Presbyterian | 288/290 | 285 | 85/85 | 1,245 | 27/115 | 722 | 39/97 | 4,994 | 439/587 | 1,812 | 1,591 | 88 |
| U.C.C. | 97/98 | 284 | 22/22 | 1,638 | 5/13 | 250 | 3/13 | 500 | 127/146 | 668 | 485 | 73 |
| Jewish | 84/87 | 973 | 6/6 | 21,048 | 33/150 | 3,364 | 64/170 | 14,980 | 187/413 | 10,091 | 7,923 | 79 |
| Roman Catholic | 65/66 | 546 | 12/12 | 4,109 | 3/14 | 1,750 | 4/8 | 12,810 | 84/100 | 4,804 | 4,003 | 83 |
| Total | 1,635/1,822 | 337.2 | 407/411 | 1,652 | 145/634 | 1,998 | 235/593 | 7,420 | 2,422/3,460 | 2,852 | 2,284 | 80 |

[a]The designation 164/165 means 164 active cases out of a possible 165 cases.
[b]The total variation of 80 percent is unacceptable statistically unless it can be broken down and explained. An analysis of volume holdings indicated a 7.1 percent variation due to sampling differences and bias. We can accept this percentage for expenditure, too. We also have a 60 to 70 percent inflation rate over time and something ought to be left over for true growth in expenditure.
[c]For the two ALD studies the change over time = 271 percent. Over the base of $2,852 this change of $5,422 = 190 percent. For the White and

Hannaford studies the corresponding figures were 390 percent and 46 percent. The latter statistic is much lower than its counterpart 190 percent simply because the dates are that much earlier. If the 190 percent (for two studies) is averaged with the 46 percent (for two studies), then the result is 118 percent. Of this, about 70 percent is due to inflation. This leaves 48 percent change for true growth in expenditure in real dollars (which appears to be too high to be true). Also, it is questionable if this form of logic is valid to "explain" the mean variation.

dSummary: Of the 80 percent mean variation to be explained, about 7 percent is due to sampling error. The remaining 73 percent must be divided between inflation and real growth in expenditure. This is rather difficult to achieve as it is obvious that both of the *ALD* studies were biased due to heavy No Response rates (77 percent and 61 percent), which probably had the effect of boosting the means for these studies in an unjustified and difficult-to-measure fashion. However, as it is clear that real growth has occurred, let us suppose that the variation is about equally divided: 35 percent for growth and 38 percent for inflation. The 35 percent growth is consistent with the 30–32 percent growth in volume holdings plus a little for personnel expenditure and a known 70 percent real inflation rate would produce a mean variation of about 34 percent for four studies over time, as seen in the example shown below:

| | Study 1 | 2 | 3 | 4 | Mean | Variation | Mean Variation |
|---|---|---|---|---|---|---|---|
| | | | | | | 10.25 | |
| | | | | | | 3.25 | |
| | | | | | | 0.25 | |
| | | | | | | 13.75 | |
| Dollars | $10 | $20 | $17 | $34 | $20.25 | Sum = $27.50 | Mean = 6.875 <br> or <br> Mean variation over base of 20.25 = 34% |

eThis is the best that can be done in this case, but it explains the 80% variation adequately:

| | |
|---|---|
| Variations from sampling differences and bias | 7.1% |
| Variation due to true growth | 35% |
| Variation due to inflation of the dollar (U.S. & Canadian) | 34% |
| Total variation as a proportion of the mean | 76.1% |
| Actual variation | 80% |
| Unexplained variation | 3.9% |

TABLE 6.34

Four-Study Comparison of Annual Library Expenditure on Personnel: Congregational Libraries Only[a–d]

| Denom-ination | ----White----- Number of Libraries | Mean | --Hannaford-- Number of Libraries | Mean | ---ALD-1978--- Number of Libraries | Mean | ---ALD-1988--- Number of Libraries | Mean |
|---|---|---|---|---|---|---|---|---|
| Baptist | –/165 | – | 26/26 | 753.8 | 2/83 | 5,000 | 6/71 | 9,583 |
| Christian | –/0 | – | 21/21 | – | 2/18 | 2,500 | 2/17 | 2,500 |
| Churches of Christ | –/40 | – | –/0 | – | –/0 | – | –/2 | – |
| Congrega-tional | –/15 | – | 17/17 | – | –/0 | – | –/0 | – |
| Episcopal/ Anglican | –/118 | – | 43/43 | 58.1 | 1/41 | 2,500 | 4/33 | 11,880 |
| Independent | –/0 | – | –/0 | – | –/3 | – | –/1 | – |
| Lutheran | –/560 | – | 42/42 | 17.8 | 3/53 | 6,667 | –/42 | – |
| Mennonite | –/22 | – | –/0 | – | –/3 | – | –/4 | – |
| Methodist | –/202 | – | 80/80 | 85.0 | 3/55 | 4,167 | 6/64 | 15,420 |
| Other Denom-inations | –/159 | – | 57/57 | 319.1 | 2/86 | 8,750 | 5/71 | 5,000 |
| Presbyterian | –/290 | – | 85/85 | 188.2 | 1/115 | 2,500 | 2/97 | 15,000 |
| UCC | –/98 | – | 22/22 | 636.3 | –/13 | – | –/13 | – |
| Jewish | –/87 | – | 6/6 | 5,855.0 | 16/150 | 3,750 | 43/170 | 15,000 |
| Roman Catholic | –/66 | – | 12/12 | 1,916.6 | 1/14 | 2,500 | 2/8 | 76,250 |
| Total | –/1,822 | – | 411/411 | 330.8 | 31/634 | 4,274 | 70/593 | 15,070 |

[a]The designation 164/165 means 164 active cases out of a possible 165 cases.

[b]White gave no figures for annual library expenditure on personnel broken down by denomination.

TABLE 6.34 (continued)
Four-Study Comparison of Total Annual Library Expenditure on
Personnel: Congregational Libraries Only[a–d]

---

[c]The Hannaford questionnaire categorization system assumed that if no personnel expenditure was shown, then this variable = 0. However, for the *ALD* publication the opposite method was used: if no expenditure on personnel was shown in the *ALD*, then it became necessary to register the variable as No Response or Missing as it was impossible to tell if the entry ought to have been equal to zero or if it were merely incomplete data due to partial questionnaire data submission. For the Hannaford study the author carefully followed up submissions by telephone to ensure completeness. Therefore, the Hannaford data is almost certainly more complete and more reliable for this variable than is the *ALD* data. What the *ALD* data *does* indicate for congregational libraries is libraries and denominations that incur significant personnel expenditures as part of their regular budget allocations. The Hannaford data, on the other hand, provides a reasonable picture of the true *mean denominational expenditures* and can probably be most trusted in this regard. Therefore, as shown, the denominational ranking for personnel expenditure is Jewish, Roman Catholic, Baptist, United Church of Christ, Other Denominations, Presbyterian, Methodist, Episcopal/Anglican, and Lutheran.

[d]Note that the ranking for the *ALD* denominations is Roman Catholic, Methodist, Jewish, Presbyterian, etc. Apart from the fact that Jewish and Roman Catholic are toward the top of the list there is, as expected from such an inadequate sample, little other correspondence. Indeed, the only figure worth relying on is that for Jewish libraries, which indicates (1) quite a healthy mean personnel budget ($15,000 p.a. in 1988 for 43 libraries) and (2) a budget growing strongly over time—an increase of 300 percent from 1978. Therefore, although the Hannaford data is of better quality than is that for the *ALD*, in order to compare the three samples it is necessary to remove the zero entries from the CSLA study. See table 6.35.

TABLE 6.35

Three Study Comparison of Annual Library Expenditure on Personnel: Congregational Libraries Only with Hannaford Library Results Improved for Comparability[a-f]

| Denomination | Hannaford | | ALD-1978 | | ALD-1988 | | Summary | | Rank Score ("1" having Highest Denominational Mean Expenditure) |
|---|---|---|---|---|---|---|---|---|---|
| | Number of Libraries | Mean | Number of Libraries | Mean | Number of Libraries | Mean | Number of Libraries | Total Overall Mean | |
| Baptist | 4/26 | $4,900 | 2/83 | $5,000 | 6/71 | $9,583 | 12/180 | $6,495 | 6 |
| Christian | –/21 | 0 | 2/18 | 2,500 | 2/17 | 2,500 | 4/56 | 2,500 | 10 |
| Churches of Christ | – | – | –/0 | – | –/2 | – | –/2 | – | |
| Congregational | –/17 | 0 | –/0 | – | –/0 | – | –/17 | – | |
| Episcopal/Anglican | 2/43 | 1,250 | 1/41 | 2,500 | 4/33 | 11,880 | 7/117 | 5,210 | 8 |
| Independent | – | – | –/3 | – | –/1 | – | –/4 | – | |
| Lutheran | 1/42 | 750 | 3/53 | 6,667 | –/42 | – | 4/137 | 3,709 | 9 |
| Mennonite | – | – | –/3 | – | –/4 | – | –/7 | – | |
| Methodist | 3/80 | 2,267 | 3/55 | 4,167 | 6/64 | 15,420 | 12/199 | 7,285 | 4 |
| Other Denominations | 5/57 | 3,638 | 2/86 | 8,750 | 5/71 | 5,000 | 12/214 | 5,796 | 7 |
| Presbyterian | 4/85 | 4,000 | 1/115 | 2,500 | 2/97 | 15,000 | 7/297 | 7,167 | 5 |
| U.C.C. | 1/22 | 14,000 | –/13 | – | –/13 | – | 1,48 | 14,000 | 2 |
| Jewish | 5/6 | 7,026 | 16/150 | 3,750 | 43/170 | 15,000 | 64/326 | 8,592 | 3 |
| Roman Catholic | 3/12 | 7,667 | 1/14 | 2,500 | 2/8 | 76,250 | 6/34 | 28,806 | 1 |
| Total | 28/411 | 4,856 | 31/634 | 4,274 | 70/593 | 15,070 | 129/1,638 | 8,067 | 8,067 (mean is between rank numbers 3 and 4) |

[a]The designation 4/26 means four active cases out of a possible twenty-six cases.

TABLE 6.35 (continued)
Three Study Comparison of Annual Library Expenditure on Personnel: Congregational Libraries Only With Hannaford Library Results Improved for Comparability[a-f]

[b]For this table means are calculated on the base of *only those libraries with salary expenditures*, not on the basis of all libraries in each denomination, i.e., libraries with zero expenditures whether actual or through No Response have been dropped from the Hannaford study results.

[c]The number of libraries is too small for the Christian, Lutheran, U.C.C., and Roman Catholic denominations for any true ranking to occur. Therefore, the rank values for salary/personnel expenditure indicate Jewish, Methodist, Presbyterian, and Baptist in that order for denominations of $\geq$7 libraries with salaried personnel. This order seems relatively acceptable given our knowledge of these denominations. The overall mean of $8,067 is similarly acceptable and is possibly the only really concrete statistic on the entire table (representing 129 libraries out of 1,638).

[d]In fact, the one inescapable conclusion to be drawn is that most libraries (92 percent) do not boast paid personnel! Also, Jewish libraries with their 64 contributing responses to a total of 129 libraries with paid personnel is relatively stable from one system of zero-registration to another. It represents nearly half (64/129 = 50 percent) of the active libraries and establishes the overall mean.

[e]Therefore, to a very large extent, if the overall mean is $8,067, then it is largely because the Jewish mean is $8,592. The two conclusions are (1) many Jewish librarians are paid (64/326 = 19.6 percent, or one-fifth) and (2) Jewish librarians are paid best. The overall estimated mean (using the usual procedure where each single library is given equal weight) for those libraries *not* in the Jewish group = $8,203.33 and depends heavily on the Roman Catholic and U.C.C. salary rates in 1988. Even so, for this variable and for congregational libraries, Jews lead on both calculation indicators (between $300 to $500 per library.)

[f]Overall mean = (mean 1986 + mean 1978 + mean 1988)/3 for the penultimate column.

**TABLE 6.36**
Summary of Four Congregational Library Studies: White, Hannaford, ALD 1978, ALD 1988: Selected Variables[a-d]

| Variable | White | | Hannaford | | ALD-1978 | | ALD-1988 | | 4-Study Total | |
|---|---|---|---|---|---|---|---|---|---|---|
| | Actual/ Total | Mean/ Median | Actual/ Total | Mean/ Median | Actual/ Total | Mean/ Median | Actual/ Total | Mean/ Median | Actual/ Total | Mean/ Median |
| Library age (medians) | 1,366/1,822 (456) | 19.3 (25.0%) | 376/411 (35) | 17.5 (8.5%) | 284/634 (350) | 39.4 (55%) | 339/593 (254) | 37.8 (43.0%) | 2,365/3,460 (1,095) | 23.1 (31.6%) |
| Book/volume holdings | 1,490/1,822 (332) | 1,667 (18.0%) | 405/411 (6) | 2,824 (1.5%) | 465/634 (169) | 4,540 (27%) | 569/593 (24) | 5,737 (4.0%) | 2,929/3,460 (531) | 3,692 (15.3%) |
| Filmstrip holdings | 1,137/1,822 (685) | 101.1 (37.6%) | 404/411 (7) | 39.3 (1.7%) | — | — | — | — | 1,541/2,233 (692) | 70.2 (31.0%) |
| Filmstrips (improved) | same | same | 164/411 (249) | 98 (60.6%) | — | — | — | — | 1,299/2,233 (934) | 99.6 (41.8%) |
| Library circulation charges per month | 1,581/1,822 (241) | 108 (13.2%) | 320/411 (91) | 114.5 (22.0%) | — | — | — | — | 1,901/2,233 (332) | 111.3 (14.9%) |
| Personnel expenditure per year | — | — | $411/411 (0) | $330.8 (0%) | $31/634 (603) | $4,274 (95%) | $70/593 (523) | $15,070 (88.2%) | $512/1,638 (1,126) | $6,558.3 (68.7%) |
| Personnel expenditure (improved) | — | — | $28/411 (383) | $4,856 (93.2%) | same | same | same | same | $129/1,638 (1,509) | $8,067 (92.1%) |
| Total annual library expenditure | $1,635/1,822 (187) | $337.2 (10.3%) | $407/411 (4) | $1,652 (1.0%) | $145/634 (489) | $1,998 (77%) | $235/593 (358) | $7,420 (60.4%) | $2,422/3,460 (1,038) | $2,852 (30.0%) |

[a]Missing cases or No Response shown in brackets.
[b]The designation 1,366/1,822 means 1,366 active cases out of a possible 1,822 cases.
[c]"Improved" mean refers to the minor adjustments made by the author to make two sets of similar data more comparable, usually by removing zero entries from the means to make them equal to No Response as for the two ALD studies.
[d]Medians are shown by age. All other variables show means only.

TABLE 6.37

1978 and 1988 *American Library Directory* Longitudinal Study Congregational Library Personnel Expenditures by Denomination

| Denomination | 1978 | | | | 1988 | | | | Summary | |
|---|---|---|---|---|---|---|---|---|---|---|
| | No. of Libraries | No Response | Total Libraries | Mean ($) | No. of Libraries | No Response | Total Libraries | Mean ($) | % Change 1978-88 | 2-Study Mean |
| Baptist | 2 | 81 | 83 | 5,000 | 6 | 65 | 71 | 9,583 | 92 | 7,292 |
| Christian | 2 | 16 | 18 | 2,500 | 2 | 15 | 17 | 2,500 | 0 | 2,500 |
| Churches of Christ | 0 | 0 | 0 | | 0 | 2 | 2 | | – | – |
| Episcopal/Anglican | 1 | 40 | 41 | 2,500 | 4 | 29 | 33 | 11,880 | 375 | 7,190 |
| Independent | 0 | 3 | 3 | | 0 | 1 | 1 | | – | – |
| Lutheran | 3 | 50 | 53 | 6,667 | 0 | 42 | 42 | | –100 | 6,667 |
| Mennonite | 0 | 3 | 3 | | 0 | 4 | 4 | | – | – |
| Methodist | 3 | 52 | 55 | 4,167 | 6 | 58 | 64 | 15,420 | 270 | 9,794 |
| Other Denominations | 2 | 84 | 86 | 8,750 | 5 | 66 | 71 | 5,000 | –43 | 6,875 |
| Presbyterian | 1 | 114 | 115 | 2,500 | 2 | 95 | 97 | 15,000 | 500 | 8,750 |
| U.C.C. | 0 | 13 | 13 | | 0 | 13 | 13 | | – | – |
| Summary | | | | | | | | | | |
| Jewish | 16 | 134 | 150 | 3,750 | 43 | 127 | 170 | 15,000 | 300 | 9,375 |
| Roman Catholic | 1 | 13 | 14 | 2,500 | 2 | 6 | 8 | 76,250 | 2,950 | 39,375 |
| All Protestant | 14 | 456 | 470 | 5,000 | 25 | 390 | 415 | 10,300 | 106 | 7,650 |
| Total | 31 | 603 | 634 | 4,274 | 70 | 523 | 593 | 15,070 | 253 | 9,672 |

# APPENDIX A
# ANNOTATED POPULAR
# RELIGIOUS LIBRARY
# BIBLIOGRAPHY

## Popular Religious Libraries

Association of Christian Libraries, 910 Union Road, W. Seneca, NY 14224 USA.
Publishes the *Christian Periodical Index.*
Association of Jewish Libraries, National Foundation for Jewish Culture, Room 1512, 122 E. 42nd Street, New York, NY 10168 USA. Has two sections: research and special libraries and synagogue, school and center libraries. Publishes quarterly
*Newsletter*
*Judaica Librarianship,* a semiannual journal
*Jewish Holiday Short Story Index*
*Weine Classification System,* 1982
*Basic Reference List for the SSC Library,* 1989
*Juvenile Judaica,* 1985 plus updates
*A Basic Periodical List for the Judaica Library,* 1989
*Membership Directory,* 1997
In addition, The Temple Library, University Circle and Silver Park, Cleveland, OH 44106 USA publishes useful Jewish library material.
Augsburg Publishing House, *Book Newsletter* (Minneapolis).
Berman, Margot S. *How to Organize a Jewish Library: A Source Book and Guide for Synagogue, School and Center Libraries.* New York: JWB Jewish Book Council, 1982.

*Bowker Annual of Library of Book Trade Information.* New York: R. R. Bowker.

Contains directories of international and national library and publishers associations.

Church and Synagogue Librarians Fellowship, 3800 Donerin Way, Phoenix, MD 21131 USA.

Publishes a three-times-a-year newsletter, *Cross and Star.*

Church and Synagogue Library Association, P.O. Box 19357, Portland, OR 97219 USA.

An ecumenical association of two thousand congregational librarans. Ask for their publication list. Publishes

*Church and Synagogue Libraries,* a bimonthly bulletin

Twenty 10-50 page pamphlets

Five bibliographies

Five videocassettes

Newsletters are published by many CSLA chapters also

"The Church and Synagogue Library Association." *Encyclopedia of Library and Information Science,* 4:674–76. New York: Marcel Dekker, 1971.

"Church and Synagogue Libraries," *Drexel Library Quarterly* 6 (April 1970). Entire issue.

Australian Library Association, contact Margaret Stiller, 9 Charnock Street, Largs North, South Australia, 5016. Publishes a quarterly newsletter, *Off The Shelf.*

Church of Christ, Scientist (Christian Science), 1 Norway Street, Boston, MA 02115 USA. Sponsors a network of public reading rooms in many nations where publications can be read or bought.

The Church of Jesus Christ of Latter-day Saints (LDS), E. North Temple Street, Salt Lake City, UT 84150 USA. Sponsors thousands of LDS genealogical and meetinghouse libraries around the world.

Church Library Association of Toronto, Flat 302, 10 Allanhurst Drive, Islington, ON M9A 4J5 Canada. Publishes a three-times-a-year newsletter, *Library Lines.*

Church Library Council, 5406 Quintana Street, Riverdale, MD 20237 USA. Publishes a quarterly newsletter, *News.*

Congregational Library Association of British Columbia, 38489 Old Yale Road, Abbotsford, BC V2S 4N2 Canada. Publishes a monthly newsletter, *Rare Bird.*

Evangelical Church Library Association, P.O. Box 353, Glen Ellyn, IL

60137 USA. Publishes a quarterly periodical, *Librarian's World,* containing many short book reviews.

Galfand, Sidney. "Organized Jewish Libraries." *Library Journal* 87 (January 1962): 31–34. An early description of synagogue libraries.

"Have a Church Library!" *International Journal of Religious Education* (October 1966). Entire issue.

Harvey, John F., and Shahr Azar Musavi. "Tehran Mosque Libraries and a Comparison with American Christian Church Libraries." *International Library Review* 13 (October 1981): 385–95.

Johnson, Marian. "Lutheran Church Library Association." In *Encyclopedia of Library and Information Science,* 16:363–66. New York: Marcel Dekker, 1975.

Lutheran Church Library Association, 122 W. Franklin Avenue, Minneapolis, MN 55404 USA. Has 1,800 members and 25 chapters. Publishes manuals and booklists as well as *Lutheran Libraries,* a quarterly periodical.

McMichael, Betty. *The Church Librarian's Handbook.* Grand Rapids: Baker Book House, 1984.

National Foundation for Jewish Culture, Room 1512, 122 W. 42nd Street, New York, NY 10168 USA. Publishes basic book and periodical lists.

Pacific Northwest Association of Church Libraries, P.O. Box Section 12379, Main Office Station, Seattle, WA 98111 USA. Publishes a quarterly newsletter, *The Lamplighter.*

"Periodicals to Assist Church Librarians." *Church and Synagogue Libraries* 23 (November/December 1989): 6.

*Provident Library Associates Network,* published quarterly by the Provident Bookstores of the Mennonite Publishing House, 616 Walnut Avenue, Scottdale, PA 15683 USA.

The Southern Baptist Convention Church Library Department, 127 Ninth Avenue North, Nashville, TN 37234 USA. Publishes several manuals and bulletins with information on library organization, and media and book selection, such as the quarterly *Church Media Library Magazine* which contains articles, book and media reviews, and lists of books and media for Sunday School curriculum support.

Union Nationale Culture et Bibliothèques Pour Tous, 63 Rue de Varenne, 75007 Paris, France which operates an extensive religious public library system.

White, Joyce L. "Church Libraries." In *Encyclopedia of Library and Information Science,* 4:662–73. New York: Marcel Dekker, 1970.

# APPENDIX B
# GLOSSARY AND ACRONYMS

See appendix A for other addresses.

Academic Libraries
> This term is used generically to include all junior and senior college and university libraries of all kinds.

Accreditation
> Recognition of an educational institution as maintaining good quality standards in all operating areas, thereby qualifying its graduates for admission to higher or more specialized institutions. In this study, institutions were recognized as being accredited by a regional college and university accrediting association, the Association of Theological Schools, the Association of Bible Colleges, or the U.S. Office of Education.

ACRL
> Association of College and Research Libraries, 50 E. Huron Street, Chicago, IL 60611 USA.

Active
> Those libraries reporting on a variable in some quantity, as shown in tables, as opposed to those libraries responding negatively or simply not responding to questions concerning attributes of interest, e.g., an "active" library for ILL would provide at least limited ILL service.

Additional Activities
> A special analysis that obtained a total score by adding together the library's scores for consortium memberships, OCLC membership, and local automation projects.

AJL
> Association of Jewish Libraries, c/o National Foundation for Jewish Culture, 330 Seventh Avenue, 21st floor, New York, NY 10001 USA.

**ALA**
American Library Association, 50 E. Huron Street, Chicago, IL 60611 USA.

**ALD**
*American Library Directory* (New York: R. R. Bowker Company, annually).

**Archives**
Official institutional records or correspondence in active storage.

**ATLA**
American Theological Library Association, Suite 300, 820 Church Street, Evanston, IL 60201-3707 USA.

**Book**
The term includes all types of printed and media library material.

**Born**
*See* Newly Born Libraries.

**CACUL**
Canadian Association of College and University Libraries, 200 Elgin Street, Ottawa, ON K2P 1L5, Canada.

**Cath LA**
Catholic Library Association, 1258 Pelham Parkway, Bronx, NY 10461 USA.

**Christian Science**
Church of Christ, Scientist.

**Circulation**
Loaning of library material to a user.

**City Population Level**
The population category mean for the city in which the institution is located (since population categories cover a range of specific values, the category means were used to describe all libraries falling within the category).

**CLA**
Canadian Library Association, 200 Elgin Street, Ottawa, ON K2P 1L5, Canada.

**Classification Scheme**
The plan by which books are arranged in systematic order on the shelves, usually by subject.

**CNLIA**
Council National Library and Information Associations, 461 W. Lancaster Avenue, Haverford, PA 19041 USA.

Collection
  The library's stock of print and nonprint material.
Congregational Library
  A library serving a specific church, synagogue, mosque, or other house
  of worship, a popular religious library. The term should not be confused with the Congregational denomination or with the other kinds
  of popular religious libraries, i.e., religious parochial school and
  public libraries. Many congregations have a collection of book material which does not meet the definition of a library and so should
  not be called one.
  To become a library, the collection should (1) be organized in a logical order, e.g., by author or subject, (2) have an appointed supervi-
  sor, librarian, or committee, (3) actively provide circulation, processing and reference service, (4) contain at least one hundred
  volumes of library material, (5) be established in a dedicated room,
  space or other quarters with stack shelving, (6) have a recognized
  and clearly defined user group or clientele, (7) have a functional organization plan and set of objectives, and preferably (8) be supported with an annual income from the sponsoring institution. *See
  also* Library.
Consortium
  An organized group of usually similar institutions banded together to
  carry out specific projects.
Convent
  The house of a religious order or congregation where nuns and sisters
  live, work, and pray.
CSLA
  Church and Synagogue Library Association, P.O. Box 19357, Port-
  land, OR 97219 USA.
Data
  While the words data and information often have distinct meanings, in
  this book they are generally considered to be synonymous.
Database
  In this study, equals the entire sample, or all the questionnaires com-
  pleted for one *ALD* edition.
DDC
  Dewey Decimal Classification.
Dead Libraries
  *See* No Longer Listed Libraries.

Degree, Highest
   The highest level of academic degree awarded to students by a college or university measured by years normally needed for completion.
Denomination
   Christianity is a faith and Presbyterianism is a denomination. A denomination is a religious organization uniting a number of local congregations in one single administrative body. As used in this book, the term "denomination" distinguishes each Protestant group from another and similarly, Buddhist, Jewish, and Roman Catholic groups, for instance, from each other as well as from Protestant groups. The term is used as a delimiter of organizational affinities rather than as an indicating position on beliefs, creed, or dogma.
Enrollment
   The number of students attending classes at an academic institution at one time, usually expressed in terms of full-time equivalent and covering both undergraduate and graduate credit students.
Extended Services and Collections
   A special analysis that obtained a total score by adding together for each library religious subject interests, special collections and publications.
Faculty
   Faculty members (teachers) are reported in full-time equivalent form for most of the academic institutions and their libraries that are represented in the *ALD*.
Faith
   A system of beliefs: Buddhist, Christian, Hindu, Jewish, Muslim, etc. Each faith may include several denominations.
FID
   International Federation of Documentation, P. O. Box 90402, 2509 LK The Hague, Netherlands.
Finance
   The library's income and expenditures of all kinds.
Founding
   Starting date, when the institution or the library began work.
Gross Library Growth Rating
   This special analysis aggregated numerous variables. It covers

twenty-seven (scholarly) or twenty-two (popular) variables and shows the points earned by specific libraries by virtue of summing their individual growth percentages, table by table. The twenty-seven variables are total staff members, professional staff members, clerical staff members, student assistant staff members, volume holdings, periodical title holdings, vertical file holdings, microforms, media holdings, map holdings, art reproductions, material expenditures, personnel expenditures, other expenditures, total expenditures, consortium memberships, OCLC memberships, automation projects, subject interests, special collections, publications, library age, city population size, degree years offered, faculty size, students enrolled, and cumulative expenditure.

Holdings

A library's collection of reading and viewing material. Total holdings is a special analysis that shows the aggregate by summing the volumes, periodical titles, vertical file drawers, and microforms for a specific library or a group of libraries.

House of Worship

A generic term that refers to a church, synagogue, mosque, or other meeting place for congregational service, worship, and prayer.

IFLA

International Federation of Library Associations and Institutions, The Royal Library, P. O. Box 95312, 2509 CH The Hague, Netherlands.

Independent

An institution with no denominational affiliation. In this study, the term carries a meaning similar to the terms interdominational, ecumenical, and nondenominational, though these are by no means synonyms. While the independent institutions are not denominationally affiliated, this does not mean they lack dogma or creed. Some are permeated with religion while others are not.

Junior College

The thirteenth and usually also the fourteenth year of formal schooling provided in an institution that commonly offers a program leading to an associate of arts or science degree.

LCLA

Lutheran Church Library Association, 122 W. Franklin Avenue, Minneapolis, MN 55404 USA.

**LDS**

Church of Jesus Christ of Latter-day Saints. Refers to either the church located in Salt Lake City, Utah, or the one located in Independence, MO.

**Librarians**

Narrowly, they are persons who have graduated from a library school, but broadly, and as used in much of this book, they are simply persons who are in charge of libraries. The narrow definition is used more often at the scholarly level and less often at the popular level.

**Library**

Should be interpreted in the widest possible sense, to include all types of information activities and personnel. That institution in which such material as books, manuscripts, serials, documents, and media are collected and organized for use but normally not for sale. *See also* congregational library.

**Library Age**

Refers to the library's founding date.

**Library Material**

Includes books, bound and current issues of periodicals and continuations, documents, media, art reproductions, maps, vertical file material, and microforms.

**LL**

Refers to the index to library books and periodicals, *Library Literature*.

**Longitudinal**

A statistical term referring to two or more samples taken at different points in time but which are sufficiently comparable to permit meaningful statistical comparison and analysis in order to generate trend information.

**Matched Pair**

A library that appears in both the 1978 and the 1988 *ALD* editions.

**Mean**

A statistical measure of central tendency, an average or the arithmetic midpoint of sample scores.

**Media**

Includes films, filmstrips, video- and audiocassettes, and many other audiovisual devices. Media holdings (cumulative) includes these measures of media, maps, and art reproductions. As these three variables are dichotomous, the cumulative is obtained by adding positive yes or no responses: range is 0 to 3.

**Median**

A statistical measure of central tendency in which the middle record within a range of variable values represents the median.

Micro

Microform holdings. Microforms include microfiche, microfilm, microcards, ultrafiche, or any printed material made available on film in miniaturized form.

Mode

A statistical measure of central tendency: the most frequent value in a set of data scores on one variable, i.e., the most common response or the flat top of the curve of distribution.

Monastery

The house of a religious order where priests, brothers, or monks live, work, and pray. Also may be called an abbey or priory.

Mormons

Members of the original or of the Reorganized Church of Jesus Christ of Latter-day Saints.

NCES

National Center for Education Statistics, 400 Maryland Avenue, SW, Washington, DC 20202 USA.

Newly Listed Libraries

These libraries appeared in the 1988 but not in the 1978 *ALD*, so presumably they were "newly born" in the decade preceding 1988 as far as the *ALD* was concerned.

No Longer Listed Libraries

Those libraries were listed in the 1978 but not in the 1988 *ALD*. As far as the *ALD* was concerned, they did not reply to the 1988 questionnaire nor could their information be located elsewhere, and so they were "dead," effectively and statistically, at least temporarily.

No Response

A statistical term that refers to the number of libraries which did not respond to a particular query on a questionnaire.

North America

In this author's definition, North America is that Western hemisphere continent northwest of South American that is bound by the Arctic, Atlantic, and Pacific oceans. This study omits Mexico and the Central American countries as well as the island countries constituting Cuba and the Caribbean area. That leaves Canada and the United States to be included. These two countries make up 80 percent of the land area and 70 percent of the North American population.

Number

Number is a term used in the study's tables (often shown simply as N) to show the tally of libraries (or staff members, volumes, etc.) in that

portion of the table. In the same context, the word "libraries" means
number of libraries.

OCLC
  Online Computer Library Center, P.O. Box 7777, Dublin, OH 43017
  USA. A cooperative and computerized library consortium with a
  large number of academic and other library members.

Paired Libraries
  *See* Matched Pair.

Parochial School
  A private elementary or secondary school sponsored and to some extent staffed by a religious group or church.

Percentage
  A statistical and tabular term that shows the proportion of a sample
  whole represented by a part and expressed in hundredths, e.g., in the
  *ALD* 1978 study, 6 percent of the libraries were located in junior colleges, 125 of 2,062 libraries. Percentages are often rounded in order
  not to exceed the decimal places of accuracy of the statistics from
  which the percentage was originally derived.

Periodical
  A publication issued on a regular schedule twice or more times a year.

Personnel
  The library's staff members of all ranks. In this study they are divided
  among professional, clerical, and student assistants (volunteers or
  committee members).

Popular or Popular-Level
  Generally, popular religious libraries serve users primarily at an elementary or secondary school or a public library level with an appropriate material collection. Three types of religious libraries
  are classified at the popular level: congregational (church, synagogue, mosque, or other house of worship), parochial school, and
  public. More formally, a popular-level library is an organized and
  staffed collection that may include adult, young adult, and children's material, religious periodicals, and other printed and media material. It provides educational and perhaps recreational
  reading and other library service primarily on religious themes
  and on a popular level for lay congregational members, friends,
  and for religious education centers, Sunday and synagogue
  school teachers and students, and in some cases, for the general
  public.
  Such libraries as the following are included in this group: (1) Roman
  Catholic church parish or community libraries and information

centers; (2) synagogue, temple, or Jewish center libraries; (3) Jewish, Catholic, Lutheran, or other denomination parochial or private religious school libraries; and (4) Christian Science reading rooms and Church of Jesus Christ of Latter-day Saints meetinghouse and genealogical libraries. All faiths and denominations are included as found in both countries.

Private Public Libraries
In this context, a library that provides service to the general public rather than to a specific congregation, although its own congregation members may be among its heaviest users. These libraries constitute *private public libraries*. Such a library is sponsored by a specific congregation, society, or order and provides library material for borrower or rental use.

Private School Libraries
A term that can be used in either a generic or specific sense for a religious elementary or secondary school. Almost but not quite synonymous with a parochial or synagogue school. A parochial school is a private school directly sponsored by a house of worship or a diocesan headquarters and is usually open to any student in its district who wishes to attend it. It may or may not be part of a city religious (usually Roman Catholic) school system. A private school (in the specific sense) is an independent school sponsored by a specific religious organization or board of trustees or religious order that may restrict its enrollment in any way it wishes. A synagogue school is a Jewish school at the elementary and secondary level that is sponsored by a specific synagogue or by a group of synagogues. Used in the generic sense, a private school is any school not publicly supported, so all parochial and synagogue (as well as nonreligious and non-publicly supported) schools are private schools.

There are five kinds of religiously affiliated school libraries: (1) Catholic parochial school libraries, which are sponsored by a local parish or diocese and in certain large cities form part of a system of such elementary and secondary school libraries; (2) private Catholic elementary and secondary school libraries, which are sponsored by an order of the clergy, brothers, or nuns or are independent and have their own school board of trustees; (3) Lutheran, Episcopal, Quaker, Jewish, etc., elementary and secondary parochial school libraries, which may form part of a system of denominational school libraries; (4) Protestant or Jewish elementary and secondary schools, which are similar to those in (2) above; and (5) private part-time and independent synagogue or Jewish schools, which cover parts of both elementary and secondary school levels, concentrating on teaching the Jewish history, and religion, culture, and life, which are sponsored by a specific synagogue or by a group of them.

Professional Librarian

A person who has graduated with a degree from a library school.

Public Library

In this context, a religious library that provides service to the general public rather than to a specific congregation, though its own congregation members may be among its heaviest users. These libraries constitute private public libraries. Such a library is sponsored by a specific congregation, society, or order and provides religious library material for borrowing or for rental use, e.g., a Christian Science reading room.

Publications

Serials or monographs published by a specific library.

Range

A statistical measure of distribution that calculates the maximum variation between sample records with scores on the same variable, e.g., the "highest" library in a sample has 1,295,450 volumes and the "lowest" possesses only 990 volumes. The range is 1,295,450 minus 990.

Ratio

A statistical term in which two figures are juxtaposed in order to compare them closely and show their relative magnitudes. The number of 1978 United States:Canada libraries can be compared as 1930: 116 or 16.6:1.0 in ratio form.

Reference Work

Answering readers' question, helping them locate useful information.

Region

An area of the United States including several contiguous states. For Canada, the entire nation is put into one large region due to smaller population size.

Religion

This word can be defined as the service and worship of a deity or god or an institutionalized system of beliefs and practices relating to a supreme being.

Religious

This word is used in two distinct senses here. In general, it refers to any direct or indirect connection with a congregation or a religious denomination or faith. Specifically, it is used also to refer to the members of a religious order, such as Dominican brothers or Franciscan nuns, who may be referred to collectively by the phrase "the religious."

Religious Administrative Office

Offices of a denomination or faith, usually located centrally, and administering or liaising with one or more houses of worship and other religious activities of the denomination.

Religious History Libraries and Archive Centers

Those libraries and archive centers that house and service religious historical and archival material, usually for a particular denomination, nationally or regionally. While table 1.1 calls for this category and data was collected on it from the *ALD*, relatively few of these libraries seem to exist. A revised edition of the classification scheme may place this category under Organization or Institution Administrative Libraries.

Religious Libraries

Those libraries that serve under an institution formally and officially or else informally sponsored by or affiliated or connected with a religious organization or institution, local, state, or provincewide, national or international, such as a house of worship or a denominational headquarters. To put it in a somewhat different way, a library has a religious affiliation when its parent institution, e.g., college or university, house of worship, or religious order, has a formal and official tie (sponsorship or affiliation or connection) with a specific religious group. In other situations, a formal and official tie may not now exist, only an informal and friendly connection, although probably such a connection existed previously. Both cases are recognized. Further, for this study, any library coded with an *R* in the *ALD*. Obviously this is a broad, flexible, and inclusive definition which has been interpreted liberally here. In addition, many academic institutions that presently have or had in the past a connection with a religious institution or organization are included. No distinction was made between institutions that were sponsored formally and directly with financial support by a religious group versus those affiliated with but without financial support from such a group. Nor was it important whether this affiliation was close or distant, presently extant or existing only in the past.

In other words, the definition of a religious library was sufficiently flexible to cover such examples as Canisius College in Buffalo, which was once said to have been officially sponsored by the Roman Catholic Society of Jesus but formally severed or at least redefined that connection several years ago for reasons apparently relating to institutional eligibility for state and federal government student aid. Now, as a more-or-less independent college, Canisius is controlled by a primarily lay board of trustees but still has (and perhaps always will have) a Jesuit priest as president and other Jesuit priests as faculty members. Another questionable example is Temple University in Philadelphia, which is now clearly a state government sponsored and supported institution. However, in its earlier years it was under strong Baptist influence, and its president was a Baptist minister.

This definition may seem too loose and flexible to certain readers. However, under the present circumstances where acceptable definitions have not yet been established through common usage or by previous studies, the author felt bound to select cases according to the greatest generality. Whether or not a particular religious denomination presently has influence on an academic campus (or at least did so in 1978 and 1988) was difficult for the author to ascertain without going there and closely studying the institution and its history, an impossibility for two thousand institutions. So, he had to generalize. Many marginally religious academic institutions were rejected on this basis, but others were accepted into the database. Finally, there is no implication intended here that a present or former religious connection necessarily implies any distinctive ideological, ethical, moral or religious influence on the institution.

Repeat Question

This question asked if the library was included in both the 1978 and 1988 *ALD* editions or merely in the 1988 edition.

Sample

Refers to the study's databases. The questionnaires completed for each *ALD* edition make up the samples taken for 1978 and 1988 respectively.

Scholarly

Generally, scholarly libraries serve users on a tertiary education or research level with material collections at that level. The author classifies several types of religious libraries at the scholarly level: (1) and (2) are those affiliated with colleges of both junior and senior levels, (3) with universities, (4) with seminaries, with (5) convents or (6) monasteries, with (7) denominational or (8) religious order headquarters offices, and with (9) historical or archival collections. All religious libraries can be assigned to either the scholarly or popular category based on the educational level of the library's sponsoring organization and its user groups.

Certain religious institutions' libraries were omitted from the *ALD* portion of this study. It deliberately excluded the many religious hospital libraries existing in these countries, for instance. Nor did the study include parochial elementary or secondary school libraries (except for a few). In the former case, the typical material collection contained few religious titles and the library's objectives did not involve religious material service. In the second case, the libraries fell within the popular religious library classification, but only a few of them were listed in either the American Library Directory or the Church and Synagogue Library Association membership list.

Seminary

A school for educating ministers, priests, and other religious workers. This word is used primarily in a generic sense to represent all schools or departments that educate persons for work in the ministry or religious education in any faith or denomination. So, the reader may substitute such words as "school" or "department" or faculty of theology or divinity, Hebrew college, or rabbinical college for "seminary" if desired.

Senior College

The thirteenth through the sixteenth years of formal schooling provided in an institution which commonly offers a program leading to a bachelor's and/or master's degree.

Service

Providing formal or informal advice and assistance directly to users through instruction, referring them to reference material or circulating material to them.

Small City

Those cities with population of ten thousand persons or less.

Special Collection

A library section in which are kept rare and unusual titles and narrowly focused subject collections, or the narrowly focused collection itself.

Student

Number of registered students (pupils) is reported for each academic institution represented in the *ALD* in full-time equivalent form.

Subject Interest

A subject or broad topic that becomes a primary focus for library acquisitions policy.

Sunday School Libraries

A synonym for the church or congregational library since many of these libraries serve primarily the church or Sunday school teachers and students and therefore resemble private elementary and secondary school libraries in certain ways. Generically the same as the synagogue library.

Synagogue Libraries

Among synagogue libraries there are two kinds: (1) synagogue libraries serving primarily the adult congregation and (2) synagogue or parochial school libraries serving private elementary and secondary school students and faculty members. Wherever there is a synagogue school library, it is often the principal library for any synagogue associated with it and which probably has a part-time staff member in charge and regular service hours. This study treats all synagogue, temple and Jewish center libraries as meeting the same definition.

University

An institution that provides at least five years of higher education and offers graduate degrees to students. In this study, also any institution which calls itself a university.

Unmatched Pairs

Includes all libraries not in the matched pairs group, i.e., the dead and the newly born libraries.

U.S.

United States of America.

Variable

A factor or characteristic which is under study, e.g., student enrollment (fte), OCLC membership, or volumes in the library collection.

VF

Vertical file case or cabinet. A wood or steel cabinet in which pamphlets or papers are stored. This study counts the number of drawers held, not the number of cabinets on the inventory.

# APPENDIX C
# POPULAR LIBRARY
# STATISTICAL LIMITATIONS
# AND INTERPRETATION,
# by Jo Ann Mouridou

## Qualifications

The statistics compiled on the 1978 and 1988 editions of the *American Library Directory* have been based on a number of common (although perhaps only partly justifiable) assumptions:

1. The *ALD* data collection activities used the same set of data definitions, i.e., data collected were comparable both *within* each edition and also *between* the two editions,
2. Growth projections made for all variables assume that change over time is approximately *linear*. That is, if a variable changes by a certain number of units in one year, then this change in *units per year* will be continued at more or less the same rate in subsequent years. The suggestion is that if a library adds five hundred books per year then this is the measure of *increase in units p.a.* The five hundred books may mean a 10 percent increase on a base of five thousand books for the year 1980 and only a 9 percent increase for the year 1981 (by which time the library has a base of 5,500 books). Nevertheless, the number of books added per year will tend to be constant.

The assumption of linear change in *units* rather than in *percentages* is probably quite reasonable for all variables except financial measures such as expenditure on material, personnel, "other" categories and total annual library expenditure. For this set of variables it appears more likely that true change should be in the realm of a 10 percent increment in operating costs/expenditures p.a. This tendency toward percentage-oriented change is based on the practice of organized bodies to demand budgetary increases in terms of percentages (to cover both growth and inflation) rather than in terms of number of books, etc. However, there are several factors prohibiting accurate financial forecasts of growth as percentage-based rates:

(a) The United States and Canada use different and incomparable currencies; they vary at different rates as well as being valued at differing rates of exchange.

(b) Although it is possible to calculate the past annual inflation rates, it is not possible to predict accurately the future rates of inflation for the United States.

(c) Most popular libraries are in no position to demand an increase to their budgets, as they are usually not part of organizations working on either strictly fixed or flexible budgeting systems.

(d) It is not safe to assume on the basis of the growth rates between 1978 and 1988 that annual financial change will take the form of an annual *percentage* increase. Total annual library expenditure between 1978 and 1988 "grew" by about 67 percent for all scholarly and popular libraries combined (see longitudinal table 4.178). If the average annual rate of inflation was 5 percent for this period of ten years, then more than 60 percent of the total increase of 67 percent was due to inflation alone! This means that *real* growth exclusive of inflation was between 3 percent and 5 percent for the entire decade! Contrary to appearances, it is unlikely that nearly all of the *actual* financial change was absorbed by inflation. This is obvious simply through examining the real change in volume holdings for all libraries: between 1978 and 1988 *actual* volume holdings "grew" by 17 percent overall and 21 percent for the scholarly libraries (see longitudinal table 4.73).

As the result of the contradictory trends concerning money, it has seemed wisest to project financial increases in the same way as for the other variables: change is calculated per annum in rates of dollars expected to be spent plotted against a *linear* curve, as for the other variables used.

3. The samples gathered as the foundation of the statistical analysis are representative of all the *ALD* religious libraries. Every effort has been made to ensure that this is the case.

4. The samples used for the 1978 and 1988 editions are representative, at least *to a somewhat lesser degree,* of all the religious libraries in the United States and Canada. No doubt this is true; however, it is also true that bodies responding to questionnaires tend to be those more inclined to group participation and less inclined to understaffing or inefficiency. Therefore, there will be a distinct form of bias in the samples used, even though it is difficult to predict the exact *nature* or *direction* or *extent* of the bias.

5. Data collection and publication in the *American Library Directory* does not systematically discriminate against any particular group of libraries. This assumption includes *both* that all libraries are treated equally in terms of data representation on paper *within* the two editions, and *also* that data publication policy is consistent *between* the publications for 1978 and 1988.

6. The system of data categorization used on the study questionnaires is reasonable (vis-à-vis category groups, midpoints, etc.) both in terms of the actual categories used and also with reference to the top category for each one of the operative variables. This assumption is quite valid for most of the variables, i.e., for most of those with standard deviations of approximately one sixth of the variable ranges. However, it is violated for some variables such as "other" expenditures. For this particular variable the top category maxima was much too low to represent accurately the expenditure of many libraries on "other" categories.

As a result, the S.D. for this variable runs between 25 percent and 32 percent of the variable range (see tables C-1, C-2, C-3), about 100 percent too much (this phenomenon is the result of extreme skewness toward the *upper* end of the variable range). The S.D. for popular libraries is only 25 percent—still too large, but much less so than for libraries that tend to have disproportionately larger budgets for all categories of expenditure. This distribution of popular libraries on this variable does not appear to approximate normal at all, possibly because of the disparate nature of "other" expenditure as an expense category and possibly because popular libraries may have any amount to spend on "other" items—from a tiny sum right through to enormous capital investments for facilities or construction.

## Popular Libraries: All Sample and Matched Pairs

Table 2.70 shows popular libraries as having average standard deviations of approximately 9 percent of the entire ranges of the twenty-one variables studied. This finding was expected, as the popular libraries on the whole are much smaller and poorer than their scholarly fellows. If the scholarly library average S.D. is approximately 20 percent of the range, then the 9 percent average S.D. for the popular libraries indicates that the average popular library (1) is much more clustered under a normal curve, (2) is much less bimodal than the scholarly libraries, and (3) more closely resembles other popular libraries on the twenty-one variables than do the scholarly libraries. This set of suggestions is validated by considering that there are only three subgroups of popular libraries, of which congregational is by far the largest, and by looking at table C-3.

The range of material expenditures for scholarly libraries is immense: right up to a $144,400 *mean* value for universities. This is 35.3 *times* as big as the mean popular expenditure. By contrast the popular libraries, which also need to spend money on material, have subgroup ranges between $2,691 (congregational) and $24,290 (public). The range difference within groups is $133,000 for scholarly libraries and only $21,600 for popular libraries. In fact, public libraries vary radically from congregational libraries; however, there are only six public libraries showing expenditure on material vis-à-vis 211 congregational libraries with such expenditures. The overall effect is to show popular libraries as being much more intergroup homogeneous than are the scholarly subgroups. Table 2.71 compares all popular libraries with all popular: matched pairs. As with scholarly libraries, the popular matched pairs are ahead in 1998. The pattern of increase is different, however.

In 1978 the average actual mean is 7.9 percent less for the matched pairs than for the all popular group (19,010 cf. 20,631). However, by 1988 this difference has decreased to −6.5 percent. The ten-year projected growth for the all popular group is an average of 10 percent (107 units). However, for the matched pairs this figure is actually 15 percent (235 units). Although both of these figures reduce to an average first-year increase of only one percent (rounded), by 1998 it is expected that the matched pairs will be ahead on the twenty-one variables by an average of 4.5 percent, or slightly over one thousand units.

As with scholarly samples, the popular library matched pairs sample has a lower average standard deviation than does the all popular group.

Again, this is because the subsample is both relatively more homogeneous and slightly smaller than the one for the all popular group. An examination of the average projected minimums and maximums reveals quite wide ranges (12,655: all popular, and 16,822: matched pairs, cf. approx. 7,860 and 8,440 for scholarly libraries). These figures are greatly larger than the corresponding values for the scholarly samples and are the result of the much lower response rates for popular libraries combined with the significantly smaller sample sizes. See table C-3 again: the 1988 response rate for scholarly libraries averaged 1,057/1,431, or 74 percent. The matching figures for the popular libraries were 230/643 or 36 percent—less than half.

Considering that 230/1,057 equals approximately 22 percent, we would expect that the ranges for popular libraries would be roughly twice as large as for scholarly libraries (the square root of the difference of 22 percent = approximately 47 percent) and this is precisely what we do find—sixteen thousand is twice as large as eight thousand.

However, this statistic is *merely* a *statistic* and does not reflect significantly on the expected growth rates for the two popular library samples. How they grow certainly ought to be within the 90 percent significance range indicated by the maximum, and even within the middle of the range as indicated by the 1998 projection. The 10 percent all popular ten-year projection does not compare particularly favorable with the matching 17 percent ten-year projection for all scholarly libraries; however, considering the size and funding of popular libraries on the whole, this 10 percent is certainly not bad, and even better for the Popular: Matched Pairs with a 15% ten-year expected growth rate (see table 2.71).

## Statistical Comparison: United States versus Canada

Even a quick glance at table 2.73 shows that comparison of the U.S. versus Canadian distributions can proceed along only general lines. Several profound problems arise out of a consideration of libraries from the two countries as constituting parts of the same sample; but there are even larger problems in considering them as separate, independent subsamples of the same whole. Most of the difficulties concern the Canadian libraries.

1. It is questionable if the Canadian libraries listed by the *American Library Directory* are truly representative of Canadian libraries as a population. In addition, it is clear from a look at the mean ages of Canadian libraries in 1978 and 1988 (75 years and 68 years for scholarly, and 64 and 54 years for popular) that the l composition of the groups is swinging toward younger establishments.

2. Canadian libraries show a *different profile* than do their American counterparts. For example, Canadian popular libraries tend to locate increasingly in cities of over a half million persons. Canadian scholarly libraries are found in cities of well over 400,000 persons, although the mean is dropping slightly. American scholarly libraries, on the other hand, are located in increasingly smaller cities of approximately 325,000 persons, while American popular libraries are in cities of 350,000 on the average. Similarly, Canadian library spending has always been higher than U.S. spending (in Canadian currency), but it is tending to level off whereas the American library spending curves are on a sharp incline (well over 40 percent for the United States but less than 20 percent increases for Canada, see both the scholarly and popular ten-year projections for 1998). The fact that the two countries show varying library profiles suggests strongly that these two groups ought *not* to be studied under the same sample curve.

3. The average variable response rates for Canadian libraries (over the fourteen variables for which mean numeric projections to 1998 were calculated) is *50 libraries for the scholarly subgroup* and only *7.1 for the popular libraries*. Although fifty libraries is a respectable (if small) sample, an average of seven responses is negligible and cannot be considered seriously as more than a token sample. Curiously enough, both of the Canadian groups are approximately 5 percent the size of their American counterpart groups (5.72 percent for scholarly and 4.29 percent for popular). The rule for measuring the reliability of a sample is "the size of the error is inversely proportional to the square root of the sample size." By this standard the American samples of 875 and 166 are stable, predictable, and reliable. By contrast, the Canadian groups are 4.2 times less reliable for scholarly libraries and 4.8 times less so for the popular group! When it is considered that the *American popular libraries* are 2.3 times less reliable than their *scholarly* counterparts, this is a serious qualification indeed. However, the fact that the reduced reliability pattern displayed by the Canadian scholarly libraries is so closely replicated among that country's popular libraries suggests that the Canadian samples, if not overwhelmingly similar in profiles to the American samples, are at least *randomly representative of all Canadian libraries in the same proportions as are the U.S.*

*scholarly and popular libraries.* This stands as one indicator that the *American Library Directory* is unbiased toward either scholarly or popular libraries within the U.S.-Canadian distribution.

## Interpretation of the Statistics

Despite the limitations placed on interpretation as the result of the small Canadian sample sizes, the figures show distinct trends that will probably be continued into the future. Table 2.73 contains two columns of projection data that are valuable indicators of *present profiles* and *future developments.* For the two U.S.-based samples, the column labeled "projection 1998" shows how slowly or rapidly changes can be expected to affect the fourteen major variables listed.

For American popular libraries, total annual library expenditure will also increase, largely as a result of the push toward higher personnel expenses and greater volume holdings. The number of library staff members is expected to increase at about the same rate of growth as for volume holdings (20.3 percent vs. 17.7 percent); consortium memberships are projected to increase (but may not) by about the same amount (16.7 percent), and extra services in the form of subject interests, special collections, and library publications are also predicted to rise, although at a slower rate. This slight discrepancy may be a function of the need for libraries to achieve a certain minimum size (minimum threshold value) before they can afford the luxury of special collections and publications.

American popular libraries also grow at a slightly slower rate: 16.2 percent on average over the set. For this group library age and city population size decrease somewhat accompanied by slight decreases in periodical subscriptions and microform holdings. The reason for these latter two decreases is unexplained: the predictions may prove spurious.

The Canadian popular library group is hardest to interpret as it contains so few libraries. The "ten-year percentage change" column indicates that there will be decreases in library age, total library staff, library professionals, and volume holdings. The same pattern of newer, smaller libraries is indicated here as for the Canadian scholarly sample. Mean sample age actually *fell by ten years* between the 1978 and the 1988 editions of the *ALD.* This one fact in itself is characteristic of this group of libraries (70 percent response rate). If we combine with this fact the average variable growth projection of 12.2 percent for the upcoming ten years, cf. the break-even projection for the Canadian scholarly libraries, it appears that the northern popular sample may make great strides indeed. The only other variables (with sufficient responses to support this thesis) are volume holdings and special collections for Canadian popular libraries which are higher than for their American counterparts.

It is significant that *only Canadian popular* libraries (among the four subsamples) show a trend toward locating in bigger cities. The implication is that the popular libraries from Canada reporting to the *ALD* tend to be the largest and most prominent within the Canadian library population (only large Canadian cities have populations sufficient to draw large, affluent congregations to support large popular libraries). There is no other *statistical* evidence to support this conclusion except that the twenty-one libraries reporting volume holdings showed a mean for Canada 468 percent above their American counterparts, and this single fact alone is more than sufficient to justify such an idea as a working hypothesis! That it is not a fluke is verified by the whacking 738 percent superiority reported by twenty-one libraries in 1978.

TABLE C-1

*American Library Directory* Statistical Summary for All Popular
Libraries

| | Variable Range from 0— | Value of 1 Standard Dev'n | Percentage of Range | Value of 1 Standard Error of the Means |
|---|---|---|---|---|
| Library age | 270 | 24 | 9 | 3 |
| Library city population size | 5,000,000 | 629,196 | 13 | 60,806 |
| Institutional degree years offered | 8 | 0 | 0 | 1 |
| Total library staff size | 69 | 4 | 6 | 2 |
| Library professionals | 16 | 2 | 11 | 1 |
| Library clerks | 16 | 4 | 25 | 1 |
| Library student assistants | 37 | 1 | 3 | 2 |
| Faculty size | 360 | 60 | 17 | 71 |
| Students enrolled | 5,500 | 141 | 3 | 221 |
| Total annual library expenditure | 610,000 | 22,772 | 4 | 5,350 |
| Annual expenditure on material | 182,000 | 4,324 | 2 | 1,303 |
| Annual expenditure on personnel | 350,000 | 7,576 | 2 | 8,234 |
| Annual expenditure on "other" | 22,000 | 5,404 | 25 | 4,993 |
| Library volume holdings | 640,000 | 12,847 | 2 | 1,319 |
| Library periodical subscriptions | 1,800 | 131 | 7 | 21 |
| Library microform holdings | 280,000 | 81,110 | 29 | 62,488 |
| Library vertical file drawers | 145 | 8 | 6 | 2 |
| Library consortium memberships | 9 | 0 | 0 | 1 |
| Library subject interests | 7 | 1 | 17 | 1 |
| Library special collections | 12 | 1 | 9 | 1 |
| Library publications | 7 | 0 | 0 | −1 |
| All variable total | | | 188.9 | |
| All variable mean | | | 9.0 | |

TABLE C-2

*American Library Directory* Statistical Summary for All Popular
Libraries: Matched Pairs

| | Variable Range from 0— | Value of 1 Standard Dev'n | Percentage of Range | Value of 1 Standard Error of the Means |
|---|---|---|---|---|
| Library age | 270 | 23 | 9 | 4 |
| Library city population size | 5,000,000 | 595,639 | 12 | 67,110 |
| Institutional degree years offered | 8 | 0 | 0 | 1 |
| Total library staff size | 69 | 4 | 6 | 2 |
| Library professionals | 16 | 2 | 11 | 1 |
| Library clerks | 16 | 4 | 25 | 1 |
| Library student assistants | 37 | 1 | 3 | 3 |
| Faculty size | 360 | 60 | 17 | 70 |
| Students enrolled | 5,500 | 141 | 3 | 135 |
| Total annual library expenditure | 610,000 | 23,537 | 4 | 6,479 |
| Annual expenditure on material | 182,000 | 4,055 | 2 | 1,486 |
| Annual expenditure on personnel | 350,000 | 7,663 | 2 | 10,024 |
| Annual expenditure on "other" | 22,000 | 5,404 | 25 | 5,460 |

TABLE C-2 (continued)
*American Library Directory* Statistical Summary for All Popular
Libraries: Matched Pairs

|  | Variable Range from 0— | Value of 1 Standard Dev'n | Percentage of Range | Value of 1 Standard Error of the Means |
|---|---|---|---|---|
| Library volume holdings | 640,000 | 11,485 | 2 | 1,509 |
| Library periodical subscriptions | 1,800 | 141 | 8 | 25 |
| Library microform holdings | 280,000 | 86,287 | 31 | 86,194 |
| Library vertical file drawers | 145 | 9 | 6 | 3 |
| Library consortium memberships | 9 | 0 | 0 | 1 |
| Library subject interests | 7 | 1 | 17 | 1 |
| Library special collections | 12 | 1 | 9 | 1 |
| Library publications | 7 | 0 | 0 | −1 |
| All variable total |  |  | 190.6 |  |
| All variable mean |  |  | 9.1 |  |

TABLE C-3
1978 and 1988 *American Library DIirectory* Longitudinal Study All
Library Expenditure on Material by Library Type

| Library Type | Number of Libraries | No Response | Total Libraries | Mean Dollars | Number of Libraries | No Response | Total Libraries | Mean Dollars | Percentage Change 1978–88 |
|---|---|---|---|---|---|---|---|---|---|
|  | ----------1 9 7 8---------- | | | | ----------1 9 8 8---------- | | | | |
| Scholarly | 749 | 626 | 1,375 | 49,430 | 1,057 | 374 | 1,431 | 81,500 | 65% |
| Junior college | 52 | 73 | 125 | 16,980 | 73 | 35 | 108 | 37,200 | 119% |
| Senior college | 435 | 269 | 704 | 46,300 | 579 | 126 | 705 | 82,180 | 77% |
| University | 113 | 41 | 154 | 113,100 | 169 | 20 | 189 | 144,400 | 28% |
| Seminary | 105 | 128 | 233 | 29,060 | 162 | 68 | 230 | 64,570 | 122% |
| Convent/ monastery | 7 | 28 | 35 | 3,393 | 6 | 19 | 25 | 10,750 | 217% |
| Denomina- tional HQ | 18 | 59 | 77 | 4,181 | 29 | 57 | 86 | 14,540 | 248% |
| History/ archives | 19 | 28 | 47 | 3,566 | 39 | 49 | 88 | 12,990 | 264% |
| Popular | 110 | 577 | 687 | 1,811 | 230 | 413 | 643 | 4,085 | 126% |
| Congrega- tional | 100 | 534 | 634 | 1,128 | 211 | 382 | 593 | 2,691 | 139% |
| Parochial | 3 | 24 | 27 | 9,083 | 13 | 12 | 25 | 17,380 | 91% |
| Public | 7 | 19 | 26 | 8,464 | 6 | 19 | 25 | 24,290 | 187% |
| Total | 859 | 1,203 | 2,062 | 43,330 | 1,287 | 787 | 2,074 | 67,670 | 56% |

# APPENDIX D
## *AMERICAN LIBRARY DIRECTORY* RELIGIOUS LIBRARY DATA FORM (Harvey)

1. Edition and lib number? (1) 31 _____ (2) 35 _____ (3) 36 _____ (4) 37 _____ (5) 41 _____ (6) 42 _____
2. Institution? _____
3. Library name? _____
4. Library type? (1) Scholarly _____: (2) Junior col _____ (3) Senior col _____ (4) University _____
   (5) Seminary _____ (6) Convent/Monastery _____
   (7) Denominational HQ _____ (8) History/Archives _____
   (9) Popular _____: (10) Congregational _____ (11) Parochial _____
   (12) Public _____
5. Accreditation status? (1) Regional _____ (2) Denominational _____ (3) Other _____ (4) AABC _____
   (5) ATLA _____ (6) ATS _____ (7) U.S. Dept. of Education _____
6. Formal religious denomination affiliation? (1) Yes _____ (2) No _____
7. Nation? (1) USA _____ (2) Canada _____
8. (1) State _____ (2) Province _____
9. Region? (1) NE _____ (2) MA _____ (3) SE _____ (4) SW _____ (5) W _____ (6) RM _____
   (7) MW _____ (8) Can _____
10. City? _____ 11. Repeat? (1) Yes _____ (2) _____ (3) _____
12. City popul? (1)    0– 5000 _____    (5) 50001–100000 _____    (9) 700001–1000000 _____
      (2) 5001–10000 _____    (6) 100001–300000 _____    (10) 1–2 million _____
      (3) 10001–30000 _____    (7) 300001–500000 _____    (11) 2–3 million _____
      (4) 30001–50000 _____    (8) 500001–700000 _____    (12) 3+ million _____
13. Questionnaire returned? (1) Yes _____ (2) No _____
14. Departmental library? (1) Yes _____ (2) No _____
15. Age?    (1) 0–1800 _____    (5) 1861–80 _____    (9) 1941–60 _____
      (2) 1801–20 _____    (6) 1881–1900 _____    (10) 1961–70 _____
      (3) 1821–40 _____    (7) 1901–20 _____    (11) 1971–80 _____
      (4) 1841–60 _____    (8) 1921–40 _____    (12) 1981+ _____
16. Highest degree? (1) Associate _____ (2) Bachelors _____ (3) Masters _____ (4) Doctors _____
17. Director named? (1) Yes _____ (2) No _____ 18. Director's sex? (1) Male _____ (2) Female _____
19. Director's religious order status? (1) Priest or brother _____ (2) Nun or sister _____ (3) Neither _____
20. Denomination?
      (1) Adventist _____          (12) Congregational _____          (23) Pentecostal _____
      (2) Assemblies of God _____  (13) Eastern Orthodox _____          (24) Presbyterian _____
      (3) Baha'i _____             (14) Episcopal/Anglican _____         (25) Reformed _____

703

Page:

**704  Popular Religious Libraries in North America**

(4) Baptist ____   (15) Friends ____   (26) Roman Catholic ____
(5) Brethren ____   (16) Independent ____   (27) Salvation Army ____
(6) Christian (D of C) ____   (17) Jehovah's Wit ____   (28) Theosophist ____
(7) Christian Science ____   (18) Jewish ____   (29) Unit Univer ____
(8) Church of Canada ____   (19) Lutheran ____   (30) United Ch of Ch ____
(9) Church of Christ ____   (20) Mennonite ____   (31) Unknown ____
(10) Church of God ____   (21) Methodist ____
(11) Church of The Nazarene __   (22) Mormon ____
(32) Other _____

21. Staff? *Profess* (1) 1 ___ (2) 2 ___ (3) 3 ___ (4) 4 ___ (5) 5 ___ (6) 6 ___ (7) 7 ___ (8) 8 ___
(9) 9 ___ (10) 10+ ___

22. Staff? *Clerk* (1) 1 ___ (2) 2 ___ (3) 3 ___ (4) 4 ___ (5) 5 ___ (6) 6 ___ (7) 7 ___ (8) 8 ___
(9) 9 ___ (10) 10+ ___

23. Staff? *Stud Asst*  (1) 1–2 ___   (5) 9–10 ___   (9) 17–18 ___   (13) 25–26 ___
(2) 3–4 ___   (6) 11–12 ___   (10) 19–20 ___   (14) 27–28 ___
(3) 5–6 ___   (7) 13–14 ___   (11) 21–22 ___   (15) 29+ ___
(4) 7–8 ___   (8) 15–16 ___   (12) 23–24 ___

24. Enrollment? (1) 0–300 ____   (5) 1201–1500 ____   (9) 2401–2700 ____   (13) 4001–4500 ____
(2) 301–600 ____   (6) 1501–1800 ____   (10) 2701–3000 ____   (14) 4501–5000 ____
(3) 601–900 ____   (7) 1801–2100 ____   (11) 3001–3500 ____   (15) 5001+ ____
(4) 901–1200 ____   (8) 2101–2400 ____   (12) 3501–4000 ____

25. Faculty?  (1) 0–20 ____   (6) 101–120 ____   (11) 201–220 ____   (15) 281–300 ____
(2) 21–40 ____   (7) 121–140 ____   (12) 221–240 ____   (16) 301–320 ____
(3) 41–60 ____   (8) 141–160 ____   (13) 241–260 ____   (17) 321–340 ____
(4) 61–80 ____   (9) 161–180 ____   (14) 261–280 ____   (18) 341+
(5) 81–100 ____   (10) 181–200 ____

26. Expenditures? *Material*
(1) $0– 500 ____   (6) $10001–18000 ____   (11) $88001–110000 ____
(2) $501– 1000 ____   (7) $18001–28000 ____   (12) $110001–122000 ____
(3) $1001– 2000 ____   (8) $28001–47000 ____   (13) $122001–142000 ____
(4) $2001– 6000 ____   (9) $47001–67000 ____   (14) $142001–162000 ____
(5) $6001–10000 ____   (10) $67001–88000 ____   (15) $162001+ ____

27. Expenditures? *Personnel*
(1) $0– 5000 ____   (6) $50001– 65000 ____   (11) $160001–195000 ____
(2) $5001–10000 ____   (7) $65001– 85000 ____   (12) $195001–230000 ____
(3) $10001–20000 ____   (8) $85001–105000 ____   (13) $230001–265000 ____
(4) $20001–35000 ____   (9) $105001–130000 ____   (14) $265001–300000 ____
(5) $35001–50000 ____   (10) $130001–160000 ____   (15) $300001+ ____

28. Expenditures? *Other*
(1) $0–1000 ____   (5) $6001– 8000 ____   (9) $14001–16000 ____
(2) $1001–2000 ____   (6) $8001–10000 ____   (10) $16001–18000 ____
(3) $2001–4000 ____   (7) $10001–12000 ____   (11) $18001+ ____
(4) $4001–6000 ____   (8) $12001–14000 ____

29. Expenditures? *Total*
(1) $0– 500 ____   (5) $20001– 45000 ____   (9) $220001–310000 ____
(2) $501– 1500 ____   (6) $45001– 95000 ____   (10) $310001–410000 ____
(3) $1501– 7500 ____   (7) $95001–150000 ____   (11) $410001–510000 ____
(4) $7501–20000 ____   (8) $150001–220000 ____   (12) $510001+ ____

30. Holdings? *Volumes*
(1) 0–1000 ____   (5) 20001–50000 ____   (9) 240001–340000 ____
(2) 1001–3500 ____   (6) 50001–100000 ____   (10) 340001–440000 ____
(3) 3501–10000 ____   (7) 100001–160000 ____   (11) 440001–540000 ____
(4) 10001–20000 ____   (8) 160001–240000 ____   (12) 540001+ ____

31. Holdings? *Periodicals*

(1)    0–100 ____        (5)  601– 800 ____        (9) 1401–1600 ____
(2) 101–200 ____        (6)  801–1000 ____        (10) 1601+ ____
(3) 201–400 ____        (7) 1001–1200 ____
(4) 401–600 ____        (8) 1201–1400 ____

32. Holdings? *VF*

(1)  0– 5 ____        (5) 31–40 ____        (9)  86–100 ____
(2)  6–10 ____        (6) 41–55 ____        (10) 101–115 ____
(3) 11–20 ____        (7) 56–70 ____        (11) 116–130 ____
(4) 21–30 ____        (8) 71–85 ____        (12) 131+ ____

33. Holdings? *Microforms*

(1)    0–  100 ____        (5) 10001– 20000 ____        (9) 120001–180000 ____
(2)  101– 1000 ____        (6) 20001– 40000 ____        (10) 180001+ ____
(3) 1001– 5000 ____        (7) 40001– 80000 ____
(4) 5001–10000 ____        (8) 80001–120000 ____

34. Holdings? *Other*   (1) Media ____    (2) Maps ____    (3) Art Reproductions ____

35. Use?   (1) Circulation to members only ____    (2) Reference service to members only ____

36. Consortium memberships?                     37. Local automation projects? (1) Yes ____

(1) 1 ____ (2) 2 ____ (3) 3 ____ (4) 4 ____ (5) 5 ____ (6) 6 ____ (7) 7 ____ (8) 8+ ____
(9) OCLC? ____

38. Religious subject interests?   (1) Relig studies ____      (2) Others _____

_____                     Number: (3) 1 ____ (4) 2 ____ (5) 3 ____

_____                     (6) 4 ____ (7) 5 ____ (8) 6+ ____

39. Religious special collections? (1) _____

_____ Number: (2) 1 ____ (4) 3 ____ (6) 5 ____ (8) 7 ____ (10) 9 ____
(3) 2 ____ (5) 4 ____ (7) 6 ____ (9) 8 ____ (11) 10+ ____

40. Publications? (1) _____

Number: (2) 1 ____ (3) 2 ____ (4) 3 ____ (5) 4 ____ (6) 5 ____ (7) 6+ ____

41. Notes _____

# APPENDIX E
# CSLA LIBRARIES
# (Hannaford) STATISTICAL
# DATA FORM

Dear CSLA Member,

If you're like me, you often wonder how your congregational library compares with others in budget, circulation, and so forth.

We will appreciate your cooperation in providing the data called for on this form. The information will enable us to know and serve you better. We will send each one of you who participates a report of the tally. It will provide you with a basis for comparison of your library with others of a similar size and situation.

Give approximate numbers if specific figures are not available; then fold to show the mailing address, affix the stamp (saving CSLA funds), and return it by April 30.

Thank you for your time and assistance.

Claudia Hannaford, Chairman
CSLA Continuing Education Committee

CHURCH/SYNAGOGUE NAME _____

    Address _____ City _____ State/Province _____ Zip _____

    Setting: Urban _____ Rural _____ Suburban _____

    Size of congregation (including children): (1–199) _____ (200–499) _____ (500–999) _____ (1000–1999) _____ (2000–4999) _____ (Over 5000) _____ (Over 10000) _____

    Church/Synagogue TOTAL annual budget $ _____ (See other side for library budget)

CHURCH/SYNAGOGUE LIBRARY

    Years in operation _____

    Library Head's Name _____ Title _____

    Home address _____ City _____ State/Province _____ Zip _____

    Home telephone: Area code ___-_____ Years of congregational library experience___

PERSONNEL (Include Head):

    Number on committee or staff: Professionally trained _____ Volunteers _____

HOLDINGS

    BOOKS: Total volumes, including duplicates and bound periodicals

        (1–199) _____ (200–499) _____ (500–999) _____ (1000–1499) _____

        (1500–2999) _____ (Over 3000) _____ (Over 5000) _____ (Over 10000) _____

    PERIODICALS: Number being received, both subscriptions and gifts

        Newspapers _____          Magazines _____

    NON-BOOK AND AUDIOVISUAL MATERIALS (Number owned)

| _____ Cassette tapes | _____ Kits | _____ Recordings |
|---|---|---|
| _____ Filmstrips | _____ Maps | _____ Video tapes |
| _____ Games | _____ Paintings | _____ _____ |
| _____ Picture file | _____ Pamphlet file | _____ _____ |

        (Number of boxes or drawers in above)

SUBJECTS

    Main focus of collection (i.e., Devotional, Reference, Children's, etc.):

    Unique or distinctive holdings (Please describe):

    What do you consider your library's greatest strengths?

    Describe any areas in which your library needs help or information:

    Other remarks:

### LIBRARY SERVICES (Please check all that apply)

CATALOGUE

| _____ Author list | _____ Title list | _____ Subject list |
|---|---|---|
| _____ Shelf list | _____ Accession record | |

    _____ Non-book and Audiovisual items cataloged

CLASSIFICATION

    _____ Not classified _____ Dewey Decimal System _____ Locally designed arrangement

    _____ Other (Please identify or describe) _____

    _____

CIRCULATION

    _____ Congregation only may borrow      _____ Open to outside users

    _____ Open to outside users with restrictions (Describe) _____

    _____

    _____ Library self-serve when open

    _____ Library staffed part of the time; self-serve other times

    _____ Library always staffed when open

    _____ Number of hours staffed per week (if applicable)

    _____ Average monthly circulation

        Adults _____          Children _____

    _____ Library also serves a school

AUTOMATED OR COMPUTERIZED OPERATIONS (If applicable, please specify system and describe briefly):

PUBLICATIONS

    _____ Newsletter published by church/synagogue sometimes includes library news

    _____ Library issues separate newsletter (We would appreciate receiving a copy)

    _____ Frequency of issue (i.e., Monthly, quarterly, irregularly, etc.)

    _____ Library described in church/synagogue leaflet or separate brochure (We would appreciate receiving a copy)

FINANCES
$_____ Library's annual budget allocation from church/synagogue
$_____ Funds received as gifts and memorials (annual average)
$_____ Funds received from congregational organizations or departments (annual average)
$_____ Proceeds from fundraising activities of library (annual average)
       Please describe: _____
       _____

$_____ Other source(s) - Please identify _____
       REPORTED BY (Name, Title): _____

Please
affix
stamp


TO:  CSLA Continuing Education Committee
     c/o Claudia Hannaford
     4684 Brittany Road
     Toledo, Ohio 43615
     USA

# APPENDIX F

# CSLA (White) DIRECTORY QUESTIONNAIRE

RETURN BY
Date Due: _____

Identification

(1)   Name of Church or Synagogue: _____
(2)   Address: _____

City

(3) Denomination: _____

(4) Telephone: _____

State      Zip      (area)   (exchange)   (number)

(5) Year the Library was Established: _____

Library Collection
(check appropriate block in each column)

| Category of Resources | 0–100 | 101–300 | 301–500 | 501–1000 | 1001–5000 | 5001 up |
|---|---|---|---|---|---|---|
| (6) Books (Volumes)* | | | | | | |
| (7) Periodicals (Magazine Subscriptions)** | | | | | | |
| (8) Filmstrips | | | | | | |
| (9) Films | | | | | | |
| (10) Phonograph records | | | | | | |

Definitions:
    *A BOOK is any volume which is catalogued and stands on the shelf with a call number. It includes all bound volumes of periodicals.
    **Periodical means the number of different titles which the library receives. It does NOT MEAN the number of individual issues which the library has.

Library Staffing
(mark specific number in appropriate block)

| (11) Person specifically in charge. | | | | (12) Library Committee or Helpers. | | | |
|---|---|---|---|---|---|---|---|
| If Professional | | If Non-Professional | | If Professional | | If Non-Professional | |
| Paid | Volunteer | Paid | Volunteer | Paid | Volunteer | Paid | Volunteer |
| | | | | | | | |

## Library Finances

(13) Amount of money spent annually for the library is
                    ____less than $100.00    ____$101–$500    ____$501–$1000    ____More
(check appropriate block)

## Library Services

(14) Whom does the Library serve?
____Mostly clergy.    ____Mostly children.    ____Whole Congregation    ____Local Community
(check appropriate block)
(15) How often is the library accessible?

| One day per week only | | Before & after meetings | | Whenever the building is open. | |
|---|---|---|---|---|---|
| staffed | self-service | staffed | self-service | staffed | self-service |
|  |  |  |  |  |  |

(16) How much does the library serve? (check average number of books borrowed each week)

| less than 10 | 11–25 | 26–50 | 51–100 | more than 100 |
|---|---|---|---|---|
|  |  |  |  |  |

# Index

# LIST OF TABLES

# 730

List of Tables

# About the Authors

**John F. Harvey** attended Dartmouth College, the University of Illinois, and the University of Chicago Graduate Library School (Ph.D., 1949). A former Presbyterian church deacon, he held several positions as a university library director and the dean or chairman of a graduate library school in such notable institutions as the University of New Mexico, Hofstra University, Drexel University, the University of Chicago, the University of Tehran, and Mottahedin University. He has published extensively and held office in several national and state library associations as well as several American university alumni associations. He founded the Church and Synagogue Library Association in the United States, the Iranian Documentation Centre, and the Tehran Book Processing Centre in Iran in the late 1960s. He has been listed in publications such as *Who's Who in America* and *Who's Who in the World*. Much of his time now is spent working on the Internet, on alumni association activities, in book editing, in book reviewing of library science and mystery and detective novels, and in library consulting. He has lived and worked in Cyprus since going there as a refugee in 1980.

    **Jo Ann Mouridou** earned a master's degree in political science and research methods from Canada's most prominent Lutheran university. She followed with doctoral work in Edmonton, Alberta. Mouridou also holds formal U.K. qualifications in communications studies, marketing, advertising, and systems analysis and design. In addition to having worked in two large North American libraries and as head of the business studies department of a local Cypriot senior college for five years, Mouridou has worked as accountant, program analyst, and researcher for several religious agencies. She designed and compiled the statistical analysis sections of Harvey's books *Scholarly Religious Libraries in North America* and *Popular Religious Libraries in North America* and is the author of several college-type study manuals, short articles, book reviews, and two unpublished volumes for children—one in verse and one in prose.

# Books Edited or Written
# by John F. Harvey

*The Library Periodical Directory*, with Phillips Temple, Betty Martin Brown, and Mary Adele Springman (Pittsburg, Kans.: 1955 and 1967).

*The Librarian's Career: A Study of Mobility*, ACRL Microcard Series, no. 85 (Rochester, N.Y.: University of Rochester, 1957).

*The Library College*, with Louis Shores and Robert Jordan (Philadelphia: Drexel, 1964).

*Data Processing in College and Public Libraries* (Philadelphia: Drexel, 1966).

*Comparative and International Library Science* (Metuchen, N.J.: Scarecrow, 1977).

*Church and Synagogue Libraries* (Metuchen, N.J.: Scarecrow, 1980).

*Librarians' Affirmative Action Handbook*, with Elizabeth M. Dickinson (Metuchen, N.J.: Scarecrow, 1984).

*Austerity Management in Academic Libraries*, with Peter Spyers-Duran (Metuchen, N.J.: Scarecrow, 1982).

*Internationalizing Library Education: A Handbook*, with Frances Laverne Carroll (Westport, Conn.: Greenwood, 1987).

*Scholarly Religious Libraries in North America; A Statistical Examination* (Lanham, Md.: Scarecrow, 1999).

*Popular Religious Libraries in North America: A Statistical Examination* (Lanham, Md.: Scarecrow, 1999)

*World Directory of Theological Libraries*, 2d ed., 2 vols. (in process)

HIEBERT LIBRARY

3 6877 00161 8973

Z
675
.R37
H46
1998